D1426447

THE MALATESTA OF RIMINI AND
THE PAPAL STATE

THE MALATESTA OF RIMINI
AND THE PAPAL STATE

A POLITICAL HISTORY

P. J. JONES
Fellow of Brasenose College, Oxford

CAMBRIDGE UNIVERSITY PRESS

Published by the Syndics of the Cambridge University Press
Bentley House, 200 Euston Road, London NW1 2DB
American Branch: 32 East 57th Street, New York, N.Y.10022

© Cambridge University Press 1974

Library of Congress Catalogue Card Number: 72-87178

ISBN: 0 521 20042 3

First published 1974

Printed in Great Britain
at the University Printing House, Cambridge
(Brooke Crutchley, University Printer)

Contents

Preface vii   Abbreviations ix
Map of Romagna and the Marche in the later Middle Ages x–xi

1 The Papal State and Romagna in the thirteenth century   *page* 1

2 Rimini and the rise of the Malatesta   21

3 From commune to papal vicariate   42

4 Galeotto Malatesta, 'ecclesie pugil'   79

5 The prime of Malatesta rule: Carlo Malatesta   102

6 The pontificate of Martin V   149

7 Sigismondo Pandolfo Malatesta, 'fex Italiae'   176

8 The papal reconquest   240

9 The government of the Malatesta: I. The papal vicariate   262

10 The government of the Malatesta: II. The *signoria*   289

Appendix 339   *Bibliography* 347
Index 361

FOR CARLA

Preface

This work was originally written, some twenty years ago, as a doctoral thesis in the University of Oxford. The reason for publication after so long an interval is the growing evidence of demand for a general account of the Malatesta of Rimini based on modern research. No extended history of the Malatesta has appeared since the nineteenth century, nor has anything of the sort been published or promised in the past few years. Outside a small number of specialised articles, new information has been mainly added in writings on other, related subjects: on neighbouring states and dynasties, like the Montefeltro and Polenta, or on Romagna and the Papal State in general. Little rewriting has therefore been necessary to bring the book up to date. Only the introductory chapter, handling themes subsequently discussed in works on papal government and Romagna in the thirteenth century, has been wholly recast and cut. Otherwise the original text is essentially unaltered, and revision has been mainly confined to work of abbreviation, especially of footnotes. To facilitate this, references have been minimised and almost all authorities quoted in brief, full titles being listed in the Bibliography.

At this date acknowledgements for help received must carry an obituary note. But I am bound to recall the obligations incurred, from a very early stage, first to the late Professor E. F. Jacob, who suggested the subject (Carlo Malatesta and church unity) from which the finished study developed, and to the late Cecilia Ady, who acted as supervisor and placed at my disposal her intimate knowledge of fifteenth-century Italian political history. In Italy too there are debts to record: to Professor Emilio Re, for help in Rome, to the Conte Piercarlo Borgogelli, who introduced me to the archives at Fano, and most of all, to Professor Augusto Campana of the Vatican Library, whose special lifelong interest has been Romagna and Rimini (not to speak of Santarcangelo), and whose completed edition of the *Cronache malatestiane* is the most awaited contribution to Malatesta studies.

Brasenose College, Oxford   P. J. JONES
July 1973

Abbreviations

ARCHIVES

ACF	Archivio Comunale, Fano
ASF	Archivio di Stato, Firenze
Arch. vat.	Archivio segreto vaticano
Bib. Gamb.	Biblioteca civica Gambalunga, Rimini
Bib. sen.	Biblioteca del senato, Roma

PERIODICALS

AMM	*Atti e Memorie della Deputazione di Storia Patria per le Marche*
AMR	*Atti e Memorie della Deputazione di Storia Patria per le provincie di Romagna*
AR	*Archivio della Società Romana di Storia Patria*
ASI	*Archivio Storico Italiano*
ASL	*Archivio Storico Lombardo*
ASN	*Archivio Storico per le provincie Napoletane*
BU	*Bollettino della Deputazione di Storia Patria per l'Umbria*
QF	*Quellen und Forschungen aus italienischen Archiven und Bibliotheken*
RQ	*Römische Quartalschrift*
SP	*Studia Picena*
SR	*Studi Romagnoli*
SS	*Studi Storici*
VSWG	*Vierteljahrschrift für Sozial- und Wirtschaftsgeschichte*
ZRG	*Zeitschrift der Savigny-Stiftung für Rechtsgeschichte*

COLLECTIONS AND HISTORIES

MGH	*Monumenta Germaniae Historica*, Hannover, 1826–.
RIS	*Rerum Italicarum Scriptores*, ed. L. A. Muratori, Milan, 1723–51.
RIS²	*Rerum Italicarum Scriptores*, ed. G. Carducci, V. Fiorini, Città di Castello, 1900ff.

Theiner   *Codex diplomaticus temporalis S. Sedis,* ed. A. Theiner, Rome, 1861–2.

Battaglini   *Zecca*: F. G. Battaglini, *Memorie istoriche di Rimino scritte ad illustrare la zecca riminese,* Bologna, 1789.
Vita: F. G. Battaglini, *Della vita di Sigismondo Pandolfo Malatesta,* Rimini, 1794.

Clementini   C. Clementini, *Raccolto storico della fondatione di Rimino,* Rimini, 1617.

Tonini   L. and C. Tonini, *Storia civile e sacra riminese,* Rimini, 1848–82.

For other works cited in abbreviated form see Bibliography.

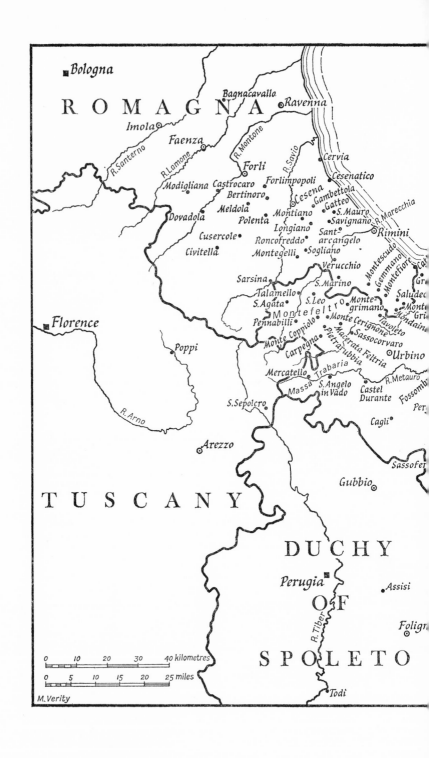

ADRIATIC

SEA

ro
ilara

a

Mondolfo

arina   Sinigaglia

ndavio

•Corinaldo

•Montalboddo

Ancona

Iesi   •Offagna

ontrada   R. Esino   •Osimo

Staffolo   •Castelfidardo

Serra   •Filottrano

S. Quirico   •Recanati

iano   R   •Cingoli   •Montecassiano

Matelica   ⊙Macerata

. Severino•   R. Chienti

                •Tolentino

erino

⊙   •S. Ginesio   •Fermo

              Ripatransone

Amandola• H

              •Offida

        Ascoli
        ⊙

E

N

I

The Papal State and Romagna in the thirteenth century

The Malatesta of Rimini possess a double history. They belong to a class of princes who appear in Italian politics during the later Middle Ages endowed with a composite character: as despots, *signori*, ruling urban communes, and as temporal subjects of the pope. At every stage of their history, from their rise in the later thirteenth century to their fall in the early sixteenth, they illustrate larger changes occurring in two forms of political life peculiarly Italian: city state and Papal State. And this especially in their rise. For both institutions, the establishment of despotism marked a critical turning-point.

For the popes the power of despots represented a new phase to an old problem: of making good their claim to rule and found a state in Central Italy. State-building, certainly, was not in 1300 a specially papal problem, but nowhere was it so intractable as in the *patrimonium S. Petri*. The area covered by that date was nominally large. It extended, in theory, from Bologna (or Ferrara) in the north to Terracina in the south, comprising principally the regions of Romagna and the March of Ancona, the duchy of Spoleto, the 'Tuscan' March or Patrimony, and the Roman Campagna and Marittima. But in none of these provinces was papal authority secure or uncontested, as self-interested contemporaries were quick to point out. To the Frenchman Pierre Dubois, writing at the turn of the century, it was a matter of general scandal and called for a drastic remedy: alienation or enfeoffment to a secular (French) prince. The case was unambiguous:

'Although [he said] in the kingdom of Sicily, the city of Rome, Tuscany, and other lands, maritime and mountain, which he holds by the gift of the first catholic emperor, Constantine, the pope should have and fully exercise all imperial prerogatives, yet on account of the malice, cunning, and deceit of these places, he cannot now and never could enjoy complete control of them.'[1]

It was a just if summary judgement, well warranted by current events. As analysis, however, it was also overemphatic, sounder in

---

[1] *De recuperatione Terre Sancte*, 33, 98, 105–6; Waley, 301–2.

politics than history. Full imperial rights the papacy should certainly
have had and was unable to enforce. But the fact is overlooked that
only very recently, partly in Dubois' own lifetime, had the popes
managed to claim possession of the lands that were their due and
organise a government at all. A century before, the Papal State had
existed more in title than in fact. At the same time the impression
of inveterate weakness was further enhanced when Dubois, following
popular tradition, chose to derive the papal claims from a gift of the
emperor Constantine, a thing the Roman *curia* almost never did.[1] More
prudently the popes themselves, when not invoking divine right,[2] preferred to base their title on later, more authentic privileges. And in
practice it was over these that the first and greatest obstacles had arisen
to the growth of a Papal State. Historically, papal authority rested on a
series of royal and imperial donations (*privilegia, promissiones*), of the
eighth and later centuries, which transferred to Roman suzerainty lands
in time identified with the duchies of Rome and Spoleto, the Tuscan
Patrimony, the Pentapolis and the Exarchate of Ravenna.[3] But for the
space of some four hundred years, as long as imperial authority retained some force in Italy, the awards, despite renewal, were not upheld. In the twelfth century the Patrimony comprised little more than
the duchy of Rome. Of other provinces, the Exarchate (coming to be
called Romagna) had passed, as an imperial fief, under the archbishops
of Ravenna, and with the Pentapolis (now termed the March of Ancona)
and much of the duchy of Spoleto, had been practically lost if not
relinquished by the papacy.[4]

Created by the empire, the Papal State only became a reality with the
failure of the empire at the end of the twelfth century, and its final
collapse in the mid-thirteenth. Between 1197 and 1202, exploiting
imperial schism, the papacy claimed and secured submission from the
March of Ancona, the duchy of Spoleto and the Tuscan Patrimony.
Ratified from 1201 by a succession of new donations from rival
German kings, and reinforced by administrative intervention, this
marked the effective beginning of the medieval Papal State, though in a

[1] G. Laehr, *Die konstantinische Schenkung in der abendländischen Literatur des Mittelalters*
(Berlin, 1926). Belief in the Constantinian origin of the Papal State was and
remained widespread in Italy: Dante, *Inf.*, xix, 115; Petrarch, *Sonetti*, n. cxxxviii;
Gasperoni, 'Savignano', 270.

[2] As for example Gregory IX: J. Rivière, *Le problème de l'église et de l'état au temps de
Philippe le Bel* (Louvain, 1926), 38. Cf. *Cost. Egid.*, 158.

[3] L. Duchesne, *Les premiers temps de l'état pontifical* (Paris, 1898); T. Sickel, *Das
Privilegium Otto I. für die römische Kirche vom Jahre 962* (Innsbruck, 1883); Ficker,
Forschungen, ii. 328ff.; Waley, 1ff.

[4] Buzzi, *AR* 1915; Waley, 3ff. For changes in regional terminology, virtually complete by the thirteenth century, outside the imperial chancery: Ficker, ii. 161–3,
444ff., 487ff., 499ff.

form not yet complete or unquestioned.[1] In particular Romagna, though regranted with the rest, was left unclaimed and ceded provisionally to the church of Ravenna.[2] In the other provinces also reconquest was checked for a time by renewed Hohenstaufen interference from Frederick II and, more briefly, Manfred. But once begun papal influence persisted, especially after 1250, then invading also Romagna;[3] and by 1274, from another embarrassed emperor elect, the popes felt strong enough to demand, not simply further renewal, but the full and final implementation of the royal *promissiones*, by the transfer, *de facto* as well as *de iure*, of Romagna and Bologna.[4] With this transaction, concluded in 1278, the Papal State became territorially complete and free, except for one short interval, free from imperial violation. Foreign influences – Angevin, French, Italian – periodically intruded. But henceforward the threat to papal sovereignty no longer lay outside. It arose from 'malice' and 'deceit' within.

At no stage, in fact, was the defeat of the empire in Central Italy the work of the papacy alone. It depended as much, if not more, on the action of local powers, feudal and urban, equally anxious with the popes, and better equipped, to inherit imperial prerogatives.[5] Collectively they presented to papal rule a challenge more formidable than the claims of rival sovereigns. From the earliest days the papacy had been faced with the problem of internal insubordination, first from landed magnates, then increasingly, from the eleventh century, from towns and city communes. And with both also from an early stage, in the small area they commanded, the popes had been forced to adopt a policy, which soon became habitual, of concession and compromise: with magnates by the use of feudal contracts,[6] with towns by charters of privilege, also semi-feudal, through all of which, in return for specified duties of fealty, service and counsel (*parlamentum*), the *curia* sought to safeguard for more propitious times (*tempore opportuno*) reserves of effective sovereignty.[7] This abnegatory policy prevailed even more in the new provinces occupied after 1197, where feudal lords and communes,

[1] Waley, 30–67.
[2] Ficker, *Forschungen*, ii.444–57, iii.450–3; Waley, 31, 34–5, 43, 184.
[3] From 1247, in collaboration and quasi-condominion with papalist archbishops of Ravenna: Vasina, *Romagnoli*, ch. 1.
[4] Theiner, i.194ff.; Vicinelli, 'Inizio'; Waley, 184ff., 194ff.; Vasina, *Romagnoli*, ch. 11. On the boundaries of Romagna and the position of Bologna: Comelli, *AMR* 1907–8; Waley, 18, 92–4; Vasina, *Romagnoli*, 2, 77; Larner, 205–7; below p. 12 n. 2.
[5] Thus by some contemporaries the acquisition of Romagna was attributed more to local than to papal initiative: below p. 8 n. 2, 34.
[6] To replace (though never with complete success) the laxer relation of emphyteusis: Jordan, 'Eindringen'; Paradisi, in *Studi C. Calisse* (Milan, 1939), i.249ff.; Waley, 7–8.
[7] Falco, 'Amministrazione', *passim*; 'Comuni' 1919; Koelmel; Vehse, *QF* 1929–30; Waley, 6–26.

already generously enfranchised, proceeded like the popes to seize regalian rights. Papal reconquest turned into a piecemeal process of negotiation and treaty over reciprocal rights and duties.[1] And the need to bargain for allegiance was aggravated further in the confused period which followed of conflict with the Hohenstaufen and virtual interregnum, when empire and papacy bid against each other with grants of fief and privilege.[2] But practice did not alter much when foreign pressure withdrew. In Romagna, where by 1278 local powers had a long accumulation of franchises and could even appeal in some cases to the peace of Constance, the papacy was compelled to acknowledge existing rights and negotiate in detail.[3] To an exceptional degree, authority in the Papal State came to rest on compact, a confusion of agreements over alleged liberties and customs (*bonae consuetudines*) with individual lords and communes. As between lords and communes, there does not appear in papal policy any sign of special preference. The only consistent distinction drawn was a juridical division between lands immediately subject (*immediate subiectae*) and those held by a mesne lord or city (*mediate subiectae*).[4] For the rest, the papacy's main concern was to secure, for now or later, the maximum of effective sovereignty, and incorporate the territories immediately subject into some administrative system.

It was not without success. In the space of barely a century, when the empire was breaking down, the popes created a *regnum*, partly copied from the empire, with a regular administration and advancing all the claims of contemporary monarchy. The administration, complete and largely standardised by 1300, was a system based on provinces, each entrusted to a 'rector' (or rectors, lay and clerical, 'in temporalibus' and 'spiritualibus'), endowed normally with plenipotentiary authority (*liberum arbitrium*) and supported by a small but expanding *curia* of judges and officials, and in time also a police force of *stipendiarii*.[5] The rights of government (*regalia S. Petri*) also expanded, at least in definition. As disclosed particularly by acts of submission and official inquisition,[6] they were typical for the time. Secured by an oath of fealty[7] and a claim to counsel (*parlamentum*), they came to

---

[1] Ermini, 'Libertà'; Waley, 31–43.
[2] Papal policy was 'a long trail of privileges derogating from papal rights': Waley, 150, cf. 59ff., 130–64, 260, 286, 294.
[3] Waley, 196; Vasina, *Romagnoli*, 68ff.; below pp. 7, 23, 31.
[4] Ermini, 'Relazioni', 'Aspetti', 'Caratteri', *passim*. There were also some places in papal 'demesne': Waley, 69.
[5] Ermini, 'Rettori', 29–58; 'Caratteri', 322ff., 343ff.; 'Aspetti', 8ff.; Eitel, 62ff.; Waley, 37, 42, 51ff., 91ff., 289.
[6] For repeated inquests, *quo waranto* or otherwise: Theiner, i.273, 324–5, 465; Rondini, 'Monte Filottrano', 26–7. Cf. *Cost. Egid.*, 118–19.
[7] Feudally phrased, as in the oath from Romagna in 1278: Fasoli, *ASI* 1933.

include: judicial sovereignty (*merum et mixtum imperium*), comprising appellate jurisdiction and commonly certain reserved cases (heresy, treason, homicide etc.) as well as other justice; the power to legislate, generally or locally, by rectorial constitution; military levies (*exercitus, cavalcata*) or their money commutation (*stipendia* or *tallia militum*); and a variety of fiscal charges: profits of justice and administration, tolls and other indirect payments, including a lucrative salt-tax,[1] and a medley of direct taxes, regular and irregular (rectorial procurations, *census, affictus,* and hearth-tax or *focaticum*).[2] In harmony with contemporary practice, if not one step ahead, the custom was also early developed of convening for government purposes estates of nobles, clergy and communes in representative parliaments: on the first occasion (1207) centrally, but from the middle of the century in mainly provincial assemblies.[3] In all its forms this growth of papal government naturally took time, and there were varieties of detail (especially fiscal detail) between different provinces, and even in the definition of provinces themselves.[4] The greatest advance took place in the last decades, from around 1270, when central control was sharpened and regional bureaucracies enlarged.[5] But at no time, however troubled, did administration wholly fail, nor were there serious regional divergencies in rights and forms of rule. To Romagna, on its acquisition, the system was applied complete: of rectorial administration, justice, legislation, military and money levies, and provincial parliaments. It was after 1278, in fact, and especially in Romagna, that parliaments became a regular feature of papal government.[6] With such resources and institutions the papal dominion on a summary view might seem to have offered all the makings of a state, a *Ständestaat* like others of the age, in and outside Italy,[7] which, but for the removal to Avignon, the papacy could in time have made efficient.

Such was not, then or later, the opinion of outsiders. Combined with resentment at the misdirection of papal energies into temporal ambitions, there went, as seen, a feeling that the effort had miscarried,

---

[1] At least in Romagna, based on the Cervia *saline*, from around 1290 (Waley, 255; Vasina, *Romagnoli*, 218–19), about which time salt taxes were becoming widely established elsewhere in Italy and Europe: *Le rôle du sel dans l'histoire*, ed. M. Mollat (Paris, 1968).

[2] Eitel, 66ff.; Ermini, 'Caratteri', 318, 332–3; 'Relazioni', 184–200; Loye, 97; Antonelli, 'Registri'; Fabre, 'Registre'; Calisse, 'Costituzioni', 29ff., 52ff.; Schäfer, *Ritter*, i. 20–36; Waley, 68ff., 253ff., 276ff.; below pp. 28off.

[3] Ermini, 'Parlamenti', *passim*; Waley, 52ff., 110ff.; Marongiù, 6ff., 256ff.

[4] Ermini, 'Rettori', 36ff.; Waley, 91ff.; above p. 2 n. 4.

[5] Waley, 106ff., 120ff., 220–1, 237; Vasina, *Romagnoli*, 260ff.

[6] Waley, 112, 195ff.; Vasina, *Romagnoli*, 24, 65ff. In Romagna at least 17 parliaments met between 1278 and 1302: Waley, 112, 305–6; Vasina, 201 n.3, 249, n.3, 260 n.1, 263 n.1.

[7] Leicht, 'Staatsformen'.

and eventually a belief that the papacy (like the empire) was driven from its Italian territories by a breakdown of authority.[1] It is easy to see why. In no part of Europe were public rights more widely divorced from actual power. Viewed through official records, as one historian notes,[2] papal government presents the appearance of an ordered state, equipped with laws, yielding arms and revenue, attractive to ambitious officials, of growing importance to cardinals and *curia*;[3] viewed from the ground, through chronicles and local records, it creates an impression of anarchy: a remote influence, scarcely meriting notice.[4] To be exact, the same impression emerges from official records also: beginning with the fact that a number suffered loss through seizure or destruction by insubordinate subjects.[5] Rectorial justice consisted largely of proceedings for disobedience; the bulk of constitutions published in provincial parliaments were concerned with disorder and 'rebellion';[6] and, after admonitory legislation the main business of parliament (when not obstructed or evaded by refusals to attend, to invest proctors with sufficient powers, or to accept its decisions) was raising troops and taxes to suppress revolts or combat wars and alliances among the provincials themselves.[7] Government remained a process of incessant reconquest, absorbing all the resources of the State; and for this the self-evident reason was that no state had previously existed. Each province passed to the pope in a condition of virtual independence. And the most independent of all was the newest province – Romagna. It came to the papacy after more than a generation of undisturbed anarchy. Of the twenty-five years which followed, nearly half (1279–83, 1296–9, 1300ff.) were spent by the papal government in open war, on unequal terms, with large parts of the province, and the rest of the time in contending with concerted disobedience, resistance to taxation, and local strife. The frequency of parliaments was significant of unrest. Rectors had to perambulate to find a place to stay. In 1290 one was abducted, in 1302 another nearly murdered. And more than once authority almost totally collapsed.

[1] Dubois, 101; Petrarch, *Opera* (1554), 1172; Waley, 294–5, 298ff.
[2] L. Simeoni, *Le signorie* (Milan, 1950), i.322.
[3] By the later thirteenth century the cardinals had acquired a say in grants of papal territory and the nomination of rectors: Theiner, i.468; Ermini, 'Rettori', 53–4; Waley, 122–3. Towns also found it worthwhile to subsidise patrons and maintain proctors at the *curia*: Waley, 224.
[4] As for example in urban statute: Waley, 171.
[5] In Romagna on several occasions: Vasina, *Romagnoli*, 249.
[6] See the parliamentary constitutions for various provinces published by Sella, in *ASI* 1925, 1927, *Riv. stor. dir. it.*, 1929, and *Studi E. Besta* (Milan, 1937–9), iii; Ermini, *Riv. stor. dir. it.*, 1932; Falco, *AR* 1927; L. Colini-Baldeschi, *N. studi medievali*, ii (1925).
[7] Ermini, 'Parlamenti', 40–4 and *passim*; Waley, 118ff., 220, 295–6.

From the history of these years Romagna acquired the reputation of the most turbulent part of Italy: 'mai sanza guerra'.[1] By comparison other papal provinces were more settled, enough at least to provide support for campaigns in Romagna. But it was a difference only of degree. Disturbance and defiance were everywhere recurrent, though partly, in the later years, by contagion from Romagna.[2] To be effective, papal government had to create some habit of obedience. And what this meant, in practical terms, was reaching a *modus vivendi*, a clarification of rights and duties, with the two powers of urban and feudal immunity, communes and lords.

For most of the thirteenth century, in outward form at least, papal sovereignty was regulated more by communes than by lords. Towns had won predominance in the local balance of power. It was from towns, primarily, that the papacy sought oaths of obedience when taking over provinces.[3] And it was against insurgent towns, *civitates rebelles*,[4] that rectorial prosecutions were principally directed, for all possible kinds of misdemeanour: for building unlicensed fortifications, exporting corn illegally, withholding troops and taxes, harbouring outlaws, evading justice, but most commonly of all, for waging war on neighbours.[5] Inter-city war, the result of urban expansion into the country (*contado*), against feudatories, or to subdue other towns, was a tradition as old as the communes; and almost equally old was civil war within towns, of party and class. All the warfare of Romagna, before and after 1278, arose from these two sources. And both there and everywhere else, one immediate concern of papal government was to put an end to it. The first papal act in Romagna – and the first occasion of defeat – was an attempt to pacify towns and factions, and stop aggression in the *contado*: an effort renewed many times and with repeated lack of success.[6] The most elementary failure of papal sovereignty was inability to impose peace.[7] But not only the communes were to blame. On the principle of 'divide and rule', the popes frequently

---

[1] Dante, *Inf.*, xxvii, 37–8; Waley, 100–1, 111–12, 194ff., 211–12, 227–9, 236ff., 264ff., 271, 289; Larner, 26–7, 41–2, 45–55, 71ff.; Vasina, *Romagnoli*, chs. i–vii, *passim*. Vasina (45, n.1) questions, unconvincingly, the ill reputation of Romagna.

[2] Especially in the March of Ancona, the next most troublesome province. To safeguard government there was one motive for taking over Romagna: Vasina, *Romagnoli*, 28–9, 33, etc. Cf. Waley, 178, 186, 245, 247, 287.

[3] As in Romagna, 1278: Vasina, *Romagnoli*, 69ff.

[4] In the formula of William Durand, recalling his troubled rectorship (1284–6, 1295–6) in Romagna: Waley, 295, n.1.

[5] Cf. Waley, 79, 159, 161, 265.

[6] Notably in 1280, 1291, 1295, 1297 and 1301: Ermini, 'Rettori', 45–9; Fasoli, *ASI* 1933; Vasina, *Romagnoli*, 66–106, 108–17, 252ff.; Waley, 103, 111, 195–9, 236, 247–8.

[7] Or even withhold the right of war, granted for example to Rimini in 1294: Tonini, iii.677–89.

indulged in the self-defeating practice of backing one town against another,[1] thereby aggravating war. By their general position in Italian politics they were also, though in differing degrees, inclined to be partisan. In Romagna, from 1250 and again, according to Ghibelline sources, in 1278, the way was prepared for papal rule by collusion and coalition with local Guelf interests.[2] The policy was resumed with passion by the French pope Martin IV, who between 1281 and 1283, using French and Angevin forces and a French-staffed administration, succeeded for a time in banishing all Ghibelline organisation from Romagna and installing a Guelf-based régime.[3] In the event the *pars ecclesie*, antagonised by the *francigeni* and by continuing demands for troops and taxes for which it saw no further need, proved as unsubmissive as the evicted imperialists. The papalist communes formed a peace federation directed against the government; and only from 1293, when Ghibelline (and White Guelf) forces revived, did papal authority partially recover, in an association with Guelf powers that had more of dependence than alliance, and even less of rule.[4] Analogous situations are found in other provinces. Papal power, like imperial power earlier, was controlled by a casual coincidence of interest with overmighty subjects. To turn partnership into government, whether on a party or a peace basis, was to invite resistance for invasion of urban liberty.

This was the crucial issue: to reconcile 'sovereignty' and 'liberty'. With monotonous regularity towns invoked their franchises against the claims of papal government. In 1278 all the communes of Romagna published 'protestationes' reserving their liberties, over city, *contado* and district, and a number repeated the action on subsequent occasions.[5] On similar grounds there also arose a continuous flow of appeals to Rome against the 'tyranny' (*durities*) and misgovernment of papal officials.[6] One of the commonest grievances was the rival *libertas*

---

[1] Or exploiting divisions between towns and barons: Waley, 65, 87, 151ff., 158, 160, 170–83, 187–8, 284. Communes in turn sued one another or feudatories in papal courts: *ibid.* 79, 187.

[2] Vasina, *Romagnoli*, 9, 14, 23, 36ff. In the Ghibelline version, the Guelf leaders, then losing ground in the province, engineered the transfer to the papacy: below p. 34.

[3] Vasina, *Romagnoli*, 124–64; Waley, 202–4.

[4] Vasina, *Romagnoli*, 91, 99ff., 106–7, 126–7, 130ff., 165–288; Waley, 211–12, 217–19, 227–8, 242, 300; below pp. 31, 34.

[5] Especially Bologna and other 'Guelf' cities: Theiner, i.365–9; Cantinelli, 28; Vasina, *Romagnoli*, 72–3, 243–4, 258, 268; below p. 31. Exactly analogous was the position of Guelf Perugia, represented in a late thirteenth-century patriotic poem as devoted to the papacy, but undiminished in all its liberties, including freedom to dominate the whole of Umbria: Galletti, *ASI* 1970, 334.

[6] Notably again in Romagna, as in 1287–8 and 1292: Vasina, *Romagnoli*, 180ff., 234ff.; below p. 32. Cf. Waley, 155, 166. Rectorial 'abuses' figure largely in three papal reforming codes, for Campagna (1295), Tuscan Patrimony (1300), and March of Ancona (1303): *ibid.* 233ff.

claimed on behalf of the church. This was an ancient question, older than the papal reconquest,[1] and prominent among rectorial enactments were laws to uphold ecclesiastical privilege, rescind anti-clerical statutes, combat heresy, and check communal encroachments on church land and lordship.[2] But under papal dominion *libertas ecclesie* denoted more than clerical immunity. It meant the sovereign rights of Rome (*iura Romane ecclesie*) – as threatening in practice to clerical as to communal freedom.[3] And the tyranny which occasioned urban protest was the exercise of rights deriving from the *regalia S. Petri*. Of these larger prerogatives, among the most contested, especially in Romagna, were the interrelated claims to money, military service, and attendance at parliament. In law, none could be rejected; the only valid objection, frequently invoked, was breach of chartered privilege in the manner and forms of demand – expressed in time through parliament itself, but at first more by protest or defiance.[4] But there were other causes of friction, more general to the Papal State, and more compromising of urban liberty, than taxation.[5] One was the requirement, widely accepted by the fourteenth century, to include some reference to papal lordship in the oath of communal officials, and to incorporate rectorial constitutions in municipal statute.[6] Another, more contentious, was the exercise of papal appellate jurisdiction and, through right of *preventio*, of concurrent ordinary jurisdiction.[7] But most provocative of all was the attempt by papal government to establish, or more exactly extend from smaller to larger communes, control over the nomination of the chief communal officials: *podestà* and *capitano*. Although not generally enforced against the greater cities, except during moments of papal peace-making, no action caused more trouble: in Romagna it contributed to the Guelf revolt of 1287–90 and 1292. Also, more than any other claim, it was certainly interpreted as a deliberate attack on urban franchise.[8]

---

[1] Below p. 24.
[2] Above p. 6 n. 6. Cf. Theiner, i. 324–5, 583; Waley, 133–4, 142ff.; Larner, 41, 186ff.; Vasina, *Romagnoli*, 152, 190, 230.
[3] At least in Romagna, by reason particularly of increasing papal appointment to bishoprics (including Ravenna, which sank into subordination) and control and taxation of the lower clergy, which became as disaffected as the 'pars ecclesie': Ermini, 'Stato', 606ff.; Vasina, *Romagnoli*, 95ff., 177–8, 186, 202ff., 229–32, 246ff., 274.
[4] Ermini, 'Parlamenti', *passim*; Vasina, *Romagnoli*, 219–20, 243–4, 258, 268; below p. 53.
[5] Which in some provinces (the Tuscan Patrimony and duchy of Spoleto) does not seem even to have been a parliamentary matter: Waley, 115–16.
[6] Ermini, 'Libertà', *passim*; *Cost. Egid.*, 84ff.; Waley, 73.
[7] Ermini, 'Libertà'; Waley, 75ff., 145, 161, 205, 211, 230–1, 249.
[8] Ermini, 'Libertà'; Waley, 70ff., 161, 205, 211, 230–1; Vasina, *Romagnoli*, 82ff., 97–8, 104, 170ff., 252ff.

That the popes did in fact, as is sometimes said, foster an 'anti-communal' policy is questionable. No doubt in extreme cases they were prepared to suppress at least temporarily, all municipal liberties.[1] Individual popes, and still more rectors, may also have acted with authoritarian harshness, or sought to over-centralise.[2] But if this reflected policy, it was not consistently maintained. Rather would it seem to have been reversed. In the later years of the century, particularly from the pontificate of Nicholas IV, it is possible to see in the relations of popes and communes a distinct trend towards accommodation, an effective *modus vivendi* in various issues of government, especially touching jurisdiction and election of officials. In jurisdiction, the popes began to acknowledge, with a new spirit of realism and unprecedented generosity, extensive, even full powers (*merum et mixtum imperium*), reserving only certain major cases.[3] In the interests of peace and precision, a similar clarification was reached, largely by papal concession, in conflicting claims to nominate *podestà*. In numerous communes the right to elect was released in return for an annual *census*.[4] But this was not all. Reciprocating papal action, many towns, from the later 1280s began to present the *podesteria* to the pope himself or his representatives, and even, by the fourteenth century, the outright *regimen et dominium* of the city.[5] Papacy and communes seem suddenly to have found a reason for alliance.

Various reasons are attested.[6] But one, possibly the principal, is not easy to mistake. By the end of the thirteenth century, the office of *podestà* (and equally *capitano*) had become an office for sale; and in city after city, in almost all states of the Church, the papacy was beginning to enter into rivalry for the legacy of communal independence with a new power, no less hostile, which was rising to replace it: of *signori*, *tiranni*, petty urban despots.

The motive, to be sure, is more apparent in papal than in communa attitudes. In February 1290 Nicholas IV took the first step in a long papal counter-offensive against nascent *signoria* with a law condemning nobles who had got control of towns by repeated election to high municipal office, and cancelling all elections beyond one year.

---

[1] As with the Ghibelline towns of Romagna in 1282 and certain Guelf towns later: *Reg. M. IV*, nn.266, 279, 462; below p. 32.
[2] As argued by Vasina of the first phase of papal government in Romagna: *Romagnoli, passim*.
[3] Such as treason, heresy, adultery, rape of a virgin: Waley, 76, 223, 230ff.
[4] The origin of the *census* paid by a large class of communes: Waley, 70ff., 222ff., 230ff., 253.
[5] Theiner, i.516, 535, 544; Ermini, 'Libertà'; Waley, 72, 221ff.
[6] Waley, 222–3, 233.

Papal authority and urban liberty are treated as interdependent.[1] That the communes, diversified by class and party interests, felt equal concern to uphold papal government is more debatable. There are cases where, for a time, a town seems to have preferred papal to despotic rule.[2] But there are others which suggest the population had an equal distaste for both.[3] While of Romagna it has been argued that communes rallied behind despots the better to resist papal government.[4] However that may be, Romagna certainly provides proof that, although they were prepared on occasion to collaborate with *signori*, for the popes the rise of despotism represented a marked change for the worse. The trouble-centre of the Papal State was also the province most early addicted to despots. Already in 1278 the majority of communes were succumbing to *signorie*. By 1300 only one, Cesena, survived precariously, in Dante's words, 'between tyranny and freedom'.[5] Romagna, in fact, was chosen by Dante to exhibit the character of rising tyranny. One by one, in scathing terms, he lists its towns by catalogue of despots (*Inferno*, XXVII). And its chronic war he rightly sees as the feuding of *tiranni*.[6] With the exception of Bologna, the *civitates rebelles* were towns run by despots, replaced by despots in dealings with the pope and, by 1300, in parliament. And failure to control the despots was the main cause of the papal weakness deplored by Pierre Dubois.[7]

It was a sign of things to come. For the next two centuries papal government would have to struggle principally with despotism. At the same time the change from commune to *signoria* was also, in certain ways, a return to things past, a revolution in form as much as substance. The new despotic families were not *parvenus*, newcomers to power. Independently of citizenship, or their place in urban politics, they were all without exception, by origin and status, also feudal lords, magnates endowed for generations with property and jurisdiction, who had emerged and prospered side by side with the communes. Behind the *signoria*, together with urban autonomy, lay the older *seigneurie*: a backward shift in the balance of power confronting papal authority, from town to feudatory.

It was the same all over Italy. After two centuries of freedom and constitution-making, communes everywhere were surrendering in

---

[1] *Reg. N. IV*, 7245; Waley, 122, 190, 220; Vasina, *Romagnoli*, 212.
[2] As Forlì in 1290: Vasina, *Romagnoli*, 212 (but cf. 225).
[3] As possibly Rimini in 1290: Vasina, *Romagnoli*, 208; below p. 32.
[4] Larner, 44, 80–1.   [5] 'tra tirannia si vive e stato franco': *Inf.*, XXVII, 54.
[6] 'mai Sanza guerra ne' cor de' suoi tiranni' (*Inf.*, XXVII, 37–8) – with Benvenuto da Imola's gloss: 'intellige postquam coepit habere tyrannos': *Comentum super Comoediam*, ii.304.
[7] Waley, 114, 117ff., 219–20, 274, 296; Vasina, *Romagnoli*, 12, 23, 166–8; Larner, 47.

form or fact, to the *signoria* of feudal lords and dynasties. And every-where the ultimate cause was the same: the aristocratic nature of the Italian city-state – the effect of ancient urban tradition – and the con-sequent failure of most, through faction, war or economic weakness, to achieve, or even attempt, effective control of the landed nobility in town and *contado*. In Italy, unlike transalpine Europe, the community of the antique *civitas*, embracing town and territory, was never permanently broken, divided up between feudal territory and 'bourgeois' town; but neither was it fully re-established. Feudal and urban society co-existed and commingled. For a time, it is true, a regional contrast developed between a 'communal' Italy in the north, and a 'feudal' Italy in the south. The Papal State, coming between, participated in both, the Roman region being feudal, the other provinces communal.[1] But the division was never sharp. In the urban and commercial north agrarian influences also prevailed widely. In particular, landed interests pre-ponderated in the formation and government of most urban communes, and survived, with feudal lordship, in the adjacent *contado*. Communal Italy was not Florence, Venice, Genoa or even Milan. In the great majority of towns commercial growth was too restricted and plebeian to attract the noble class (*milites, magnati*), or to endow the commoner class (*pedites, popolo*) with strength enough to capture the commune and subjugate the country. The attempt by the *Popolo* to achieve this in many communes during the thirteenth century was generally of limited or short-lived effect. The most inveterate divisions in urban politics, the cause of faction and of much inter-city war, arose not from class but from aristocratic conflicts, frequently involved with the territorial rivalries of feudal magnates. And the main effect of expansion in the *contado* was to transfer to feudal magnates, as nominal citizens and subjects, the leadership of party and eventually, through party, the domination, *signoria*, of the communes themselves.

These processes were nowhere better exhibited than in Romagna and the adjacent areas of the Montefeltro and March of Ancona.[2] Communes here were all primarily aristocratic creations, of the lesser knightly nobility (*milites, capitanei, valvassores*). They were 'born seigneurial'. And such essentially they remained: communities directed by a landed and professional (legal) ruling class (*maiores*).[3] Except at Bologna (the largest city of the Papal State), and to some

[1] For a recent survey: Waley, 8off.
[2] The Montefeltro, in fact, and even at times Urbino, were treated as part of Romagna, while Rimini looked as much to the March as to Romagna: Waley, 93–4; Larner, 207; Vasina, *Romagna*, 140, 142, 187; above p. 3 n. 9, below p. 21.
[3] Taurino, *Studi medievali*, xi (1970), 663; Luzzatto, 'Sottomissioni' 1906, 114ff. (cf. 1907, 212ff.); Colini-Baldeschi, 'Comuni'; Vasina, *Romagna*, 168ff. Only at Imola, owing to very particular circumstances, has it been suggested that the merchant class originated the commune: Fasoli, *AMR* 1942–3, 134.

extent Ancona, their development, by Lombard and Tuscan standards, was comparatively modest. In the March, communes of a kind were numerous, but for the most part they were small, in status more *castella* than *civitates*, populated by landholders of different degree. In Romagna the major cities may on average have been larger, but, with the possible exception of Rimini, are thought unlikely to have exceeded 10,000 souls.[1] Economically both provinces were predominantly agrarian, producers and exporters to the more urbanised parts of Italy of food and raw materials.[2] But the prime profits of this 'colonial' traffic went not to native traders and entrepreneurs but to landlords and foreign buyers. Local merchants and artisans, though of growing number, enterprising, and by the thirteenth century, guild organised, were mostly confined to local markets;[3] they produced no money aristocracy, no powerful 'bourgeoisie', few 'ricchi populari merchatanti'.[4] The export trade was commandeered by outsiders, in the first place Venetians, who from the twelfth century, if not before, as part of a general policy of economic hegemony in the Adriatic and *terra ferma* hinterland, imposed a series of increasingly restrictive trade pacts on the leading towns of Romagna and the March (Ravenna, Faenza, Fano etc.). In Romagna Venetian encroachment was challenged for a time in the thirteenth century by Bologna, which to economic added territorial ambitions, particularly against Imola, and exerted a potent influence in the politics and urban alliances of the region. But the Bolognese counter-offensive was abruptly checked by the outbreak in 1274 and 1279 of savage civil faction – a major cause of the warfare which then convulsed the whole province. And in the last decades of the century competition with Venice, in Romagna and Bologna itself, passed to another 'foreign' power: the commercial and banking interest of Tuscany and Florence.[5]

---

[1] Waley, 89–90; Larner, 10, 220ff., 225ff.

[2] Grain, wine, oil, meat, cheese, salt and, by the later Middle Ages, flax, hemp, woad and saffron. Food exports, especially of corn, therefore figured as one more contentious issue between the papacy and communes and despots: Larner, 11–12 etc.

[3] By the late Middle Ages both regions, however, had developed an export industry (which awaits investigation) in cheap cloth (*panni romagnoli*, *bigi* etc.) based on sheep-farming in the hills and, possibly, transhumant grazing in the lowlands: cf. Feliciangeli, *AMM* 1912; Ferranti, 123–4.

[4] A phrase used, exceptionally, in the Statutes of Ascoli (ed. L. Zdekauer and P. Sella, Rome, 1910), 221. The mass of *populares*, in the March at least, were smallowners, even yokels ('protorustici'). Cf. generally: A. Schaube, *Handelsgeschichte d. romanischen Völker* (Munich, 1906), 494–7, 669ff.; Spadoni, *Le Marche* 1906, 2ff.; Mondolfo, *ibid.* 1912, 12ff.; Marcucci, *ibid.* 1908, 36ff.; Colini-Baldeschi, *Vita maceratese* (Macerata, 1900), 16–17, 5off., 77; Balduzzi, *AMR* 1875, 158; Larner, 1ff., 129ff., 147ff.; Vasina, *Romagnoli*, 5–7; Waley, 87–8, 162, 193, 274.

[5] For details: Fasoli, *AMR* 1942–3, 136ff., 166ff.; Vasina, *Romagnoli*, 4–6, 9–10, 22, 30, 35–6, 45ff., 121ff., 169ff. etc.; *Romagna*, 196; Larner, 10–11, 16, 23, 26; Torre,

Political conformed to economic development. In power and prestige most communes of Romagna and the Marche remained of second rank. Of the smaller towns some were barely enfranchised from feudal overlordship: Bagnacavallo and Castrocaro, and several in the March.[1] For the rest, they made their mark if at all – like Rimini or, even more, Urbino – only when feudal combined with urban power in despotism. Before then their progress is little documented or chronicled.[2] There is enough, certainly, to show that each evolved a typical urban constitution, though partly, in Romagna, under influence from Bologna: the standard structure of great and small councils under consuls, then *podestà*, administering the familiar forms of statute law, jurisdiction and municipal taxation. In addition, during the thirteenth century, following earlier disputes between *milites* and *pedites*, some attempt was made in many towns by the class of *popolani* to democratise the government, by securing guild participation, tying citizenship to guild membership, and even in places creating a popular constitution, with laws restraining magnate privilege, and a separate magistracy of *anziani* under a *capitano del popolo*. But in few communes outside Bologna (here again a model to Romagna) and some larger towns in the March (Ancona, Ascoli, Macerata), did the *popolo* establish effective control, still less develop a ruling class distinct in composition or interest from the feudal elements of city and *contado*. If anything it provoked a noble reaction, of benefit to despotism. Even with popular representation, the magnate class preserved its authority and influence in both church and state, penetrating the guilds, manipulating the *popolo*, or contending independently to impose party and personal rule.[3] Stronger than democratisation or the effect of social struggle was the contrary pressure, equally old and, in Romagna, far more evident, of aristocratic faction. All over Romagna, in fact, from the late twelfth century, the nobility is found divided and cities disputed between rival factions: clan groups and *clientele*, generated by family feuds and property interests (including ownership of the commune), and known by family names (the Tuscan terms 'Guelf' and 'Ghibelline', with

Polentani, 33–61, 94, 126 etc.; below pp. 20, 323. For parallel developments in the March, opposing Venice and Ancona: Waley, 184, 186.

[1] In some larger towns also communes continued formally bound to the former suzerain for the exercise of certain *regalia*: as Ravenna, to the archbishop, for the right of coinage: Torre, *Polentani*, 95.

[2] Significantly in Romagna chronicles (with one exception) first appear late, toward the end of the thirteenth century, and are already partly apologies for emergent *signorie*: Vasina, *Romagna*, 158–9. Urbino has none at all until long after court replaced commune.

[3] Fasoli, 'Ricerche sulla legislazione anti-magnatizia', *Riv. stor. dir. it.*, 1939, 109ff., 120ff.; Vasina, *Romagnoli*, 5, 7, 281; *Romagna*, 176ff.; Larner, 1off., 59–60, 132, 147, 204; Luzzatto, 'Sottomissioni' 1906; Spadoni, *Le Marche* 1906; *Stat. Ascoli* (ed. Zdekauer).

their ideological undertones, being later and adventitious). And already then, in one town, party was turning precociously into personal domination. Between the late twelfth and mid-thirteenth century, the commune of Ravenna was governed in hereditary succession by the Traversari family. This first, proto-*signoria* was cut short in 1240 by the sudden death without male heirs of Paolo Traversari (only the Traversari name and connection surviving for a time). But in many ways it typified the despotisms to come. In form it was anonymous, a *de facto* tyranny, based not on election but on influence and wealth. By contemporaries the Traversari were called in fact 'barons'. And the recorded source of their double dominion, baronial and despotic, was a long accumulation of land, lordship and vassalage, acquired largely by usurpation or grant from local churches. Their only possible singularity was their ancient civic status. Descended from *capitanei* of the pre-communal archiepiscopal *curia*, they belonged by origin to the nobility of the town, not, like later despots, to the more recently urbanised nobility of the *contado*.[1]

In the *contado* also, from motives and by methods common throughout the city states all the communes of Romagna and the March (with the peculiar exception of Imola)[2] asserted urban control and, in the thirteenth century especially, with growing popular influence, sought to supplant rival lordships, lay and ecclesiastical, most notably, in these parts, the archbishopric of Ravenna. In increasing number *comitatini* of all classes accepted communal suzerainty: lords to become citizens, owing certain obligations, particularly urban domicile; their *homines* to become 'free' subjects, bound to urban justice, taxes, war service and *corvées*. To further enfranchisement, various towns also acted to suppress serfdom or to attract and emancipate immigrant dependants.[3] But once again the old landed order (backed, in the case of the church, by papal authority) proved indestructible, and to the extent that in the end it was the *contado* that conquered the town. Urban expansion was never complete, either in range or depth.[4] In Romagna particularly, where all the larger city communes lay along the lowlands, most of the mountain

---

1 Torre, *Polentani*, 6ff., 30ff., 62ff., 71, 82ff., 111; Larner, 25, 36–7, 66, 129; Vasina, *Romagna*, 168, 177. The Traversari were 10 times *podestà* of Ravenna between 1180 and 1220.
2 Where, through the opposition of bishop and count, the *contado* was never subdued, and came to form a federal commune of its own: Fasoli, *AMR* 1942–3, 120ff.
3 Luzzatto, 'Sottomissioni' 1906, 129ff.; Colini-Baldeschi, *Riv. bib. archivi*, 1900, 17ff., 112ff.; Torre, 'Controversie'; Vasina, *SR* 1967, 333ff.; Larner, 3ff., 17; Waley, 134 n.1.
4 For what follows cf. Luzzatto, 'Sottomissioni' 1906; Colini-Baldeschi, *Vita*, 98ff.; Ferranti, iii.21ff.; Fasoli, *AMR* 1942–3; Larner, 14ff., 45, 76–8, 105ff.; Torre, *Polentani*, 31, 33, 41; Vasina, *Romagnoli*, 7ff., 23; Vicinelli, 'Famiglia' 1925, 194ff.

interior, but also parts of the plain, remained under feudatories, or immunists like the church of Ravenna. Some were comital families, of ancient stock: the counts of Bagnacavallo, Castrocaro, Cunio, or the Guidi. But others were new, or newly emerged, in process of building up land and lordship, largely, like the communes, at the expense of the church. Land and lordship still went together. Throughout the thirteenth century, and in places beyond, forms of serfdom persisted, or of rustic 'vassalage' on occasion combining rent with military service, and yielding regular retinues of *fideles*, *seguaces*, *homines de masnata*.¹ Too many townsmen were serfowners for communes to attack villeinage wholesale;² and the towns collectively were too small, underdeveloped and divided to pursue any consistent antiseigneurial policy. They had to compromise. In the March of Ancona, where peasant immigration brought communes and feudatories into frequent conflict, a settlement was usually arranged whereby lords received part of the tenants' holdings and other compensations – often including tax immunity and tenure of the *podesteria*. In Romagna too, many acts of feudal submission have the character of contract, alliances based on common interest, in peace and still more war. Intercity war and faction were of all things the salvation and opportunity of the feudal class. From start to finish the wars of Romagna were fought by coalitions, not of towns against lords but of towns and lords together; and the forces engaged were commonly hired troops, *milites* of the highlands, recruited as vassals by Apennine warlords who combined the trade of *condottieri* with feuds and leagues of their own.³ Still greater was the confusion of town and feudal rivalries when compacts of citizenship brought territorial magnates into urban civil war. Installed in the communal councils, and even the guilds, and with their land, wealth and feuding habits all unimpaired, they became the natural leaders of faction and party *signoria*. By the mid-thirteenth century, in all towns of Romagna, feudal families had gained control of one or both parties, and were beginning to add urban to rural lordship. One early example were the counts of Bagnacavallo who as Ghibelline leaders briefly ruled Ravenna between 1249 and 1252.⁴ Exactly similar was the early history of all other *signori*, except perhaps in the one point of pedigree. As a class the lords of Romagna seem to have belonged

¹ For example Fantuzzi, iii. 110, 258, 263; Larner, 107ff.
² Even to immigrant serfs it was rare to grant freedom within a short term as at Amandola (Ferranti, iii. 106) or Rimini (below p. 25 n. 4) and emancipation was generally withheld from serfs of citizens, friendly lords or lords who became citizens.
³ The beginning of a long tradition in which the uplands of Romagna became famous for soldiers: Franceschini, *Montefeltro*, 19, 27–8, 32; Larner, 32.
⁴ Ravaglia, *SR* 1956, 275ff.; Torre, *Polentani*, 10–11; Larner, 36–7.

principally to the newer, 'recent feudality'.[1] Such at least were the families who eventually prevailed: the counts of Montefeltro in Urbino, the Alidosi, Manfredi and Ordelaffi at Imola, Faenza and Forlì, and, on the frontiers of the province, the Polenta at Ravenna and the Malatesta in Rimini.

In later days courtly propaganda was to fabricate for *signori* illustrious antecedents, Germanic and Byzantine, biblical or Roman,[2] testimonials of legitimacy, if not divine right. In prosaic fact their ancestry in every case barely covers three generations, and their sole title to dominion was, in all cases, right of conquest, in urban war and faction.

The only partial exception were the counts of Montefeltro, the earliest and, with brief interruptions, the longest to rule, whose *signoria* at Urbino was formally instituted by imperial investiture in 1226 and is unique in Romagna in that it seems to have been based on no civic party or office.[3] Substantially, however, their career was typical.[4] Descended, by reputation at least, from the widely ramified Apennine dynasty of the counts of Carpegna, they first emerge, and were first themselves made counts, in the reign of Barbarossa. Their strength was founded on concentrations of land and jurisdiction, much of it ecclesiastical, of the see of S. Leo, which from the late twelfth century they virtually appropriated for nearly a hundred years. And the lordship of Urbino they owed primarily not to any imperial act, but to the slow growth of territorial influence, the support of a wide affinity of local lords and their *fideles* (the Brancaleoni, Bernardini, counts of Montedoglio etc.), and, in the last stage, to conquest, in an eight-year war (1226–34), secured by partisan alliance and treaty of citizenship with the neighbouring rival commune of Rimini. In the same period by similar means they extended their influence also into other adjoining areas, first toward Umbria, the March and the upper Tiber valley, then in the later thirteenth century toward northern Romagna, to the cities of the plain. This transformation of local into regional *signoria* was mainly the work of one man: the warlord and Ghibelline leader Guido da Montefeltro (1220–98) who, sustained by two great victories over Guelf and papal forces (at S. Procolo in 1275 and Forlì in 1282) imposed his rule, for some ten years (1274–83) on Forlì, Cervia and Cesena, and, through party affiliation, on almost the whole province. Based on local faction

[1] Torre, *Polentani*, 111. It was the same in the March of Ancona: Colini-Baldeschi, 'Comuni'.
[2] In order of fashion: Larner, 18–19; below p. 26.
[3] With the marginal exception of the counts of Bagnacavallo, there is no case either in Romagna, unlike the March, of former feudal lords of a town recovering power later in the new character of *signori*: Luzzatto, 'Le finanze di un castello (Matelica) nel secolo XIII', *VSWG* 1912.
[4] For what follows: Franceschini, *Montefeltro*, 11–172.

and tenure or control of municipal office (*podesteria*, *capitanato*),[1] this compound despotism was virtually the first true 'tyranny' to be formed in Romagna.[2] It showed also the potentialities of war-captaincy, and the instinct of *signorie* to expand. At the same time it failed to strike root. Dispossessed of all his lordships by the Guelf Martin IV, Guido returned to Urbino in 1293 (adding nearby Cagli); and from there he and his successors continued to intrigue for dominion in Romagna. So also, in response to his example, did two other Ghibelline war-leaders of the feudal highlands: Maghinardo Pagani da Susinana, who at the end of the century governed Faenza, Forlì and Imola till his death without male heirs in 1302;[3] and Uguccione della Faggiola, captain-general in 1297 of the Ghibelline league of Romagna and *capitano* of Cesena, 1300–1.[4] But again there was no sequel. With different *fortuna* both might have founded lordships. But the general experience of Italy suggests that at this stage alien *signorie* by intrusive warlords lacked stability. In Romagna, certainly, all the despotisms which prospered were initially, like Urbino, of native growth.

The first of these in Romagna proper was once again the lordship of Ravenna, established in 1275 by the Polenta family. The Polenta, like the Traversari, belonged by origin to the curial feudality of the arch-bishopric of Ravenna, of which during the thirteenth century they became, with great profit, the leading lay administrators. They took their name from the mountain *castrum* of Polenta, near Bertinoro, which along with earlier lands they came to hold from 1182 of the monastery of S. Giovanni Evangelista; and their subsequent pro-gress is marked throughout by the steady occupation, by fief, lease or encroachment, of ecclesiastical property in Ravenna and neighbour-ing territories. Politically they rose first as clients of the Traversari, sharing a place by 1215 in the council of the commune with member-ship of the episcopal *curia*; and with the 'pars Traversariorum' they continued to long collaborate after its fall in 1240, in opposition to the Ghibelline counts of Bagnacavallo. But eventually, in the way of all Italian faction, the party divided. In 1274 the Traversari were expelled; and the following year the Polenta, armed with outside help (from the Malatesta), seized power (*dominium*) forcibly in Ravenna, at the same time taking Comacchio. From that time, despite some papal inter-ference, they ruled without serious break, increasing their wealth with

[1] Supported also and, to some extent, prepared by the acquisition of feudal posses-sions in the region (notably an interest in the county of Ghiaggiolo): Vasina, *Romagnoli*, 253; Franceschini, *Montefeltro*, 48, 74–5, 87–8, 106.

[2] Larner, 35–6.

[3] 'Grande e savio tiranno e della contrada fra Casentino e Romagna grande castel-lano a con molti fedeli': G. Villani, vii. 149. For details and older works: Torre, *SR* 1963; Larner, 49–51; Vasina, *Romagnoli*, 172–3, 179–80, 185–6.

[4] P. Vigo, *Uguccione della Faggiola* (Leghorn, 1879).

additional church holdings (especially those of the Traversari and other discredited 'usurpers'), and exercising a *de facto*, untitled tyranny, occasionally as 'consuls' or 'rectors', more regularly as *podestà*, but sometimes without office at all. From 1283 they also controlled Cervia.[1]

Hardly different, if slightly more protracted, was the progress of the three neighbouring dynasties of Manfredi, Alidosi and Ordelaffi, all of whom, like the Polenta, first appear distinctly in the late twelfth or early thirteenth century, as minor nobles, tenants of church land, involved in urban affairs; by the later thirteenth century had become leaders of faction; and by the early fourteenth, after temporary eclipse or subordination by Guido da Montefeltro and Maghinardo Pagani, were assuming predominance, with or without office, in the adjacent cities of Faenza, Imola and Forlì.[2] At the same time others of the sort were coming up in the March of Ancona: the Varani at Camerino, the Attoni at Matelica.[3] And in all city states similar *maiores* were grappling for domination. Beneath republican forms, a seigneurial society was again taking shape: a hybrid society, part feudal, part urban, linked closely with the past; but, for upholders of the past – the 'buon tempo antico' – a degenerate, 'bastard' society, dead to old ideals of chivalry, honour, civic pride, grounded on the single principle of fitness (for Dante, unfitness) to survive.[4] In the crude contest for *signoria* no differences of creed divided victors from vanquished, no policy or programme beyond domination or elimination. 'Ghibelline' and 'Guelf' were names without political or social significance. Tenure by *tiranni* of the office of *capitano* implied no popular affinity.[5] As Machiavelli saw (*Discorsi*, i.55), *gentiluomini* were natural enemies of all true self-government (*repubblica*), all *civiltà*, all 'vivere politico'. Not before the fourteenth century did *signori* in Romagna bother to legalise their lordship by formalities of election and hereditary title.[6] Of an ideological conflict between republicanism and tyranny there is barely

---

[1] A town originally subject to the archbishop, intermittently to Ravenna, most recently to Guido da Montefeltro: Torre, *Polentani, passim*; Larner, 21–2, 37, 51–2.

[2] Larner, 20–1, 49–50, 82–3, 86; Maltoni, *SR* 1960. Chronicle references of the thirteenth century to the Manfredi and to urban faction in Faenza as early as 1100 savour of anachronism: *RIS*[2] xxviii/1925–7, 57.

[3] Luzzatto, *VSWC* 1912; Waley, 89, 219.

[4] 'Oh Romagnoli tornati in bastardi' etc.: *Purg.*, xiv, 99ff.; and the whole invective canto on the decay of antique chivalry (with the 'casa Traversara' etc.) and civic virtue.

[5] As argued, for rexample, by Vasina of Maghinardo at Faenza and Forlì and of the Montelfeltro and Malatesta at Cesena: *Romagnoli*, 236, 240–1, 281.

[6] Saving, briefly, the Polenta at Comacchio in 1275: Torre, *Polentani*, 75; Larner, 32, 77–8, 82–5. They were more concerned with extending their influence to positions of authority in the local church (a further reason for papal interest to control episcopal elections): Vasina, *Romagnoli*, 231–2; Franceschini, *Montefeltro*, 172–3, 186, 198, below pp. 61, 300.

a hint in contemporary writing. The only genuine struggle (to echo Salutati on Caesar's Rome) was to determine, not whether one should rule, but who the one should be.[1] It was a pure fight for power and wealth, so intimately personal that, well before 1300, almost all the ruling families had themselves fratricidally split, over property and dominion, into rival 'Guelfs' and 'Ghibellines'.[2] And, as everywhere in Italy, the means to power were not votes or manifestos, but force, fraud, proficiency in gang war – a Machiavellian mixture of *fortuna* and *virtù*.

In thirteenth-century Romagna, the family, on Dante's testimony, most outstanding for these qualities were the Malatesta of Rimini.

[1] 'non omnino ne quisquam, sed uter regeret, certabatur': *De Tyranno* (ed. A. V. Martin, Berlin, 1913), xxvii.

[2] The Montefeltro (from *c.* 1250), the Polenta (from 1279), the Ordelaffi (1276), the Manfredi (with a particularly foul murder in 1285: Dante, *Inf.*, xxxiii, 109ff.), and the Malatesta: Franceschini, *Montefeltro*, 41–2, 63ff.; Torre, *Polentani*, 83ff.; Larner, 32, 37; below p. 37. It was a dissident branch of the Polenta that obtained Comacchio in 1276, and of the Montefeltro that first reoccupied Urbino after papal dispossession in 1283.

2

Rimini and the rise of the Malatesta

Rimini, before the Malatesta, played no remarkable part in the history of either the papal or the Italian city state. Though greater, possibly, than neighbouring towns in size and commercial growth, it rose to no pre-eminence in regional life or politics.[1] Incorporated from the beginning into the States of the Church, first as part of the Maritime Pentapolis, then as the boundary city of Romagna,[2] it became, with Romagna, effectively papal only in the later thirteenth century. Previously, for two hundred years, it was imperial and imperialist, and remained so for as long as the empire continued in Italy to be more than a partisan symbol. In the twelfth century it was quick to embrace the Hohenstaufen interest, fighting on their behalf and accepting the rule of their local counts and margraves. Under Frederick II it welcomed the return of imperial government in 1221, surrendering the *contado* to the count of Romagna, and allowing an imperial *vicecomes* to be appointed in the city. Even after the Council of Lyons Rimini continued Ghibelline and only abandoned Frederick when he was routed at Parma in 1248 and Romagna as a whole withdrew allegiance from him. After that it remained a predominantly Guelf community. Its history blends imperceptibly with that of the Guelf Malatesta. And inside the commune the struggle of party is one for local dominion alone.[3]

As a commune, too, Rimini developed along typical lines. Despite vestiges of antique urban organisation, surviving in the office of 'Pater, Civitatis' or 'Parcitade',[4] in Rimini as everywhere a communal constitution first matured in the twelfth and early thirteenth centuries. The long period of imperial supremacy presented no serious obstacle to the progress of municipal franchise; and by 1278 the city possessed all the

---

[1] About economic development, in fact, little information survives. Vasina detects signs of a flourishing 'bourgeoisie' with wide trading connections, but what mainly emerges, here as elsewhere, is growing Venetian and then Florentine influence: *Romagna*, 254, 277ff.; below p. 323.

[2] 'Ista civitas cum suo comitatu est finis Romandiole': Theiner, ii.534 (*a.* 1371). Cf. *Liber Censuum*, i.86 n. 1; Vasina, *Romagna*, 142.

[3] Clementini, i.249–464; Battaglini, *Zecca*, 1–54; Tonini, ii.206–385, iii.1–94.

[4] Clementini, i.249–50; Tonini, ii.154–62, 217–18, 232, 234, 274–8, 317–24.

machinery of effective self-government. The first surviving collection of statutes derives from the fourteenth century, but it is possible to trace the main outlines of earlier organisation. The ultimate source of authority resided, though with diminishing vigour, in the *consiglio generale*, which had possibly replaced an earlier *parlamentum* or *arengum*, and which down to the fourteenth century every 'paterfamilias' may have been entitled to attend. Presided over by the *podestà* or his vicar, whose proposals it discussed and voted, it elected all ordinary officials of the commune.[1] Alongside it existed also a smaller *consiglio di credenza, de' Savj* or *degli Anziani*, an offshoot of the larger body charged with the particular duty of checking the *podestà*. It seems to have had no fixed composition, its numbers varying in the thirteenth century from six to twenty-two.[2] The chief magistrate was the *podestà*, a 'foreigner' elected for the term of six months. During the twelfth century the 'Proceri', successors of the 'Patres Civitatis', had persisted for a time, but they were later eclipsed by elected 'consoli', until at the close of the century the new office of the *podesteria* was established with full civil, military and judicial powers.[3] From then on the series of *podestà* became regular and survived the rector's attempt in 1278 to make the office a papal appointment.[4]

There is little evidence in Rimini of any sharp struggle between 'milites' and 'populares', nor are the references to *compagnie* in Rimini as full as they are in other towns of Romagna. Yet Rimini possessed its guilds, and from as early as 1232 there is mention of 'Capitularii ordinum', officers of various societies and trades, being summoned to assemblies of the general council, together with the 'baillitores Capellarum', officials representing each *contrada* of the city, who had jurisdiction over offences committed at night. The pretensions of the popular 'Capitularii' probably grew, and in 1254 they appear as 'capitanei populi et ordinum', having power to deal with peace and war. Evidently they were normally four in number, and from about the year 1278 they assumed the name of 'Quatuor Officiales', which was to

---

[1] Battaglini, *Zecca*, 181. The number of people authorised to attend the *consiglio* is not known, and what lists there are give only about 100 names (see Tonini, iii, XII, XX; 397–8, 411); but Tonini (*ibid.* 196) was of the opinion that the head of every family was free to attend, and this is supported by a document of 1290 which speaks of members being eligible 'according to the extimum' (or property tax), 'scilicet unus de familia tantum' (*ibid.* 157; cf. below p. 36 n. 3). In the fourteenth century however the number was limited to 300, 'ut melius rei publicae provideatur per numerum competentem quam per consiliariorum multitudinem onerosam' (*ibid.* 196).

[2] Tonini, iii. 209, 213, XVII, XXXII, XXXIV, XXXIX, XLVI, LVI, LXVII.

[3] For the obscure beginnings of the *podesteria* at Rimini: Battaglini, *Zecca*, 40, 126; Tonini, ii. 394–6, 589–90; Ficker, *Forschungen*, iii. 434.

[4] Tonini, iii. 102–3, 605–8; Cantinelli, *Chronicon*, 29.

remain permanent. By that time their authority had become considerable. Elected every month by the general council, they were to prose-
cute the affairs of the commune, together with the *podestà* and the two
councils. Without their assent the *podestà* could propose nothing,
whereas they could propose any measures they wished, independently
of him and his justices. They were further authorised to appoint all
extraordinary officials – ambassadors, syndics and proctors, the custo-
dians of the gates and of the *castelli* – and to nominate the *consiglio di
credenza*; and their fiscal powers were correspondingly wide. As
established at the end of the thirteenth century, they formed the principal challenge to any would-be despot.[1]

These institutions, with the powers exercised, were primarily the
product of spontaneous growth and usurpation. Though charters
attributed to Barbarossa have been preserved which grant privileges of
full self-government in Rimini,[2] these have been exposed as spurious.[3]
Spurious or not, however, the commune was careful to have them
ratified by both pope and emperor, and to legitimise rights it had
cumulatively seized: of jurisdiction, taxation, coinage and so on. By
Innocent IV and William of Holland in 1250, by Tommaso da Fogliano,
imperial count of Romagna, in 1255, and again by the pope in 1284, the
grants were renewed or extended; and at the same time the Riminese
were taken into the 'speciale demanium' of the church.[4]

Equipped with a system of government and with privileges it could
appeal to, when the papacy resumed control of Romagna the commune
of Rimini had been acting for over a century with increasing autonomy
and self-consciousness, despite the presence of imperial officials –
engaging in wars and concluding treaties, contesting the limits of
ecclesiastical jurisdiction, encroaching upon the *contado*, and, as it grew in
importance, taking under its protection the neighbouring lords and town-
ships. In war the most obstinate enemies of Rimini were the citizens of
nearby Cesena. In the conflict of jurisdictions, they were the local bishop
of the diocese and the church of Ravenna. But common to all these
disputes was the attempt by Rimini to conquer the surrounding *contado*.

---

[1] Battaglini, *Zecca*, 175, 181; Tonini, iii.103, 196–7, LXVII, LXXVI, LXXIX, LXXX,
LXXXI, LXXXVII, XCII, C, CVII, CXXVIII, CXXIX, CXLV. One document, of 1290 (*ibid.*
CLXIV), also speaks of an 'arengum societatum ordinum Arim'. Cf. generally
Tonini, ii.386–96, iii.193–221.
[2] *Ann.* 1156 or 1157, and 1167: Tonini, ii.576.
[3] Giordani, *Gradara*, 14; Ficker, *Forschungen*, ii.218. Cf. Massèra in *RIS²* xv/2.243.
[4] Collectively the rights conferred comprised 'Civitatem Suburbia et Comitatum
cum portubus portis nundinis et moneta honoribus iurisdictionibus' (in one case,
1255, equated with *merum et mixtum imperium*). The earliest reference to Riminese
coinage is 1265: Clementini, i.491; Battaglini, *Zecca*, 54, 58, 171; Tonini, iii.434–5,
553, 640; Theiner, i.438; *Reg. M. IV*, 523.

Conquest of the *contado* and its subordination to the city, with obligations in men and money, were a natural consequence of the independence to which the charters of Barbarossa, whether forged or not, bore
testimony, and it was probably during the period of confusion after the
death of Henry VI that Rimini first proceeded to occupy the 'comitatus'
hitherto pertaining to the empire, and so became involved in a series of
wars with Cesena.[1] This act of invasion was premature, and not until
the defeat and death of Frederick II was the possession of the contado
made secure; after that, in the privileges, papal and imperial, of 1250
and later, the grant of the 'comitatus' was given a regular place. This
put the claims of the commune upon an authoritative foundation; but
in practice it was not only against pope or emperor that Rimini had to
safeguard its ambition to govern the contado. It had also to overcome the long-established franchises of other powers in Romagna
itself.

The first of these was the bishop of Rimini, who during the twelfth
century had preserved a considerable temporal authority and was
unwilling to let it go.[2] From the beginning the Italian communes had
challenged ecclesiastical privilege, and not all of the struggles in which
Rimini engaged with the church were confined to territorial or juridical
rights.[3] But even when they were not, they may be taken as symptoms
of a deeper opposition which turned upon the possession or jurisdiction
of castles and properties in the locality of the city. A conclusion to this
source of unrest came in 1255 when the bishop gave up his remnant of
the 'passagia' in Rimini itself, and surrendered all jurisdiction and fiscal
rights over Santarcangelo and other disputed territories. An attempt
to reverse this decision twenty years later met with no success.[4]

Beside the pretensions of the church of Ravenna the rights attributed
to the bishops of Rimini were modest. From earliest times the archbishops of Ravenna had patrimonies only less extensive than those of
the see of Rome, and the lands confirmed to them by the emperor as
late as 1220 still included the 'comitatus' of Cesena, Fano and

---

[1] Ficker, *Forschungen*, ii.289; Savioli, *Annali*, ii.275.

[2] See for example Battaglini, *Zecca*, 124–5.

[3] Tonini, ii.589–90. In 1223 the city was placed under interdict for anti-clerical
ordinances (*Reg. Hon. III*, ii. n. 4961; Battaglini, *Zecca*, 136–8). In 1226 the imperial
decrees on heresy provoked tumults in Rimini (Theiner, i.140; *Reg. Hon. III*, iii,
n. 5768), and in 1243 the count of Romagna had to lend his protection to the
cathedral canons (Tonini, iii.87).

[4] Fantuzzi, v. 348ff.; Tonini, iii.133–6, 547–53, 592–6, 608–31. This is not to say
that all the places involved acquiesced peacefully in Riminese government.
Santarcangelo in particular seems to have been as often independent as submissive,
until granted by the papacy to the Malatesta. At the end of the thirteenth century
it formed one of a number of 'vicariates' established by the papacy in the *contado*
of Rimini and other Romagnol towns: Vasina, *Romagnoli*, 284–5; Marini, *Malatesta*;
Castellani, *Santarcangelo*.

Sinigaglia, and many places in the dioceses of Rimini and Pesaro.[1] Differences between the commune of Rimini and the church of Ravenna occurred throughout the thirteenth century, in which the advantage fell increasingly, if not consistently, to the commune.[2] But the archbishops did not easily yield their rights, vestiges of which they were able to uphold for another two hundred years.[3] The traditional claims of Ravenna, though enfeebled by a century of conflict with the communes, confronted the future powers of despotism everywhere in this region.

Subjugation of the *contado* took time to accomplish, and in the early decades of the thirteenth century the commune was only one of several authorities claiming obedience there. While some lands were subject to Rimini, others were directly administered by the emperor, some were in the possession of the church, and others in the hands of private lords. Most of the private lords were at this time bound in some way to the city by individual compact, for willingness to seek or to accept the protection of the commune grew with its importance. In increasing number from the late twelfth century, local communities commended themselves to Rimini, usually assuming in return military and fiscal obligations;[4] while the nobility of the district also began to come to terms with the new authority, sometimes accepting similar obligations for themselves or their *homines*, but sometimes contracting rather treaties that safeguarded their jurisdiction and involved no more than an oath of obedience and residence in time of war.[5]

Among the earliest to conclude such agreements were the Malatesta.

---

[1] *Regesto della Chiesa di Ravenna* (ed. V. Federici, G. Buzzi, Rome, 1911–31), n. 215. In 1228 the pope renewed this privilege in a reduced form (*ibid.* n. 277). S. Appolinare in Classe also had possessions in the Riminese and Cesenate which had been confirmed by Otto IV and led to transactions with Rimini: Tonini, iii. 14, 433.

[2] Torre, 'Controversie'. The conflict of Ravenna with Pesaro was no less acute (Giordani, *Illustrazione*; Vaccai, 226) and in 1271, to obtain peace, certain of the disputed castles, with the consent of the archiepiscopal viscount, submitted to Rimini, which was to share the jurisdiction with Ravenna: Clementini, i.482; Battaglini, *Zecca*, 140; Tonini, iii.120–3, 588–92.   [3] Below p. 294.

[4] For examples, including Urbino (1202) and certain communities of the Montefeltro (1233), see Clementini, i.333–5; Tonini, ii.385–6, iii.503–5, 516–17. From the same period (1220) comes a decree freeing immigrant serfs after a year and a day; but excepted were the *servi* of Riminese citizens and taxpayers (now coming to include feudal lords) and it does not seem to have been rigorously enforced, e.g. against the archbishop of Ravenna: Tonini, iii.24–5; Tarlazzi, i.171.

[5] Compare for example the two contracts, of 1228 and 1232, with the counts of Montefeltro and of Carpegna, the first mainly a treaty of alliance, the second imposing an annual oath, *census* and *collecta* of £50 *Rav.*, 'hostis et cavalcata', subjection to communal justice, and work (presumably *corvées*) from the communities submitted. The commune made the counts citizens and promised to accept none of their subjects as such: Tonini, iii.450–4, 492–5.

Of the Malatesta, as of neighbouring dynasties, the precise origins are obscure. But if the legend of their Germanic ancestry be set aside,[1] they may be identified in the second half of the twelfth century as local magnates of the Riminese hinterland, exercising a certain jurisdiction, and perhaps ascribed as citizens to the commune.[2] Although the chroniclers and early writers all agree in deriving them from Penna Billi, a castle in the Montefeltro,[3] the oldest documents link them with Verucchio and il Trebbio near S. Marino.[4] They were active in extending their properties and patrimonial connections. The first notable member of the family, Malatesta di Giovanni, was married to a daughter of the Ravenna lord Pietro Traversari,[5] and in 1186 is recorded buying land at Scorticata, between the Marecchia and the Rubicon, and from the sea to Sogliano. By 1210 the Malatesta had possessions in Rimini as well.[6]

The tradition that Verucchio had been given to the Malatesta by Rimini cannot be ignored,[7] but it should be noted that when the Malatesta submitted Verucchio to the commune in 1197, the recent death of Henry VI had for the first time allowed the Riminese to extend their authority over the contado. In that year, the record states, there had been prolonged conflict – 'discordia et guerra iamdudum' – between Giovanni, the son of Malatesta, and the citizens of Rimini. Induced by the example of other subjects of the *contado*, Giovanni therefore addressed letters of peace and submission to the commune, and on 21 December, in the name of himself and his nephew, together with the 'maioribus Veruculi et totius sue Terre Comitatus Arimini',

---

[1] Or their descent from Noah, the Tarquins or Scipio Africanus: *Cron. mal.*, 141; Battagli, 73; Clementini, i.253–72, ii.49–50; Amiani, i.122; Sansovino, 221.

[2] Clementini mentions a document of 1150 describing Malatesta di Giovanni as 'civis Arim.': i.276, 280. In April 1164 a 'Johannes Misoni Malatesta' appears as witness to a charter in Rimini (*Regesto S. Apollinare*, n. 96). He might be Malatesta's son (Tonini, ii.401). In 1197, finally, Giovanni di Malatesta, when writing to the Riminese, says of himself: 'de sanguine Vestro esse me recolo': Tonini, ii.603.

[3] Battagli, 27; *Cron mal.*, 3; Branchi, 141–2; *Chron. Bon.*, ii.127; Benvenuto da Imola, ii.309–10; Clementini, ii.682; but all these writers are speaking of Malatesta della Penna (below p. 27). Cf. Aeneas Sylvius Piccolomini: 'Haec origo gentis, haec familiae vetustas, haec nobilitas generis, cuius laudatores nesciunt invenisse principium ... Decepti sumus. Novum est nomen, nova familia; neque ab Ilis venit, neque Francorum sanguis est, neque Germanicus. Ex Penna venit, vili oppidulo et paucis cognito; nec per virtutem crevit. Prima tyrannidis fundamenta in proditione iacta fuerunt': *Opera ined.*, 538.

[4] As affirmed later in a papal letter of 1320 (*Lettres, Jean XXII*, 11, 148) and by Biondo in the fifteenth century (Flavio Biondo, *Italia illustrata* (Basle, 1531), 343).

[5] Imperial *comes Ariminensis* in 1186: Tonini, ii.402.

[6] For the early Malatesta properties see Fantuzzi, vi.242; Tonini, ii.402, 404–7, 591–2; iii.407–8, 511ff.

[7] Benvenuto da Imola, ii.310; Massèra, *RIS*² xvi/3.27. Branchi (146) says it was Malatesta della Penna to whom Verucchio was given.

he formally surrendered the castle of Verucchio in the presence of the consul and people of the city, and swore to obey them in everything.[1] There is no indication that the Malatesta were or now became citizens of Rimini, but in 1206 Giovanni Malatesta appears in the general council.[2]

The terms of 1197 were neither precise nor elaborate, and this may explain why twenty years later further conditions were imposed by Rimini on the Malatesta. In March 1216 a new agreement was concluded, whereby Giovanni and his nephew, Malatesta, undertook to live in Rimini, continuously in time of war, and for three months each year in time of peace, to go to war as directed by the commune, and to surrender whenever required 'omnia sua castra sive castella et loca ad defensionem commis Arimini'. In return the *podestà* declared the Malatesta citizens of Rimini. They were promised the protection of the commune, and were confirmed in their immunity from all taxes, which, it is affirmed, their family had not been accustomed to pay, while their private jurisdiction was safeguarded by the undertaking that none of their subjects should be received as citizens of Rimini.[3] A few weeks later, early in April, Malatesta was given money by the commune to buy a house in the city for himself and his family.[4]

With this covenant Giovanni Malatesta retires from the recorded history of his family. Dying in 1221 he left descendants of no conspicuous importance,[5] and his place was taken by his nephew, popularly known as Malatesta 'della Penna'.[6] Possessed of Verucchio and other lands in the *contado*, Malatesta della Penna won wide esteem in Rimini.[7] According to later chroniclers he performed great services for

[1] Tonini, ii.603–7: 'Concordia inter dominos de Malatesta et Veruculenses ex una, et Comune Arimini ex altera, in qua Johannes de Malatesta se submittit Comuni Arimini et pro offensis dat eidem Comuni Castrum Veruculi.' Giovanni was to maintain or destroy the castle as the consuls directed, and the 'Veruculenses' were to take an oath to the commune every 5 or 10 years.

[2] Tonini, iii.397–8. Cf. Savioli, *Annali*, iv.280.

[3] Clementini, i.359–65; Battaglini, *Zecca*, 164; Tonini, ii.405–6, iii.15–16, 408–11. The Malatesta are described as possessing 'terrae, castra, villae, loca et homines'. A similar exemption from 'gabelle' was accorded the counts of Montefeltro and Carpegna in 1228, but in general the convention is lighter than most others.

[4] Tonini, iii.412–13.

[5] His son, Ramberto, and grandson, Giovanni, survive obscurely in the records of the thirteenth century: see Tonini, ii.405–6, III, LXXXI, p. 520; Loevinson, 'Sunti', 355–6; below p. 31.

[6] Already in 1210 Malatesta appears independently of his uncle, when conceding certain emphyteutic property in Rimini: Tonini, iii.407–8. In 1221 he received further properties emphyteutically in the Riminese from the archbishop of Ravenna (Tarlazzi, i.114–15). Why he was called 'della Penna' is unknown.

[7] 'Isto autem tempore imperium tote Ytalie dominabatur et tunc Ariminum camera imperii vocabatur et ibi nobiles de patria pro suis negotiis se multotiens conferebant, et presertim dominus Malatesta de Penna cum filiis, sicut civis de

the commune, receiving in return extensive properties and immunities;[1] but the detail of their narrative is too confused to show what manner of services these were, and all that can be said with certainty is that before his death about the year 1248, Malatesta had held the office of *podestà* in Pistoja (1233) and in Rimini (1239), and may have obtained besides the distinction of knighthood from Frederick II.[2] Other spare notices of the Malatesta appear at this time, but the family becomes prominent in the annals of Rimini only when, in the middle of the thirteenth century, leadership passed to Malatesta's son, Malatesta da Verucchio, who was to lay the foundations of the *signoria*.

Although the chronicler Baldo Branchi, writing more than two centuries afterwards, describes Malatesta della Penna as 'capo de parte ghelfa',[3] the Malatesta are not seen as yet to follow any obvious party loyalty. As late as 1230 they appeared beside the imperialist Parcitadi, later their bitterest enemies, and swore with them to observe the league formed at the emperor's command between Rimini and other cities of Romagna. Still later, in 1247 or 1248, Malatesta da Verucchio took as his wife Concordia, whose mother was one of the Parcitadi, and whose father, Enrighetto, had been imperial *vicecomes* in the *contado*.[4] The marriage is revealing of the place now occupied by the Malatesta in Rimini, but it also suggests that as long as the Hohenstaufen and the 'Ghibelline' leaders retained control of the city the Malatesta were content to unite with them. They were gaining influence and wealth, but the time had not come for them to act alone. Not until 1248,when Romagna was lost to Frederick II, did they suddenly step forward as captains of the 'Guelfs', bent on seizing power for themselves. The anonymous chronicler of Rimini relates that the 'parte guelfa' at this time was strong in numbers but 'little feared because it had neither head nor leader' – 'and looking around for a leader who would be loyal and respected, they chose *misere* Malatesta, who dwelt at Verucchio, and sent for him and made him head and rector of the party'. Malatesta's marriage with Concordia had brought him a rich dowry, with rights and properties in Giovedia and S. Mauro 'et alia loca plurima infinita' in the Riminese *contado*, and this increased his power and pre-

---

Arimino et in Monte Feretro ac in Veruculo predilectus': Battagli, 27–8. In an embassy to Cesena in 1230, complaining of attacks on Riminese territory, the only citizen mentioned by name is 'dominus Malatesta': Tonini, iii.474–7.

[1] Benvenuto da Imola, ii.309; Branchi, 142, 144–6; Battagli, 29, 80; Tonini, iii.17; Massèra, RIS² xvi/3.29.

[2] Clementini, i.458, 462; F. G. Battaglini, *Zecca*, 166–7; A. Battaglini, *Saggio*, 34; Tonini, ii.407, iii.523; Massèra, RIS² xv/2.3, xvi/3.28. Clementini says he was *podestà* of Rimini in 1247 also.

[3] RIS² xv/2.144–6.

[4] Battagli, 28; *Cron. mal.*, 4–5; Branchi, 146–7, 149; Broglio, 185; Massèra, 'Note', 3–17.

tension – 'comenza a cresere la spesa e fare de grandi coredi e sempre onorare la parte ghelfa'.[1] Already therefore in 1248 Malatesta may have been in secret accord with the Guelfs.

In February of that year Frederick II was heavily defeated at Parma – a defeat which undid his power in Italy – and this must have decided Malatesta da Verucchio, who was in command of the Riminese militia, to carry through a long-meditated change of allegiance The Cesena annals relate that when he was with his contingent in the neighbourhood of Imola, as directed by the imperial count of Romagna, he surprised a messenger from the *podestà* of Rimini who wrote urging the count to detain him in prison as a suspect member of the Guelfs. Malatesta at once returned to Rimini, arrested the *podestà*, and with the assistance of friendly citizens gained control of the whole city, excepting only the houses of Ugolino Parcitade and a few others. Most of the Ghibelline leaders were driven out, while the Guelf families who had been exiled eight years before were readmitted into the city with the help of the papal legate, Ottaviano degli Ubaldini. The pope without delay released the commune from interdict, and wrote expressing his gratitude to the knight 'Malatesta de Veruculo', upon whom henceforward, as its leader, the 'parte guelfa' began to bestow all its favour and its wealth.[2]

The eminence to which Malatesta da Verucchio adroitly raised himself in 1248 forecast his ultimate dominion, and some of the oldest writers date from this time the beginnings of the Malatesta *signoria*.[3] But it was not until nearly fifty years later that the power of the Malatesta was securely founded. First the opposing faction of the Parcitadi had to be abased, whose leader was 'omo richissimo e potentissimo in detta città de Arimino'.[4]

The formal leaders of party in Rimini were two families of the old urban nobility: the Omodei, Ghibelline, and the Gambancerri, Guelf. The chronicler who records the return of the Guelfs to Rimini in 1248 therefore refers to the 'pars Gamancerra'.[5] But notices of both these families are scanty, though the Omodei still appear in 1267 to represent collectively the Ghibelline interest; and the active leadership of the factions seems to have passed in the middle of the thirteenth century to

---

[1] *Cron. mal.*, 4–5; Battagli, 28.

[2] 'Hoc autem tempore imperium cepit vacare et minui et ecclesia in Ytalia exaltari; unde ob hoc dominus Malatesta, imperium deserens, partem ecclesie est secutus': Battagli, 29; *Ann. Caes.*, 1101; Cantinelli, 6; Tonini, iii.92–5, 527–8; *Reg. Inn. IV*, n. 4272.

[3] Battagli, 29: 'Et hic incipit habere in Arimino partem maximam et sequaces': *Chron. Bon.*, ii.127: 'Anno Christi Mccxl9 huius Frederici tempore fuit origo illorum de Malatestis.'

[4] Branchi, 147.

[5] Battagli, 29.

the Malatesta and the Parcitadi. This second family, whose name, deriving from the office of Pater Civitatis, implied long-established prominence in the city, had become the most powerful Ghibelline partisans in Rimini, and under Frederick II Ugolino Parcitade had held the office of *vicecomes* in the Riminese *contado*. The same Ugolino was the uncle or the grandfather of Concordia Parcitade, and he is said to have designed her marriage with Malatesta da Verucchio in order to prevent the defection of Malatesta to the Guelfs. But events were to uphold the truth of Machiavelli's observation that 'intra gli uomini che aspirano ad una medesima grandezza, si può facilmente fare parentado, ma non amicizia',[1] and Concordia's death about 1265 was soon to remove what frail restraint upon hostility she may have been.[2]

The struggles of faction were not so violent in Rimini as in some large and wealthy communes like Bologna, but they were destined to recur until one party had overthrown the other. In 1251 the exiled Omodei combined with the Ghibellines of Urbino and the Montefeltro to devastate the Riminese *contado*, until a peace was made in January 1252. In the same year there is fragmentary record of a treaty between the Omodei and their allies, and the Gambancerri and commune of Rimini, by which it was agreed that municipal offices should in future be divided equally between the rival families and their followers. Malatesta da Verucchio does not appear in these transactions, but there are facts enough to show that he was still deemed a leader of the Guelfs. It was the Guelfs who helped him to extend his *palazzo* in the city, which was later to be incorporated in the Rocca Malatestiana, and it was doubtless in obedience to his Guelf alliance that in 1261 Malatesta refused to serve in Savignano with Parcitade as *vicecomes* of the archbishop of Ravenna. At the same time he was active as Guelf captain in Romagna, and when Charles of Anjou entered Italy in 1265 there were signs of a movement among the Ghibellines of Rimini, directed in particular against the Malatesta. It seems to have been inevitable that after a further peace between the parties in 1267, and the expulsion yet again of the imperialists in 1271, Malatesta da Verucchio should emerge as the dominant Guelf in Rimini.[3]

The advance of the Malatesta to power was not therefore unchallenged or smooth. There were others to rival their pre-eminence even among their allies. Until his death fighting the conte Guido in 1282, the leader of the Guelf Montefeltro, Taddeo Novello, seems to

[1] *Istorie Fiorentine*, lib. vi.
[2] Tonini, ii.397–8, iii.117, 225–40; Massèra in *RIS*² xvi/3.28 (n. 6). Cf. above p. 28 n. 4.
[3] *Ann. Parm.*, 683; *Cron. mal.*, 5; *Chron. Bon.*, 173; Clementini, i.469–70, 479, 482; Rubeus, 419E; Battaglini, *Zecca*, 140, 170–1; Fantuzzi, ii.428, vi. 240; Tarlazzi, ii, n. LIII, p. 67; Tonini, iii.100–2, 112, 113–14, 116, 118, 123, 535–7, 538–40, 581–3.

have been only less favoured a person in Rimini than his friend Malatesta.[1] But this can have been of small importance beside the direct
opposition to be overcome, which finally led in 1288 to the expulsion
of the Malatesta from the city.

On assuming control of Romagna in 1278 the papacy, as already
seen, quickly learned how conditional was the allegiance even of communities professedly Guelf, and in the prevailing suspicion of Rome
and her legates Rimini and the Malatesta came to share. While Rimini,
like the other towns, reserved its liberties when acknowledging papal
overlordship, Malatesta da Verucchio was forbidden by the pope in
1281 to conclude a profitable alliance between his daughter and a son
of Guido da Montefeltro.[2] These irritations were premonitory of the
dogged quarrel with the papal government which broke out in 1287.
At the beginning of that year Malatesta da Verucchio asserted his
growing influence by negotiating a peace with the principal families of
Forlì and Faenza, in company with his sons Giovanni and Malatestino,
and Giovanni di Ramberto Malatesta. Formally the peace was declared
to be to the honour of Mother Church, the pope, and the provincial
rector; but already in itself a threat to the authority of the papal
count, it seems also to have been a treaty of defence against the
papal administration, recently freed by victory over Guido da Montefeltro.[3] Whatever the provocation, the rector Pietro di Stefano, alleg-
ing that Malatesta had acted without his licence, prepared an ambush
to take him on his way back from Forlì. Malatesta himself was able to
escape, but others were captured, including Giovanni di Ramberto,
and their punishment was prevented only by the payment of heavy
fines by the communes of Rimini, Faenza and Forlì (14 June 1287).[4] A
further source of unrest came at the end of November: the syndics of
Rimini and Ravenna opposed requests for troops and money made by
the rector at a parliament in Imola, and were consequently thrown into
prison. There followed in January and February the publication of
formal charges against the Polenta and the Malatesta: against Malatesta da Verucchio, who was *podestà* of Rimini, and who was accused
of treason, both as municipal magistrate and as private individual. The
communes also were threatened; and when they and the families
accused failed by the stated term to answer the charges against them,
the rector proceeded to punishment. Rimini was placed under interdict
and subjected to a severe fine, while Malatesta da Verucchio, his sons
and his adherents were fined, deprived of all office, and pronounced

[1] Battaglini, *Zecca*, 168, 174; Tonini, iii.116, 118–20, 138–9, 200–21; *RIS*² xvi/3.35.
[2] Tonini, iii.601–5, 631.
[3] 'Et iste tales concordie fuerunt facte contra dictum dominum comitem Romandiole': Cantinelli, 56. Cf. Tonini, iii.144–6, 642–5.
[4] Cantinelli, 56; Clementini, i.490; Tonini, iii.146–8.

outside the protection of the law. These sentences were not repealed for several years.[1]

Following his election to the papacy on 22 February 1288, Nicholas IV attempted to reconcile the Malatesta and Pietro di Stefano, and although Malatesta da Verucchio expressed suspicion of the rector 'propter eius duritiem', he seems to have entered into some negotiations with the church, for on 5 May, despite his tenure of the office of *podestà*, he and his family were expelled from Rimini as showing too great an anxiety to recover the favour of Rome. Clementini speaks of an agreement concluded with the rector which the commune was unprepared to fulfil, involving as it did the disbursement of £4,000. But the movement was also Ghibelline and the imperialist leaders hastened to strengthen their position by demanding submission of the *contado*.[2]

In April Pietro di Stefano had been replaced by another rector, Ermanno dei Monaldeschi. To him Malatesta now turned for help, and for the next two years, as ally of the church against the commune, he directed all his energies to recovering Rimini by force or treaty. While his son attacked the *contado* the pope tried to impose a peace. But the commune was obstinate, declaring Malatesta 'rebel and capital enemy of the commune of Rimini'; and its leaders, among them Malatesta's bitterest opponent, Montagna di Parcitade, entered successive protests to the pope against the rector and his Malatesta confederates.[3] Not until the winter of 1289 were peace negotiations begun and it was not until March 1290 that agreement was finally reached, after the commune and the Malatesta had surrendered into the hands of a new legate, Pietro Saracino, bishop of Grosseto, the *contado* castles each had occupied. By the sentence of the rector damages were remitted on both sides, and the Malatesta subjected to modest confinement outside the city at the pleasure of the papal representatives.[4]

The reinstatement of the Malatesta was formally incomplete, but it was a signal reverse for their opponents, who now, out of resentment, may have helped to instigate the revolt which broke out in June against the rector, Stefano Colonna. Through the intercession of both Montagna Parcitade and the adherents of the Malatesta the rector was permitted to escape from Rimini, but once in safe retirement he proceeded to deprive the commune of its privileges in city and *contado*. His

---

[1] Clementini, i.494–5; Battaglini, *Zecca*, 174–5; Tonini, iii.646–51, 681–9.
[2] *Reg. N. IV*, 6962; Cantinelli, 57–8; Branchi, 147–8; Clementini, ii.495–6; Tonini, iii.651. Vasina (*Romagnoli*, 192–4) would also see, in the expulsion of the Malatesta, hints of a 'popular' movement against aristocratic power and incipient *signoria*.
[3] *Reg. N. IV*, 6966, 6979, 7150, 7192–3; Clementini, i.497; Tonini, iii.149–55, 653–63.
[4] Cantinelli, 59–60; Clementini, i.497–8; Tonini, iii.155–7, 663–7. Once again, in the resistance of Rimini to a Malatesta restoration, Vasina (*Romagnoli*, 207; *Romagna*, 257, 283–4) sees evidence of popular revolt against the threat of despotism.

sentence may have been just, but the course of events is obscure. The subsequent insurrection of Romagna and the imprisonment of the rector in Ravenna show his conduct to have been provocative, and the most that may be said is that in Rimini the general agitation turned momentarily to the advantage of the Parcitadi, ultimately to the advantage of the Malatesta.[1] The rectorial vicars were expelled and Malatesta da Verucchio resumed his influence by having elected as *podestà* Rodolfino da Calliscese of Cesena.[2] According to Cantinelli this marked the beginning of the Malatesta *signoria*. But another five years were necessary to make it stable; for, as Branchi remarks, 'niente di manco era l'odio infra el predetto miser Parcitado e suoi aderenti et el prefato miser Malatesta e suoi aderenti'.[3] During that period, and as part of a general peace in Romagna, which preserved papal authority from all but total eclipse, the hostile proceedings of Pietro di Stefano and Stefano Colonna were reversed, in July 1924 and January 1295, and ample privileges bestowed on the city.[4]

Precedence then fell sharply to events within the commune.

Governing elements in the Malatesta's rise to power are not difficult to distinguish: increasing private wealth and jurisdiction, a wide though not always concordant family, tenure of municipal office, and a discriminating loyalty to the church, all contributed.

As partisan of the Guelfs, Malatesta da Verucchio had made himself their most capable and respected captain in Romagna, receiving from the papacy many tokens of esteem, and coming forward as a worthy opponent of the Ghibelline Guido da Montefeltro. When *podestà* of Rimini in 1263 he had been commended by the pope, 'quia semper fuit fidelis et devotus Ecclesiae', for having sent to Rome intercepted letters from the emperor Baldwin to Manfred.[5] The arrival in Italy of Charles of Anjou and his campaign in the south threw Malatesta into greater prominence. Further letters of congratulations were sent him by the pope, and in 1268-9 he acted with papal assent as Angevin vicar in Florence.[6] Shortly afterwards, in the summer of 1271, the long conflict between the Malatesta and Guido da Montefeltro, which was to continue intermittently until the end of the century, began with an

---

[1] Cantinelli, 61; Clementini, i.499–500; Tonini, iii.155–7, 690–5.
[2] Branchi, 148–9; Clementini, i.501; Tonini, iii.162.
[3] Cantinelli, 62 ('accepit et habuit dominium ipsius civitatis'); Branchi, 149.
[4] Including right of war: Cantinelli, 74–5; Tonini, iii.164–6, 677–95.
[5] Martène and Durand, *Collectio*, ii.23. In the same year the pope collected church money in Romagna for Gianciotto and Paolo, Malatesta's sons, at that time students: Tonini, iii.567.
[6] Ptolomaei Lucensis, *Annales* (Florence, 1876), 86; Manni, 127–8; Martène and Durand, *Collectio*, ii.361; Tonini, iii.116–20, 569–72, 574–8, 583–4; Davidsohn, *Forschungen*, iv.301, 538.

engagement in the March of Ancona from which Malatesta da Verucchio brought back the conte Guido as prisoner to Rimini.[1] But four
years later the count avenged his defeat when he routed Malatesta at
S. Procolo.[2]

Malatesta and the conte Guido were already the recognised leaders
of their factions in Romagna. It was as Guelf and Ghibelline leaders
that they appeared in 1276 in an attempt to pacify Romagna, and a
Ghibelline poem of this period sets out to contrast the two captains,
Guido 'leone' and Malatesta da Verucchio 'veltro'. The occasion of
the poem, which is an invocation to the Ghibellines, seems to have been
the offer of Romagna to the Roman *curia* made by Malatesta da
Verucchio, Guido da Polenta and others in 1277.[3] Malatesta was therefore no rebel to the restoration of papal government, and when on the
death of Nicholas III disorder became general in the province, he
received from the pope's successor a series of letters which reveal him
to be still an ardent and unwavering Guelf.[4] Captaining the Guelf
forces under Guy of Montfort, he helped in 1283 to repair the disaster
of the conte Guido's victory at Forlì, and once again received a letter
of personal tribute from the pope. By this time Malatesta da Verucchio
had succeeded in winning the peculiar favour of the papacy. But the
anxiety of Rome or its lieutenants to make the papal authority everywhere felt in the States of the Church was to drive him, as it did most
others, into open rebellion. In 1288, as already mentioned, he incurred
the penalties of treason, and although he obtained support from the
church in compelling Rimini to receive him back, he nevertheless took
part in the general revolt of Romagna which broke out immediately
after. Jealousy of his influence had not subsided when peace was
re-established. And in 1295 when Malatesta finally became supreme in
Rimini, the papal legates were still suspicious and hostile. But because
he thought it a victory for the Guelfs, or because he was impotent to
undo events, the rector William Durand merely ratified the revolution,
and in the following year the provincial parliament was convened in
Rimini. Malatesta da Verucchio now resumed his character of Guelf
captain in Romagna, and was conspicuous in promoting the general
peace which Boniface VIII strove to introduce there (1296–9). For this
he was rewarded with possessions in Pesaro. And never again during
his lifetime was the power of his dynasty seriously challenged.[5]

[1] Tonini, iii.123; Massèra, 'Note', 20–5.   [2] Cantinelli, 19; *Chron. Bon.*, 191–2.
[3] *Ann. Caes.*, 1104–5; Battagli, 14, 29; Tonini, iii.127–8. Cf. Fasoli in *ASI* 1933;
Massèra, 'Serventese'; Waley, 194–5; above p. 8.
[4] Tonini, iii.631, 634: 1281.
[5] *Ann. Parm.*, 720; Lünig, iv.43–60; Clementini, i.488–9, 506–7, 521; Battaglini,
Zecca, 180; Tonini, iii.140–1, 162, 168, 169, 175–81, 187–91; Theiner, i.502; *Reg.
Bon. VIII*, 1556–8, 3299, 3345. The Pesaro properties were those of Bernardo dei
Bandi: below p. 54.

Commanding the influence he did in the province, Malatesta da Verucchio could not help but come to dominate in his own commune, but the ultimate and original resources of his authority had to lie there. The first Malatesta had prospered as local magnates and landowners, and as an undertone to the political events of the time, they are seen from the late twelfth century to be adding unostentatiously to their properties and jurisdictions, sometimes by purchase or exchange, sometimes by new investitures, like that of Ghiaggiolo in 1262–3 or that of Gradara in 1283; within a hundred years their patrimony had come to spread everywhere in the neighbourhood of Rimini, Verucchio and Santarcangelo. In addition they received gifts, as when the lands of certain persecuted heretics were transferred to them by the commune about 1259, and they obtained further increments of wealth by making profitable marriages.[1] Malatesta's first wife, Concordia, brought him rich endowments, enhancing both his status and his influence.[2] But his second wife, Margherita de' Palterieri da Monselice, must have encouraged his ambition still more. Related by blood to a cardinal of the church, she brought to her husband not merely a large dowry in money, but also alliance with an ecclesiastic who at the time of the marriage in July 1266 was rector and apostolic legate in the March of Ancona and duchy of Spoleto. Malatesta da Verucchio may have hoped to receive the cardinal's inheritance, but he was disappointed.[3]

With the eminence deriving from wealth, military leadership and the favour of a powerful party, went also from time to time the authority of municipal magistrate and a growing influence in the government of the commune. At various times and with increasing frequency from the year 1239 Malatesta della Penna, and after him his son, had held the office of *podestà* in Rimini, and in 1282 Malatesta da Verucchio assumed it for six successive years before his expulsion from the city. Soon after his return, in the winter of 1290, he may have been re-elected, and in the following year his son Gianciotto. In 1294 Bernardino da Polenta, son-in-law of Malatesta and a member of a friendly dynasty, was appointed, although in the next and critical year no Malatesta is recorded as *podestà*.[4] The principal office of the commune had not yet come under the family's control, but other signs of their growing ascendancy in communal affairs indicate how close this was. Already by 1271 their name had become prominent in the public acts of Rimini;[5] and when the church took over Romagna in 1278 Malatesta

[1] Battaglini, *Zecca*, 172; Tonini, iii.563–5; Theiner, i.269; Battaglini, *Vita*, 691; Giordani, *Gradara*, 68.
[2] Above pp. 28–9.
[3] Fantuzzi, vi.242; Tonini, iv/2.26, 27; Massèra, 'Note', 18–19.
[4] Tonini, iii.200–21; above p. 28.
[5] Tonini, iii.120–1, 246.

da Verucchio and Gianciotto were chief among the citizens acknowledging papal supremacy. Two years later Malatesta was the leading
representative of the Riminese 'parte Guelfa' when Bertoldo Orsini
tried to pacify the factions of Romagna; and in 1281 he attended the
provincial parliament of the rector Jean d'Eppes. These sparse records
of Malatesta's activity suggest he was already becoming the most
important citizen of Rimini; and Martin IV on his election in 1281
showed by his greater care in writing to Malatesta than in writing to
the commune, that he was more concerned to flatter him than to
conciliate the city. To the pope it may have seemed enough to keep the
Malatesta loyal.[1]

Control of the office of *podestà* followed naturally upon this personal
predominance, and along with the *podesteria* may have gone certain
other means of influence and privilege which there was some attempt
to abrogate when in 1290 the Malatesta were restored to Rimini. By
the terms concluded then the Malatesta were compelled to surrender
their immunity from taxes, and to pay all 'dues personal and real for
their possessions in the city, contado, district, and diocese of Rimini
. . . as do other citizens'.[2] At the same time Malatesta da Verucchio,
Giovanni di Ramberto and other *extrinseci* were readmitted to the
council, but only according to the recognised number, 'scilicet unus
de familia tantum', while all officials, it was laid down, were to be
elected in the council 'secundum formam statuti civitatis Arimini'.[3]
Whether the Malatesta had neglected these rules is conjectural, but if
they accepted the new conditions, it cannot have been for long.

In every way that Malatesta da Verucchio strove to extend his power, he
was strengthened by the family raised from two fruitful marriages. Most
important were the sons born of his first union, Malatestino, Giovanni
and Paolo; but Maddalene also, daughter by his second wife, procured
him a useful ally in neighbouring Ravenna by marrying Bernardino da
Polenta, while from Pandolfo, likewise born of Margherita, was to
proceed the principal line of the Malatesta of Rimini. His other
daughters, Rengarda and Simona, were married into the Manfredi and
the conti di Cunio, extending the influence of the Malatesta still further
in Romagna. Giovanni Sciancato (the Lame), or Gianciotto, also
married one of the Polenta, Francesca, the daughter of Guido di
Lamberto, perhaps as a reward for the help the Malatesta gave the
Polentani in seizing the *signoria* of Ravenna. But his marriage ended
disastrously with the adultery and murder of his wife and brother, Paolo
il Bello – the two 'anime affannate' of Dante's most celebrated canto.

[1] Tonini, iii.121, 129–31, 601, 631–7; Theiner, i.369; Fasoli, *ASI* 1936.
[2] 'solvent collect [a et fac]tiones personales et reales sicut alii Cives Arimineses':
Tonini, iii.663–7.   [3] Clementini, i.498; Tonini, *loc. cit.*

For his part Paolo made secure the possession of Ghiaggiolo by marrying in 1269 Orabile, the daughter and heir of the last count, Uberto. He was less active than the other members of his family, but he was a loyal Guelf and held the office of *capitano* in Florence. His premature death, and the manner of it, were to make his principal legacy to the Malatesta of Rimini the resentment and hostility of the neighbouring counts of Ghiaggiolo.[1] The most resourceful and the most consistent allies of Malatesta da Verucchio were his other sons, Malatestino dall'Occhio (the One-eyed) and Gianciotto, both of whom were warriors, ambitious, able and ruthless, as portrayed in the pages of Dante, and one or other of them was always present with him at the critical moments in his rise to power. It was they who began systematically to extend their authority over the adjacent cities of Romagna and the March. But although Malatesta da Verucchio had himself held offices outside Rimini,[2] when this became regular practice at the close of the thirteenth century, it foreshadowed a further phase of Malatesta expansion, representative of a later period, and one with which he had less directly to do than his successors, however much he may have approved it.

In their expulsion from Rimini the Malatesta had suffered a bitter reverse. Resolutely they fought their way back to restitution in 1290, and after that nothing but a complete and uncompromising decision to the contest for supremacy in Rimini could follow. Five years later the two factions came to grips and in the dexterity then displayed by Malatesta da Verucchio and his son must be seen the ultimate cause of their success, for the Parcitadi were fatally outwitted.

Some premonition of impending struggle there must have been, for both the legate Peter of Monreale and his successor, William Durand, interposed to arrange a peace. In October 1295 William was in Rimini, and in his company came Guido da Montefeltro, to whom the Parcitadi appealed for help.[3] It was a well-calculated step. The old alliance with Rimini, through which the Montefeltro had acquired Urbino,[4] had depended largely on friendship with the Ghibelline

---

[1] Fantuzzi, ii.376; Tonini, iii.247–9, 253–4, 260–73, 585–8; Massèra, 'Note', 4; Davidsohn, *Forschungen*, iv.552. Along with Ghiaggiolo went Valdeponde and Cusercole which together became the regular patrimony of the Malatesta counts of Ghiaggiolo, although, in the early fourteenth century at least, subject to the church of Ravenna: Fantuzzi, ii.377, 378; Tonini, iv/2.146, 332.

[2] As vicar in Florence in 1268–9 (above p. 33), as *capitano del popolo* in Bologna in 1275 (Cantinelli, 12, 18), and as *podestà* in Cesena in 1292 (Fantuzzi, v.383; Tonini, iii.219–20). In harmony with this Malatesta claimed in 1293 to have many friends outside Rimini, at S. Leo, Pesaro, and elsewhere: Tonini, 676.

[3] *Ann. Caes.*, 1111, 1112; Cantinelli, 50–1; Clementini, i.566–7.

[4] Above p. 17.

Parcitadi. With the Guelf Malatesta the Montefeltro had long-standing differences, personal and public. One early cause of quarrel was a joint claim to the lordship of Ghiaggiolo. But behind this local issue (settled in 1269) lay a deeper antagonism, of territorial ambition, which from this time began to develop into one of the bitterest rivalries of Italian regional politics. Even the Guelf branch of the Montefeltro, after a ong period of alliance (1265–85), the Malatesta eventually estranged by intrigue in Urbino. Hostility was invincible. And from the conte Guido the Parcitadi obtained a ready promise of help.[1]

Already during the summer Malatesta da Verucchio had caused the institutions of the commune to be ominously adjusted in favour of himself and the 'parte Guelfa'. For some years military authority had been lodged with the four Ufficiali, and these alone with the *podestà* could authorise the arming of the populace, a provision which, as the events of 1288 had shown, could be to the disadvantage of the Guelfs. Malatesta therefore obtained two radical amendments at a session of the general council. By the first the powers of the four Ufficiali were restricted in such a way as to put part of them into his own hands.[2] By the second the power to arm the people was transferred from the four Ufficiali to the *consiglio di credenza*, over which the Malatesta had a surer control. At the same time it was provided that the decisions of the *consiglio di credenza* were to be ratified by the general council, where the number of Guelfs could be expected to predominate, and where secret voting was now to prevail.[3] After these measures the 'parte Guelfa' could take greater heart and wait for its leaders to act.

Various accounts are given by the chroniclers of what took place on the decisive day, 13 December 1295, but that of the anonymous chronicler, is the most circumstantial, if contrived.[4] His story is that for some time the whole city had looked like an armed camp. The Parcitadi, having contacted the count of Montefeltro, restrained their hand while awaiting his arrival. Malatesta da Verucchio also restrained his hand, expecting to gain nothing, when suddenly an uproar arose in the piazza

---

[1] Clementini, i.504, 518, 543, 583; Battaglini, *Zecca*, 172, 193; Tonini, iii.163–6, 184, 675–7, 709–11; Franceschini, *Montefeltro*, 19, 29, 33, 41, 48, 52–3, 63ff., 74–5, 87–8, 122ff.

[2] Tonini, iii.170.

[3] Tonini, *loc. cit.*: 'Statutum et ordinatum est in Millio ducenteximo nonagesimo quinto die XVIII Augusti, quod per Comune Arim. non possit nec debeat fieri aliqua expensa vel solutio de debitis imposterum contrahendis a quantitate centum sold. supra, vel aliqua coletta vel prestantia imposterum imponi, vel cavalcata sive exercitus fieri, vel guerra aliqua inchoari, nisi primo facta proposita in Conscilio credentie fuerit adfirmatum ad conscilium et ad bussolas et palottas per omnes de Conscilio.' For the probable influence of the Malatesta in the *consiglio di credenza*: Battaglini, *Zecca*, 177; Tonini, iii.707–9. Already, it may be supposed, the government of affairs was passing to the smaller council (cf. below pp. 62, 318).

[4] *Cron. mal.*, 5–7; Battagli, 30; Branchi, 149–52; *Ann. Forl.*, 52; *Ann. Parm.*, 718.

from an attempt by two asses to mate, which 'made such a disturbance that everyone ran to arms, thinking it was the *signori*. A certain miser Lodovico dale Caminate', a loyal adherent of the Malatesta,

'hurried at once in arms to the piazza shouting "Viva miser Malatesta e la parte ghelfa". At that moment the followers of miser Parcitado arrived and discharging a crossbow-bolt, killed the said miser Lodovico. As soon as miser Malatesta heard this, he went to the Piazza: and the followers of miser Parcitado departed and went their way, while in the middle of the "strada reale" in the "riolo dela fontana" barricades were thrown up by each side, and here a great fight took place which lasted three days. Meanwhile someone had come from Verucchio and secretly informed miser Malatesta that at San Marino preparations were being made by the Conte Guido, who was coming with three hundred horsemen from Pietramala, Fermo, and Fabriano, to the help of miser Parcitado. At this he grew afraid, and at once summoning to him four trustworthy men, began: "Gentlemen, I marvel greatly that miser Parcitado should be willing to lay waste Rimini, and without any reason that I can see. I didn't begin this brawl and I'm very much grieved at it." Then they departed and went to confer with miser Parcitado, and he said just the same. They laboured so much with each side that the barricades were taken down and miser Malatesta went out to meet miser Parcitado, and they spoke together and embraced. Herodes et Pilatus facti sunt amici. Then the crowd of citizens raised them up on their shoulders and carried them to the Palazzo del Comune shouting "Viva miser Malatesta e miser Parcitado". Whereupon it was published in all directions that every stranger should leave ... and miser Parcitado wrote to the Conte Guido thanking him and explaining that peace had been made so that for the present he need not come. The count mocked at the wisdom of this [but he disbanded his troops] ... Miser Malatesta divided his following; one part, the Guelf, he concealed within his house, while the other, with trumpets and banners, left in the direction of Verucchio, and went just so far that day as to reach by evening the bridge over the Mavone, which is nearly three miles; but with the descent of night, they turned back to the city, arriving at the porta del Gattolo. Then the company of miser Malatesta issued out crying "Viva miser Malatesta e la parte ghelfa, e mora miser Parcitado e i ghebilini", and miser Parcitado, being without support, sought safety in flight together with his family: but many of his house and following were killed or taken, among them Montagna di Parcitade who was thrown into prison and there put to death ... Miser Parcitado and his adherents made for San Marino, where the Conte Guido greeted him with the words, "Ben venga, miser Perdecitade". And this was in the year 1295, in the month of December, on the feast of Santa Lucia.'

From this defeat the Parcitadi never recovered. Ugolino, called 'Cignatta', had fallen in the fighting, but the death of his brother, Montagna, was delayed, as Benvenuto da Imola relates in a concise note that may serve as appendix to the verbose story of the chronicler. He had been imprisoned by Malatestino, and shortly after Malatesta asked his son

'what had been done with Montagna. To which Malatestino answered, "My lord, he is well taken care of, so well that should he wish to drown himself he could not, although close to the sea." And again [Malatesta] asked and kept on asking, always receiving the same reply, until he said, "I begin to doubt whether indeed you do know how to take care of him." Then Malatestino, marking his sense, had Montagna done to death – cum quibusdam aliis.'[1]

The sons of Cignatta and Montagna, Giovanni, Galassino and Parcitadino, with their associates, were deprived of their properties by the commune,[2] and to these penalties the papal rector, who was in Rimini ten days after the skirmish, added the censures of the church. Later in the autumn of 1297 Galassino, who was in the custody of the Malatesta, was exchanged through papal mediation for Alberghettino Manfredi, the grandson of Malatesta da Verucchio.[3] Meanwhile the new signori of Rimini could not afford to be indifferent to the repercussions of the revolution in Romagna. In April of the following year the citizens of Faenza described their triumph as 'notorium . . . tam finitivis quam remotis',[4] and for some time the exiled Ghibellines, who were gradually dispersed all over Italy, could invoke the support of powerful neighbours in Romagna.[5] Among these was the relative of Malatesta, Giovanni, who was lord of Sogliano, and who, perhaps by marriage into the family of the Faggiola, had entered the orbit of the Ghibelline party.[6] Only when a general peace was concluded in the province by Boniface VIII was the menace from outside removed.

'Fo facto el sopraditto miser Malatesta signore dela città d'Arimino

[1] Benvenuto da Imola, ii. 311.
[2] Bib. sen., Stat. Rim., fo. 269v; Tonini, iii. 175. The family does not fade at once from historical record: ibid. iii. 718–19, v/1. 528–9; below pp. 62, 71.
[3] Cantinelli, 52. Reg. Bon. VIII, 1978; Tonini, iii. 175, 699, 711.
[4] Tonini, iii. 705.
[5] Ann. Caes., 1113, 1114, 1115; Clementini, i. 511; Tonini, iii. 177–81, 185–6, 187–90.
[6] Cron. mal., 7; Branchi, 152. On the origins of the Malatesta of Sogliano: Battaglini, Zecca, 308ff.; Tonini, ii. 407–8, iii. 177–8, 243; Massèra in RIS² xv/2.3 (n. 2), 7 (n. 5).

e del contado':[1] Malatesta da Verucchio was now lord of Rimini and its territories. But no overt emblems, no new titles were assumed to proclaim this, and in 1296 a certain Guido de' Luisini appears as *podestà* of the city. The *signoria* remained for the moment nameless. It was none the less real. It was acknowledged everywhere. And Clementini, writing in the early seventeenth century, was induced at this point to pause and draw a stern picture of saddened faces and vestments of mourning, to speak of imprecations and oaths and the presence of a foreign soldiery, and to deplore 'la soggettione de' Riminesi e la perdita della dolce libertà'.[2]

Although he survived for another seventeen years, the events of 1295 may be held to conclude the achievements of Malatesta da Verucchio. The impetus was declining, and at the beginning of the fourteenth century the personalities that dominate are those of his sons to whom the conduct of policy seems now in the main to have fallen, although in the last months of his life, when a hundred years old or more, he may have tried to control relations with the Malatesta of Sogliano. He died in 1312 after only three days of sickness, maintaining almost to the end the habits of a warrior. In February of the preceding year he had made his will, by which he left as his principal heirs Malatestino and Pandolfo, whom he enjoined always to remain united. In the same place he testified to his affection for the Order of S. Francis and his bequests to religious houses were liberal. He provided for the holding in Rimini of a General Chapter by the Franciscans, as had been several times requested, and he gave instructions that he should be buried in the Franciscan church, clothed in the habit of a Tertiary. Malatesta da Verucchio, as Clementini remarks, was 'buonissimo Cattolico'.[3]

---

[1] *Cron. mal.*, 7. Cf. Battagli, 30: '. . . tunc inceperunt dominationem liberam possidere, quod usque illud festum minime poterunt'.

[2] Clementini, i.506, 511, who adds (512) that Malatesta da Verucchio had himself declared *podestà* and 'Difensore del ben publico della Città di Rimino', but Battaglini rejects this (*Zecca*, 177) and his view is supported by the analogy of other *signorie*: above p. 19.

[3] Clementini, i.528, 531, 534, 535, 536; Battaglini, *Zecca*, 182; Tonini, iv.27–9, iv/2.20–35.

3

From commune to papal vicariate

With the election of Bertrand de Got as pope in 1305 began the long exile of the papacy from Italy, during which the Malatesta of Rimini and other 'tyrampni' of the States of the Church were to consolidate their power. Though moved to the frontiers of the French kingdom, ruled by a succession of French pontiffs, and subject to the persistent pressures of French policy, the papacy of Avignon in no way relaxed its interest in Italy, or in the immunities and government of the Papal State. On the contrary, Italy and the Papal State remained throughout its first concern. The laconic testimony of papal finance would suffice to prove this,[1] were there not also the last great struggle of papacy and empire, in which once again care for the autonomy of the States of the Church is seen to predominate. As before, the relations of pope and emperor turned upon Italy, and not until the middle of the fourteenth century was the imperial threat finally removed. Not only did the German kings revive their inherited Italian claims; they also meddled in the territories of Rome. Clement V had to warn Henry of Luxemburg against interference in Bologna,[2] and in 1313, as the quarrel developed between the emperor and Robert of Naples, Henry declared his enemy dispossessed of all titles and offices, including the rectorate of Bologna and Romagna, which he pronounced subject to imperial jurisdiction.[3] This renascent Hohenstaufen policy was carried still further by Lewis of Bavaria who invaded the Papal State and challenged its autonomy. Through his creature, Nicholas V, he was able to control legations into the papal provinces,[4] he nominated vicars in papal

---

[1] From the figures of Göller, *Einnahmen*, and Schäfer, *Ausgaben*, for income and expenditure under the Avignonese popes it becomes evident that the most expensive pontificates were those marked by an active and militant Italian policy. Cf. G. Mollat, *Les papes d'Avignon* (Paris, 1930), 137–295.   [2] Vitale, 131.

[3] Schneider, 288, 293–4; R. Pöhlmann, *Der Römerzug Kaiser Heinrichs VII und die Politik der Kurie* (Nuremberg, 1875), 105; Fasoli, *AMR* 1939, 48ff.

[4] G. Villani, x.75, 98, 99, 123; A. Mussato, *De gestis Henrici VII*, i.183, in F. Böhmer, *Fontes Rerum Germanicarum* (Stuttgart, 1843); Müller, i.204; Ficker, *Forschungen*, ii.448; Chroust, 164ff.; Eubel, *Hist. Jahrb.*, xii (1891). Chroust (159, 165–6) suggests there was an agreement between Nicholas V and Lewis of Bavaria to restore the *dominium temporale* to the empire.

cities;[1] and more than once he questioned the very title of the papacy to a number of important territories.[2] Even the complaisant Charles of Bohemia aroused suspicion in his papal patron; and relations between them had cooled by the death of Clement VI.[3]

Provocation from the empire, however, was slight when compared with the papal counterblast, which was to assert more explicitly than ever before the supremacy of pope over emperor, and try to exclude imperial influence once for all from the whole Italian peninsula. Declaring the empire vacant, and assuming a superior right to administer during vacancy, the popes, with strong Angevin backing, proceeded to exercise authority, directly or by vicariate to local *signori*, in Lombardy and Northern Italy.[4] That the policy was restricted mainly to Italy reveals again the primary concern of the papacy with Italian affairs and the defence of its own dominions. In the event, the papal counter-offensive, which commanded the support of so pacific a pope as Benedict XII, was not sustained. But while it lasted, few Lombard cities escaped its influence. The papal vicariate 'vacante imperio' was a reality.[5] And when the church finally withdrew from Northern Italy it was not by surrender to the empire.

For the Papal State it was a better safeguard if emperors could be induced to renounce any suspect claims to land in Central Italy. And, in fact, at various times, Henry of Luxemburg, Lewis of Bavaria and Charles of Bohemia all made or offered promises which ratified the old imperial donations and limited the rights traditionally due to emperors elect when entering papal territory for coronation.[6] It was under Charles IV that this entente was finally established, and with it papal

---

[1] Theiner, i.726–8; Ugolini, ii.498–500 Preger, *Politik*, Urk. 618; *MGH Const.*, v.629ff., 696 sec. 5; Antonelli, 'Vicende' 1903, 258, 262; Fumi, 'Eretici' 1899, 8ff. There is also the perplexing statement of Biondo that some time early in the pontificate of Clement VI Lewis bestowed vicariates on most of the *signori* in the Papal State, including the Malatesta in Rimini, Fano and Pesaro (*Hist.* 362). Though accepted by de Vergottini ('Ricerche', 301) it is corroborated by no documentary evidence.

[2] Chroust, 165; Müller, i.204, 331; ii.13–14, 144, 190, 192, 204.

[3] Werunsky, *Karl IV*, ii.493–5, 500ff.; Biscaro, 'Relazioni' 1928, 17, 35, 43–4, 57.

[4] In 1309 Clement V's cardinals even claimed that all Italy was subordinate to the pope: *Acta Arag.*, ii, n. 354. For details, in addition to the general works of Müller, Preger etc., see Ciaccio, 'Bertrando del Poggetto'; Otto, *QF* 1911; Biscaro, 'Relazioni' 1919, 1920, 1927, Bock, *RQ* 1936.

[5] There is evidence that *signori* (the Scaligeri, the Visconti) paid their *census*: Göller *Einnahmen, Ben. XII*, 16; Biscaro, 'Relazioni' 1927, 89; *Lettres, Ben. XII*, 3268.

[6] Theiner, i.607, 612, 626; ii.156, 165, 288–9, 291–2, 296; Bonaini, doc. 25; *MGH Leg.*, IV, viii.96ff.; Müller, ii.205–8, 215–17; Werunsky, *Karl IV*, i.409–20, ii.578; Otto, *RQ* 1906.

encroachments in Lombardy quietly ceased. On all sides the papacy sought to protect its territories by sworn agreements of this kind,[1] and by the death of Clement VI it could rest satisfied that its rights were incontestably recognised. But juridical victory alone was little enough. The contest of papacy and empire was largely one of words, and its solution contributed nothing to effective authority in the papal patrimony itself, where more was needed than solemn concordats to govern with success.

During the first half of the fourteenth century the constitution of the Papal States did, it is true, continue to develop,[2] and something was forecast, if only ineffectually, of the stable and uniform government planned by Albornoz, whose laws were in part a digest of earlier enactments.[3] But the task of papal government was severe; and however mistaken the belief that the pope quitted his dominions to escape their violence and disorder,[4] the retirement to Avignon certainly reduced still further his power to control them. If the papacy succeeded in resisting the wider Italian ambitions of France and Anjou, within its own territories the French invasion was universal, and French officials entered everywhere to aggravate the inherited deficiencies of papal administration.[5] Often appointed for a short period, and strangers to the country, the papal rectors were concerned above all to make their office lucrative. They were followed in this by their subordinates, and the tale of their abuses is long: of the sale of ecclesiastical rights, embezzlement, extortions and forced gifts; of maladministration of justice, bribery and too prompt a readiness to accept money composi-tions; of local nepotism, and even the issue of adulterate coin.[6] The chorus of protest against church officials was loud and persistent, and

---

[1] For example from the Visconti, when invested with the vicariate: Biscaro, 'Relazioni' 1920, 221, 223, 234–6. The same condition was prominent in the Sicilian oath of homage: Caggese, i.107.

[2] The main constitutional feature of the period seems to have been a growing urge to centralisation and, particularly under John XXII, increasing preoccupation with revenues, both illustrated by the mounting importance of the provincial treasurer: Theiner, ii.222; Aloisi, *AMM* 1904, 407, 1905, 343, 1906, 324–5, 1908, 282–5; Ermini, 'Ordinamenti', 234ff.

[3] Aloisi, *AMM* 1904, 317–68, 393–422; 1905, 369–421; 1906, 307–30; 1907, 129–67; 1908, 261–310; Zdekauer, in *Riv. it. scienze giur.*, xxix.200–8, xxxi.65–76.

[4] Above p. 6.

[5] Cf. for example G. Villani's description of papal government as 'la signoria de' Caorsini e di Lingadoca': *Croniche*, x.228, xi.6. Schäfer (*Ritter*, i.43–4) re-marks that the French predominance became less after the pontificate of John XXII.

[6] *Reg. Clem. V*, 7582–3; Theiner, i.694, ii.1, 12, 32, 66, 70–1, 73–4, 77; Tonini, iv/2, LXXXI; Riezler, 39ff.; Preger, *Politik*, xvi, doc. 23; *Lettres, Ben. XII*, 561–6, 592–7, 911, 913, 973, 978–80, 984–5, 1080, 1096, 1098ff., 1109, 1111, 1126, 2166–70, 2190, 2192, 2201, 2218, 2273, 2275, 2366–7, 2375, 2459, 2505.

did not spare the most exalted legates such as Bertrand du Pouget and Astorgio di Duraforte, who attracted the odium of states outside the government of the church.[1] The popes themselves were not without responsibility. Only Benedict XII abstained from rewarding *nipoti* and favourites with the emoluments of an Italian legation or rectorate.[2] It was Benedict also who made the most strenuous attack, before Albornoz, on papal maladministration. He appointed two reforming legations and dismissed many officials.[3] But he had little success. When Innocent VI came to undertake the reconstruction of papal government, he had to begin by replacing the chief officials in every province but one.[4]

Misgovernment by officials was only one theme in reforming constitutions of the fourteenth century. Inseparable from it in most cases was a further complaint: against the despots or *tiranni* – and often against collusion between the two.[5] An inquest held in the March of Ancona in 1343 to determine the state of government there, and find out what people thought of it and what improvements they desired, disclosed the great advances recently made by despots and *signorotti*. With the demand for impartial justice, light taxation, and other reforms, it also elicited from the more hardy witnesses a charge to defend communal institutions, dethrone the *tiranni* – Varani, Montefeltro, Malatesta and others – and check rectorial connivance at their excesses: in short, to establish good and strong government, and make obedience safe. The dual problem could not have been better stated.[6] It was not merely that Ghibellinism, to which some witnesses ascribed the strength of the despots, persisted in the Papal States as elsewhere in Italy: a Ghibellinism almost emptied of meaning, but now often bewilderingly confused with heresy in such a way that papal authority, if not denied in

---

[1] Benvenuto da Imola (ii.305): 'Primum est avaritia pastorum ecclesiae, qui nunc vendunt unam terram nunc unus favet uni tyranno, alius alteri, secundum quod saepe mutantur officiales.' Cf. Cola di Rienzo, letter of 24 May 1347: *Briefwechsel*, iii; Ciaccio, 'Bertrando del Poggetto', 109–10, 127–56, 482ff.; Vitale, 189; Biscaro, 'Relazioni' 1919, 111–12, 166, 174, 176, 219, 224; 1920, 206; Sorbelli, *Signoria*, 335–6.

[2] Cf. Eitel, 72ff., 86; Göller, *Einnahmen, Ben. XII*, 5*, 510; M. Villani, i.53; Antonelli, 'Vicende' 1904, 342–4.

[3] *Vitae pap. av.*, i.230; *Lettres, Ben. XII*, above p. 44 n. 6, and 2531, 2586, 2619, 2634, 2716ff., 2785, 3038; Otto, *RQ* 1928, 59–110; Antonelli, 'Vicende' 1903, 308–9; Aloisi, *AMM* 1906, 413–39; Nucci, *AMM* 1913, 138ff.

[4] Theiner, ii.250–2, 256; Filippini, *SS* vi.195; *Cardinale*, 10–11.

[5] 'pastoribus et tyrannis cum pastore tyrannizantibus': Cola di Rienzo, iii, n. 57; Aloisi, *AMM* 1907; Otto, *RQ* 1928, Beilage 16; Theiner, ii.117; Filippini, *SS* vii.407; *Cost Egid.*, 45–8, 103–6, 160–3.

[6] Theiner, ii.218 (conjecturally dated 1341, but it must be later than the summer of 1343: below p. 71).

principle,[1] was not less imperilled in practice.[2] Everywhere in the Papal States, but especially in Romagna and the March, the authority of government was flouted, independently of faction. The prohibitions common in the thirteenth century were repeated;[3] disobedience produced the need for armed repression, and with that sank the revenues of the province.[4] The Papal States in the first half of the fourteenth century were turbulent without example, and for this the despots who ignored their superior and, in the words of Albornoz, oppressed their subjects 'tamquam thauri in vaccis', were held more responsible than anyone.[5]

It fell to cardinal Egidio Albornoz, appointed 'reformator pacis' of the Papal State in June 1353,[6] to pursue with success the policy implied in the inquest of 1343: to correct misgovernment and bridle the despots. By 1350 the situation had become grave for papal government. Rome

[1] As for example by Pierre Dubois (Bock, *RQ* 1936) or Marsilius of Padua (*Defensor Pacis*, ed. R. Scholtz, Hannover, 1932–3, 481). The Ghibelline notion of the separation of temporal and spiritual powers was current in the Papal States (Bock, 'Processi'), as is shown by the Malatesta chronicler Battagli who deplored the Donation of Constantine and denounced clerical greed (*RIS*² xvi/3, p. xiv).

[2] Fumi, 'Eretici' 1897, 257–85, 429–89; 1898, 221–301, 437–86; 1899, 1–46, 205–425. The doctrines of the Fraticelli could easily be used to impugn the temporal dominion of the church, and were encouraged by the turbulent like Federigo d'Urbino. Fumi also alleges the complicity of the Malatesta, but does not cite an authority for it and there is no other evidence (1897, 276), although Francesco Ordelaffi, and Giovanni and Guglielmo Manfredi were condemned as heretics by Innocent VI (*Cost. Egid.*, 1 off.) and the Varani were charged with protecting Fraticelli (1343: Werunsky, *Excerpta*, n. 39). Much of this heresy was mere anti-clericalism, much mere irreverence (Bock, 'Este-Prozess', VII; *Cron. mal.*, 39.)

[3] Against unlicensed warfare, illicit 'fortillitia', usurpation of ecclesiastical rights etc.: Theiner, i.640, 667; *Lettres, Ben. XII*, 1520; *Cost. Egid.*, 106–8, 110–12, 118–19, 165–9; Fabre, 'Registre', 161; Falco, 'Comuni' 1926, 153–4, 284.

[4] The revenues from the Papal State recorded as reaching Avignon were, until Albornoz, negligible, engrossed by local war: Göller, *Einnahmen, Joh. XXII*, 67*–70*, 308, 310, 340, 495; *Einnahmen, Ben. XII*, 16*–17*; Mohler, *Einnahmen, Klem. VI*; Schäfer, *Ritter*, i.20–3, 27–9, 33–4, 41–2; Antonelli, *AR* 1902, 308 nn. 1, 2; 'Relazione'; 'Ribellione', *AR* 1896; Cessi, *AR* 1913, 150, 185. Albornoz had to sustain almost alone the expenses of the war against the Malatesta (Filippini, *SS* vii.541). In this same period rectorial stipends were reduced almost everywhere: Ermini, 'Rettori', 99.

[5] *Cost. Egid.*, 91. Incorporated in the *Cost. Egid.* are a whole series of enactments by papal government against tyranny and the abrogation of communal freedoms: 90–2, 109–10, 169–70. Benedict XII urged the rector of the March to assemble the communes against the *tiranni* (*Lettres*, 2512; cf. 2534, 2716–26), and still earlier John XXII's *nuncii* reported popular aversion to them (Preger, *Politik*, Auszug 23, pt. iv). In 1321 the rector of Romagna exclaimed that only a 'rector ferox' and the 'armatae Militiae bracchium' could overcome the despots: Tonini, iv/2.41. Yet the communes were equally insubordinate.

[6] Theiner, ii–242, 243 (wrongly printed 'II Kal. Iunii).

and the Campagna were given over to a licentious feudal nobility. The Tuscan Patrimony was divided by unruly cities and aspirant *signori*. Spoleto was threatened by Perugia, while the cities of Romagna and the March, the peculiar nursery of despotism, were surrendering on all sides to *signorie*.[1] Some of these – the Este, the Pepoli and the Alidosi – had been recognised by the papacy.[2] But most had only the sanction of its weakness. At the beginning of 1350 the papacy lost Faenza to the Manfredi, but the ensuing campaign to recover the city, and then to dispossess the Pepoli of Bologna, worked only to the discredit and humiliation of the rector, Astorgio di Duraforte, and his patron, Clement VI. The struggle was soon overshadowed by the greater quarrel between Giovanni Visconti and Mastino della Scala, in which the first was victorious, and Bologna passed to the Visconti with reluctant papal assent.[3]

Such was the situation that Albornoz was sent to repair. Why he was successful where others had failed is not at once apparent. Chance favoured him, as did the quarrels of his enemies. But much was due to his personal qualities, his integrity and circumspection, and above all his ability to compromise and wait. His encounter with the Malatesta particularly showed this. The first year and more of his legation was spent in subduing the Tuscan Patrimony and establishing his influence in Umbria and Spoleto.[4] But by the end of 1354 he was free to move against the *tiranni* north of the Apennines, and first and before all against the family which by arms and by cunning was threatening to subjugate an entire province of the church, the Malatesta.

During the previous half century the Malatesta had advanced greatly in strength and prestige. They had firmly established their authority in Rimini, and were bent on extending their control over the cities to the north and south. The wars of rival communes had now become the wars of rival despots, and behind the phantom titles of Guelf and Ghibelline the new *signori* fought to subjugate the towns which were still independent. In this perpetual conflict the Malatesta soon outdistanced other dynasties and by 1354 they were predominant in Romagna and the March. But their rise to supremacy was not easily achieved. Not only did they have to face resistance from the legates of

---

[1] Werunsky, *Karl IV*, ii.423–71, 515–16; Biscaro, 'Relazioni' 1928, 12.
[2] The Este as temporal vicars of the church, and probably the Alidosi also (Theiner, i.737ff., ii.135, 214; *Lettres, Jean XXII*, 62, 901; de Vergottini, 'Ricerche'). Taddeo Pepoli had also received authority from the papacy although not as vicar: Rodolico, 138ff.
[3] M. Villani, i.54–5, 58–71, 77; *Ann. Caes.*, 1179C–1180A; Theiner, ii.195–9, 205, 220; Werunsky, *Excerpta*, 247; A. Pepoli, *Doc. stor. del secolo xiv* (Florence, 1884), n. 53; Biscaro, 'Relazioni' 1928, 13.
[4] Filippini, *SS* vi.192, 343–78; vii.481; *Cardinale*, 18, 71–3; Theiner, ii.259, 267.

the church and a host of minor lords, but for many years they had also to settle fratricidal differences among themselves. Their conquests were often shortlived, and had constantly to be renewed, while personal jealousies crept ever closer to the centre of the family, at one time threatening their power in Rimini itself, and only papal weakness then preserved them from premature extinction.

Already late in the thirteenth century, the Malatesta had begun to push their influence into neighbouring towns, through the office of *podestà* or *capitano*, and to effect there the same transition from temporary to permanent control that they were accomplishing in Rimini. At various times they held high office in Forlì, Bertinoro and Faenza. But the two communities which engaged their attention most were Pesaro and Cesena. At the close of the century Cesena passed to the Montefeltro and their ally, Uberto Malatesta, count of Ghiaggiolo. In Pesaro however, Giovanni Malatesta possessed the office of *podestà* continuously from 1296 until his death in 1304.[1]

The first of the cities in Romagna to submit to the Malatesta should, by situation, have been Cesena. Yet not until the late fourteenth century were they destined to govern it permanently. Against them were not only the Ghibelline Montefeltro and Ordelaffi, but also their traditional allies, the Polenta of Ravenna, as well as the legitimate papal rulers of the city. In 1301 Federigo da Montefeltro and Ugguccione della Faggiola were expelled from Cesena. The conte Uberto now made peace with his cousins of Rimini, and from 1303 to 1309, as *podestà* and *capitano*, held Cesena for the Malatesta, until the machinations of the Guelf faction, stirred by fear of his ascendancy, compelled him to leave the city.[2] His place was taken as *podestà* by Bernardino da Polenta, but since the Polenta, like the Malatesta, were Guelf, Bernardino's election caused no estrangement between the two families. Rather he helped the Malatesta to subdue the castle of Sogliano in 1312 with forces from Cervia and Cesena.[3]

Before surrendering Cesena the Malatesta also made their first short-lived advances into the March of Ancona, to them as natural a field of expansion as Romagna. In 1304 Pandolfo Malatesta followed his brother Gianciotto as *podestà* of Pesaro, and shortly afterwards was

[1] Lünig, iv.43–6, 51–4; *Ann. Caes.*, 1120; Cantinelli, 70; Clementini, 1.486, 501, 519, 543, 581–3, 612–13; Chiaramonti, 232–3, 235–6, 244–6, 251; Giordani, *Porto*, 25; *Novilara*, 33–4; *Orazioni*, vi, vii. Gianciotto also held Gradara and in 1297 obtained from the archbishop of Ravenna the hereditary grant of Monte Cagnano: Giordani, *Gradara*, 72; *Novilara*, 35, App. iii.

[2] *Reg. Bon. VIII*, 5001; Theiner, i.566; *Ann. Caes.*, 1121, 1124, 1131; Clementini, 1.612–13, 651; Chiaramonti, 248, 263–6; Tonini, iv/1.1–5, 19–20; Zazzeri, 173; Davidsohn, *Geschichte*, iii.229.

[3] *Ann. Caes.*, 1133–4. There were however differences between the Malatesta and Polenta in 1305 (*ibid.* 1126).

elected *podestà* of Serrasanquirico, and *podestà* and *capitano* of Fano, where for some time the Malatesta had been intervening in the quarrels of Ghibelline and Guelf. At the same time, his nephew, Ferrantino, was appointed *podestà* and *capitano* of Sinigaglia, and *podestà* of Cingoli. Fossombrone also seems to have passed under the control of the Malatesta; and an attempt was made to capture Iesi, with the help of one of the citizens, Tano Baligano, brother-in-law of Ferrantino. Taken by force and held by force (Dante, *Inferno*, xxvii, 76–81), these cities were lost in the same way; and in 1306 the Malatesta were driven from the March by a popular insurrection, which was strengthened by papal arms. In 1307 and 1313 they may have repeated their attacks, but with no better success.[1]

It was as Guelfs that the Malatesta made their sudden conquest in the March of Ancona, and it was as Guelfs that they were forced to retire.[2] Their party allegiance remained what it had been. Malatestino dall'Ochio, who now led the family, was said to have only one defect: 'che non voleva né udire né vedere nissuno ghibillino e molto glie persiguiva'.[3] In 1301 he entered Florence with Charles of Valois,[4] and two years later he was elected captain of the Guelf league of Tuscany. From that time on his relations with the Tuscan Guelfs were intimate,[5] and at the end of 1306 Rimini, with Cesena and Ravenna, formally joined the Guelf league. Meanwhile in 1304 Malatestino had supported the papal representative in Romagna against Forlì.[6] But the papacy of Clement V did not at first share the animosities of Ghibelline and Guelf; and the legate sent in 1306, Napoleone Orsini, was mistrusted as a Ghibelline sympathiser. His partisan conduct at once offended Florence and Bologna, and drove the smaller Guelf powers, including Rimini, Cesena and the Malatesta, into open opposition. The Orsini replied with anathema and interdict, but 'suono di campane' and 'fumo di candele'

---

[1] For details see *Reg. Clem. V*, 430, 883–8; Vernarecci, *Fossombrone*, i.284–6; *Ann. Caes.*, 1127; Gritio, 32; Chiaramonti, 258; T. Baldassini, 50–3; G. Baldassini, doc.37; Siena, 117–19; Amiani, i.229–30, 233, 237–41, 243, 285–6; ii.348; Giordani, *Gradara*, 69–70; *Orazioni*, viii–ix; Colini, 28–9; Mariotti, *Serrungarina*, 8; Gaspari, 104; Valeri, *Arch. stor. Marche Umb.*, 1885, 304; Mazzatinti, *Archivi*, Ser. 1, ii.169, 204; Ser. 2, ii.281, n. 836; *Inventari*, xxxvii.84; Marcucci, 48; Nucci, *AMM* 1913, 116–17; Zdekauer, *AMM* 1916, 224, 228, 229.

[2] Göller, *RQ* 1905. The expulsion of the Malatesta left the March of Ancona open to the Ghibellines who established there what was almost a rival administration: Eitel, 140.

[3] *Cron. mal.*, 7; Branchi, 154: 'e solo attese al governo de parte ghelfa, intermittendo ogn'altra cura'.

[4] Dino Compagni, *RIS*² ix/2.102.

[5] He was also in close touch with the Guelfs of Bologna and Perugia: Davidsohn, *Forschungen*, ii.n. 2034; *Geschichte*, iii.331; Ghirardacci, i, *sub* 1306; Pellini, i.344; Vitale, 125; Eitel, 158–60.

[6] Bonoli, 125.

produced small effect, and the legate's military measures all miscarried. At the beginning of 1307 he left Romagna with Federigo da Montefeltro, to humble the 'Blacks' in Tuscany, only to be thwarted again by a Guelf army under Ferrantino Malatesta, *podestà* of Florence.[1]

The legation of Orsini enheartened the Ghibellines, and forced the Malatesta into revolt against the church.[2] But with Orsini's withdrawal from Italy departed the anomaly of a papal legate who was a Ghibelline. A general peace was concluded in Romagna,[3] and the Malatesta were soon able to renew their alliance with the papacy. In 1308 they were summoned to help resist the Venetian invasion of Ferrara, and shortly afterwards Rimini was absolved from interdict.[4] The Malatesta also gave support to the papal governor in the March, while in Romagna they became the closest allies of the new rector, Robert, king of Naples. 'With the help of King Robert', says Battagli, Malatestino was able at this time to make himself 'virtual lord of all Romagna'; and in 1311, when the province rose in rebellion, he was one of the few to remain faithful to the Angevin administration.[5]

The tradition of his house compelled Robert of Naples to become the wavering leader of the 'parte Guelfa' in Italy. He had already shown his colours in Romagna, making the province unsafe for the exiled 'Whites' of Tuscany.[6] The descent of Henry of Luxemburg reunited, under his feeble tutelage, the Guelfs on both sides of the Apennines. The Malatesta were still friendly with the greater Guelf communes,[7] and in 1312, following desperate appeals from Florence, they sent a contingent to Tuscany to protect the Guelf capital.[8] They are recorded as taking no other part in the contest with Henry VII. The Ghibellines of the March were active and well-organised under the leadership of

[1] *Reg. Clem. V*, 4401–2, 5271; Degli Azzi, ii, n. 137; *Ann. Caes.*, 1128; G. Villani, viii.89; Davidsohn, *Forschungen*, iv.543; *Geschichte*, iii.338–41; Eitel, 26ff., 161–2; Veronesi, *AMR* 1910, 118; C. A. Willemsen, *Kardinal Nap. Orsini* (Berlin, 1927), 29–51.

[2] On 6 Aug. 1307 Rimini, Cesena and the Malatesta were heavily defeated at Bertinoro by the Ghibelline Scarpetta degli Ordelaffi: *Cron. mal.*, 8; *Chron. Bon.*, ii.283–4; Cobelli, 82.

[3] Sept. 1308: *Ann. Caes.*, 1130; Tonini, iv/1.22–3.

[4] Followed by Cesena: *Reg. Clem. V*, 4401–2, 5001, 5084, 5271; Theiner, i.595; *Acta Arag.*, ii.645–6.

[5] Battagli, 30–1; Rubeus, 535; *Acta Arag.*, i.188; Eitel, 145–6; Caggese, i.133–5.

[6] Battagli, 43; *Ann. Forl.*, 62; Davidsohn, *Geschichte*, iii.454. For Florentine refugees in Rimini: Garampi, *Beata Chiara*, 255.

[7] In 1309 Ferrantino was *podestà* and then arbiter of Bologna: *Chron. Bon.*, ii.305, 307; Tarlazzi, i.471; Ghirardacci, i.526.

[8] Kern, 259; Bonaini, ii, docs.201, 214–15; Davidsohn, *Geschichte*, iii.441, 490; Caggese, i.137, 148.

Federigo da Montefeltro;[1] and this may have prevented the Malatesta from heeding the other Florentine demands for help which continued to reach Romagna until the sudden death of Henry at Buonconvento in August 1313.[2]

For their loyalty to Robert and his vicars, the Malatesta were rewarded in 1312 with help from the Angevin rector, Gilbert de Santillis, against Sogliano. During 1314 fresh discord broke out in Romagna, and again the Malatesta profited. In alliance with the rector, Malatestino was able to replace Guido da Polenta, one of the insurgents, as *podestà* of Cesena, and re-establish control by his family. Placing Ferrantino there as lieutenant, he was next appointed *podestà* of Forlì; but despite Angevin and papal patronage he was driven out by the Ordelaffi in September 1315. Possessed of Cesena, and for a time of Forlì, Malatestino was also successful in securing office in Cervia, which was governed by the Malatesta until 1316. All these were advantages accruing to the one dynasty that upheld Roberto's government in Romagna.[3]

In 1317 Pandolfo Malatesta took over as leader of the family. He was no less violent a Guelf than his brother, and according to Battagli, 'quasi omnes Gebellinos cun favore ecclesie delevit de patria'.[4] Under him the Malatesta were principally employed against the rebel cities of the March, Osimo, Fano, Fermo and others, which were led by Federigo, Guido and Speranza da Montefeltro;[5] and it was the Malatesta more than anyone who caused the defeat and death of Federigo in 1322 which finally gave ascendancy to the Guelfs.[6] The value of their services is eloquently attested by the long succession of letters sent by the pope,[7] and was commemorated locally by the

---

[1] Kern, 235; Bonaini, i, docs.193, 352; Doenniges, i.52, 67. Battaglini (*Vita*, App. LXIX, 690) prints a late sixteenth-century record in Rimini which runs: 'Bolla overo Privilegio d'Enrico Imperadore a Malatesta da Verucchio confermandoli tutte le terre della diocesi di Arimino et di Montefeltro'; but it stands alone.

[2] Bonaini, ii.288, 334, 343.

[3] *Ann. Caes.*, 1133–5; *Cron. mal.*, 7; Branchi, 153; Battagli, 30–1; *Chron. Bon.*, ii.320, 340–1; Fantuzzi, iii.342; Predelli, i, nn. 637, 690–1, 696, 715; Caggese, i.216, ii.2. In the summer of 1316 the Malatesta combined with the new Angevin vicar, Diego de la Rat, to reduce Forlì to obedience: *Ann. Caes.*, 1136–7.

[4] Battagli, 31.

[5] Theiner, i.643–5, 649–50, 655, 658, 661, 703, 716; *Lettres, Jean XXII*, 14, 219; Ugolini, i.115, 119.

[6] Tonini, iv/2, XVII, XXII, XXXII, XXXVII; Fumi, 'Eretici' 1897, 453; *Chron. Bon.*, ii.353; Davidsohn, *Geschichte*, iii.667–8; F. Guardabassi, *Storia di Perugia* (Perugia, 1933), i.168–9.

[7] *Lettres, Jean XXII*, 12030–1, 14959–60, 22638; Tonini, iv/2, XVIII, XIX, XXII, XXIV, XXXII, XXXVII–VIII, XLI, XLIII, XLVI. In commiserating with Ferrantino, Malatesta and Galeotto on the death of Pandolfo, John XXII wrote (19 May 1326) urging them to imitate him, 'fidelis pugil et devotus athleta' of the church: Tonini, iv/2, LV. Pandolfo exhibited conventional piety in gifts of land to the Minorites: *Bull. Franc.*, v, nn. 393, 538; *Lettres, Jean XXII*, 11148, 19773.

betrothal and marriage of Galeotto di Pandolfo with Hélise, niece of the papal rector Amelius de Lautrec. The marriage was solemnised in May 1324 amidst great festivity, and it was attended by many from the nobility of Tuscany, Lombardy, Romagna and the March. Pandolfo, his family and his friends were created knights with the sanction of the church, and gifts were sent in their honour from Florence, Bologna, and other wealthy communes.[1]

During the same period the Malatesta were active outside the Papal States as well, and the presence of so many representatives at the marriage of Galeotto was a tribute to their reputation. There is no mention of their sending help to Florence against Ugoccione della Faggiola; but Romagna's relations with Robert of Naples and the commune of Florence remained close,[2] and at the end of 1324 Ferrantino Malatesta was elected captain of the Tuscan league.[3] A year later he seems to have been employed in the same capacity by Guelf Perugia, though not in every way to her satisfaction.[4] In 1325 also his cousin Malatesta was engaged unsuccessfully against the Este, and his son, Malatestino, was severely defeated when leading the forces of Bologna against the Ghibellines at Zappolino.[5] The confederated factions of Italy were still in no way becalmed when Lewis of Bavaria entered Lombardy in 1327, and the Malatesta were called upon again to serve the Guelfs. As before during the campaign of Henry of Luxemburg, Florence became the centre of preparations for a common defence, but as before the Malatesta could take little notice of the circular letters from Tuscany,[6] being occupied in Romagna and the March, where the presence of an imperial rector, the count of Chiaramonte, and the influence of Nicholas V stirred up the Ghibellines to new activity.[7]

---

[1] The bride brought a dowry of 1,600 gold florins: Tonini, iv/2.121; *Cron. mal.*, 8; Branchi, 155; *Ann. Caes.*, 1141; Battagli, 32; *Ann. Forl.*, 64; *Chron. Bon.*, ii.357, 360–1; Davidsohn, *Geschichte*, iii.726. The celebrations were soon after marred by a heavy defeat at Urbino: G. Villani, ix.265; *Ann. Caes.*, 1142; *Chron. Bon.*, 358–9.

[2] In March 1318 Robert, preoccupied with the affairs of Genoa, appealed for contingents from among others the Malatesta: Caggese, ii.29–30.

[3] G. Villani, ix.286.

[4] 'Regesto Città di Castello', nn. 51, 54, 59, 70, 123; *Cron. Perug.*, 88, 90; Fumi, 'Eretici' 1898, 441. There is no report of the Malatesta at Altopascio, though the Romagna Guelfs were represented there, and the Ghibellines of Romagna and the March supported Castruccio: G. Villani, ix.344–6; Davidsohn, *Geschichte*, iii.733–5; Vitale, 179–80.

[5] Malatestino was taken prisoner, but in January 1326 peace was made and all but two prisoners released: G. Villani, ix.322; *Ann. Parm.*, 758; *Ann. Caes.*, 1144; *Chron. Est.*, *RIS*² xv/3.94–5; *Chron. Parm.*, *RIS*² ix/9.180; etc.

[6] Ficker, *Urkunden*, nn. 53, 58, 63; *MGH Leg.*, IV, vi/1.176–7.

[7] The papal censures on Lewis of Bavaria were published in Rimini 27 Nov. 1323, May and June 1324, and Dec. 1324: *Lettres, Jean XXII*, 20346, 23273; Riezler, 178.

Chiaramonte commanded a numerous following,[1] and in 1328 the Ghibellines delivered an assault on Rimini. The city stood firm, the attack was beaten off, and soon after the Malatesta were able to lend some help to the church against the rebels in the March.[2] In 1329 their ally Tano Baligano, lord of Iesi, was deposed and done to death at the count's order, and fresh incursions followed into Romagna and the Riminese *contado*. But this was the last Ghibelline success, and the movement died away amid papal fulminations and censures, although the rebels were slow to atone and reconciliation was long delayed.[3]

When Lewis of Bavaria abandoned Italy, the Malatesta had for twenty years been acting in constant association with the papacy as loyal and respected subjects. But this close union with the church was not untroubled by the usual conflict over franchise and privilege. While the commune of Rimini continued as before to defend its traditional autonomy, the Malatesta fought for the pope as paid *condottieri* no less than as vassals.[4] This helps to explain the occasional remittances of tallage and other dues which the records disclose.[5] But normally the church was too precise in the exercise of its fiscal rights to allow the communes or *signori*, ever jealous of their liberties, to forget the limits of their loyalty. The endless campaigning in Romagna and the March made *tallia militum* a regular imposition,[6] and this gave rise to continual disputes with the communes. The Angevin governors of Romagna met with opposition to their taxes, and in 1318 the Riminese, who were particularly intractable, were placed under censure for refusing to pay *tallia*.[7] During the rule of Aimery de Châtelus, successor to Robert of

---

[1] Including in Romagna the Ordelaffi and Polenta, in the March Niccolo da Busca-reto, the Simonetti of Iesi, with Fermo, Osimo, Urbino, Sinigaglia etc.: *Ann. Caes.*, 1151; Theiner, i.745; Schäfer, *Ritter*, i.13, ii.124–30; Martorelli, 151; Colini, 30.

[2] Branchi, 157; G. Villani, x.93; Tonini, iv/1.74–5, iv/2, LXVII–VIII, LXXII; Massèra, *RIS²* xv/2.157 n. 4.

[3] Branchi, 157; G. Villani, x.123; *Chron. Bon.*, ii.411; Ficker, *Urkunden*, n. 238.

[4] The treaty between Pandolfo Malatesta and the rector of the March in Feb. 1321 suggests a *condotta* (Tonini, iv/2, XVII); between 1 April and 1 Oct. 1322 he received 2,700 fl. as pay for himself and a troop of 50 horse (*ibid.* XXI), and in November a clerical tenth raised in Rimini was paid over to him: Mazzatinti, *Archivi*, Ser. 2, ii.297. Merely to call out the provincial *exercitus* was futile: Aloisi, *AMM* 1908, 270–1. For his services in Tuscany and elsewhere Ferrantino was also paid: Battaglini, *Zecca*, 200 n. 55. Already the Malatesta were *condottieri*.

[5] Below p. 54; cf. Tonini, iv/2, XLIV–V.

[6] Partner, 111ff.; Larner, 221ff.; below p. 92.

[7] In 1311 there were differences with Robert of Naples over *tallia* when Rimini took the opportunity of asserting its ancient privileges, 'quod pax Constantie dicitur', by which it had been granted 'expresse quod Comune ipsum et populus possint sibi rectores eligere ac iudices appelationum habere, qui de appelationibus usque ad summum vigintiquinque librarum imperialium causas audiant et decidant':

Naples in Romagna, the conflict became acute, and early in 1321 the rector was moved to write a scathing indictment of the *tiranni*, of whom, he said, Pandolfo Malatesta was the worst, since he had halved the rate of tallage and challenged payment even of that. Pandolfo's argument was that since the imperial grant of *merum et mixtum imperium* Rimini was subject to no exactions, and he sent as proof a copy of its immunities.[1] This was the beginning of an inconclusive dispute lasting several years. Stung by the importunacy of the rector and the admonitions of the pope, the commune decided in 1322 to send an embassy to Avignon, rejecting unreservedly all obligation to pay tallage, complaining of the distribution of the tax, and reminding the pope of the good service Rimini was rendering the church. No settlement had been reached when at a parliament in Bertinoro in 1326 the quarrel broke out afresh.[2] To the request for a *tallia* all assented but the communes of Forlì and Rimini, which sent a representative with insufficient powers. For a second time Rimini pleaded its imperial privileges, but the rector, invoking still older Carolingian memories, replied that these were forfeit, since the commune had long left its annual *census* unpaid, and in any case had contributed to tallage before. Once again an embassy was appointed, but John XXII remained inflexible, until in September 1327 he finally excused the Malatesta from all arrears of *tallia*, with a caution against evasion in the future.[3]

In itself the dispute over taxes would not have caused a breach between the Malatesta and the church, for at the same time the pope was writing to acknowledge their loyalty and service. But in the next few years, when the constitutional controversy was still unsettled, a situation began to develop in Romagna and the Papal State which drove the Malatesta to rebellion.

They had not abandoned their designs on neighbouring towns, and the war with Federigo da Montefeltro and the Ghibellines of the March

Caggese, i.129, 147, 192, 216. There were also disputes between the Malatesta and the church at this time, first concerning a sum of 3,700 fl. deposited with Pandolfo Malatesta by the rector of the March (*Reg. Clem. V*, 9969–70; *Lettres, Jean XXII*, 8138, 8197; Tonini, iv/2, LVIII; Aloisi, *AMM* 1908, 280; Bock 'Processi', 22 and App. I); secondly, over the grant by Boniface VIII of the lands of Bernardo Bandoni (above p. 34), which Clement V and John XXII tried to revoke (*Lettres, Jean XXII*, 7655; *Reg. Clem. V*, App. I, 324, 384, 470, 546, 629, 686, 716; Göller, *Einnahmen, Joh. XXII*, nn. 9, 43, 66, 92, 110, 131; Giordani, *Gradara*, 66; Tonini, iv/2, XXIV; Mazzatinti, *Inventari*, xxxvii.84, 91.

[1] Above p. 46 n. 5; cf. *Lettres, Jean XXII*, 12050, 12051, 14343.

[2] Tonini, iv/2, XXX, XXXIII; Delfico, ii, App. XII. The commune said that all previous payments had been voluntary and that, by its privileges, it was bound to pay only £300. In 1321 the commune was also instructed to repeal certain anti-clerical statutes: Tonini, iv/1.39. In 1325 Rimini and the Malatesta were again withholding *tallia*: *ibid.* 61, iv/2, n. 1.

[3] Fantuzzi, v.398, 408; Tonini, iv/1.63, iv/2, LIII, LVI, LXII, LXV.

gave them every opportunity for conquest. In this they were favoured, if not encouraged, by the papacy, and in 1321 the pope approved a plan to weaken the Montefeltro by surrendering part of the land round Urbino, together with S. Marino, ostensibly to Rimini, in fact to the Malatesta.[1] Later, in 1326, again with papal favour, the Malatesta may have won impermanent control of Santarcangelo.[2] But these were slender gains beside their successes in Pesaro and Fano.

By 1320, if not before, the Malatesta were re-established as *podestà* of Pesaro. This time it was for good; and when Malatesta di Pandolfo succeeded there in 1326 he had a special statute passed declaring him and his heirs citizens of Pesaro, with the right to settle in the city and compete for public office.[3] At the same time the Malatesta renewed their attempt on Fano. In 1321 Fano had surrendered to Federigo da Montefeltro, and it was as Guelf captains of the church that the Malatesta captured control of the city at the beginning of the next year. The republic of Venice, intent on extending its influence further in Romagna and the March, tried to resist their encroachment, but was checked by the remonstrances of John XXII, who explained that the Malatesta acted by his command. Ferrantino Malatesta became *podestà*, and to placate the city appointed as his vicar a prominent Fanese, Guido di Carignano; but in 1324 Pandolfo Malatesta was made *podestà*. Disputes between the city and *contado* of Fano had long been bitter, and in this year Pandolfo Malatesta was nominated papal *gubernator* of part of the *contado*: 'olim Comitatus Fani ad Ecclesiam spectantium'. This was an affront to the commune of Fano and may have contributed to the expulsion of the Malatesta in 1326 by Giacomo di Carignano, Ghibelline brother of Guido. Shortly afterwards, in 1328, the two brothers were reconciled, and after a period of interdict, Fano returned to the church independently of the Malatesta.[4]

Finally, in Cesena too the Malatesta maintained an uneasy supremacy. Internally the city was torn by faction, while from outside an offensive by the Ghibelline Ordelaffi perpetually threatened.[5] When the Malatesta

---

1 Tonini, iv/2.76; Delfico, i.112–20, ii, App. xii–vi; Fattori, 34; Pochettino, 'S. Marino', 363–6; Bock, 'Processi', 41.

2 *Ann. Caes.*, 1144; Branchi, 155–6; Marini, *Santo Arcangelo*, 44. In 1324 Pandolfo Malatesta may have been contemplating buying S. Leo: Tonini, iv/2.57.

3 Giordani, *Gradara*, 70; *Orazioni*, x–xi; Vaccai, 12.

4 *Ann. Caes.*, 1140, 1141; G. Villani, x.140; *Chron. Bon.*, ii.352; Tarlazzi, i, n. ccclxxxviii; Theiner, i.685, 712; Tonini, iv/2, xxviii, xxix, xlvii; Predelli, ii, n. 311; *Bull. Franc.*, v, n. 451; Amiani, i.250–7, 348; ii, lxviii–ix; Castelucci, 184–5. In 1327, when they had lost Fano, the Malatesta were largely instrumental in the confiscation of part of the *contado* by the papacy, which was later to cause them irritation: Amiani, i.257.

5 There seems to have been no comparable threat from the Polenta. What hostilities there had been were composed at the end of 1317 (Ghirardacci, i.598), and although the Malatesta were guilty of interference in the salt-works of Cervia, and pro-

recovered Cesena in 1314 the extreme Guelf party of the Callisesi had
withdrawn, but four years later they were readmitted as a counterpoise
to the rival Ghibelline family of the Artechini, at that time probably in
secret alliance with the Ordelaffi. This threw the Malatesta into dependence upon the Guelf party, who in the absence of Ferrantino, *podestà*
and *capitano*, drove their adversaries from the city. Thenceforward
Cesena was troubled by the Ghibelline exiles allied with the Ordelaffi,
but their attacks were unsuccessful, and when in 1326 Cesena slipped
from the grasp of the Malatesta, it was to the rector that it finally
submitted.[1]

It was no mere chance that both Fano and Cesena were lost to the
Malatesta in close succession. To make effective or permanent a complex
signoria extending over many cities, unity of purpose if not of leadership
had to be preserved. Malatesta da Verucchio had warned his successors
to remain united, and at first his counsel had been obeyed.[2] But ten
years after his death disharmony began to appear among his numerous
descendants and soon endangered the political power of the Malatesta,
which still lay rather in personal ascendancy and influence than in
formal or public prerogative.

. The first to break away was Uberto, count of Ghiaggiolo, who had
once already been an ally of the Ghibellines; after serving the Malatesta
for a time in Cesena, he became a close confederate of the Ghibelline
Ordelaffi. For fifteen years he conspired and fought against the
Malatesta, making their authority in Cesena insecure, until in 1324,
perhaps despairing of peace, they sent him an invitation to come and
confer at a place near Roncofreddo. He foolishly accepted and paid for
his folly with his life. The Malatesta murdered him as he entered for
dinner, and his body was removed in a sack. But he left a son, Ramberto, to carry on the feud.[3]

moted the coup d'état of Ostasio in 1322, they remained at peace with the Polenta
(Fantuzzi, iii.343; *Lettres, Jean XXII*, 14315; Theiner, i.671; Tonini, iv/1.37–8;
Chiaramonti, 285, 289; Rubeus, 549–50; G. Villani, ix.169). Between Dec. 1322
and Nov. 1323 Pandolfo Malatesta was vicariously *podestà* of Ravenna (Fantuzzi,
v.180n., 181), and when in 1326 the Malatesta began to lose control of Cesena,
Bernardino da Polenta was *podestà* there (Zazzeri, 184). Malatestino Novello was
married to Polentesa da Polenta (Tonini, iv/1.71, 309; Massèra, 'Note', 31; *Ann.
Caes.*, 1145B).

[1] *Ann. Caes.*, 1140–1, 1142, 1144–6; *Ann. Forl.*, 64; *Chron. Bon.*, ii.359; G. Villani,
ix.266; *Lettres, Jean XXII*, 8348; *Stat. Caes.* (1589), 243; Ghirardacci, ii.4;
Chiaramonti, 266–78, 282, 286–7, 291, 293–7.
[2] Only in 1312 did the Malatesta of Rimini dispossess the Ghibelline Malatesta of
Sogliano: *Cron. mal.*, 7; Tonini, iv/2.26–9. In September of the same year it is
recorded that Roberto of Naples attempted to compose peace between Malatestino
and 'alcuni consorti': Caggese, i.182.
[3] Cobelli, 88–9, 94, 96–7; *Ann. Caes.*, 1135, 1136–7, 1139, 1140–1; *Cron. mal.*, 8–9;
Branchi, 155; *Chron. Bon.*, ii.357.

The line of Paolo il Bello was perhaps fated to treachery and the vindication of a crime. It fell to the heirs of his assassin, Gianciotto, to begin the quite different struggle which now developed among the three remaining branches of the family to gain the political inheritance of Malatesta da Verucchio entire and undivided. Even before the death of Pandolfo, the youngest son of Malatesta, in April 1326, Ramberto di Gianciotto had betrayed a design to capture the *signoria* for himself,[1] but as long as Pandolfo lived, outward harmony was preserved. It was the second generation, the *consorteria* of cousins, that fell into murderous strife, until one had emerged victorious over the rest. Pandolfo's place in Rimini was taken by Ferrantino Malatesta, the son of Malatestino dall'Occhio, but the elevation of Ferrantino was resented by his relatives, and in July 1326, by 'uno laido tradimento', Ramberto took him prisoner, with his son Malatestino, and Ferrantino Novello, his grandson. As a result Cesena was lost to the Malatesta, and Fano rose in revolt.[2] Ramberto retained the *signoria* for only three days. While Rimini stood by Ferrantino, Ramberto was forced to abandon the city by Malatesta di Pandolfo, his other cousin, who had been absent fighting the Ghibellines of the March. The prisoners were then released, and a long war followed. The pope had declared against Ramberto, but did not despair of reconciling him with his family. Ramberto himself was anxious for peace, and this anxiety was his undoing. In January 1330 he agreed to meet Malatestino, who had craftily encouraged his overtures, and by him was stabbed to death when kneeling to entreat pardon. His castles were then destroyed, and his nephew and associate, Giovanni di Tino di Gianciotto, wandered into exile: 'se partie et andò per lo mondo per spazio de tempo'. For this murder Malatestino was banned by the church.[3]

It only remained now for the successors of Malatestino dall'Occhio and Pandolfo, of the eldest and youngest sons of Malatesta da Verucchio, to grapple for supremacy.

The occasion of their quarrel was the papal offensive to recover authority in Romagna. Both Fano and Cesena had passed to the control not of other despots but of the church. The papal representative at this time was the bellicose legate Bertrand du Pouget, who between 1326 and 1331 was able to force the whole of Romagna into outward submission. Bologna was the first to surrender its liberties in February 1327. Imola, Faenza, Ravenna and Forlì all followed in close succession; finally in May 1331 the intestine animosities of the Malatesta gave him the possession of Rimini as well.[4]

---

[1] See Tonini, iv/2, xlviii–ix.   [2] Above p. 55.
[3] *Cron. mal.*, 9–10, 11; Branchi, 156; *Ann. Caes.*, 1145, 1151; G. Villani, ix.351; Tonini, iv/2, lxii, lxiv.
[4] Ciaccio, 'Bertrando del Poggetto', 119, 159–60, 170, 181, 462–3, 466–9.

United against the machinations of Ramberto in 1326, Ferrantino and Malatesta di Pandolfo had soon become estranged. Malatesta was clearly the more resolute and ruthless of the two, and proved himself willing to go to any length that might make him sole lord of Rimini. Although only *podestà* of Pesaro, his name quickly appeared beside that of Ferrantino in letters addressed to the Malatesta,[1] and his formal ascendancy could not be long delayed. The pope tried to prevent an open schism in the family,[2] but Malatesta was not to be moved. Instead he planned to make adroit use of the papal restoration in Romagna, and overthrow his rivals with the blessing of the church. Once already he may have offered Rimini to the papacy,[3] and when in April 1331 the cardinal-legate sent command for Rimini to be surrendered, Malatesta may have been in secret alliance with him.[4] Ferrantino seems at first to have contemplated resistance, and took counsel with his family, summoning Malatesta also to attend, 'che stava a Pesaro el più tempo, perché non se fidava di soi consorti'. The debate was long and heated, but with cunning obstinacy Malatesta refused to become a rebel of the church, and Ferrantino had no choice but to invite the legate to enter Rimini. When the papal representatives arrived in May, Malatesta at last revealed the full extent of his design by driving out Ferrantino, who was forced to withdraw with his family into the *contado* where he held the castles of Roncofreddo, S. Giovanni in Galilea, Mondaino, and Monlione. Futile negotiations followed for the surrender of these places, and while Ferrantino retired into safety in Friuli, Malatesta, created *capitaneus guerre* by the legate, with his brother Galeotto harried Ferrantino's family 'tamquam capitales inimicos'. Malatestino resisted him, strong in the support of Perugia, Fermo, Arezzo, Fabriano and Urbino, until in 1332 an agreement was reached by papal intercession. Ferrantino was allowed to keep all but Mondaino, and a 'firm truce' was made.

'Per la qual cosa fu guasta la detta casa', says Villani, who saw in this the characteristic perfidy of the Romagnoli, 'che volentieri sono traditori tra loro', and from that time forward Malatesta carried the name of 'Guastafamiglia'.[5]

---

[1] Tonini, iv/2, LX, LXVII–III; Ficker, *Urkunden*, n. 63.

[2] See Tonini, iv/2, LXXI.   [3] *Chron. Bon.*, ii. 381; Chiaramonti, 299.

[4] Thus already on 21 April 1331 the sequence of papal favours to Malatesta had begun with letters legitimising Giovanni, the bastard son of Pandolfo Malatesta, and granting dispensation for the marriage of his own son Pandolfo to Luppa Francesca, daughter of Bernardo, count of Marsano in the diocese of Perugia *Lettres, Jean XXII*, 53465–6; Tonini, iv/1.328, iv/2, LXXIV). Tonini thinks the marriage did not take place, but he may be mistaken: see Mascetta-Caracci, *Zeitsch. f. Roman. Philologie*, 1907, 63.

[5] *Ann. Caes.*, 1152; *Cron. mal.*, 11; Branchi, 157; Battagli, 32; Griffoni, 39; G Villani, x. 180; Tonini, iv/2, LXXV, LXXVIII; Ciaccio, 'Bertrando del Poggetto', 195 and n. 5.

For the moment the Malatesta had lost control of Rimini, and the church governed in their stead. But their influence remained as strong as before, and 'il Guastafamiglia' cannot have expected to remain dispossessed for long. He and Galeotto retained their place in Pesaro, and may also have been given the custody of Fossombrone with a number of castles in the *contado* of Fano.[1] They were not disturbed in their patrimonial lordships, at Gradara and elsewhere,[2] and they were still possessed of sufficient power in Rimini itself to be granted by the commune certain parts of the *contado*.[3] Having used the papal legate to humble his enemies, Malatesta found it wise or necessary to remain on cordial terms with the church, and in return for his politic display of obedience was awarded a series of gifts and favours by the grateful pope.[4] But he and other *fideles* of the church were constantly 'molested and oppressed' by the officials created by the legate,[5] and like the other *signori* of Romagna he can only have been awaiting the chance to re-establish power.

The chance soon came. Bertrand du Pouget had achieved his last successes, and his patient campaign to put down the *tiranni* was nearing its end. Only Ferrara remained unsubdued under the government of the Este, and in March 1332 a parliament was held at Faenza to vote troops for an attack on the city. In October Malatesta was sent to defend Castelfranco against the Este, and in the following spring he and Galeotto were summoned with other *signori* to lead the papal army. But the 'caporali di Romagna' were conscripted against their will; their forces were heavily defeated, and they themselves were all taken prisoner, the Malatesta among them.[6] At once the legate's authority, so laboriously acquired, began to crumble everywhere, and within a year Romagna had returned to its usual independence. The captive lords went over to the Este and their allies, and during the summer Galeotto, and then Malatesta, were allowed to go free. Without delay they set about recovering Rimini. Encouraged by successes in the *contado*, and supported by Pietro Tarlati, lord of Arezzo, they assembled a large force to reduce the city, which was strongly garrisoned by the church.

---

[1] Amiani, i.259; Tonini, iv/2, LXXIX; Vernarecci, *Fossombrone*, i.292.

[2] Giordani, *Gradara*, App. XV; Theiner, i.764; *Lettres, Jean XXII*, 57149.

[3] 30 May 1332 (with papal sanction): Tonini, iv/2, LXXIX.

[4] *Lettres, Jean XXII*, 57145ff., granting Malatesta, Galeotto and their wives plenary indulgences 'in articulo mortis', licensing an exchange of lands with the bishop of Rimini' etc.; cf. further Theiner, i.766. Malatesta was also in direct touch with Avignon, whence he received in June 1332, a gift of 1,000 fl.: Schäfer, *Ausgaben, Joh. XXII*, 116–17, 531.

[5] Tonini, iv/2, LXXXI.

[6] 14 April 1333: *Cron. mal.*, 11; Branchi, 158; Battagli, 32; *Ann. Caes.*, 1152, 1153; *Chron. Est.*, RIS² xv/3.101–2; *Cron. sen.*, 509–10; *Chron. Bon.*, ii.425–6; G. Villani, x.217–18; Ficker, *Urkunden*, 155; Ciaccio, 'Bertrando del Poggetto', 468–73, 478.

The siege continued for more than a month until on 22 September, reinforced by the populace, 'et omine e femine', they were able to force an entry, expelling the legatine vicar and overpowering his troops. At the same time the other lords of Romagna were restored to power, and in January 1334 they and Malatesta attended a parliament at Peschiera to renew the alliance against the legate. As a result Argenta and then Bologna threw off papal control, and the first deliberate offensive against the *tiranni* ended in ignominious failure.[1]

Romagna and the March persevered long in rebellion, unaffected by the appeals of Robert of Naples and the election of a conciliatory pope, Benedict XII. Whether Ghibelline or Guelf, lords and cities alike expressed their revulsion against the legate and his policy by a general indifference to papal admonition and entreaty. The Malatesta of Rimini shared this attitude, and during the next twenty years their close alliance with the church was broken. They turned instead to giving their supremacy in Rimini the institutional clarity it lacked, while outside the city the enfeebled communes of the March fell one by one into their control, threatening to create from a province of the church the foundations of a wide principality.

The first concern of Malatesta and Galeotto, once securely reinstated in Rimini, was to restrict all political authority to themselves. Their anxiety to recover the city in 1333 had reunited momentarily the two conflicting branches of the family, and as long as Bertrand du Pouget remained in Romagna the coalition stood firm; 'ma . . . como el ditto legato fo partito, andò a male'. The old rancours revived and as before were settled by treachery and violence. At the beginning of June 1334 Malatesta Guastafamiglia, in concert with Ostasio da Polenta, suddenly seized Ferrantino, his son Malatestino and his grandson Guido, and confined them to the castle of Gradara. Ferrantino was later released in January 1336, but the others were removed to Fossombrone and there put to death. Ferrantino Novello, who had been absent at Paderno, hastened to establish himself at Mondaino, Roncofreddo, and the other castles of the Riminese *contado* which were held by his family, and a contest began which dragged on for more than ten years. Ferrantino was formidable in alliance with Perugia, the Montefeltro, the Carrara and the Pepoli.[2] He was also consistently favoured by the legates of the

---

[1] G. Villani, x.228; Cobelli, 104; *Ann. Caes.*, 1153–4, 1155–6, 1158; *Cron. mal.*, 11–13; Branchi, 158; Battagli, 33; *Chron. Est.*, *RIS* xv.395; *Chron. Bon.*, 428–30, 487; Ciaccio, 'Bertrando del Poggetto', 482–9. With the Este the Malatesta may for some time have been related: *Chron. Est.*, 188–9; *Chron. Bon.*, iii.22, 24, 25. Tonini (iv/1.315) does not pronounce on the question whether Malatesta Guastafamiglia had an Estense wife, Costanza.

[2] Ferrantino was married to Anna, sister of Nolfo da Montefeltro, and in 1340 the granddaughter of Ferrantino vecchio, also Anna, married Ubertino da Carrara.

church. But he was never able to recover power in Rimini, either by negotiation or by force. On his side Guastafamiglia was supported by Imola, Ravenna and Forlì. He refused to contemplate any agreement with his enemies, and fought remorselessly for their total dispossession. In 1337 a truce was arranged, and in 1343 the papal legate imposed a formal peace, but Malatesta disregarded both. For another five years he pursued the war, and was not satisfied until in February 1348 he had captured Mondaino, the last remnant of Ferrantino's power in the *contado*. Shortly afterwards Ferrantino Novello was killed when leading a Ghibelline attack upon Perugia, while his father, Ferrantino 'vecchio', now a very old and harmless man, was allowed to return to Rimini. There he died in November 1353, and death completed Guastafamiglia's work.[1]

'Et in questo modo comincionno li predetti miser Malatesta e miser Galeotto chiarmarsi signori de Arivino etc., ché sempre prima erano bene stati i maggiori e come capi dela terra, ma non signori a bachetta.'[2]

Long before this family quarrel had been fought to a decision, Malatesta had acted to remove all other impediments to the formal supremacy of his line, and it cannot have been an accident that in the very years of his attack on Ferrantino Guastafamiglia was first created 'signore a bachetta'. It was the natural result of his resolve to rule alone. It was also perhaps a natural sequel to the short interval of government by the church; and although the Malatesta seem to have been restored to Rimini with the active approval of their fellow-citizens, they did not allow many months to elapse before seeking a final and statutory definition of their authority. Hitherto this may have been wanting. The practical ascendancy of the family was evident enough but its constitutional nature was vague, as the curt language of the chroniclers indicated.[3] In the contest with the papacy over tallage it is impossible to separate the Malatesta from the commune or the commune from the Malatesta; and throughout this period letters

---

[1] *Cron. mal.*, 13–14, 15, 17; Branchi, 159, 160, 162–3; Battagli, 33–5; *Ann. Caes.*, 1160, 1161, 1163, 1165, 1173, 1174, 1176; *Chron. Bon.*, ii.438, 440, 457, 495–6, 503–4, 509, 511; *Chron. Est.*, RIS² xv/3.147; Giordani, *Gradara*, 73; L. Bonazzi, *Storia di Perugia* (Perugia, 1871–9), i.436; Tonini, iv/1.86–8, 93, 95–9, 115–19, 129–30; Vernarecci, *Fossombrone*, i.294–6; Massèra, 'Note', 25–48.

[2] Branchi, 159.

[3] Of each successive Malatesta they simply say: 'fo facto signore' (*Cron. mal.*, 7, 8, 9) or 'fo levato capo de parte ma era onorato come signore' (Branchi, 154, 155, 156). Clementini describes Malatestino as 'Difensore' (i.547–8) though he appears only as *podestà* in documents, and he uses similar terms of Pandolfo (ii.3). To support him is a rubric in the Riminese statutes: 'Quod querela aliqua a modo non admictatur de processibus factis vel obmissis per magnificos viros malatestinum dominum pandulfum et ferantinum de Malatestis olim potestates et *deffensores* civit. arimini' (Battaglini, *Zecca*, 177).

continued to be addressed as regularly to the magistrates of Rimini as to the Malatesta.[1] Yet, as has been seen, the commune seems already to subserve the private ambitions of the Malatesta.[2] The lands held by the Malatesta in the Riminese *contado* were rapidly increasing,[3] and already they seem able to make decisions affecting communal statutes and revenue. In 1325 Pandolfo Malatesta granted the people of Cattolica a general immunity from taxation;[4] and when in the time of Ferrantino the exiled Parcitadi combined with the Romagnol Ghibellines to cause disturbances in Rimini, the laws were at once re-enacted, no doubt at the wish of the Malatesta, which had been passed in 1295 to dispossess and banish them.[5] The power of the Malatesta was formal mainly by their control of the *podesteria*. In every year between 1301 and 1320, with the possible exception of 1309, a member of the family was *podestà*, and again in 1325; and even when others held office, Malatesta influence was present.[6] Possession, as distinct from control, of the appointment denoted only the initial phase of the *signoria*, and the fact that the Malatesta withdrew from it during the third decade of the fourteenth century may imply a greater consciousness of power. At the initiative of his father, Ferrantino Malatesta was certainly awarded the distinct office of 'Conservator Civitatis et Comitatus Arimini', together with the presidency of the *consiglio dei Savj*, both of which he retained.[7] This council had been from the beginning peculiarly dependent on the Malatesta. From 1295 it seems to have become increasingly prominent in the government of the city; and when Ferrantino received this privileged position, a development was already fore-

---

[1] See Tonini, iv/2; if a letter were sent to the commune, it was accompanied by another to the Malatesta: Ficker, *Urkunden*, n. 277, *a*.1329.

[2] Above p. 55. The rectorial complaint of 1321 and the embassy of the Riminese to Avignon in 1322 both reveal the complete ascendancy of the Malatesta: above p. 55.

[3] Above p. 59; below p. 290.

[4] Clementini, ii.18; cf. Tonini, iv/2, XII.

[5] The *Ann. Caes.* (1133) record that in 1310 the Angevin vicar in Romagna re-admitted the Parcitadi to Rimini; but soon after they appear among the Lombard Ghibellines (*MGH Leg.*, IV, vol. v, doc. 742; Schwalm, *Neues Archiv*, XXV, 1900, doc. VIII), and about the time of Ramberto Malatesta's coup d'état they were stirring up trouble in Rimini. For this they were declared 'baniti', and the statute states that they had been rebels of the church and Rimini 'a tempore novitatis facte in civitate ariminj in festo sancte Lucie quod fuit in Millio. ducentessimo nonagesimo quinto vel idcirca quando fuit mortuus dictus Cignata' (Bib. sen., *Stat. Rim.*, fo. 269r; Tonini, iii.175 n. 1). They remained with the Ghibellines of Romagna after the return of the Malatesta in 1333: Branchi, 160; Rodolico, 151.

[6] See Tonini, iv/1.254, iv/2, XXXVI; Battaglini, *Vita*, 566.

[7] Clementini, i.555. Battaglini, *Zecca*, 195 (March 1316); Tonini, iv/2, XIII (March 1317), XV (Dec. 1320). In 1330 the *consiglio dei Savj* assembled 'in Camera magnifici militis Domini Ferrantini' (Tonini, iv/2, LXX), where it continued to meet even during the period of papal government (*ibid.* LXXVI: March 1332).

shadowed which it was left for Malatesta Guastafamiglia to resume and complete in 1334, after his restoration.

The various enactments of that year were decisive in the assumption of formal power by the Malatesta in Rimini. Their order is not easy to determine, but collectively they represent an unreserved surrender by the commune of *plenitudo potestatis*. It was provided in the first place that Malatesta, Galeotto and their descendants should be absolved from all obedience to communal statutes and ordinances, and allowed to proceed against anyone 'ad sui comodum pro libito voluntatis'.[1] A further statute laid down that only Malatesta and Galeotto should in future hold the office of *podestà*, which was to be closed to every other 'civis vel comitatinus districcualis vel forensis dicte Civitatis'.[2] The two brothers were next empowered to unite whatever number of friends they pleased in a 'consilium credentie parvum vel magnum', the deliberations of which, even if unstatutory, were to be held as binding. No further conciliar ratification was to be necessary, nor was the assent of the four Ufficiali, and this was to apply as much to fiscal as to other measures.[3] Even after the limits imposed in 1295, the powers of the four Ufficiali had remained extensive. They had been the dominant institution of the commune, and it was inevitable that the prerogatives of these 'popular' magistrates should succumb to the new authority of the *signoria*.[4]

None of these acts makes any mention of Malatesta Guastafamiglia as *defensor* of Rimini. But the last of them alludes to the 'dominium liberum et perpetuum' recently granted him by a *reformatio* of the general council; and it is certain that at about this time he was given the 'dominium et defensoria' for life ('ad vitam'). This is proved by another statute confirming the 'Baylia' and 'arbitrium' which had been conveyed to him, and acknowledging his unrestricted control of communal revenues and jurisdiction.[5]

On 26 November 1334 all these decisions were ratified in a new edition of the statutes published and approved by the *consiglio generale*;[6] and in April of the following year the prerogatives of the *signori* were

---

[1] Below App. I; cf. Bib. sen., *Stat. Rim.*, fo. 206r. Already in 1334 there was a provision that anyone guilty of treachery to the Malatesta should be tried summarily, and condemned to death: Salvioli, *Statuti di Rimini*, 26.

[2] Below App. II. Battaglini (*Zecca*, 217) mentions a statute by which the two Malatesta were to be *podestà* whenever they wished; they were not obliged like the *podestà* to reside in the 'Palatium Comunis'. Otherwise a different *podestà* and *judex mallefitiorum* were to be elected.

[3] Below App. III.

[4] Battaglini, *Zecca*, 181; below p. 308.

[5] Below App. IV. The same act confirmed the 'gratie' made by Galeotto in respect of all criminal cases then pending or concluded.

[6] Bib. sen., *Stat. Rim.*, fo. 253r.

further defined when a formal session of the general council, at which
the Malatesta were not present, referred the impending election of a
new *podestà* to the *defensor*, Malatesta de' Malatesta, to determine with
what *sapientes* he chose to consult.[1]

By this revolution Malatesta Guastafamiglia was raised to the summit
of power in the commune. The ultimate authority, the *defensoria*, was
his (Galeotto for the moment remaining a simple 'miles');[2] and whatever the means by which he attained supremacy, it is certain that if any
single man firmly established the government of his family it was
Malatesta. His personality may only be inferred from the terse entries
of chroniclers. There were no humanist panegyrists to commemorate
him, no court poets or painters. The *tiranni* had still to be generally
acknowledged by publicists. But he remains the most challenging
figure of his dynasty before the accession of Sigismondo a century
later; and it was natural that under him the dominion of the Malatesta,
now strengthened at its source, should also have reached its greatest
territorial limits.

Pesaro and Fossombrone they already held in 1333,[3] and during the
rebellion of that year, in which they recovered Rimini, the Malatesta
also tried to occupy Cesena, only however to lose it to Francesco
Ordelaffi, who remained in possession until deprived by Albornoz.[4]
No more successful was an attempt to capture Urbino in 1340. But
these reverses were exceptional. Otherwise the record of the Malatesta
at this time is one of swift and persistent conquests.

Their first important acquisition was Fano. Here, from 1334, they
cultivated a close association with the leading local family, the Carignano, united with them in common hostility to the Montefeltro; and
when, late in the following year, the rector tried to depose from power
Giacomo da Carignano, then absent fighting with the Este, Malatesta sent
his son Pandolfo to help the Fanesi, and succeeded in intruding him as
podestà. This established his influence, though it took several years to consolidate. For a short time (1337–8) he lost his hold on Fano; but by stirring up the *contadini* against the city, he managed to force the commune
to offer the *signoria* to his brother Galeotto, who sent a vicar to govern
beside the *podestà*. The Carignano were now driven into opposition,

---

[1] Below App. v. All these changes were carried through by the *consiglio generale*.
There is no evidence of a *parlamentum* or *arengum* such as confirmed similar elections in other Italian cities, even in the fourteenth century: Salzer, 42, 44–6, 173,
223–4, 227.

[2] Battaglini, *Saggio*, 47 (a. 1336).

[3] Early in 1334 the rector of the March occupied Fossombrone, but the Malatesta
recovered it in the same year: *Ann. Caes.*, 1159; Vernarecci, *Fossombrone*, i. 292.

[4] *Ann. Caes.*, 1154–5; *Ann. Forl.*, 65; Griffoni, 43; Cobelli, 103, 105. Ramberto,
count of Ghiaggiolo, cooperated with the Ordelaffi in gaining Cesena.

and under them Fano rose in revolt against the Malatesta in 1340 and again at the end of 1342, when part of the Grand Company of Duke Werner was used to subdue the city. Fano was compelled to surrender 'a patti', and Galeotto was established as 'Protector, Gubernator, Defensor, Dominus, ac Vicarius Generalis Civitatis Fani, eiusque Comitatus Fortiae et Districtus'.[1]

Other cities quickly followed,[2] and between 1348 and 1350 by influence or force the Malatesta imposed their government upon Ascoli,[3] Osimo, Ancona,[4] Iesi,[5] Cingoli,[6] and a great number of smaller places,[7] assuming the various titles of 'Lord,' 'governor' and 'Defensor'. The Black Death in no way hindered their advance, for although in Rimini, as the anonymous chronicler testifies, 'morì de tre persone le doe', of the 'tiranni e grandi signuri non morì nissuno'.[8] The effect of this sudden expansion was not only to arouse papal anxiety.

---

[1] For these complicated events see Amiani, i.261–2, 264–6, 269; ii.349; *Ann. Caes.*, 1157, 1159; *Cron mal.*, 14–15; Branchi, 160; *Chron. Est., RIS*² xv/3.115; *Chron. Bon.*, ii.510–11; Ricotti, 51–6; Mariotti, *Serrungarina, passim*. In 1343 Galeotto took measures to strengthen his authority, reserving election of the *podestà*, assuring control of revenues and the watch, and making generous payments to all officials. Later he set to eradicating all memorials of the Carignano (ACF, *Depos., Collette* I, II; *Depos., Catasti* I; Amiani, 1.269, 272; Zonghi, 474–8, 483, 488). Meanwhile the papacy continued to withhold the part of the Fanese *contado* confiscated by John XXII (above p. 55). After the final acquisition of Fano the Malatesta may have proceeded to partition their state, Galeotto taking Fano, Pandolfo di Malatesta Pesaro, and Malatesta Rimini and Fossombrone: Tonini, iv/1.113; Vernarecci (*Fossombrone*, i.297) puts it earlier.

[2] Or preceded: about 1340 the Malatesta must have occupied Sinigaglia: Theiner, ii.115.

[3] In May 1348 Galeotto seems to have been called in to captain the Ascolani; his election as *signore* followed with the support of the popular party: *Chron. Est., RIS*² xv/3.163; *Chron. Bon.*, ii.592; Battaglini, *Vita*, 692; G. Rosa, *Disegno della storia di Ascoli Piceno* (Brescia, 1869–70), 118–19; Luzi, 106–8. At the same time Galeotto and Malatesta took over Ripatransone as 'Gubernatores et Defensores': Colucci, xviii.30–1.

[4] Ancona in Dec. 1348, following depopulation of the city by plague and fire, and with the support, in this case, of nobles against popolani: Bernabei (Oddo de Biagio), 62–3, 72–3; *Chron. Est., RIS*² xv/3.164; *Chron. Bon.*, ii.594–5. When precisely the Malatesta took Osimo does not emerge but in 1347 they were helping Ancona to subdue the city: Martorelli, 156–7; Compagnoni, *Osimo*, v. 93; Tarlazzi, ii.307–8.

[5] 10 Jan. 1349, displacing Lomo dei Simonetti, lord of the city since 1342, who however came to terms: *Chron. Est., RIS*² xv/3.164–5; *Chron. Bon.*, ii.596; G. Baldassini, 105; Compagnoni, *Reggia Picena*, 215; G. Cecconi, *Cenni storico-genealogici della famiglia Simonetti di Osimo*, 13–14.

[6] In 1350 or 1351: Amiani, i.275; Gaspari, 195; Avicenna, 168; Menicucci, in Colucci, xx, pt. 1, 74–5; Nucci, 'Arte dei notari', 144–5.

[7] For various estimates (Pergola, Roccacontrada etc.): Amiani, i.273–5; Nicoletti, 154; Calvi, *AMM* 1904–5, Tav. xxix; Battagli, 34–5; Tonini, iv/2.180–4; below p. 66 n. 2.

[8] *Cron. mal.*, 17.

By imperilling their puny powers it combined in fear of the Malatesta a crowd of *signorotti* of the March, resolved at all costs to resist the threat to their independence. With more powerful lords like the Varano of Camerino and the Montefeltro of Urbino were associated lesser despots who had only lately risen to power, and who were now in some cases dispossessed. Such were Ismeduccio of S. Severino, Bartolomeo Cima of Cingoli, Niccolo da Buscareto of Corinaldo, Lomo dei Simonetti of Iesi, the Chiavelli of Fabriano, the Gabrielli of Gubbio, and others besides; and by 1354 the Malatesta had been compelled to surrender many of their secondary conquests to them.[1] Of the March of Ancona at this time the Riminese chronicler could say without exaggeration: 'la quale Marca regeva miser Malatesta, fora que Fermo';[2] and it was the lord of Fermo, Gentile da Mogliano, who was most strenuous in opposing the Malatesta. He had come to power in 1348, and in that same year had threatened Ascoli and Fano, but he was taken in ambush by the Malatesta who were able to exact from him what terms they pleased.[3] Hostilities were not long interrupted; and in 1353 Galeotto and Malatesta attempted to conquer Fermo. Success may have been near, but Gentile da Mogliano, with Francesco Ordelaffi, invited the intervention of Fra Moriale, then the most dreaded of the foreign captains, with a large company of horse and foot. Malatesta was forced to retire from the siege, promise the payment of a large fine, and surrender his son, Malatesta Ungaro, as hostage.[4]

Such was the state of the March of Ancona when the cardinal-legate Albornoz was sent to bring peace and order.

In challenging the power and dominion of the Malatesta Albornoz was no longer confronted with the wavering authority of the petty despot, but with a dynasty which had won recognition and respect among the greater states of Italy. Particularly close was the alliance of the Malatesta with Florence, in part a legacy of the Guelf confederation of earlier days. Reminiscent of that tradition was the league of mutual defence concluded in 1336 between Florence and Bologna, the Malatesta and Polenta, which was renewed in 1338 at the instance of Malatesta and Ostasio da Polenta.[5] It may have been to satisfy the

---

[1] For the territories allegedly lost (Mondolfo, Pergola, Umana, Castel Fidardo etc.): Amiani, i. 276–8, 280; Colucci, xviii. 32.

[2] *Cron. mal.*, 18. Cf. Re, 233: 'la maiure parte de la Marca di Ancona ... si pe amore si pe forza'; Benvenuto da Imola, ii. 308: 'Malatesti ... diebus nostris habuerunt fere totam Marchiam.'

[3] *Chron. Est.*, RIS² xv/3.164; *Chron. Bon.*, ii.594–5; Amiani, i.272–3; Tanursi, 30.

[4] *Cron. mal.*, 18; Branchi, 163; *Chron. Est.*, RIS² xv/3.187, 188; *Chron. Bon.*, iii.22–3, 26; M. Villani, iii.89, 110; Cobelli, 110; *Cron. Perug.*, 170–1; Amiani, i.279.

[5] Ammirato, 410, 425.

terms of this league that Malatesta sent help to Florence against Lucca in May 1337; while in October, released by the temporary truce with Ferrantino, he himself entered Florentine service for a period of six months.[1] In return the Signoria, which was anxious to prepare defences against Lewis of Bavaria, and so reconcile the papacy with its subjects, sent an embassy in 1340 to press Malatesta's interest at Avignon.[2] Nothing was obtained, but Malatesta was grateful,[3] and in January 1342 agreed to become *capitano di guerra* in the Florentine war with Pisa. From this developed a temporary estrangement. Malatesta's conduct of the war may have caused dissatisfaction, and at the same time differences arose concerning his pay as captain. By way of reprisal he detained Florentine merchandise in Pesaro and Romagna, and an agreement was not reached until the middle of 1345, when he was compelled to make indemnity.[4] Relations were not again troubled, and a friendship was resumed, invaluable to the Malatesta but useful also to the Florentines, who were reluctant to forfeit any means of influence across the Apennines in Romagna.

It was here in Romagna and in the March of Ancona that the Malatesta were bound to figure most prominently. Romagna in particular had already become the closely-knit community it was to remain for more than a century, a community of nobles who were also *signori*, still at times using the titles of Ghibelline and Guelf, still in part governed by traditional animosities, but swayed more usually by the sympathies and antipathies of the moment, the promptings of immediate ambition, all aspiring to territorial gain yet all united by an intricate society of intermarriage – the Ordelaffi, the Manfredi, the Alidosi, the Polenta, and a swarm of lesser lords. This too was the native community of the Malatesta. The legation of Bertrand du Pouget had threatened to destroy this dynastic society, driving the *signori* into instinctive union against him, and for some years the alliance of 1333 persisted.[5] But with the passing of all danger local jealousies revived. At first the particular allies of Malatesta were

---

[1] G. Villani, x.63, 74; Ammirato, 424. Florence had been trying to arrange a peace between Ferrantino and Malatesta: *ibid.* 412.

[2] G. Villani, xi.103; Theiner, ii.110; Rodolico, 118–19, doc. 17; Canestrini, 'Documenti', 356–9; below p. 71. In 1340 Boccaccio was a justice in Pesaro: Giordani, *Orazioni*, XI.

[3] 'Ego absque dubietate cognosco meam vitam et statum a vestra dominatione et ... omnis spes mee exaltationis et vite in vestris paternis bracchiis conquiescit': Caggese, ii.258 (*a.* 1341).

[4] G. Villani, xi.135, 138–9; *Cron. Perug.*, 124; Stefani, rub. 546, 548, 550–3; *Cron. sen.*, 530; *Chron. Est., RIS*[2] xv/3.112; *Chron. Bon.*, ii.500, 504–5; *Ist. Pistolesi, RIS*[2] xi/5.171–2; Rodolico, doc. 79; F. Baldasseroni, *Pace; Capitoli, Firenze*, ii.XIII, 39–40.

[5] At Bologna early in 1336 a general alliance is reported of the lords of Romagna, including the Malatesta; *Chron. Bon.*, ii.461–2.

Francesco Ordelaffi and the Polenta of Ravenna, and in 1338 he married his daughters, Taddea and Caterina, to Francesco's sons, Giovanni and Ludovico.[1] It was the war for the possession of Lucca between Guelf Florence and Ghibelline Pisa which, by renewing old political loyalties, dissolved this alliance, and introduced Taddeo Pepoli into the place of the Ordelaffi as ally of the Malatesta. While Francesco supported Pisa, Taddeo stood by Florence, and his contingent served with Malatesta in the campaign of 1342.[2]

The Pisan war was also responsible for extending the relations of the Malatesta outside Romagna, for the Florentine league was wide, including Perugia, Siena, the Este and the Scaligeri, and this alliance was given new life when in the autumn of 1342 the German company of Duke Werner, lately released from the service of Pisa and fresh from devastating parts of Tuscany, proceeded 'sopra Arimino per fare vergogna a messer Malatesta stato nostro capitano di guerra'.[3] With the help of the Varani and the rector of the March, the Malatesta had averted an invasion of Perugia and, encouraged by Ferrantino Malatesta and the Ordelaffi, the company turned instead on Rimini. Malatesta at once opened negotiations and eventually arranged to take the mercenary leaders into the pay of the Este, the Pepoli and himself. The della Scala also joined the alliance; and at the end of January 1343, after helping to reduce Fano, the whole force moved off toward Modena.[4] This league of lords, Lombard and Romagnol, lasted several years,[5] and resulted in the marriage of Malatesta's daughter Masia with Obizzo Pepoli in 1350.[6] A few months later however the Pepoli were driven from Bologna. The papal rector, Astorgio di Duraforte, was resolved to dispossess them, and although supported by the Malatesta and other lords, they only saved themselves by selling the city to the Visconti.[7]

The Pepoli had been in alliance with the Visconti as early as 1347, and at the close of 1349, perhaps at their wish, the Malatesta were also brought into contact with Milan.[8] For more than a year Malatesta remained an ally of the Visconti,[9] but by no diplomatic dexterity could

---

[1] Branchi, 159; Cobelli, 419; G. Villani, xi.103.
[2] Rodolico, 152–3, 159. At the same time the alliance with the Polenta continued: *Chron. Est.*, *RIS*² xv/3.149, 154; Branchi, 161; *Chron. Bon.*, ii.566–7; Rubeus, 574–5.
[3] G. Villani, xii.9.
[4] *Cron. mal.*, 15; Branchi, 160; *Ann. Caes.*, 1178; *Chron. Est.*, *RIS*² xv/3.115; *Chron. Bon.*, ii.509, 511–15; *Cron. Perug.*, 125–7; Cipolla, 'Documenti', cxxxviii; Pellini, i.554; Ricotti, ii.51–6; Rodolico, 168–9.
[5] *Chron. Est.*, *RIS*² xv/3.121–2, 124–5, 162–3, 166–7.
[6] Branchi, 162.
[7] *Chron. Bon.*, ii.602, 604, 609; Sorbelli, *Signoria*, 11.
[8] Cipolla, clxxxxix–cc; Lattes, *Repertorio*, n. 403; Amiani, i.275.
[9] In April 1351 Malatesta arrived in Bologna after conferring with archbishop Giovanni in Milan: *Chron. Bon.*, iii.5–6.

he expect to preserve the friendship of both Milan and Florence. Florence was alarmed by the loss of Bologna, and in 1351 tried to form a defensive league against the Visconti. On his side archbishop Giovanni made ineffective approaches to the Florentines 'per ambassadori de' Marchesi [di Ferrara], di messer Malatesta da Rimino, e per molti mercatanti nostri cittadini che là trafficano'.[1] By late September Florence had won over Siena and Perugia and was seeking further allies in Romagna. The lords of Rimini were asked to join, but after some delay Malatesta refused, and, although elected, declined to serve as 'capitaneus comunis tallie'.[2] That others also refused shows rather a general fear of the Visconti, then arbiters of Italy, than any affection for them. The Malatesta certainly avoided any part in the offensive launched in the Papal State by Giovanni d'Oleggio and the Visconti; and in the peace finally arranged between Florence and Milan in March 1353 they appear among the allies of neither side. But beside the adherents of archbishop Giovanni are recorded their local enemies, among them Gentile da Mogliano, and it was with Visconti complicity that the discontented lords of the March attacked the lands of the Malatesta at this time.[3] It did not come to an open breach with the Visconti, but there was nothing strange in the fact that the Malatesta were expected to join the league against Milan formed in 1353–4 by Venice and Charles IV.[4] Nor could the rapprochement then developing between the Visconti and the papacy promise any calculable help to the Malatesta in the imminent decision with Albornoz.[5]

A more profitable alliance which the Malatesta had recently established was with Queen Giovanna of Naples and her consort, Louis of Taranto. The former Guelf union with the Angevin house of Naples had withered away, and it was with a prince denounced by the papacy, Louis of Hungary, that the Malatesta first reopened their relations with the kingdom. In December 1347, near the end of a triumphant advance through Italy, the king was received magnificently in Rimini on his way south to vindicate the murder of Andreas. Here he was met by the envoys of Florence, and the festivities were dignified by the customary

---

[1] Velluti, *Cronica*, 198.

[2] Ammirato, 521; Amiani, i.277–8; Baldasseroni, 'Guerra' 1902, 382, 388, 391, doc. 8; Sorbelli, *Signoria*, 90, 102–3. In Sept. 1351 Pandolfo di Malatesta was at the 'bagni' of Siena, where he was ceremoniously received: *Chron. sen.*, 563.

[3] M. Villani, i.78–9, iii.2; Lünig, i.2295ff.; F. Ughelli, *Italia sacra*, iv (Venice, 1719), 242; *Capitoli, Firenze*, ii.xiii.44; Baldasseroni, 'Guerra' 1903, 79, doc. 9; Amiani, i.277–8.

[4] In which the Carrara, the Este and the Manfredi all accepted a place: Winkelmann, ii, n. 1191. In July 1353 Giovanni Visconti had arranged a short truce between Gentile da Mogliano and the Malatesta, but refused his help to the lord of Fermo: *Chron. Est.*, *RIS*² xv/3.187; *Chron. Bon.*, 22.

[5] Biscaro, 'Relazioni' 1927, 62.

granting of knighthood, from which Malatesta Novello received the popular title of 'Ungaro'.[1] Louis' intervention in the kingdom of Naples was indecisive, but he abandoned there on his retreat a number of companies of Hungarian troops which Louis of Taranto, left in possession, had to subdue or drive out. For this purpose he summoned to his help Galeotto and Malatesta, who during 1351 and later cooperated with the king and his minister, Niccolo Acciaiuoli, in dispossessing the Hungarian captains. In recognition of their services Louis supported the Malatesta in their war with Gentile da Mogliano, and created them vicars of certain castles in the Abruzzi which, in the pope's indignant words, were 'quasi claves quedam euntibus de Aprucio in Marchia Anconitana et de Marchia ipsa in provinciam Aprutinam', and extended their possessions even beyond the March.[2]

The Malatesta advance seemed irresistible. They had powerful allies outside Romagna and seemed likely to overcome present disadvantages: insecurity of some of their conquests, the resentment of the petty *signori*, the obstinate resistance of Gentile da Mogliano, and the reverse inflicted by Fra Moriale. Yet 1353 marked the summit of their power. The papacy, under the resolute leadership of Innocent VI, now intervened to make these disadvantages permanent, resuming with quite different success, in the legation of Albornoz, the work ineptly begun by Bertrand du Pouget and Astorgio di Duraforte. The king of the Romans and all the major Italian states were summoned to help put down the rebel *tiranni*, and the Malatesta and other despots were bidden to make submission. The Malatesta preferred to risk a war, but it went against them, and in the end they were forced to surrender all but a part of their ample territories, and accept terms imposed by their papal sovereign.

Until it came to open conflict the relations of the Malatesta with the church had been erratic, not consistently hostile but never for long composed. The papacy had begun in 1335 by commanding them to restore to the rector the properties and rights they had usurped in the March of Ancona. They were reminded that although 'peccare est humanum, perseverare tamen in peccatis diabolicum est', and for a time Benedict XII may have hoped for a reconciliation.[3] The Malatesta were represented at the parliaments of Faenza in 1336, and provincial

---

[1] G. Villani, xii.105, 106, 107; *Cron. mal.*, 15–16; Branchi, 161–2; *Chron. Est.*, *RIS*[2] xv/3.156–7; *Chron. Bon.*, ii.580. Francesco Ordelaffi, Malatesta and others may have accompanied Louis to Naples.

[2] M. Villani, ii.38, 39; *Chron. Est.*, *RIS*[3] xv/3.185; Branchi, 162; *Chron. Sic.*, 17–18; L. Tanfani, *Niccola Acciaiuoli* (Florence, 1863), 85–6; Gaye, i.58; below p. 74.

[3] *Lettres, Ben. XII*, 257, 345–56, 358, 662–70, 687–91, 1036; Theiner, ii.6; Tonini, iv/2, LXXXVII, LXXXIX.

taxes were paid.[1] But their encroachments in the March, and especially against Urbino, stirred the papacy to fresh protests, until late in 1340 Malatesta and Ostasio da Polenta, strongly supported by Florence, sent a peace embassy to Avignon. Their overtures were repelled, the pope proving 'multum austerus et durus, ex mala informations assumpta'.[2] Hostilities continued, and the rector of Romagna, Philip de Antilla, acted with such energy, appealing to the powers of Tuscany, Lombardy and the Papal States, that in May 1343 Malatesta was compelled to make peace with Ferrantino, and in July to submit to the church. The keys of Rimini were surrendered, by Pandolfo Malatesta, and representatives of the commune swore fealty to the pope, and accepted a heavy fine. The rector was empowered to appoint the *podestà* for a year, and it was agreed to reinstate all but certain exiles. The Malatesta with many notables of Rimini then appeared before the legate Aimery de Châtelus to beg and receive absolution from all ecclesiastical censures.[3] With this the Malatesta were restored to papal favour; and in the survey of the March later that year they are reported holding Fano, Pesaro and Fossombrone 'ad mandata Ecclesie'.[4]

No attempt seems to have been made by the rector to reverse the revolution of 1334. He ratified the statutes issued that year, rescinding only those injurious to the church, he acknowledged that the Malatesta were 'governing' Rimini, and the exiles whose return to the city he forbade were probably Ferrantino and his adherents.[5] Certainly the Malatesta continued as before to dominate the city and dispose of every department of municipal administration. In 1345 Malatesta, with full powers of revision, caused a reassessment to be made of the *extimum* or

[1] *Ann. Caes.*, 1173. Galeotto attended for Rimini and Teresino da Carignano was sent by Pandolfo Malatesta for Fano: Amiani, i.264. For taxes: Tonini, iv. 100ff.

[2] *Lettres, Ben. XII*, 2794, 2805, 2834–7, 2955, 2988, 3209, 3261; Theiner, ii.95–6, 106, 110, 117, 119; Tonini, iv/2.150–2; Gorrini, 'Lettere ined.' 1884, 170–1, 1885, 329–31; Canestrini, 'Documenti', 356–9; Otto, *RQ* 1928, 109–10. Amiani (i.270) states the Malatesta wrote to the pope in 1342 requesting a grant of vicariate. This is near the time of the supposed vicariates of Lewis of Bavaria: above p. 43 n. 1.

[3] Tonini, iv/2.155–64; *Vitae pap. av.*, ii.352.

[4] Theiner, ii.128. Similar conditions seem to have been imposed on the Malatesta in these cities also, for the rector writes: 'de civitatibus Fani, Pensauri et Forosinfronii michi pro uno anno Potestarias presentarunt et omnes exititios dictarum divitatum volentes intrare debent reintromictere': *ibid.* 115.

[5] It was now perhaps that certain of the Parcitadi were allowed to return to Rimini, though under a different name: A. Battaglini, *Saggio*, 54. The Malatesta may have felt secure enough to readmit some exiles at least, in that way repudiating the partisan basis of their power. Thus around 1334 the Malatesta of Sogliano were rehabilitated as adherents of Malatesta Guastafamiglia (F. G. Battaglini, *Zecca*, 311–12); and there are numerous provisions in the *Statuto di Rimini*, from the time of Malatesta *dominus defensor*, which deal with the return of rebels and 'baniti' (Bib. sen., fos. 317rff.).

land tax, excepting only the properties of his family and *fideles*: a reservation reminiscent of the tax immunity contested in the time of Malatesta da Verucchio.[1] And a few years later, in 1349 and 1351, with the help of certain Savj, he introduced a number of 'provisions' supplementary to the statutes.[2] One of these, in 1349, suggests that Galeotto Malatesta had now been given powers as wide as those of Malatesta, amending as it does a statute which had bestowed on both brothers complete *arbitrium* and *baylia*, and disposed that their 'simplex verbum et volumptas sint perfectissima lex'. This statute had granted them the right to appoint all leading officials and control all revenues, to 'give, sell, and alienate' the income of the commune, 'impose, increase, and moderate' all *datia* and *gabellae*, and acquitted them from all duty to render accounts.[3] It was a further sign of their power in Rimini that, like other despots, the Malatesta were now hiring German mercenaries.[4] In recognition of this, the present statute granted them power of 'stipendarios conducendj', at the expense of the commune.[5] These fresh enactments show that the Malatesta *signoria* was assuming institutional stability, and had they remained at peace with the church their authority need never have been challenged.

The campaign against Osimo in 1347 first heralded a renewal of war.[6] Then, by supporting Louis of Hungary, and also perhaps Cola di Rienzo,[7] both rejected by the papacy, the Malatesta further offended the church. But what irreparably broke the peace and made compromise impossible was the part they played, in Romagna, in the resistance to Astorgio di Duraforte, and, most of all, their conquests in the March. In the summer and autumn of 1354, with the papal reconquest a year under way and its object unmistakable, Innocent VI opened his offensive against the despots of Romagna. On 4 July he cited Malatesta and Galeotto to appear at Avignon as rebels against the constitution of John XXII, many times reiterated, which forbade the lawless occupa-

---

[1] Tonini, iv/1. 122–6; above p. 36. In 1341 a small committee of lawyers had been commissioned by Malatesta Ungaro to revise the statutes 'super immuniatate datium': Battaglini, *Saggio*, 3 n. 5; *Corte*, 122.

[2] Bib. sen., *Stat. Rim.*, fos. 262v ff., 326r ff.

[3] *Ibid.* fo. 339r; for further 'provisiones', 'deroghationes' etc. in the statutes *temp.* Malatesta *defensor*: fos. 286r ff., 320v, 323v, 324r.

[4] Schäfer, *Ritter*, i.79, ii.134 n. 6; G. Villani, xi.135.

[5] Bib. sen., *Stat. Rim.*, fos. 262v ff., 326r ff. At the same time Pandolfo Malatesta was consolidating influence in Pesaro, since he was probably responsible for new statutes drawn up there in 1343, creating a small council of 60 and reducing membership of the *consiglio generale*: Vaccai, 13, 27; below p. 317.

[6] Above p. 65. In the interval relations seem to have been good, on the evidence at least of tax payments: Theiner, ii.144–5; Amiani, i.271.

[7] Re (117) says the Malatesta, after spurning Rienzo's overtures, finally sent an embassy, but there is no confirmation of this in Burdach and Piur, *Briefwechsel*.

tion of the patrimonies of the church.[1] No offer of submission followed. And on 12 December they were condemned as contumacious, leaving it for Albornoz to assemble his companies and enforce the sentence by arms.[2]

The Malatesta did not let the threat go unheeded, or without some effort to come to terms. Among their allies the Florentine republic, suspicious of all attempts to increase authority in the Papal State, was particularly active on their behalf. As early as 1351, during negotiations for a Tuscan league against Milan, it tried to reconcile the Malatesta with the church.[3] Two years later the threatened descent of Charles IV into Italy and the approach of Fra Moriale with his marauding companies again brought Florence into close relations with Romagna and the Malatesta. In September 1353 Malatesta and Galeotto sent representatives to Albornoz, but they were given a cold reception.[4] The Malatesta therefore appealed to Florence, which at the end of October sent an agent to talk with their envoys and arrange some peace with the legate. The Florentines also tried independently to mediate between the lords of Rimini and Forlì, and persuade them to submission.[5] But in neither embassy were they successful, and in February 1354 Albornoz wrote indignantly that the emissaries of the Malatesta and Ordelaffi had only come to sound his intentions, and were fit to be treated 'as spies rather than ambassadors'.[6] Even so the Florentine government did not at once abandon its policy of appeasement. When, in the middle of April, Boccaccio was sent as envoy to Avignon, he was given instructions, at the desire of the Malatesta, to urge the pope to peace.[7] In July a further embassy was sent, this time carrying proposals from the Malatesta that their extensive dominions in the March should be created a papal vicariate;[8] and in November the republic made yet

---

1 Tonini, iv/2.180–4. On the same day Gentile da Mogliano was also cited: Werunsky, *Excerpta*, n. 305. On 20 June Francesco Ordelaffi had been summoned: *ibid.* n. 304; cf. Theiner, ii.260.

2 Fantuzzi, iii.349; Werunsky, *Excerpta*, n. 318. On 10 Oct. Gentile da Mogliano and the Manfredi were condemned: *ibid.* nn. 315–16. On 15 Dec. Albornoz was instructed to publish excommunication of the Malatesta: Theiner, ii.283.

3 Sorbelli, *Signoria*, 101, 122, 340; Baldasseroni, 'Guerra' 1902, 369.

4 Filippini, *SS*, vi.208.

5 Baldasseroni, 'Relazioni', 10, docs. 4, 5.   6 Filippini, *SS*, vi.101, vii.504.

7 Canestrini, 'Documenti', LIV; above p. 67.

8 The proposals of the Malatesta were merely an extravagant anticipation of the vicariate finally granted them. They demanded an hereditary vicariate, with an annual *census* of 10,000 fl. (9,000 for the cities of the March, 1,000 for Rimini, 'actento quod civitas Ariminensis non est manualis nec subdita Ecclesie, prout sunt alie civitates, de Romandiola') and an obligation to furnish 200 knights for 3 months or 300 knights for 2. If possible, the envoy was to press for the inclusion of Fermo, then bound according to report to fall into the hands of the Malatesta, and to discuss the restoration of the contado of Fano: Baldasseroni, 'Relazioni', 10–11, docs. 6–7.

another attempt, at the request of the Malatesta, to dissuade Albornoz and the pope from making war. But all to no effect. Innocent was inflexible, the Malatesta impenitent, and Florence in the end gave up.[1]

Of no greater help to the Malatesta was their alliance with Naples;[2] and by the end of 1354 their choice lay between outright submission or war. During January and February appeals and fulminations were issued in every direction by the pope, to Florence, Siena, Perugia and Arezzo, to Venice, the Visconti, and the Este, to Louis of Taranto and Charles, king of the Romans.[3] Charles promised armed support. And in January 1355 Albornoz moved from Orvieto to Foligno, to commence operations.[4]

His first concern was to win over a number of the lesser *signori* of the March, the dispossessed or discontented under Malatesta aggression, Lomo di S. Maria of Iesi, Alberghetto Chiavelli of Fabriano, Ungaro of Sassoferrato, Neri della Faggiola, Ismeduccio of S. Severino, the counts of Carpegna, Niccolo da Buscareto of Roccacontrada, and many more, whom he left for the moment undisturbed in return for support against the Malatesta.[5] He was also at first successful in gaining the support of the lord of Fermo, Gentile da Mogliano, allowing him to keep for an annual *census* some part of his dominions, and even making him Gonfaloniere of the Church.[6] But Francesco Ordelaffi, who had concluded a temporary alliance with the Malatesta against the papal threat, interposed to reconcile them with Gentile, and, reassured by this in his possession of Fermo, he immediately changed sides.[7] Ordelaffi also joined the Malatesta in approaches to Charles IV; but the pope was

---

[1] *Ibid.* 23–7, docs. 9–10, 13; Degli Azzi, i, n. 243; Canestrini, 'Documenti', LXIV, LXXXIII.

[2] Innocent had written to Louis of Taranto as early as 13 Nov. 1353, censuring him for keeping as vicar in his kingdom a member of so rebellious a family as the Malatesta, who by their oppressions of the clergy rivalled Pharaoh and Totila (Tonini, iv/2, CIX, 178–80; Cerasoli, *ASN* xxii.368–70). This refers to the detention of the bishop of Ascoli for seven months by Galeotto, who, although absolved, did not make any amends (see Tonini, iv.139–40, iv/2, CVIII). On 27 Dec. 1354 Louis of Taranto was told to remove the custody of Civitella and Mecla from Galeotto and Malatesta (Tonini, iv.141; Cerasoli, 510–11); and again in Jan. 1355 (*ibid.* 511–12).

[3] *Capitoli, Firenze,* ii.XVI.86–7; Predelli, ii, v, nn. 69, 72, 83; Tonini, iv/2, CXI–II; Theiner, ii.278, 285; Werunsky, *Excerpta,* n. 322; Filippini, *SS* v, doc. 14; Baldasseroni, 'Relazioni', doc. 17. The papal letter to Charles IV (Theiner, ii.285) speaks of the Malatesta oppressing their subjects: 'variis angustiis et pressuris angariarunt et angariant'.

[4] Filippini, *SS* vii.503; *Cardinale,* 69.

[5] Filippini, *SS* vii.507, 515, 526; *Cardinale,* 74, 82–3; Werunsky, *Karl IV,* ii.579–80.

[6] M. Villani, iv.33; *Cron. mal.,* 19, 49; Branchi, 163; Filippini, *SS* vii.505–6; *Cardinale,* 68; Theiner, 11.282.

[7] M. Villani, iv.52; *Cron. mal.,* 19; Branchi, 163–4; Filippini, *SS* vii.516; *Cardinale,* 74–5; Werunsky, *Karl IV,* ii.578.

prompt in warning him against their deceits, and at the end of February he sent a small force of German knights to collaborate with the legate.[1]

At first the Malatesta and their allies were strong in reinforcements they attracted from the Grand Company by generous promises of booty,[2] and until the end of April 1355 they enjoyed some military success. As a result Malatesta was emboldened to break a promise he had made to meet Albornoz in Siena, and, greatly incensed at his duplicity, the legate returned to Perugia to continue the war.[3] Malatesta's presumption however was premature, and the tide soon turned against him when insurrection and unrest began to spread among the conquered cities of the March. Recanati had already rebelled in January and submitted to the church, and when Galeotto attempted to recover the city, the *contado* of Ancona, oppressed by 'le impositione de le colte', also rose in revolt. At once Galeotto prepared to suppress the rising, and it was while besieging the rebel castle of Paderno that on 29 April he was suddenly attacked and heavily defeated by the papal army under Niccolo da Buscareto and Rodolfo of Camerino. At the end of a fiercely fought battle, in which he was twice taken prisoner and his horse was killed under him, Galeotto was wounded and captured by a German constable when making his way from the field.[4] He was taken to Gubbio, where the legate had established his quarters, and there he learned that the castellan of Ascoli, Giovanni di Tino Malatesta, had been expelled from the city. Galeotto's defeat decided the campaign, and the dissolution of the Malatesta state followed rapidly. Iesi and Macerata hastened to make their peace with the church, Ancona also broke away, although only to declare its independence, while Ramberto Malatesta, count of Ghiaggiolo, in alliance with the papal Gonfaloniere, stirred up revolt in the *contado* of Rimini and tried to take the city.[5]

Further resistance was impossible, and Malatesta, 'conoscendo . . . che la pace piuttosto che la guerra potea mantenere il loro stato' (M. Villani, v. 46), now sued for peace, first visiting the emperor in

[1] M. Villani, iv.67; Filippini, *SS* vii.517ff.; *Cardinale*, 77–81; Werunsky, *Karl IV*, ii.536, 579; Theiner, ii.285.

[2] Baldasseroni, 'Relazioni', doc. 11.

[3] M. Villani, v.6, 15; Theiner, ii.374; Filippini, *SS* vii.527ff.; *Cardinale*, 83–5.

[4] M. Villani, iv.18; Bernabei, i.75–9; *Cron. mal.*, 19; Branchi, 164; *Chron. Bon.*, iii.52–3, 58–9; Theiner, ii.380; Schäfer, *Ausgaben, Ben. XII*, 570, 573. Rodolfo da Camerino was among the first of the Marchigiani to swear obedience and offer aid against the Malatesta; in March 1355 he was appointed 'Vexillifer ecclesie Romane'; Filippini, *SS* vii.507.

[5] M. Villani, v.24; *Ann. Caes.*, 1182–3; *Cron. mal.*, 20; Branchi, 164; Bernabei, i.75–9; Filippini, *SS* vii.534; Annibaldi, 'Podestà', 141. On Ramberto di Ghiaggiolo at this time see *Capitoli, Firenze*, i.VIII, n. 2; M. Villani, i.80; *Ann. Caes.*, 1180.

Pisa at the beginning of May to obtain a safe-conduct.[1] With this he proceeded to Gubbio, and there on 2 June, after concluding a truce with the legate, negotiated the heads of an agreement. That the terms reached were not severe must partly be ascribed to the prevailing unrest in Italy, which did not favour an intransigent papal policy, partly again to the pope's desire for peace, and partly to intercession by Niccolo Acciaiuoli and Albertaccio Ricasoli, envoys of Naples and Florence.[2] But it may also be that the legate realised that to try to destroy the Malatesta was impolitic, and that by concessions redoubtable allies could be won for the church. As the Riminese chronicler remarked: 'per certo, se non fosse i Malatesti, ello non poria avere obtinute ale grande imprese, che ello fé', and therefore he showed them 'più grazia, che agli altri'.[3]

Subject to papal ratification or amendment it was established that the Malatesta should surrender all their territories except Rimini, Fano, Pesaro and Fossombrone, over which they were to exercise a vicariate for ten years, in return for an annual *census* of 8,000 florins, and the equipment for three months each year of 150 knights to serve in Romagna and the March. For this they were to receive absolution, and meanwhile, until 1 August, a truce was to run during which the castles and fortresses of Ancona and Ascoli were to be surrendered into the custody of Giovanni degli Alberti and Albertaccio Ricasoli; one of Malatesta's sons was to be given as hostage, and Galeotto released into the keeping of Niccolo Acciaiuoli. In the event of papal confirmation, the Malatesta were to make the promised restitutions, and the imprisoned members of the family would be liberated; if the pope demurred, the negotiations would be cancelled.[4] Malatesta raised objections to the proposed tribute and service, complaining that even his former lands would not have supported as much, and made it clear that in the visit to the pope, which he had promised to make, he would try to renegotiate those points.[5] On the following day Albornoz communicated the terms to Avignon, and at the end of two weeks (20 June) Innocent authorised the vicariate, at the same time reducing the *census* from 8,000 to 6,000 florins, a sum dismissed by Villani as 'certa piccola

[1] *Ann. Caes.*, 1182; *Cron. Pisana*, *ASI* vi/2.130; Filippini, *SS* vii.535–6; *Cardinale*, 87; Massèra, *RIS*[2] xvi/3, xxiv.

[2] As admitted by Albornoz, though many of his advisers tried to prevent an agreement, as did the Ordelaffi and Gentile da Mogliano: Filippini, *SS* v.380–1, vii.536–40; *Cardinale*, 88–91; Tonini, iv/2.196.

[3] *Cron. mal.*, 30. Re (242) says Ludovico Ordelaffi pointed out to Francesco, his father, how well the legate had treated the Malatesta, and urged him to submission too: 'como bene hao trattati li Malatesti, cosi bene trattarao noa'.

[4] Theiner, ii.303; Tonini, iv/2, cxiii.

[5] *Ibid.* On 3 June Albornoz wrote: 'Dominus Malatesta parat se ad eundum personaliter ad pedes domini nostri . . .': Filippini, *SS* v, doc.18.

quantità di pecunia'.[1] The general council of Rimini, attended by Galeotto and Giovanni Malatesta, and assembled with traditional formality by order of the *podestà* and consent of the four Ufficiali, then (28 June) appointed a representative to swear obedience to the legate, and obtain absolution, a ceremony completed on 2 July in the presence of Malatesta and Pandolfo. The delegate confessed to having connived at the crimes of the Malatesta, and to having illegally appointed them 'protectores, defensores, et rectores . . . absque Sedis Apostolice licentia speciali'. This was never to be repeated, though the right to elect other communal officers was left unimpeached. The commune engaged forever to obey the pope, his legate or his vicar, and the interdict was lifted.[2]

Finally on 8 July formalities were completed at Gubbio between Albornoz and the Malatesta for setting up the vicariate. Each of the Malatesta first personally acknowledged the supremacy of the papacy over his territories and over those he had occupied. Then restitution was made and the penitent *signori* were absolved from censure. The vicariate of the four cities was granted for ten years, with full judicial, legislative, administrative and fiscal powers, though with certain conditions annexed. Political exiles were to be reinstated, and the Malatesta were to govern 'secundum Iura et consuetudines et Statuta', to repeal statutes against the liberty of the church, and avoid 'talias illicitas' or 'exactiones indebitas'. Although they were to be subject to no tallage or general imposition, they were not exempt from *parlamentum generale*, the payment of *focatio* in Romagna, or of *census* and *afflictus* in the March, while the appellate jurisdiction of provincial *curiae* was also saved. They were further bound to surrender their vicariate peacefully at the end of the term of years, though the papacy might resume direct government at any time. In return the Malatesta were engaged to pay the annual *census* of 6,000 florins, and furnish for three months' service a contingent now reduced to 100 knights, while an oath of allegiance to the papacy was to be taken by every male subject of fourteen years or more within a month of being required to do so.[3] This oath was first sworn by Malatesta on behalf of the dynasty, and a few days later (13 July) Galeotto gave his assent as well, and the solemn treaty was closed.[4]

The *signoria* of the Malatesta had now been legitimised. The four communes they governed could be distinguished henceforward from

[1] M. Villani, v.46; Tonini, iv/2, cxv; Battaglini, *Zecca*, 211–12; Werunsky, *Excerpta*, n. 344.
[2] Tonini, iv/2, cxvi, cxvii. The same ceremony was performed on 7 July by a representative of Fossombrone in the same way: Vernarecci, *Fossombrone*, i.306–9.
[3] Tonini, iv/2, cxviii; Giordani, *Gradara*, 63.
[4] Tonini, iv/2, cxix.

those 'que tenentur sine titulo tyrampnice de provincia Marchiae Anconitane', like Camerino, Fabriano and many others;[1] and beside the popular origin of their authority they could now place the delegated privileges of the papacy. Within a year Malatesta was able to proclaim himself not merely 'honorabilis defensor et dominus . . . arimini', but also 'vicarius generalis eiusdem pro S.R.E.', deriving his title both 'a conscilio et commune arimini quam etiam a Reverendo . . . domino domino Egidio . . . apostolice sedis legato et vicario generali'.[2] For the moment, however, the church was not so generous in its formulae; the lords of Rimini had first to expiate their long rebellion, before the papacy would fully acknowledge their new status.

[1] Theiner, ii.342. Cf. Aeneas Sylvius Piccolomini, *Commentarii*, 255: 'et hic tandem legitimus Malatestarum titulus coepit, cum autem sola tyrranide imperarent'.
[2] Battaglini, *Zecca*, 213.

4

Galeotto Malatesta, 'ecclesie pugil'

The compromise of 1355 marked the beginning of a long and close association with the church, which was to bring the Malatesta a rich succession of titles, honours and gifts of territory, and become in time the first condition of their survival as *signori*. Inflexibly loyal to the papacy, but favoured also by events in Italy and Europe, they were able again, and this time with the goodwill of the church, to win control of a wide dominion only less extensive than that which they had quickly and precariously conquered during the years of rebellion. Each new pope had occasion to praise or reward their services, often using phrases of a more than formal gratitude which distinguished them from other and less powerful subjects. But before the alliance was finally established, the Malatesta were obliged to give active proof of their fidelity, and satisfy the papacy that their submission was sincere by helping the legate to overcome the same independent spirit which they had lately fought to defend.

By the end of 1355 the March of Ancona, which Albornoz had found 'volubilis velut rota et labilis ut anguilla', was nearly all subdued, the provincial administration was returning to efficiency, and the legate was free to resume his work of reconquest in Romagna, where the Manfredi of Faenza, and Francesco Ordelaffi at Forlì, Cesena and elsewhere, persisted in revolt. During the winter months a crusade was preached against the *tiranni*. A full remission of sins was assured to all who took up arms and served for one year. The papal collectors were prodigal of still more generous promises; and the response to their appeal was wide. Among those who took the cross were Malatesta Guastafamiglia, his son Malatesta Ungaro, and more than six hundred Riminese. Support came also from the Este, the Carrara and the lords of Romagna and the March, among them Roberto Alidosi whom Malatesta Ungaro persuaded to join. To these were added a number of mercenary troops, and in April 1356 the command of the whole force was given to Galeotto Malatesta, created Gonfaloniere of the Church with a monthly stipend of 300 florins.[1]

---

[1] *Cron. mal.*, 21; M. Villani, vi.14; Cobelli, 113; Amiani, i.283; Filippini, *SS* viii. 307–13; *Cardinale*, 110–14. Malatesta Ungaro was also paid, at the rate of 150 fl.

The details of the ensuing war are unimportant, but they show at least how prominent the Malatesta now became as papal captains. Between the summer of 1356 and the summer of 1359, first the Manfredi, then the Ordelaffi were forced to surrender to the legate, and the success was due primarily to the Malatesta.[1] It was the Malatesta again who gave most help to Albornoz and the legate who temporarily replaced him, Androin de la Roche, in coming to terms with the German companies which continued to trouble Italy and the Papal State in the constant search for booty and pay.[2] It was therefore not inappropriate that the solemn parliament called by Albornoz in 1357 should have met in Fano, and that the constitutions destined to form the fundamental laws of papal government should have been 'publicate et lecte ... in generali parlamento Fani celebrato ... in domibus magnifici domini Galeocti de Malatestis de Arimino'.[3]

After the capitulation of Forlì and the settlement of Romagna, only Bologna remained unconquered. But here the ambitions of the papal legate clashed with legitimate claims upheld by the Visconti, and at the end of 1359 a war broke out with Milan, in which once again the Malatesta were called to play a leading part. Most of the responsibility fell as before upon Galeotto Malatesta and his nephew Malatesta Ungaro. Galeotto was first employed in driving Francesco Ordelaffi from Romagna,[4] and then during the summer of 1360 in suppressing disorders in the March, stirred up by the conflict with Bernabò Visconti;[5] but by September he was back with Malatesta Ungaro fighting in the Bolognese and was able to accompany Albornoz in his ceremonial entry into Bologna at the end of October.[6] Here, despite recent

[1] M. Villani, vi.20; vii.33, 34, 79, 83, 94; viii.84; *Ann. Caes.*, 1183, 1184; *Cron. mal.*, 21–3, 24, 25, 26–7; Branchi, 164, 165, 166; Cobelli, 114–22, 127–8, 422; Filippini, *SS* viii.313–16, 324–5, 333–5, 473–7, 484–5; xii, doc.6, p. 300; *Cardinale*, 114–15, 124–5, 131–9, 145–9, 155, 165–82, 191–200.

[2] Sighinolfi, 209–10, 242, 254; M. Villani, viii.105; Cobelli, 124–6; *Cron. mal.*, 25–6; Amiani, i.284–5; Vernarecci, *Fossombrone*, i.332–3; Filippini, *Cardinale*, 183–91.

[3] *Cost. Egid.*, 236; Filippini, *SS* viii.345ff., 465ff.; *Cardinale*, 426.

[4] Cobelli, 150–2. It was now perhaps that Galeotto Malatesta and Francesco Ordelaffi degraded themselves, in the eyes of the poet (and their former teacher) Antonio da Ferrara, by the unknightly and unprincely act, especially in men of their years, of challenging each other to personal combat: (T. Bini), *Rime e prose del buon secolo della lingua* (Lucca, 1852), pp. xvi, 60–1.

[5] M. Villani, ix.106, 111; Lilii, ii.96; Amiani, i.285–6; Filippini, *Cardinale*, 219–20, 228–9; Franceschini, 'Stato d'Urbino', 10. Ghirardacci (ii.246) speaks also of Pandolfo Malatesta as active in the March at this time; while a document of April 1361 in the Archivio Capitolare of Ascoli (B Busta, n.39) would suggest Malatesta Guastafamiglia was employed there as well (I owe this reference to Professor Charles Mitchell).

[6] Griffoni, 63; M. Villani, x.6; Ghirardacci, ii.246–9; Filippini, *Cardinale*, 233, 236, 253–4; Vancini, 'Bologna', 269, 273; Tonini, iv/1.168, iv/2, cxli.

reverses, he was created military commander beside the civilian governor, Gomez Albornoz, and in June 1361 the Malatesta saved the city for the church when they defeated the Visconti army in a memorable engagement at S. Ruffilo (20 June 1361).[1] In describing this victory the chroniclers forsook their usual brevity, but the strategic effect was slight; and throughout the war neither side achieved decisive successes. Early in 1362 Albornoz was able to include the della Scala, the Carrara and the Este in a general league against the Visconti, which the Gonzaga later joined, and the alliance was strengthened by the betrothal of Malatesta Ungaro to Costanza, the sister of Niccolo d'Este, and the marriage of his daughter to Niccolo's brother Ugo.[2] Malatesta Ungaro was also appointed captain of the league, and although replaced by Feltrino Gonzaga on 1 April 1363, he was present as *vicecapitano* at the defeat of the Visconti near Solara a few days later, and in May attended with Malatesta 'senex' a general parliament of the league in Ferrara.[3] At this time a successful outcome to the war seemed promised, but the Visconti resorted to bribery and intrigue at the court of Avignon, and by July peace negotiations had taken over. The final treaty was not drawn up till March 1364, and before then Albornoz' authority in Italy had been drastically curtailed, and the control of affairs restored to cardinal Androin. On 7 February Androin entered Bologna, and Gomez Albornoz withdrew from the city with Malatesta, to the regret, it is said, of the population.[4]

The Milanese war had stopped far short of the triumph planned by Albornoz, but within the narrower politics of the Papal State it enabled the Malatesta to seal their alliance with the church. Already during the Romagna campaigns the pope wrote expressing gratitude for their services, urging them to persevere in effacing all their guilt.[5] At the

---

[1] M. Villani, x.53, 56, 59–60, 74; Griffoni, 63–4; Branchi, 166; *Chron. Bon.*, iii.123–5, 127, 132–3; *Chron. Est.*, RIS xv.484–5; *Ann. Forl.*, 68; *Chron. Plac.*, 506; Velluti, 225; Filippini, *Cardinale*, 236, 238–9, 254, 261–9; Vancini, 'Bologna', 273, 277, 292ff. At this time Galeotto Malatesta is described as 'capitaneus guerrae pro sancta Romana ecclesia' and Malatesta Ungaro as 'vexillifer provintie Romandiole': Filippini, *SS* xii, doc.15.

[2] M. Villani, x.96, 99; Griffoni, 64–5; *Chron. Est.*, RIS xv.485, 486; *Chron. Bon.*, iii.145, 146; Ghirardacci, ii.261; Werunsky, *Karl IV*, iii.278; Filippini, *Cardinale*, 276–9; Vancini, 'Bologna', 299, 302, 304. The marriage of Malatesta Ungaro took place in July 1363, Fano paying the *sposo* 200 gold ducats (Amiani, i.287); no doubt other cities paid a contribution.

[3] M. Villani, xi.44; *Chron. Est.*, RIS xv.486; Branchi, 166; *Chron. Bon.*, iii.146, 147, 154–7; *Diario d'anon. fiorent.*, 296–7; Theiner, ii.378; Schäfer, *Ausgaben, Urban V und Gregor XI*, 17; Filippini, *Cardinale*, 280ff., 308ff.; *SS* xiii, doc. 33; Vancini, 302ff.; Romano, 'Spinelli' 1899, 386–7.

[4] Ghirardacci, ii.275; Werunsky, *Karl IV*, iii.283–94, 297; Filippini, *Cardinale*, 316–34, 337, 340–1; Vancini, 311ff., 318ff.; Theiner, ii.387.

[5] July and Nov. 1356: Tonini, iv/2, cxx, cxxi; Filippini, *SS* viii.319; *Cardinale*, 121.

same time the new vicars punctually paid their *census*.[1] But the formality of a visit to Avignon had still to be fulfilled; and in the autumn of 1357 Malatesta accompanied Albornoz on his return to the papal court. Here he was fully reconciled ('plenarie reconciliatus') with the pope, and on 8 January 1358 the vicariate was renewed to himself and Galeotto for seven and a half years, the unexpired term of the original grant. Under the same conditions a number of villages and castles were added in the dioceses of Rimini, Fano and Fossombrone, with the obligation to pay 300 florins *census* and equip fifty foot-soldiers for three months each year. This was a generous mark of favour, but it did not give Malatesta all he hoped for. His purpose had been to recover possession of the castles in the Riminese which had rebelled in 1355 and had since been governed by the church, but only some were surrendered. Others, and the more important, led by Santarcangelo and Savignano, were reluctant to return to the Malatesta from fear of retribution, and sent envoys to Avignon at the time of Malatesta's visit to counter his demands. The pope, perhaps persuaded by Albornoz, gave in, and in March 1358 established these places as a separate vicariate, depending on Santarcangelo, and independent of Rimini; and for twenty years more the Malatesta had to hold their claims in check.

By the middle of February Malatesta was back again in Rimini, bringing letters for the legate, and the new bulls of investiture.[2]

The Malatesta do not appear among the people richly recompensed upon the taking of Forlì,[3] but this was due to no decline in papal favour; and their loyal response to the pope's appeal for help against the Visconti[4] at last brought to a close their period of probation.[5] In the winter of 1359–60 Albornoz petitioned Avignon for an extension of the vicariates 'ad quinquennium vel circa', 'et hoc propter servitia que ultra debitum impenderunt vicarii' – though he added, 'et quia etiam esset impossibile omnia immediate ad manus ecclesie revocare'. In reply the pope promised to act when more of the current grant

---

[1] Bib. Gamb., *Cod. Pand.*, fos. 107, 117, 119, 123–6; Tonini, iv/1.14.

[2] *Cron. mal.*, 23–4; *Vitae pap. av.*, i.322, 337, 345; *Liber Pontificalis*, ii.493; Theiner, ii.533; *Mem. Santarcangelo*, nn. 10–11; Marini, *Santo Arcangelo*, doc. B; Tonini, iv/2, CXXII–III, CXXXIII; *Imposte*, 19; Filippini, *SS* viii.490–1; *Cardinale*, 158–9, 165. The restored places of the Riminese were now held separately by the Malatesta as papal vicars, not lords of Rimini. In the *contado* of Fano only 4 castles were transferred of the 21 detained by the church, the rest being withheld for some time: Theiner, ii.342; below p. 98. In 1356 the Malatesta were granted further castles round Rimini and Pesaro by the archbishop of Ravenna: Fantuzzi, iv.447–8.

[3] Filippini, *Cardinale*, 201–2.

[4] 10 May 1360: Theiner, ii.345; Tonini, iv/2, CXXV; Vancini, 263; Filippini, *Cardinale*, 230–2.

[5] On 9 July 1361 the pope congratulated Galeotto and Malatesta Ungaro upon their victory at S. Ruffilo: Martène and Durand, *Thes. nov.*, ii.1023, 1025.

had elapsed, thinking the request for the moment premature.[1] And in the event it was not Innocent but his successor Urban V who took the final step in absolving the Malatesta from the last taint of rebellion.

At the beginning of 1362 Albornoz published a declaration that the Malatesta had fulfilled all obligations incurred in 1355, in particular of fighting in person against the enemies of the church, and were now wholly free from penalty;[2] and at the end of the year the new pope turned to consider their case. Although he wrote warning the cardinal to dissuade anyone hoping to obtain a vicariate of papal territory from coming to Avignon,[3] he was evidently well disposed towards the Malatesta,[4] and on 15 February 1363 he issued a bull extending their vicariate for another ten years, though the earlier grant had not yet expired. This he did, he said, because when 'in minoribus' he had observed their good and equitable government.[5] On the same day he dispensed Galeotto from the duty to visit Avignon and take the oath of fidelity due within a year of a new papal election, directing him instead to swear the oath to Albornoz.[6] But Guastafamiglia went, 'ad fatiendum reverentiam domino nostro', and returned with a number of valuable gifts from the pope.[7]

It was now also that the papacy began fully to recognise the Malatesta as temporal vicars. During the earlier part of the fourteenth century the popes had addressed the Malatesta variously as 'nobiles viri', 'milites', 'domini', 'cives', or 'familiares nostri',[8] and this practice persisted even after the investiture of 1355.[9] But in his letter of 18 December 1362 Urban V finally accorded the Malatesta the title of vicars, employing a formula which thereafter became habitual: 'Dilectus filius nobilis vir Malatesta etc. miles Arim. pre nobis et Romana Ecclesia in Ariminen. et certis aliis civitatibus Vicarius'.[10] Thenceforward, too, papal letters to the commune almost wholly ceased. The years of trial were over, and the anomaly of a vicariate imperfectly acknowledged was removed.

---

[1] Filippini, *SS* xii.301–2.

[2] 29 Jan. 1362: Tonini, iv/2, cxxx. For a similar letter, 10 Nov. 1365: Bib. Gamb., *Cod. Pand.*, fo. 123.

[3] Theiner, ii.371 (29 Dec. 1362).   [4] 18 Dec. 1362: Tonini, iv/2, cxxii.

[5] Tonini, iv/2, cxxxiii; L. Muratori, *Antiquitates Italicae* (Milan, 1738–42), vi.189. Cf. Filippini, *Cardinale*, 349ff.

[6] Tonini, iv/2, cxxxiv.

[7] Filippini, *SS* xiii, doc. 50; *Cardinale*, 349ff.; Schäfer, *Ausgaben, Urban V und Gregor XI*, 70–1. The troops who fought at Solara were paid with money brought back by Malatesta from Avignon: Filippini, *Cardinale*, 317.

[8] For example, letters of 1325, 1326, 1331, 1335, 1342–3, 1353: Tonini, iv/2, xlviii, li, lii, lv, lxxiv, lxxvii, xc, c, cviii.

[9] For example the letters of 1356, 1358, 1360, 1361: *ibid.* cxx, cxxii, cxxv, cxxviii; Filippini, *SS* xii, doc. 15.

[10] Tonini, iv/2, cxxxii. Cf. 1363: 'Vicarius et Gubernator', *ibid.* cxxxiv.

It was natural that immediately following the agreements of 1355 the church should have had most claim on the services of the Malatesta, but it was not the only power to do so. There is first to be recalled the sorry record of Pandolfo Malatesta, elder son of Guastafamiglia and the friend of Petrarch, as a captain of the Visconti and then of Florence.[1] During 1356 and the first half of 1357 he was appointed Galeazzo Visconti's representative in Milan and commander in the war with Montferrat in 1356–7. But an indiscreet intimacy with Bernabò Visconti's mistress, Giovannina Montebretto, brought his employment to an abrupt end. The Milanese chronicler Azario speaks slightly of his services ('cum infinitis expensis nichil vel parum fecit'); and adds that although he was so maltreated ('vituperatus') by Bernabò as to become a lifelong enemy, enmity was nothing new. The Malatesta had always been Guelf, with little love for the Visconti; and consequently, when elected to a papal captaincy Pandolfo did all he could to deprive them of Bologna. A letter to Bernabò from Louis of Hungary, with appropriate classical allusions and stressing Pandolfo's youth, seems to have had no effect.[2]

From Lombardy Pandolfo passed into the pay of Florence, reaffirming what was by now a traditional friendship with the Malatesta, but here he was to draw from the Tuscan chroniclers comments no less bitter, only of a graver kind. During his first term of service in 1358–9 against the company of the conte Lando he acquitted himself honourably and well.[3] It was when he resumed command of Florentine forces during the war with Pisa that he lost all credit. Elected *capitano* in October 1363, he at once aroused suspicion by demanding powers of corporal jurisdiction. Similar demands had been made by the duke of Calabria in 1326,[4] and there was the more recent example of the duke of Athens to encourage him to think of seizing political power in Florence. This at least is the charge made against him by the chronicles: that he was less intent to wage war than to draw authority to himself. The *signoria* of Pandolfo Malatesta might then have taken its place beside the other shortlived despotisms established in fourteenth-century Florence. But the Priori were vigilant, and at the end of April

---

[1] In 1357 the Venetians offered to take Pandolfo Malatesta into service, but nothing resulted: Tonini, iv/1.156.

[2] M. Villani, vii.48; *Chron. Plac.*, 501, 502; Azarius, 86, 147–8, 154; T. Rymer, *Foedera* (London, 1816), vi.17; *Calendar Patent Rolls* (1354–8), 563; Salutati, ii.146; Giulini, ii.41–2, 46; F Novati, in F. *Petraca e la Lombardia* (Milan, 1904), 42, 46–7, doc. III, who rejects Villani's imputation of political motives for Pandolfo's retirement.

[3] M. Villani, ix.20, (31) 29; Manni, 181; Degli Azzi, i. nn. 342–3; Sighinolfi, 253–4, 258. In 1361 Pandolfo appears as a knighted citizen of Florence: Gamurrini, II.128.

[4] Caggese, ii.90.

the would-be dictator was forced to leave, and 'inhonoratis ab omnibus abiit cum suis militibus'.[1]

Pandolfo's misconduct did not disturb good relations between Florence and the Malatesta, for his place was taken by Galeotto, who was able to bring the war to a quick and successful conclusion, atoning for the folly of his nephew. Shortly before (1362-3) Galeotto had held the post of captain-general and *riformatore di giustizia* in the kingdom of Naples, but with evident reluctance, and in the spring of 1363 he quitted Angevin service despite pressure from the pope.[2] A year later, when attending a provincial parliament, he received permission to go with his troops into Florentine service.[3] Elected captain-general on 12 July, he set out against the English company employed by Pisa on the 23rd, and five days later won a complete though unpremeditated victory over it at Cascina. Peace followed soon after (29 August), and on 6 September Galeotto re-entered Florence, ceremonially surrendering the insignia. Yet in the festivities which followed he himself took no part. A few days before (27 August) his brother Malatesta had died, and so, in the words of Antonia Pucci, 'non volle nè palio nè festa'.[4]

Guastafamiglia had already renounced the government of Rimini in the previous October, and evidently had some presentiment of death, for during his visit to Avignon in 1363 this hardened *tirannus*, notable for *virtù*, had obtained a bull allowing him to choose a confessor with whom to devise ways of restoring all his extortions from churches and religious houses, from God and from man, in peace and war, during a life of tyranny and sin, and so receive absolution.[5] He died piously, requesting to be buried in Franciscan habit in the chapel he himself had built for his family in the Franciscan church, and with instructions to discharge all debtors' obligations and amnesty all prisoners. The pope

---

1 Sozomenus, 1073-7; M. Villani, xi.67, 69, 70, 73, 85, 87; cf. Velluti, 227-34; Tonini, iv/2, cxxxviii.
2 On this episode: *Capitoli, Firenze*, ii.xvi, n. 333; Branchi, 166; Filippini, *SS* xiii.9-12; Romano, 'Spinelli', xxv.176; Tonini, iv.172, iv/2, cxxxv-vi. Galeotto remained in touch with Naples: Rondini, *Monte Filottrano*, 41; *Doc. arch. Caetani, Reg. Chart.*, ii.290.
3 Amiani, i.288.
4 M. Villani, xi.96.7; Sozomenus, 1078-9, 1081; *Cron. sen.*, 608-9; Bonincontri, 10-16; *Diario d'anon. fiorent.*, 219, 297, 298; Velluti, 238-41; Sercambi, i.125-6; 'Diario del Monaldi', in *Ist. Pistolesi, RIS* xi.324-5; *Cron. pisana, ASI* vi/2. 151ff.; Manni, 186-7; A. Pucci, 'Guerra pisana', 262, in *Delizie degli eruditi toscani*, ed. Ildefonso di S. Luigi, xx (Florence, 1785); Salutati, i.16. According to Gianozzo Manetti this victory was still being commemorated in his time; but there was some resentment that Galeotto had exacted double pay for his troops.
5 Filippini, *SS* xiii, doc. 50.

at once sent condolences (15 September) for the loss of a man 'fidelitate praeclarum prudentia praepollentem'.[1]

There remained the problem of succession. The papal vicariate was granted originally to Malatesta and Galeotto, or to their heirs in case of death before the term expired. This condition did not hinder them from dividing up their territories for convenience of government, and such a division may already have occurred.[2] when shortly before his death Guastafamiglia proceeded by lot to partition his share of the inheritance to prevent disputes between his sons Pandolfo and Malatesta Ungaro. The first was assigned Pesaro, Fano and Fossombrone, the second Rimini. Malatesta's personal properties were also divided, Gradara being expressly given to Pandolfo and Montefiore to his brother. Galeotto alone however was papal vicar, and the two brothers were instructed by Malatesta in his will to respect and obey him in everything. Galeotto seems to have taken most practical part in the management of Fano, sharing the administration of Fossombrone and Pesaro with his nephew Pandolfo, but he remained without question the dominant force in the family.[3]

The peace of 1364 between Bernabò Visconti, the church and the Lombard allies settled nothing. But for the moment hostilities took the indirect form of negotiation, intrigue and alliance in restraint of the foreign mercenary companies. Albornoz had already tried to fight them, but it was Urban V who, from the beginning of his pontificate, became most active in pressing for a united effort to put them down. The Lombard powers were no less alert, and from the first Bernabò Visconti seems to have been envisaged as the ultimate enemy.[4] This may explain his self-restraint during 1366 when Malatesta Ungaro and

[1] F. Villani, xi.102; *Chron. Est.*, *RIS* xv.487B; *Cron. mal.*, 27-8; Tonini, iv/2, CXLI, CXLII; Battaglini, *Zecca*, 219; Amiani, i.288-9; Filippini, *SS* xiii, doc. 50.

[2] Niccolo Spinelli, writing in 1393, claimed that Albornoz had given Rimini to Guastafamiglia, Fano to Galeotto, Pesaro to Pandolfo, and Fossombrone to Malatesta Ungaro: Durrieu, *Royaume d'Adria*, i.48. This is inaccurate, but it may imply an act of partition.

[3] Tonini, iv/2, CXLI; 'Descriptio Romandiole' (1371): Theiner, ii.514-15, 534. In a papal letter to all three Malatesta in Feb. 1371 only Galeotto is called 'vicar of Rimini' – his nephews merely 'milites Ariminenses' (*Lettres, Grég. XI*, n. 42), and only Galeotto payed the papal *census* (Bib. Gamb., *Cod. Pand.*, fos. 107ff.). In Pesaro Pandolfo was evidently expected to collect the revenues 'vice . . . Galeoti Vicarii Pontificii', retaining £500 *Rav.* for himself each month, and resigning the remainder to Galeotto; but his he failed to do and there were recriminations on his death in 1373: Tonini, *Imposte*, 37-9; Mazzatinti, *Inventari*, xxix.16, n. 30.

[4] As shown by approaches to the Malatesta from the Lombard allies and Florence (1364-5): Ghirardacci, ii.285; Amiani, i.289. Late in 1364 Galeotto Malatesta was appealing for help against Hawkswood: Tonini, iv/2.270-1.

Niccolo d'Este were invited to attend the baptism of Gian Galeazzo's firstborn in the spring, before passing on to Avignon to discuss the preliminaries of a general league against the companies.[1] But the invasion of the Papal States by Ambrogio Visconti and Hawkwood betrayed Bernabò's insincerity, and in September a league was formed between the church, Naples and the Tuscan communities against any future 'compagnia di ventura', which in the summer of 1367 was converted into a military alliance, uniting the pope, the emperor, the Este, the Carrara, the Gonzaga, and a little later Siena, Perugia and Queen Giovanna of Naples. By the end of that year the resumption of war with the Visconti was clearly impending.[2]

These preparations for a fresh offensive had been greatly helped by the return of the papacy to Italy. Such a restoration had been meditated by nearly every Avignonese pope, but Urban V was the first to put it into effect as the natural and necessary conclusion to the work of Albornoz. Leaving Avignon in April 1367, he reached Corneto early in June, and thence moved to Viterbo to pass the summer.[3] Here on 20 August he was joined by the three Malatesta, who had lent him money for the journey, and he at once summoned them to try to settle unrest in the city.[4] The Malatesta may have stayed with the pope at Viterbo, for they were prominent in the large military company which, with other notables of the Papal State, Niccolo d'Este and Rodolfo da Camerino, escorted Urban into Rome in the middle of October;[5] and a few months later, as a token of esteem, the pope created Galeotto a Roman senator. Despite encouragement from cardinal Anglico, however, he does not seem ever to have assumed office.[6] Instead he took part in the campaign against Bernabò Visconti in the spring and summer of 1368. In January he and Pandolfo had accompanied the cardinal-legate to Bologna, and one of them went on with him to Ferrara,

---

[1] Corio, ii.222; Clementini, ii.78; Tonini, iv.177-8, iv/2, CXLIV; Muratore, *ASL* 1905.

[2] Sautier; Pirchan, i.4-49; Muratore, *ASL* 1905; Fumi, *AR* 1886, 154ff.; Werunsky, *Karl IV*, iii.313ff., 337ff., 346-8, 358, 361, 366; Filippini, *SS* xiii.68; Pellini, i.10, 18; Vernarecci, *Fossombrone*, i.333; Amiani, i.291; Theiner, ii.405; *Cron. mal.*, 30; Franceschini, 'Stato d'Urbino', 3. The Malatesta and their cities were involved in the campaign against Ambrogio Visconti in 1366 and 1367.

[3] Mirot, 6-7; Filippini, *Cardinale*, 391, 422; Dupré-Theseider, 122ff.; Kirsch, 'Rückkehr', xiii-xv.

[4] Fumi, *AR* 1886, doc. VI; Kirsch, 'Rückkehr', 55 n. 5; Amiani, i.290-1. Six cardinals came independently by way of Romagna and Rimini: *Cron. mal.*, 29; Werunsky, *Karl IV*, iii.357.

[5] Kirsch, 'Rückkehr', xvi; *Cron. mal.*, 30-1; *Chron. Bon.*, iii.218; Pirchan, i.47.

[6] He was appointed 27, 30 Jan. 1368: Theiner, ii.439, 446, 447; Tonini, iv/2, CXLVI, CXLVII; Pirchan, ii, Erläut. XXVI; A. Salimei, *Senatori e statuti di Roma nel medioevo*: *Senatori* (Rome, 1935), 153.

Padua and Venice during the following month.[1] At the same time the pope sent Malatesta Ungaro to Bologna, as likely to give more valuable service there. He urged the legate to appoint one of the Malatesta commander of the league, but this post was finally held by Gomez Albornoz, and then by Niccolo d'Este.[2]

The lords of the Papal States assembled their forces quickly, and by May, when the emperor arrived to lend support, hostilities in Lombardy had begun.[3] Since his meeting with the pope in 1365 Charles IV had been very close to papal policy. But his wide and vague ambitions which had then included the return of the papacy to Rome, the pacification of Italy and the conduct of a crusade, soon narrowed under papal influence into the single, practical purpose of a war of aggression.[4] The emperor was forced to acquiesce and, after renewing the imperial grants and privileges to the Roman church, left Vienna in April, to reach the theatre of operations in the middle of May.[5] The campaign which followed, in which both Galeotto and Malatesta Ungaro played a part, was expected to lead to a great decision. But very little was achieved against either Bernabò or Cansignore della Scala. By the second half of July Charles and the enemy were coming to terms. And on 27 August a peace was arranged which the pope was persuaded to accept, though suspicion of the Visconti remained, and with good reason, until a second treaty was made at Bologna in February of the following year.[6]

Among the witnesses to the peace of August was Malatesta Ungaro, who at this time, as other imperial documents show, had temporarily joined the imperial retinue.[7] The troops under his command remained Angevin and papal, but this did not stop Charles appointing him imperial lieutenant in Siena at the beginning of September. Here, following the regular cycle of communal politics, an aristocratic régime had just replaced a government of middle-class guilds, and Malatesta Ungaro was only able to gain admission through a rising of the *popolo minuto*, instigated by the magnate Salimbeni. On 23 September he entered the city and installed a popular government ('del popolo minuto'). Supreme power he reserved to himself as imperial *referen-*

---

[1] *Chron. Bon.*, iii.219–21, 223; Ghirardacci, ii.294; Vancini, 'Bologna', 520; Pirchan, i.50–1, 56.
[2] Tonini, iv/2, CXLVIII; Pirchan, i.71, 162–3.
[3] *Chron. Bon.*, iii.227, 230–1, 234; Corio, ii.230; Ghirardacci, ii.295; Pirchan, i.63–75.
[4] A change of policy censured by Sacchetti: *Rime*, n.cxli; *Lettere*, 99; cf. Pirchan, i.4, 90–1; Werunsky, *Karl IV*, iii.322, 344, 346–7, 355.
[5] Lünig, ii.791; Theiner, ii.443; *Chron. Bon.*, *locc. citt.*; Werunsky, *Karl IV*, iii.381.
[6] Pirchan, i.149–87, 313, 368–71; ii, Erläut. LXX, LXXIII, LXXVI; Ghirardacci, ii.296; *Chron. Bon.*, iii.229–31.
[7] Pirchan, ii, Erläut. LXXVI, 116.

darius and *locumtenens*, but it depended wholly on partisan alliance with the new régime and the Salimbeni. For a time his administration brought peace to the city. And it was a submissive community that welcomed Charles on his arrival in October. Even so, Malatesta Ungaro was no more capable of permanently restraining communal factions than any other ill-equipped outsider. When Charles returned from Rome in mid-January, he found Siena in a fresh state of agitation. Malatesta was forced to leave, and the emperor only saved the vestiges of authority by granting the commune a vicariate.[1] The Sienese chronicler says Charles complained of treachery by Malatesta Ungaro, but Malatesta reappeared in his following at Bologna and Ferrara during his return journey,[2] and the same writer even adds that he received Siena 'a tirannia da lo imperadore per xx mila fiorini d'oro l'anno'.[3]

In working for the empire the Malatesta did not neglect the papacy. Pope and emperor were still allies.[4] And with the operations in Siena were combined other services, now and later, on behalf of the church. About this time Pandolfo Malatesta was papal governor in Città di Castello (1368–9) and then in Urbino (1370).[5] The Malatesta were also parties to the peace with the Visconti in February 1369; and when war broke out a third time, they were again called on for help.[6] During 1370 they joined in defending the Papal States against John Hawkwood, while Malatesta Ungaro was sent into Tuscany to resist the Visconti there.[7] The return of Urban to Avignon in September and his death at the end of the year in no way affected the course of events.[8] Galeotto and Malatesta Ungaro were directed by the new pope, Gregory XI, to lend aid to Niccolo d'Este; and in April a company was formed in Tuscany on behalf of the church, Florence, Ferrara, the

---

[1] *Cron. sen.*, 159, 160, 618–26; Sozomenus, 1084, 1085; Velluti, 264–5; *Chron Bon.*, iii.232, 238; Canestrini, 'Documenti', 430; J. Luchaire, *Documenti per la storia dei rivolgimenti politici del comune di Siena dal 1354 al 1369* (Lyon, 1906), docs. 51–85; Banchi, *ASI* Ser. 3, xi.1.91–4; Pirchan, i.262–89, 328, 336–62; ii, Erläut. CII, CXX–CXXIII; Sacchetti, *Rime*, 134.

[2] July 1369: Griffoni, 68; *Chron. Est.*, *RIS* xv.491; Pirchan, i.431.

[3] *Cron. sen.*, 626.

[4] 31 Oct. 1368; Urban urged Malatesta Ungaro to keep Siena obedient to the emperor: Tonini, iv/2, CLI.

[5] *Ibid.* CXLIX, CLIV. The Montefeltro had been recently expelled from Urbino: Franceschini, *Montefeltro*, 286ff.

[6] *Chron. Est.*, *RIS* xv.491; Clementini, ii.78. Amiani, i.293.

[7] Tonini, iv/2, CLIV–VII; Amiani, i.293; *Lucca, Regesti*, ii/2, n. 24. In 1369 Giovanni Malatesta was Florentine war-captain: Sozomenus, *RIS* xvi.1086–7.

[8] One or more of the Malatesta may have done homage to the new pope and attended the funeral of Urban in Bologna: Clementini, ii.79, 93–4, 134; Rubeus 591; Ghirardacci, ii.301; Amiani, i.294. Malatesta Ungaro was in Avignon in April 1371: *Lettres, Grég. XI*, nn. 176, 180.

Malatesta, and other lords.[1] At the same time it seems to have been as a result of Urban's death that the town of S. Sepolcro was now sold to Galeotto Malatesta. Since 1358 S. Sepolcro had been under Città di Castello. But in 1370, to accommodate the pope, Charles IV had entrusted it to cardinal Anglico and William of Grisac. Their tenure may have been insecure, and Gregory XI, to avoid the scandal of seeming to usurp imperial rights, gave them permission to sell the town to any ally or friend of the church. In July 1371 S. Sepolcro was accordingly sold to Galeotto Malatesta for 18,000 florins. He took possession at once, but not until November 1378, just before his death, did the emperor ratify the sale, together with that of Citerna Castella.[2]

During this year and the next papal demands on the Malatesta in diplomacy and war were frequent and importunate;[3] but their strength was seriously reduced when Malatesta Ungaro suddenly died in July 1372, and his brother Pandolfo only six months after him.[4] Henceforward Galeotto remained in sole command of the family dominions, for the first of his nephews, Malatesta, left only a daughter, Costanza,[5] while Malatesta, Pandolfo's heir, was still only a child.[6] When Guastafamiglia died in 1364, Galeotto was still himself without male issue. His wife Hélise had borne him a daughter, Rengarda, married to Masio da Pietramala, but no sons. In 1366 Hélise died,[7] and in the following year Galeotto took a second wife, Gentile, daughter of Rodolfo da

---

[1] *Lettres, Grég. XI*, n. 42; Tonini, iv/2.188; *Chron. Est.*, *RIS* xv.493; Ghirardacci, ii.303; Amiani, i.294.

[2] Muzi, i.222; Coleschi, 55–9; Franceschini, 'Galeotto M. a San Sepolcro', 39ff. Both places were fiefs requiring performance of homage.

[3] Sept.–Nov. 1371 Malatesta Ungaro was back in Avignon on diplomatic business, and on 2 Nov. Galeotto was nominated captain-general of the league (renewed Oct. 1372): Tonini, iv/2, CLXI, CLXIX; Theiner, ii.528; Segre, *ASI* 1909.

[4] *Cron. mal.*, 34–5; *Chron. Bon.*, 268, 276, 284; Mazzatinti, *Inventari*, xxxvii.123, xxxix.225; *Archivi*, Ser.2, ii.340. Malatesta Ungaro, like his predecessors, left many bequests to the Franciscans, and a request to be buried in the Franciscan habit: Tonini, iv/2, CLXVII. For further details on Pandolfo, his marriage ties with the Orsini, his relations with Petrarch: Savio, *BU* 1895; Antonelli, *AR* 1942, 160; Tonini, *Coltura*, i.58–62.

[5] Married to Ugo d'Este who died in 1370. She misspent the remainder of her life and was put to death for improper conduct by order of Galeotto in 1378: *Il Pecorone di Ser Giovanni Florentino* (Milan, 1804), i.140–9; Letterio di Francia, *Gior. stor. lett. it.* 1909, 371–4; Massèra, *RIS²* xv/2.34.

[6] Born in 1368 (Feliciangeli, 'Notizie', 12 n. 2), Malatesta is described as 'pupillus' in a case between himself and Galeotto before a papal official in the winter of 1373–4. Galeotto was claiming revenue from Pesaro owed by Pandolfo and got it (34,650 ducats: Tonini, *Imposte*, 37–9). He and Galeotto were also part heirs of Malatesta Ungaro and seem to have reached some agreement on that as well: Bosdari, 'Giovanni da Legnano', doc. XXI.

[7] 18 Aug.: *Cron. mal.*, 28. In Dec. Rengarda also died: *ibid.* Cf. Franceschini, 'Gal. da Pietramala', 375ff.

Camerino.[1] By her he was presented in the next ten years with four sons, who were destined to continue the Riminese line: Carlo (1368), Pandolfo (1370), Andrea Malatesta (1373) and Galeotto Belfiore (1377).[2]

The pope sent the usual condolences to Galeotto on the loss of his two nephews;[3] but demands for money and service were not relaxed. During 1373 Galeotto was closely involved with papal policy in Romagna and Lombardy, for a time governing Bologna in the absence of the legate, guiding his decisions in the campaign against the Visconti, and cooperating with Hawkwood, now a captain of the church, in the victory on the Chiese at the beginning of May.[4] From that time the Visconti war languished, dragging on to a truce in the summer of 1375. No sooner had peace been made in the north, however, than other enemies appeared, perhaps less strong and united than the Visconti, but much more dangerous to the reconstituted Papal State.

By 1375, within ten years of the cardinal's death, the Papal States had fallen a long way from the 'grande e prospero stato'[5] established by Albornoz. All the old malpractices of papal rule had revived. Albornoz himself predicted the decline, and more than once protested to the papacy. Not only did he formulate the conditions of good government, in the *Constitutions* and elsewhere.[6] He raised objection to particular abuses as they began to reappear: against the invasion of the Papal States by French bishops, against the speculators who left Avignon endowed with wide privileges, against the persistence of heavy taxes which only war had justified. And he forecast the troubles that would

---

[1] With whom political relations, strained after 1355, had recently improved: Filippini, *Cardinale*, 229; Lilii, ii.96; Amiani, i.290; Tonini, iv.320. Rodolfo was a lord after the Malatesta stamp: when asked why he had married 'una giovane a un vecchio? Rispondea: occelo fatto per noi, e non per lei': Sacchetti, *Novelle*, XLI. The children of Galeotto's nephew, Pandolfo, also married into the Varani: Giordani, *Orazioni*, XVII, XXI–II.

[2] *Cron. mal.*, 28–9. The name Carlo was possibly meant to commemorate links with Charles IV.

[3] Tonini, iv/2, CLXVIII, CLXXII.

[4] Sozomenus, 1094; Theiner, ii.551; Tonini, iv/2.192, iv/2, CLXIX, CLXXIII–VI, CLXXX; Poggio, 219; Ghirardacci, ii.321–4, 333; Temple-Leader and Marcotti, 61. Some time now Galeotto seems to have incurred censure for being late with his *census*, but in Feb. 1374 he paid the 3,150 fl. for the preceding June and Dec., and in April 1374 not merely 3,150 fl. for the coming June and Dec., but a gift of 3,000 fl. toward the Visconti war: Bib. Gamb., *Cod. Pand.*, fos. 114–15. There is also an obscure record that on 5 Aug. 1374 the pope renewed the Malatesta vicariates, but there is no confirmation of this in later grants: Giordani, *Gradara*, 71; Battaglini, *Zecca*, 214; *Vita*, App. LXIX, 691.

[5] Sacchetti, *Novelle*, CLXII.

[6] *Cost. Egid.*, *passim*; Filippini, *SS* v, doc.44, viii.345ff., 465ff.; *Cardinale*, 141–4, 426–33; above pp. 44ff.

follow if his advice was disregarded.[1] A few years later in 1371 cardinal Anglico also submitted recommendations for equitable government, remarking that 'homines istarum partium sunt passionatissimi'.[2]

In one direction, certainly, against local independence, communal and signorial, pope and legates continued Albornoz' work.[3] In later retrospect, indeed, the middle decades of the fourteenth century may be seen to foreshadow a radical change in the balance of power within the Papal State, by which, in commune after commune, the papacy took over or began to imitate the rights of *signoria*, an official 'despotism' unthinkable a century before.[4] At the same time the papal reconquest, while involving, on the pope's admission, a new burden of taxation,[5] also widened the opportunity for oppression and misgovernment. Once again the popes had to check official abuses,[6] and once again complaints were raised against 'mali pastori e rettori che attossicano e imputridiscono questo giardino'.[7] Some of the sharpest criticism came, as before, from outside: from Caterina of Siena, the Florentine Sacchetti,[8] or anonymous writers like the Piacenza annalist who, in a notable parenthesis on papal maladministration, laid the blame on the nepotism of officials, and their short terms of office which led them to think of one thing only: 'scilicet quod efficiantur divites'.[9] The justice of these complaints was proved by the reckless misrule of Gérard de Puy, abbot of Marmoutier, in Perugia,[10] and by the growing discontent of Bologna which in 1360, for the first time ever, had surrendered unconditionally to the church.[11] Only one feature of previous conditions was lacking: the omnipresence of *tiranni*. Not all, however, had fallen to the offensive of Albornoz, and those who had were only awaiting an opportunity to recover power.[12]

---

[1] Filippini, *Cardinale*, 295, 343.

[2] Theiner, ii. 539; cf. n. 527.

[3] Thus (1368–70) Urban V profited by the revolt of Città di Castello from Perugia to assume control of the first and reduce the second to surer subordination: *ASI* xvi/1.208; *Cron. mal.*, 33; Pellini, i.963, 1037, 1080–5; Muzi, 166, 178; Pirchan, i.424, ii, Erläut. CXLIII, CXXV; Theiner, ii.467.

[4] Towns recovered from despots were rarely reaccorded their former liberties: Partner, 14, 95, 124, 159.

[5] Theiner, ii.430. On intensified taxation cf. Larner, 220; Partner, 111; Favier, *Finances*, 688–9.

[6] Cocquelines, iii/2.353–4; Mirot, 42–5.

[7] S. Caterina, iii.159; cf. 75, 172, 225. Similar sentiments were expressed by Giovanni da Legnano: *AMR* 1901, 57.

[8] Who attacks the temporal dominion generally: *Rime*, 200–4, 255.

[9] *RIS* xvi.527. Cf. Mirot, 40–1.

[10] *Cron. Perug.*, 217–20; *Chron. Reg.*, 85.

[11] Filippini, *Cardinale*, 215–16, 371–3; Vancini, 'Bologna', *passim*.

[12] It is notable how generously the Malatesta had been treated compared with other *signori* who came to terms with the church. They alone retained their principal cities. The Montefeltro were granted some slight control in Urbino and Cagli, but

Their chance came in 1375 with a general revolt of the Papal State, stirred up, not by themselves, however, or by merely papal action, but by a foreign power, proclaimed enemy of despots: the republic of Florence.[1] Relations between Florence and the church had been cooling ever since Innocent VI's attempt to restore papal government.[2] The papal alliance with Charles IV also aroused Florentine suspicion, particularly when, in 1368, cardinal Guy of Boulogne was appointed imperial vicar in Tuscany. This measure recalled the one-time Tuscan ambitions of the papacy, which Albornoz himself may have contemplated reviving; and when, therefore, following the truce of 1375 between the church and the Visconti, the papal captain Hawkwood appeared in Tuscany, it was rumoured that the pope had designs on the province.[3] This, with other Florentine grievances, has been exposed as false;[4] and the Eight Saints war which now broke out between Florence and the papacy can only be explained by the long irritation these grievances betray. No more credible was the idea propagated by the Florentines that they were acting merely as liberators of the Papal State from the despotism of foreign prelates.[5] Misgovernment there was and also dispossession; and Florence made dexterous use of both.

Strengthened by alliance with the despot Visconti, Florence succeeded in the space of a few weeks at the end of 1375 in raising almost the whole papal dominion in revolt.[6] Those lords and communities who remained loyal were soon outnumbered by *tiranni* returning from exile or re-establishing power: the Ordelaffi, Montefeltro, Brancaleoni, Manfredi, and others.[7] Even the Alidosi forsook the

---

no vicariate (Franceschini, *Montefeltro*, 28off.); nor were the Varani at Camerino, Ismeducci at S. Severino, Manfredi at Faenza, or Ordelaffi at Forlì, all of which places were kept 'libere ad manus ecclesie' (Werunsky, *Karl IV*, iii.182, 186, 242; Filippini, *SS* vii.548-9, viii.333; Theiner, ii.336, 340). By 1375 the Manfredi and Ordelaffi had both been dispossessed again and so, virtually, had the Montefeltro: Cobelli, 133-7, 141; Theiner, ii.527; Filippini, *Cardinale*, 345, 369-70; Franceschini, *loc. cit.*

[1] The Riminese chronicler attributes the rising to the 'grande sapere e malicia di Fiorentini', as much as 'la grande avarizia e luxuria e lo so male reggimento' of the papacy: *Cron. mal.*, 37, 38. Cf. *Chron. Est.*, *RIS* xv.499C; S. Caterina, iii, ccvii, 163.

[2] Mirot, 25ff.; Sautier, 94ff. and Anhang. 44; Fumi, *AR* 1886, 129.

[3] Pirchan, i.324-7; Filippini *Cardinale*, 243; Gherardi, 'Guerra', *ASI* (1867) v/2.38ff.; Vancini, *Rivolta*, 8-11.

[4] Mirot, 25, 31, 45, 72; Gherardi, 'Guerra', *ASI* (1867), v/2, doc. 49.

[5] Gherardi, *ibid. passim*; Duprè-Theseider, 178; Degli Azzi, nn. 434, 441, 449, 494-5; Sacchetti, *Rime*, 205.

[6] Gherardi, 'Guerra', *ASI* (1867) v/2.45-6, 54; *Cron. mal.*, 37-8; *Chron. Est.*, *RIS* xv.499; *Cron. Perug.*, 220. In March 1376 Bologna joined: Vancini, *Rivolta*, 17-18.

[7] *Cron. mal.*, 37, 38; *Ann. Forl.*, 69; Cobelli, 114-17, 148; Gherardi, 'Guerra', *ASI* (1868) vii/1, docs. 127, 129, 145; Torelli; Colucci, xiii.177; Franceschini, 'Stato'

church. The Varano were divided. And of all the leading families only the Malatesta stood firm.[1] All this added urgency to papal plans for returning again to Italy. In September 1376 Gregory XI left Avignon and, after a difficult journey, entered Rome in January the following year.[2] This time, however, there was no papal escort of subject *signori*. Not even Galeotto Malatesta was there.

Galeotto may have been absent because he doubted the loyalty of his own subject cities.[3] From the first, however, he assumed the defence of papal government. The position he had come to occupy in Romagna, even though informal, was not one lightly to compromise; and the pope very soon turned to him for help.[4] In December 1375 he tried to prevent the return of the Montefeltro to Urbino, and for a time the people of Cagli elected him lord.[5] By resisting the Montefeltro he aroused the resentment of the Florentines, who numbered Antonio da Montefeltro among their allies against the papacy, and from as early as September had been trying every expedient to win Galeotto to their side.[6] Their specious letters do not seem to have had effect. Instead Galeotto may have helped to resist the Florentine troops which were everywhere penetrating the Papal States. Nothing, however, came of it. In May 1376 a truce was arranged between them, which the Montefeltro later joined;[7] and from that time, though Florence secured Rodolfo da Camerino as *capitano di guerra*, and Galeotto Malatesta continued to serve the pope, the real arbiters of the struggle became the mercenary soldiers: Hawkwood, who later deserted to Florence, and the 'gens barbara, gens immanis' of the Breton companies, just taken

---

40–1; 'Signoria', 86; *Montefeltro*, 300ff. Among the reinstated were some displaced by the Malatesta in their earlier expansion, e.g. the Simonetti of Iesi: Amiani, i.299.

[1] 'sola Malatestarum domus in fide permansit, Galeotto partes Ecclesiae iuvante': Aeneas Sylvius Piccolomini, *Commentarii*, 256. Cf. Gherardi, 'Guerra', *ASI* (1868) vii/2, doc. 189; viii/1, docs. 219, 331.

[2] *Chron. Est.*, *RIS* xv.499E; Kirsch, 'Rückkehr', xvii–xxii; Dupré-Theseider, 157ff.; Mirot, 10, 86, 104; Tonini, iv/2, CLXXXIV.

[3] Amiani, i.299.

[4] 1 Oct. 1375: Tonini, iv/2, CLXXXVII. The *Cron. mal.* (43) remarks that it was Galeotto's loyalty which enabled the pope to return to Italy.

[5] *Ibid.* 37; *Chron. Bon.*, iii.316–17; *Diario d'anon. fiorent.*, 308; Gherardi, 'Guerra' *ASI* (1868) vii/1, docs. 127, 129; Franceschini, 'Signoria', 86. Cagli soon expelled the officers of Galeotto and offered allegiance to the Montefeltro: Franceschini, 'Stato', 40–1; *Montefeltro*, 300.

[6] Gherardi, 'Guerra', *ASI* (1867) vi/2, doc. 47; (1868) vii/1, docs. 105, 116, 125, 127; vii/2, docs. 179, 200; Salutati, i.41; Franceschini, 'Signoria', App. 4; Stefani, 297.

[7] Degli Azzi, 134; Gherardi, 'Guerra', *ASI* (1868) viii/1.264; Amiani, i.298; *Cron. mal.*, 41; Franceschini, 'Signoria', App. 5–6.

into papal pay.¹ These *condottieri* profited no one who employed them, though it was they who were responsible for the only two notable events of the war: the double sack of Faenza and of Cesena.

With the first, the sack of Faenza by Hawkwood in March 1376, Galeotto Malatesta had nothing to do; but he may have played some minor part in the second. At the beginning of 1376 he saved Cesena for the church, sending a garrison to keep it loyal;² and in August, when the Breton mercenaries reached Romagna, Galeotto met their commander, cardinal Robert of Geneva, and surrendered the government of the city.³ But the misconduct and violence of the soldiery soon incensed the population, and in February 1377 they rose in revolt, putting a number of Bretons to death. Galeotto, it is said, interposed to obtain them pardon from the legate, but the promise was not kept. Robert called in the English company from Faenza, and Cesena was subjected to savage punishment. Many thousands were killed; many more escaped into Malatesta territory and there took refuge until the Bretons finally left in August, and Galeotto had them escorted back to their crippled city.⁴ The sack had no effect on the war, and the Breton companies merely moved on to intimidate other papal regions, until Gregory summoned them to Rome for his own security.⁵

Hawkwood was giving the Florentines little better service, and the war was clearly losing what momentum it ever had. Florence continued to fight but there was nothing to bind the allies to her side, particularly after the pope had returned to Rome and was able to negotiate with them directly. The rebel cities and *signori* had followed their own interests. And this was equally true of Bernabò Visconti, whose alliance throughout was unsure. It was his defection more than anything that brought the war to a close. By the end of 1377 negotiations for a peace were in train.⁶ Before this Galeotto Malatesta had been

¹ Gherardi, 'Guerra', *ASI* (1867) v/2.89, 91, 95–6, 109, 111; Stefani, 297; *Diario d'anon. fiorent.*, 310; Temple-Leader and Marcotti, 97–9; Lilii, ii.105; Bonincontri, 27; Degli Azzi, i.136; Sacchetti, *Rime*, 207.
² *Cron. mal.*, 39; Chiaramonti (372–3) detects a design by Galeotto on the *signoria* of Cesena.
³ *Diario d'anon. fiorent.*, 314; *Chron. Bon.*, iii.316. The *Cron. mal.* says (42–3): 'El populo de Cesena remase mal contento' at this 'perchè amava forte, et anco ama, lo regimento e la signoria de misere Galeotto'.
⁴ Gherardi, 'Guerra', *ASI* (1867) v/2.105–6; *Cron. mal.*, 43–4, 46, 47; *Chron. Est.*, *RIS* xv.500; *Cron. sen.*, 666; Niem, *De scismate* (ed. G. Erler, Leipzig, 1890), 125–6. It is Sozomenus who says Galeotto interposed (*RIS* xvi.1100A); but he adds that Cesena was sacked 'consentiente secrete dicto domino Galeotto de Malatestis, ut postea faciliter posset consequi dominationem dictae civitatis destructae, sicut consequutus fuit' (1100B).
⁵ *Cron. mal.*, 46, 47; *ASI* xvi/1.225; Durrieu, *Gascons*, 187ff.; Valois, *Schisme*, i.16–17.
⁶ Gherardi, 'Guerra', *ASI* (1867) v/2.106; Mirot, 48–9, 85; Romano, 'Spinelli' 1901, 51–2; Vancini, *Rivolta*, 61.

himself employed in trying to bring the pope and the Signoria to an agreement.[1] He was present at the negotiations finally opened at Sarzana; and when peace was at length arranged in July 1378 he, with the marquis of Este and Guido da Polenta, was given a special exemption from one of its clauses.[2] By this time, however, events had occurred which were to affect far more than the provincial politics of the Papal State. A new papal election and a revolt among the cardinals was threatening a schism in the church itself.

Galeotto Malatesta was among the mediators who tried to avert the Schism, visiting Rome in May and later taking part in the negotiations between Urban VI and the cardinals at Anagni.[3] His attitude was not shared by every *signore* of the Papal State. More typical was the reply of his father-in-law, Rodolfo Varani, when Galeotto rebuked him for encouraging the election of an anti-pope: 'Aiolo fatto perchè abbiano tanto a fare de' fatti loro, ch'e nostri lascino stare.'[4] And such certainly was the effect of schism on the States of the Church. Here, as everywhere else in Italy and Europe, there was division. But more important was the enfeeblement of the papacy, its resources impoverished, its territories threatened, and its powers reduced to the purchase of allegiance by concessions and immunities.[5] The Papal State once again assumed the condition in which Albornoz had begun his work. The last principles of his policy had to be discarded. And the history of the Malatesta to the end of the Schism is a history mainly of this decline, with the privileges and honours they gained from it. As formal vicars of a helpless government they grew in power, strength and prosperity.

Although it was by his influence that the Malatesta were reconciled to the church, Albornoz himself had never been reckless in favours to them. During the later years of his legation they had hoped for new grants of territory in Romagna and the March, but the legate consistently avoided concessions which might have imperilled his work later.[6] In particular he was anxious to keep free, as possible centres of

[1] Salutati, *Epist.*, ii.21; Tonini, iv/2, CLXXXIX–CXC; Gherardi, 'Guerra', *ASI* (1868) viii/1, doc. 298.

[2] Romano, 'Spinelli' 1901, 53; Gherardi, 'Guerra', *ASI* (1867) v/2.123–5; Franceschini, 'Signoria', App. 7.

[3] *Cron. mal.*, 44, 46; *Chron. Sic.*, 31.

[4] Sacchetti, *Novelle*, XLI.

[5] The threat to its territories is illustrated best by the 'kingdom of Adria' projected by adherents of the anti-pope, which was to comprise Bologna, Ferrara, Romagna, the March of Ancona, Massa Trabaria, Perugia and the duchy of Spoleto: Lünig, ii.1167; Valois, *Schisme*, i.167–8, 187–8; Boüard, 38–9, 52; A. D'Ancona, *Il regno d'Adria*. The idea of secularising the Papal State also revived: Romano, 'Spinelli' 1901, 484.

[6] Tonini, iv/2, CXL, CXLIV; Filippini, *Cardinale*, 349–51.

resistance against the Montefeltro or the Malatesta, strategically placed communities like S. Marino, S. Leo, Cagli and Santarcangelo.[1] Yet cardinal Anglico's survey of Romagna in 1371 showed that the Malatesta had not forgotten their former power in this region,[2] and during the war with Florence they were able at last to recover and extend it. Galeotto Malatesta's tenure of Cagli was only shortlived, but it revealed the range of his ambitions, for the city had never before been subject to his family. In Santarcangelo and Cesena, however, his conquest was complete. During 1376 Galeotto intervened to keep both places loyal to the church by assuming personal control of them.[3] Cesena, it is true, he had for a time to surrender, but at the end of 1378 he was finally given the vicariate of the city. And the reason for this must be sought in papal weakness.

The rebellion of the Papal State gravely embarrassed papal finance and government,[4] and throughout the war Gregory XI found it difficult to pay his troops.[5] In 1377 Robert of Geneva was reduced to pawning his silver, his mitre and his rings in Rimini to pay the Breton companies. Money was borrowed from Galeotto Malatesta and Guido da Polenta, and to Guido, in the face of Galeotto's indignant protests, the town of Cesenatico was assigned in pledge.[6] The condition of Cesena was serious. The citizens too had to borrow money from the Malatesta and the Polenta to pay for reconstruction;[7] and this may have led the pope to consider granting it in vicariate. Galeotto petitioned for investiture, but he was not the only candidate. Astorgio di Manfredi also tried to get possession, but was prevented by Sinibaldo Ordelaffi with whom Galeotto was now on friendly terms. Guido da Polenta, too, had adherents in Cesena who were plotting to give him the *signoria*. It was in defence against them that the papal governor at last called in Galeotto in October 1378. Galeotto was able to reduce the commune to obedience, and on 20 December was given the government of the city: largely, Chiaramonti believes, because the papacy was so deeply in debt to him for the payment of mercenaries. In January

[1] Filippini, *Cardinale*, 288, 293.
[2] Theiner, ii.503–4; Tonini, iv/2, CXLIV.
[3] *Cron. mal.*, 39, 40. Santarcangelo was surrendered to Galeotto 'de volentà e licenzia del papa' by Mucciolo dei Balacchi, of the principal family in the town, which had inspired the revolt of 1355 (*Ann. Caes.*, 1182). Shortly after Galeotto married one of his bastard daughters to Mucciolo's son, perhaps to keep him loyal (*Cron. mal.*, 41; Marini, *Santo Arcangelo*, 88). With Santarcangelo itself Galeotto probably took over the whole vicariate established in 1358, this former district of the Riminese *contado* now returning direct to the Malatesta.
[4] As shown by renewed concessions to local powers: Theiner, ii.599, 600, 604, 607, 608.
[5] Temple-Leader and Marcotti, 81; *ASI* xvi/1.223–4.
[6] *ASI* xvi/i.225; Chiaramonti, 380–1; Tonini, iv/2, CXCIV.
[7] Chiaramonti, 381–2.

the citadel surrendered and Galeotto had control of Cesena.[1] The Riminese chronicler reports, without confirmation, that at the same time Bertinoro made him *signore*, and that he established authority there. It is also possible that he was holding Senigallia as well:[3] this was certainly soon the case. By March 1380 Galeotto numbered among his 'colligati, adherentes, et recomendati' not merely the four cities of the original vicariate but, in addition, Santarcangelo, Cesena, Senigallia, S. Sepolcro, S. Leo, the detached parts of the *contado* of Fano and many smaller places. Bertinoro is not mentioned, but instead Meldola appears, 'cum eius curia et districtu'.[4] During the turbulent years after 1375, and possibly before, Galeotto must have been quietly extending his possessions, and building up a territorial estate which in the sequel was to make his family dominant in Romagna, Montefeltro and the March of Ancona throughout the Schism. He was safe in the favour of a distracted and destitute papacy, and the pope did nothing to check the expansion of the Malatesta *signoria*; if anything he gave it his sanction.[5] Certainly he did not repudiate Galeotto, but endowed him with new dignities, and even encouraged him to seize new territories.

In September 1378 Urban created cardinal a nephew of Galeotto, Galeotto de' Tarlatti da Pietramala.[6] It was probably also from consideration for the Malatesta that in 1379 he granted the vicariate of Forlì to Sinibaldo Ordelaffi. The family ties of Malatesta and Ordelaffi had long been broken by the death of Giovanni and Lodovico di

---

[1] *Cron. mal.*, 48; *Ann. Forl.*, 70; *Chron. Est.*, RIS xv.503; Chiaramonti, 384–8; Tonduzzi, 442; Pedrino, 426ff. Cf. Valois, *Schisme*, i.164–5. Chiaramonti (366) mentions an earlier attempt of the Malatesta on the *signoria* of Cesena late in 1364; cf. Braschi, 277; Zazzeri, 219.

[2] *Cron. mal.*, 48.

[3] Amiani, i.301, 302.

[4] Corinaldo, Finigli, Donato, Citerna, Pieve de Sestino, Castellacia, Carpegna and Montebello are also listed: Ansidei, 'Tregua', 36–9; Battaglini, *Zecca*, 215, 222; Cimarelli, 26ff. In 1393 Niccolo Spinelli wrote of Montenovo, Mondolfo and Corinaldo: 'Ista habebam in concessione ab Ecclesia; et possedi pacifice usque ad novitatem factam per Florentinos contra Ecclesiam [1375]; nunc tenet Karolus de Malatestis', which suggests again that the Malatesta profited by the Eight Saints war to extend their influence: Durrieu, *Royaume d'Adria*, ii.56. As to Bertinoro, this and Castrocaro were conferred in vicariate on the Neapolitan Francesco Tortello in 1381: Valois, *Schisme*, i.91.

[5] There are indications in a later papal privilege (1399: below p. 104) and in certain statutes of Galeotto (ACF, *Cod. mal.* 3, fo. 19v) that around 1380 Urban VI may have granted him the vicariate of many of the new lands then listed as in his possession: cf. Battaglini, *Zecca*, 221–2; *Vita*, 590–1, 692–3. However, a tax-table of 1389/90 records only Fano, Pesaro and Fossombrone as held by the Malatesta in the March at that time: *ASI* 1866, 191–2.

[6] Franceschini, 'Gal. da Pietramala', 375ff. The new cardinal later joined the antipope.

Francesco,[1] and political relations had ceased when the Malatesta made their peace with the church. But with the return of the Ordelaffi to Forlì during the Eight Saints war their friendship was renewed. Sinibaldo helped Galeotto win Cesena. His own investiture with Forlì soon followed; and the alliance was confirmed by his betrothal with Paola Bianca, daughter of Pandolfo Malatesta.[2]

The old power structure of the States of the Church was everywhere reviving behind the forms of papal vicariate. Yet the privilege awarded Galeotto in the following year was almost without precedent. Giovanni da Olaggio, on surrendering Bologna in 1360, had been made rector of the March; and Rodolfo of Camerino may have held the same appointment shortly before the death of Gregory XI.[3] Otherwise, in a tradition of government by mainly ecclesiastical rectors there is little to parallel the nomination of Galeotto Malatesta as rector of Romagna in 1380. It was much more a tribute to his place in the province, and to recent services of the Malatesta to the church, than a concession to political necessity. For nearly fifty years he and his son Carlo were to retain control of the office, at the head of the provincial administration. During that time the Malatesta reached the summit of their power.[4]

Galeotto's relations with the papacy during the last five years of his life were particularly close, and he and his allies were continuously employed by Urban in carrying out the intricate policies devised to put down the followers of Clement VII. In 1380 he was involved in the enterprise of Charles of Durazzo, whom he entertained in Rimini at the beginning of August.[5] Later in the year, at the request of the pope, he followed Charles to Rome, and there, according to one report,

[1] *Ann. Caes.*, 1183; *Cron. mal.*, 27 n. 5. Their sons, Cecco and Pino, Giovanni and Tebaldo, were grandsons of Malatesta Guastafamiglia: above pp. 67–8. Taddea, daughter of Guastafamiglia and wife of Giovanni Ordelaffi, had died in 1363, probably of the plague: *Cron. mal.*, 27.

[2] *Ibid.* 50; Pedrino, 430, rub. 1969; Cobelli, 148; *Ann. Forl.*, 70; Clementini, ii.148.

[3] Lilii, ii.116. Other instances were Onorato Gaetani, made rector of the Campagna and Marittima by Gregory XI: *AR* 1926, 258–9, and Rinaldo Orsini, made rector of the Patrimony by Urban VI in 1378 (Valois, *Schisme*, ii.127); another Orsini was rector of the Patrimony in 1353.

[4] Theiner, ii.629; Fantuzzi, iii.351, v.197; Tonini, iv/2, cxciii; Mazzatinti, *Inventari*, xlv. 218.

[5] Where Galeotto must have witnessed the snub to the envoys of Florence: *Cron. mal.*, 51; Stefani, rub.867; Bonincontri, 30–1. Though in 1380 Rimini was a centre of Florentine exiles (*RIS*² xviii/1, iii.66), relations with Florence were not unfriendly: Stefani, 380–1; Sozomenus, 1118; Bonincontri, 31; Gherardi, 'Guerra', *ASI* (1868) viii/1, docs. 407, 408 (which reveal that the Malatesta had owed Florence 3,000 fl. since 29 Aug. 1354; Degli Azzi, i, nn. 621, 622, 636; *Lucca, Regesti*, ii/2, nn. 883, 886, 889.

asked for the grant of his vicariate in 'terza generatione'. The pope was disposed to assent, but first demanded the payment of 200,000 florins. Galeotto had offered half this sum, and it was expected that 150,000 florins would be the total finally agreed. The result of the bargaining is not recorded, but it may be that some concessions was obtained.[1] During 1382 Romagna was again disturbed by papal policy in Naples. Queen Giovanna had soon been overcome by Charles of Durazzo, and to defend her claims she appealed to Louis of Anjou. Clement VII made Louis duke of Calabria, and in the spring of 1382 he set off for Naples with a large French force, supported by Amadeo of Savoy. The expedition left Turin in July, and by August was near Bologna. The lords of Romagna and the March generally neither opposed Louis nor actively supported him. Galeotto Malatesta alone, as papal rector, offered resistance, and an armed encounter was only avoided when the Angevin troops passed on through the March of Ancona.[2]

It was probably this Angevin invasion that decided Urban in the following year to sharpen proceedings against the followers of Clement still holding out in his own dominions. Prominent among these was Guido da Polenta; and when the pope commissioned Galeotto Malatesta to deal with him, he must have known that the task would be particularly welcome. Ill-feeling between Malatesta and Polenta had been growing ever since Guido received Porto Cesenatico in pledge from Robert of Geneva.[3] Rival claims to Cesena drove them further apart; and when Galeotto was invested with the city (including probably Cesenatico) a war soon broke out between them. A provisional peace was arranged at the end of 1380 by which Guido seems to have kept Cesenatico.[4] But early in 1382 Galeotto, as rector of Romagna, repaid the debt of 6,000 florins owing to the Polenta, and since the money was his own, assumed control of Cesenatico himself.[5] This did not end the friction. Guido, as a Clementine, joined Louis of Anjou, and in 1383, with papal support, Galeotto opened the campaign. In August the pope instructed him to expel the Polenta from Ravenna and all their other territories, and take over their vicariate.[6] For some years Galeotto had been in almost ceaseless conflict with the mercenary captains still marauding in the Papal State: the conte Lucio Lando, Giovanni

[1] Amiani, i.304; *Lucca Regesti*, ii/2, n. 801 (Jan. 1381).
[2] *Cron. mal.*, 52–4; Bernabei, 103–4; Pedrino, rub. 1997; *Ann. Forl.*, 71–2; *Lucca, Regesti*, ii/2, nn. 1061–5, 2104; Valois, *Schisme*, ii.8ff., 38ff.; Boüard, 45ff.; Feliciangeli, *AMM* 1907, 370–1, 374–81, 447, 452. In 1381 Clement VII tried to establish relations with Galeotto through the Manfredi: Valois, *Schisme*, ii.45.
[3] Above p. 97.
[4] *Chron. Bon.*, iii.361; Pedrino, rub. 1976; Chiaramonti, 386, 388; Amiani, i.304.
[5] Feb. 1382: Tonini, iv/2, cxciv, cxcv. Cf. Rubeus, 596–7; Chiaramonti, 388.
[6] Bib. Gamb., *Cod. Pand.*, fo. 137; Fantuzzi, iii.352; Tonini, iv/2, cxcvi, cxcviii.

GALEOTTO MALATESTA   101

d'Azzo degli Ubaldini, Hawkwood and Richard Romsey;[1] and at last
a chance seemed offered of making use of them. Hawkwood had
helped Galeotto at an earlier stage of the war;[2] now the two lords of
Rimini and Ravenna entered into competition for the services of a
foreign captain. Neither succeeded in hiring Romsey's company, but
it was with the help of the conte Lucio that at the end of October
Galeotto occupied Cervia. Ravenna was his second objective; but it
resisted all attack. and he had to be content with the smaller gains of
Polenta and Culianello.[3] After that the war dragged on inconclu-
sively. From the beginning other *signori* of Romagna had been implicated, the Manfredi as enemies, the Ordelaffi as allies of Galeotto. And
perhaps it was a sign of slackening energy when the four papal vicars
of Faenza, Imola, Forlì and Rimini united in alliance late in 1384.[4]

Galeotto Malatesta was himself nearing his end.[5] In January 1385
he was too sick to attend the marriage in Forlì of Pino Ordelaffi and
Venanza Brancaleoni.[6] He was also very advanced in years.[7] His wife,
Gentile, was already dead,[8] and Rodolfo of Camerino had recently died
too.[9] The personalities of Italian politics were changing. This was the
year in which Gian Galeazzo Visconti seized control of Milan to prepare the way for the greatest bid made by his family for the hegemony
of North and Central Italy. And Galeotto had long survived most of
his contemporaries when he finally died at Cesena on 21 January 1385.[10]
He left his dynasty near the height of its power and reputation, and
little was to be added to his achievement and the respect he had won
from Italian statesmen.[11] A year later Sacchetti mourned him as one
of the 'sei signori saggi ed alteri' who had just departed the world.[12]

---

[1] *Lucca, Regesti*, ii/2, nn. 971, 1031, 2048, 2072; 'Regesto Città di Castello', 138;
Predelli, viii, n. 82; Pellini, i. 1261; Amiani, i. 305–6.

[2] 1379: Temple-Leader and Marcotti, 123–4. Amiani (i. 306) says Galeotto, with
Perugia and the Montefeltro, took Hawkwood into their service in 1382 against
Louis of Anjou. Hawkwood, Romsey, and Giovanni d'Azzo were certainly in
Galeotto's territories in Sept.: *Lucca, Regesti*, 11/2, n. 971). At that same time
Galeotto may have hired Alberigo da Barbiano: *ibid.* n. 1061.

[3] *Lucca, Regesti*, ii/2, nn. 1113, 1116–17, 1119, 1124, 1172–3, 1177, 2110, 2113,
2117a; Pedrino, rub. 2013–14; Griffoni, 78–9; *Chron. Est., RIS* xv. 508; *Ann. Forl.*,
72; *Chron. Bon.*, iii. 371; Rubeus, 597.

[4] Temple-Leader and Marcotti, 123–4; *Lucca, Regesti*, ii/2, n. 1128; Pedrino, rub.
2013; Tonduzzi, 442–3; Tonini, iv/1. 228, iv/2, cc.

[5] *Cron. sen.*, 701 (1384): 'portava al collo la testa della morte'.

[6] Pedrino, rub. 2035.   [7] Pedrino (rub. 2036) says he was 85 at his death.

[8] June 1383: Pedrino, rub. 2009.

[9] Lilii, ii. 120. Galeotto's sons shared in his inheritance: cf. Benadducci, *Arch. stor.
Marche Umb.*, 1886, 705–16.

[10] *Cron. mal.*, 54. The subject cities paid for the friars who preached at his funeral:
Vernarecci, *Fossombrone*, i. 339.

[11] Salutati, ii. 173 (describing Galeotto as 'Ecclesiae pugil'); Pedrino, rub. 2036.

[12] *Rime*, 273. cf. *Lettere*, 97. Vergerio, 52.

5

The prime of Malatesta rule:
Carlo Malatesta

It was after Galeotto's death, and during the Great Schism, that the Malatesta of Rimini attained their greatest prominence, if not their greatest power, in the Papal State and in the politics of Upper Italy. While throughout the period they were never without the firm support of the papacy, the gradual emergence now in Italy of a few great territorial states, with regional or wider, Italian ambitions, compelled them also, with other minor despots who had thriven unmolested for a century or more, to look beyond their parochial alliances and feuds and take sides in a larger, general contest. This was the last age of the small *signore*, adventurer and *condottiere*. The expansion of the Visconti in the early fourteenth century had revealed the threat to lords of second rank, who could now expect to prosper, or even survive, only as clients or allies of a greater power. With other *signori* of their kind, the Malatesta, of Rimini and Pesaro, were caught up and forced to participate in a struggle for dominion that began at this time to divide all Lombardy, Tuscany and Romagna, and nearly the whole of Italy. But first of all they have to be seen in their local relations, with the Roman papacy and with the neighbouring lordships of their region.

Galeotto Malatesta left four sons to succeed him, each of whom, for administrative purposes at least, assumed particular control of part of the Malatesta vicariate. Carlo took over Rimini, Pandolfo Fano, with both the *contado* and vicariate (Mondavio), Mondolfo and Scorticata, while to Andrea Malatesta were assigned Cesena, Fossombrone and Roncofreddo, and to Galeotto Belfiore, the youngest, Cervia, Meldola, S. Sepolcro and a number of lesser places.[1] Pesaro was now a separate dominion, though relations between the two families for long continued cordial, and in 1391 Malatesta di Pandolfo received the city from Boniface IX as an independent vicariate.[2] It is not clear how soon

---

[1] Borghi, 86–7; Branchi, 171; Guerriero, 26. There was some dispute for a time over Fossombrone between Pandolfo and Andrea, settled in 1388 by Gian Galeazzo Visconti: Branchi, 172; Clementini, ii. 174; Vernarecci, *Fossombrone*, i. 339.

[2] 2 Jan. 1391: Mazzatinti, *Inventari*, xxxvii. 92, n. 56; Guiraud, 213. None the less in 1386 the Malatesta of Rimini were still paying *census* for Pesaro (Bib. Gamb.,

after Galeotto's death the partition among the Malatesta brothers took place, though it may have been in obedience to his own last wishes.[1] The exact nature and implications are also obscure. According to one chronicler, 'ciaschuno faceva corte da per se'.[2] Local government in each district must have been managed separately. It is probable too that the papal *census* was divided and apportioned.[3] But cooperation remained very close, particularly since, until 1392 at least, Galeotto Belfiore was held to be 'in pupillari etate'.[4] The arrangement was, as Battaglini says, a 'fraterna convenzione'.[5] Each brother could support the others in routine administration,[6] or replace them during absence;[7] while in external relations they continued to act as one, as in 1392 when all four Malatesta submitted an appeal to Rome on behalf of the Friars Minor of Fossombrone.[8] Partition was at most an expedient of government. It certainly did not divide the brothers in their dealings with other states or with the papacy.

With the papacy no change of relations followed the death of Galeotto. Carlo Malatesta at once replaced him as rector of Romagna.[9] Soon after, in 1386, he was also created Gonfaloniere of the Church;[10] and it was while holding this appointment that he furnished the pope with an armed escort through Tuscany, and accompanied Urban in autumn of the following year from Lucca to Perugia.[11] About the same

Cod. Pand., fo. 138), in 1392 a papal document still refers to Malatesta of Pesaro as 'domicellus Ariminensis' (Theiner, iii. 47), and in 1398 he was member of the general council of Rimini (Tonini, iv/2, CCXVII, p. 423). Cf. below p. 166.

[1] Battaglini, *Zecca*, 219; Chiaramonti, 392–3, 395–6.

[2] Guerriero, 26.

[3] Amiani, i. 327.

[4] Theiner, iii. 17. He was represented by his brothers in the peace of 1392 with the Montefeltro: below p. 109. Similarly, between 1390 and 1400 the *cancellarius* or *depositarius* in S. Sepolcro is described as acting for Carlo and Pandolfo: Mazzatinti, *Archivi*, Ser. 2, iv. 106.

[5] Battaglini, *Vita*, 274; which may explain the very confused accounts of the partition in chronicles and early histories.

[6] Amiani, i. 308.

[7] Thus in 1392 Carlo replaced Pandolfo at Fano during his absence: Amiani, i. 316–17. Again, while Pandolfo was in Brescia and Lombardy after 1403, petitions in Fano appear endorsed by a great variety of relatives: Carlo, Malatesta, Galeotto, Isabetta Gonzaga, Polissena da S. Severino. Between 1411 and 1415 Carlo and Malatesta took over in Fano, though Pandolfo was still lord: Zonghi, 13–15; *Commiss. Albizzi*, i. 225.

[8] *Bull. Franc.*, vii, n. 84 (13 Jan. 1392).

[9] 16 March 1385: Clementini, ii. 227–9; Battaglini, *Vita*, LXIX, 692; Tonini, iv/2, CCII; Fantuzzi, 352, 354–6.

[10] Amiani, i. 311.

[11] Pedrino, rub. 2084; *Diario d'anon. Fiorent.*, 473 and n. 1; *Cron. Perug.*, 229; Ser Naddo, *Memorie*, 88; Sozomenus, 1134; etc. Clementini (ii. 230) says Carlo Malatesta did homage to Urban in Lucca.

time (1385–6) Pandolfo Malatesta was also employed by the church, against Taddeo Pepoli, then besieging Meldola.[1]

The pope whom the Malatesta served remained the pope of Rome; with Avignon they formed no relations. And any inclination they might have had to do so was quickly checked in 1387, when Clement VI invested Louis of Touraine with all the lands lately held by Galeotto Malatesta: Rimini, Pesaro and Fossombrone.[2] This grant extended also to Faenza, Imola, Bertinoro and Forlì,[3] but did not include Ravenna. Here, Guido da Polenta still followed the schismatic allegiance; and once again the Malatesta were enlisted against him. War between the two families, partly instigated by the pope, continued intermittently down to 1388.[4] But it was not until Guido was overthrown and then assassinated by his sons two years later that Ravenna finally adopted the Roman obedience and relations with the Malatesta improved.[5]

Boniface IX, who succeeded Urban in November 1389,[6] continued and further fostered the Malatesta alliance. In 1390 he confirmed Carlo as Gonfaloniere,[7] and early in 1391 elaborately reaffirmed all the Malatesta vicariates. On 2 January bulls were published granting (or renewing)[8] to the four Malatesta for nine years the vicariate of Cesena, Sinigaglia, Meldola, Santarcangelo, Pergola and certain other places.[9] And on 3 January the vicariates of Rimini, Fano and Fossombrone were also confirmed and expanded for the term of their lives and the lives of their sons.[10] At or about the same time similar grants were

---

[1] Amiani, i.309–10. In 1388 Pandolfo and Malatesta may have attended a parliament summoned in Rome by Urban: *ibid.* 312.

[2] Jarry, 35–6, 406–7; Valois, *Schisme*, ii.139. In 1393 N. Spinelli used this as a precedent for the projected kingdom of Adria: Durrieu, *Royaume d'Adria*, 52.

[3] Jarry, *loc. citt.*, who misinterprets the document, supposing these places also to have been held by Galeotto Malatesta.

[4] Branchi, 172; *Cron. Volg.*, *RIS*² xxvii/2.49; Rubeus, 599; Bonoli, 183; Amiani, i.311; Vernarecci, *Fossombrone*, i.337; Collino, 'Preparazione', 242–3, 251; 'Guerra veneto-viscontea', 327–9.

[5] Pedrino, rub. 2123; Rubeus, 601; Durrieu, *Royaume d'Adria*, 54.

[6] A few months before his death Urban seems to have had difficulty in obtaining *census* owed by the Malatesta: Theiner, ii.652; Mazzatinti, *Inventari*, xxxvii.92. Boniface IX was less exacting: Tonini, iv.235.

[7] Amiani, i.314. He also remitted the *census* of the Malatesta (and Ordelaffi) for help in recovering Bertinoro: Bib. Gamb., *Cod. Pand.*, fo. 139 (23 Oct. 1390).

[8] Above p. 98; cf. *Stat. Caes.* (1589), 252.

[9] Mucciolo, i.5; Battaglini, *Zecca*, 221; *Vita*, 558, 692; Marini, *Santo Arcangelo*, 59; Castellani, *Malatesta*, 23; Tonini, iv/2.396, 433; Mazzatinti, *Archivi*, Ser. 1, i.325.| Battaglini would add Montefeltro and the vicariate of Mondavio, but his reference could apply equally to the grant of these places in 1399: below p. 116.

[10] Theiner, iii.13; Battaglini, *Vita*, 558 and App. 1; Tonini, iv/2.385–96.

made to Malatesta of Pesaro and to a great many other families of the Papal State.[1] Such compromise concessions were once again, over large areas, the only means of safeguarding papal sovereignty. In the duchy of Spoleto, joining other adventurers, Malatesta of Pesaro seized Todi in 1392 and then obtained a vicariate.[2] In the March of Ancona there was also revolt; and here in 1393 Pandolfo Malatesta acted as papal captain until a settlement was reached.[3] In the following year Carlo Malatesta was placed over Roccacontrada and made rector and reformer of the town.[4] In every way the pope was dependent on the cooperation of his subjects, whether freely given or purchased. Papal revenues were too reduced for any resolute government; and they were further depleted by borrowing on the security of regalian rights. In this way the town of Bertinoro was pledged in 1394 to Carlo and Galeotto Malatesta for a loan of 22,000 florins.[5]

The purchase of Bertinoro was no mere transaction between the Malatesta and the pope. It was an event with wide repercussions in provincial politics. One immediate effect was to aggravate a growing estrangement between the Malatesta and the Ordelaffi, who in 1393 had arranged a similar loan contract with the papacy only to be violently ousted by the Malatesta.[6] The previous friendship of the two families had perhaps begun to deteriorate when Cecco and Pino Ordelaffi dispossessed their great-uncle, Sinibaldo, at the end of 1385 and then put him to death.[7] However, no serious quarrel arose until the pope in 1392 transferred the castle of Roversano from Ubaldino degli Ubaldini to the Malatesta. Ubaldino retorted by offering it himself to Pino Ordelaffi, as a result starting a war in which Carlo and Pandolfo Malatesta eventually came off best.[8] This was followed by the difference over Bertinoro which threw the two families into prolonged antagonism. The Malatesta, it is true, found some counter-support in

---

[1] Above p. 102 n. 2; Raynaldus, viii, 1390, n. XVIII; Guiraud, 224–6.
[2] See below p. 116. In Nov. 1388 Orte was mortgaged to him for a loan of 10,000 fl.: *AR* 1938, 174–5.
[3] Amiani, i.318–19; Guerriero, 30–1; Mazzatinti, *Archivi*, Ser. 1, ii.205; Theiner, iii.26; Sozomenus, 1154, 1155.
[4] Tonini, iv.241.
[5] Theiner, iii.33; Guerriero, 31; *Ann. Forl.*, 77; Amiani, i.319; Fantuzzi, iii.353; Tonini, iv.241; Favier, 554, 603.
[6] Following a sharp engagement and Malatesta victory on 8 Aug. 1393: Pedrino, rub. 1956–8; Cobelli, 155–6; Sozomenus, 1155; *Cron. Volg.*, 178; *Ann. Forl.*, 77; *Chron. Bon.*, iii.449.
[7] Pandolfo Malatesta married his widow, Paola Bianca, after papal dispensation: Pedrino, rub. 2055, 2067–8, 2073, 2106; Cobelli, 150–3; *Ann. Forl.*, 73.
[8] On this and relations generally between the Malatesta and Ordelaffi: Pedrino, rub. 2089, 2161, 2169; Cobelli, 153–5, 447; *Ann. Forl.*, 76.

alliance with other despots. In 1391 Malatesta of Cesena married Rengarda, daughter of Bertrando Alidosi,[1] and a year later Malatesta and Manfredi were on the same side in the general alliances then forming of North Italian powers. Astorgio Manfredi also intervened against the Ordelaffi in 1393, and in 1396 Gian Galeazzo Manfredi was betrothed to Gentile, Carlo Malatesta's sister.[2] But none of these things lessened the gravity of the breach with Forlì, which came at the culmination of another and much larger feud, overshadowing these years, between the Malatesta and the counts of Montefeltro.

Rivalry between Malatesta and Montefeltro had continued unbroken from the last years of the thirteenth century, an almost unfailing feature in all political events. Though rarely fighting alone, the two families are consistently found, almost by instinct, pursuing contrary interests: in regional wars, in the larger alliances of Guelf and Ghibelline politics, and even, at times, providing opposite commanders in the wars of other states.[3] In the family division of the Malatesta, at the time of Guastafamiglia, the Montefeltro intermeddled as allies of Ferrantino. Later, during the papal reconquest, the Malatesta in turn collaborated with the church in the humiliation of the Montefeltro and in the Eight Saints war tried to prevent their return to Cagli and Urbino.[4] From then on a tense conflict for territorial influence seems to have developed. Whether the Malatesta profited by the dispossession of the counts of Urbino is not recorded. But there is clear evidence that, while in 1371 their lands in the district of Montefeltro were still inconsiderable, by the year 1380 Galeotto had built up a large *clientela* there of 'allies' and 'recomendati'.[5] Driving further into Montefeltro territory the Malatesta were also trying to extend their influence over the adjacent up-

---

[1] After papal dispensation: Pedrino, rub. 2161; Tonini, iv/2, ccv. In 1398 Malatesta found his wife guilty of adultery and sent her back to her father who had her poisoned: Chiaramonti, 403; Zazzeri, 255–6. Clementini (ii.181) puts this in 1401 and says Malatesta starved two of her lovers to death.

[2] Tonduzzi, 448–51; Mittarelli, *Accessiones*, 570–1; Chiaramonti, 400; Vecchiazzani, ii.53; Sacchetti, *Rime*, cclxviii. For earlier hostilities between Malatesta and Manfredi: below p. 113.

[3] As in the Florence–Pisa war of 1341–2: Franceschini, *Montefeltro*, 237ff.; above p. 68.

[4] For details: Franceschini, *Montefeltro*, 179, 184ff., 215ff., 234ff., 289ff.; Clementini, ii.136–7; Amiani, i.296; above p. 94. In 1357 the Malatesta tried to seize Cagli but were checked by Albornoz: Ugolini, i.143. Contention here was aggravated by a long tradition of boundary disputes between Cagli and Fossombrone: Vernarecci, *Fossombrone*, i.322–5.

[5] Including S. Leo, Macerata, Pietrarubbia, Carpegna and Montebello: Theiner, ii.504; Tonini, iv/2.316; Ansidei, 'Tregua', 37–8; Franceschini, 'Signoria', 87.

lands of the Massa Trabaria and its leading feudal family, the Brancaleoni.[1] The main focus of quarrel, however, was at this time the Umbrian city of Gubbio.

Here the family of Gabrielli were conspiring to become *signori*, and in 1378, with the election as bishop of Gabriele de' Gabrielli, their authority seemed established.[2] But Antonio, count of Montefeltro, also coveted Gubbio; and but for the Malatesta he might at once have gained it. For some time allies of the Gabrielli,[3] no doubt in opposition to Urbino, the Malatesta now backed them against the count and precipitated a war. Florence tried anxiously to mediate, but without success, and not till March 1380 was a truce arranged by the Perugians, friends and allies of both Malatesta and Montefeltro.[4] The truce was inconclusive; and in July Florence and Perugia were complaining of renewed assaults by Galeotto on Montefeltro territory.[5] In Gubbio this was a period of confusion and uncertainty. For a brief interval (August 1380) Charles of Durazzo was elected *signore*, but with his departure the clandestine struggle revived.[6] Perugia remained on friendly terms with Feltreschi and Malatesta, and may have prevented war again in 1382, when it was rumoured that Alberigo da Barbiano was about to attack Urbino 'a piticione di messer Ghaleotto'.[7] For another two years this unsettled situation continued, until at last in 1384 a decision was reached. On 24 March the general council of Gubbio pronounced for Francesco Gabrielli, who with the help of Florence and the Malatesta had been trying hard to make the commune submit; and a commission of nobles was appointed to create him lord. Antonio da Montefeltro got wind of the proposal, and, whether or not through his influence, the commission decided to offer the

---

[1] Of Castel Durante. One-time clients of the Montefeltro (above p. 17), they had become, from the later thirteenth century, with the rise of the Montefeltro *signoria* in Urbino, uncompromising enemies: Franceschini, *Montefeltro*, 188, 194, 217, 233, 290. At this time the family was divided, one branch, under Branca and his sons, allied with the Malatesta, others with the Feltreschi. For details: Bib. Gamb., *Cod. Pand.*, fos. 68, 120; Torelli, 172–3, 177–8; Colucci, xxvii.15–6; Ansidei, 'Tregua', 21, 37–9; 'Regesto Città di Castello', 320–1, 323–5; Guerriero, 14; Cobelli, 149; Pedrino, rub. 2035; Theiner, ii.526, 535; iii.43; Tonini, iv/2.283; Osio, i.285; Delfico, ii, App. xxv.
[2] Pellegrini, 'Gubbio', 148.
[3] Filippini, *SS* v, doc. 44; Mittarelli, *Ann. Camald.*, vi.126; Franceschini, 'Signoria', 93–5, 108–9, 116–19.
[4] Ansidei, 'Tregua'; Pellini, i.1166, 1241, 1246; Guerriero, 21; Amiani, i.301–2, 304–5; 'Regesto Città di Castello', 315, 321, 322; Franceschini, 'Signoria', 100–7, 110–11.
[5] Degli Azzi, n. 560. Cf. Pellini, i.1251; Amiani, i.304.
[6] The Malatesta again supporting the Gabrielli: Stefani, rub. 869; Pellegrini, 'Gubbio', 148; Guerriero, 21–3.
[7] Pellini, i.1255, 1261, 1265, 1267–8, 1286; 'Regesto Città di Castello', 138, 139, 345, 349; Ansidei, 'Tregua', 22; *Lucca, Regesti*, ii/2, n. 2099, p. 464.

signoria to him instead. Seven days later the count entered Gubbio.[1]
From lassitude or sickness Galeotto acquiesced and in November,
through the mediation of Gian Galeazzo Visconti, he agreed to peace
with the Montefeltro.[2] Grievances enough remained, however, to re-
kindle the war under his sons; and already in the following April
Antonio was forcing them to look to the defence of Pergola.[3]

One continuing source of contention was Francesco Gabrielli, now
established in Cantiano with other Gubbio exiles, and exposed to
interference from the Montefeltro. To check this the republic of
Florence, which favoured the Gabrielli, though not unfriendly to
Urbino, in 1386 mounted a short admonitory campaign against the
count, inviting the Malatesta to lend support.[4] With their object once
gained, the Florentines withdrew. They did not forsake the Gabrielli,
but they had no wish to alienate Antonio, particularly when, a little
later, they came into conflict with Urban VI in the Tuscan Patrimony.
In August 1387 they formed an alliance with the count against Urban;
and after that their main concern was to avoid any further outbreak of
trouble.[5]

The Florentine–papal quarrel gave the Malatesta opportunity to
reopen war with Antonio. The Gubbio peace of 1384 had evidently
left unsettled a large number of territorial claims in the Montefeltro
and elsewhere.[6] The pope empowered the Malatesta to seize Antonio's
lands, and it was in his name that they once more attacked Urbino in
the spring and summer of 1388. Florence again protested; but more
effective was the further intercession of Gian Galeazzo Visconti. In
November he succeeded in re-establishing peace between the rival
families. The Malatesta and the Feltreschi both became his *raccomandati*;
and for the next few years their common alliance kept them at peace.[7]

Shortly before, Perugia, which had fought for the pope, also made
peace with the count, and the papacy soon followed by restoring him

---

[1] Guerriero, 23–5; Pellegrini, 'Gubbio', 148–50; Pedrino, rub. 2016.
[2] 7 Nov. 1384: Tonini, iv/2, cxcix, 365–6; Franceschini, 'Gian Galeazzo', 292 and
App. *passim*; *Montefeltro*, 313ff.
[3] Amiani, i. 308; Pergola too had been the object of rivalry between the Malatesta
and Montefeltro. The Malatesta had recently gained possession: Nicoletti, 162–3.
[4] Collino, 'Politica', 135, 139, 166, 168–70, 171–2, 175–6, 180; Degli Azzi, i,
nn. 640, 642–6; ii, n. 720; *Cron. Volg.*, 15–16; Bonincontri, 48; Pedrino, rub. 2060;
Ser Naddo, 84–5; Pellini, i. 1342–3; Frati, 'Raccolta', 139; Pellegrini, 'Gubbio',
151–5.
[5] *Cron. Volg.*, 40; Guerriero, 25; Degli Azzi, i. 182, 185, 187, 189, 193; ii. 182.
[6] The peace of 1388 mentions 'Montefeltro' (S. Leo), Montebello, Pietrarubbia,
Ripalta, and other places, all in the district of Montefeltro: Franceschini, 'Gian
Galeazzo', 313. The first three appear among the Malatesta 'colligati' in 1380 and
may have have been held by them: Ansidei, 'Tregua', 37, 38.
[7] Guerriero, 25; Battaglini, *Vita*, 692; Pellegrini, 'Gubbio', 159; Franceschini,
'Gian Galeazzo', 300–1, 304–25; Mazzatinti, *Inventari*, xxxix. 133, n. 973.

to favour. In June 1390 Boniface IX, more conciliatory than Urban, created Antonio papal vicar in Urbino, Cagli and Gubbio.[1] And by this impartial attitude towards the two families he was able to act as arbiter when the final phase in the Malatesta–Montefeltro feud flared up in the following year.

In the summer of 1391 a Florentine chronicler relates that between Rimini and Urbino 'per piccole cagioni nacque non piccola discordia, donde sequie non piccola guerra'.[2] To the Florentines, locked in mortal contest with the Visconti, the causes, which were of the usual sort, must certainly have seemed trivial: the situation of Cantiano and the Gabrielli, the independence of Sassoferrato, protected by the Malatesta and threatened by the Montefeltro, and the possession of scattered communities in the *contado* of Cagli and March of Ancona. Yet the war was fought ferociously.

At the end of 1390 Antonio da Montefeltro reopened his attacks on Cantiano, but negotiations were started under the auspices of certain lords (Giovanni di Ungaro degli Atti of Sassoferrato, the Simonetti of Iesi, and Sforza of Buscareto) who were commissioned to draw up an agreement. As a result Francesco Gabrielli was freed to accept the *podestà*-ship of Bologna, which he did early in 1391, meanwhile surrendering Cantiano to the care of the Malatesta. To this provocation the Montefeltro replied with a double threat, against Cantiano and Sassoferrato. Carlo Malatesta protested; and, getting no satisfaction, retaliated by occupying another castle, Ripalta.[3] The war, which Malatesta of Pesaro also joined, continued stubbornly for five months, neither side making much progress.[4] The Venetians and Gian Galeazzo both offered mediation, but with no effect, and even the pope and his envoys were at first rebuffed. Only in January 1392 was Boniface able to conclude a temporary settlement, which uncovered a whole tangle of territorial disputes, extending to Corinaldo and Mondolfo in the March, and various castles and villages round Cagli.[5] The Malatesta may now actually have entered into alliance with the Montefeltro,[6]

[1] 4 June 1390: Theiner, iii.8; Mazzatinti, *Inventari*, xxxix.129. This investiture included Ripalta and Montebello, but not S. Leo and other places disputed in 1388: above p. 108 n.6, below p. 110 n.2.

[2] *Cron. Volg.*, 137.

[3] On Sassoferrato, its lords the Atti, and their relations with the Malatesta and Montefeltro: Guerriero, 27–8; Pedrino, rub. 2154; *Chron. Bon.*, iii.435; Ansidei, 'Tregua', 38; Osio, i.285.

[4] Though *Cron. Volg.* (137) says: 'Fu questa guerra fatta con vergogna e danne de' Malatesti in tutte le parti.'

[5] Guerriero, 28–9; *Cron. Volg.*, 137; Sozomenus, 1147; Theiner, iii.17; Mazzatinti, *Inventari*, xxxix.129, xxxvii.146. Corinaldo was among Galeotto's 'colligati' in 1380 (Ansidei, 'Tregua', 36, 37), while Mondolfo is mentioned as falling to Pandolfo Malatesta in the partition after Galeotto's death: above p. 102.

[6] 28 April 1392: Pellegrini, 'Gubbio', 159.

but if so it was not sufficient to prevent further disagreements arising at the end of the year, nor a renewal of hostilities during 1393, when the Ordelaffi, bent on seizing Bertinoro, helped revive the war. The campaign was no more conclusive than the last. If the count of Urbino was finally successful in buying up Cantiano,[1] in the conflict with the Malatesta he was worsted.[2] Both sides must by now have been worn out by a quarrel which offered profit to neither. When the pope again intervened in October 1393, he was at last able to make a permanent peace.[3] In December Carlo Malatesta and the count met and conferred: 'and not a soul could ever find out what they settled together, except that they went off in the very best of spirits (molto alegri insieme)'.[4] The new-found friendship was later confirmed by the marriages of Galeotto Belfiore with Anna, Antonio's daughter (1395), and of Rengarda, Carlo's sister, with Guid'Antonio, Antonio's son (1397).[5] And for many years the relations of the two houses remained unshakably close.

Though of little general importance, these 'wars of mice' in Romagna did not proceed unnoticed or without interference by the major Italian states. At the time of the peace between Rimini and Urbino, the first 'world war' of city states between Florence and Milan had already begun, and essential to both powers was an assured following in Romagna. However averse the pope himself was to becoming implicated, this small papal province, flanked by Tuscany and Lombardy, could not escape the conflict. And every city, however governed, by commune or *signoria*, was forced by fear or interest to enrol in the leagues and combinations which developed during the struggle.

With Florence the Malatesta had a long, if not unbroken, tradition of friendship, and at the death of Galeotto they were still reckoned among

---

[1] Guerriero, 30; Degli Azzi, ii, nn. 770, 774, 784–5, 806, 808. The Gabrielli withdrew to Florence, but were not finally subdued until 1420: Pellegrini, 'Gubbio', 179.

[2] He lost Montegello and Montebello (Guerriero, 30), both included in the Montefeltro vicariate of 1390. The second was kept by the Malatesta (Zonghi, 18), the first must have reverted to the counts: *Stat. di Montefeltro* (Ciavarini, iii), 334.

[3] 13 Oct. 1393: Mazzatinti, *Inventari*, xxxix.129; Guerriero, 30; Amiani, i.318–19; Tonini, iv/2, CCVIII–XI; R. Reposati, *Della zecca di Gubbio* (Bologna, 1772–3), i.115. It was probably now that the Atti allies of the Malatesta were restored to Sassoferrato (Pedrino, rub. 2154); they remained clients (Broglio, 188) and in 1402 Giovanni Malatesta of Ghiaggiolo (now reconciled with his relatives: below p. 296) married into the family: Clementini, i.625. With the Brancaleoni also the Malatesta remained on friendly terms: Tonini, iv/2.422; Zonghi, 39; Torelli, 181–3, 189–90; Vitali, 414.

[4] Guerriero, 33–4.

[5] *Ibid.* 31, 32; Amiani, i.320; Biondo, *Triumphantis Romae*, ii; *Scritti ined.*, xxiii–iv. On 12 March 1396, when granting fiscal privileges to settlers in Cervia, Galeotto Belfiore adds: 'purchè non sia traditore e ribello alla prefata casa de Malatesti né al magnifico Signore Conte Antonio de Urbino': Battaglini, *Zecca*, 222.

the 'adherents' of the republic.[1] Salutati, the Florentine chancellor, wrote at once to Galeotto's heirs, urging them to unity,[2] and in the next year the Signoria enlisted them in the war with the Montefeltro.[3] So far nothing had happened to estrange Florence and Rimini. But at the same time the Malatesta were establishing a new connection in Lombardy, a region where previously they had appeared more as papal captains than as independent princes. A marriage alliance between Galeotto's sister and Cansignorio della Scala created a relationship which seems to have survived Cansignorio's death in 1375.[4] With the Visconti also Galeotto had intermittent dealings before Gian Galeazzo's peace-making in 1384.[5] And there had evidently been close relations between the Malatesta and Mantua[6] when, in 1386, Carlo married Isabetta, sister of Francesco Gonzaga, forming a friendship which was to last many years.[7] Most of all, however, it was the tireless intrigue of Gian Galeazzo Visconti which finally involved the Malatesta in the wider world of Lombardy and general Italian politics. In fact, though not his first excursion into peninsular affairs,[8] Gian Galeazzo's arbitration of 1384 between Malatesta and Montefeltro first clearly marked the resumption of Visconti policy in Central Italy, checked at Sarzana thirty years before.[9] Nor was this his only intervention in Romagna.[10] In 1386 he may have succeeded for a time in holding back the Malatesta from giving help to Florence.[11]

At first the Malatesta remained aloof from these general political manoeuvres. Like other neighbouring *signori* they remained preoccupied with mainly local issues. Quite early however, they showed signs of preferring the Visconti to Florence. With the Este, Montefeltro and Ordelaffi, they were represented in a league against the companies

---

[1] Degli Azzi, i, n. 636; above p. 99 n. 5.

[2] Above p. 101 n. 11.

[3] See above p. 108. In Jan. 1386 Pandolfo Malatesta was in Florence: *Diario d'anon. fiorent.*, 468.

[4] By Cansignorio's will Galeotto was appointed tutor to his sons, Bartolomeo and Antonio (Sansovino, 230; Clementini, ii.139; Tonini, iv/2, CLXXXVIII; Gatari, i.140–1), and on at least two occasions (1373, 1378) he borrowed large sums from the Scaligeri: Bib. Gamb., *Cod. Pand.*, fos.68, 129; Clementini, ii.137–8, 146. Cf. Amiani, i.305.

[5] Amiani, i.301, 305; Tonini, iv/1.224.

[6] *Arch. Gonzaga*, ii.180.

[7] *Cron. Mant.*, 149; Platina, *Hist. Mant.*, RIS xx.753C; *Chron. Est.*, RIS xv.514; *Arch. Gonzaga*, i.51; A. Maffei, *Annali di Mantova* (Mantua, 1675), 723; Pedrino, rub. 2059, 2072, who says: 'la ditta donna era picholla asae, brutta, [d'] etade d'anni 17 o circha'.

[8] Mesquita, 84ff.; Boüard, 85ff.

[9] Franceschini, 'Gian Galeazzo', 292.

[10] Above p. 102 n. 1. Cf. *Cron. Volg.*, 17; Mittarelli, *Accessiones*, 567; *Chron. Reg.*, 94; Ghirardacci, ii.406–7.

[11] Collino, 'Politica', 139 and doc. XCIV; but cf. doc. CIX.

promoted in October 1385 by Gian Galeazzo, Florence, Bologna and other states; but they took no part in the separate alliance of Bologna, Perugia and the Tuscan communes immediately following it.[1] In the diplomacy preceding Gian Galeazzo's war with the Scaligeri their names do not appear. All the same, in 1387 they helped to prevent the *condottiere* Bernardo della Salle from going to the relief of the della Scala.[2]

Their immediate reward was discouraging. At the end of 1387 Giovanni d'Azzo degli Ubaldini and Giovanni Ordelaffi, lately Visconti captains, entered Romagna, probably with the count's connivance, and proceeded to harass the territories of Bologna, Forlì, Cesena and Ravenna. Bulgaria, Polenta, Casalbone and Culianello, the four *castelli* of the archbishop of Ravenna taken by Galeotto Malatesta,[3] were already in their hands, when the two marauders quarrelled, Giovanni Ordelaffi taking service with the Malatesta, Giovanni Ubaldini with the Polenta. These events cannot have pleased Gian Galeazzo, for in February 1388 he took steps to reconcile the Malatesta and the Ubaldini, to prevent them from siding with Bologna, traditional ally to Florence. In May a truce was arranged, the disputed castles being assigned in temporary custody to the lords of Forlì;[4] and immediately after, the Malatesta dropped all caution and joined the Visconti. First, following the truce, Pandolfo Malatesta and Giovanni d'Azzo combined to form a single mercenary company, and, disregarding Florentine protests, invaded Tuscany.[5] Then, in July and August, Carlo Malatesta took a small contingent of lances to Lombardy to fight with Gian Galeazzo against Padua and Treviso, returning only in the autumn for the peace negotiations between the Malatesta and Montefeltro, in which both families became Visconti clients.[6]

Milanese diplomacy was producing results, and the Florentines were not slow to react. They complained to Bologna that the Malatesta were forsaking the ways of their father. They also tried to include the Malatesta in an alliance of 20 August with Bologna and the lords of Ravenna, Faenza and Imola. Then, at the end of the new year, they warned them against molesting the Polenta.[7] All without result. The

---

[1] Collino, docs. LXIX, LXXIII; Sozomenus, 1129; Degli Azzi, ii.177–8; Seregni, *ASL* 1911, pt. ii, 162ff.

[2] Novati, *ASL* 1912, pt. 11, 574–7. Antonio da Montefeltro was in the Visconti league against Verona: *Cron. Volg.*, 31.

[3] Above p. 101; Ansidei, 'Tregua', 38.

[4] They were not recovered by the Malatesta until 1392: Guerriero, 29; Pedrino, rub. 2085, 2090; *Cron. Volg.*, 49; Rubeus, 599–600; Bonoli, 183; Collino, 'Preparazione', 234, 242–3, 251.

[5] Sozomenus, 1137; *Cron. Volg.*, 61; Collino, 'Preparazione', 264–6, 270–3, 277, 279.

[6] *Lucca, Regesti*, ii/2, n. 1386; Pedrino, rub. 2096, 2098, 2103. Cf. Collino, 'Guerra veneto-viscontea', 49.

[7] *Ibid.* 22, 32, 36, 327–9, 357–8; *Capitoli, Firenze*, ii.XII.46.

Malatesta stood by Gian Galeazzo.[1] In 1389 they figured among his followers in the time-wasting general league of October between the Visconti, Florence and their allies;[2] and when war finally broke out next spring, they fought on the Visconti side, defeating the Bolognese captain, Giovanni da Barbiano.[3] That they failed to do more was doubtless due to their troubled relations with the Montefeltro, though Cesena continued to be harassed by Astorre Manfredi, a follower of Florence,[4] and both Pandolfo and Malatesta seem to have served the Visconti alliance in 1391.[5] Occupied with the Ordelaffi and Montefeltro, they played no part in the negotiations that resulted in the general peace of January 1392. Nor did they join the combination between Florence, Bologna, the Este, and the Carrara, Manfredi and Alidosi in April of that year.[6] They may have been reluctant to abandon the Visconti interest. All the same, when the lord of Mantua also went over to Florence in September 1392, they agreed to accept an informal place at his side; and for the next four years, although without much enthusiasm, they remained with him in the Florentine camp.[7] The Gonzaga connection was shortly afterwards strengthened by a further marriage: of Francesco to Carlo's sister, Margarita.[8] It was mainly due to this connection, though the pope also indicated his approval, that the Malatesta separated from the Visconti. They attended meetings of the

---

[1] *Cron. sen.*, 724; *Cron. Perug.*, 235; Pellini, 1372; *Lucca Regesti*, ii/2, n. 1412. Cf. Mesquita, 106; Gatari, i.387, 397.

[2] Osio, i, CCI; *Registri visc.*, 17, nn. 1, 122; *Cron. Perug.*, 237; Pedrino, rub. 2119; *Cron. Volg.*, 81; Mesquita, 104–10.

[3] Frati, 'Lega dei Bolognesi', 17, 23; Zambeccari, *Epist.*, 113; *Lucca, Regesti*, ii/2, n. 1467; Gatari, 770A; *Chron. Bon.*, iii.402–3; Branchi, 173; *Cron. Volg.*, 91–2; etc. Florence addressed a letter of stilted reproval to the Malatesta, reminding them of their youth and the uncertainties of fortune, yet expressing willingness to renew the old friendship: 10 April 1390: Tonini, iv/2, CCVI; Dainelli, 'Uzzano', 44.

[4] Pedrino, rub. 2142; Chiaramonti, 395–6; Tonduzzi, 446–7. The *Chron. Bon.* (iii.428) states that in Feb. 1391 Bologna and Astorre Manfredi made peace with the Malatesta; and Messeri and Calzi (126) that a commercial treaty was then concluded between them; but only in 1392 was a firm peace established: above p. 106.

[5] Zazzeri, 252; Amiani, i.315.

[6] Florence at least debated whether the Malatesta should be included: Salutati, ii.362.

[7] *Capitoli, Firenze*, ii.XII.50; Sozomenus, 1151; *Cron. Volg.*, 163; Guerriero, 29; Pedrino, rub. 2169; Muzi, i.192.

[8] Nov. 1393: *Chron. Bon.*, iii.452–3; Nerli, 13; *Cron. Mant.*, 154–5; *Ann. Est.*, 909. Francesco had beheaded his first wife, Agnese, daughter of Bernabò Visconti, for adultery (1390); nonetheless remarriage to one of her sisters was proposed, and was prevented only by his estrangement from Gian Galeazzo: *Chron. Plac.*, 553; Mesquita, 144–5. The *Arch. Gonzaga* (i.51) records in 1394 the marriage of a Ramberto Malatesta with an Alda di Febo Gonzaga.

allies (October 1392, May 1393),[1] resumed friendship with Florence,[2] and composed local differences with Florentine confederates.[3] But they did not hasten to act openly against Milan. In July 1395, Carlo Malatesta excused himself from attending Gian Galeazzo's investiture as duke.[4] Yet in the same year he declined the offer from Francesco Gonzaga of the captaincy of the league.[5] Only at the end of 1396 when war threatened between Mantua and Milan did he finally drop all reserve.[6]

In September Florence concluded an alliance with France against the Visconti, reserving a place in it for her allies, including the Malatesta.[7] Gian Galeazzo was forced to act without delay and concentrated his attention on Francesco Gonzaga, who for several years had been carrying complaints to the Florentines against Milan. While the republic appealed to the lords of Romagna,[8] Visconti troops began to overrun Florentine and Mantuan territory,[9] and at long last events seemed to be moving toward a final military decision. At the same time the Malatesta and other members of the league were busy assembling troops. Malatesta of Cesena was in Bolognese pay.[10] From Rimini, Carlo also joined the enterprise, and possibly Pandolfo and Galeotto as well. In the conduct of the campaign Carlo quickly took first place. In July and August he paid a rapid visit to Ferrara, Venice, Florence and Bologna to mobilise contingents for the defence of Mantua. With these reinforcements he advanced to the relief of Governolo, and there, on 28 August, inflicted a crushing defeat on Jacopo dal Verme. It was a victory which, if followed up, would certainly have decided the war. As it was the leaders fell out, Giovanni da Barbiano and the conte di Carrara refusing to go forward and attack Brescia. In disgust Carlo hastened to Florence to demand the powers of captain-general; but he seems to have been disappointed. He retired from Florence to Romagna, while

---

[1] Gatari, i.439; *Chron. Est.*, *RIS* xv.530; *Chron. Bon.*, iii.447; Guerriero, 30. Cf. Niccolo Spinelli (1393) of Carlo Malatesta: 'fuit adherens domini comitis Virtutum, sed nunc puto quod concurret cum aliis et sit colligatus cum Florentinis': Durrieu, *Royaume d'Adria*, 55.

[2] In June 1393 Carlo was in Florence with Francesco Gonzaga: Salutati, iii.536; *Cron. Volg.*, 175.

[3] Cf. the letter of P. Zambeccari (Oct. 1393) exhorting Carlo Malatesta to keep peace with the Ordelaffi: *Epist.*, 146–7.

[4] Amiani, i.320.

[5] *Cron. Mant.*, 156. Amiani (i.319–20) says that in 1394, despite papal opposition, Pandolfo Malatesta entered Milanese service.

[6] In a general league of May 1396 the Malatesta appear among the allies of Florence: *Capitoli, Firenze*, ii.xi.40, 43.

[7] Lünig, i.1093.

[8] Dec. 1396: Degli Azzi, i.233.

[9] Early 1397: *Cron. Volg.*, 212–13; Sozomenus, 1163; Mesquita, 210ff.

[10] Ammirato, ii.855; *Lucca, Regesti*, ii/2, nn. 1636, 1684, 1686–9, 1695.

Gian Galeazzo resumed his Mantuan offensive until checked by winter.[1]

There are signs that with this rebuff Carlo Malatesta began to reconsider a rapprochement with the Visconti,[2] when dissatisfaction with the allies decided Francesco Gonzaga also to attempt a compromise. For this purpose he sent Carlo, whom both policy and temperament inclined to impartiality, as emissary to Pavia; and on 11 May 1398, largely through his mediation, a ten-year truce was settled between Gian Galeazzo and the league, by which Carlo was given custody of the disputed Mantuan territories until conclusion of a general peace. In this way Carlo Malatesta attracted respect from both sides.[3] He continued to represent the Gonzaga in negotiations over the Mantuan castles in his keeping;[4] but he also won the confidence of Gian Galeazzo, possibly by revealing the alleged treacheries of the duke's secretary, Pasquino Capelli.[5] In the summer of 1399 the Visconti in turn offered to mediate in a war between the Malatesta and Ordelaffi.[6] A safe neutrality was probably Carlo's object. While welcoming Milanese friendship, therefore, he did not let it prejudice communications with Florence.[7] And even less did it affect relations between the Malatesta and the papacy, which through all this period continued undisturbed by the tumult of Italian politics.

Boniface IX did not take much part in the Visconti wars: his attention was sufficiently claimed by events in the States of the Church. Here his

---

[1] For details: *Lucca, Regesti*, ii/2, nn. 1698, 1704–5, 1707–8, 1740, 1742, 1747, 1789, 1791, 1792, 1794, 1798, 1808, 1811–13, 1820, 1824; Sercambi, ii.36; Sozomenus, 1164; *Ann. Est.*, 940; *Cron. Mant.*, 157–8; Bonincontri, 74–5. *Cron. Volg.*, 215; Bruni, 273–4; Gatari, i.53–63; Morelli, *Ricordi*, 5; Mazzei, i.182; A. Medin, 'Le rime di Bruscaccio da Rovezzano', *Gior. stor. lett. it.*, 1895, 224–5 (Cançon); Mesquita, 211.

[2] Thus he was not in the Florentine alliance with Venice of March 1398: *Capitoli, Firenze*, ii.XII.51, XIV.77; Predelli, i.88), though it seems about that time he was disclosing to the Florentines Gian Galeazzo's plan to stir up their Tuscan neighbours: Dainelli, 'Uzzano', 56.

[3] Dumont, ii/i.266–9; *Capitoli, Firenze*, ii.XI.44–5; Predelli, ix.109; Romano, 'Regesti C. Cristiani', 282–3; Sercambi, ii.165; *Cron. Volg.*, 223–4; Guerriero, 32; *Ann. Est.*, 940; Sozomenus, 1165; Zambeccari, 183–4. Goro Dati (65) suggests Carlo induced Francesco Gonzaga to change sides.

[4] Osio, i, CCXXVIII.

[5] Corio, ii.415; but cf. Giulini, iii.8–9; Mesquita, 235. Osio (i.328) prints a will by Gian Galeazzo which includes among the counsellors of his heirs Carlo and Pandolfo Malatesta with Malatesta of Pesaro, Francesco Gonzaga and Antonio da Montefeltro, and which he dates to 1397; it cannot be earlier than the summer of 1398 and according to Romano belongs to 1399 or even later: *ASI* 1897; *Boll. Soc. Pavese di Stor. Pat.*, 1917.

[6] Corio, ii.418; below p. 117. In the same year Carlo Malatesta introduced a relative of his into the service of the Visconti: Clementini, i.624–5, ii.251.

[7] Degli Azzi, i.236. But cf. Tonini, iv/2, CCXX; Muzi, i.194.

policy was advanced once more by service from the Malatesta. In 1395 they persuaded their cousin of Pesaro to surrender Todi which with Narni and other places he had usurped some years before.[1] In the same year they kept aloof from the disturbances in Romagna caused by a Florentine attempt to occupy Castrocaro.[2] During the next three years they or their companies were further employed by the pope in the March of Ancona, Romagna and the Tuscan Patrimony;[3] and in 1398 Malatesta of Cesena was appointed senator of Rome. Unlike his father he took up the office, and administered it well to the end of his term.[4]

This proof of papal confidence was confirmed shortly afterwards, in January 1399, by a renewal of the vicariates granted on 2 January 1391, together with those of Cervia, Culianello, Polenta, Mondolfo, Corinaldo, Montevenere, the vicariate of Mondavio, and the lands held in the Montefeltro – this time for two generations.[5] In addition Boniface invested the Malatesta for five years with the government of Osimo, Montelupone, Castelficardo, Montefano, Monte Filottrano, and other lands.[6] To these possessions Galeotto Belfiore added Montalboddo later in the year when fighting for the church with Pandolfo in the March, though he did not live long to enjoy it, for he died there in August 1400. Montalboddo then passed to Pandolfo, and Galeotto's other territories were partitioned among the brothers.[7] Nevertheless the place was left in their keeping by the compliant pope.

Gian Galeazzo Visconti could not then have found a more suitable person than Carlo Malatesta to send as envoy to Boniface at the

[1] For details: Theiner, iii. 19, 34; Rayaldus, vii, 1392, n. IV; *Cronaca inedita d'Orvieto* (ed. F. A. Gualterio, Turin, 1846), i. 74–5, 77–8, 80–2; Degli Azzi, i, nn. 812, 824–5, 857, 859; Tonini, iv/2, CCXIV; Ceci.

[2] On which: Theiner, iii. 35; *Capitoli, Firenze*, ii. 282; Sozomenus, 1158, 1159; *Cron. Volg.*, 197–9: Bolognini, *N. arch. ven.* 1895, 81–95.

[3] In 1396 troops of the Malatesta were active on behalf of the church in Romagna and the March: Lilii, 132; Amiani, i. 320–1. The following year (5 Sept. 1397) saw Pandolfo Malatesta constituted captain-general of the church, 'cum . . . emolumentis consuetis' (Tonini, iv/2, CCXVI) and rector of the duchy of Spoleto as well (*ibid.* iv. 247: 16 Sept.); and during the winter, supported by Malatesta of Cesena, he led an offensive against Biordo Michelotti, usurper of Perugia (*Lucca, Regesti*, ii/2.1855, cf. 1887, 1890, 1959; Sozomenus, 1165–6; Sercambi, ii.161; *Cron. ined. Orvieto*, i.87–8, 90; Muzi, i.234; cf. Ceci, 23–4, who says Pandolfo was papal vicar in Todi, March 1397). For his services, 1397–8, Pandolfo was paid handsomely by the church ('Codici malatestiani', *Le Marche*, i, ii; Bartoccetti, 'Traduzione'; Favier, 639).

[4] Theiner, iii. 46, 49; A. Salimei, *Senatori e statuti di Roma nel medioevo: Senatori* (Rome, 1935), 154; Compagnoni, *Reggia Picena*, 269; *Cron. ined. Orvieto*, i.91; Chiaramonti, 402; Braschi, 284; Zazzeri, 256.

[5] 26 Jan. 1399; Battaglini, *Vita*, App. II; Tonini, iv/2, CCXIX; Castellani, *Malatesta*, 40; Mazzatinti, *Archivi*, Ser. I, i.326.

[6] Ottrano, Staffolo, Offagna: Battaglini, *Vita*, App. III, IV.

[7] *Cron. Volg.*, 239–40; Rossi, *Monte Alboddo*, 94–5; Clementini, ii.171–3, 252; Amiani, i.325; *Copia cronicae Terrae Montis Bodii*, in Menchetti, i.21, 24.

beginning of 1401: 'pero che era fama il Papa credere a lui piu che ad un'altra persona'.[1] This embassy showed that Carlo was still in ducal favour. The year before, the truce of 1398 had been turned by Venice into a general peace, and Carlo had restored to Francesco Gonzaga the Lombard castles in his custody.[2] This did not bring to an end Gian Galeazzo's dealings with the Malatesta; but at this time their relations had less to do with Lombardy than with Romagna. Here, in 1399, conflict had blazed up afresh between the Malatesta and Ordelaffi, both families finally referring the dispute to the Visconti.[3] During this squabble Astorre Manfredi, the neighbouring lord of Faenza, helped the Malatesta, and when at the end of the year a more serious struggle broke out between him and the commune of Bologna, he was able to count on their support. The Bolognese on their side were strengthened by the diplomacy of Florence and the arms of the Ordelaffi; and to redress the balance Carlo Malatesta tried to win over Gian Galeazzo in the autumn of 1400, when the war was well advanced and Faenza seriously threatened. At the same time Astorre himself, who had quitted the city, leaving defence to the Malatesta and to his son, Gian Galeazzo, secretly offered to become Visconti's vassal. But the duke, with his eye on securing Bologna, had intervened on the other side, through his captain Alberico da Barbiano, and was not disposed to change. He did instruct Carlo Malatesta to have Gian Galeazzo sent to Milan; and some arrangement might have been made, had not Niccolo d'Este, to settle an old grievance against the Manfredi, seized on their journey north (and in violation of his own safe-conduct) the young Manfredi, his wife and mother, and Isabetta, wife of Carlo Malatesta.[4] After that nothing more is heard of negotiations with Milan. But the Malatesta kept up their fight for the Manfredi and against the Ordelaffi,[5]

---

[1] *Cron. Volg.*, 239–40. In 1400 Carlo attended the jubilee in Rome (Amiani, i.325) and was able some time that year to obtain ecclesiastical privileges for S. Sepolcro: Mittarelli, *Ann. Camald.*, vi.217–18, 221–2, 627–8.

[2] 21 March 1400: Predelli, ix.174; Sozomenus, 1169; *Cron. Volg.*, 247; *Ann. Est.*, 959. According to Clementini (ii.251) Carlo Malatesta was in Lombardy and Milan during the winter 1399–1400, and certainly he may be traced in Mantua in Feb. (Battaglini, *Vita*, App. III). Clementini (ii.252) also states that the reconstruction of the port of Rimini, begun in April, was conducted under the direction of the duke's engineer, Domenico. Later in the same year, contrary to the sympathies of the pope and Florence, Pandolfo Malatesta ostentatiously accepted service with Gian Galeazzo (Amiani, i.325).

[3] Corio, ii.418; Messeri and Calzi, 130.

[4] Griffoni, 90; *Ann. Est.*, 934, 959–60; Corio, ii.425–6; Clementini, ii.252; Messeri and Calzi, 131.

[5] During this war the Ordelaffi managed to stir up a rebellious movement in Cesena against the Malatesta under certain Ghibelline families who appealed to the pope to resume direct dominion; but Boniface was too dependent on the Malatesta to heed them: Clementini, ii.179; Chiaramonti, 406–7.

until the coup d'état of Giovanni Bentivoglio in Bologna (March 1401) and his treaty of peace with the Manfredi (July) brought the war to an abrupt and unforeseen end.[1]

Though divided over this imbroglio in Romagna, Carlo Malatesta and the Visconti remained on friendly terms. In 1401 Carlo undertook a mission to Rome, to persuade the pope to join Milan against Rupert of Bavaria, though he put in a word also for the Manfredi.[2] The embassy was unsuccessful, and in March Carlo left with the intention of bringing the Papal States onto the Visconti side.[3] Once again the Malatesta were aligning themselves with Gian Galeazzo. In September the Gonzaga and Niccolo d'Este also entered into secret agreements with the duke; and the alliance of powers began to form for the great offensive against Bologna that developed in 1402. Meanwhile in October, Carlo and Pandolfo Malatesta fought for the Visconti against Rupert, embarked at last on his harebrained and futile incursion into Italy, on which Florence placed so many unsatisfied hopes.[4]

The Malatesta did not desert the interest of the Manfredi, but the political situation was radically changed when Giovanni Bentivoglio as lord of Bologna, and courted at once by Milan and Florence, pronounced finally for the Florentines. After that Gian Galeazzo had only to prepare to humiliate and dispossess him by force, and he gathered his strength to do this in the spring of 1402. On 20 March, Florence concluded an alliance with the Bentivoglio, and almost immediately war broke out.[5]

Carlo, Pandolfo and Malatesta opened the campaign by sending formal defiance to Bologna, and then accepting the *signoria* of S. Giovanni in Persiceto, a community long, if insecurely subordinate to the city. Some months before the people of S. Giovanni had revolted, and now, in April 1402, they called in the Malatesta to be their lords. The contingents of the Visconti followed up to defend them in their conquest, and the general operation against Bologna began. A formidable army, commanded by Francesco Gonzaga, with Pandolfo and Malatesta, Antonio de Montefeltro and many other

[1] In this year, 1401, Cobelli (156) reports that Pino Ordelaffi put to death two assassins sent to murder him 'con tractato de' Malatesti'; but this does not seem to have prevented Carlo Malatesta and Pino Ordelaffi being present at a tourney in Cesena during June, when peace with the Manfredi was impending: Rubeus, 604; Clementini, ii.180, 254.
[2] *Cron. Volg.*, 260-1; Sozomenus, 1171, 1172; Clementini, ii.254.
[3] Bosdari, 'Bentivoglio', 228, 233.
[4] Sozomenus, 1173-4; Gatari, i.472-3; *Cron. Volg.*, 264-9, 275; *Ann. Forl.*, 78; Bosdari, 'Bentivoglio', 240; Mesquita, 269-70. In this enterprise the Malatesta were on opposite sides from the pope: *Deutsche Reichstagsakten*, iv.44, 74.
[5] Bosdari, 'Bentivoglio', doc. xi; *Cron. Volg.*, 272, 273.

signori of the Papal States among the secondary captains, advanced against the city in May, and on 26 June secured a decisive victory over the enemy at Casalecchio. The Bolognesi rose to depose and murder their ruler, and three days later Bologna was being governed by Pandolfo Malatesta as 'vizio signore' on behalf of Gian Galeazzo Visconti.[1]

Carlo Malatesta does not appear to have taken part in the concluding stages of the campaign, and he may already have been entrusted by the duke of Milan with the delicate commission of bringing the pope to accept this disquieting return of the Visconti to Romagna. Certainly, early in August, through the bishop of Cervia, the Malatesta emissary in Rome, the duke was proposing terms of a compromise with Boniface, offering to surrender Perugia in return for his investiture with Bologna as a marquisate or duchy; and an agreement to be arranged by Carlo Malatesta seemed to be impending.[2] Once again Carlo was the obvious man to choose, and there is proof that he was still in the papal confidence.[3] Yet it is a strange commentary upon conditions of sovereignty in the Papal States at the turn of the fourteenth century, that a papal subject and a papal officer, rector of Romagna, could negotiate with his overlord a partial dismemberment of his dominions which he himself had helped to bring about.[4] It is uncertain which side Carlo Malatesta would have declared for had it come to a war between Gian Galeazzo and the pope, though there are signs that his intimacy with the Visconti was weakening.[5] On 5 September the Florentine envoys in Rome were still able to report the progress of the negotiations, but two days earlier the duke of Milan had died, and Carlo Malatesta was spared a testing conflict of his loyalties.

---

[1] Mattiolo, *Cron.*, 109; Griffoni, 91; *Chron. Bon.*, 477–9, 483, 486; *Cron. Volg.*, 270–2, 275–8; *Ann. Med.*, 835ff.; *Ann. Est.*, 966–71; Gatari, i. 478ff.; Bonincontri, 87–8; Bosdari, 'Bentivoglio', 251, 256ff.; Pastorello, 'Copialettere', 279–80, 295; Mesquita, 278ff.

[2] Mesquita, 282–3, doc. 16. Gozzadini, *Nanne Gozzadini*, 173; *Deutsche Reichstagsakten*, v. 408.

[3] Theiner, iii. 61, 63; Tonini, v/2, 11.

[4] The Malatesta did not neglect their own interests in this affair: on 29 Aug. a letter of Gabione Gozzadini addressed from Rome states: 'qui se dize che al signor messer pandolfo rimane san giovanni [Persiceto] e manziolino...': Gozzadini, *Nanne Gozzadini*, 170–1.

[5] For example just at the time when Bologna was being taken Carlo Malatesta allowed Florence the use of the port of Rimini, although earlier in the same year he had refused the same privilege in Cesenatico (*Commiss. Albizzi*, i. 10–19). He may, it is true, have discouraged Astorre Manfredi, then threatened by Alberico da Barbiano, from placing himself under Florentine protection (*Cron. Volg.*, 279–80; Tonduzzi, 454; Mesquita, 290–1); but he was at loggerheads with Alberico himself, a leading Visconti commander, and with the other captains of Milan is recorded as leaving the Visconti camp in disgust through lack of money to pay the troops (Morelli, *Cron.*, 315; cf. Mesquita, 292).

With the death of his powerful patron, and the political confusion resulting, Carlo Malatesta resumed service with the papacy, and having helped to bring the Visconti into the States of the Church, now helped to drive them out. In October the pope, abandoning his hesitation, and the republic of Florence, anxious to avenge the humiliations of the last ten years, came together in an alliance against the distracted dominions of Milan; and Carlo Malatesta, with his brother of Cesena, and the contingents they commanded, were taken into their pay.[1] Other lords of the Papal States, the Polenta, Niccolo d'Este, Paolo Orsini and Alberico da Barbiano, joined in, and in June 1403, under the resolute direction of the new legate, Baldassare Cossa, they advanced against Bologna and the north. An early attempt on Bologna was unsuccessful and the offensive was diverted against Lombardy, now convulsed with revolt. Cossa may have been meditating the total destruction of the Visconti state, but if so he was quickly thwarted. Carlo Malatesta favoured no such grand design, and immediately interposed to negotiate with the enemy. Without any reference to his Florentine paymasters, he conferred secretly with Francesco Gonzaga, his relative and representative of the duchess of Milan, and together they drew up terms whereby, subject to papal ratification, Bologna, Perugia and Assisi were restored to Rome (August). At once the Bolognese rose against the ducal administration, and in September the legate assumed control in their city. Carlo Malatesta was given possession and command of the citadel, and remained an influence in the government until an attempt by the Gozzadini a month later to seize the *signoria* of Bologna made it politic for him to retire and go to Rome.[2]

The Florentines, already dissatisfied with the slow beginning of a campaign most of which they were paying for, were outraged by Carlo's action, and did everything to stop the pope from sanctioning the peace. Carlo and the legate kept them entertained with insincere encouragements to occupy Pisa while Boniface debated his decision. But at last he accepted the compromise, and Carlo returned to Rimini.[3]

---

[1] Morelli, *Cron.* 310; *Ricordi*, 8; Sozomenus, 1176; *Cron. Volg.*, 282–3; *Commiss. Albizzi*, i.20ff.

[2] *Cron. Volg.*, 288–9, 294–7, 298–9; Bonincontri, 89; Sozomenus, 1177, 1178, 1179; *Ann. Est.*, 976–84; Morelli, *Cron.*, 318; Griffoni, 92–3; Gatari, i.506; *Ann. Forl.* 79–80; *Chron. Bon.*, iii.490, 491, 493, 496, 501, 504–6; *Commiss. Albizzi*, i.22–3; *Deutsche Reichstagsakten*, iv.105. Once again the Malatesta safeguarded their own interests, and a clause in the terms discussed in Aug. assured to Pandolfo Malatesta the possession of Persiceto (*Ann. Est.*, 984). In Sept. Malatesta of Cesena also entered Bologna where he met a girl 'de la quale tenacissimamente se accese': Volpi, 'Serdini', 13–14.

[3] *Commiss. Albizzi*, i.20–2, 32; J. Salviati, *Cronica*, 214–17, in *Delizie degli eruditi toscani*, ed. Ildefonso di S. Luigi, xx (Florence, 1785); *Cron. Volg.*, 298; Clementini,

Not for several years did his relations with Florence recover. Apart from alarming Florentine encroachments in Romagna, there were differences over pay still owed him by the Signoria, over the dispossession by Florence of the counts of Bagno and of Andreino degli Ubertini in 1404, and over the inheritance of Francesco da Calpolo, Salutario, which was claimed by Malatesta, count of Dovadola, relative and *accomandato* of Carlo. Yet in 1404 Rinaldo degli Albizzi was *podestà* of Rimini. At the same time Florence was inviting Carlo to mediate between herself and Milan. And although nothing seems to have come of this, the squabble over Salutario was composed peacefully in 1406.[1]

A year from the death of Gian Galeazzo Visconti the papacy was reinstated in three of its leading cities, while in Romagna the Alidosi were again obedient to Rome.[2] Nonetheless unrest continued in the province, and the legate, Cossa, even if no Albornoz, was not a man to slumber over these first achievements. When, as now happened, opportunities for intervention arose in Faenza, Forlì and the territories of Alberigo da Barbiano, he resumed the work begun in Bologna, calling in the Malatesta to help.

Ever since Astorre Manfredi conspired with the murderers of his brother Giovanni da Barbiano, Alberigo, the *condottiere*, had vowed vengeance, resolving if possible to drive him from Faenza. Gian Galeazzo Visconti quietly played on his feelings, and as soon as Bologna fell Alberigo turned on the Manfredi. The death of the duke of Milan, and a season of service in the 1403 campaign, did nothing to temper his violence. He pursued his vindictive war against Faenza, and by the autumn of 1404 the city and its lord were at the end of their resources. It was now that the pope and legate interfered; and Astorre Manfredi was compelled 'propter guerrarum angustias' to surrender his ancestral *signoria* to the church. What part Carlo Malatesta played in this transaction is not clear, but he was probably reduced to obtaining the best conditions possible for his relative. By the terms agreed Astorre resigned Faenza for ten years, and his other territories for five, in return for an annual pension from the papacy. Carlo Malatesta went surety for Cossa and the pope, as well as assuming custody of the strongholds in

---

ii.257–8; Boüard, 287. At this time harsh words by Carlo Malatesta against the Florentines are reported by the chroniclers, calling them a 'congregatio rusticorum', 'una colombaia di villani': Sozomenus, 179; *Cron. Volg.*, 299.
[1] *Commiss. Albizzi*, i.23–6, 34, 36–50, 152; *Cron. Volg.*, 311. Cf. Boüard, 293–4; Cutolo, i.298, ii.149.
[2] Bologna (above p. 120), Perugia and Assisi (*ASI* xvi/2.570–1; *Cron. Volg.*, 284, 291, 297; Sozomenus, 1178; Pellini, ii.138–40). For the Alidosi see *Ann. Est.*, 982; *Deutsche Reichstagsakten*, iv.105.

Faenza and its *contado*. And it was to Rimini that the Manfredi then withdrew to spend their exile.[1]

The loss of Faenza bitterly angered Alberigo, and in the summer of 1405 the legate had to take steps to bridle him also. Here again Carlo Malatesta, 'requisitus ad ea ecclesiae servitia', after defeating Barbiano in June, helped to conclude a peace and, perhaps as rector, assumed the custody of lands in dispute.[2] In this provincial war Astorre Manfredi also played a part, but it did not save him from death at the hands of Cossa at the end of the year. In November 1405 the cardinal had him seized and beheaded in Faenza, on suspicion of treasonable intrigue in Forlì.[3]

Forlì at this time was another trouble-spot of Romagna, and one where the church might have been thought assured of ready Malatesta support. For over ten years they had been at feud with the Ordelaffi, and no peace measures had been successful. During 1403 Carlo Malatesta arranged the marriage of his brother Malatesta to Lucrezia, daughter of Cecco Ordelaffi, the ruling lord of Forlì. But Malatesta merely made this the occasion of a clumsy attempt to foment disaffection in the city and unseat his father-in-law from power: a miscalculation for which Lucrezia paid with her life in October 1404, shortly after giving birth to a daughter, Parisina. Even so, the Malatesta seem to have commanded substantial support in Forlì. Cecco, who was reported neither 'cauto nè malicioso nè homo de regimento', succeeded only in alienating both factions of the city, Guelf and Ghibelline, and when he fell mortally ill in August 1405, the Forlivesi rose and put him to death. Despite a promise to make his illegitimate son, Antonio, *signore*, they expelled the rest of the family from the city, and instead set up a communal régime, 'sub populari statu et dominio rei publicae'.[4] With a revolution of this kind the Malatesta could have no sympathy. They offered refuge to Giorgio Ordelaffi in Cesena, and when the pope and legate prepared to punish the city, Malatesta of Cesena took part in the campaign. In May 1406 the people of Forlì at last came to terms with Cossa, allowing him to nominate the *podestà* and *capitano*, but the Malatesta were not party to the pact, and for another year they continued to harass the commune. They seized a number of places: le

---

[1] *Ann. Est.*, 1004; Mittarelli, *Accessiones*, 572; Griffoni, 94; Theiner, iii.67; Tonduzzi, 454–9; Messeri and Calzi, 133; *Cron. Volg.*, 317–18, 339.

[2] Mattiolo, 168–9; Griffoni, 94, 95; *Ann. Est.*, 1032–3; *Chron. Bon.*, iii.513–15; Amiani, i.327–8; Messeri and Calzi, 133.

[3] Mattiolo, 178; *Ann. Est.*, 1032–4; Griffoni, 95; Sozomenus, 1186; *Ann. Forl.*, 81; Sercambi, 119–20; Tonduzzi, 460. The *Cron. Volg.* (339) remarks justly that Astorre Manfredi was notoriously a master of deceit, 'ma il pugliese [Cossa] le seppe più di lui a questa volta'.

[4] Cobelli, 156, 158–60; *Ann. Forl.*, 80–1; *Chron. Forl.*, 875ff.; Clementini, ii.182–3; Vecchiazzani, ii.60–1; Bonoli, 194–5, 198; Zazzeri, 258–60.

Caminate, Belfiore, Ranchio and Campiano; and might even have taken Forlì itself, if the legate had not managed in July 1407 to get unconditional control of the city and re-establish quiet.[1]

This unlicensed action does not seem to have troubled relations between the Malatesta and the papacy. These years are marked by the customary concessions;[2] and in January 1407 Gregory XII confirmed to them for five years the government of Osimo and neighbouring places granted eight years before, adding also Montalboddo and Serra dei Conti.[3] As it turned out this inconspicuous act was the first of a pontificate exceptional in the history of the Malatesta.

The conquest of Forlì was the last of cardinal Cossa's important exploits in Romagna. Nothing notable arose to claim his attention before developments in the papal Schism took him to Florence in the summer of 1408. For the moment Romagna was quiet. Where not directly governed by the church, it was in the power of friendly dynasties; and although across the border, in the March of Ancona, all was still unrest, the immediate disturbance was local. For Carlo Malatesta it was an occasion to leave the Papal State once more for the troubled politics of Lombardy and Milan.[4]

Here, since Gian Galeazzo's death, order had yielded to anarchy, unity to local independence, and everywhere, in the general collapse of the composite Visconti state, private cupidity and ambition were in control. The principal beneficiaries were the captains and *condottieri* of Gian Galeazzo's wars; and prominent among them was Pandolfo Malatesta, a restless, impetuous adventurer, far removed in every way from the sober character of Carlo. Nominated by Gian Galeazzo's will to the ducal council of regency, Pandolfo promptly left Bologna for Milan to see what fortune would offer.[5] While his brothers withdrew

---

[1] Mattiolo, 178; *Chron. Forl.*, 875–7; *Ann. Forl.*, 81–2; Griffoni, 95; *Cron. Volg.*, 344–5; *Ann. Est.*, 1033, 1038–9; Pedrino, rub. 29: Vecchiazzani, ii.66–7, 69–70; Bonoli, 199. Immediately the Malatesta invested their captain, Belmonte dei Belmonti, with the captured places: Vecchiazzani, ii.70. In July 1417 they were transferred to Carlo da Montalboddo: Pedrino, *loc. cit.*; Rossi, *Monte Alboddo*, 94, 97.

[2] Mazzatinti, *Archivi*, Ser. 1, i.334.

[3] Battaglini, *Vita*, App. v; Tonini, v/2, vi; Cecconi, 'Sommario', 47; Mazzatinti, *Archivi*, Ser. 1, iii.299. Cf. ACF, *Cod. Mal.* 21, fo. 177r.

[4] What follows is the barest outline, based on printed sources, of the Malatesta in Lombardy 1402–21. For fuller detail cf. Valeri, *Eredità*; I. Bonardi, *Pandolfo M. signore di Brescia* (1930); Zanelli, *ASL* 1931.

[5] *Deutsche Reichstagsakten*, v. 409; *Ann. Med.*, 839; Guerriero, 33; Tonini, v. 8–9; Santoro, *Registro Besozzi*, ii.19; Corio, ii.436; Giulini, ii.74; Romano, 'Regesti C. Cristiani', ii.359. Pandolfo Malatesta was present at the funeral of Gian Galeazzo, whereas his brothers only sent representatives: *RIS*² xvii/1, i.494; xvi, 933, 1027–8, 1033–4; Amiani, i.326. But Carlo Malatesta, with Peter of Candia, was among the guardians of the young princes.

into papal service, Pandolfo stood with the Visconti, braving papal censures, and already no doubt nourishing plans of territorial conquest.[1] In 1404 he seized Brescia, and set to founding a new Malatesta *signoria* in the north. But it was a formidable undertaking. There were many others – Facino Cane, Ottobuon Terzo, Gabrino Fondulo – all bent on building states from the debris of the duchy. Nor were these the only competitors. By tradition, Pandolfo was tied to one of two contending parties, Guelf and Ghibelline, which had revived with all their ancient bitterness once the hand of despotism had relaxed.[2] Last of all, there were heirs to the duchy, still young and untrained in politics, yet unlikely to acquiesce in permanent dismemberment of their territories, particularly if one survived to inherit undivided claims. The rivals had to fight for the counsels of Giovanni Maria Visconti, and try to bind this wayward prince to their own ambitions. None was more than momentarily successful. They were defeated by their own jealousies, and by insufficient strength. And the Visconti duchy was able to survive fifty years more, before falling to another mercenary captain, Francesco Sforza.

The depth of these differences was not as yet clear, however, and when Carlo Malatesta in 1407 came to join his brother, the fortune of their family seemed secured. It was not his first visit. He had come, briefly and uninvited, in the previous year to try to repair the Guelf party, by reconciling its leaders among themselves and with the Visconti. But by the beginning of 1407 he had left, either through disillusion or because fresh demands suddenly called him to Mantua.[3] There, early in March, Francesco Gonzaga had just died, entrusting his son, Gianfrancesco, then not twelve years old, to the Malatesta and the republic of Venice. The Venetians left the greater share in the regency to their partners, and it fell to Carlo Malatesta to administer the change of government. This he seems to have managed easily, at the same time including the Gonzaga in an alliance recently made between Pandolfo Malatesta, Venice and Niccolo d'Este; and soon he was free to return to Milan and resume his attempt to restore order and

[1] At first Pandolfo was employed giving help to Siena, then held by the Visconti; he returned to Milan on the collapse of the state in the summer of 1403: Bonincontri, 89, 90; Sozomenus, 1177; *Ann. Forl.*, 79; *Cron. Volg.*, 286, 289, 300; Santoro, *Registri provv.*, 3, n. 263; *Commiss. Albizzi*, i.21. On 1 June 1403 Boniface IX threatened Pandolfo with excommunication and the loss of his vicariates, for his service with the Visconti: Lünig, iv.123.

[2] See for example the letter of Florence to Pandolfo Malatesta (12 Jan. 1407), urging him to promote the Guelf name: L. Muratori, *Antiquitates Italicae* (Milan, 1738–42), iv.645.

[3] *Chron. Berg.*, 990–2; Lünig, iii, n. XLIX; Mazzatinti, *Inventari*, xiv.157; Morbio, 52; *Registri statuti*, 17; Santoro, *Registri Provv.*, v, n. 25, 203; Giulini, iii.155-6.

stabilise the Guelf régime.[1] It was now that the Malatesta, strong in Mantua and Milan, achieved their greatest, if impermanent, influence in Northern Italy.

Until August 1408 Carlo Malatesta was actively occupied in trying to maintain the political system of Gian Galeazzo Visconti. He has been described as the 'spiritual heir' of Gian Galeazzo, a man who had known the duke and was anxious to perpetuate his achievement. In the end, not even he could subdue the disorders of the Visconti state or restrain the incalculable temper of Giovanni Maria, but for several months at least he was effective as governor of the duchy. Any pact with the Ghibellines had proved untenable, and in January 1408 Carlo proceeded to reduce their garrison in Milan by force. Then powerlessly he had to watch the prisoners die on the scaffold, or perish between the teeth of Giovanni Maria's mastiffs. In other, more constructive ways his administration was also vigorous, particularly in financial reform and in a peremptory reduction of the Milanese general council from 900 members to 72. His dealings with the Ghibelline rebels outside Milan were less successful. Some were kept inactive by truce, but Facino Cane and Ottobuon Terzo, usurper of Parma, were irreducible. Carlo resolutely faced the situation, and in May an alliance was struck against the lord of Parma between Pandolfo Malatesta, Giovanni Maria Visconti, Venice, Niccolo d'Este, Gabrino Fondulo and Gianfrancesco Gonzaga. At this point events still seemed to favour the Malatesta, and it was while Carlo Malatesta was governor that Pandolfo succeeded in purchasing the *signoria* of Bergamo. Carlo himself had later been voted an ample endowment by Giovanni Maria, and now, in July 1408, he took the step of arranging the marriage to the young duke of Antonia, daughter of Malatesta of Cesena. This, however, marked the peak of his success. Giovanni Maria was beginning already to escape capriciously from his control, entering into secret relations with the French, and in August Carlo abandoned Milan to his brother of Cesena, leaving behind a summary list of precepts and recommendations for continuing the administration, by which the duke, 'non come duca, ma come pazzo' (Valeri), was subjected to a kind of tutelage. Malatesta of Cesena was not long in following him. Falling out with a favourite of Giovanni Maria, Antonio Torriano, he too withdrew, and only Pandolfo, jealous to keep his territorial conquests, fought another ten years and more the independent fight of his own ambitions.[2]

[1] *Cron. Mant.*, 168; *Ann. Est.*, 1042; Platina, *Hist. Mant.*, *RIS* xx.796; *Chron. Bon.*, iii.521; Predelli, x.43, 51, 53, 54; A. Maffei, *Annali di Mantova* (Mantua, 1675), 747, 748, 750; Romanin, iv.55; Tarducci, 'Gianfr. Gonzaga', pt. i, 311ff.

[2] *Ann. Est.*, 1049, 1050, 1052–3, 1054–5, 1061; *Chron. Tarvisinum*, *RIS* xix, 807, 810; *Cron. Mant.*, 168; Billii, 32–3; *Chron. Berg.*, 1000–2; *Chron. Bon.*, iii.525; Osio, i.401, 406; Predelli, x.62; Morbio, 69ff.; Santoro, *Registri Provv.*, v, vi *passim*;

When Carlo left Milan, greater matters than the Guelf and Ghibelline squabbles of Lombardy had been agitating for some time the diplomacy of Italy and Europe. After thirty years of papal Schism it seemed at last, in the pontificates of Gregory XII and Benedict XIII, that unity was to be restored through the goodwill of the rival popes themselves. Bound by oath in the conclave of November 1406 to remit no effort to end the Schism, Angelo Correr, who took the title of Gregory XII, at once proposed a meeting with the Avignonese pope; and in April 1407 his envoys in Marseilles agreed to appoint Savona as the seat of conference.[1] In Italy, where all serious resistance to the Roman papacy had long ceased, this attempt at reunification only served to revive disunity. Ladislas of Durazzo, the young king of Naples, who ruled with the support of the Roman popes, was unshakably opposed to a policy which could threaten his throne by elevating the pope of Avignon with his French and Angevin affinities, and from this cause and through native ambition, had established a control over Rome and the Papal State. In 1394, and again ten years later, he intervened as arbiter between the Romans and the papacy, winning from the pope, Innocent VII, the rectorial office in Campagna and Marittima. Innocent also promised to do nothing for unity of the church until Ladislas had been universally acknowledged king of Naples; and from that time on the Neapolitan influence at Rome was unflagging. From the start Ladislas was a declared enemy of the negotiations begun by Gregory XII, and in June 1407 he made a first and unsuccessful attempt to occupy Rome and prevent the meeting at Savona. Not until nearly a year later, in April 1408, and months after the pope had left for Tuscany, did he finally capture the city and launch his campaign against the work of union.[2]

Ladislas' interference was not confined to the western provinces of the Papal State. During the same period he won power and influence in the March of Ancona too. After a brief tenure of authority in Ascoli (November 1404 to January 1406)[3] he began, with the pontificate of Gregory XII, systematically to invade the province, helped and encouraged by Ludovico Migliorati, nephew of the late pope, Innocent VII, who had made him rector of the March. Unsure of his position under the new pope, Ludovico fortified himself in Fermo and Ascoli, and was at once degraded by Gregory. Arrayed against him were the

Cagnola, 26; Odorici, vii.289–91, 294; Giulini, iii.160–1, 166, 168–76, 178, 612–17; Tonini, v/2, vii; Valeri, *Eredità*, 'Insegnamento'; Salvelli; Belotti, i.570ff.
[1] Valois, *Schisme*, iii.485–6, 493–4, 502–5.
[2] Sozomenus, 1157; *Cron. Volg.*, 368–9; Gregorovius, *History of the city of Rome*, tr. Hamilton (London, 1894–1902), vi/2.569–70, 572–3, 579, 583, 590, 593ff.; Cutolo, i.296–9, 302–4, 309–10; Valois, *Schisme*, iii.522–4, 580–4; Theiner, iii.89–91.
[3] Theiner, iii.81

Varani, the Chiavelli and the papal rector, joined by the rising young *condottiere* Braccio da Montone, and to strengthen himself Ludovico had to buy the support of Ladislas with a grant of Ascoli. From here the king moved on to other conquests. Gregory issued protests until early in 1408 a peace was arranged. But Ladislas continued to harass the March through his captains, Martino of Faenza and others, at the same time taking Rome and then Perugia (June 1408).[1]

It is difficult to estimate the Malatesta's involvement in this obscure struggle. Some sources claim they were engaged against Camerino in the war of 1407,[2] but only one event is clear. In March 1408 the city of Iesi rose and expelled the Simonetti family, *signori* and papal vicars. While Gregory XII revoked their vicariates, the king of Naples sent help. But the decisive action did not come from them. The neighbouring lords, Chiavello of Fabriano, Onofrio Smeducci of S. Severino and Giovanni Cima of Cingoli, together with Braccio, gathered at once to rob the city of its territories. The entry of Braccio must have annoyed the others, for they joined up against him, and the *condottiere* was compelled to retire and sell the city to the Malatesta. This is the first certain appearance of the Malatesta in the conflicts of the March at this time, an appearance which, while flattering to their interests, does not yet show them to be the determined adherents of Ladislas they were shortly to become.[3]

Usurper of Rome and invader of the March, Ladislas was denounced by the partisans of union as their principal enemy. How far pope Gregory was in secret understanding with him has never been agreed, but the warlike action of the king certainly enabled him more easily to evade the meeting with Benedict, which fear, lack of decision or mere self-interest made him increasingly reluctant to attend.[4] At last, in May 1408, disgusted by his equivocation, the cardinals of his obedience began to desert him, inviting those of Avignon to join them and arrange for a general council. Slowly the defection spread among Gregory's adherents. In August, September and October still more prelates and cardinals abandoned the discredited pope, among them Baldassare Cossa, the legate of Bologna, and Peter of Candia, archbishop of Milan; and Gregory's situation in Tuscany became less and

---

[1] *Cron. Volg.*, 357, 361–2, 366–9; Bonincontri, 87; Campanus, 25–31; *Cron. Ferm.*, 30ff.; Adami, 37–9; Lilii, 133–4; Theiner, iii.105; Valois, *Schisme*, iii.558.

[2] Campanus, 31–2; Lilii, 133–4.

[3] Campanus, 40; Gamurrini, iii.439–40; Gritio, 44; T. Baldassini, 66ff.; G. Baldassini, 117–19, doc. 43; Amiani, i.332. In 1408–9 Braccio was receiving pay from the Malatesta: ACF, *Cod. mal.* 21, fo. 240.

[4] On the relations of Gregory and Ladislas, 1407–8, and the supposed sale of the Papal State to the king: *Cron. Volg.*, 369–70, 378; Sozomenus, 1193; Bonincontri, 100; Gregorovius, *History of the city of Rome*, vi/2.598–9; Valois, *Schisme*, iii.522–4, 550, 558–60, 579, 580–4, 586–7; Cutolo, i.303, 305, 308–10; ii.151, 153.

less secure. It was precisely at this juncture that he received an invitation from Carlo Malatesta to remove with his *curia* to Rimini. He accepted at once, travelling through S. Sepolcro, and arrived on November, welcomed in Carlo's absence by the clergy and people of the city.[1]

Carlo's action at this time, in calling the pope to Rimini, was evidence of an interest to take some part in efforts to end the Schism, for which both character and conviction seem to have fitted him. He came of a family which by now had long redeemed its early disobedience by service to the church, had avoided taint of heresy and been regular in the observance of pious practices: gifts to religious houses,[2] pilgrimages to the Santo Volto at Lucca,[3] to the Holy Land,[4] even to Saint Patrick's well.[5] Carlo was equally generous to the religious, and when in 1399 the penitential companies of the Bianchi passed through Romagna, 'devotissimo e amatore de Dio', he joined and accompanied them, with Isabetta his wife, and Francesco Gonzaga.[6] But unlike his predecessors he seems also to have been interested in religious erudition. The tribute to his learning, both sacred and profane, is too emphatic to be dismissed as courtly adulation. Zambeccari,[7] Salutati,[8] Poggio,[9] Bruni,[10] Sant'Antonino,[11] and others besides,[12] all unite in exceptional

---

[1] *Chron. Forl.*, 377; *Cron. Volg.*, 370–7; Sozomenus, 1193; Platina, 299; *Cron. sen.*, 764; *Ann. Est.*, 1049, 1051; *Cron. Ferm.*, 34; Sercambi, iii.144–5; Valois, *Schisme*, iii.587; Cutolo, i.313; Tonini, v.26.

[2] Above pp. 41, 85, 90; cf. Clementini, ii.157; Mittarelli, *Ann. Camald.*, vi.64. Clementini (ii.153) says Galeotto Malatesta at the end of his life gave himself wholly to works of piety. Even the device of Moor's head with a star in seals of the Malatesta may be a religious motif: Battaglini, *Zecca*, 216.

[3] *Lucca, Registri*, ii/1, n. 915/2 (30 Aug. 1361).

[4] Though the dates are difficult to determine, it seems that Galeotto Malatesta, Malatesta Ungaro and Pandolfo di Galeotto all visited the Holy Land: *RIS*[2] xv/ 2.17, 162; xvi/3.34, 87; Guerriero, 33; Clementini, ii.76–7, 153, 179, 194; Tonduzzi, Amiani, i.321–2; Tonini, iv.249; Sacchetti, *Novelle*, x.

[5] By Malatesta Ungaro, perhaps to commune with a departed mistress: *RIS*[2] xv/2.24–5; Rymer, *Foedera* (London, 1816), vi.107; *Calendar Patent Rolls* (1358–61), 108; Levi, in *Atti Mem. Dep. Ferrar. S.P.* 1909, 103–8; Massèra, in *Giorn. stor. lett. it.*, 1914, 174–5.

[6] Broglio, 190–1; Clementini, ii.238, 241, 249, 257, 283; Tonini, v/1.659, v/2, xxxi; Tarducci, 'Gianfr. Gonzaga', pt. i, 343.

[7] *Epist.*, 40–2 ('naturalis sapientia cum altissima doctrini concreta' etc.).

[8] *Epist.*, iii.285–94 ('ad studia divina conversus' etc.).

[9] *Hist.*, 331 ('studiis literarum deditissimus et disserendi cum viris doctrina et ingenio prestantibus quibus admodum utebatur, cupidus' etc.).

[10] *Hist.*, 439; *Epistolae* (ed. L. Mehus, Florence, 1741), i.81–3, ii.52–2; *Humanistisch-philosophische Schriften* (ed. Baron, Leipzig, Berlin, 1928), 17 ('studiorum litterarumque peritissimus', a deft verse-maker, rapid reader, accomplished orator and debater, in every way modelled after the ancients).

[11] *Chronicon, Tertia pars* (Lyon, 1586), 479 (echoing Bruni).

[12] Biondo (*Hist.*, 416), Loschi (Battaglini, *Corte*, 55, 126), Guarino da Verona (*Epistolario* (ed. R. Sabbadini, Venice, 1915–19), i.24–5, iii.17–18); *Cron. Mant.*,

praise of him. But while commending his military and other qualities, they tend also to dwell particularly on the 'gravity' of his manners. So Poggio for example writes: 'maxime in eo erat auctoritas tum plurimis virtutibus, tum morum optimorum gravitate contracta'; the chronicler Andrea Biglia: 'homo supra modum gravem se ferens, nec alteri in Italia de virtute aut continentia plus creditum'; and Flavio Biondo: 'litteris moribusque et gravitate conspicuus'.[1] It is not difficult to believe that in 1397, outraged by what he considered a pagan idolatry, he had the statue of Virgil in Mantua, an object of local devotion, removed and thrown in the river: an action which infuriated the humanists and was long commemorated as an exhibition of barbarism. He was alleged to have insulted the dignity of Cicero and dismissed Virgil and the other Latin poets as 'histriones'. Bruni reproves his obstinacy in argument, citing by way of illustration: 'is ergo quia quandoque negavit poetas esse legendos, usque ad mortem tunc errorem prosequitur'.[2] In the same puritan spirit Carlo Malatesta in his legislation seems to have been particularly intent to punish blasphemers and idolators, and to enforce observance of holy days.[3] When addressing him the poet Simone Serdini, who exchanged amorous verses with Carlo's brother, chose to deplore the sins of the flesh:

'Esser non può che nel terrestre sito
il miser corpo l'anima non gravi . . .'[4]

Isabetta Gonzaga, Carlo's wife, was no less devout.[5] And it is perhaps memorial enough of their character that the nephew whom they educated, Galeotto Roberto, Pandolfo's eldest son, was the one member of the Malatesta family to grow up and practise the austerities of a saint.[6]

Such was the man from whom Gregory XII accepted protection and asylum in 1408. The pope must already have been well disposed, for the year before he had named Rimini, Fano and Pesaro among the alternative cities to Savona.[7] And Carlo must have commended himself

170 ('Signor Karlo di gran sapir famato'). To be noted also are Carlo's plans for a public library: Battaglini, *Corte*, 56, 128.

[1] Poggio, 331; Billii, 116; Biondo, *Scritti ined.*, 175.
[2] Bruni, *Epistolae*, i.81–3, ii.51–2; Salutati, iii.285–94; Vergerio, n. LXXXI; Battaglini, *Corte*, 54–6; J. Voigt, *Wiederbelebung des Classischen Altertums* (Berlin, 1893), i.573–5; J. Pontanus, *Opera* (Basle, 1556), 101–2; A. Possevinus, *Gonzaga* (Mantua, 1628), 485–6; *Arch. Gonzaga*, ii.180 (n. 3). Pius II saw only one fault in Carlo: 'superbia': *Commentarii*, 257.
[3] Bib. sen., *Stat. Rim.*, fos. 352r–353v, 355r–356v, 359v; Bagli, 79–82, 84.
[4] Volpi, 'Serdini', 14.
[5] *Bull. Franc.*, vii.17.
[6] Below p. 175.
[7] Valois, *Schisme*, iii.561 (n. 6). Amiani (i.328, 329) says Angelo Correr was a friend of Carlo before his election.

still more when, in the following July, he warned the pope of a design
by cardinal Cossa to abduct him.[1] While inviting the pope to his
territory, Carlo was active elsewhere on his behalf, an envoy of his
being in Venice urging the republic to collaborate in reuniting the
church. Rimini may have been discussed and accepted by the Venetians
as meeting-place for the council.[2] Like Venice, Florence and Sigismund of Hungary, Carlo's aimed at reconciling Gregory with his
cardinals as nucleus of a combined council, but by January 1409 this
had proved impracticable. In a bull dated the 14th, censuring their
indifference to the appeals of Sigismund, Venice and Carlo Malatesta,
the pope excommunicated and degraded them.[3] Carlo was not discouraged by this initial failure, still less shaken in his Gregorian
allegiance. Throughout his conviction was to be that just and sufficient
reason must be shown for deserting the Roman pope. When at this
time the University of Paris tried to win him over, he was deaf to all
persuasions.[4] When Florence now, and later Venice and Sigismund
abandoned Gregory he stood loyally by him. At the same time he did
not exclude all contact with the pope's enemies. As soon as the Council
of Pisa met, in March 1409, he renewed attempts towards an agreement.

His first approach was through Malatesta of Pesaro, who had also
played some part in the negotiations of the last two years, and was at
this time Florentine general. A letter was sent to the Council rehearsing
Carlo's acitivities on behalf of unity: how, while still in Lombardy, he
had been invited to join Gregory, had finally left for Rimini, pausing
in Venice to preach the cause of reunion, and then pressed for a general
council to meet in Bologna, Forlì, Mantua or Rimini. His sole concern
was: 'quod fiat unicum et generale concilium in quo concurrat voluntas
dicti domini Gregorii pariter et vestra'; and this could be met by a
council summoned in a place agreeable to Gregory. The fathers replied
that such was the council they had called, and that the two popes had
only to acknowledge an assembly which was supported by most of
Christendom. They also warned Carlo against the pope's deceit and
urged him to bring Gregory to Pisa. But at this point Carlo himself
arrived.

Shortly before, on 15 April, an embassy from Rupert of Bavaria had
presented a series of captious articles on behalf of Gregory which had
done nothing to make the Council more compliant. Carlo Malatesta

[1] Raynaldus, 1408, n. 42.
[2] *Deutsche Reichstagsakten*, iv.602; E. Piva, 'Venezia e lo Scisma', *N. arch. ven.*, 1897,
   148.
[3] Raynaldus, 1409, nn. 1–4; Hefele-Leclerq, vi.1376–7, 1389–90; *Ann. Est.*, 1061,
   1062; Griffoni, 97.
[4] Valois, *Schisme*, iv.58.

was better received, but no more successful. For several days he debated, argued and declaimed before the representatives, among them the archbishop of Milan and later Pierre d'Ailly, delegated to negotiate with him. His object was unchanged: to have the Council removed to some other city where Gregory could cooperate in overcoming the Schism, even offering himself as hostage and surety for the pope's good faith. He pointed out that in the council 'non esse utramque obedientiam sed unam quae ex duabus facta est', that the way of concord was surer than that of juristic scruple, while it would, by removing the grievances of Ladislas, put an end to any war fought on religious pretexts. Carlo Malatesta already foresaw the conflicts which would arise from any religious schism in Italy. On their side the conciliar delegates applauded the loyalty of Carlo and his ancestors to the church, and commended his sincerity, the archbishop of Milan recalling talks they had had on the Schism when Carlo was in Lombardy. But they were not prepared to yield. Instead they pressed Carlo to use his influence with Gregory and persuade him to resign the papacy, offering in compensation some legation in Friuli, the March of Treviso, or the province of Ancona. In reply, acting upon his own authority, Carlo Malatesta promised to deliver their arguments to the pope and submit their proposal of a meeting with Gregory in Pistoia. With this, and an undertaking to bring or send an answer within fifteen days, he finally left the council, 'quasi desperatus', and after an exchange of courtesies with the republic of Florence, re-entered Rimini on 26 April.

The next day he spent in discussion with Gregory and his nephews, reserving for private audience the offers made by the Council. To the pope's indignant astonishment he urged him to go to Pistoia, and recommended abdication as the only means to union; otherwise a 'trischisma', even a 'quartischisma', would be threatened. Gregory confessed himself 'totus stupefactus', and complained that Pisa had altered Carlo's opinions. Carlo rebutted this charge, explaining that his only purpose was the peace of the church. And he made the same answer when Gregory asked what was to become of his adherents, clerical and lay. Beside this, he said, the convenience of cardinals and *curiales* was of no account. The pope was immovable. He only declared he would abandon Rimini to celebrate the council he had appointed nearly a year before to assemble in Friuli. And the interview closed cheerlessly with Carlo Malatesta repeating that there was now only one way to peace, 'cognita partium voluntate'.[1]

In this profitless negotiation Carlo Malatesta had at least made clear the principles of his policy: a peaceful settlement of the Schism which

---

[1] Martène and Durand, *Collectio*, vii.966–1078; Mansi, xxvii.96–9, 245ff., 256; *Acta Const.*, iv, LXX; *Deutsche Reichstagsakten*, v.331–2; Sauerland, *RQ* 1897, 450; Schmitz, *RQ* 1894, 232–3; *Chron. Bon.*, iii.530; Sercambi, iii.152.

would safeguard Gregory's claims but did not exclude abdication, and he adhered to this inflexibly in the years that followed.

Three weeks later, on 16 May, Gregory XII left Rimini for Cividale where his council was to assemble.[1] But Carlo did not leave his work towards ecclesiastical union. Sometime in June he sent a further letter to Pisa, profuse with biblical quotations, allusions to canon law and to Roman history, in which he returned to the danger of a threefold schism. The conclave he feared had already opened when this letter arrived; and on 26 June the archbishop of Milan, Peter Philarges, was elected pope, taking the name of Alexander V. The 'trivisio' was consummated.[2] An appeal from Carlo to the new pope complaining that the Council had failed in zeal for unity, had failed, that is, to show that Gregory XII 'incorrigibilis reputari debeat et haereticus condemnari', and urging him to the 'via cessionis', had no effect. Alexander merely reminded him that the Council had deposed the two contending popes and declared them heretics.[3]

Gregory's case could not have appeared more forlorn. Disheartened by his *conciliabulum* at Cividale, which only exposed his weakness and the insecurity of his position, he fled in disguise on 6 September to the dominions of Ladislas, travelling by sea and land to Ortona, Fondi and Gaeta. However, the previous day he solemnly announced his readiness to adopt the way of abdication, and summoned Rupert, Ladislas and Sigismund to give heed to Carlo Malatesta, 'qui est valde avidus ad sacratissimam unionem'.[4]

Not for nearly a year after Pisa was Carlo Malatesta able to renew his efforts for 'the most sacred union'. At the beginning of May 1410 the conciliar pope died in Bologna, restoring, as it appeared to Carlo, the previous situation. He at once sent an envoy to the cardinals, repeating his arguments of a year before and deprecating a second election. Cossa took it on himself to answer, dwelling in defence of a new election on the political inconveniences it would avoid: arguments which Carlo Malatesta swept aside in a vehement letter of high principle and religious eloquence. Once again his intervention was wasted. On 17 May Cossa was elected pope, assuming the title of John XXIII and a week later proceeding to his coronation. This did not end the negotiations. For a further two months Carlo Malatesta kept a representative in Bologna pleading to the new pope the alternatives of 'via cessionis'

---

[1] *Chron. Forl.*, 877. Among the six cardinals attending Gregory's council was bishop Bandello of Rimini, elected cardinal on 19 Sept. 1408: Schmitz, 245; Eubel, RQ 1896, 100.

[2] Martène and Durand, *Collectio*, vii.1143; Valois, *Schisme*, iv.105.

[3] Martène and Durand, *Collectio*, vii.1136–41.

[4] *Deutsche Reichstagsakten*, v.573–4; Hefele-Leclerq, vii.63–4; Cutolo, i.335. By this time Carlo Malatesta's interest in union was becoming well known: *Deutsche Reichstagsakten*, v. 693.

and 'via concilii generalis', and promising even to resign Rimini in the cause of religious peace. John may have hoped by these protracted negotiations to keep Carlo friendly, for he confessed at one point he would rather have his allegiance than that of Hungary, Sweden or any other state he expected to win, but by July talks were broken off.[1]

Thereafter, in Italy at least, Carlo Malatesta was concerned less with principles and devices for church unity than with organisation of war.

The Council of Pisa and the papal election made the Schism a graver reality for Italy than perhaps it had ever been before. One argument advanced by Cossa for electing a successor to Alexander V was that it would preserve Rome from the king of Naples,[2] against whom he and his allies, Florence and Louis of Anjou, had been fighting for nearly two years. In December 1409 they recovered Rome from Ladislas, but the campaign did not end with this success. Even after Florence made a separate peace in 1411, John XXIII and the Angevin claimant made preparations to continue the struggle alone.[3]

Up to then any relations between the Malatesta and Ladislas must have been slight.[4] During his negotiations with John XXIII Carlo Malatesta touched on the Angevin claims to Naples.[5] Only at the end of 1410, when the talks had broken down, and Gregory had been for some time under the king's protection, did the Malatesta finally go over to Ladislas. In the Florentine peace with Naples (7 January 1411) they appear already among the king's allies.[6] Soon after, Carlo Malatesta became captain-general of the Neapolitan army, and was also perhaps appointed Gonfaloniere of the Church by Gregory XII.[7] Gregory at least contributed to the expenses of his *condotta*.[8]

On both sides the campaign that followed was inglorious. On 19 May Louis of Anjou defeated Ladislas at Roccasecca, but he failed to develop his victory, and what might have been another Benevento remained a mere passage of arms. After that hostilities languished, and

---

[1] Martène and Durand, *Collectio*, vii.1141–2, 1162–79; Raynaldus, 1410, n. 27; Niem, *Vita*, 361–2. Cf. Finke, 'Vorgeschichte'; Valois, *Schisme*, iv.129–30; Blumenthal, 'Johannes XXIII', 490–3.

[2] Martène and Durand, *Collectio*, vii.1164. Carlo replied: 'si ecclesia in hoc trischismate permanebit, amittet Romam et plus quam Romam': 1167.

[3] Cutolo, i.341–66; Gregorovius, *History of the city of Rome*, tr. Hamilton (London, 1894–1902), vi/2.608; Valois, *Schisme*, iv.115.

[4] Sometime in 1408 Andrea Malatesta of Cesena married the Neapolitan Polissena, *nipote* of Ladislas and daughter of Wenzel, duke of Vanosa: Bonincontri, 87; Clementini, ii.185, 265; Amiani, i.333; Zazzeri, 263.

[5] Martène and Durand, *Collectio*, vii.1168.

[6] *Capitoli, Firenze*, ii.xvi.61.

[7] Bonincontri, 105. In the same month Ladislas was requesting Venice to send supplies for Perugia 'ad partes Fani vel alias terras dominorum de Malatestis': Cutolo, ii.184. Cf. further: Pellini, ii.186–7; Cutolo, i.367, ii.185.

[8] Fedele, *ASN* 1905, 187; Eubel, *RQ* 1896, 100.

at the beginning of August Louis abandoned Italy for Provence.[1] From then until the following June events moved perversely toward a compromise between Ladislas and John XXIII.

Even before Roccasecca Ladislas, to the distress of the Perugians, gave signs of readiness to desert Gregory XII if John would forsake Louis of Anjou.[2] Nothing came of this immediately and Perugia continued to be intimately, if anxiously, united with the king.[3] But with the retirement of Louis, and the successes Ladislas enjoyed at the end of 1411 and early in the next year, John XXIII was forced to think of negotiations. On 17 June 1412 what Gregory denounced as 'pestifera pactio' was quietly arranged between them near S. Felice, which assured to Ladislas his territorial conquests in the Papal States as well as his Neapolitan throne, and engaged him to repudiate Gregory. A synod of Neapolitan bishops hastened obediently to discover Gregory guilty of heresy, and in October the schismatic pope was banished from the kingdom.[4] Without delay he escaped from Gaeta, and after a crippling voyage arrived in December at Cesenatico, whence he proceeded again to Rimini, 'dove disse di volere stare e morire'.[5]

In these events Carlo Malatesta played no part. Instead, perhaps foreseeing the rapprochement between Ladislas and John XXIII, or because encouraged by the king of Naples, to whom as much as to Venice the king of the Romans was an enemy, he entered Venetian service against Sigismund. The *condotta* was concluded between December 1411 and January 1412, and in the spring the campaign opened. Carlo was supported by his brother Pandolfo, and succeeded twice in defeating the Hungarians. But in the second engagement, at Motta (24 August), he was too severely wounded to continue and had to surrender the command to Pandolfo. Under him the war was resumed, until in April 1413 a truce was concluded for five years, in which the Malatesta were included. Pandolfo and his heirs were awarded Venetian nobility, and he himself was given an annual allowance, a *condotta in aspetto*, and a house on the Canalgrande. The title of duke of Crete which was offered him he decided to decline. In

[1] Cutolo, i.370–4; Valois, *Schisme*, iv.138. There is no statement that the Malatesta took part in this campaign. They were occupied elsewhere: below p. 136.

[2] Cutolo, i.368–70. In May Perugia sent to Carlo Malatesta and Guidantonio da Montefeltro to ask for help in the event of a peace between John and Ladislas: *ibid.* ii.187.

[3] Concerned, among other things, to obtain the service and maintain the alliance of Carlo Malatesta with Ladislas: Pellini, ii.188–9, 192; Cutolo, ii.192, 193, 198.

[4] Fedele, *ASN* 1905; Cutolo, i.377–85; Valois, *Schisme*, iv.142–5.

[5] Sanudo, 874; *Chron. Forl.*, 883; Raynaldus, viii, 1412, n. 4; Niem, 369–70. For this deliverance Gregory granted a plenary indulgence in perpetuity to 'omnibus vere penitentibus et confessis de civitate comitatu et territorio Arimini oriundis vel alias incolis', visiting the cathedral of S. Colomba (22 March 1415): Broglio, 191; Clementini, ii.280–3; Tonini, v/2, xxv.

the interval Carlo Malatesta was given leave, because of his injuries, and reached Rimini about the same time as Gregory arrived there in flight from Gaeta.[1]

Ladislas of Naples did not long maintain his peace with John XXIII. He mistrusted the pope, fearing a secret accord between him and Sigismund, and in June 1413, deaf to the remonstrances of Florence, occupied Rome. The Malatesta now resumed service with him, and Malatesta of Cesena may have been present in the Roman campaign. But they were mainly active as his confederates in Romagna and the March of Ancona.[2]

It was here, beside their own dominions, that the Malatesta from the beginning fought most for Gregory XII. More than any part of Italy the Papal States were tormented by division after the Council of Pisa. As before, following 1378, each pope tried to win allegiance, only now, when the rivals were Italian, the contest was sharper and the forces more balanced. Baldassare Cossa had been deposed from his legation in Bologna by Gregory XII (October 1408), but Alexander V, when elected, extended his commission to the Papal States generally.[3] Both popes solicited support from communes and *signori*,[4] and both sent rectors into the March of Ancona.[5] The struggle went on for five years, and it was still undecided when the Council of Constance began to assemble.

In Romagna the conflict turned on the obedience of Bologna, Forlì and Faenza, the three cities earlier subdued by the papal legate,[6] and then withdrawn by him from the authority of the suspect pope (August 1408).[7] Early in his pontificate (August 1407) Gregory XII contemplated investing some of his relatives with Faenza and Forlì.[8] But now, in 1410, another course was forced on him. Calling in the dispossessed *tiranni*, he appointed Gian Galeazzo Manfredi vicar in Faenza and hereditary count of the Val di Lamone, and gave the vicariates of Forlì and Forlimpopoli to Giorgio and Antonio degli Ordelaffi, on the

---

[1] Predelli, x.148, 150, 154–5, 175–6, 178–9, 192; Sanudo, 858–80; *Chron. Tarvisinum*, *RIS* xix.836, 839–40, 842; Romanin, iv.57–62; H. Kretschmayr, *Geschichte von Venedig*, ii (Gotha, 1920), 264. In this war Carlo Malatesta may have lost the use of one arm: *Acta Const.*, iii.307.

[2] Cutolo, i.388–404; Valois, *Schisme*, iv.230–1; Sercambi, iii.211–12.

[3] Compagnoni, *Reggia Picena*, 284.

[4] For example to the commune of Fano: Amiani, i.333 (1410).

[5] Compagnoni, *Reggia Picena*, 285–6. Later (1413?), in opposition to Carlo Malatesta, Gregorian rector of Romagna, John XXIII created Paolo Orsini legate in Romagna and the March of Ancona: Niem, ii.366.

[6] The Alidosi adhered to Alexander and John. Niccolo d'Este vacillated: Theiner, iii.108, 117.   [7] *Ann. Est.*, 1050.

[8] Sauerland, *Zeitschr. f. Kirchengeschichte*, 1895, 413. On 1 June 1409 he made his nephew Paolo vicar in a number of places in Romagna: *ibid.* 414.

understanding that all should take up arms against Cossa.[1] The Ordelaffi had already occupied Forlimpopoli (January 1410) and were only checked from taking Forlì by the armed intervention of Florence. Not until June 1411, after a year of skirmishing, did they finally enter the city.[2] The Malatesta took little part in this enterprise, but they gave their help, and just after Giorgio Ordelaffi took Forlì Carlo Malatesta went to visit him. Later, in 1413, Malatesta of Cesena prevented Guido da Montefeltro from molesting the Ordelaffi; and in the treaty of June 1414 between Ladislas and Florence, the lord of Forlì appears among the Malatesta *colligati*.[3] There was no wavering in his allegiance to Gregory XII.

With the simultaneous recovery of Faenza by Gian Galeazzo Manfredi the Malatesta had more to do and it was with their support and the help of the Ordelaffi that he was restored to power in June 1410.[4] Gian Galeazzo complained that Cossa had broken the agreements of 1404, and so refused when Carlo Malatesta, in negotiations with John XXIII that month, offered to arrange a compromise.[5] Momentarily Gian Galeazzo did enter into relations with John, but he soon returned to the alliance of the Malatesta, among whose *colligati* he also appears in 1414.[6]

The return of *signori* friendly to Gregory XII in Forlimpopoli, Faenza and then Forlì, was enough to establish his strength in Romagna. But to dominate the province he needed also to supplant his enemy in Bologna. For this he employed the rector Carlo Malatesta. A first engagement came in the spring and summer of 1411 when Carlo was in the service of Ladislas, and John XXIII had abandoned Bologna to conduct the campaign of Roccasecca. Pope Gregory, from Gaeta, gave what support he could,[7] and success seemed assured. At the end of April John's representatives in Bologna were attacking the Malatesta castle of S. Giovanni in Persiceto, taken in 1402. But on 12 May the Bolognese rose again in revolt against papal government. Carlo Malatesta had addressed to them an appeal (16 April), disavowing

[1] Tonduzzi, 462–3.
[2] Cobelli, 160–2; Pedrino, rub. 1–2; *Chron. Forl.*, 878–81; *Ann. Forl.*, 83–4; Griffoni, 97–8; *Chron. Bon.*, iii.533; *Diario Ferrar.*, 56–7; Sozomenus, 1197; *Cron. Volg.*, 400; Niem, 360.
[3] Pedrino, rub. 2, 8; Cobelli, 162; *Chron. Forl.*, 881; *Ann. Forl.*, 83; Cutolo, ii.226.
[4] Sercambi, iii.180; Griffoni, 98; Bonincontri, 103; *Ann. Est.*, Addenda to p. 1096; Sozomenus, 1198; *Diario Ferrar.*, 56–7; Niem, 59.
[5] *Cron. Volg.*, 400–1; Martène and Durand, *Collectio*, vii.1173, 1176–7.
[6] Clementini, ii.266; Theiner, iii.121; Messeri and Calzi, 141; Mazzatinti, *Inventari*, xxvi.17; Cutolo, ii.226.
[7] In April he issued a plenary indulgence to everyone joining Carlo against Cossa, and in May, and again October, arranged for payment of Carlo's expenses: Raynaldus, 1411, n. 1; Eubel, *RQ* 1896, 100. For further detail: ACF, *Cod. mal.* 21, fo. 293r; Maraschini, nn. 26, 30–1, 33–4, 38, 42, 47; Cutolo, ii.198.

designs of personal aggrandisement and claiming to act only on behalf of Gregory XII. This, with the irritations of war, may have started the rising. But it was soon apparent that the Bolognese were no allies of the Malatesta. What they wanted was their old autonomy and territorial strength. They repelled Carlo's approaches and resumed the assault on Persiceto; and the noble enterprise against Bologna issued finally in a meagre convention, arranged by Venice and Florence, which confirmed Carlo Malatesta in possession of S. Giovanni and obliged the Bolognese to pay him 10,000 ducats' reparation (June 1411).[1] A year later Bologna returned to the attack; and in September 1412 the population of S. Giovanni expelled the Malatesta garrison, and followed the Bolognese in submitting to John XXIII, then back in Emilia, who sent Luigi da Prato as governor.[2] Carlo Malatesta continued the campaign,[3] and in the summer of 1413, as ally of Ladislas, succeeded in forming a Romagnol alliance against Bologna. Niccolo d'Este was put in command by the king of Naples, and this time the city would certainly have fallen had not Niccolo been induced by Florence to change sides (October 1413). His defection forced Malatesta of Cesena to retreat before the enemy captain, Braccio. And when in the next season, 1414, Carlo Malatesta resumed the offensive, he suffered a similar check; though only Ladislas' death in August finally freed the Bolognese from danger.[4] After that John was secure in their allegiance.

This was the situation of Romagna when the first delegates began to arrive at Constance. And in the March of Ancona, where the 'way of arms' was also the most favoured mode of conversion, things were little different.

Here, since the death of Galeotto the Malatesta had managed through papal generosity greatly to extend their dominions; and after the purchase of Iesi in 1408 they were in a strong position to enforce their influence in whatever cause they followed.[5] In 1411 Carlo Malatesta, on behalf of Gregory XII, accepted the return to obedience of Monte Cassiano which then 'commended' itself to him. In June he

[1] Griffoni, 98–9; *Chron. Bon.*, iii.537–9; *Diario Ferrar.*, 10–12; Mattiolo, 233–6; Sercambi, iii.188–9, 192–4; Ghirardacci, ii.588–9; *Acta Const.*, i.24–5; Martène and Durand, *Collectio*, vii.1206–8.
[2] *Chron. Bon.*, ii.539–42; Griffoni, 99–100, 101; *Ann. Forl.*, 84; *Chron. Forl.*, 882; Mattiolo, 241–2; Clementini, ii.268–9; Ghirardacci, ii.592, 594.
[3] In 1413 a conspiracy was detected at Bologna to give the city to the Malatesta: *Chron. Bon.*, iii.544; Ghirardacci, ii.598.
[4] Battaglini, *Vita*, 566; Tonini, v/2, xvi; *Cron. sen.*, 776–7; Campanus, 66–7; *Cron. Mant.*, 178; *Chron. Bon.*, iii.546–7; *Diario fiorent.*, *ASI* 1894, ii.252; Mattiolo, 257–8; Niem, 385–8; Minuti, *Vita*, 169.
[5] For Pandolfo Malatesta's territories in the March c. 1410: Zonghi, 22–32; Bartoccetti, 'Liber'.

took over Montolmo, again for Gregory; and later in the same year he was receiving excuses from Macerata for its occasional disloyalty to the pope. Here too within a few months he was able to extend his 'protection' over the city.[1] But these were small affairs beside the contest with Ludovico Migliorati, who had been created vicar of Fermo by Alexander V and rector of the March by John XXIII.[2]

At the end of December 1412, the township of Monte Rubbiano in the territory of Fermo rose in revolt and proclaimed Carlo Malatesta lord. Ten days later Malatesta of Cesena[3] came and 'reformed' the community, and a stubborn war broke out with the adherents of John XXIII, led by Paolo Orsini, cardinal Orsini and Ludovico Migliorati. Locally Malatesta had the alliance of Recanati which surrendered to him as representative of Gregory XII;[4] but he was also strengthened by contingents from Ladislas of Naples, captained by Sforza, and with these he soon had Paolo Orsini besieged in Roccacontrada. In August Paolo escaped to Urbino, abandoning the command to Ludovico, and Malatesta then attacked him, occupying Francavilla and a number of minor places. But in November Rodolfo Varani interceded to arrange a truce and refer matters to arbitration by the king of Naples.[5] A few months later Migliorati's troops were taken into Neapolitan service.[6]

The peace was brief. In the March as in Romagna, the result of the Pisan Council was a territorial conflict in which personal rivalries and religious divisions were inseparably confused; and they still awaited

---

[1] Bartoccetti, 'Liber', 56; Maraschini, 40, 47–8, 54; Colucci, xxviii.54–6, 63–4; Compagnoni, *Reggia Picena*, 288–9. At the same time, unconnected with the Schism, the Malatesta were engaged in other, minor wars with the Cima of Cingoli, Smeducci of S. Severino, and the Varani: Campanus, 32–4; G. Baldassini, 120–1; Lilii, ii.138–9; Amiani, i.333.

[2] Adami, 40; Compagnoni, *Reggia Picena*, 290. Gregory still had a rector in the March also.

[3] Who had married a daughter to the brother of Ludovico Migliorati: *Cron. Ferm.*, 39.

[4] *Cron. Ferm.*, 39; Theiner, iii.132; Maraschini, nn. 40, 62, 69; Adami, 42; Angelita, 14–15; Cutolo, ii.226. In Oct. 1413 a similar agreement seems to have been reached between Malatesta as vicar of Gregory XII and Montegiorgio: F. Filippini and G. Luzzato, 'Archivi marchigiani', *AMM* 1912, 407.

[5] Earlier, in 1410 or 1411, Malatesta of Cesena had married his son Galeotto to Niccola di Rodolfo of Camerino: Pedrino, rub. 5–6; Sanudo, 856; Maraschini, n. 60; *Carteggio Guinigi*, 479, App. 50–1; Clementini, ii.185; Amiani, i.335: Zazzeri, 269.

[6] *Cron. Ferm.*, 39–41; *Ristretto d'Urbino*, 50; *Cron. sen.*, 773–4, 776; Bonincontri, 106; Campanus, 67–8; Niem, 366; Minuti, 169–70; Adami, 41–3; Compagnoni, *Reggia Picena*, 292–4, 296; Anselmi; Cutolo, ii.226. The whole operation may be considered a success for Gregory XII and his adherents. It was also used by the Perugians as occasion to repay their debt of gratitude to the Malatesta: Cutolo, i.414.

settlement when the reformers assembled at Constance to repair the Council's mistakes in ecclesiastical policy. Their first concern was with the church, not the Papal State, which only later occupied their attention. And the same was true, in his modest place, of Carlo Malatesta, who throughout these years had continued to work for religious unity and peace.

Carlo contributed nothing directly to the summoning of the Council of Constance, but his policy helped to prepare the way. Though an avowed partisan of Gregory XII,[1] he acknowledged and was ready to discharge a superior duty to the church as a whole. After the Council of Pisa, it has been said, the Gregorian party alone showed interest in ending the Schism;[2] and the active influence behind this was Carlo Malatesta. More than anyone he intervened to exert pressure on the vacillating pope, particularly after Gregory became dependent on his protection at Rimini.[3] While fighting locally to uphold and extend the Gregorian obedience he was increasingly engaged between Pisa and Constance in negotiations for ecclesiastical reunion: with John XXIII, with Benedict XIII and with Sigismund, king of the Romans.

With John XXIII Carlo cannot have expected to have further dealings after the failure at the time of his election. It came as a surprise therefore when John expressed an interest in the 'via concilii generalis', on leaving Bologna in the spring of 1411. His object no doubt was to detach Carlo from the alliance with Ladislas of Naples, which threatened his hold on Bologna; and he tried to gain his sympathy through Malatesta of Pesaro, one of his firmest supporters. But Carlo merely repeated his earlier arguments in favour of the two 'modi'; that all three popes should abdicate or together summon a council; and John's manoeuvres finally came to nothing.[4] Even less sincere were the negotiations indirectly opened, early in 1413, by Luigi da Prato, 'che a quel tempo governava papa Ioanni XXIII'. The intermediary was Rinaldo degli Albizzi, who soon sensed the deceit of a man who had nothing to gain by agreement, and complained of being 'menato per lo naso'. John, whose subjects, it was stressed, were much the more numerous, would only consider abdication by his rival, to which Carlo Malatesta persistently replied by reasserting Gregory's

---

[1] In Milan, for example, he was instrumental in keeping out the archiepiscopal candidate of Alexander V in favour of the Gregorian candidate: Giulini, iii.184–5. In Mantua his influence was less effective: in 1413 Gianfrancesco became a captain of John XXIII: Tarducci, 'Gianfr. Gonzaga', pt. i, 336–56, pt. ii, 34–5.

[2] Hollerbach, 'Gregorianische Partei', 137.

[3] Reporting on Gregory to Ferdinand of Aragon (30 Aug. 1414), Berengar de Muntmany wrote: 'Car no ha que despendere sino tant com lo dit Carlos li vol donar': Acta Const., i.260.

[4] Martène and Durand, Collectio vii.1186ff.

claims. By March it was clear that further talks were useless, and Carlo was not again troubled by Cossa.[1]

No more pliable was Benedict XIII, but with him too Carlo Malatesta and Gregory XII conducted a long, if intermittent, negotiation, lasting from 1410 to 1413 or later. Like everyone else who dealt with him, Benedict commended Carlo's good intentions, 'que in paucis hodie reperitur', and gracefully alluded to an earlier association of their families.[2] But in the subsequent exchange of letters and embassies his well-known obstinacy soon began to show. He would countenance no relations with John XXIII, the schismatic pope of Pisa, and he would offer only a promise to meet personally with Gregory XII, who, controlled by Carlo Malatesta, insisted for his part on a general council, to assemble in Rimini or Fano. There was never even an approach to agreement, and all Carlo's eloquent pleadings went for nothing. This was in 1413, and although some contact may have been maintained, by then the preliminaries of Constance were beginning to claim all attention.[3]

After Pisa, only intervention by a secular power could achieve unity or reform in the church. The power to which it fell was the empire, 'advocatus et defensor ecclesiae'. Carlo Malatesta's efforts produced no success; and although he may have had some influence on Sigismund, the initiative in reunion now passed to the king of the Romans.[4] In the summer of 1411 Carlo sent Sigismund an account of his negotiations with John XXIII. In this he laid stress on the need to summon a council, and in a place 'safe and free'. However, no answer survives to show what effect this had upon the king.[5] Sigismund was busy with other things, war with Venice and in Lombardy, until October 1413, and in any case had reserved his favour for John XXIII, whose insecurity in Italy finally compelled him (November 1413) to join with the king and summon a council at Constance. Gregory's imperial ally had always been Rupert of Bavaria, and then his son Ludwig.[6] In March 1413 Gregory had communicated the 'modi' to Ludwig; and

---

[1] *Commiss. Albizzi*, i.xxx.220–34. Cf. *Acta Const.*, i.13–14, 75–8, 81–8. In 1414, as a move against Gregory and the Malatesta, John granted the vicariate of Fano to one of his followers: Castelucci, 'Regesto', 187.

[2] Lopez de Luna, archbishop of Saragossa (1351–82), accompanied Albornoz on his first legation to Italy: *Acta Const.*, i.34, n. 2.

[3] Martène and Durand, *Collectio*, vii.1132–6; *Acta Const.*, i.10–13, 33–74, 316, 319; iv, lxx.

[4] Finke, *Vorgeschichte*, 2–3; Hollerbach, 'Gregorianische Partei', 137ff.

[5] Martène and Durand, *Collectio*, vii.1176–1206. Finke conjectures that this letter was written late in July or in August, and infers from a similar fragment addressed to an Italian city that Carlo may have approached several states at this time: *Acta Const.*, i.7–8, 25–33.

[6] Finke, *Vorgeschichte*, 3–13; *Acta Const.*, i.15–20, 170–9; Cutolo, i.407–9; Valois, *Schisme*, iv.228–9. Cf. Göller, *Kirchenpolitik*, 59ff.

during the following autumn and winter he tried to win his support against the 'conciliabulum Constanciense'. But Ludwig was probably turning already to Sigismund.[1] A project of union issued by Gregory in the spring of 1414 was savagely treated in a reply by Simon Cramaud, which showed how insignificant and isolated the pope in Rimini had become.[2] Long after starting negotiations with the other popes, and with the secular rulers of Europe, Sigismund made an approach to Gregory in June through Amadeus of Savoy, but without any evident result.[3]

At last, early in August, Gregory received an invitation to the Council, dated, to his indignation, December of the previous year. Within a few days archbishop Andrea of Spoleto appeared in Rimini curtly demanding the presence at Constance of 'Angelo Correr, formerly named Gregory XII'. A series of discussions followed in which Carlo Malatesta certainly took part, ending with the quick departure of the archbishop and a protest from Gregory XII (14 August) that he was not impeding reunion, but must have safe-conducts for himself and his supporters before any voyage to Germany.[4]

No further choice remained to Gregory but to arrange the best terms of submission he could with Sigismund and the Council. In this he must have been encouraged, if not directed, by Carlo Malatesta, who seems now increasingly to have controlled negotiations. In September or October he had envoys with Sigismund debating the conditions which would enable Gregory to come uncompromised to Constance, among them a bull from the pope authorising the king to call a council, safe-conducts from Sigismund and Frederick of Austria, security and maintenance in the city itself. In his reply (4 October) Sigismund merely urged Carlo to persuade the pope to attend, or at least to attend himself in Gregory's name.[5] The suggestion confirms the dominant influence, noted by other contemporaries, now exercised by Carlo

---

[1] *Acta Const.*, i.78–81, 184–7; Hardt, ii.466–7. The letter betrays the influence of Carlo Malatesta, who sent Ludwig the materials from which were compiled Job Verner's 'Plura Scripta et gesta circa unionem per Karolum de Malatestis'. The work applauds 'magnificus Carolus de Malatestis . . . magnarum litterature, experienie, prudencie, et potencie ac pre ceteris Ytalie magnatibus animi probitate, constancia et aliis virtutum insigniis est multipliciter commendatus': *Acta Const.*, iv, lxix–lxx.

[2] Finke, *Vorgeschichte*, 15–22; *Acta Const.*, i.192–6 and nn. 67–70. Cramaud claimed that Gregory's obedience was reduced to Carlo Malatesta, 'quem forte propter sua peccata Deus exceccavit': *ibid.* 285.

[3] *Ibid.* 196. Cf. Bourgeois du Chastenet, *Nouvelle Histoire du Concile de Constance* (Paris, 1718), Preuves, 498–500.

[4] Finke, *Vorgeschichte*, 22–4; *Acta Const.*, i.294–307, iii.318–19; Clementini, ii.276. The protest was issued in the presence of Carlo Malatesta, Galeotto di Malatesta of Cesena, Galeazzo di Malatesta of Pesaro.

[5] *Acta Const.*, i.308–10, iii.323–6; cf. i.201, iii.319–23.

Malatesta in the Gregorian party.[1] Gregory had sent representatives to Constance to safeguard his interests, but not every decision was left to them. The central issue at the Council was the position of John XXIII: was he to preside over the assembly, or were all three popes to abdicate? Was Pisa to be upheld or repudiated? Already on 20 January 1415, Carlo Malatesta was able to send an embassy to Constance announcing Gregory's readiness to resign his office. A few days later (26 January) Ludwig Count Palatine together with Gregory's envoys was urging the procedure of triple cession. He was not without support; and by February this policy, a victory for the Gregorian party, was beginning to prevail. In March even John XXIII was persuaded to acquiesce. It remained only for Gregory to prepare and communicate his abdication.[2]

For this he chose, or accepted, Carlo Malatesta as his proctor.[3] In the second week of March he drew up bulls authorising the Council, appointing proctors in Constance, among them Carlo and the Count Palatine, and finally entrusting special powers of representation to Malatesta as 'procuraterem nostrum . . . specialem', free to treat of renunciation 'si, ubi et quando tibi videbitur pro unione huiusmodi expedire', and to do 'quae nos ipsi facere possemus, si personaliter interessemus'. On 25 March, after a solemn session of the Riminese general council, Carlo left by way of Cesenatico for Ravenna and Venice.[4] In Venice he was pressed to abandon the journey, the government emphasising the 'small love' between Pandolfo Malatesta and Sigismund, and the ill-feeling of the king of the Romans towards all Italians.[5] But Carlo continued on his way to Brescia. Here, in his brother's city, he was detained by disorder following the flight from Constance of John XXIII (20 March). He wrote to the Council explaining his delay and revealing that two of his envoys had been captured, one in the Trentino, the other near Friuli, and not until safe-conducts had been supplied by Filippo Visconti and Frederick of Austria was he able to resume his journey late in May.[6]

---

[1] Which explains the dramatic narrative of Platina, according to which Carlo Malatesta was too precipitate in resigning the papacy; Gregory XII wished, like Benedict XIII, to procrastinate, and the sudden deprivation killed him: Platina, 302. In the time of the Council of Basle a similar opinion circulated: John of Segovia, ii.1127–8.

[2] Hollerbach, 'Gregorianische Partei', 21–2, 24; *Acta Const.*, iii.325–6; Hardt, ii.206ff., vi.38; Mansi, xxvii.439; Valois, *Schisme*, iv.275; Hefele-Leclerq, vii–182–4.

[3] Sanudo wrote of Carlo Malatesta when in Venice during March: 'Non ha voluto che il papa vadi in persona': *Vite*, 993.

[4] Hardt, iv.177–8, 192–3, 369ff.; *Acta Const.*, i.190, 270–1; Hollerbach, 'Gregorianische Partei', 28; *Ristretto d'Urbino*, 50; Pedrino, rub. 16; Clementini, ii.283–4.

[5] *Acta Const.*, iii.362–7, cf. 333.

[6] *Ibid.* iii.327–33; Hardt, 179–80; Martène and Durand, *Thes. nov.*, ii.1533, 1637; Hollerbach, 'Gregorianische Partei', 30–2.

He entered Constance on Sunday, 15 June, with a large and splendid following, and was met by a company no less impressive, which escorted him to his residence. The next day, since Gregory had not yet formally recognised the Council, he presented himself before Sigismund, and there ensued a dogged negotiation with the heads of the nations which lasted over two weeks, Carlo inflexibly defending the rights of his obedience. He was even anxious to defer any act of renunciation until Sigismund had met Benedict XIII at Nice, offering to go along with the king 'ad videndum quid vocatus Benedictus facere vellet', and he only agreed to it when the cardinals had accepted Gregory's bulls of convocation and authorisation: 'et visum fuit concilio pro tanto bono pocius admittendam, quam cessionem non fieri' (Fillastre). Carlo also insisted on provision for Gregory, his cardinals and his officials. When all these conditions had been met he was free to surrender the papacy, as Gregory's proctor; which he did in a ceremonial session, in the presence of Sigismund, 'tanquam praesidens', on 4 July 1415, prefacing the act with a 'beautiful dissertation' on the biblical text, 'facta est cum angelo multitudo militiae coelestis . . .' (Luke, ii.13). The hopes of six patient years had at last been realised.[1]

The fourteenth session of Constance did not end Carlo Malatesta's interest in ecclesiastical unity: he could still find spirit to write to Benedict XIII and the king of Aragon.[2] Even less did it dissolve his connection with Gregory XII, for whom he had already exacted concessions from the Council: he was present at the session of 15 July in which Angelo Correr was pronounced cardinal-bishop of Porto, as well as *legatus a la tere* and vicar-general in the March of Ancona.[3] Ten days later Carlo left Constance.[4] But his achievement was not as secure as he thought. Correr's legation was resented by many Italians, particularly in the March, and in a letter to the Council from Brescia (17 August) Carlo, while reporting the deposition of his insignia by Gregory (20 July), complained of rumours in Italy that the legation was disliked in Constance, and urged prompt despatch of an embassy.[5] In October Angelo was still expecting the arrival of envoys from the Council;[6] and as late as April 1416 Sigismund had to remind the fathers

---

[1] Hardt, iv.369–82; Martène and Durand, *Thes. nov.*, ii.1638; *Acta Const.*, ii.41, 46–7, 251; iii.337–9; *Frankfurts Reichskorrespondenz* (ed. Janssen, Freiburg, i. B., 1863–72), i.291, 293–4; Sanudo, 896; Hollerbach, 'Gregorianische Partei', 32–9. Throughout his stay Carlo Malatesta seems to have shown a taste and some ability for religious discourse: *Acta Const.*, ii.375.

[2] *Ibid.* iii.340–51; Hollerbach, 'Gregorianische Partei', 122–3, 127.

[3] Hardt, i.169–70, ii.413, iv.474–81.

[4] *Acta Const.*, ii.255.

[5] Hardt, ii.413–14; *Acta Const.*, 33–7, 352–5; Sanudo, 896; Hollerbach, 'Gregorianische Partei', 123–5; Mercati, *AR* 1. 234–5.   [6] Hardt, iv.550–3.

of their undertakings to the late pope.[1] But most revealing of all is a letter addressed to Barcelona from Florence (11 December 1415). In this even revocation of the legateship is mentioned: Angelo Correr is wholly governed by the Malatesta, of whom 'tots les altres senyors de la Marca son enemichs mortals e no han volgut james consentir en aquesta legacio. E per co lay han levada.'[2] The other Marcher lords certainly had grievances against the Malatesta. It was natural to suppose Correr's legation would increase their influence further.

Among the numerous charges levelled against John XXIII at Constance was a complaint that he had alienated many lands of the church.[3] Gregory XII could have incurred the same accusation. Records of his generosity to the Malatesta are few; but his good will is evident enough. As we have seen, the Malatesta had extended their possessions in the March as secular representatives of the pope, at Monte Cassiano, Montolmo and elsewhere.[4] Other benefits followed. In February 1414 Gregory granted Carlo a large assignment on monastic revenues in his territory, in discharge of expenses. In June of the following year he bestowed on Malatesta of Cesena the vicariate for ten years of numerous castles belonging to the church of Ravenna in the dioceses of Rimini, Cesena, Bertinoro and Sarsina.[5] And a little later (1 July) when reserving the *census* due to the treasury in the March of Ancona and Massa Trabaria, he excepted a proportion promised to the Malatesta.[6] The association became even closer when Carlo Malatesta, on returning from Constance, accompanied Correr into the March late in 1415.[7] Memories of 1355 must by then have become dim, but it seemed the Malatesta were about to recover their previous power in the March, and it aroused the same protest and revolt.

The main aggressor was Malatesta of Cesena who, after serving Ladislas in Umbria until the king's death in August 1414, launched an offensive of his own in the March of Ancona. He first attacked Ludovico Migliorati, conquering part of the territory of Fermo. Then, after

[1] *Acta Const.*, ii.287.
[2] *Ibid.* iv.669. Correr settled as legate in Recanati, a city commended to the Malatesta: Compagnoni, *Reggia Picena*, 299.
[3] E.g. *Acta Const.*, iv.791: lands alienated to Ladislas, Paolo Orsini, Giovanni da Montefeltro and Malatesta of Pesaro.
[4] By March 1415 the Malatesta had also secured Amandola which in June 1413 was being held by a vicar of Ladislas, pending settlement of disputes between the Malatesta and Rodolfo of Camerino: Zonghi, 19; Bartoccetti, 'Liber', 54.
[5] Cecconi, 'Sommario', n. xxxvi; Fantuzzi, iv, clxi; Battaglini, *Vita*, 691; Tonini, v/2, xxvii. It seems Malatesta had been fighting to recover or defend these for the church (at his own expense) and been holding them 'iam per annos'.
[6] *Acta Const.*, iii.311.
[7] Clementini, ii.288–9; Sanudo, 897; *Acta Const.*, iii.355–6. Battaglini thinks Carlo was made rector of the March: *Zecca*, 224.

a truce (April, May 1415) he turned against the Varani and the city of Macerata, until halted again by a temporary peace in August.[1]

Among the parties to this second peace was a new and threatening personality in Central Italian politics: the Perugian *condottiere* Braccio da Montone, who had been entrusted by John XXIII with defence of the Papal State. He soon made his presence felt. After trying to levy tribute from the province of Romagna, he proceeded in the spring of 1415 to lay waste the territory of Forlì, and then – in sympathy if not in alliance with the enemies of the Malatesta – of Cesena, Fano, Rimini and Pesaro as well.[2] For the Malatesta Braccio's intervention was to have serious consequences. But in the autumn of 1415 events were suddenly complicated by the arrival, in Romagna and the March, of delegates from Constance.[3]

The lords of the March lost no time in enlisting their support. In November Migliorati sent envoys to them at Gubbio, and in December two of the legates visited him in Fermo.[4] At the same time he and Rodolfo Varani, with the city of Ancona, had representatives at Constance, exchanging charges and counter-charges with an ambassador of Carlo Malatesta and to some possible effect.[5] Certainly the legates on the spot seem to have been convinced. In response to their complaints, they agreed to join with Migliorati, the Varani and the commune of Ancona in an alliance against the Malatesta and the cardinal-legate Correr. By the spring their forces had overrun a number of territories and they were pressing Malatesta of Cesena hard

---

[1] Bonincontri, 108–9; *Cron. Ferm.*, 42–3; Adami, 43–4; Lilii, ii.143; *Mem. M. Cassiano*, 56–62. In Oct. 1414 the Malatesta of Pesaro, allies of Rimini during this whole war, made a futile attempt to take Ancona: Pedrino, rub. 12; *Ristretto d'Urbino*, 50; *Cron. Ferm.*, 42; Bernabei, 149ff.; Bonincontri, 107; Sanudo, 891, 892. In this campaign the dependants and allies of the Malatesta included, with many other places: Osimo, Iesi, Amandola, Castelfidardo, Filottrano, Offagna, Montolmo, Civitanova: Amiani, i.339. Matelica imposed a 'datium' in May, 1415 to pay the stipend of Malatesta of Cesena: Mazzatinti, *Archivi*, Ser. 2, ii.341; S. Severino seems also to have been at their command (Lilii, ii.148–9), as were Recanati and perhaps Cingoli (*Mem. di M. Cassiano*, 56). Roccacontrada refused submission: Zonghi, 17; Anselmi, pt. i.

[2] Campanus, 75–6; *Chron. Forl.*, 884; Bonincontri, *loc. cit.*; Guerriero, 39; *Ann. Forl.*, 85; *Ristretto d'Urbino*, 50; Pedrino, rub. 17–18; Cobelli, 164. Perugia helped the Malatesta: Pellini, ii.212, 214.

[3] They left on 17 Aug., commissioned among other things to compose peace, particularly in the March. They reached Forlì 23 Sept., then passed through, Rimini and Fano to Gubbio and Macerata to install Correr: Hardt, iv.493; *Chron. Forl.*, 885; Amiani, i.340; *Ristretto d'Urbino*, 51; *Codice Dip. S. Vitioria*, cxxv. On 25 Dec. the Malatesta wrote to Macerata to re-establish friendly relations (Compagnoni, *Reggia Picena*, 298–9), and on 6 Jan. 1416 ordered Osimo to elect a representative to swear fealty to the legates (Martorelli, 230).

[4] Adami, 44.   [5] Hardt, iv.558–61.

when a disaster occurred which suddenly faced the Malatesta with a threat of total ruin.[1]

It arose from their part in a long conflict between Perugia and Braccio, who was trying to make himself *signore* of the city. This he finally did in 1416, but not without a bitter struggle involving the Malatesta. Relations between Carlo Malatesta and Perugia had lately become very close, and early in 1416 the Priors besought his help against Braccio. After some negotiation he accepted command of their army and began organising a campaign. But on 12 July he was decisively routed by Braccio and Tartaglia da Lavello four miles from Perugia, and was taken prisoner with Galeazzo Malatesta of Pesaro and many others.[2]

This was the worst crisis for the Malatesta since 1355. Carlo Malatesta was a captive, Malatesta of Cesena was infirm (he died in September 'di quartana')[3] and Pandolfo Malatesta far away, embroiled in Lombardy. Only intercession by friends and allies preserved them from destruction. Isabetta, cut off in Rimini, appealed at once to the Council and to Venice.[4] Malatesta of Pesaro and his son Carlo hastened to give support, perhaps feeling endangered themselves; while Obizzo da Polenta, close ally of the Venetians, and since November 1414 married to a daughter of Malatesta of Cesena, was prompt with help and advice to Isabetta. Above all he pressed Pandolfo Malatesta to free himself from Lombardy and come south to save his possessions.[5] Pandolfo needed no urging. On 4 August he concluded a hasty truce with Filippo Visconti,[6] begged release from Venice, though his *ferma* was not yet expired (24 August),[7] and then, followed by his captain,

---

[1] Compagnoni, *Reggia Picena*, 300; *Cron. Ferm.*, 44–5; Adami, 44–5; Lilii, ii. 149. Amiani (i. 341) says an attack by Carlo Malatesta on Camerino provoked the alliance; also that Migliorati was created rector of the March.

[2] B. Pitti, *Cronica* (Bologna, 1905), 196–7; Morelli, *Ricordi*, 28; Minuti, 190–1; *Ristretto d'Urbino*, 51; F. Rinuccini, *Ricordi storici* (Florence, 1840), liv; Pedrino, rub. 21; *Cron. sen.*, 785–6; *Cron. mal.*, 57; etc. Campanus (91–103) hints at a design on the *signoria* by Carlo Malatesta also; he certainly demanded *merum et mixtum imperium* in Perugia in the place of pay: Pellini, ii. 220–1.

[3] 20 Sept.: *Chron. Forl.*, 886; Borghi, 87; Branchi, 174. He had already lost his son Galeotto, the only legitimate heir to the Malatesta *signoria*, in Oct. 1414: Pedrino, rub. 11; *Ristretto d'Urbino*, 50; Mazzatinti, *Inventari*, xxxix. 226, n. 279k. Polissena, his widow, married Michele Attendolo Sforza: Zazzeri, 267. On the succession to his territories: below p. 154.

[4] Finke, *Forschungen*, 180; *Acta Const.*, ii. 64, iii. 307. At this time Carlo's troops were carrying Venetian standards, the Malatesta being *raccomandati* of Venice: *Cron. sen.*, 786.

[5] Clementini, ii. 105, 188, 291; Zazzeri, 270; Rubeus, 614.

[6] Osio, ii, xxxvii, 58–9; Morbio, 185; Sanudo, 910; Predelli, x. 214, 217.

[7] Sanudo, 910. On 24 Aug. Pandolfo tearfully besought the Venetian senate to release him 'ad partes Marchie pro liberacione sui sanguinis et pro deffensione status sui in partibus Marchie, qui est antiquus nidus domus sue, nam clare videbat omnia loca sua esse perdita nisi illuc se transferat': *Acta Const.*, iii. 307 n. 1.

Martino da Faenza, hurried to Romagna with a force of 3,000 men.[1]
Here he arrived in time to prevent the total dissolution of the Malatesta state.

After Carlo's defeat the Marcher allies, with the conciliar legates,
took Braccio into their service, and mounted a combined offensive
against the Malatesta territories. Malatesta of Cesena's recent conquests
soon fell away. Osimo rose in revolt, and on 17 September, a week
before Pandolfo's arrival, Braccio was writing to Orvieto that he had
reduced the *contado* of Fano and would shortly be holding the *contado*
of Iesi as well. With these advantages he hoped to conclude a quick
agreement with the Malatesta. But he reckoned without the reinforcements from the north. In November Pandolfo advanced into the
March, recovering many castles of Fano, together with Osimo,
Montelupone and Civitanova, and was soon stirring up trouble for
Braccio in Perugia. On 4 December he secured a truce with the Varani
and Ludovico Migliorati; and although hostilities went on, the only
task outstanding was to negotiate Carlo's release.[2]

Agreement was not easy. Venetian intervention effected nothing, for
Braccio demanded payment of a heavy ransom which he claimed the
Malatesta were rich enough to pay.[3] More successful were Florence
and Guidantonio da Montefeltro,[4] who, with the legates, were able to
arrange articles of peace between Braccio, the Marcher lords and the
Malatesta in February 1417. Carlo Malatesta was burdened with a
ransom of 60,000 ducats, 30,000 to be paid at once, the remainder in
annual sums of 10,000, Guidantonio undertaking to contribute a part.
Braccio was to keep Iesi with Monte Cassiano and Montalboddo, while
Ancona was to surrender Sinigaglia, and the Malatesta the castles they
held round Recanati. After paying the first instalment of ransom Carlo
was released and allowed to return, at the beginning of April, to
Rimini, where he was visited and congratulated by the neighbouring
signori.[5]

---

[1] By 24 Sept. he was in Rimini: *Ristretto d'Urbino*, 51; Mattiolo, 283; *Chron. Forl.*,
886. Pandolfo received help from Gianfrancesco Gonzaga: *RIS* xx. 800; Tarducci,
'Gianfr. Gonzaga', pt. ii, 54–5.

[2] *Cron. Ferm.*, 45–6; *Ristretto d'Urbino*, 51; Campanus, 115–18; Sanudo, 913;
Adami, 45–6; Lilii, ii. 149–55; Amiani, i. 341–2; Compagnoni, *Reggia Picena*, 301;
Martorelli, 230; Bartoccetti, 'Liber', 45–7, 51–2; Valentini, *BU* 1923, 11–13,
docs. 26–9. Carlo had been committed by Braccio to the custody of the Varani.

[3] Sanudo, 910, 912–13; Campanus, 116–18. The Venetians refused Pandolfo a loan
for the release of his brother: Sanudo, 913; *Acta Const.*, iii. 307 n.1.

[4] *Ibid.*; *ASI* xvi/2.579; Guerriero, 39; Sozomenus, 7; Ammirato, ii. 976–7;
Pedrino, rub. 21; *Ristretto d'Urbino*, 51; *ASI* 1894, 256.

[5] The ransom is variously assessed and cannot be established exactly: *Chron. Forl.*,
886: Sanudo, 913ff.; Campanus, 118; *Cron. sen.*, 788; *Cron. Ferm.*, 46; Pedrino,
rub. 25ff.; *Ristretto d'Urbino*, 51–2; Adami, 46; Lilii, ii. 155–6; Compagnoni,
Reggia Picena, 302–3; Amiani, i. 342; Fabretti, v. 125; *Mem. M. Cassiano*, 62–3,

For the moment Romagna and the March were composed.[1] The restless presence of Braccio certainly remained a threat, both to peace and to papal authority. But with the death of Angelo Correr in September 1417,[2] and the election at Constance two months later of an unquestioned pope, a new period at last seemed impending in the history of the church, of the papal domains, and of those who had held them for so long.

65–6; Rossi, *Monte Alboddo*, 97; *ASI* xvi/2.580; Valentini, 17. One legacy of this peace may have been the arrest and execution by Carlo Malatesta of Pandolfo's captain, Martino da Faenza, after Pandolfo's departure in April 1417. According to some the design was simply to take treacherous possession of Martino's wealth as a contribution towards the ransom; but more probably, it was retribution for a plot to occupy Rimini.

[1] In May Ludovico Migliorati was betrothed to Taddea Malatesta of Pesaro, whom he married in January 1418: Sanudo, 915; *Cron. Ferm.*, 47.

[2] Who remained to the end on friendly terms with the Malatesta: Martorelli, 237–41; Cecconi, 'Sommario', n. XL.

6

The pontificate of Martin V

The Great Schism is commonly seen as the darkest period in the history of the Papal State, an interregnum of impoverishment, debility and decay. That the papacy had to fight for recognition of its authority, and conciliate the power of lords and communes was certainly characteristic of the time. But it is not easy to show that such conditions were greatly different from those prevailing before or after the legation of Albornoz, or that they were insuperable.[1] If, during the Schism, the office of rector was burdensome,[2] or taxes difficult to collect,[3] the elements of provincial government survived intact,[4] even though abuses were grave and needed time to eradicate.[5] Boniface IX in particular was successful in asserting papal authority, and could be described at the end of his pontificate as ruling 'like a strict emperor'.[6] His achievement, it is true, must be largely explained by his liberality, more particularly his readiness in granting both to cities and *signori* the authority of temporal vicariate, which normally bestowed 'auctoritate apostolica' without the express assent of the cardinals, became most widespread under him. Not only did earlier grantees continue to hold the title. New claimants also appeared, and among them some of the greatest papal cities: Ascoli, Fermo, Bologna, Città di Castello.[7] Most numerous, however, were lords:

---

[1] Partner, 16ff.; Guiraud, ch. 1, who neglects to emphasise earlier anarchy. It must be recalled that dilapidation of the Papal State was possibly the greatest inducement to the popes to return to Rome – and so, according to N. Spinelli, was the real cause of the Schism: Durrieu, *Royaume d'Adria*, 50; Romano, 'Spinelli' 1901, 484ff.; Valois, *Schisme*, i.10.

[2] E.g. Lilii, ii.130. [3] E.g. *Cron. Volg.*, *RIS*[2] xxvii/2.172.

[4] Cf. Fumi, 'Inventario'. For taxation: Favier, 181ff.; Amati, Notizie', 191–2; Theiner, iii.72; Adami, 31; Castellani, *Malatesta*, 40; for parliaments: Theiner, iii.72, 104; Amiani, i.325–6; Favier, 190ff.

[5] Hofmann, i.1ff.

[6] Gregorovius, *History of the city of Rome*, tr. Hamilton (London, 1894–1902), vi/2.546–7, 554, 561; Ermini, 'Relazioni', 258ff.; Finke, 'Papstchronik', 349; Cf. Gabione writing to Nanne Gozzadini in 1403: 'Gia longissimo tempo non fu la Santa ghiexia magior da Roma qui [Bologna]': Gozzadini, *Nanne Gozzadini*, 276–82.

[7] Between 1390 and 1412 (in addition to those previously noted) vicariates were granted at various times to the Este, Montefeltro, Manfredi, Alidosi, Ordelaffi,

vicar-despots, whose depredations of pope and people were denounced by some contemporaries as bitterly as the tyrants of Dante's day.[1] Because of them, towns now began to stipulate in agreements with the pope that they should never be granted, without consent, to lords or vicars: a provision increasingly recurrent during the fifteenth century.[2] There was little enough to check the liberty of despots.[3] Yet a grant of vicariate did not imply total abdication of papal power. It kept alive the distinction between unlicensed and illegitimate authority.[4] It envisaged an ultimate restoration of direct papal government. Above all, it carried obligations, at least in money, often in service, and was normally limited to a term of years, even when regranted on petition.[5] It is to be noticed too that at this time the oath imposed on vicars became more stringent and elaborate, and to the older oath of fidelity were added new clauses, of which the most revealing bound the vicar and his subjects to observe the constitutions of John XXII and his successors against the usurpation of papal lands 'tyrannice' by any emperor, king, prince, or lesser secular lord.[6] That the popes intended these obligations to be taken seriously is proved not only by the particularity of the terms of investiture themselves, but also by the bulls

Polenta, Brancaleoni, Simonetti, Migliorati and (for some of their lands) the Varani, and to Fermo, Ascoli, Bologna, Città di Castello, Siena and Perugia: Theiner, iii. 3–4, 7–8, 22, 70, 127; Fantuzzi, iii, cxxiv; *Cron. Ferm.*, 37; Raynaldus, vii, 1390, n. xviii; Ghirardacci, ii.459; G. Baldassini, App. xli; Lilii, ii.145; Torelli, 180–1; Guiraud, 225; Pellegrini, 'Gubbio', 168. There were also many feudal grants.

[1] Thus Niccolo Spinelli, in 1393: 'quia omnia per pecuniam facta sunt, et est vulgare proverbium in Italia: la glesia de Roma voli botti e denari . . . illi qui expulerunt officiales Ecclesie, cum pecuniis, quas eviscerant a miseris populis subditis . . . concredant cum Summis Pontificibus, qui sunt pro tempore, qui curant magis de pecuniis quam de salute subditorum, et concedunt terras eis in vicariatum ad certum tempus et cum aliquo censu quod promittunt Ecclesie, et tenent ipsos subditos per tirampniam' etc.: Durrieu, *Royaume d'Adria*, 44; cf. *Chron. Plac.*, 530.

[2] E.g. Theiner, iii.51 (Anagni, 1399), 60 (Viterbo, 140–1). A similar promise was made to Recanati as early as 1372: *ibid.* ii.540. Cf. below pp. 258, 336.

[3] Best illustrated perhaps by the relations of semi-dependence on other Italian powers contracted by many vicars: as when Antonio da Montefeltro in 1399 swore fealty to the Visconti (Romano, 'Regesti C. Cristiani', 320), or the Montefeltro, Alidosi and Trinci became *raccomandati* of Florence in 1413 (Ammirato, ii.969), or the Polenta, in 1409 (or 1407) formed a similar alliance with Venice (Rubeus, 607; Romanin, iv.55). The practice continued long after the Schism.

[4] Thus the Varani did not obtain the *gubernatio* of Camerino until the Council of Constance granted it in 1416: Theiner, ii.338, 527; Feliciangeli, 'Relazioni', 396–7.

[5] Even during the Schism vicariates for life or more were only exceptional, being limited to the Este, Malatesta, Montefeltro and Alidosi. Cf. Vergottini, 'Note', 365.

[6] E.g. vicariates to Ascoli, Fermo, Bologna, Città di Castello, the Alidosi, Montefeltro, and others: above p. 149 n. 7.

issued under Boniface IX and Innocent VII against invalid grants of vicariate and the danger of such grants to papal revenue.[1] If the policy denoted weakness, neither the weakness nor the policy was new. The reformers of Constance did not reverse it,[2] and it was destined to last for years.

After the Council of Pisa brought the Schism closer to Italian politics, conditions sharply worsened in the Papal State. It was now that *signori* like Guidantonio da Montefeltro, as ally of one Italian pope, and the Malatesta, as allies of another, were able to extend their dominions in the name of religious allegiance.[3] And it was now that neighbouring powers were able to occupy, with show of legitimacy, parts of papal territory.[4] The threatened disruption of the patrimony, never so serious since the war of Eight Saints, offered opportune support to the advocates of reform in papal administration and particularly papal finance, which it was hoped would be taken up at Constance. The reformers of the Schism period did not accept the thirteenth-century papal theory which traced back the temporal power to Christ himself, but derived the *patrimonium* from Constantine's Donation. Their concern however was not to challenge the existence of the Papal States, or to have them secularised, but much more to see them prosper under a careful government, that the church universal might be relieved of taxation.[5] It was in this spirit that the Council denounced the dilapidation of papal territory by John XXIII,[6] and later proposed that the pope before election should swear never to alienate the church's temporalities: 'nec in feudum novum seu emphyteosin dabit'.[7] The Council of Basle reaffirmed the prohibition on enfeoffments and other grants, at least without the consent of the college of cardinals.[8] And it is only with reference to these decrees, and the reluctance they expressed to supporting the papacy financially, that we can explain the growing importance that temporal revenues began

---

[1] Theiner, iii.83–4; *Magnum Bull. Roman.*, iv.642–3.

[2] As shown by grants to Città di Castello (Muzi, i.199, 201, 202) and the Varani (Lilii, ii.145, 147–8).

[3] For Guidantonio: *Ristretto d'Urbino*, 49; *Ann. Est.*, 1049–50; Theiner, iii.128, 130; Guiraud, 36.

[4] In 1409 or 1410 Florence was invested with a number of small places in Romagna 'in perpetuum et honorificum feudum': Sugenheim, 312. And in 1412 John XXIII granted Siena the vicariate of Radicofani for sixty years: Theiner, iii.127.

[5] See Laehr, *QF* 1913. Cf. Freidrich Reiser's *Reformation des Kaisers Sigmund* (ed. W. Boehm, Leipzig, 1876), 163.

[6] May 1415: Hardt, iv.201–2, 232; *Acta Const.*, iii.184.

[7] Hardt, i.655–6, ch. v.

[8] *Concilium Bas.*, ii.298; John of Segovia, ii.291, 851, 998, 1000, 1004, 1024; iii.84, 90. On 26 Sept. 1437 the Patrimony was asserted to be for the maintenance of the pope and the cardinals: *ibid.* ii.1024; cf. 1128, 1179

to assume in papal income after the Council of Constance. The pope was to live of his own.[1]

It was the opinion then of many churchmen in Europe that the papacy could and should set its house in order, whatever the powers of its subjects; and this foreshadows another feature of the period now impending. During the fifteenth century once again the greatest embarrassment to papal government came not from within but from without: not from turbulent *tiranni* but from aggressive neighbours, or from *condottieri* in search of territory, as well as from the dynastic policy of the popes themselves. The origin of all three evils may be traced to the years of Schism. The career of Biordo dei Michelotti in Orvieto and Todi, of Braccio in the Marches and Umbria, forecast the later incursions of Niccolo Fortebraccio, Francesco Sforza, and the Piccinini, which were to help to break up for ever the compact society of Romagna and the March. Filippo Visconti and the Aragonese kings of Naples had only to follow the example of Gian Galeazzo and Ladislas. And the papal *nipoti* could claim precursors, if not in the brother of Boniface IX who became 'Marchio Marchie',[2] then in the nephew of Innocent VII, Ludovico Migliorati, lord and vicar of Fermo.

Martin V was the first pope to apply the conciliar principles of papal government urged by the Council of Constance. It remains to see how far in a pontificate of fourteen years he was able or disposed to do so. Only then can the decline be appreciated which now, so soon after their influence was at its height, began to overtake the Malatesta of Rimini, and brought them within several decades to the verge of political extinction.

Little has changed in the traditional picture of Martin V as a ruler successful in restoring a large part of papal authority, and at the same time the most nepotistic of popes since Boniface VIII.[3] Elected in November 1417, he did not long conceal his attitude to the vicar-despots of the papal patrimony. In Article XII of the reform proposals he published two months later, he revoked all alienations of land, all

[1] And this, as a result of the councils, the papacy in the fifteenth century was largely obliged to do: Favier, 689; Nina, i.68ff., iii.9ff.; Bauer, 'Epochen', 473–98; Göller, 'Untersuchungen', 251; Miltenberger, *RQ* viii.393. By the pontificate of Eugenius IV the Camera Apostolica was the governing authority of the Papal State: Gottlob, 71. In March 1433 the Council of Basle ordered an assessment of the papal patrimony to be made, and four years later it was stated that the popes had never before derived so much from their temporalities: *Concilium Bas.*, ii. 377; cf. 490, 493; John of Segovia, ii.1128.

[2] Sozomenus, 1145.

[3] A. V. Reumont, *Beiträge zur Ital. Gesch.* (Berlin, 1853–7), v.51ff.; Partner, 193ff. and *passim*.

vicariates and similar concessions since Gregory XI, 'ultra quinquennium sine Concilii consensu et subscriptione maioris partis
cardinalium illius obedientiae'. In addition he expressed the intention
that rule over papal land should in future be given only to cardinals or
to other prelates and that vicariates should not be granted for more
than three years, and then only with the consent of the cardinals.[1] This
was no empty declaration. During the opening months of his pontificate
many lords and towns of the papal states petitioned the pope for confirmation or extension of their vicariates, and although to most he gave
way,[2] nearly all were limited to the term of three years, and previous
grants were cancelled.[3] Even the investiture of Braccio with Perugia,
Todi, and other places, which Martin was compelled to make in 1420,
carried this provision.[4] Braccio outlived the three years, but died soon
afterwards, and the pope was able to reclaim his inheritance.[5] Rome
he had already recovered from the Neapolitans, Bologna had submitted, and by 1430, though not always by his own endeavours, he
had managed to restore papal government in Imola, Forlì, Fermo,
Ascoli and S. Severino.[6] In that year, 'esendo del nostro signor papa
Martino pacifficho regimente per la Ghiexa de Roma, ciò da Roma
fima a Imola ogne terra al suo dominio o veramente hobediente ad essa
Ghiexa, salvoché Bologna avea certa diferencia con le Ghiexa',[7] the
pope might feel satisfied. Not every family had been dispossessed, it is
true, nor every enterprise successful. In 1424 Martin tried and failed to
expel from his dominions Corrado Trinci, lord of Foligno, and the
undertaking ended characteristically with the marriage of Corrado's
daughter Faustina with the papal *nipote*, Giovanni Andrea Colonna.[8]
In this compromise Martin had perhaps acquiesced reluctantly.[9] But
it harmonised well with other marriages concluded under his rule,
which united his family with the lords of Montefeltro, Piombino and

---

[1] Hardt, i.1020. On 3 March 1418 he revoked all concessions of tallages or subsidies
to captains and vicars in the March of Ancona: Theiner, iii.154.

[2] Bologna notably failed to obtain an extension of its 25-year vicariate: Ghirardacci,
ii.620; M. Longhi, 'N. Piccinino in Bologna', *AMR* 1905–6, 153, 1906–7,
284–5; Theiner, iii.166.

[3] This condition appears in vicariates granted, between 1418 and 1421, to Città di
Castello, the Alidosi, Ordelaffi, Orsini and Trinci: Theiner, iii.157–8, 171; *Chron.
Forl.*, 888; Pedrino, rub. 33; Dorio, 204. Cf. Partner, 47ff.

[4] Theiner, iii.183; Contelorio, 49.

[5] Theiner, iii.225; Partner, 78ff.

[6] Despite protests, he also continued the work of tightening authority over towns
recovered from despots, especially in control of the *podesteria*, jurisdiction and
finance; papal succeeded to domestic *signoria*: Partner, 67ff., 84ff., 98–9, 124ff. and
passim; *Cron. Ferm.*, 57–60; Adami, 49–50.

[7] Pedrino, rub. 446.

[8] Dorio, 207–11.

[9] Morici, 'Vicariato', 260–2.

Camerino.[1] In this way, as the Malatesta of Rimini were to find, where the ambitions of the *signori* could not be overcome, they might at least be exploited. And nothing was more revealing of this than the relations of Martin with the Malatesta, which showed at once his aspirations as pope and his frailties as a dynast.

If the lands ruled by the Malatesta of Rimini had already, in 1418, suffered some curtailment, they still formed the largest lordship in papal territory north of the Apennines and, because of that alone, were a serious challenge to any design of papal restoration. If the castle of S. Giovanni in Persiceto had returned to Bologna, and Iesi, Monte S. Maria in Cassiano, and Montalboddo, all had been lost to Braccio, the gains made over the years at the expense of Forlì, the Polenta and the counts of Urbino, which the papacy had subsequently sanctioned or condoned, continued safely to encircle the cities on which the Malatesta had originally based their power. The death of Malatesta of Cesena in 1416, like that of Galeotto Belfiore sixteen years before, merely released his lands to the surviving brothers, Pandolfo taking Cesena and Meldola, where Carlo controlled the government in his absence.[2] Andrea Malatesta had been an energetic member of his family; and his presence may well have been missed when the lords of Rimini looked to the first intimations of policy from the new pope.

Whether Martin V before his election had had any communication with Carlo Malatesta at Constance can only be surmised, as also his attitude to Carlo's activities during the Council. But certainly his relations with the Malatesta during the first years of his pontificate were cordial and benevolent. At the very beginning he received tokens of their obedience;[3] and it agreed also with his policy when the Malatesta, in April 1418, accepted an invitation from Giovanna of Naples to collaborate against Braccio in the March of Ancona.[4] In his turn the pope tried to make terms between Pandolfo Malatesta and Filippo Maria Visconti, and preserve the Malatesta lordship in Lombardy.

When Pandolfo Malatesta hurried south in 1416 to save the Malatesta state he had already been fighting for several years to save his own. The control which he and his brother had established in Milan in 1408 scarcely survived Carlo's departure. Giovanni Maria Visconti

[1] Lilii, ii.157, 161; Lanciani, 'Patrimonio'; Partner, 77 etc.; below p. 160.

[2] Braschi, 286–7; Zazzeri, 271, 276: cf. *Commiss. Albizzi*, i.464, 470, and n. XL *passim*. Of Malatesta's other lands Fossombrone came into the possession of the Malatesta of Pesaro: below p. 166.

[3] Thus on the election of Martin the *consiglio generale* of Fano appointed representatives to swear obedience to the bishop of Teramo on behalf of the church, the Council and the new pope. Later (Feb. 1419) two more envoys did obedience to Martin in Forlì: Amiani, i.345,347.

[4] *ASI* xvi/2. 508; Tonini, v/2. 120–2.

soon withdrew his uncertain support and Malatesta of Cesena left Lombardy in disgust (1409). At the same time Giovanni Maria called in Bouciquault, the French governor of Genoa, against the brothers Malatesta, and when this failed had to submit to the equally uncomfortable domination of Facino Cane. Even so, the assassination of Giovanni Maria and the death of Facino Cane in 1412 only served to make Pandolfo's situation more precarious. Filippo Maria, who took over Milan within a month, never pretended he would tolerate the permanent seizure of Visconti territory by alien *condottieri*. He allowed Antonia Malatesta to retain a share in the government for a few months; she then found it necessary to retire to Cesena, though retaining her title of 'Duchessa di Milano'. Though willing enough to use Pandolfo, it was only a matter of time before Filippo Maria expelled all usurpers from the duchy. Neither the intercession of Venice, which had Pandolfo in its pay, nor Filippo's worries with the king of the Romans and other enemies at Rome, could induce the duke to consider a lasting settlement with the Malatesta. Martin V's intervention was to be no more successful.[1]

The decisive war with the Visconti captain Carmagnola for the possession of Brescia and Bergamo had already begun when the pope arrived in Brescia during October 1418. For the length of his passage through the Milanese a short truce had been declared, and this Martin tried to make permanent. From Brescia he moved to Mantua, in company with Pandolfo, and there, joined by Carlo Malatesta, he drafted terms of peace by which, in brief, the two cities were to remain for life to Pandolfo and then revert to the Visconti. At the end of January Filippo Maria accepted the award. And on 22 February, after Martin had left for Forlì and Florence, the peace was made public.[2] But if Martin thought his decision was final he was quickly undeceived. Neither side probably expected the peace to last. Neither side observed its terms. And when Pandolfo went to the defence of another usurper, Gabrino Fondulo, threatened by the Visconti *riconquista*, he condemned himself to destruction. In July Bergamo with most of the

[1] Fuller detail, with references, on Visconti-Malatesta relations, 1408–18, may be found in the standard histories of Milan, Brescia and Bergamo; cf. also Romano, *ASL* 1896. Among the side-effects was one of the more dramatic and best recorded episodes of Malatesta family history: the marriage alliance, in 1418, of Niccolo III d'Este with Parisina di Andrea Malatesta, terminated violently 7 years later with the trial and death for adultery of Parisina and Ugo, eldest of Niccolo's innumerable bastards: Solerti, N. *Antologia*, Ser. 3, 45–6 (1893); Lazzari, *Rassegna Nazionale*, Feb.–April 1915.

[2] Filippo Visconti was also to pay Pandolfo an annual pension and settle 65,000 ducats on his heirs, when the cities reverted: Morbio, 197; Osio, ii, XLV, 70–1; *Commiss. Albizzi*, i. 308; Romano, *ASL* 1897, i. 117; Sanudo, 924–5; Sercambi, iii. 239; Odorici, viii. 303ff.; Miltenberger, *Mitteil. Inst. Oest. Geschichtsforsch.*, xv, 1894.

castles of the Bresciano were occupied by Carmagnola and a fortnight later Filippo Maria sent his first commissioners to negotiate for Brescia. But this was premature. Another year elapsed before Pandolfo's final defeat, and during that time one more effort was made to save the remnant of his state.

A further approach to Martin V now proved unavailing.[1] But the Venetians agreed to lend Pandolfo 10,000 ducats 'sopra certi suoi argenti'; while in Romagna during the autumn of 1420 Carlo Malatesta assembled a force under Ludovico Migliorati, vicar of Fermo, which he sent to the help of his brother.[2] But there was no campaign. Carmagnola intercepted the army in October, inflicted a heavy defeat, and took its captain prisoner.[3] Diplomacy could not now succeed where arms had failed, particularly when in the new year (February 1421) Venice, deaf to appeals from the Malatesta, deserted them for the Visconti. In March 1421 Pandolfo Malatesta had finally to surrender Brescia for the paltry sum of 34,000 florins. A month later he passed through Ferrara on his way home.[4] In the space of a few years Filippo Maria Visconti had accomplished what it was to take the papacy a century and more to do: made himself master in his own dominions.

The example may not have been lost on Martin V, but for the moment he let it rest. If he gave no further help to Pandolfo Malatesta in the north, it was probably from resentment at his previous failure. In other ways he was ready enough with favours to the Malatesta. He began in May 1419 by regranting to Carlo Malatesta, after a brief interruption, the rectorship of Romagna.[5] It was perhaps partly for their sake also that he renewed the vicariate of the young Manfredi in Faenza, where Gentile Malatesta, sister to Carlo and Pandolfo, was governing as regent.[6] The vicariates of the Malatesta themselves, in Rimini, Fano, Cesena and elsewhere, did not, since the grants of 1391 and 1399 for two generations, require formal repetition, unless the pope chose to challenge them. But in October 1419, by remitting arrears of *census* due, he gave them implicit recognition. And in the same year, at a parliament in the March, proctors of Fano swore

---

[1] Sercambi, iii.253–5; Billii, 54.

[2] Carlo also appealed to Florence: Biondo, *Hist.*, 399; Billii, 54; Capponi, 1157–8.

[3] *Registri visc.*, 26; Romano, *ASL* 1897, i.123, 124; Guarino da Verona, *Epistolario* (ed. R. Sabbadini, Venice, 1915–19), i.300; Decembrio, 94–5, 142, 145; *Cron. sen.*, 794; *Cron. Ferm.*, 50; *Ristretto d'Urbino*, 79; Adami, 47; Giulini, iii.325, 334, 341; Carmine di Pierro, *ASL* 1920. Pandolfo's jewellery was redeemed from Venice in Feb. 1429: Predelli, iv, xii, no. 100.

[4] Santoro, *Registri provv.*, 325; Predelli, iv, xi, n. 68; Giulini, *locc. citt.*; Sercambi, iii.280; *Diario Ferrar.*, 17.

[5] Theiner, iii.167, 168; Fantuzzi, iii.357; Battaglini, *Vita*, 691; Partner, 44, 55, 99. Carlo was also given power to judge all appeals, and it may have been now that he received the revenues of the rectorate of S. Agata: Battaglini, 692.

[6] Since 1417: Griffoni, 104; *Chron. For.*, 887; *Ristretto d'Urbino*, 52.

obedience to the church and to the Malatesta as vicars.[1] Over Osimo, however, and the other places enumerated with it, Pandolfo Malatesta had received from Boniface and Gregory not the vicariate but only the 'government' for a space of years; and this would now have lapsed, had not Martin, according to one report, chosen during 1420 to convert it into a vicariate to be held in common by Carlo and Pandolfo.[2] If he did so, it may have been from recognition of services rendered by Carlo early in that year in helping to subdue Bologna, in collaboration with the other vicars of Romagna, and with Braccio, now reconciled with the pope.[3]

The friendship of Malatesta and pope seemed as firm as ever. Nor had anything yet occurred to endanger it in the spring of 1422 when Martin nominated Pandolfo Malatesta captain-general of the church.[4] And the threat, when it came, was the effect as much of Italian power politics, as of provincial rivalries in papal territory or the temporal policy of the pope.

It was during the fifteenth century that the concentration of political power in five great states was finally perfected in Italy, though it was to take thirty years of incessant war before the peace of Lodi in 1454 introduced some measure of uneasy balance and quiet. Nationwide warfare was not necessarily destructive to the *signori* of the Papal States. It was after peace was established that they were most exposed to papal counter-attack. But it involved them as allies or clients in struggles dangerous to their independence and often at variance with the policies of the pope. The reconquest of his duchy by Filippo Maria Visconti seemed already to portend the revival of his father's aggressive ambitions. Territorial jealousies reappeared into which the Adriatic lands of the papacy were once more inevitably drawn, and it was in Romagna that war was first provoked.

In January 1422 the papal vicar of Forlì, Giorgio Ordelaffi, died, leaving a son, Tebaldo, and widow, Lucrezia Alidosi, to inherit the *signoria*. But before his death, he is reported to have left his heir in wardship to Filippo Maria Visconti. In doing this he may have feared interference from the Alidosi, for Lucrezia at once had Tebaldo

[1] Theiner, iii.178; Castelucci, 'Regesto', 187; Amiani, i.348. Both Coleschi (66) and G. Marini (*Saggio*, 188) speak of a grant or regrant of the Malatesta vicariate in S. Sepolcro, the Montefeltro and elsewhere in 1417 or 1418, and Clementini (ii.208) alludes to a similar renewal to Carlo Malatesta in 1421.
[2] Battaglini, *Vita*, App. LXIX, p. 692; Clementini, ii.297. In 1421 they paid 20,000 fl. for two years' *census*, though the same year their obligation was reduced from 10,000 to 8,000 fl. *p.a.*: Partner, 69–70, 189.
[3] *Chron. For.*, 889; Griffoni, 105–6; Campanus, 149; *Chron. Bon.*, iii.563–5; Sercambi, iii.253–4; Ghirardacci, ii.632–3; Partner, 65.
[4] Theiner, iii.212; Sercambi, iii.295. Cf. further: Castellucci, 'Regesto', 187.

removed to Imola, and contrived, in the words of Cavalcanti, 'che messer Lodovico [Alidosi] ne fusse più tosto l'attore che il Duca ne fusse il tutore'. For some twelve months the people of Forlì submitted with growing resentment to control by Ludovico. Then in May 1423 the city rebelled and called in the Visconti.[1] This was no chance event. Shortly before, embassies from both Milan and Florence had been in Forlì, and since Lucrezia favoured the republic, her subjects followed the duke.[2] Already Filippo Maria had occupied Lugo, and from this point a general conflict revived for domination of Romagna.

The first concern of the Florentines was to nominate a war-captain. As early as September 1421 their envoy in Rome had sounded Pandolfo Malatesta 'per la faccenda', and not without effect.[3] But when Lucrezia Alidosi appealed for help to the Malatesta, and fled to Rimini with Tebaldo, no final agreement had yet been reached.[4] The choice to be made was difficult. The pope was an ally of Filippo Maria, and although in general sympathy with Florence, and not averse to attacking Forlì, Carlo Malatesta, with whom the decision rested, was reluctant to bind himself to any contract without papal sanction.[5] Pandolfo was more impulsive.[6] He may also have welcomed a chance to avenge the loss of Brescia. Hastily he withdrew from papal service and in August was elected Florentine captain,[7] though not before the pope had complained of his conduct in a letter to Milan. Martin wished to retain his service, 'quamvis eius expensa Camere Apostolica gravis esset'; but so insistently had he begged for discharge that no argument would dissuade him, and 'tandem a nobis licentiam non obtinuit, sed extorsit'.[8]

From the very start the Florentine connection went badly for the Malatesta. While Pandolfo was defeated in his first engagement near Forlì,[9] the republic proved less prompt in sending troops than in advice on how to use them. Carlo Malatesta continued to avoid a formal alliance, but he rejected overtures from Milan, he was active in trying to bring in Mantua and Faenza, and it was also largely due to

[1] Griffoni, 107; Capponi, 1162; Billii, 68; *Chron. For.*, 890–1; Cobelli, 165; Pedrino, rub. 51, 54–6, 58–9; Cavalcanti, i.32–5; *Ristretto d'Urbino*, 80; Bonoli, 207–8; Partner, 76ff.
[2] *Chron. For.*, 890; Cobelli, 165; Bonoli, 209.
[3] *Commiss. Albizzi*, i.321, 355.
[4] Cobelli, 165; *Chron. For.*, 891.
[5] *Commiss. Albizzi*, i.401, 417, 430–2; Guicciardini, 163, 164, 166, 167.
[6] So the Florentine envoy at the end of the year: 'ma il signor Carlo he la pelle più dura': *Commiss. Albizzi*, i.572.
[7] Capponi, 1162; Sozomenus, 11; Poggio, 329–30; *Cron. sen.*, 799; Sercambi, iii.370; Cavalcanti, 40–1; Biondo, 403–4.
[8] Tonini, v/2, xxxii.
[9] 6 Sept. 1423: *Cron. sen.*, 800; *Ann. Forl.*, 86–7; Cobelli, 165; Pedrino, rub. 66; *Ristretto d'Urbino*, 80; Cavalcanti, i.41; *Commiss. Albizzi*, i.468–71.

him that the legate in Bologna joined Florence in November.[1] This
was the only success of importance the Malatesta could claim, and the
new year brought only fresh reverses. In February Imola fell to the
duke of Milan,[2] and in July, when about to besiege Forlì, Pandolfo
Malatesta had to turn aside and relieve Zagonara, a castle in the
Faentino, threatened by the Visconti captain Angelo della Pergola.
Carlo was directed to join him, and on 28 July the two brothers
engaged with the enemy. Their defeat was overwhelming, and for the
second time in his life Carlo Malatesta was taken prisoner. Pandolfo
managed to escape to Cesenatico and Ravenna, but Carlo was sent to
Milan, and the Malatesta territories were thrown open defencelessly to
the advance of the ducal armies.[3]

Once again it was a critical moment for the Malatesta of Rimini.
Both the Ordelaffi and Alidosi had just been dispossessed by Filippo
Visconti; and there was little now to prevent him from evicting them
as well. It was hoped that Martin V might provide some decisive help.
But, to aggravate the danger, an appeal to him as overlord resulted
instead in a further, and equally serious, threat to the Malatesta
dominion. At first the pope replied with a promise of immediate armed
support; and early in September revealed an undertaking to help the
Malatesta, with an offer to leave them undisturbed in their vicariates,
'eziandio faccendonegli chiari per scrittura'.[4] But a week later no help
had yet been sent. And the *vicepodestà* of Rimini, who had been to the papal
court, protested that nothing would be done, because the pope 'wanted
possession of Rimini and all other strongholds'.[5] No more may have
been intended than an expedient of defence. But if it was Martin's
purpose to reclaim the Malatesta lands, no occasion could have been
better. What prompted the plan does not appear, whether papal interest
alone, or the Malatesta alliance with Florence. The simple opportunity
would seem argument enough, were there not reason to suspect as well
another, extraneous, influence: of Guidantonio da Montefeltro, lord of
Urbino.

Guidantonio was an old ally and intimate of Martin V, who for
many years had been bishop of Urbino, and from an early stage he set
about cultivating his favour. When still at Constance the pope had

[1] *Ibid.*, i.461–2, 465, 471, 472–4, 493–6, 498–9, 514, 522, 528, 541, 558, 563–4.,
569, 571–2, 589.
[2] *Ann. Forl.*, 87; Griffoni, 108; *Chron. For.*, 891; Cobelli, 169–70; Pedrino, rub.
67, 69, 73–5, 81–3.
[3] *Cron. mal.*, 58; *Chron. Bon.*, iii.575–6; *Chron. For.*, 892–3; *Ann. Forl.*, 87;
Guerriero, 42; Billii, 68–9; Griffoni, 108; *Commiss. Albizzi*, ii.17, 119, 130, 135,
137, 141–4; Sozomenus, 11, 15 (commenting acidly on Carlo Malatesta's gift for
defeat in war).
[4] *Commiss. Albizzi*, ii.138–9, 149–50, 153–4, 162, 171.
[5] *Ibid.* 177, 178.

received an embassy from him; and later, at a meeting in Mantua, Martin created him duke and rector of Spoleto. During 1419 he was employed at papal command against Braccio, and when peace with Braccio was finally made in the following year, Guidantonio was awarded territorial compensation for the loss of Assisi and honoured with the golden rose.[1] That the count was an ally and *raccomandato* of Florence when war broke out in Romagna did not affect his papal relations. In January 1424, only shortly after the death of his first wife, Rengarda Malatesta, Guidantonio was married to the pope's niece, Caterina di Lorenzo Colonna.[2] By this the union of Martin with the Montefeltro was unshakably established; and it was a tribute to the position that the count had come to occupy at the papal court. While the Malatesta were organising their disastrous campaign against the Visconti, Guidantonio was engaged on the pope's behalf in recovering the cities freed by the death of Braccio, and in arranging an agreement between the papacy and Corrado Trinci.[3] All this was naturally part of his office as rector of Spoleto. But the combination of papal service and alliance with the pope's family encouraged him to aspire to greater rewards.

Sometime before, in 1411 or thereabouts, the Brancaleoni family, who for a generation had been holding the vicariate of Castel Durante, S. Angelo in Vado, Mercatello, Sascorbaro and other castles in the Massa Trabaria, arranged a partition of territories between Bartolomeo di Gentile Brancaleone, who took Mercatello and S. Angelo in Vado, and his cousins Galeotto and Alberigo di Niccolo Filippo Brancaleone. In March 1424 Bartolemeo died, leaving a daughter of tender age, Gentile, and Guidantonio da Montefeltro, resuming the hereditary claims of his house, obtained the government of Massa Trabaria from Martin V as guardian to Gentile (12 May). At the same time proceedings were opened by the treasurer of the March against Galeotto and Alberigo for failure to pay their *census*, and in September the count of Urbino expelled them from Castel Durante, in which he was placed as substitute vicar by the accommodating pope.[4] By tradition the allies of the Brancaleoni were the Malatesta of Rimini, and it was in Rimini that Alberigo finally took refuge. All this was more than

---

[1] Theiner, iii.162, 170; Mazzatinti, *Inventari*, xxxix.86; Amati, 'Notizie', 201; Bernardy, 'Archivio', 133; Guerriero, 40; *Ristretto d'Urbino*, 52, 79; Pellini, ii.237; Lazzari, 52–4; Fumi, *BU* 1900, 377–9, 379, 381–2. In compensation Guidantonio received lands near Narni (*ibid.* 382–3). For further privileges granted him by the pope: Theiner, iii.190.

[2] Guerriero, 42; Scalvanti, 'Cronaca perug.' 606; Baldi, *Federigo*, i.10; Lazzari, 55; Ugolini, i.223; Dennistoun, i.45. Fumi, *BU* 1900, 384.

[3] Theiner, iii.225; Dorio, 210; Fumi, *BU* 1900, 383.

[4] *Ristretto d'Urbino*, 80; Guerriero, 42; Torelli, 180–2, 193; *Cron. Castel delle Ripe*, 20–1, 60–1; Franceschini, 'Gentile Brancaleone', 493; Fumi, *BU* 1900, 382–3.

enough to revive suspicions between Malatesta and Montefeltro. But there were other grievances besides; and Guidantonio, confident of papal sympathy, was anxious to have them settled.

Just what these other grievances were, and how they arose, can only be surmised. After the agreements of 1393, the relations of Montefeltro and Malatesta had for years continued not merely peaceful but amicable, strengthened by marriage and identity of political interest,[1] and confirmed by mutual privilege.[2] Guidantonio's accession in 1404 did nothing to disturb the friendship, even when after Pisa he followed the conciliar popes; and in his treaties with John XXIII the Malatesta were expressly excepted from attack.[3] In 1416, as 'bono amigho', he mediated between the Malatesta and Braccio, pledging payment of part of Carlo's ransom. And in return the Malatesta provided support when, two years later, Braccio also attacked him, on the pretext that he had been dilatory over the ransom.[4]

There is insufficient evidence to explain why from this time the connection began to break up, but the question of the ransom may have played a part. At all events, in 1421, when the count was still at loggerheads with Braccio,[5] the pope had to restrain him from invading Malatesta territory.[6] A further disagreement is recorded, on the death of Rengarda, which was composed when Guidantonio passed through Rimini in November 1423.[7] Like the Malatesta he was an ally of Florence, and like them he tried to win Gentile Malatesta of Faenza to the Florentine side. But in the summer of 1424 Rinaldo degli Albizzi disclosed to the *signoria* that serious differences continued to divide the families.[8] What the causes were he does not say, though his hint that a payment of money might settle them could again refer to the ransom; but it might equally well imply the revival of older disputes, previously adjusted by the marriage with Rengarda, who had recently died without issue, or composed by the settlement of 1393. The details of that settlement were never made public.[9] But it ratified and acknowledged one thing: the place the Malatesta had won in the district of Montefeltro.

If the counts of Urbino had conquered Cagli and Gubbio, the Mala-

---

[1] Both were allies of Gian Galeazzo Visconti: e.g. Corio, ii.436; above pp. 111ff.

[2] 12 March 1396: proclamation by Galeotto Belfiore in Cervia placing Antonio da Montefeltro in the same privileged position as the Malatesta: *Stat. Cerviae*, 111; cf. above p. 110 n. 5. Oct. 1405: treaty between the families to exclude fugitive criminals from their dominions: Pellegrini, 'Gubbio'; *Boll. Umb.*, xi, 1905, 170.

[3] Theiner, iii.128, 142.

[4] Campanus, 131; Pellini, ii.234–5; Fumi, *BU* 1900, 379; Amiani, i.346, 348.

[5] Mazzatinti, *Inventari*, xxxix.129.

[6] 18 March 1421: Mazzatinti, *Inventari*, xxxix.86.

[7] *Commiss. Albizzi*, i.555–7.

[8] *Ibid.* ii.155–6.   [9] Above p. 110.

testa had at least kept abreast in extending influence over the mountainous region from which both families sprang.[1] Down to the Eight Saints war the Malatesta had found it easier to expand in the March of Ancona, and although, as seen, this still remained their policy, by the end of the fourteenth century they had also acquired possession of many places in the Montefeltro, among them S. Leo, all former dominions of the Feltreschi.[2] The wars concluded in 1393 had not dislodged the Malatesta, and they were still there, strengthened by papal mandate, at the election of Martin V. During the same period they may also have made their influence secure in the adjoining lands of S. Agata and Macerata Feltria.[3] Only over S. Marino did the Montefeltro retain traditional ascendancy.[4]

After the Council of Constance it was the Feltreschi's turn to prosper. A new era opened, for them as for the papacy; and the death of Braccio, with the dispersal of the Brancaleoni, offered Guidantonio the chance for quick and fertile conquests. In this he was bound to expect resistance from the Malatesta who, indifferent though they may have been to the Umbria lordships of Braccio, had long been confederates of the Brancaleoni[5] and may even have coveted their lands for themselves. But after the defeat of Zagonara they had little power to act. It was for Guidantonio to exploit his opportunity.

During the autumn of 1424 the Visconti forces under Angelo della Pergola and Guido Torelli occupied and laid waste the territories of the Malatesta and their dependants, 'plura castra comitatus Arimini subjiciendo', and at the end of August the Florentine envoy in Rome forecast the total submersion of their state.[6] His pleas to the pope were unheeded. And precisely now Guidantonio seized Castel Durante and possessed himself of 'la magior parte dele castella de Montefeltro, le quale teneva el prefato signore Carlo'.[7] Early in October the Malatesta ambassador in Rome protested to the *curia*, but 'con poco frutto'. The

---

[1] Their possessions apart, sufficient proof of this is given by the list of their 'colligati, adherents, recomandati' in 1380, of their adherents in 1389, of their 'colligati et adherents' in 1414, who included the Brancaleoni, the Pietramala, the Malatesta of Sogliano, the Atti of Sassoferrato, the counts of Carpegna and many others: Ansidei, 'Tregua'; Osio, i, CCI, 278ff.; Cutolo, ii.226.

[2] The places in the Montefeltro later described by the Venetians as having belonged to Sigismondo Malatesta 'de lo antiquo patrimonio' are very numerous, but difficult to corroborate in detail at this period: Sanuto, v. 606–7; Tonini, vi/2.832.

[3] Borghi, 88; Branchi, 175; Ansidei, 'Tregua', 37; Cutolo, ii.226; above p. 156 n. 5.

[4] Delfico, i.184–93; Bernardy, *ASI* 1900, pt. 2. The war with Braccio involved Carlo Malatesta in disputes with S. Marino which were not composed until 1422.

[5] Cutolo, ii.226; Torelli, 183.

[6] *Cron. mal.*, 58; Guerriero, 42; *Ann. Forl.*, 87–8; Poggio, 331; Billii, 69–70; *Chron. For.*, 893–4; *Cron. Ferm.*, 54; Cobelli, 170–1; Biondo, *Hist.*, 416; *Cron. Perug.*, 302; Pedrino, rub. 89; Coleschi, 66ff.; *Commiss. Albizzi*, ii.170.

[7] *Cron. mal.*, 59. Cf. Franceschini, 'Notizie', 171.

count of Urbino was then in Rome, where his influence seems to have been dominant; and policy had not yet persuaded the pope to defer his plans for evicting the Malatesta.[1]

The Florentines feared such a course could only drive the Malatesta into the arms of Filippo Visconti, and pointed out that the pope might still prevent this if only he did not insist on confiscation of the Malatesta lands, or a promise 'per scrittura di renderle'.[2] In the end Martin agreed, though from what motives is not clear; and at the beginning of November he sanctioned an attempt by Rinaldo degli Albizzi to mediate between Guidantonio and the Malatesta. But he had delayed too long. According to Guidantonio the Malatesta had already come to terms with the Visconti, swearing fealty and contracting to become allies and stipendiaries of Milan.[3] His report was not mistaken. By calculated generosity and courtesy to his captive,[4] Filippo Maria had won over the Malatesta, and in a short time arranged an agreement with them.[5] The duke called off his captains in Romagna; and at the end of January 1425 Carlo was back in Rimini where, at the desire of the Visconti, the 'Capitula, pacta, et federa' were submitted for confirmation to the commune. In March, again at Filippo's wish, Pandolfo Malatesta went to Milan to ratify the treaty.[6]

The Malatesta now had powerful protection. They were also back in arms and free to fight once more. It was probably this that decided the pope to try again, this time with better success, to negotiate a settlement between Rimini and Urbino. A peace was reached in his presence on 28 June, and incorporated in a papal bull of 14 July. The agreements of 1393 were re-enacted and confirmed, and Guidantonio was ordered to restore all his conquests from the Malatesta and their allies. At the same time the pope betrayed some partiality by reserving to himself disposal of Castel Durante, Pietrarubbia, Pennabilli and other castles.[7]

---

[1] *Commiss. Albizzi*, ii. 200. Guidantonio was in Rome between 25 Sept. and 16 Nov. 1424 (*Ristretto d'Urbino*, 88), where, on 7 Oct. Martin publicly professed his 'love' of the conte: *Commiss. Albizzi*, ii. 214.

[2] *Ibid.* ii. 269. The Florentines offered to guarantee obedience from the Malatesta.

[3] *Ibid.* ii. 281–3, 205, 290–313.

[4] Decembrio in the chapter of his life of Filippo Visconti entitled 'De clementia eius in bello' adds another motive: 'quod virum puer observaverat': *RIS*[2] xx/1.96–8, 100ff.

[5] The first word of the duke's proposals reached Rome in Sept.: *Commiss. Albizzi*, ii. 178–80.

[6] Griffoni, 108; *Ann. Forl.*, 88; *Chron. For.*, 894; Cobelli, 172–3; *Cron. Ferm.*, 54; Pedrino, rub. 115, 129–30; Poggio, 331; Billii, 69–70; Biondo, *Hist.*, 416; Amiani, i. 354; Tonini, v/2, xxxiii. For this treaty the subject communes of the Malatesta had all to go surety.

[7] Theiner, iii. 232; Mazzatinti, *Inventari*, xxxvii. 146, xxxix. 129; Battaglini, *Vita*, 693; Fumi, *BU* 1900, 394–5; Morpurgo-Castelnuovo, *AR* 1929, 15. Cf. Guicciardini, 184; *Commiss. Albizzi*, ii. 386.

Soon afterwards he granted Guidantonio the vicariate of Castel Durante, and further helped the count by encouraging the betrothal to Gentile Brancaleone, heiress to Mercatello and S. Angelo in Vado, of Guidantonio's bastard son Federigo.[1] Nevertheless the Malatesta had won their immediate object: they were reinstated in the Montefeltro. And as long as Carlo Malatesta lived they were not again openly threatened by the count or by Martin V.

Throughout the early months of 1425 Carlo and Pandolfo Malatesta remained in close relation with the Visconti,[2] but it does not appear that they performed any service, and when peace was made with the Montefeltro, the need for Milanese patronage was removed. Carlo Malatesta may have been uncomfortable in an alliance imposed by force. On his side Filippo also became less friendly and confiding,[3] while the Florentines now tried as much to break the agreement as they had previously tried to prevent it. In a draft of peace terms in October and December they proposed the release of the Malatesta from their contract to Milan; but Filippo Maria was at that time intractable, and declared the question matter for the pope.[4] During the following year Florence, now allied with Venice,[5] continued negotiations, trying to induce Venice as well to prevail on the Malatesta, if necessary by threat of force 'verso la marina che sarà a loro e a' loro sudditi di gravissimo danno'.[6] The pope also, to whom the duke of Milan had recently surrendered Imola and Forlì, was not opposed to peace and closely followed all proceedings. But not till April 1428 did Filippo Visconti finally absolve Carlo Malatesta from his obligations.[7]

In all this activity on their behalf the Malatesta themselves seem to have played little part. In place of foreign entanglements, other more intimate issues had suddenly arisen, affecting the welfare and possible

---

[1] It was certainly about this time that the pope legitimised Federigo and granted dispensation for his marriage to Gentile: Baldi, *Federigo*, i.11; Colucci, xxi/1.116, 143; Fumi, *loc. cit.*; Franceschini, *Montefeltro*, 431ff.

[2] Pedrino, rub. 117, 134, 145, 154; *Chron. For.*, 894; *Commiss. Albizzi*, ii.325; *Atti canc. visc.*, i, nn. 954, 1149.

[3] At the end of the year he refused the Malatesta a loan of 10,000 ducats; *Atti canc. visc.*, i, nn. 1536, 1550, 1560. Already while still at Milan Carlo Malatesta is reported to have persuaded the Manfredi to go over to Florence, arguing that the life of a republic was surer than that of a despot: Guicciardini, 170–5; Ammirato, ii.1019–20; Tonduzzi, 477; Vecchiazzani, 96. Cf. *Commiss. Albizzi*, ii.327.

[4] *Ibid.* ii.414–15, 419, 420, 500, 506.

[5] By a treaty (Dec. 1425) which permitted Venice to occupy Malatesta territory if they adhered to Filippo Maria: Predelli, iv, xi, n. 197. In April 1426 all Riminese were told to leave the Venetian dominions and all Venetians to leave those of the Malatesta: Sanudo, 984.

[6] *Commiss. Albizzi*, ii.568; iii.7–8, 21, 36, 43, 132–3, 141, 145; Predelli, iv, xi, n. 232.

[7] *Ibid.* xii, n. 15; *Atti canc. visc.*, ii, n. 822; Guicciardini, 193.

survival of their state. On 3 October 1427, when on his way to fulfil a vow to visit the Madonna of Loreto, Pandolfo Malatesta died in Fano, 'cum grandissimi pianti de citadini, perché era molto dilecto da tutto el populo'. He died also 'cum bona contrizione e disposizone' in the arms of friar Giacomo della Marca, 'frate predicatore dela observanza de san Francesco', and was buried 'cum grandissimo onore' in the Franciscan convent at Fano.[1] However contrite his last hours, in his lifetime Pandolfo had been of very different temper from his austere elder brother. Unlike Carlo, he had patronised the humanists;[2] while in private life he had the reputation of a libertine, inclined to 'donne leggiadre'.[3] Though three times married,[4] he had no legitimate off-spring and left at his death three bastard sons, Galeotto Roberto (born in 1411), Sigismondo Pandolfo (born 1417), and Domenico, later known as Malatesta Novello (born 1418).[5] Since Carlo Malatesta also was childless, and the son of Andrea Malatesta had died, these were now the only heirs to the Malatesta *signoria*. Illegitimate sons were normally excluded from the succession to Italian despotisms, as well as to papal vicariates. But they were also so frequently the sole heirs that it became customary to seek and secure their legitimation from emperor or pope.[6] Martin V had recently accorded this privilege to Federigo, the chosen successor of Guidantonio da Montefeltro. And Carlo Malatesta might justly have hoped to assume undivided command of the family dominions and, with a similar bull for his nephews,

---

[1] *Cron. mal.*, 59; Branchi, 174–5; Borghi, 88; *Chron. For.*, 901; *Ann. Forl.*, 89; Pedrino, rub. 276; Decembrio, 578; Amiani, i.355–6.

[2] Filelfo, *Epist. fam.*, 76; Tonini, *Coltura*, i.76ff.

[3] Volpi, 'Serdini', 12–13.

[4] To Paola Bianca, dead many years before (above p. 105), to Antonia da Varano (between 1421 or 1422 and 1424) and to Margherita, de' conti di Poppi (1427): Clementini, ii.222–4; Amiani, i.350, 355–6; Zazzeri, 280; Tonini, v/i.463.

[5] Clementini, ii.211, 217, 218; Amiani, i.344–5. Pius II gives a colourful account of Pandolfo, and tells a story which casts doubts on Sigismondo's paternity, similar to those surrounding the birth of Federigo d'Urbino, his lifelong rival. Of Pandolfo he says: 'In bello fugax, trepidus domi, temulentus et audax et ganeo, quasi ac turpissimus leno inter scorta victitans. Cum senuisset nec pro voluntate libidini posset operam dare, se coram nudas adduci iubebat foeminas et adolescentes, qui eis admiscerentur, ut ex aliorum coitu suum provocaret. Inter scorta, quibus frequentur abutebatur, unum fuit forma egregium, quod prae caeteris amavit, huic cum satisfacere non posset vetulus, Marchesinum ... Bergomensem aetate florida, moribus scurrum, qui suam vicem adimpleret, introduxit, concubinumque concubinae adiecit, et saepe medium dormire permisit. Hinc nobilissima soboles nata, Sigismundus ac Pandulphus [*sic*] at Dominicus Malatesta, qui Malatestarum hodie principes habentur.' Marchesino for a long time boasted of the relationship, but Francesco Sforza warned him against doing so lest Sigismondo should hear of it: *Opera ined.*, 538–9.

[6] Salzer, 231–2.

provide for their inheritance. But in this he was faced with sudden opposition from two of his neighbours: the count of Urbino, and Malatesta, vicar of Pesaro.

Like the Montefeltro, the Malatesta of Pesaro had for many years previously cultivated a close alliance with Rimini. On Galeotto's death in 1385, Malatesta di Pandolfo had served against the Montefeltro and then, after conclusion of peace, made a marriage alliance with them.[1] When necessary he had assisted in the government of Malatesta lands outside Pesaro; and although subsequently he aligned himself with the Council of Pisa and its popes, and supported Florence against Ladislas,[2] this did not affect his relations with the Malatesta of Rimini, with whom he sought to profit from the troubles of the March of Ancona. Here, in 1411, the Malatesta of Pesaro were given Iesi by Pandolfo,[3] and when Andrea Malatesta died they entered into possession of Fossombrone too.[4] In 1418 the two families still appear united;[5] and once again it was only during the pontificate of Martin V that, from motives none too clear, they began to drift apart.

From the first Malatesta di Pandolfo was among the lords more generously treated by Martin,[6] and one reason for this is certainly that Carlo Malatesta, his youngest but most active son, was married to the pope's niece, Vittoria Colonna.[7] In 1424 the choice fell on Malatesta to disperse the remnants of the Council of Siena.[8] Whether or not he was implicated in the designs against Rimini that year is not disclosed. He was in Rome when the news came through of Zagonara, and left at once to protect his own territories, though to no great effect.[9] There must have been some growing dissension between him and the Malatesta of Rimini, for he was allotted no place in the peace treaty between

[1] Theiner, iii.17; cf. above p. 109. In 1405 Galeazzo, his eldest son, married Battista da Montefeltro, celebrated as one of the first Italian ladies to excel in humanist learning.

[2] *Chron. Bon.*, iii.535; Martène and Durand, *Collectio*, vii.1168–71; Mattiolo, 212; *Capitoli, Firenze*, ii.xvi.61; Ammirato, ii.946, 949, 951–6, 969; Valentini, *BU* 1923, 85; Valois, *Schisme*, iv.123, 125, 126.

[3] Zonghi, 27; Gritio, 44; Pedrino, rub. 614.

[4] Zazzeri, 293; Vernarecci, *Fossombrone*, i.344–5; cf. Theiner, iii.199. In 1417 Pandolfo Malatesta left the provisional administration of Fano to Malatesta of Pesaro: Amiani, i.342.

[5] Both were in the league with Giovanna of Naples against Braccio: above p. 154; Campanus, 126.

[6] 18 Dec. 1418 Martin renewed his vicariate (Mazzatinti, *Inventari*, xxxvii.124, n. 28), and 29 Jan. 1419 confirmed Gregory XII's reduction of his *census* (Theiner, iii.163). 30 May 1422 the pope empowered him to divide his lands among his sons in order to avoid disputes (Mazzatinti, *ibid.* n. 30).

[7] According to Clementini (ii.105) since 1416. Cf. Guiraud, 50–1, 53, 215.

[8] *Cron. sen.*, 802–3; Valois, *Pape et concile*, i.69–75.

[9] *Commiss. Albizzi*, ii.139, 141, 157, 318; Billii, 69–70; *Ristretto d'Urbino*, 80; Giordani, *Notizie*, 18–19; Vernarecci, *Fossombrone*, i.347.

Filippo Visconti and Carlo Malatesta, and he had angrily to send his son Carlo to Milan to secure a similar agreement.[1] On 23 February 1425 the Malatesta of Pesaro became the *raccomandati* of the Visconti, and at the same time asked for help in recovering certain lands and privileges from Carlo and Pandolfo of Rimini. The duke chose to excuse himself on the plea of his recent alliance;[2] and although throughout the following years Malatesta remained closely leagued with Milan,[3] he seems to have gained no encouragement there for his aims in the Papal States.

More promising for his purpose was the Colonna alliance, with its assurance of papal support,[4] and the kindred aims and interests of Guidantonio da Montefeltro with whom in the 1420s the Malatesta of Pesaro became cordial confederates.[5] Common jealousy of Rimini brought the two together and combined them in common action which, by the time of Pandolfo Malatesta's death in 1427, was evidently threatening dramatic results. In February of the following year it is related that Carlo Malatesta,

'having certain differences with the Count of Urbino and the lord Malatesta of Pesaro, both of whom had violently accused and vilified him to Pope Martin, their relative, since the said lord Carlo was suffering the displeasure of the said Pope, at his command went to Rome, taking the road of S. Sepolcro, of which he was lord. And he remained many days in Rome, and was greatly honoured by the Pope, the cardinals and the whole court, and was given the Golden Rose. The Count of Urbino likewise went to Rome, and they met, so that the lord Carlo was restored to the good will of the Pope, and also established a good peace with the said lords, and on his return he passed through Urbino with great festivity.'

To the Riminese chronicler Carlo's Roman visit appeared an unqualified triumph. He was reconciled again with Urbino, he obtained a bull legitimising his three nephews, and another granting him the power to dispose of his lands by will, and he was treated with every demonstration of respect by the pope. Yet it is almost certain that these

---

[1] *Commiss. Albizzi*, ii. 283.

[2] Osio, ii. 124–9.

[3] See especially *Registri visc.*, 10, nn. 6, 7, 8, 14, n. 12; *Atti canc. visc.*, i, nn. 48, 57, 59, 894, 938, 1008, 1015, 1038–9, 1050–1, 1073–6, 1082–3, 1089, 1091, 1100, 1102, 1128, 1169, 1174, 1254, 1309, 1310, 1314, 1325, 1345, 1490; ii, nn. 101, 228–9, 819, 827; Osio, ii, LXXV, LXXXI.

[4] 3 April 1426 Martin V reduced the *census* of the Pesaro vicariate still further: Mazzatinti, *Inventari*, xxxvii. 87.

[5] Malatesta of Pesaro appears beside Carlo and Pandolfo Malatesta of Rimini in the peace with Guidantonio da Montefeltro arranged in 1425: above p. 163. On the close cooperation of Pesaro and Urbino: Franceschini, 'Poeta', 122–3.

concessions had to be bought, and that some secret undertaking was
negotiated with Carlo that a proportion of Malatesta territories, including Cervia, Osimo, Sinigaglia, Mondavio, Pergola, Corinaldo and
Castelfidardo, should revert to the church on his death. A reckoning
with the papacy had only been deferred.[1]

The last few months of Carlo's life were quiet and untroubled. When
Bologna rose in further revolt during 1428 he gave some help against
the Canetoli rebels,[2] but no other demands were made on his services.
If the conte Guidantonio was still on the watch for territorial prizes,[3]
with Carlo Malatesta he lived on more than peaceful terms. He was
even appointed one of the guardians of Carlo's nephews.[4] The other
was the marquis Niccolo d'Este. Parisina's adultery and execution had
not estranged Rimini and Ferrara. Only recently, in 1427, the marriage
had been arranged between Galeotto Roberto and Niccolo's daughter
Margherita, who received the same dower lands Parisina had held.[5] In
every way Carlo had tried to safeguard the Malatesta *signoria*, and by
the time of his death, in September 1429, could hope to have ensured
under difficult conditions an undisturbed succession to his state. He
died at Longiano on 14 September and was brought at once to Rimini,
where he was sumptuously buried in the church of S. Franceso: 'e di
lì a pochi dì glie fo facto uno solenissimo officio, al quale cie fo el
signore marchese de Ferara, e tuti quilli, che portonno i dopieri,
fonno vestiti de niro e anche tutta la sua fameglia . . . El quale offizio
fece fare el nostro magnifico signore Ruberto di Malatesti e li soi
magnifici fradelli.'[6]

When his uncle died Galeotto Roberto was only eighteen, Sigismondo
not more than twelve, and Domenico a year younger. Government was
therefore shared with Elizabetta, Carlo's widow, and a regency council
of twelve nominated by Carlo. Prominent among its members were
Giovanni di Ramberto Malatesta, a descendant of Gianciotto, 'vir
maxime reputationis Arimini propter longam consuetudinem et
societatem quam habuerat cum Carolo principe',[7] Pandolfo de' Mengardoni, a grandson of Pandolfo III Malatesta, and Leonardo Roello, a

[1] Pedrino, rub. 293; *Cron. mal.*, 59; Clementini, ii.219–20, 222, 231–2; Battaglini,
  Vita, 277, 691, 692, 693; Tonini, v/1.77–9; Müntz, *Arts*, i.19.
[2] Biondo, *Hist.*, 447; Battaglini, *Zecca*, 225.
[3] He had his eye on the remaining fragments of the Brancaleoni inheritance (below
  p. 171), and was still trying to win part of the lands released by Braccio: Rossi,
  Monte Alboddo, 97–8; *Cron. Perug.*, 325.
[4] Below p. 171.
[5] Fantuzzi, v.423–6; Tonini, v/2, xxxiv; Rubeus, 621.
[6] *Cron. mal.*, 60; Borghi, 88; Billii, 116; Biondo, *Hist.*, 448; *Ristretto d'Urbino*. 89;
  Pedrino, rub. 389.
[7] Borghi, 89. On this line of the Malatesta family: below p. 296.

member of a local gentry family long in Malatesta service.[1] Public acts were issued in the name of all three brothers, and at first of Elizabetta as well,[2] though it is probable at the same time that a partition of territory was soon projected, like that of 1385, by which Galeotto Roberto took Rimini, Sigismondo Cesena, and Malatesta Novello Fano.[3] Besides these domestic arrangements, the new government could also look to some support outside: from Niccolo d'Este, from Venice,[4] and, among neighbouring *signori*, from the Manfredi and the Polenta, close allies still of the Malatesta.[5] More significantly, a few weeks after Carlo's death, the *condottiere* Niccolo Fortebraccio, a nephew of Braccio with grievances against Urbino, visited Rimini and offered his services to the regent.[6]

His approaches were well timed. No sooner had the three Malatesta succeeded in Rimini than it became clear that their political enemies had merely been awaiting this chance to resume their previous aggressions. The first to move were the Malatesta of Pesaro, though with small awareness of the consequences. Once before, during the legation of Bertrand du Pouget, a division between two branches of the family had nearly overwhelmed the Malatesta. In the fifteenth century a dissension still more bitter developed, destructive in the end to both sides. Malatesta of Pesaro died at Gradara in December 1429,[7] but already on the news of Carlo Malatesta's death he had begun to assemble troops, and filed a claim in Rome to the whole inheritance of Carlo's nephews as properly due to himself.[8] His claims passed to his three sons, Galeazzo, Pandolfo and Carlo Malatesta; but before they had time to act, the *curia* itself, with their interests partly in view, instituted proceedings against the Malatesta of Rimini. The plan probably was for the pope to proclaim sentence and censure, and the Malatesta of Pesaro to execute papal justice in arms.

[1] Clementini, ii.233; Battaglini, *Vita*, 286-7; Tonini, v/1.79-81.
[2] Amiani, i.360-1, 368-9; ii, pp. lxxv-vi; Zonghi, 128-9; Braschi, 291; ACF, *Cod. mal.*, 4, fo. 206r; *Canc., Cons.* 5, fo. 9v. In Fano officials all acted 'on behalf of' the three brothers in common: Amiani, ii, p. lxxv; Zonghi, 403. According to one tradition it was now that three heads were added to the Malatesta coat of arms: Clementini, i.460-1, ii.224; Amiani, i.358, 359.
[3] As on the previous occasion, the precise allocation of lands is variously reported: Billii, 116; Anon. Veron., 101; Amiani, i.365-6; Tonini, v/1.79; *Mem. Santarcangelo*, n.xvi.
[4] In June 1428 the Malatesta of Rimini were listed among Venetian allies (Predelli, xii, n. 27), and in Nov. the next year Elisabetta obtained a loan from the republic of 15,000 ducats: Sanudo, 1006.
[5] Rubeus, 621; Zazzeri, 270; Fantuzzi, vi.243.
[6] Pedrino, rub. 389.
[7] *Cron. mal.*, 60; Pedrino, rub. 407; Mazzatinti, *Inventari*, xxxix.226; Clementini, ii.102.
[8] Pedrino, rub. 407; Billii, 116; Fumi, 'Inventario', 293. Cf. Partner, 93-4.

Whatever the agreements concluded between Carlo Malatesta and the pope in 1428, it was certainly not consistent with their spirit when Martin V, in January 1430, addressed to the Riminese government a solemn letter declaring the Malatesta lands forfeit for non-payment of *census*. This was to become a standard pretext for action against vicars of the church, normally backward in their dues, and it always concealed an intention to evict. In Rimini it provoked a popular riot. The life of the papal emissary was endangered; and a street orator rehearsed the loyal services of the Malatesta to the church, stressing particularly Carlo's part in securing renunciation of the papacy from Gregory XII. Roberto replied with an energetic protest, and the leading cities were at once laid under contribution to produce the money needed. A deputation from the cities was sent as well to prevail on Martin V to relent. Niccolo d'Este and Fortebraccio also threatened pressure.[1] At last the pope consented to negotiate. In the middle of March[2] a pact was arranged which renewed the terms previously granted Carlo. Galeotto and his brothers were confirmed in the tenure of Rimini, Fano, Cesena, Bertinoro and other places in the neighbourhood, but were obliged to surrender S. Sepolcro, Cervia and most of the cities and castles they held in the March of Ancona, 'in tutto forse L castelle e bone comunançe'.[3] According to Giovanni Pedrino, 4,000 ducats were sent in addition to Rome, 'per romanere in la segnoria per ereditate'.[4] In May further privileges were conferred upon the Malatesta and their subjects, clarifying the original treaty.[5] And in July the pope formally commanded Rimini, Fano and Cesena to obey the papal vicars.[6] The bulls of investiture did not arrive until September.[7] Meanwhile the church took possession of S. Sepolcro, Montefano, Osimo, Serra dei Conti, Sinigaglia, Corinaldo, the vicariate of Mondavio and Pergola; and on 5 August Astorgio, bishop of Ancona and Umana, papal lieutenant-general of the papacy in the March, issued letters declaring that the Malatesta of Rimini, in obedience to bulls published in the preceding May, had relinquished the 'pacificam,

---

[1] *Commiss. Albizzi*, iii.405.
[2] News of the agreement reached Fano by 16 March: ACF, *Canc. Cons.* v, fo. 18v.
[3] Borghi, 88; Branchi, 175; Billii, 116; Pedrino, rub. 439, 446, 447; Clementini, ii.234ff.; Chiaramonti, 418; Battaglini, *Vita*, 279–81, 688; Amiani, i.361–3; Tonini, v/1. 81–3, 667.
[4] Pedrino, rub. 439. Cf. Battaglini, *Vita*, 281.
[5] Zonghi, 175–6; Battaglini, *Vita*, 693.
[6] Amiani, ii, pp. lxxiv–v; Mazzatinti, *Archivi*, Ser. 1, ii.235.
[7] Tonini, v/1, 81–3, 667. Included was a temporary vicariate of S. Agata Feltre, and other places in the Montefeltro: Marini, *Saggio*, 19; Partner, 98. Cf. Nicholas V's confirmation of papal grants to the Malatesta (1450), from which it might be inferred that S. Leo and Penna Billi were also conceded: Battaglini, *Vita*, 626; Tonini, v/2.176–7.

liberam, et corporalem possessionem' of Cervia, Osimo, Sinigaglia, Offagna, Pergola, Montelupone, Castelfidardo, and a whole crowd of other places in the March.[1] Most of these territories Martin V kept under the direct government of the church, but Sinigaglia he handed over to the Malatesta of Pesaro,[2] and Guidantonio da Montefeltro also had some pickings.[3]

Nearly thirty years later, in the confrontation with Federigo d'Urbino arranged by the marquis of Este, Sigismondo Malatesta complained that in breach of his trust as guardian, the count of Montefeltro had instigated this papal attempt to dispossess the Malatesta. Federigo replied that, as existing documents could prove, the deprivation would have been just, but denied his father had proposed it to the pope. And in fact it does not appear that Guidantonio did at this time act openly against the Malatesta.[4] Instead he contented himself with expelling Alberigo de' Brancaleoni from his remaining castles in the Massa Trabaria (Sascorbaro, Lunano and Montelocco) and with establishing himself firmly in Castel Durante.[5]

Sigismondo charged him also with a no less serious betrayal: with having helped foment a rising which now broke out in Rimini under the leadership of Giovanni di Ramberto Malatesta.[6]

The Malatesta were barely freed from the papal threat and adjusting to their new condition when they were faced with a sudden challenge to their authority from within. The insurrection which developed during May 1431, and was complicated by disturbances in Fano and Cesena, though accompanied by the destruction of fiscal and judicial records, was not a popular rebellion against oppressive government or outrage to private rights, of the kind which troubled *signori* of other towns, but an attempt by one man with a slender following to depose

---

[1] Battaglini, *Vita*, App. VII. Cf. Mazzatinti, *Archivi*, Ser. 2, iv.125; Fantuzzi, iii.358; Mittarelli, *Ann. Camald.*, vi.339; *Cron. Ferm.*, 62; Fumi, 'Inventario', 297; Cecconi, *Castelfidardo*, 110; Nicoletti, 165. Osimo wished to remain under the Malatesta, but this was not granted: Martorelli, 244–6.

[2] Bonincontri, 137; Clementini, ii.237. Pedrino adds: 'E ancora [the Malatesta of Rimini] non romaneno troppo buoni amixe con gli figluoli del signor de Pexaro, perché puo' la morte del signor Carlo avo piatido nanço al papa. A pare a ogne persona che de raxone quigli da Pexaro dovè soçedere a ogne cosa, percio l'una e l'altra parte à piatido, quello che non bisogna perchè finalmente è de la Giexa': rub. 439.

[3] Battaglini, *Vita*, 281–2.

[4] Clementini, ii.233; below p. 216.

[5] *Ristretto d'Urbino*, 89; Guerriero, 47; Pedrino, rub. 422; Lazzari, 55; Ugolini, i.256. Alberigo now came to Rimini, where he was to enjoy the favour of Sigismondo, marry into the line of the Malatesta of Sogliano, and no doubt keep alive his grievances against the counts of Montefeltro: below pp. 191, 299.

[6] Below p. 216. Federigo also repelled this accusation and, as far as is known, rightly.

the established rulers from power. It was a coup d'état, and it failed from miscalculation and inadequate support.[1]

Giovanni di Ramberto first came under suspicion of disloyalty when Niccolo d'Este, or his daughter Margherita, urged Galeotto Roberto to replace the council of twelve, to which he had left increasing responsibility, by other advisers, more trustworthy and appointed from outside. Giovanni at once began to organise opposition and encouraged the discarded counsellors to resist the new men. On 5 May 1431, with a catchword cry against over-taxation and other abuses, he succeeded in raising a riot in the streets of Rimini. So far he carried the city with him. But when he betrayed ambition to seize control himself, his colleagues deserted him, he was left without adherents, and the Malatesta, 'by the goodwill of the majority of citizens, and against the ill-disposed (*cativi*) were restored to power (*ritornati insignoria*)'. Sigismondo was absent in Cesena, where he had gone on the first day for fear of disorder there. His arrival was sufficient to quieten the excitement and, collecting a force of men from city and *contado* (*totos nudat cultoribus agros*), he started back to help his brothers, 'only to find them reinstated (*in signoria*)'. The *novità* was already over, and the appearance of Sigismondo's army quickly drove off Carlo Malatesta of Pesaro who had drawn near to profit by the tumult, which his agents in Rimini had secretly helped to stir up. Florence, Venice and the new pope, Eugenius IV, all declared for the Malatesta.[2] And it was a Venetian envoy who roused the Riminese to demand the conspirators' expulsion. At first Giovanni had been pardoned, but now, 'at the entreaty of the citizens', he and Leonardo Roello were sent into exile: 'and if they hadn't gone, the population would have torn them to pieces, for bringing such shame to the city, which at all times had been devotedly loyal (*fedellissima*) to the noble house of Malatesta'.[3]

At the end of May there was a belated rising in Fano which Domenico Malatesta was able to suppress,[4] and in October a second outbreak, led by a priest, Don Matteo Buratelli de Cuccurano. Sigis-

---

[1] For a slightly different interpretation: Vasina, *Romagna*, 269–70.

[2] In March Malatesta Novello had been elected to the Venetian nobility: Tonini, v/2, XXXVII.

[3] *Cron. mal.*, 60–2; Branchi, 175; Borghi, 89; *Ristretto d'Urbino*, 90; Pedrino, rub. 509–11; Basini, *Opera Hesperides*, lib. IV, vv. 103–71; Clementini, ii.243–55; Chiaramonti, 418ff.; Battaglini, *Vita*, 285–95, 608; *Zecca*, 227–8; Tonini, v/i. 84–8. In his *Commentaries* (but not his official charges) Pius II was to accuse Sigismondo of complicity in the revolt against the pious Galeotto Roberto who 'dies et noctes in templis ageret': *Commentaria*, 257; Soranzo, 'Invettiva' 1911, 154ff. Leonardo Roello was later readmitted to favour by Sigismondo, but Giovanni di Ramberto, whose property was confiscated, remained a perpetual enemy of the Malatesta of Rimini: *RIS*[2] xv/2.61–2.

[4] *Ristretto d'Urbino*, 90; Chiaramonti, 419; Amiani, i.367; Zonghi, 399. According to Giovanni Pedrino (rub. 509–11) there was also a fresh disturbance in Cesena.

mondo was sent with three hundred foot to restore order, when on 3 November Don Matteo, 'with certain ribald peasants, raised a disturbance in the piazza'. The *locumtenens*, Guido da Monte Vecchio, the *podestà*, Ungaro da Sassoferrato, and certain others, among them count Giovanni of Carpegna, were all killed, and Sigismondo himself had a lucky escape; 'even so the city stood firm and attempted no rebellion (*mutazione*)'. Don Matteo, with the other ringleaders, was sent to Rimini, where he was degraded by a court of three bishops, surrendered to the *podestà*, and hanged in the *piazza del Comune*.[1]

Meanwhile, at the bidding of Elisabetta, the three brothers rode ceremonially through Rimini, and were again acclaimed *signori*.[2] Few insurgents were executed, though for several months punitive proceedings were continued on various pretexts, perhaps under the influence of counsellors, sent at this time by the marquis of Este to support the Malatesta.[3] All cause for revolt had departed with Giovanni Ramberto, and the next twelve months are passed over in silence by the chroniclers.

Galeotto and his brothers were now securely established. The careless action of a few ill-affected notables had revealed their general popularity, and the danger of papal interference was at the same time removed by the death of Martin V, in February 1431. His successor, Eugenius IV, as a nephew of Gregory XII, enemy of the Colonna, and Venetian, was bound in several ways to the Malatesta, and was reported to be 'amicissimo' of the family, from affectionate contacts formed as cardinal with Carlo Malatesta.[4] A series of bulls in the summer and autumn of his first year as pope expressed both his friendship and a desire for their alliance;[5] and in 1432, like his uncle earlier, he thought of Rimini as a possible meeting-place for a general council.[6] At the same time with favour to Rimini went disfavour to Pesaro. Under Eugenius IV the situation developed during the previous pontificate was reversed in every detail. Now it was the Malatesta of Pesaro who had to face a partisan pope.

[1] *Cron. mal.*, 62–3; Pedrino, rub. 586. *Ristretto d'Urbino*, 90; Clementini, ii.261, 298–9; Chiaramonti, 419; Amiani, i.367–9; Battaglini, *Vita*, 298; Tonini, v/i.90–1. On 9 Jan 1432 the Malatesta sent a general pardon to Fano: Amiani, *loc. cit.*, who adds that the Venetians sent help which arrived after suppression of the revolt.

[2] Battaglini, *Vita*, 291.

[3] Clementini, ii.255–6; Battaglini, *Vita*, 295.

[4] *Cron. mal.*, 60.

[5] Raynaldus, 1431, n. xxxii; Battaglini, *Vita*, App. ix; Tonini, v/1.89, v/2, xxxviii–ix. On the death of Martin V the Malatesta sent troops to the governor of Forlì, and then in Aug. to the papal governor in Imola, both moves, it seems, against the Colonnesi: Pedrino, rub. 488, 552; Marchesi, 384–5; Battaglini, *Vita*, 298.

[6] Valois, *Pape et concile*, i.192.

Toward another Colonna ally, the count of Montefeltro, Eugenius was at first less severe. Although, according to Filippo Visconti, Guidantonio was no certain friend of the new pope, he and his state were at once taken into papal protection.[1] He was also employed by Eugenius to reoccupy Città di Castello, seized by Niccolo Fortebraccio during the papal vacancy. And even when the count tried to establish power there, an agreement was reached safeguarding his interests in the city and regranting him for ten years lands received from Martin V without the title of vicar.[2] Though equally compromised by association with the Colonna pope, it was Pesaro, not Urbino, which was to feel most strongly the reaction in papal policy.

In the middle of June 1431, following disturbances in Fossombrone and only a month after the Rimini rising, the population of Pesaro rose against Galeazzo, Pandolfo and Carlo Malatesta and drove them out. The occasion was the reimposition of certain dues (*gabelle*) recently suppressed, but it is likely that the pope or his legates, together with other anti-Colonnese, Venice and Ferrara, helped stir up disaffection. Eugenius repelled with fair words Pandolfo's appeal for assistance, evaded all negotiation, and let papal troops occupy Pesaro. Galeotto Roberto of Rimini tried to mediate and even, according to Clementini, rejected an offer of the *signoria* from the people of Fossombrone, an action which Carlo Malatesta later rewarded by helping to check insurrection in Fano. With no hope of treaty with the church, the Malatesta of Pesaro were obliged to muster resources from the lands they still held and attempt recovery by force. In October, supported by the Montefeltro, they opened attack from Gradara; and a struggle began which soon widened from a simple contest between papacy and Malatesta for possession of Pesaro into part of a larger conflict in Italy between papalists and professed adherents of the Council of Basle.

In this war, as long as Galeotto Roberto lived, the Malatesta of Rimini followed the pope. In January 1432 they obtained a papal *condotta* of which the command fell to Sigismondo, and sometime during the spring, at Serrungarina, he engaged and defeated a joint force of the count of Urbino and Malatesta of Pesaro, reinforced possibly from Lombardy. Galeotto Roberto himself meanwhile repelled approaches from the Malatesta of Pesaro, inviting him to reclaim his own recent losses to the church and recover S. Costanzo with the vicariate of Mondavio. But he did not break off relations; and

[1] 19 Feb. 1431: Mazzatinti, *Inventari*, xxxix.129; Franceschini, 'Poeta', 124.
[2] 29 Jan., 20 Feb. 1432: Theiner, iii.255, 257; Guiraud, 173–4, 195–6; Fumi *BU* 1900, 387–95.

according to some accounts he was party to an interim peace arranged by Vitteleschi which gave him custody of Gradara.[1]

The papal war with Pesaro continued into the next year, but this was Galeotto Roberto's last recorded part in it. On 10 October, when still only twenty-one, he died at Santarcangelo. In his short life, the chronicler adds, 'he had become known to all for his exemplary goodness and purity, and was believed by all to be certain of salvation'.[2] Since childhood Galeotto Roberto's absorbing ambition had been to become a 'povero di Cristo', and for two years before his death he was a dedicated Tertiary of the Franciscan Order. Though married by the will of his uncle, he kept his vow of chastity. So too, to the end of her life, did his wife Margherita, who returned to Ferrara and entered a nunnery. Despite warnings from the pope to moderate his religious practices, Galeotto Roberto devoted himself more and more to the contemplative life, so that his name and memory became in time the object of local legend and cult. But with his discipline of prayer and fasting his two brothers, and particularly Sigismondo, can have had little sympathy. Pius II, whose *Commentaries* incorporated all that might be said or believed to the discredit of the Malatesta, reports the story that Sigismondo had him poisoned.[3]

In 1430 an astrological almanack circulated in Romagna which predicted of the lord of Rimini that he would rise to great things: 'dominus vester ad magnum transibunt [*sic*]'.[4] The three years' rule of Galeotto Roberto had bitterly belied it. The reverses suffered may not have troubled a prince unworldly enough to refuse the *signoria* of a rival's city. But to Sigismondo, into whose hands government now passed, a man impassioned in the pursuit of secular ambition, to be commemorated in the works of distinguished artists and *litterati*, and to be denounced as an infidel and burned in effigy as a heathen, they represented an obligation and challenge. He had grown to manhood at a time when, as it appeared to him, the papacy was bent on robbing his dynasty of its legitimate rights to enrich greedy neighbours. To recover those losses or avenge them was a duty to his family and to his pride.

[1] Borghi, 89–90; *Chron. Bon.*, iv.52; Bonincontri, 138; *Ristretto d'Urbino*, 90; *Cron. Perug.*, 355; Pedrino, rub. 611, 614, 526, 528–30; Biondo, 466, 473; Pastor, *Acta*, i.20–1; Sansovino, 233v; Clementini, ii.255–6, 263; Giordani, *Gradara*, 78ff.; Battaglini, *Zecca*, 228; *Vita*, 295–7; Amiani, i.369–70; Vernarecci, *Fossombrone*, i.351; Guiraud, 216–19; Fumi, *BU* 1900, 395; Franceschini, 'Poeta', 125.
[2] *Cron. mal.*, 63. Elisabetta Gonzaga, who had exercised such great influence over him from his childhood, died a few months before, on 31 July: *ibid.* 63–4; Pedrino, rub. 648.
[3] Pedrino, rub. 657; Raynaldus, 1431, n. XXXII; Clementini, ii.228, 231; Battaglini, *Zecca*, 229–30; Tonini, v. 93–5, 675–94; Bartolucci, 'Legenda'; Giovanardi, 'Vitae duae'; Pius II, *Commentaria*, 257.   [4] Pedrino, rub. 418.

7

Sigismondo Pandolfo Malatesta, 'fex Italiae'

Sigismondo Malatesta is one of history's reprobates, a man burdened for centuries with the character of moral outcast. According to Jacob Burckhardt, 'unscrupulousness, impiety, military skill and high culture have been seldom so combined in one individual as in Sigismondo Malatesta'. Similarly, for J. A. Symonds, Sigismondo embodied the 'true type of the princes who united a romantic zeal for culture with the vices of barbarians': in his personal conduct 'a mere savage', in his patronage of art and letters 'a Neo-Pagan', in his career as *condottiere* 'the most accomplished villain of his age'.[1] It is the traditional judgement, maintained through generations by all but devout historians of the Malatesta dynasty. And even these, from an early stage, have had their reservations.[2]

Modern opinion is more circumspect. It is now understood that Sigismondo Malatesta, like other bad characters of the past, owes much of his evil reputation to hostile testimony, and especially, as often in the Middle Ages, the testimony of the church. The worst allegations against him were all transmitted to posterity by one authority: the Piccolimini pope Pius II, whose interests as ruler, and possibly as Sienese, envenomed him against the Malatesta, and whose published anathemas and, still more, his widely read historical *Commentaries*, represented Sigismondo with medieval gusto and indiscriminacy as a monster guilty of every possible public and private outrage. Many of these charges can be dismissed at once as the conventional invective of *curia* and church.[3] Others, among the most grave, convicting him of the murder of his first two wives, Ginevra d'Este and Polissena Sforza, and of killing and dishonouring the corpse of a German noblewoman, were either inaccurate, improbable, or the offspring of

---

[1] J. Burckhardt, *Civilisation of the Renaissance in Italy* (tr. Middlemore, London, 1878), i.45; J. A. Symonds, *Renaissance in Italy*, i (London, 1897), 134.

[2] Thus the court historian of Sigismondo, Gaspare Broglio, writing after his death: 'L'aspetto suo era feroce e rigido: crudelissimo contro li suoi nemici' – words hardly qualified by the sequel: 'era di persona più che communale; el suo referire era un altro Tullio: assai competentemente era dottato di scientia e di senno naturale': Clementini, ii.473; Tonini, v. 324.

[3] Cf. John XXII's indictment of the Este: Bock, 'Processi' and 'Este-Prozess'.

malicious rumour.[1] Incontestable, on the other hand, were certain other offences, like the pillage of churches for the rebuilding of S. Francesco in Rimini, or deficient respect for the virtue of his nobles' womenfolk.[2] And if the extravagant expressions of impiety attributed to Sigismondo were overdrawn by partisan judges, it is likely, as Aeneas Sylvius implied, that he was impatient of clerical government and no very devout member of the fifteenth-century church.[3]

Though thrown into relief by the self-conscious rectitude of his inveterate enemy and rival, Federigo da Montefeltro, much in Sigismondo's character was indistinguishable from the manners of his age.[4] It is enough to recall the history of his son and successor, Roberto called 'Magnificent', who was no less licentious than his father, and more obviously violent and unscrupulous, and yet enjoyed a favour both universal and lasting. It was otherwise with Sigismondo. Popular, as far as we know, with the mass of his subjects, outside his state he was destined to attract the antipathy of most rulers of his day and to be judged, against all evidence, the worst member of his family since its origin, and the scum of all Italy.[5] The contradiction suggests a vice less of character than temperament, such as contemporary science blamed on imbalance of humours or hostile conjunction of stars. The most considered opinions describe Sigismondo as a man of extremes, of wayward feeling: impulsive, imprudent, precipitate and mutable in action. And it was his capricious and incalculable conduct, his quick impetuous fantasy which, as attested by two of the acutest observers, Filippo Visconti and Cosimo de' Medici,[6] more than anything marked

---

[1] For a full analysis, disproving or discrediting the greater part of these accusations, see Soranzo, 'Invettiva', *passim*, with his supplementary studies: 'Due delitti', 'Martire del sigillo' and 'Atto pio della Diva Isotta'. Cf. further: Yriarte, 288–9; Rossi, 'Delitto'; Fumi, 'Atteggiamento'; Giovanardi, *Studi francescani*, 1915–20; Ricci, 41–4.

[2] Below p. 202; Vitali, 268–9.

[3] Even so it is worth noticing that Sigismondo had in his possession numerous theological and sacred books, perhaps inherited from Carlo Malatesta (Battaglini, *Vita*, 673–84; A. F. Massèra, *Roberto Valturio 'omnium scientiarum doctor et monarcha'* (Pesaro, 1927), 12; Mazzatinti, 'Biblioteca di S. Francesco', 347–52; Ricci, 593–5), and that the theologian Giovanni Ferrarese dedicated to him his *De immortalitate anime*: D. Fava, in *Scritti vari dedicati a M. Armanni* (Milan, 1938). Cf. also Yriarte, 393.

[4] Cf. for example another of his enemies, Alessandro Sforza: Giordani, *A. Sforza*, li; Denistoun, i.48.

[5] Below p. 225 n. 2.

[6] In 1445 Filippo Visconti had to write admonishing his captains not to mind Sigismondo's strange ways: 'debono molto ben conoscere de che testa e cervello l'è': *Atti canc. vics.*, ii.121. And again, in 1452, when Francesco Sforza's envoy in Siena proposed a violent scheme for freeing Ladislas of Hungary, in the hands of Frederick III, Cosimo de' Medici sceptically commented: 'saria cosa più tosto del Signor Sigismondo': Cusin, 'Aspirazioni', 350. Cf. the assessment by P. Cortese:

him off from his contemporaries. Few princes of the time denied themselves mistresses, not even the virtuous Federigo d'Urbino, but peculiar to Sigismondo was the ostentation with which he publicised his devotion to Isotta degli Atti and the rashness of making her his wife at a time when a dynastic marriage could have procured him a much needed alliance.

In politics, most obviously, such qualities were ruinous. In contemporary judgement they would have exactly fitted Sigismondo to Dante's description of Maghinardo Pagani: 'che muta parte dall'estate al verno' (*Inferno*, XXVII, 51). Mutability was construed as faithlessness. No complaint of Sigismondo was commoner than of his 'mobilitas', his restlessness, his uncertain loyalty. So, as a *condottiere*, much sought after for his military reputation, he became notorious for unreliability: 'et molti signuri et signorie fece la truffa, essendo suo conduttiero'.[1] His principality was small and his revenues slight. To win mercenary pay was therefore a necessity. His fickle changes of allegiance were partly those of a captain in search of a sure and lucrative contract. But only partly. They proceeded just as much from a native simplicity which hoped to follow and profit by immediate advantages, indifferent to agreements broken or animosity aroused. As a dynast, Sigismondo had interests of his own, and these to him were uppermost. Yet he also pursued his personal aims with passion rather than policy. Cosimo de' Medici was doubtless reporting general opinion when he wrote of him: 'El sinor Sigismondo ha fama ed effecto de essere tanto sfrenato a li apetiti soy, che como gli mette voglia de una cosa subito la voria et non è paziente a voglierla col tempo suo, et che faria omne cosa per condure ad effecto un suo apetito.'[2] This helps to explain why politically the reign of Sigismondo Malatesta, who has received so much attention as the architect of Renaissance court life, represents a rapid and irreparable decline. Thirty years and more after his death his bad faith was still a byword in Italy.[3]

Sigismondo was not alone in governing the Malatesta *signoria*. He was supported by his brother, Domenico Malatesta (Novello). But even Malatesta Sigismondo frequently antagonised and drove to join his enemies. By comparison, Malatesta Novello was a pallid figure, quiet, austere, scholarly, infirm of health, but not incapable of devising policies of his own or resenting injuries done to him. During the greater part of their lives their relations were rather

'Habuit hic [Sigismundus] multa contraria et diversa inter se naturae studia' etc.: *De hominibus doctis*, in *Ph. Villani liber de civitatis Florentiae famosis civibus* (ed. G. C. Galletti, Florence, 1847), 230–1.
[1] *Chron. Bon.*, iv. 384.
Fumi, 'Attegiamento', 165 (*a.* 1449).
[2] B. Feliciangeli, *Lettere di Galeazzo Sforza* (Sanseverino, 1915), 25.

those of suspicious neighbours than of partners in government. A territorial partition of the usual kind was to make this more apparent. Although not published until 1437, it was probably enforced some years before; and by it Sigismondo received all the lands south of the Marecchia, with Santarcangelo, Scorticata and the rectorate of S. Agata, Domenico all those to the north, depending on Cesena, Bertinoro and Meldola.[1] Each brother established a court of his own, but various facts show that, as in the past, the division was primarily administrative. Thus the popes continued to address Malatesta Novello as vicar of Rimini,[2] and the lord of Cesena retained at least a formal part in the government of Fano.[3] Had the two princes managed to act together, an easy condominium might have prevailed as under Carlo Malatesta and his brothers. In fact, they were as often enemies as friends.

At the death of Galeotto Roberto the mischief to arise from Sigismondo's character had not yet appeared. Pope Eugenius wrote congratulating the brothers on their loyalty to the church in which, he said, they imitated the illustrious example of their ancestors, and commended the Riminese in a separate letter for constancy in obedience to the Malatesta: 'cum enim plerumque decedentibus Civitatum ac Terrarum Rectoribus nonnulli in Populis motus exoriri consueverint'.[4] On the same day he wrote thanking the Venetian doge for help in securing a peaceful succession for the Malatesta, and recommending them to his protection.[5] Another firm supporter was the marquis of Este. Though one of Sigismondo's first acts on assuming power in Rimini was to restore many of the recent exiles, particularly Leonardo Roello,[6] Estense influence remained strong.[7] And it was reinforced early in 1433 by a marriage alliance between Sigismondo and Ginevra, daughter of Niccolo d'Este by Parisina Malatesta.[8]

[1] Together possibly with the Ravenna church lands granted by Gregory XII: Borghi, 89; Branchi, 175; Zonghi, 134; *Stat. Caes.* (1494); Clementini, ii. 276, 304; Amiani, i. 377; Tonini, v. 95; Zazzeri, 291; Antonini, *Supplemento*, 11; Guiraud, 223. Before 1437 there is more evidence of joint rule (ACF, *Cod. mal.* 3, fos. 20–1, 4, fo. 206v; Zonghi, 261), though this did not wholly cease: below n. 3.

[2] Guiraud, 221–2 (*a.* 1438); Chiaramonti, 429 (*a.* 1451).

[3] Anon. Veron., 101. In 1440 the communal chancellor and financial officials of Fano, and in 1441 the *podestá*, are described as representing both Malatesta, and in 1449 Malatesta Novello was managing affairs in Fano and *contado* in Sigismondo's absence: ACF, *Depos., Entrata/uscita* 80, fo. 80r; *Cod. mal.* 95, fo. 2r; *Canc., Reg.* ii, fo. 33r.

[4] 6 Dec. 1432: Battaglini, *Vita*, 611–12; Tonini, v/2. 141–2; Guiraud, 221.

[5] Battaglini, *Vita*, 610; Tonini, v/2. 140–1. The Venetians were still formal allies of both Malatesta: Predelli, iv, xii, nn. 193, 201.

[6] Clementini, ii. 301–2; Battaglini, *Zecca*, 231.

[7] Battaglini, *Vita*, 302.

[8] An earlier plan to marry him to a daughter of Carmagnola having collapsed with the *condottiere's* disgrace and execution: Borghi, 90; *Cron. mal.*, 65; *Diario Ferrar.*,

To the end of his life Venice and Ferrara were Sigismondo's two best allies. One of their earliest interventions was to promote an agreement, in 1433, between the Malatesta of Pesaro and the papacy, in which Sigismondo and Malatesta Novello also took part. Sigismondo surrendered some minor conquests (notably S. Ippolito), and may have retained the custody of Gradara.[1] In the same way Venice was temporarily assigned Pesaro and Sinigaglia, until conditions in the March of Ancona were more settled. Shortly after (September) Pesaro rose and called back the Malatesta. But not for another two years did the pope relent sufficiently to regrant them their vicariates.[2]

In early September 1433 the emperor Sigismund came from Rome to Rimini where he was festively received, and knighted the two Malatesta, in the company of numerous local lords, including Giovanni Malatesta of Sogliano, the conte Niccolo Malatesta of Ghiaggiuolo and the conte Francesco of Carpegna.[3] He then left for Basle – 'al concilio, dove s'era congregato contro papa Eugenia' – where events seemed to be moving toward a new schism, between general council and pope. The effect of this in Italy, and especially the Papal States, was to revive the disorders partially subdued by the legates of Constance and Martin V. In Italy the council canvassed for support, and in the Papal States prepared to take over the government.[4] The duke of Milan, no friend of a Venetian pope, and resolute ally of no power, chose to adopt the council and use it to justify a covert offensive on the dominions of the pope. In November 1432 an attempt by Antonio Ordelaffi to expel the papal government from Forlì had the support of Astorre Manfredi, then in Milanese pay.[5] At the same time the duke obliquely helped the Montefeltro and Malatesta of Pesaro in their conflict with the pope; and in December 1433 he promoted another attempt by the Ordelaffi on Forlì and Forlimpopoli, which a popular insurrection made successful.[6] In the Tuscan Patrimony he sent

20; Tonini, v.96–7, 101–2. From the Carmagnola connection arose an accusation, by Pius II, that Sigismondo had received and kept a dowry while repudiating the marriage; in fact the Malatesta had been advanced a loan which was, reluctantly, repaid: ACF, *Cod. Mal.* 76, fo. 33v; Zonghi, 132; Predelli, *Libri*, iv, XII, n. 209; Tonini, v.96; Soranzo, 'Invettiva' 1911, 150–4; A. Battistella, *Il conte Carmagnola* (Genoa, 1889), 370–1.

[1] Biondo, 473; Raynaldus, *sub anno*; Clementini, ii.108; Battaglini, *Vita*, 305; Tonini, v.99; Theiner, iii.268; Vernarecci, *Fossombrone*, i.367; *Comune di S. Ippolito*, 50–1; below p. 187 n 2.

[2] Pedrino, rub. 756; *Cron. Ferm.*, 67; *Ristretto d'Urbino*, 91; Biondo, 474; *Cron. mal.*, 64; Giordani, *Gradara*, 84; *Notizie*, XXIII; Theiner, iii.275.

[3] *Cron. mal.*, 64–5; Branchi, 175; Borghi, 89; *Chron. Bon.*, iv.66; Pedrino, rub. 726.

[4] *Concilium Bas.* ii.356; John of Segovia, 326, 566–7 (21 Feb. 1433).

[5] Cobelli, 175–7. In this encounter Sigismondo may have acted on the side of the church: Battaglini, *Vita*, 304.

[6] Cobelli, 178, 183; Pedrino, rub. 778, 798, 800.

Niccolo Fortebraccio to beleaguer Rome;[1] while for the conquest of
the March of Ancona he chose his most capable captain, Francesco
Sforza. Outwardly Sforza was not in Visconti service, but it was at the
duke's instigation that he came south in November 1433 to invade
the March, proclaiming the authority of the council and censuring the
pope. On 28 November he passed by Rimini with an army of 3,000
horse, and within two months had conquered nearly the whole
province, including numerous places not long before under the rule of
the Malatesta.[2]

In this attack only lands directly governed by the pope seem to have
been singled out. The *signori* were left alone. At Rimini the Malatesta
remained on the alert, without evidently siding with either pope or
council. Filippo Maria, who was anxious to win over the dynasties of
the Papal States, had thoughts of tempting the Malatesta with the lands
they had lost to the church.[3] But like their neighbours they preferred
to profit directly by the prevailing unrest, and in December 1433
quietly occupied Cervia.[4] Only in the following year, when Sforza
made peace with the pope and became marquis of Ancona and Gonfaloniere of the Church, did they begin to show their hand. Enraged by
Sforza's treachery, the duke of Milan sent another captain, Niccolo
Piccinino, into papal territory, and the two Malatesta may have joined
with Sforza to resist him.[5] It is also reported to have been against
Piccinino that at the end of 1434 an alliance was concluded between the
Malatesta and Guidantonio da Montefeltro, now reconciled with the
papacy; and that Sigismondo arranged the betrothal of his brother to
the count's daughter, Violante. The month of November passed in
convivial visits between Rimini and Urbino.[6]

In their century and more of power the Malatesta had been little
troubled by invading mercenary captains. The passage of Fra Moriale
and, later, Braccio, though causing alarm and suffering, were without
permanent effect. Under Sigismondo this was changed. More than
once his life was to be decisively affected by the unwelcome aims and
actions of powerful *condottieri*, then at the height of their influence in

---

[1] M. Creighton, *History of the Papacy*, ii (London, 1914), 232.
[2] *Cron. mal.*, 65; Simonetta, *Commentarii*, 41 ff.; Decembrio, 631 and n. 3, 640–1;
Pedrino, rub. 773; Biondo, *Hist.*, 475 ff.; Cagnola, 42–3; Compagnoni, *Reggia
Picena*, 324–5; Valois, *Pape et concile*, i.294.
[3] 24 Jan. 1424: Osio, iii.112; *Atti canc. visc.*, ii.93–4; Decembrio, 657–8. Pergola
and Roccacontrada were to go to the conte d'Urbino.
[4] Malatesta Novello took control there: Pedrino, rub. 784; Borghi, 90; Branchi, 176;
Ann. Forl., 91; Chiaramonti, 421; Battaglini, *Zecca*, 232–6; *Vita*, 309–10, 612–15;
Tonini, v/2. 143–6; Biondo, *Hist.*, 476, who adds that about the same time the
Malatesta of Pesaro seized Sinigaglia with part of the vicariate of Mondavio.
[5] Simonetta, 52; Battaglini, *Vita*, 314.
[6] *Cron. mal.*, 66; Chiaramonti, 422; Braschi, 295; Amiani, i.377; Zazzeri, 269.

Italy. The first of them to have dealings with him was Francesco Sforza, whose companion in arms he now became almost uninterruptedly for the next ten years. For a time this was to involve him in conflict with the pope; but for the present it offered no hindrance to papal favour or a papal stipend. In March 1435, after swearing fealty to Eugenius in Florence, he was taken into the service of the church for six months with 200 lances.[1] During the spring and summer he and Malatesta, supported by Sforza, were employed against the Ordelaffi in Forlì, who were supported in turn by Piccinino, until in August the marquis of Este succeeded in making peace between the pope and Milan.[2] Sigismondo was then sent to enforce papal government in Bologna, recently recovered by the church.[3]

Among the beneficiaries of peace was Antonio Ordelaffi, who was left in possession of his territories and began negotiations for obtaining a vicariate. But he failed to comply with the pope's conditions and investiture was withheld. He could not raise the money for buying the title, and at the same time fell out with the papacy over the bishopric of Forlì. So, in 1436 Sforza and the Malatesta were enlisted once more against the Ordelaffi, and this time they drove them out. In July Forlì was taken, and in August they attacked Lugo.[4] But Eugenius, then living in Bologna, was suspicious of Sforza's conduct of the campaign. Shortly before this he had been in secret correspondence with the Ordelaffi, and the pope now sent a spy, Baldassare da Offida, to watch Sforza and if possible arrest him. The plot was discovered and Baldassare thrown into prison.[5] What part if any Sigismondo took in this is not clear; but in a letter written from captivity in Fermo, Baldassare claimed the pope was planning to destroy the Malatesta as

[1] Battaglini, *Vita*, 615–18; Tonini, v/2. 147–51; Amiani, i.378; Wolkan, *Briefwechsel Eneas Sylvius*, i.39 (which reports a rumour that the pope will go to Rimini if no peace is reached with the Visconti: *ibid.* 40). Battaglini (*Vita*, 318) adds that the vicariate of Cervia was now granted Sigismondo, but cf. below p. 201. Between 1435 and 1440 cardinal Antonio Correr held the see of Cervia 'in admin.': Eubel, ii.141.

[2] *Cron. mal.*, 66–87; Biondo, *Hist.*, 493, 496; Pedrino, rub. 895, 897 ff., 904–5, 907–23; Cobelli, 185 ff.; Marchesi, 402–3. For these services it seems Eugenius contemplated restoring the vicariate of Mondavio to Fano, and Sigismondo instructed the Fanese to commence negotiations with the *curia*: Amiani, i.378.

[3] *Cron. mal.*, *SS* xv/2. 68–9; Battaglini, *Vita*, 562; *Chron. Bon.*, iv.80; Biondo, *Hist.*, 501; Ghirardacci, iii.43.

[4] Pedrino, rub. 920, 945, 951 ff., 967, 975; Cobelli, 180 ff.; Simonetta, 62–3; *Cron. mal.*, 69; Marchesi, *Supplemento*, 404–5, 409–10, 412 ff. In this war the antagonisms of the local peasantry in the border regions between their own territory and that of the Ordelaffi was used by the Malatesta whom a crowd of *contadini* followed in the campaign.

[5] *Cron. mal.*, 69–70; *Chron. Bon.*, iv.86–7; *Ann. Forl.*, 92; Simonetta, 63 ff.; Pedrino, rub. 977; Ghirardacci, iii.47–8; Battaglini, *Vita*, 323–5; Tonini, v.106–8; Valois, *Pape et concile*, ii.91.

well.[1] This may explain why the following year, despite papal pressure, Sigismondo refused to renew his *condotta*, and left it to his brother.[2] Instead he himself took service with Venice, and was present at the victory over Piccinino at Calcinara in September. He remained in Lombardy till the end of the year, and was only free to return to Rimini in January 1438.[3]

At this juncture a second, final, dispute broke out between pope and council over union with the Greek church. In January 1438 the conciliar leaders declared Eugenius suspended and assumed control over papal government. All vicars and other papal subjects were absolved from their oaths of fealty to the pope and commanded to obey the council.[4] At the same time the duke of Milan again embraced conciliar principles, and again unleashed his *condottieri* on the States of the Church. Scarcely had Eugenius left Bologna for Ferrara to await the Greek envoys, than Niccolo Piccinino appeared in Romagna with a powerful army, and by the end of May had occupied Ravenna, Forlì, Imola, Castel Bolognese and finally Bologna, from which he expelled a Malatesta garrison.[5] He also threatened Cesena, but Malatesta Novello seems to have bought him off with supplies. In June and August Niccolo and Francesco Piccinino extended their conquests further to Forlimpopoli and S. Sepolcro. But they did not disturb the Malatesta. With Domenico Malatesta at least their relations were friendly; and while Sigismondo continued to follow Sforza, his brother entertained Francesco Piccinino in Cesena, and at the end of the year was allowed to intercede with Niccolo Piccinino on behalf of the Polenta.[6]

Already perhaps Malatesta Novello had begun to feel the sympathy he was later to show with the Piccinini. Nevertheless he accepted service under Sforza with the league concluded against the Visconti in

---

[1] 26 Oct. 1436: 'Anchora era intentione de N. S. de desfar el Signor Malatesta et so fratello': *ASL* 1885, 756.

[2] Osio, iii. 318; *Atti canc. visc.*, ii. 96. In this year Sigismondo began construction of the *rocca* in Rimini which was to bear his name. It took nine years to complete: *Cron. mal.*, 70; Borghi, 90–1; Tonini, v. 108–10.

[3] Both in 1435 and 1436 the Malatesta of Rimini were numbered among the Venetian allies: Predelli, iv, XII, n. 233, XIII, nn. 12, 18, 19. The *condotta* was concluded on 3 April 1437 (*ibid.* XIII, n. 23), for 6 months service with 200 lances, and 6 'di rispetto', Sigismondo stipulating that he should not be obliged to fight the pope. Cf. *Cron. mal.*, 71; Pedrino, rub. 1038, 1048; Battaglini, *Vita*, 328, 563; Tonini, v. 110–11.

[4] John of Segovia, iii. 28 ff.

[5] Pedrino, rub. 1045, 1048, 1055, 1071 ff., 1081; Cobelli, 194; *Cron. mal.*, 72–3; *Ann. Forl.*, 92; Sanudo, 1057–9; *Diario Ferrar.*, 23; Biondo, *Hist.*, 522–3; Ghirardacci, iii. 52; Longhi, *AMR* 1905–6, 165. Antonio Ordelaffi received Forlì and the Manfredi Imola and Bagnacavallo with Massa di Romagna.

[6] Pedrino, rub. 1067, 1081, 1096, 1100, 1112; *Ann. Forl.*, 93; Amiani, i. 382.

January 1439 between Florence, Venice and the pope.[1] During May he was campaigning with Sigismondo in Romagna against Forlì and Forlimpopoli; and when Sforza left for Lombardy, they continued the contest with Guidantonio Manfredi. At the end of June, however, hostilities reached their usual inconclusive issue in a series of local truces with the Polenta, Manfredi and Ordelaffi.[2] Not until November did Malatesta Novello make a fresh but futile incursion into the general war, only to be taken prisoner in Lombardy by Niccolo Piccinino and the marquis of Mantua. He was released at the end of three months in exchange for the captive son of the Gonzaga, and made his way back to Cesena.[3]

For several seasons the Malatesta of Rimini had persevered in alliance with Sforza and the papacy, and almost escaped as princes the consequences of their allegiance as *condottieri*. In 1440 they had to combine and defend their own possessions. Years before, Braccio's invasion had shown that, even when at its grandest, their tiny state had no resources to resist a strong mercenary army. When Piccinino turned now against their territories with a company of 6,000 horse, they had no choice but to capitulate. Though Sforza, Florence and Venice all sent help and money, the campaign had not lasted more than two weeks before Sigismondo, in mid-March, went to Polenta and arranged an agreement. By the terms outlined the two Malatesta were each to receive a *condotta* from Piccinino. For the moment they were not obliged to fight either Sforza, Venice or Florence, and were dispensed altogether from serving against the church. In addition they were to recover all the lands once held by Carlo Malatesta in the March of Ancona, and were permitted, subject to approval from Milan, to accept the government of any other cities in the province. Offering as they did the prospect of territorial reparation, the conditions were generous, and were clearly intended to bind the Malatesta to the Visconti.[4]

It was probably during the same negotiations that Piccinino concluded a peace between the Malatesta and the count of Montefeltro. What the origins of the quarrel were is again unrecorded. The only

[1] Sanudo, 1068; Palmieri, 145; Predelli, iv, xiii, n. 45.
[2] Sanudo, 1073, 1076, 1089 (who says Sigismondo was in Venetian pay); *Chron. Bon.*, iv.95; Palmieri, 145; Pedrino, rub. 1137, 1140–1, 1151, 1153, 1161, 1164; Cobelli, 202; Ghirardacci, iii.58.
[3] Santoro, *Registri provv.*, 10, n. 25; *Arch. Gonzaga*, ii.181; Pedrino, rub. 1185; *Cron. mal.*, 76, 77, 78; Simonetta, 91; Biondo, *Hist.*, 557.
[4] The duke was to ratify the agreement by 15 April: *Atti canc. visc.*, i, n. 560, ii, n. 643; *Cron. mal.*, 78; Palmieri, 146; Capponi, 1191–3; Sanudo, 1090–1; Simonetta, 92–3; Biondo, *Hist.*, 562–3; Pedrino, rub. 1193–4, 1196, 1206; Cobelli, 203–4; *Cron. Perug.*, 449; Valeri, 'Signoria di Fr. Sforza', 73–4; Benadducci, 177–9; Longhi, *AMR* 1905–6, 467.

certainty is that in 1439 and 1440 was fought the opening round in the lifelong mortal feud between Sigismondo Malatesta and Federigo d'Urbino. Guidantonio was still the reigning count, but for several years Federigo, who had at last married Gentile Brancaleone in 1437,[1] had himself been making a modest entry into the wars and diplomacy of Romagna. As a relative of the Manfredi he was on the side of Milan, which put him at once among the formal enemies of the Malatesta of Rimini. Apart from this there seems to have been no special cause of friction, when Sigismondo with Malatesta Novello, early in October 1439, made a sudden attack 'proditorie' on the Feltreschi, 'pace extante inter eos', seizing the castles of Casteldelce, Sanatello and Faggiola. In November Federigo retaliated by laying waste Tavoleto in the Riminese *contado*, which provoked Sigismondo to occupy another group of castles in the Montefeltro, all traditionally subject to the rule or influence of Urbino.[2]

It was the first encounter between the rivals and the responsibility lay with Sigismondo. Writing to the citizens of S. Marino, his allies during the war, Guidantonio reminded them, with a certain inaccuracy, that for forty-seven years there had been no differences between the two families and that the present breach had not occurred 'per nostro defecto'.[3] All the same he was not opposed to negotiation, and willingly became party to the treaty between Piccinino and the Malatesta. A peace was published on 26 March. Each side gave up its conquests, and a month later Sigismondo was splendidly received in Urbino by the conte Guidantonio. There seemed no premonition yet of the bitter conflict to come.[4]

The Malatesta should now have been public allies of the Visconti. But when, in the late summer and autumn of 1440, Sigismondo reappeared beside cardinal Scarampi and the Florentine captains in an offensive against the Polenta, the Ordelaffi and the Manfredi, it was evident he did not hold himself bound by the compact with Piccinino. On his side, Malatesta of Cesena kept faith with Milan. And during the next four years the brothers were engaged to opposite alliances: perhaps, as Simonetta claimed, that 'victor postea victum apud victores

---

[1] 2 Dec. 1437. The dowry comprised 20 castles in the Massa Trabaria, among them Mercatello and S. Angelo in Vado: *Ristretto d'Urbino*, 92; Baldi, *Federigo*, i.16; Dennistoun, i.72; Bernardy, 'Archivio', n. 47; Delfico, i.191.

[2] Castelnovo, Montefotogno, Tausano, Pietramaura, Savignano di Rigo, Pennarossa, Viano, Rontagnano, Montegello: *Cron. mal.*, 76–7; *Ann. Forl.*, 93; Guerriero, 56; Pedrino, rub. 1179–80, 1187–8; *Ristretto d'Urbino*, 92; *Cron. Perug.*, 447.

[3] 23 April 1440: Delfico, ii, pp. lxxxv-vi; Bernardy, 'Archivio', 140–2; 'Frammenti sanmarinesi', 352–4, which shows the intense animosity of S. Marino against the Malatesta, an animosity which persisted.

[4] *Cron. mal.*, 77–9; *Cron. Perug.*, 449; Cavalcanti, ii.58; Baldi, *Federigo*, i.30; Amiani, i.385.

servaret'.[1] So in 1441, until a general peace was negotiated at Cremona at the end of the year, Sigismondo and Malatesta Novello fought in Romagna on different sides.[2] Sigismondo entered the service of Sforza. And in July, having lost his first wife Ginevra the year before,[3] he made the union closer by betrothal to Sforza's illegitimate daughter, Polissena. The betrothal ceremony took place in Fermo during September, and their marriage at Rimini in April the following year.[4]

Meanwhile, during 1441 Sigismondo's relations had once again worsened with the Montefeltro. This time it took the form of a clear conflict of territorial interest, which was to result three years later in his first serious political defeat, and make the dominant purpose of his whole life the humiliation of Urbino. On 21 April 1441 Pandolfo Malatesta, archbishop of Patras, died at Pesaro: 'cuius prudentia ipsa civitas iustissime gubernabatur'.[5] Three years before Carlo Malatesta of Pesaro had also died.[6] The city now passed in sole command to the youngest son of Malatesta di Pandolfo, Galeazzo, a man totally unfitted for government. 'Animo longe impar generi fuit', was Borghi's judgement of him, 'maluitque privatus cum dedecore quam dominus cum timore vitam agere . . . unus quidem indignus qui in catalogo principum Malatestarum nominaretur.' This was not the partisan opinion of a Malatesta historian. Filelfo, in his life of Federigo d'Urbino, says much the same of him: 'haebeti ingenio et animo effaeminato ac meticuloso'.[7] No ruler could have differed more from his neighbour of Rimini; this, together with the fact that he was with-

---

[1] As early as May the marquis of Este was trying to reconcile Sigismondo with the Venetians (Sanudo, 1094, 1096), and the defeat of Piccinino at Anghiari (29 June) may have decided Sigismondo to desert the Visconti, though in July he with Malatesta Novello signed a fresh agreement with Francesco Piccinino and Guidantonio Manfredi, and only at the end of August went over to his original allies: Pedrino, rub. 1267–8, 1275, 1286–7, 1289–95, 1310; Cobelli, 204–5; Biondo, *Hist.*, 576–7; *Cron. mal.*, 80–2; Simonetta, 100; *Ann. Forl.*, 93–4; *Diario Ferrar.*, 25.

[2] Pedrino, rub. 1311, 1320, 1324, 1329–30, 1338, 1359, 1370, 1392: Cobelli, 205–6, 209; Biondo, *Scritti ined.*, 11–12; *Cron. mal.*, 83, 85; Capponi, 1197; *Ann. Forl.*, 94; Predelli, iv, xiii, n. 188.

[3] Not without an unfounded suspicion of poisoning, which Pius II later published in his charges against Sigismondo: *Cron. mal.*, 81; Clementini, ii.319; Yriarte, 288–9; Soranzo, 'Invettiva' 1911, 157–9.

[4] *Cron. mal.*, 84, 86–7; Borghi, 91; Decembrio, 561, 578 (n. 3), 583 (nn. 2, 3), 584 (n. 1); Simonetta, 113; Amiani, i.388, 389; Benadducci, 193, 198, 200. Polissena was first offered to Malatesta Novello to win him over to Sforza, but nothing came of it (Decembrio, 584 n. 1). In Feb. 1442 Vannetta Toschi of Fano had given birth to a son Roberto, later Roberto il Magnifico, conceived at a time when both she and Sigismondo were 'soluti' from any marriage: Clementini, ii.483; Soranzo, 'Vanetta Toschi', 171 ff.

[5] *Cron. mal.*, 82, n. 10.

[6] *Ibid.* 74; Pedrino, rub. 1113.

[7] Borghi, 85, 86; Filelfo, *Commentarii*, 137.

out legitimate heir, to a state also enfeebled by poverty and economic decay,[1] was more than enough to encourage Sigismondo to claim the succession of Pesaro for himself. But he went wrongly about it. Recent relations had been fairly friendly between the two houses[2] and some arrangement might have been reached. Instead, within two days of Pandolfo Malatesta's death, the Montefeltro, kinsmen and allies of Galeazzo,[3] were in Pesaro with a force of men to defend it.[4] No action followed immediately, though attack from Rimini was expected.[5] Sigismondo chose to manoeuvre underhand. In August, with his covert support, the exiled Alberigo Brancaleone, long resident in Rimini, invaded the Montefeltro. Several castles were taken, and Federigo d'Urbino, then fighting for the Visconti, had to hurry from Faenza to organise defence. During the autumn, in alliance with S. Marino, he raided Riminese territory, and even succeeded by ruse in capturing the impregnable citadel of S. Leo. Sigismondo attempted no reprisal, but rather, as was to become his habit when worsted by his rival, accepted mediation from a friendly power. Through Alessandro Sforza, brother of Francesco, a truce and then a peace was made on 20 November. Once again all conquests were exchanged.[6]

In this second brush with the Montefeltro Sigismondo acted alone. Malatesta Novello did not, as far as is known, share his brother's ambition for Pesaro and took no part; he may indeed have supported the other side. In June 1442, just after Sigismondo's marriage to Polissena, he celebrated his own marriage with Violante da Montefeltro in Urbino.[7] Personal grievances more than divergent policy seem to have kept the brothers apart, and to the point of requiring formal

---

[1] Below pp. 286, 326.
[2] In 1435 or 1437 they are said to have renegotiated agreements (Battaglini, *Vita*, 618–19; Tonini, v/2. 151–2), and some time before his death Pandolfo is reported to have granted Sigismondo Gradara (Battaglini, *ibid.* 688). The position regarding Gradara is obscure. It seems likely Sigismondo was holding it, but whether by grant, force, or in virtue of the papal treaty of 1433 (above p. 180) is uncertain: Giordani, *Gradara*, 84–5, 91; *Notizie*, xix-xx; Vernarecci, *Fossombrone*, i.371; Feliciangeli, 'Notizie', 21–4. Generally at this time the internal weakness of the Malatesta of Pesaro was such that they played scarcely any part in events. In 1435, for a loan of money, they had even to pledge the *rocche* of Pesaro, Fossombrone and Montevecchio to their relative Gianfrancesco Gonzaga: *Arch. Gonzaga*,i i.181; Vernarecci, *Fossombrone*, i.369–74.
[3] Since Oct. 1438: Feliciangeli, 'Notizie', 22.
[4] *Cron. mal.*, 82–3.
[5] Bernardy, 'Archivio', 145–7.
[6] *Cron. mal.*, 83–5; Sanzio, *Cronaca*, 1, 24–7; Pedrino, rub. 1381, 1384–5; *Ristretto d'Urbino*, 92; *Cron. Perug.*, 471; Baldi, *Federigo*, i.37–54; Clementini, ii.277, 323; Amiani, i.389; Battaglini, *Vita*, 343–7; Delfico, i.197–200, ii, pp. lxxxvii–viii; Bernardy, 'Archivio', 147–50; Franceschini, *Montefeltro*, 403–4, 437.
[7] *Ristretto d'Urbino*, 92; *Cron. Ferm.*, 76; *Cron. mal.*, 88; Bernardy, *ASI* 1900, pt. 2, 138; 'Archivio', nn. 124–5; Lazzari, 58; Zazzeri, 289.

compromise. At the end of 1442 a written agreement was made between them, the first of several to follow, by the terms of which their original partition of land was confirmed, all injuries pardoned, and provision made for common defence and a common approval of alliances.[1] Notwithstanding this the two Malatesta continued to fight in the service of different captains, Sigismondo for Sforza, Domenico for the Piccinini. And they were kept employed.

The peace of Cremona brought no settlement to the Papal States. The principal obstacle was Sforza and papal refusal to recognise his *condottiere* state. Throughout 1442 and 1443 he was kept busy defending his lands in the March of Ancona against papal reconquest, while his properties in Southern Italy were threatened by Alfonso of Aragon. In this at first Sigismondo Malatesta gave him the best of his support.[2] But when in June 1443 Eugenius and Alfonso made a formal alliance to evict Sforza, and in a few months he had lost all but Fermo, Ascoli and Roccacontrada, Sigismondo began to waver; and it may only have been Sforza's presence in Fano, and generosity with money to him, that prevented him from defecting.[3] Whether willing or not, it was his loyalty alone which at this moment saved Sforza from total defeat, and it was his territory which had to face the combined attack of the Neapolitan and papal armies. By themselves they could not have resisted long. But luckily Alfonso was persuaded by Filippo Visconti to withdraw his troops; reinforcements from Florence and Venice began to concentrate around Rimini; and in September an alliance was formed between them and Milan, which engaged Filippo to send help to Sforza and Sigismondo.[4] The papal generals, Niccolo Piccinino, Federigo d'Urbino and Malatesta of Cesena, were now in their turn at a disadvantage, and on 8 November a bitter battle was fought at Monteluro, forced on by Sigismondo against the cautious advice of Sforza. Sigismondo fought 'ferociously' ('alexandrino animo et nestoreo consilio') and the rout of the enemy was complete. Piccinino and Malatesta retreated hastily southward, while Federigo fell back on Pesaro; and Sforza was free to begin reconquest of his territories.[5]

[1] *Cron. mal.*, 91; Clementini, ii.277–8; Battaglini, *Vita*, 353; Tonini, v.132; Zazzeri, 293.

[2] *Cron. mal.*, 86, 88–80; Simonetta, 118–19; Pedrino, rub. 1409, 1427, 1438, 1451, 1458, 1464, 1483; Cobelli, 213, 216; Osio, iii–276–8; Cagnola, 58, 60; Amiani, i.390; Battaglini, *Vita*, 350; Benadducci, 220–2, 213, 226.

[3] Pedrino, rub. 1522–3; *Cron. mal.*, 91–3; Borghi, 91; Simonetta, 124, 128; Sanudo, 1110; Benadducci, 243, 248–9, 251, 258; Fazio, 118.
    Cron. mal., 93–4; Sanudo, 1111; *Ann. Forl.*, 94; Simonetta, 129; Pedrino, rub. 1525, 1530–2; *Cron. Perug.*, 538; Cagnola, 62–3; Clementini, ii.329; Giulini, iii.545; Predelli, iv, xiii, nn. 244, 246, 283.

[5] *Cron. mal.*, 95; Borghi, 91; *Ann. Forl.*, 94–5; Sanudo, 1112; Broglio, in Tonini, v. 144; Simonetta, 133; *Cron. Perug.*, 540–1; Pedrino, rub. 1535–6; Sanzio, ii, ch. viii, 29; Cagnola, 63; Baldi, *Federigo*, i.54; Benadducci, 271.

His object was to exploit his success, but Sigismondo, for whom the Malatesta chroniclers claim all merit for the victory, had other ideas in mind. Already suspected during the spring of conspiracy to overthrow Galeazzo of Pesaro,[1] he thought the time propitious for seizing the city by force, and claimed it was his due for having stood by Sforza and let his own state be ravaged by enemy and allied troops. With irritated reluctance Sforza gave way, and an attack was begun. But the season was late, Pesaro and its *contado* were well defended, and only a few small places were taken. At the end of November Sforza resumed his own campaign in the March, in which Sigismondo joined him and success-fully recovered some of the territory lost earlier beyond the Metauro.[2] It was the first time Sigismondo had clearly placed his interests as *signore* before his duties as *condottiere*.

For Sforza the year which now opened was a season of complete, if impermanent, triumph. In August he inflicted a heavy defeat at Montolmo on a papal army under Francesco Piccinino and Malatesta Novello, and a month later Eugenius, yielding to Florence and Venice, at last granted him peace. For Sigismondo, however, it was a period of unrelieved calamity. After ten years of obscure campaigning in other people's wars, his life begins from this point to assume its own turbu-lent character, of misfortune and mismanagement, hasty scheming and erratic execution, which if partly natural to a petty prince in a world outgrowing his type, was also peculiar to him. The wearisome chronicle continues of wars, truces and *cavalcate*, but it now becomes more obviously related to the fate and fortune of Sigismondo himself. After a fresh attack on the *contado* of Pesaro in which he took one village, he accepted a short truce with Galeazzo at the end of March 1444.[3] He had no intention of relinquishing his claims until fought to a decisive finish. But with the approach of spring his obligations as hired captain demanded attention once more, and in April he left for Venice to claim arrears of his father-in-law's pay. Formally, he was still as much an ally of Sforza as his brother was of Piccinino,[4] and for this he was now excommunicated by the pope.[5] But the alliance, already put to the test, was showing signs of strain. His actions in the next few months made

[1] Bernardy, 'Archivio', n. 140; Pedrino, rub. 1492; *Cron. Ferm.*, 82.
[2] *Cron. mal.*, 95–7; Simonetta, 135–7; Broglio, in Tonini, v. 142–5; Cagnola, 63; Amiani, i.395; Benadducci, 274, 276, 279, 284.
[3] *Cron. mal.*, 97–8; ACF, *Canc.*, *Carteggio*, *Bandi*, i.iv; Mariotti, *Bandi di tregua*, 6–7.
[4] *Cron. mal.*, 98.
[5] April 1444; Sanudo, 1114. Sometime in 1443 or 1444 the eminent citizen of Fano, Ugolino de' Pili, and his sons suffered imprisonment and confiscation of goods for traitorous relations with the pope. The punishment seems to have been merited, but this did not prevent Pius II from accusing Sigismondo of having put them barbarously to death for being friendly with the pope: Battaglini, *Corte*, 79–81: Castelucci, 'Regesto', 188; Soranzo, 'Invettiva' 1911, 159–68.

a breach inevitable. First, he kept the Venetian money, as due to him-self for pay and expenses on Sforza's behalf in Fano the year before.[1] At the same time, preoccupied with Pesaro, he failed to join Sforza in the March.[2] For the moment, fearing his total defection, Sforza was compelled to humour him, even granting a demand for the *rocca* of Sinigaglia, taken long before from the Malatesta of Pesaro, and held by Sforza's wife Bianca.[3] But after his victory in August the need for caution passed. Though Sigismondo, as captain-general, sent a report of the battle to Bologna,[4] and received a place in the treaty with the pope,[5] when he appeared to make his excuses Sforza impatiently brushed them aside.[6]

Embroiled with Galeazzo of Pesaro, and estranged from Sforza, Sigismondo had meanwhile also rekindled the resentment of the Montefeltro. In February 1443 the conte Guidantonio had died, to be succeeded by his son, Oddantonio.[7] Galeazzo Malatesta, whose relations with Urbino were particularly close, and Malatesta Novello, as son-in-law of the dead count, both attended the funeral.[8] Malatesta was also present in Siena when Oddantonio was invested by the pope with the new title of duke.[9] Sigismondo, however, took part in none of these proceedings. He and Federigo, Oddantonio's half-brother, were in the pay of different captains, and at the end of 1443 had a preliminary clash over Pesaro.[10] Fresh conflict soon followed. It was raiding by Federigo which forced Sigismondo to his truce with Galeazzo in the following spring.[11] In May and June a similar agree-ment was arranged with Urbino by the marquis of Este.[12] But then, in July, Oddantonio was assassinated. Federigo, then in Pesaro, at once became ruler in his place. And, whether or not with his approval,

---

[1] Simonetta, 141; Sanudo, 1114; *Cron. mal.*, 98; Fumi, 'Attegiamento', 170.

[2] *Cron. mal.*, 98–9; Simonetta, 143–4, 145; Fumi, 'Attegiamento', 171.

[3] *Ibid.* 171. Since 1438, by this or other means, Sigismondo seems also to have reacquired, in the March of Ancona, Mondavio and possibly Pergola, Rocca-contrada and S. Lorenzo in Campo: ACF, *Canc., Reg.* ii, fos. 34v, 45–6; *Cod. mal.* 103; *Cron. mal.*, 74–5; Amiani, i.383–4, 392, 395; Nicoletti, 665–6.

[4] *Cron. Bon.*, iv.123; Ghirardacci, iii.99; Zazzeri, 295; Benadducci, 302. On the battle itself, in which Francesco Piccinino was killed and nearly all Malatesta Novello's forces taken: *Cron. mal.*, 100–1; *Ann. Forl.*, 95; Simonetta, 145; etc.

[5] Osio, iii.312, cf. 329; Predelli, iv, xiii, n. 369; *Cron. mal.*, 102. Sigismondo was absolved from censure and reinstated in his vicariates.

[6] Clementini. ii.337; Benadducci, 318.

[7] *Cron. mal.*, 91; *Rissretto, d'Urbino*, 93; *Cron. Ferm.*, 82; Pedrino, rub. 1489; Baldi, *Federigo*, i.54; Dennistoun, i.47, 57.

[8] *Cron. mal.*, 91.

[9] Franceschini, 'Poeta', 130. On returning to Urbino Malatesta Novello was knighted by the duke.

[10] Baldi, *Federigo*, i.63.

[11] Baldi, *Federigo*, i.66–7; Bernardy, 'Archivio', nn. 150, 153; Delfico, i.201–2.

[12] *Cron. mal.*, 99; ACF, *Canc., Carteggio, Bandi*, 1.2r, 3r; Mariotti, *Bandi de tregua*, 7–9.

reports issued from Urbino that Sigismondo had played a devious (and implausible) part in causing Oddantonio's death.[1] The rumour was prophetic. Rebutted by Sigismondo with a countercharge against Federigo, it was the first hint of what was to become, in the next twenty years, the most notorious feud in Italy between two reigning princes. Previously, in their brief early encounters, there was nothing to indicate whether rivalry had yet turned to personal hate. There are no stories or *novelle* about their opinions or relations: only a contrast of character, of cold wiliness with hot impatience, may have forecast the enmity to come. But within a few months the two lords had initiated a 'press war', incessant thereafter, in a defamatory exchange of circular letters, first by Sigismondo, then by Federigo, each questioning the other's paternity, and piling up abuse. The provocation was a turn in events at the end of 1444.[2]

The truce concluded by Lionello d'Este did not lapse with Oddantonio's death; and unless Federigo was a covert influence behind the reconquest in the summer by Galeazzo Malatesta of certain places in the *contado* of Pesaro,[3] it was Sigismondo who was the first to violate it. In September Giovanni Gabrielli, with the connivance if not open support of Sigismondo, seized the castle of Frontone in the Montefeltro;[4] and a few months later, in December, the two Malatesta of Rimini accepted the commendation of Niccolo de' Perfetti, who held a number of other castles in the same region.[5] But to these petty irritations Federigo was already in the process of preparing a more than suitable reprisal.

Nothing was more natural than that the three lords whom Sigismondo had antagonised, Sforza, Galeazzo Malatesta of Pesaro and Federigo d'Urbino, should combine to frustrate his ambitions. It was Federigo, perhaps the least affronted, who took the initiative in bringing them together. At the end of 1444 he arranged a series of secret treaties, by which Galeazzo sold Pesaro and Fossombrone to the Sforza and Montefeltro, and Alessandro Sforza, married to Costanza Varano, became lord of Pesaro in his place. Alessandro Sforza had long wanted to marry Costanza Varano, granddaughter of Galeazzo Malatesta,

---

[1] By giving encouragement (where none clearly was needed) to the profligate conduct which occasioned his murder: *Ristretto d'Urbino*, 93; Pedrino, rub. 1553; *Cron. mal.*, 99; Guerriero, 59; *Cron. Perug.*, 552–4; Sanzio, II, ch. VIII, 29–30; Lazzari, 60; Dennistoun, i.53–4.

[2] Franceschini, *Montefeltro*, 431, 445ff.

[3] *Cron. mal.*, 98–100.

[4] *Ibid.* 101; Guerriero, 59; Sanzio, II, ch. VIII, 31.

[5] *Cron. mal.*, 102; Guerriero, 60; Sanzio, II, ch. IX, 31. In 1448 Niccolo surrendered his rights to the castles to Sigismondo: *Cron. mal.*, 102; Battaglini, *Vita*, 688. On 27 Nov. 1444 Alberigo da Brancaleone had died in Rimini but favours to his family continued: Clementini, ii.379.

whose family had recovered Camerino in 1443 after nine years of exile. But as a mere adventurer and *condottiere* he was possessed of no dominion or estate, and this Federigo d'Urbino undertook to get him.[1] On 19 October Federigo made an alliance with Francesco Sforza, which included both Galeazzo of Pesaro and the Varani.[2] Galeazzo was at this time about to negotiate an agreement with Sigismondo. The recent peace between Sforza and the pope had stipulated as one condition that the dispute between Rimini and Pesaro should be arbitrated by Sforza and the cardinal of Aquileia.[3] On the same day that Sforza and Federigo became allies, Galeazzo Malatesta drew up his peace proposals. The quarrel, he claimed, was on account of 'Castri Gradarie Castrorum et lochorum tam Comitatus Civit. Pisauri, quam etiam Forisempronij, nec non Civitatis et Comitatus Senegalie a prefato Magn. Dno. Sismundo Pandolfo retentorum et occupatorum'. The castles taken by Sigismondo in the *contado* of Pesaro and Fossombrone were to be surrendered, but the possibility was acknowledged that Sforza might decide to leave Gradara and Sinigaglia to Sigismondo in which case Galeazzo said he would be content to 'promettere al sig. Sigismundo di non m'impacciare de Gradara'.[4] These terms were never seriously examined. Soon after they were drafted Galeazzo must have learned of Federigo's scheme for buying his abdication, and given his approval. At the end of November Federigo concluded the betrothal of Alessandro and Costanza, and on 8 December they were married in Camerino.[5] Three days later, as 'procuratore et commissario por lo magnifico signor Galeaç di Malatesti', Federigo arranged certain *capitoli* with Francesco Sforza at Fossombrone,[6] and on 15 January 1445 the details were finally formulated for Galeazzo's surrender of his state. Pesaro was to be sold to Francesco Sforza and assigned to his brother Alessandro, while Fossombrone was to be sold to Federigo.[7] The treaty was quickly

---

[1] As early as 8 Oct. 1444 Alessandro may have empowered Federigo to negotiate his betrothal to Costanza (Giordani, *Zecca*, 215), and later in the same month Federigo undertook to secure him both Costanza and Pesaro: Feliciangeli, 'Notizie', 42.

[2] Daverio, 175; Osio, iii.319.

[3] Predelli, iv, xiii, n. 269.

[4] Giordani, *A. Sforza*, xix–xxiii; *Zecca*, 214–15; Vernarecci, *Fossombrone*, i.375; Mazzatinti, *Inventari*, xxxvii.163.

[5] *Cron. Ferm*, 88; Lilii, ii.191–2; Giordani, *A. Sforza*, xxiii–xxiv; *Zecca*, 215, Feliciangeli, Notizie', 42–3.

[6] Daverio, 176; Mazzatinti, *MSS di Francia*, ii.287; Vernarecci, *Fossombrone*, i.375; Bernardy, 'Archivio', nn. 163–4. As late as 4 Dec. Sigismondo was still writing to Sforza from Rimini.

[7] Simonetta, 151–2; Guerriero, 60; *Ann. Forl.*, 95; Filelfo, *Commentarii*, 291–2, 315; Baldi, *Federigo*, i.87–8; Giordani, *Zecca*, 215–16; *Gradara*, 86; Ugolini, i.339; Mazzatinti, *Inventari*, xxxvii.201. By the chroniclers' account Pesaro was sold for

implemented and in March the new *signori* took possession. The nerveless Galeazzo retired to lead the life of private citizen and rentier in Florence, his wife to a religious house in Foligno, while Pesaro and Fossombrone passed for ever from his family after a century of Malatesta rule.[1]

Sigismondo's impatience to seize by force a part of his ancestral lands which with forbearance he might have obtained by negotiation, had resulted only in the permanent loss of his prize. Henceforward, behind all his shifts of policy, all his intercourse and contracts with other powers, was to lie the inflexible purpose to avenge and undo the treacherous treaties prepared by Federigo. It was the sale of Pesaro which turned their rivalry into unappeasable enmity, and in the first access of fury Sigismondo sent a personal challenge to Federigo.[2]

It was following the sale of Pesaro that certain differences appeared also between Federigo and Malatesta Novello arising from the dowry due to Violante, Malatesta's betrothed. Already when still only a child, Violante, as a legitimate daughter of the conte Guidantonio, had received a grant of lands from the pope within the vicariate of Urbino, and these with other territories she demanded as heiress of the count on the death of her brother Oddantonio in 1444. In the following year she abandoned her claims, but there remained unsettled the concession of her dowry as determined by Guidantonio at the time of her marriage; and in September 1445 or 1446, as compensation for the lands which were still withheld by Federigo, the cardinal of Aquileia, in a sentence ratified by the pope, assigned her the *contado* of Montefeltro, and particularly the castles of Montegello, Savignano, Rontagnano and Monteboaggine. The decision did not terminate the dispute. Malatesta still had to enforce surrender of the castles, and for twenty years more his wife's claims in the Montefeltro, which she relinquished only in 1466 several months after his death, were to keep him from any lasting alliance with the count of Urbino.[3] As a result he was once more his brother's ally in the war which now broke out in the March of Ancona.

Sigismondo did not wait for the entry of the Sforza into Pesaro

20,000 gold fl., Fossombrone for 13,000, but this is rejected by Giordani (*Zecca*, 215), and Vernarecci (*Fossombrone*, i.377); the treaty published by Giordani (*A. Sforza*, xxv–ix) does not mention the purchase money.

[1] *Cron. mal.*, 104; Borghi, 86; *Cron. Ferm.*, 88; Pedrino, rub. 1562; Giordani, *A. Sforza*, xxix–xxx; *Zecca*, 215–16; Franceschini, *Montefeltro*, 447–9.

[2] 21 Feb. 1445; Gaye, *Carteggio*, i.179–80; Osio, iii.363–5; Ugolini, i.337; Yriarte, 277–8; Tonini, v/2.162–3. Federigo accepted but no duel was fought.

[3] Lazzari, 58; Colucci, xxi/1.137–8; Dennistoun, i.76; Ugolini, i.353; Zazzeri, 289; Soranzo, *Pio II*, 498; Massèra, *RIS*[2] xv/2.111, 114, 119; Madiai, *Le Marche* iii, 125–7; Mazzatinti, *Inventari*, xxxix.131–2; Franceschini, *SR* 1950.

before preparing retaliation. In March he offered his services to Alfonso of Aragon, and sent envoys to Eugenius, the duke of Milan and Lionello d'Este.[1] Each one welcomed his overtures. During June and July Neapolitan ships began to arrive along the Adriatic coast to join with the Malatesta against the Sforza, while Filippo Visconti, since May in alliance with the pope, took Sigismondo and his brother into his pay, and sent a number of his captains in support. Meanwhile, early in July, Francesco Sforza, helped by Florence and Venice, invaded Malatesta territory, creating a fear in some quarters that he would drive them out and make way for the count of Urbino. Candelara was taken, la Pergola was sacked, and many places of the *contado* of Fano suffered devastation. Sigismondo at first replied with an attack in the Montefeltro, and then in October, after a brief visit to the Abruzzi to seek help for the church from Alfonso, led the troops of Milan, Naples and the papacy, of which cardinal Scarampi made him standard-bearer, in a general assault on the March. Roccacontrada fell, and Fermo, and by December he was master of the whole province. At the same time Carlo Fortebraccio, who had entered his service in the spring, and Malatesta Novello made an indecisive attack on Urbino, which issued in the usual truce.[2]

For Sigismondo this and the following year were a period of high success. It was now that he commissioned Pisanello and Matteo de' Pasti to strike their commemorative medals, and that the Castel Sigismondo, in progress since 1437, was ceremonially inaugurated; while in verse the humanist poet Basinio of Parma was to celebrate at length the conquest of Roccacontrada.[3] The pope added his tribute to the military reputation which Sigismondo now began to enjoy in Italy, and during a visit to Rome at the end of 1445 received him honourably, and 'glie donò la spada et el capello'.[4] In April he issued a bull of

[1] Battaglini, *Vita*, 373, 620; Tonini, v-2.163; Ametller, *Alfonso V*, ii.539–40.

[2] Since July Federigo was Sforza's captain-general: Osio, iii.372; *Atti canc. visc.*, i.222–3, ii.117, 121; Theiner, iii.306; Della Tuccia, 199–201; *Cron. Ferm.*, 88–90; Filelfo, *Commentarii*, 292; Pedrino, rub. 1569; *Cron. mal.*, 106–9; Guerriero, 60–1; Simonetta, 152ff.; Sanzio, ii, ch. x; Cagnola, 66–7; Giordani, *A. Sforza*, xxxi–ii; Ugolini, i.350–1 (says Federigo challenged Sigismondo to a duel); Ametller, iii.663–4; Benadducci, 328, 337–8; Bernardy, 'Archivio', nn. 172ff.; Fumi, 'Atteggiamento', 172 (n. 1); Gianandrea, 'Potestà', 87; Pellegrini, 'Gubbio', 184–5. In January 1445 Sigismondo and his heirs became *raccomandati* of Venice, but this did not make the republic any less an ally of Sforza: Predelli, iv, xiii, n. 274.

[3] Battaglini, *Zecca*, 237–9, and 'Medaglie', *ibid.* Tav. i–iii; Ricci, 26, 35ff., 148. In 1446 Guarino wrote to Tobio Borghi urging him to write a history of Sigismondo's deeds: *Epistolario* (ed. R. Sabbadini, Venice, 1915–19), ii.459–60.

[4] *Cron. mal.*, 110; Amiani, i.402; Biondo, *Scritti ined.*, 159–60. In February Bartolommeo Malatesta, whom Eugenius had elected bishop of Rimini the year before, went as Sigismondo's representative to Rome.

excommunication against Felix V and his adherents, among them Sforza and Galeazzo Malatesta, whom he denounced for alienating Pesaro and Fossombrone.[1] About the same time, he at last authorised the reunion of Mondavio and its vicariate with the *contado* of Fano, separated a century before by John XXII, and already subject *de facto* to the Malatesta.[2] A little later the cardinal-legate Scarampi ratified their tenure of Sinigaglia with a grant of vicariate.[3] The concessions showed the continuing advantages of following the papal interest in politics, and by implication the possible dangers of deserting it.[4]

The new year passed like its predecessor with Sigismondo fighting for Alfonso, Filippo Maria and the pope, against Francesco Sforza and Urbino. At the beginning a misunderstanding between Alfonso and the pope threatened delay, and Sigismondo, unwilling to face Sforza alone, in June made a truce with him, Alessandro and Federigo d'Urbino, which was limited to the Malatesta and their clients.[5] Even so, they were already at war again when during July the allied contingents at last began to assemble in Romagna and the March. The campaign that followed under the leadership of the Malatesta brothers went forward quickly. Alessandro Sforza was forced to make peace, the state of Urbino was overrun, and by the end of September Sigismondo had subdued almost all the Montefeltro.[6] Federigo was paying the price for Pesaro, and his situation remained serious until Florence, wakening to the danger, sent Simonetta and Guidaccio Manfredi to relieve him. Alessandro Sforza reverted to his old allegiance, and in October the Sforzeschi and Feltreschi were able to counter-attack. Monteluro, Pozzo Alto and la Tomba di Pesaro all fell to the conte Francesco, but he failed in a siege of over forty days to reduce the

[1] *Cron. mal.*, 111; Raynaldus, n. xi *sub anno*; Lünig, iv.181–4; Theiner, iii.308.
[2] Amiani, i.403–4; ii, pp. lxxxi–iii; Mazzatinti, *Archivi*, Ser. 1, ii.231.
[3] Some time during 1446: Siena, 135; Battaglini, *Vita*, 574. Now, or earlier they also got Monteluro, Pozzo and Granarola: Battaglini, *Vita*, 373, 688.
[4] From Rome Sigismondo went in February to Milan, barely escaping on the way an attempt by Astorgio Manfredi to capture him: *Cron. mal.*, 110; Della Tuccia, 203; Daverio, 181; *Atti canc. visc.*, i, n. 1772. In January the duke took Sigismondo into his protection: Amiani, i.402.
[5] ACF, *Canc.*, *Carteggio*, *Bandi*, 1.71 ff.; Mariotti, *Bandi di tregua*, 11–17. In March Sigismondo was suspected of complicity in a plot instigated by Niccolo dei Perfetti to assassinate Federigo in Urbino; *Cron. mal.*, 110; Guerriero, 60; *Cron. Perug.*, 578.
[6] Pergola was recaptured, while Sassocorvaro, with Montegrimano, Montecerignone, Monteboaggine and other places, surrendered to Sigismondo or the patriarch, and Malatesta and his wife occupied Monte Tassi, S. Anastasio, Soanna and Montegello: *Cron. mal.*, 111–15; Branchi, 176; Guerriero, 61–2; Della Tuccia 203; Sanzio, ii, ch. x (says Federigo challenged Sigismondo who declined to fight); Pedrino, rub. 1574–6, 1581.

fortress of Gradara. When the attempt was finally abandoned, Sigismondo felt it safe to leave Romagna for Lombardy where Filippo Visconti had sudden need of his services.[1]

The occasion was a heavy defeat recently suffered in war with Venice (Casalmaggiore, 28 September). In his dismay Filippo Maria turned everywhere for help, and the allied troops in Romagna prepared to come to his relief. In early December Sigismondo left to join them, together with the viceroy of Naples, and the next two months he passed in Lombardy in debate and negotiation.[2] One effect of the Venetian victory was to decide Filippo once again to come to terms with his son-in-law, Sforza. Some approach had already been made, and it was following this that Sigismondo concluded a temporary truce with Sforza after the siege of Gradara.[3] During the winter terms of an agreement were elaborately discussed, and they soon became part of a general initiative to establish peace in Italy, which proceeded without interruption by the death of Eugenius IV in February 1447 and the election of his successor, Nicholas V. Sforza did not yield unconditionally to the chance of a settlement with Milan. He made preliminary demands, including a stipulation that the Malatesta should restore the lands of his ally Federigo d'Urbino, and to himself the *rocca* of Sinigaglia.[4] As the exchange of letters progressed, a war of 'cavalcatelle' went on between Sforza and the Malatesta, which compelled Sigismondo to hurry home to Rimini.[5] But on 8 March the first step toward peace was taken when he and Sigismondo arranged a truce in Pesaro which also included Alessandro Sforza, the count of Montefeltro and Malatesta Novello.[6] A week later a treaty was drawn up between Sforza and the duke of Milan, in which Filippo Maria complied with each of Sforza's conditions regarding the Malatesta, though earlier he had claimed no power to command them.[7] Nor was he in practice able to make good his engagements. On 1 May, when peace terms were at last agreed between the Malatesta, Sforza and Pesaro, only a general pardon of all disputes was mentioned, without allusion to Federigo.[8] A more promising sequel to the Milanese negotiations was a final

[1] *Cron. mal.*, 116–17; Guerriero, 62; Simonetta, 167–8, 171–2; Broglio, in Tonini, v. 162–8; Della Tuccia, 205; Sanzio, II, ch. x; Anon. Veron., 3–6; Pedrino, rub. 1583–4; Fazio, 137–8; Battaglini, *Vita*, 384ff.; Benadducci, 376.

[2] *Cron. mal.*, 117; Sanudo, 1123–4; *Chron. Bon.*, iv.138–9; Pedrino, rub. 1588–91; Osio, iii.458–9; Fazio, 138c; Ghirardacci, iii.119.

[3] Guerriero, 62; Anon. Veron., 6; Osio, iii.462–3, 467–71.   [4] Osio, iii.472.

[5] Osio, iii.467–71; Rossi, *Guerra*, 24ff. Sigismondo returned on 7 Feb. (*Cron. mal.*, 118), and on his way back suffered a second attack from Astorgio Manfredi, having to hide in a marsh, in water up to his neck: Broglio, in Battaglini, *Vita*, 389–91.

[6] Decembrio, 557; Osio, iii.491–2; *Cron. mal.*, 118; *Cron. Perug.*, 591; Baldi, *Federigo*, i.102; Amiani, i.406; Pellegrini, 'Gubbio', 186.

[7] 'Comandare a li Malatesti': Osio, iii.472; Franceschini, 'Notizie', 177–9.

[8] Osio, iii.547–50, 561–2; Mazzatinti, *MSS di Francia*, ii.296. Cf. Daverio, 182.

settlement between Sforza and the papacy, with the surrender of Sforza's last possessions in the March. By August arrangements were complete. Sforza had left for Lombardy: shortly after, on the sudden death of Filippo Visconti, to press his claims to Milan. And the Malatesta and their neighbours were finally freed from a threat which had troubled them for over ten years.[1]

Though tenacious enough of his rights in his dealings with Sforza, the new pope, Nicholas, was sincerely interested in peace. By instinct and policy he was a conciliatory ruler; and one way in which he showed this, in Romagna and the March, was by withdrawing papal disfavour from the lords of Pesaro and Urbino. To the first, in July, he granted the vicariate of Pesaro, thereby ratifying with papal authority the sale of 1445;[2] and to the second, two months later, he gave absolution and provisional investiture with the castles of the Montefeltro, stipulating only that Violante's dowry be first made over.[3] Nicholas was clearly anxious to settle the divisions of Romagna, and wrote exhorting Sigismondo to live at peace with Pesaro.[4] But it was to require more than papal admonition to subdue Sigismondo's grievances, and during the autumn he made several attacks on Fossombrone and its territory, where the Malatesta could still claim a large following.[5] The papacy however was not alone at this time in wanting Romagna pacified. For reasons of general policy, the republic of Florence, which had Federigo d'Urbino in its pay, was even more concerned; and by Florentine mediation Rimini and Urbino were eventually brought together. But the arrangement was insecure; and, when it came, was part of a larger negotiation, lasting many months, which in view of the nature of the interests involved was to be of decisive importance to the survival of the Malatesta.

[1] Cron. mal., 120; Simonetta, 178; Broglio, in Tonini, v. 175–7; Pedrino, rub. 1603–4; Gianandrea, 'Signoria', 340–1.

[2] Mazzatinti (Inventari, xxxxvii.93) says 2 April, but two separate references in Giordani point to July: Gradara, 89; A. Sforza, xl.

[3] 20 Sept. 1447: Montecerignone, Montegrimani, S. Anastasio and a dozen others: Colucci, xxi/1.136; Baldi, Federigo, i.114.

[4] 28 July 1447: Giordani, A. Sforza, xl. Not that Nicholas was against the Malatesta. In this same year he gave the vicariate of Forlì to Antonio Ordelaffi, to whose son Cecco Sigismondo had recently betrothed Lucrezia, his illegitimate daughter by Gentile di Ser Giovanni da Bologna (9 April): Pedrino, rub. 1597; Cobelli, 428; Cron. mal., 118–19; Battaglini, Vita, 392, 555, 685; Amiani, i.406–7. Lucrezia was legitimated by Nicholas on 13 Dec. 1453: below p. 000.

[5] On 1 Sept. Fossombrone rose in favour of 'nostri Signori antiqui' and enabled Sigismondo temporarily to occupy all but the rocca 'per[ché] se tenea per parte gebbelina': Cron. mal., 120–2; Broglio, in Tonini, v. 178–80; Cron. Bon., iv.145–6; Guerriero, 62–3; Della Tuccia, 208; Cron. Ferm., 98; Pedrino, rub. 1600; Filelfo, Commentarii, 303; Sanzio, II, chs. XI–XII; Amiani, i.408; Mariotti, Bandi di tregua, 17.

At the beginning of 1447, when peace in the March was impending, Italy as a whole was divided between two contending alliances; on the one side Milan, Aragon and the papacy, on the other Venice, Florence, and behind them the Angevins. Each was seeking the service of reputable *condottieri*, among them the Malatesta. Sigismondo, with the natural indifference of the mercenary captain, opened negotiations with both Venice and Naples. The Venetians were not averse to hiring him, but Florence would not hear of it, with the result that in April, after several weeks of uncertainty and delay, a provisional *condotta* was concluded with Alfonso.[1] Sigismondo's state was taken into royal protection, and he was to be allowed to defend it with as many troops as the king saw fit. Payment was to begin within eight days of Sigismondo's ratification, but only if Alfonso recovered from the pope and Visconti certain sums of money he had lent them. Sigismondo, dissatisfied by these imprecise terms, may have withheld his assent. He renewed his approaches to Venice,[2] and only during the summer did he finally close with Naples.[3] Even then Alfonso was dilatory over his pay; and when in mid-October the king ordered him to Tuscany, Sigismondo, having received only 22,000 or at most 25,000 ducats, refused, and with the argument that he could do equally good service locally by attacking the Florentine captain, Federigo, renewed his interference in Fossombrone (November).[4] At this Florence, now as anxious as Venice to win Sigismondo to their side, made every effort to detach him from the king; and Sigismondo, after learning that his envoys to Alfonso had been roughly handled when demanding further payments, decided to negotiate. Early in December it was already rumoured in Siena that an agreement had been reached, and although on the ninth of the month Alfonso at last authorised the payment of the balance of the *prestanza*, he acted too late to prevent the signing of a *condotta* with the Florentine ambassadors on the following day.[5] Sigismondo was not blind to the gravity of this step. While awaiting confirmation from Florence he convened the members of his council,

---

[1] For 600 lances and 600 foot at the rate of 50 ducats for each lance and 4 for each footsoldier, amounting to 32,400 ducats in all. Sigismondo received besides 4,000 for the year: Osio, iii.491-2, 496-8, 502-3, 505, 518-20, 524-5, 528, 533-6; Rossi, *Guerra*, 24ff.; Soranzo, *Pio II*, 29ff.

[2] Osio, iii.556, 561-2, 564; *Atti canc. visc.*, ii.126.

[3] Osio, iii.577; Decembrio, 539; Fazio, 146; Soranzo, *Pio II*, 29ff. Sigismondo was evidently following the advice of the pope: Rossi, *Guerra*, 28.

[4] Filelfo, *Commentarii*, 303-5; Baldi, *Federigo*, i.115; Ugolini, i.356; Rossi, *Guerra*, 51, 61; above p. 197 n. 5.

[5] Predelli, v. 12: *Cron. mal.*, 122; Bonincontri, 154; Simonetta, 247; Capponi, 1204; Filelfo, *Commentarii*, 305-6; Della Tuccia, 209; Cavalcanti, ii.308; Anon. Veron., 99; Vespasiano da Bisticci, ii.49-50, 123-5; Baldi, *Federigo*, i.120-1; Fabronius, *Cosmi Medici Vita*, ii.187-8; Rossi, *Guerra*, 81, 85, 92-8, 465-6; Miniero-Riccio, *ASN* 1881, 255.

from whom he had kept his decision, to hear their opinions. On the one hand they stressed the danger of offending Alfonso, on the other the no less serious hazard of resisting the two republics. Those in favour of Florence urged, all the same, that Alfonso's money should be repaid. But this was opposed by Sigismondo's spokesman, Roberto Valturio.[1] When asked by Gianozzo Manetti, one of the Florentine envoys, how he would answer if Naples demanded restitution, Sigismondo replied that the money had long been owing to him, and that he had earned it by assembling troops and garrisoning his castles.[2] Nevertheless his mind seems to have wavered: a letter written by Alfonso in reply to one of his own, dictated the following January, reveals an intention to make repayment.[3] And many years later the Neapolitan ambassador to Venice attested that 6,000 ducats had in fact been handed over.[4]

Legally Sigismondo's defection may have been correct. It may also have conformed to *condottiere* practice. It was, none the less, politically mistaken. If it provoked no immediate disaster, more than any other single action it contributed to his ultimate downfall. His local quarrels with the Montefeltro were exceptional only in their virulence. The offence he had now given a powerful king could be the ruin of a princeling like himself. As the Florentine Vespasiano da Bisticci later wrote: 'Fu questa condotta la salute della libertà de' Fiorentini e la rovina della casa de' Malatesti.'[5]

Sigismondo did not set out for Tuscany at once. He and the count of Montefeltro were both now in Florentine service, but this did not improve their relations. Before leaving his state to its own defences Sigismondo insisted that some settlement with Urbino be first arranged by Florence, and on 18 December a truce with Federigo and the new *condotta* were published together.[6] This brought only momentary quiet. At the end of January the poet Angelo Galli wrote to Francesco Sforza that Sigismondo was as restless as ever: 'Cum questo vostro bon parente [Sigismondo] et nostro vicino vivono a pacti vecchi et modo usato et peggio.'[7] His present purpose was the inveterate one to occupy Pesaro. During the past two years Galeazzo Malatesta had come to repent of his hasty compact with the Sforzeschi, and in the autumn of

[1] Clementini, ii.355.
[2] Naldi, 559; Vespasiano da Bisticci, 123–5.
[3] Ametller, iii.682–3 (a. 1457).
[4] Malipiero, 205.
[5] Vespasiano da Bisticci, ii.125. Pius II stated that Sigismondo abandoned Alfonso 'novo auro inharratus' (*Commentaria*, 52), but admitted his decision saved Florence.
[6] Vespasiano da Bisticci, ii.125; Capponi, 1204; Sanzio, II, ch. XII; Baldi, *Federigo*, i.125.
[7] 31 Jan. 1440: Franceschini, 'Notizie', 182.

1447 came to live in Rimini. Nothing suited Sigismondo better. When Galeazzo made an attempt in January to recover Pesaro and took the castle of Monteluro, Sigismondo gave him full support, and even requested help from Florence and Venice.[1] The attempt miscarried, but the brothers Sforza and Federigo d'Urbino all complained to Florence; and when at last Sigismondo left Romagna in March, Alessandro Sforza persuaded Federigo to order an attack on his territories. Federigo had cautiously left a contingent of troops in the Montefeltro, knowing the habits of his neighbour, and these fell on the castles taken by Sigismondo three years before. But the government in Rimini was quick in response, and in April succeeded in re-covering most that had been lost.[2] According to Urbino sources, Sigis-mondo, chastened perhaps by his failure, now sought to win Federigo to the plan of a joint attack on Pesaro. As a bribe he offered Federigo the castles of the Montefeltro; and the upright count accepted.[3]

It may well be, as Della Tuccia says, that after Sigismondo's de-sertion the king of Naples 'pretended to be unconcerned'.[4] But he was bitterly aggrieved; and the Tuscan campaign was to make him even more so, for it was Sigismondo more than anyone who prevented his success, compelling him in September to raise the siege of Piom-bino.[5] For this victory he was acclaimed by the poets saviour of Tuscany,[6] which only inflamed Alfonso's resentment further.[7] It was as one of the most celebrated captains in Italy that Sigismondo was released by Florence in October to join the Venetian army in Lom-bardy.

If the Florentines shared this high opinion they did not express it, but first delayed, and then withheld, his pay.[8] The pope was more

---

[1] *Cron. mal.*, 121, 123; Colucci, iv.375; Giordani, *Porto*, 52; Amiani, i.408; Rossi, *Guerra*, 116–20, 212–14; Decembrio, 499.

[2] *Cron. mal.*, 125–6; Fazio, 162; Rossi, *Guerra*, 121–5, 217–19.

[3] For the alleged Malatesta intrigues behind this: Filelfo, *Commentarii*, 318–20; Sanzio, III, xv; Baldi, *Federigo*, i.138–42.

[4] *Cronache*, 209.

[5] *Cron. mal.*, 127; Palmieri, 157–8; *Ist. dell'assedio di Piombino*, 363; Capponi, 1205; Simonetta, 247; Bonincontri, 154; Filelfo, *Commentarii*, 406–10 (assigns the lion's share of the campaign to Federigo); Sanzio, III, chs. XIII–IV; Della Tuccia, 228; Fazio, 147; Rossi, *Guerra*, 126; 'Piombino', 180–3.

[6] *Basinii opera*, I.1ff., *Poesie liriche*, 114–18. Cf. Broglio, in Tonini, v. 194: 'e crediate voi leggitori, che in quel tempo in Italia non v'era il piu sufficiente nè da piu nè di maggior animo che lo Illo. Signor mis Sigismondo.'

[7] In 1452 Alfonso vowed 'ch'el farà mangiare a questo S.re [Sigismondo] certe epistole che fece uno messer Tobia da Verona [Tobia Borghi, the Malatesta chronicler] in detrazione del Re e commendazione de questo S. del impresa de Piombino': Rossi, 'Prodromi' 1905, 330. The Anon. Veron. (99) says Alfonso was more angered by the defeat than Sigismondo's desertion.

[8] Rossi, 'Prodromi' 1905, 23. They treated Federigo no better, and early in 1451(?) cancelled all credits of *condottieri*: Rossi, 'Nuove notizie', 397; 'Niccolo V', 28.

generous. In June he granted the two Malatesta the vicariate of Cervia, long held 'absque canonico titulo',[1] and before the end of the year added other favours.[2]

In September 1448 the Venetian government found itself in the same position as Filippo Visconti two years earlier. It had suffered a severe defeat by Sforza at Caravaggio, and was in immediate need of help. Within a fortnight of the battle there was talk of sending Sigismondo to her relief, and in November he left Rimini for the north with a large force of cavalry.[3] Meanwhile the Venetians abandoned the Milanese for alliance with Sforza, and during the opening months of the next year, as Venetian captain-general and in Venetian pay, Sigismondo was engaged in an unsuccessful offensive against Crema.[4] Obsessed as he still was with Pesaro, Sigismondo may well have been a lukewarm general. His particular object was to persuade Sforza to bring pressure to bear upon his brother, Alessandro, and he appealed to Cosimo de' Medici to use his influence with Francesco. His representative in Florence maintained he was ready to desert Venice if this would gain his end, and hinted that Sigismondo had means to procure the assassination of Alessandro.[5] But Sforza repelled his advances, and Sigismondo had to content himself with stirring up further trouble in the *contado* of Pesaro.[6] His rash and impracticable intrigue being brought to nothing, he became as suddenly zealous as formerly he had been cool to prevent Sforza from occupying Milan, and actively encouraged the new alliance between the Milanese and Venice concluded in September.[7] The death of Polissena in June removed all family tie with Sforza and, occurring when it did, gave quick currency to the rumour that he had caused her murder, inspired, in Sforza's own words, by personal hate (*innato odio*). The report seems unfounded. It is probable that Polissena died of plague, then prevalent in Central

---

[1] 13 or 14 June 1448: Giorgio, *Vita Nicolai V*, 81; Fantuzzi, iii.360; Battaglini, *Vita*, 620–6; Tonini, v/2.164–71.

[2] On 16 Oct. he legitimated Polissena, Sigismondo's wife (Decembrio, 584 n. 1; *Cron. mal.*, 84 n. 6). He also accorded privileges to the chapel Sigismondo contemplated building in S. Francesco in Rimini: Ricci, 585.

[3] Sanudo, 1135ff.; *Cron. mal.*, 127–8; Simonetta, 247; Sanzio, iii, chs. xiv–v; Fabronius, *Cosmi Medici Vita*, i.118; Rossi, *ASI* 1904, 159–60, 166–7.

[4] Broglio, in Tonini, v. 194; *Cron. mal.*, 128; Simonetta, 278, 305, 317, 324; Anon. Veron., 10; A. M. Sabellico, *Hist. Ven. Libri XXXIII* (Venice, 1718), ii.685; Rossi, *ASI* 1904, 161, 176. On 26 Feb. Sigismondo received a Venetian *condotta* for 12 months, Florence having refused to renew: Predelli, v. 26.

[5] Fumi, 'Attegiamento', 165–6; Soranzo, 'Due delitti'.

[6] Bonincontri, 155; Giordani, *A. Sforza*, xli; *Notizie*, xxxi–ii; Bernardy, 'Archivio', n. 205: Mazzatinti, *Inventari*, xxxv.55; Massèra, *RIS*[2] xv/2.123, n. 1.

[7] *Cron. mal.*, Simonetta, *locc. citt.*; Anon. Veron., 13; Fumi, 'Attegiamento', 166–7, 173; Rossi, 'Niccolo V', 414–15. Sigismondo even talked of marrying Filippo Maria's widow, Mary of Savoy, as a means to embarrass Sforza.

Italy. But it found its way into Pius II's catalogue of Sigismondo's crimes.[1]

The efforts of Sigismondo and Venice to impede Sforza's advance were ineffectual. In February 1450 he made his entry into Milan. But the threat to his power remained, and as a measure of defence he decided to try and divert Sigismondo from Lombardy by deceit. Since September Sigismondo had been in sole command of the Venetian army, and in January 1450 obtained extension of his *condotta* for another year.[2] Aware of Sigismondo's passion to possess Pesaro, Sforza's plan was simple: that Federigo d'Urbino, with the appearance of secrecy, should offer to help him gain the city, in return for the disputed Montefeltro castles. Success was certain. Federigo, glad of a chance to embarrass his enemy,[3] sent for one of Sigismondo's closest councillors, Goffredo da Iseo, who at once hurried to Venice with the news. Although recently taken into Venetian service, Sigismondo with agitated insistence managed to obtain from a reluctant Venice licence to leave, and in May set out for Rimini. But once informed of his departure, Sforza despatched a defensive force to Pesaro, entertained on the way by the count of Urbino, and Sigismondo, wild with indignation, had to abandon his attack.[4]

His importunate request for release may already have embittered the Venetians,[5] when a fresh scandal occurred to provoke their enmity and discharge upon Sigismondo the invective of contemporaries. 1450 was a year of jubilee, and many pilgrims from beyond the Alps were travelling through Italy. At the end of May a noblewoman, described by Sforza as 'la mogliera del dux de Bavera', was attacked, so it is said, by Sigismondo and his company, who were on their way to Rimini,

---

[1] Polissena died 1 June 1449. The charge of poisoning, upheld, though from suspect motives, by Sforza in 1461 and 1462, cannot be disproved but is very dubious: Tonini, v. 203–6; *RIS*² xv/2.129 (n. 2); Decembrio, 584 (n. 1); Soranzo, 'Invettiva' 1911, 169–75.   [2] Predelli, v. 42, 44; *Cron. mal.*, 130.

[3] In May and June of the preceding year Federigo had visited the pope in Spoleto, on what business can only be conjectured, but the Malatesta may have been concerned. The bishop of Rimini was present, and the affairs discussed required examination of bulls of Martin V: Bernardy, 'Archivio', nn. 200–1, 205.

[4] 'Infiammato disse: mis Federigo me l'ha pur calata': Broglio, in Tonini, v. 198–203; Anon. Veron., 18; *Cron. mal.*, 132; Rossi, 'Delitto', 369; G. Soranzo, 'Un fallito tentativo di Sig. Pand. Malatesta su Pesaro', *Le Marche illustrate* 1911, 221–34; 'Invettiva' 1911, 249. Again the Urbino version is different: Filelfo, *Commentarii*, 320–2, 348: Sanzio, iii, ch. xv; Baldi, *Federigo*, i. 145–8.

[5] They were certainly displeased with Sigismondo, and even contemplated awarding him the fate of Carmagnola: Filelfo, *Commentarii*, 349; Malipiero, 202–3; Rossi, 'Prodromi' 1905, 22, 309–11. A particular grievance was Sigismondo's spoliation of the churches of S. Severo and S. Appolinare in Classe for materials to help in the reconstruction of S. Francesco at Rimini, for which he had to pay compensation: Clementini, ii.368; Rubeus, 639; Pedrino, rub. 1677; Ricci, 586–7. For this he was pronounced sacrilegious by Pius II.

raped, and then, because she resisted, 'non tanto lui la spazzasse, ma fecela spazare da più de XL de li soi'. She fled to Verona, and there 'per dolore è morta'. This was the account reported to Sforza in June, but among none of the narratives of the crime is there agreement as to its place, the manner in which it was committed and by whom, or the person offended. The Venetians were outraged, because the assault was made 'sul terreno loro', and offered a high reward for the culprit. Sigismondo himself later repudiated the charge as a Venetian calumny, and said that having failed to punish him as they desired, they fell back on vituperation, 'con quela Todesca la quale mai non vide'; but at the time he threw the blame upon certain of his captains, whom he sent in custody to Venice. A judicial enquiry was begun but no decision reached, and the matter was left quiet until in 1452 the Venetians brought it before the notice of Frederick III, then in Italy – 'hanno facto instantia con lo Imperatore a rinfocolare quella novella de la Todescha' – to excite his resentment against Sigismondo. Once again it is impossible to pronounce finally on Sigismondo's guilt. But once again an equivocal accusation was adopted by Pius II.[1]

One man at least seems to have disregarded the story: the reigning pope, Nicholas V. During July and August Sigismondo was in Fabriano, where Nicholas had come to escape the plague. There he was received 'cum summa umanita', and before departing the pope renewed to him, Malatesta Novello and their heirs, the vicariate of Rimini, Fano, Cesena, Bertinoro, Cervia, Pieve di Sestino and S. Leo. To Sigismondo individually and his heirs he confirmed all grants of Sinigaglia, Pergola, Gradara, Mondaino, Penna Billi, Casteldelce, Talamello and the rectorate of S. Agata. Finally, with obvious reference to the castles taken from Federigo d'Urbino, he permitted Sigismondo to remain in possession of all other places not included in these privileges, adding only the proviso that such of them 'que ad alios de jure forsan pertinere noscuntur' should eventually be restored, after satisfaction of all expenses incurred by the Malatesta in their acquisition, repair and upkeep.[2] This did not necessarily contradict the conditional

[1] Pedrino, rub. 1634; Sanudo, 1137; Malipiero, 202–3; M. A. Sabellico, Hist. Ven. Libri XXXIII (Venice, 1718), ii.687; Tonini, v. 203–6; Rossi, 'Prodromi' 1905, 308, 310, 322; 'Delitto'; 'Nuovo documento'; Fumi, 'Attegiamento', 167–8; Soranzo, 'Invettiva' 1911, 241–56. At this same time the Venetian senate was energetically planning the murder of Francesco Sforza: Pagani, ASL 1920, 85–6. A similar charge was later made, without foundation, against Cesare Borgia: Alvisi, 162–5; Bonardi, 'Venezia e Cesare Borgia', 392, 418–20.

[2] 29 Aug. 1450. By the same document he declared the Malatesta quit of all arrears of census, and reduced the existing census from 6,000 to 4,000 fl.: Cron. mal., 133; Giorgio, 81; Giordani, Gradara, 91; Battaglini, Vita, 626–8; Tonini, v/2.176–9. At the beginning of the year (2 Jan. 1450) Montalboddo commended itself to the Malatesta: Rossi, Monte Alboddo, 144–5, 147–52.

grant of the Montefeltro castles made to Federigo in 1447,[1] but like that it declared the pope's sympathy with the claims of the Malatesta in the dispute. Two days later, on 31 August, Nicholas legitimated two of Sigismondo's sons, Roberto, born of Vanetta dei Toschi, and Malatesta, born of Isotta degli Atti, and so secured the succession to the state.[2] It was in this year of jubilee and of papal benevolence to the Malatesta that Sigismondo decided on the radical reconstruction of S. Francesco in Rimini, from which the Tempio Malatestiano was to emerge.[3]

Though treated alike by the pope, Sigismondo and Malatesta Novello were not at this time on amicable terms. Further causes of quarrel had arisen, undisclosed, but presumably settled in a fresh peace and alliance between them early in 1451.[4] This new agreement was concerned exclusively to regulate future relations. After the usual preamble, binding them to have friends and enemies in common and take no political action except by common consent, it laid down first that any conquests in the Montefeltro, by reason either of Violante's rights or by apostolic grant, should be shared between the brothers. By a further clause Malatesta received certain lands from Sigismondo, including Montegrimano, Ripalta and Monteboaggine, at the same time renouncing all claims to the territories acquired in the March or Romagna. In return Violante also was to resign to Sigismondo all her claims, by papal grant or otherwise, as in Montecerignone, S. Anastasio and elsewhere, and Malatesta was to acknowledge Sigismondo's right to assume the title of 'lord and count of Montefeltro'. Finally, no castles in the Montefeltro were to be restored to Federigo without the approval of both brothers.[5] Altogether Sigismondo could not have made clearer his preoccupation with Urbino, which was to dominate his policy in the years to come, nor the interpretation he intended to place on the recent papal concessions.

While Sigismondo was still preparing his visit to the pope in Fabriano, Florence, Venice and the king of Naples had drawn together in a precarious peace. As a preliminary condition Alfonso wished to keep out Rimini, but for the moment he had to give way, and on 22 July

[1] Above p. 197.
[2] Battaglini, *Vita*, 429; Tonini, v/2.180–1; Mazzuchelli, 11.
[3] Although for three years work had been going forward on the chapels of Sigismondo and Isotta: Ricci, 216.
[4] According to Clementini (ii. 282), followed by Chiaramonti (422–3) and Zazzeri (299), one cause of dissension was the seizure and execution by Sigismondo of Malatesta's favourite, Giovanni da Lodi. He also reports, after Aeneas Sylvius, a design by Sigismondo to possess his brother's state by putting him to death. Cf. Rossi, 'Nuove notizie', 395.
[5] Rossi, 'Nuove notizie', 169–72.

1450 Sigismondo wrote ratifying his place in the treaty between Florence and Naples.[1] He had not then relinquished the title of Venetian captain-general, and only in November, when trying to renew his *condotta* with the Signoria, did he meet with a rebuff.[2] By that time the peace recently made was already breaking up. Venice and Naples had formed an alliance for the dispossession of Sforza; and the Venetians were examining every device for getting the new duke of Milan murdered.[3]

Between Sigismondo and his immediate neighbours the normal state of clandestine hostilities continued[4] which, with the impending revival of war, and every power once more a prospective paymaster, developed into an issue of general concern. It was soon evident that the aims of Federigo and his enemy were not those of the princes they were engaged to serve. To them a *condotta* and the pay it procured were means to fighting out their own local feuds, and any government wishing to hire them had also to undertake to satisfy their private purposes.[5] Since the end of August Federigo d'Urbino had been taken into the service and protection of Francesco Sforza, who promised to ensure that the castles seized by Sigismondo in 1446, together with Pergola, Sassocorvaro and the places occupied in the territory of Fossombrone, were restored to him.[6] He may also have engaged not to hire Sigismondo himself or allow Florence to do so, until these conditions had been fulfilled; but his own necessities prevented him from keeping his word, and to the chagrin of Federigo he began, during 1451, to negotiate with Sigismondo as well. Malatesta Novello was already an associate of Sforza,[7] and Sigismondo was genuinely ready to follow his example. By hiring the lord of Rimini Sforza did not want to forfeit the loyalty of Urbino, and he was therefore obliged to try to bring them to an agreement. With Alessandro Sforza Sigismondo

---

[1] Rossi, *Guerra*, 227–8. The Malatesta appeared as *raccomandati* of the two republics in the treaty of peace between Alfonso and Florence on 21 June, and between Alfonso and Venice on 2 July: Dumont, iii/1.177; Soranzo, *Pio II*, 36. As early as 1448 Alfonso desired Sigismondo to be excluded from any peace (Rossi, *Guerra*, 131), though a year later there may have been some attempt to restore good relations between them: Colombo, *ASL* 1905, i.320.

[2] Predelli, v.57; Rossi, 'Prodromi' 1906, 207.

[3] Rossi, *ASI* 1904, 164–6, 177–9; 'Prodromi' 1905, ii.4–5, 7–8; 'Venezia Napoli, Firenze', 5–7, 11, 27; 'Niccolo V', 246.

[4] See Amiani, i.412; Tonini, v.223; Bernardy, 'Archivio', n.225; Delfico, i.205–7. On 20 June 1450 Florence sent representatives to try again to mediate between Federigo, Sigismondo, and Alessandro Sforza: Rossi, 'Federigo da Montefeltro', 142.

[5] Franceschini, 'Alcune notizie', 182.

[6] 30 Aug. 1450: Dumont, iii/1.179–80; Lünig, iii.535; Filelfo, *Commentarii*, 322–3; Sanzio, iii, ch. xv; Baldi, *Federigo*, i.150–1; Rossi, 'Federigo da Montefeltro', 145.

[7] Rossi, 'Venezia Napoli, Firenze', 286.

consented to make peace,[1] but at first he would hear of no compromise with Federigo, 'per la via del quale el non voria essere in Paradiso'.[2] Undismayed Sforza patiently urged him to evacuate the castles he had taken from the count, and in July Cosimo de' Medici, though convinced of failure, declared his willingness to mediate between the two princes, and proposed a one-year truce during which their dispute could be committed to the arbitration of authoritative and independent persons. Federigo assented, and appeared confident of a favourable decision. All he desired was the publication of a sentence, and a guarantee that it would be executed. Negotiations were opened at Florence and Milan, but neither side trusted the other. While Sigismondo tentatively sounded the feelings of Alfonso and Venice, the first of whom was willing to employ him but the second hostile, Federigo, already persuaded that Sigismondo had been taken into Milanese service, inclined in his turn to Naples. During August and early September Sigismondo was absent in Florence and Ferrara,[3] and while there proposed to Sforza that as compensation for any surrender of the contested castles he should be allowed to occupy S. Marino. On the advice of his envoy Sforza decided to offer him 'qualque speranza' in this design, though never intending to carry it out, and on this a *condotta* was at last signed on 5 September at Lodi, in the presence of the Florentine ambassador, Alessandro Sforza, and the two Riminese representatives.[4] Meanwhile the attempt to mediate between Federigo and Sigismondo had resulted only in estranging them further, and early in September, protesting that Sigismondo was plotting to occupy Pesaro, Federigo invaded Malatesta territory. His gains were slight, but he remained more than ever averse to service with the allies, and in October finally entered the pay of Alfonso. Six months of tireless negotiation had simply shown the impossibility of any power employing together the lords of Rimini and Urbino.

Sforza and Cosimo de' Medici had now to restrain Sigismondo from striking back at Federigo and giving him a 'bastonata', conscious that

[1] About May 1451 Sigismondo, at the desire of Sforza, made peace with Alessandro, even restoring Monteluro: Rossi, 'Prodromi' 1905, ii.23.

[2] 17 May 1451, report of Sforza's envoy in Rimini: *ibid.* 27, 49.

[3] While in Florence Sigismondo contemplated raising the question of the pay owed him since 1448, but the Milanese envoy thought he would be wasting his time: *ibid.* 56. Federigo had already indulged in reprisals against Florence for pay outstanding to him (*ibid.* 34), and in Sept. Sigismondo returned to Florence to renew his demands: *ibid.* 67. Dishonesty was not confined to the *condottieri*.

[4] In addition to the normal conditions of hire were included (1) a promise by Sforza to help Sigismondo seize S. Marino, provided it was not 'contra S. Chiesa' or incompatible with any agreements reached with Federigo; and (2) the mutual remission of all debts and offences 'etiam atrocissime' with the exception of what remained due to Sigismondo of Polissena's dowry: Rossi, *ibid.* 59–66.

if a local war broke out in Romagna they would never be sure of his help in Tuscany or the north; and Sigismondo had to acquiesce.[1] He failed also to detach the lord of Pesaro from Urbino, but in retaliation kept open his territories to the ambassadors of Venice, despite protests from Cosimo and Sforza.[2]

For a few months at the beginning of 1452 the outbreak of war was delayed by the quixotic journey of Frederick III to be crowned emperor in Rome. Sigismondo was anxious to meet him, and on 25 January was given a brief audience with the king at Ferrara. The subject of their talk is not recorded, but in sympathy Frederick inclined to Venice and Naples. Two months later, when in Rome, he was reported to be preparing, at the suggestion of Venice, to punish Sigismondo for the 'donna tedesca alias violata'; and in April he concluded an alliance with Alfonso for the conquest of Milan.[3] He had no power to fulfil either of these intentions, nor probably was he expected to do so. The Italian courts merely wished him to be gone, and with him went the last excuse for peace. In the middle of May the Venetian armies entered the Milanese, and on 2 June Alfonso declared war on Florence.

Sigismondo Malatesta should now have assumed his command as *condottiere*, yet not until August, after months of complaint and correspondence, did he finally leave Rimini. He feared first for the security of his own dominions. Not merely was the count of Montefeltro the leading Neapolitan captain, but as late as July it was still not known in Florence whether the army assembled by Alfonso would proceed directly to Tuscany, or advance, as Federigo desired, through the March and Romagna. Despite assurances from the Milanese envoy, Sigismondo was afraid Sforza would not support him.[4] Help from the allies arrived only fitfully, and he was compelled to enter again into what may have been only precautionary negotiations with Venice and

[1] Though there was some raiding in November and December: Pedrino, rub. 1655; Rossi, 'Prodromi' 1905, 74–5.

[2] Galeazzo Malatesta was still living in Rimini, and by the terms of the *condotta* Sigismondo was expressly allowed to keep him there, together with the rebel Gennari of Pesaro. At the same time he withdrew all claims to Pesaro, and undertook not to interfere in Monteluro, while retaining Gradara 'quanto al dominio'.

[3] Pedrino, rub. 1660; Rossi, 'Prodromi' 1905, 308; 1906, 202, 295–6; 'Delitto', 374, 378–81; Soranzo, 'Invettiva' 1911, 243–4; Cusin, 'Aspirazioni', 334, 348–9.

[4] 19 April Cusano, Sforza's representative in Rimini, urged the duke to write reassuringly to Sigismondo, so that 'per ogni cossa non se lassi mancare l'animo ne de ogni vento abbia paura e suspecto': *ibid.* doc. 30, p. 355. On the previous day he wrote: 'al parere mio, questo Signore l'ogni picolla cossa ne fa grande caso e molte volte da grande fede ad de le cosse che non saria da dare oreghie. Sono pero certo la vostra Celsitudine conosca molto meglio la sua natura de mi': *ibid.* 326. Already it seems Sigismondo was fearing the coalition of Alfonso and Federigo which was to bring on his ruin a few years later.

Naples, in order to 'tenere uno pede in cello e uno altro in terra'.[1] Malatesta Novello, who was himself in contact with the Venetians, was of the opinion they would never hire Sigismondo, 'se non fossero in la fanga fino agli occhi'.[2] But both Venice and Alfonso showed every interest in winning him to their side; and in Florence it was believed they would be successful, since Sigismondo did not wish to compromise the Adriatic trade of his subjects. As late as August Venetian and Aragonese ambassadors were tempting him with generous offers of money and support to get possession of Pesaro, and only when they learned of his *condotta* with Florence did the Venetians at last impose commercial sanctions.[3]

Sigismondo's chief complaint was the slow arrival of help or money from Florence and Milan,[4] at a time when Federigo was receiving ample and regular pay from Alfonso. In April the grievance became acute when the Feltreschi made an abortive attack on Fano, where they had traitorous adherents.[5] Sigismondo appealed at once to Sforza for troops: 'for he'd sooner lose half his state to Venice or the King than one castle to messer Federigo'.[6] Florence made over a certain sum, including part of the stipend long owed from his former term of service, but it was still insufficient, and at the beginning of July Sigismondo had to accept a six months' truce with Federigo, arranged by the Venetian envoy. The Florentines were at first suspicious, but the intervention of Venice may at last have inspired them to quicker action, and their representative in Rimini now took Sigismondo formally into his pay, with a *condotta* to run from the first day of July past to September the following year. Even then the republic was no more punctual in fulfilling its obligations, and when he set out for Tuscany on 20 August Sigismondo was still complaining of money unpaid.[7]

---

[1] Cusano to Sforza, 20 April 1452: Rossi, 'Prodromi' 1906, App. I, doc. 31.

[2] Same to same, 2 March 1452: *ibid.* doc. 20.

[3] Which the Fanesi got lifted in September: Amiani, i.416–17. It seems to have been the Venetians who deflected the Aragonese advance from the March and Romagna, although not from love of the Malatesta.

[4] In March he was still trying to obtain the pay owed by Florence for the last 4 years: Rossi, 'Prodromi' 1906, doc. 22.

[5] For details: Rossi, 'Prodromi' 1905, 88, 326–9, 334, 350–1; 1906, 201–3; Pellegrini, 'Gubbio', 187. Shortly before, Sigismondo made a suspicious request to Sforza to let him ride whenever necessary through Pesaro territory, though 'non con piu de dodece ho xv cavalli desarmeti': Rossi, 'Prodromi' 1905, 86–7, 335–9. Since 1445 the two halves of Sigismondo's state were virtually cut off except by sea.

[6] Cusano to Sforza, 3 May: Rossi, 'Prodromi' 1905, 312–14.

[7] On the foregoing section see, in addition to Rossi: Anon. Veron., 32–3, 39; Pedrino, rub. 1665–6; Pietro di Giovanni, 84–6; Amiani, i.413–16; Tonini, v/2. 181–2; Yriarte, 382–4; Bernardy, 'Archivio', nn. 241, 248, 258; Soranzo, *Pio II*, 37; Mazzatinti, *MSS di Francia*, ii.312–14, 316, 318, 431.

The campaign of 1452 was uneventful, and the following year was equally indecisive. In April fresh contracts were arranged in Rimini between Sigismondo, Milan and Florence, clarifying his conditions of service,[1] but he took offence when the captaincy-general he had claimed for himself the year before was extended to Alessandro Sforza.[2] No great demand was placed on either of them, and after the surrender of Fogliano (28 August) Alessandro, at his brother's request, retired from the campaign. Sigismondo was now again sole commander, and at the end of September Gianozzo Manetti, the Florentine envoy, with an elaborate speech in praise of the Malatesta and their noble military record, confirmed him in the title. Encouraged by the laziness and improvidence of the enemy, Sigismondo was able to reduce Vada, the last place to hold out in Tuscany, before the lateness of the season compelled him to withdraw to Romagna.[3]

Here during November he received from the pope a fresh series of privileges.[4] Among the first were bulls dated 9 and 14 November legitimising two more of his bastard children, Valerio Galeotto and Margherita Malatesta. A few days later (24 November) the pope appointed Valerio, though still under age, to the post of apostolic notary, and in December declared legitimate another daughter of Sigismondo, Lucrezia. Meanwhile, on 14 November, Nicholas extended his territorial favours to the Malatesta, and granted Sigismondo the castles of Monte Marciano and Monte Cassiano near Ancona, in return for an annual *census* of 'unius crateris sex unciarum argenti'.[5]

The pope's pre-eminent concern at this time was to bring the Italian wars to an end. One attempt at peace had already been frustrated by

---

[1] Battaglini, *Vita*, 629–31; Tonini, v/2. 184–7.

[2] At the end of 1452 and during 1453 Sigismondo also continued to negotiate with Venice, and was again slow in leaving his own dominions: *Anon. Veron.*, 48, 53; Predelli, iv, xiii, n. 321; Soranzo, *Pio II*, 37.

[3] Simonetta, 370, 391; Palmieri, 169; Sozomenus, 48; Naldi, 591; Anon .Veron., 48, 55–6, 59; *Basinii opera*, lib. xff.; Broglio, in Battaglini, *Vita*, 440–7; Tonini, v. 229–37; Vespasiano da Bisticci, 75, 171; Clementini, ii. 379, 381–2; Pastor, *Päpste*, i. 597. Battaglini thinks it was now the medal was struck inscribed 'SIGISMUNDUS PANDULFUS MALATESTA. PAN. F. POLIORCITES. ET. IMP. SEMPER. INVICT.': *Zecca*, 252–3, Tav. 3, XII.

[4] In March 1452 Sigismondo had representatives in Rome 'per lo facto di suoi censi' and other matters (Rossi, 'Prodromi' 1906, docs. 19–20), one of which was a request to be granted the marquisate of Rimini. Another may have been the desire of his brother for the union of Cervia with Cesena, which according to Giorgio (126) Nicholas authorised in a bull of 1 March 1452 (given by Fantuzzi, iii. 360, and Chiaramonti, 428 ff., as 1451, and by Soranzo, 'Cervia', 201 n. 1 as 1450).

[5] Giorgio, 144; Battaglini, *Vita*, 633–6; Tonini, v/2. 189–90; Fantuzzi, v. 197; Mazzatinti, *Inventari*, xxxvii. 7. In the preceding year (12 April 1452) Nicholas granted an indulgence to pilgrims visiting the newly consecrated chapel of S. Sigismondo in S. Francesco at Rimini, on the feast of S. Sigismondo and the first Sunday of every month: *RIS*[2] xv/2. 135.

the obstinacy of the king of Naples. But since the Ottoman conquest of Constantinople Venice, at first the most aggressive power, had become less intent to force her aims in Lombardy, and early in 1454 fresh negotiations were begun in Rome. Not least among the causes of division which demanded preliminary settlement was the claim of Alfonso to restitution of the money received and spent by the lord of Rimini in 1447.[1] According to the chronicler Broglio, Sigismondo might now with care have made his peace with the king, for it was about this time that at the mediation of Venice a provisional treaty was made between them. By this Alfonso remitted half of the money owed and promised the hand of his granddaughter to Roberto Malatesta, while Sigismondo became supreme commander of the Neapolitan forces, with permission to recover any territories formerly belonging to the Malatesta. But either in obedience to his own suspicions or restrained by the influence of Sforza and Florence, Sigismondo delayed sending his assent and, to the king's indignation, replaced the envoy who had drafted the terms. By then the peace arranged at Lodi on 5 April between Venice and Sforza had made further negotiation pointless.[2] The other Italian states were invited to participate, and by August all but Naples had done so. In May Florence and the duke of Milan, and at the beginning of June Venice, drew up lists of their allies, in each of which the Malatesta of Rimini were named;[3] and during the following weeks Malatesta Novello, Sigismondo and Federigo d'Urbino all formally adhered to the peace.[4] To preserve and perpetuate this new and sudden harmony, a general league of twenty-five years was proclaimed for the impartial repression of disorder in Italy. And to this also Sigismondo was admitted as *raccomandato* of Sforza and Venice.[5]

Only Alfonso of Naples remained angrily detached, resentful at the general unconcern for his grievances; and while his final decision was being awaited everywhere in Italy, Sigismondo, now without a *condotta*, turned where he could for employment. For several months the Sienese, supported by Venice, had been engaged in a local war with Aldobrandino Orsini, conte di Pitigliano, and in November to conclude matters they elected Sigismondo captain-general. They soon had cause for regret. Clementini reports that Sforza wrote to dissuade

[1] What Sforza called 'el facto del Signor Sigismondo': Canetta, 'Congresso', 132.
[2] Malavolti, iii.41b; Clementini, ii.382–4; Battaglini, *Vita*, 448–53; Tonini, v.239; Soranzo, *Pio II*, 37–8; Antonini, 'Pace di Lodi', 259. Amiani (i.418) says Sigismondo promised, though only verbally, as pledge of repayment to Alfonso, Sinigaglia, the vicariate of Mondavio and the *contado* of Fano.
[3] Dumont, iii/1. 208–10; Lünig, iv.1792–3, 1795, 1798.
[4] 18 June Malatesta, 4 July Sigismondo, 13 Aug. Federigo d'Urbino: Canetta, 'Pace', 559.
[5] Dumont, iii/i. 228–9; Lünig, iii.602–3; Soranzo, *Pio II*, 39.

them from hiring Sigismondo, as a man likely to prolong the war for his own profit, and a captain no state had yet found satisfactory. Almost from the beginning Sigismondo's conduct was ambiguous, although it is not clear from what motives. His desire it seems was to enter the service of Florence, no friend to Siena; but there were also advocates to propose that he make himself *signore* of the city. The weather was harsh and the terrain difficult, but instead of trying to finish the war, Sigismondo treated secretly with the count and then arranged a truce. Like the Venetians earlier, the Sienese considered putting him to death. He was discharged from their service, and had to retreat quickly through Florentine territory to Romagna, abandoning his baggage and his correspondence, which has remained in Siena ever since. There were grievances, however, on both sides, which may have persuaded the Sienese to tender excuses for their behaviour, and shortly afterwards, in 1445, re-establish friendly relations. All the same, some memory of the incident may have lingered when a few years later the Sienese Piccolomini was elected pope.[1]

Meanwhile on 26 January Alfonso and his son Ferrante had at last ratified the peace of Lodi, but only on condition that those against whom they had personal claims should be individually excluded: in particular Sigismondo Malatesta. The dispute arising from the broken *condotta* was to be investigated, and if Sigismondo was found to be the king's debtor, he was to resume his place in the league only after repayment. When the pope published his confirmation of the general league on 25 February, it was specifically provided that the king's rights against Sigismondo Pandolfo Malatesta should not be prejudiced or in any way impeded. Until Alfonso had been appeased, Sigismondo was to be outlawed from the peace system of Italy.[2]

The promised arbitration did not take place, and had Alfonso proceeded at once to exact his claim upon the lord of Rimini, there would have been none to oppose him. Though Sigismondo had won for himself

---

[1] It was certainly brought up against Sigismondo by Pius II in one of the passages of his *Commentaries* suppressed, for imprudence, by his appointed editor Campano: *Opera ined.*, 498. For details: Anon. Veron., 73, 75; Della Tuccia, 235–6; *Diari sanesi*, 769; Tonini, v. 245–50; Malavolti, iii. 46–7; Yriarte, 280–3, 406–7, 419, 444; Banchi, *ASI* 1879, 184 ff.; Soranzo, 'Invettiva' 1911, 257–69, and *N. arch. ven.*, 1907, 103; Massèra, 'Poeti Isottei', 27, and 'Sequestro'. By 1459 Siena was offering compensation: Soranzo, *Pio II*, 146–7. It was served loyally by none of its captains in this war.

[2] Federigo d'Urbino was believed to have been a strong influence in getting Sigismondo barred from the league by Alfonso. The others excluded were Astorgio Manfredi (also a debtor to the king) and the republic of Genoa: Dumont, iii/i. 234–5; Lünig, iv. 1797–1802; Theiner, iii. 384; Filelfo, *Commentarii*, 335; *Pii II Commentaria*, 52; Simonetta, 406; Baldi, *Federigo*, i. 167–8; Fazio, 188; Ugolini, i. 369.

an equivocal prominence and fame in Italy, his expulsion from the community of states in 1455 brought him little sympathy. From most he could expect indifference or at best evasive goodwill. He had only two overt enemies, the king of Naples and the count of Montefeltro, whom a common desire for retribution had already brought together. But there were other undeclared enemies, reluctant to act alone, who could hope to gain by the dismemberment of the Malatesta state. Ancona, S. Marino, Iesi, all coveted territories governed by Sigismondo. Florence disputed his dominion over Citerna; Alessandro Sforza was not yet resigned to the surrender of Gradara and neighbouring places; and the lords of Faenza, Imola and Forlì, together with Venice, all had pretensions to Cervia and other lands in the Cesenate.[1] Even the distant Gonzaga harboured grievances against Sigismondo.[2]

Against these the number of Sigismondo's calculable allies was small. Pope Nicholas V and his successor, Calixtus III, were both friendly overlords,[3] and Francesco Sforza also was well-affected towards him;[4] but their favour was not peculiar to Sigismondo, and Sforza was equally an ally of Alfonso and Federigo d'Urbino. Astorgio Manfredi, like himself banished from the society of Italian states, had been in alliance with Sigismondo since 1452;[5] and in precarious dependence upon Rimini too were certain of the petty Appenine lordships: Carpegna, where the ruling count was descended from the Malatesta, Ghiaggiolo, and Carpi. Within Sigismondo's own family, Roberto and Malatesta, his sons, had already been employed in the government of Rimini and had acted as deputies in his absence.[6] But between Sigismondo and his brother mistrust and jealousy continued to prevail. In the previous July a dispute over rights and properties had been settled by the marquis of Este. Like previous agreements, the

---

[1] Soranzo, *Pio II*, 24–5. There were already rumours that Malatesta Novello was selling Cervia to Venice: Soranzo, 'Cervia', 203; Massèra, 'Sequestro'.

[2] Later, in 1462, cardinal Gonzaga said he would be willing to see Sigismondo burned not simply in effigy, since 'tiene tre terre dell'Ill. mo mio patre che li sono obligate per denari e parte per la dote dell'Ill.ma Madonna mia ava' (Paola Malatesta of Pesaro, mother of Ludovico Gonzaga): Soranzo, *Pio II*, 318.

[3] In a defiant letter to Mahomet (1454) Nicholas named Sigismondo among the great captains of the West, with Ludovico Gonzaga, Borso d'Este and Ettore Manfredi: *Diatriba*, 596. For his part, in April 1455 Calixtus was preparing to raise the question of Sigismondo, Astorre Manfredi and Genoa, in the hope of obtaining an agreement with Alfonso: Fumi, 'Sforza', 519.

[4] On 18 Feb 1455, he wrote reassuringly to Sigismondo after his exclusion from the league: Soranzo, *Pio II*, 39. A few years earlier (1452) Sigismondo had proposed the marriage of his son Roberto with Sforza's daughter, Ippolita: Rossi, 'Prodromi' 1906, App. 1, doc. 20.

[5] *Ibid.* App 1, doc. 27b.

[6] Bernardy, 'Archivio', 267, 282–3, 290.

settlement had every appearance of a treaty between independent princes. There was no unreserved obligation on either side and no assurance of peace, and in 1456 the marquis had to intervene again and renew it.[1]

From the beginning of his reign Sigismondo had enjoyed the continuous patronage of the Estensi, and early in 1456 he took steps to strengthen it, by betrothing his daughter Lucrezia to Alberto, brother of the ruling lord, Borso.[2] Other recent marriages had also purchased him some allies: in 1451 between his daughter Giovanna and Giulio Cesare Varano,[3] and in 1454 between Margherita Malatesta and the conte Carlo Fortebraccio of Montone.[4] He himself, not yet the impoverished and excommunicate rebel he was soon to become, might also now have improved his position by taking a wife from the neighbouring dynasty. Instead, discarding policy, he chose to marry his mistress, la Diva Isotta, for many years already his true consort and companion, dutifully commemorated by his court poets and artists, and stronger in command of his loyalty or passion than any reason of state.[5]

Compared with his situation in 1432 Sigismondo, it is true, could claim to be stronger territorially. Cervia had been recovered, and the papal sanction for holding it. Pergola, Monterolo, Sinigaglia and the vicariate of Mondavio had also returned to the Malatesta. And if Pesaro had escaped his grasp, Sigismondo had kept Gradara and parts of the Pesarese, and established himself in the heart of the Montefeltro.[6] But politically he was weaker. The price paid for many of his gains was the watchful animosity of his neighbours. The tenure of his lands was insecure. And for this he alone was responsible.[7]

---

[1] Johannis Ferrariensis 46; Tonini, v/2. 191–201; Anon. Veron., 90–1.

[2] On 6 Feb 1456 Sigismondo assigned Lucrezia the dower lands held previously by both Parisina and Margherita d'Este: Fantuzzi, v.426–7; Mazzatinti, *Inventari*, xxxvii.7; Pedrino, rub. 1747; Battaglini, *Vita*, 466–7, 636–7; Tonini, v/2. 211–12; Zonghi, 152–3.

[3] Lilii, ii.203–6; Tonini, v.225, 469–70. She was the daughter of Polissena, and in 1454 Sforza's relations with his 'neza' (then in Rimini) were evidently close: Decembrio, 584 n. 1.

[4] So Clementini (ii.388, 484), but it may have been a little later (Zonghi, 152–3). At the end of 1455 Sigismondo had been seeking, without success, to arrange the marriage of one of his daughters to Braccio Baglione of Perugia: Pietro di Giovanni, 135.

[5] On whom see now, for full details and bibliography, Campana, 'Atti, Isotta degli', who agrees with Soranzo in dating the marriage to 1456.

[6] In 1454 Montalboddo, which had commended itself to the Malatesta four years earlier, decided to return to the church: Rossi, *Monte Alboddo*, 113, 153–62.

[7] By 1455 Sigismondo had done much to improve the defences of his dominions. Apart from the Castel Sigismondo at Rimini (above p. 183), he had built new fortifications at Sinigaglia, to the destruction of the cathedral church and the

Sigismondo was not the only man whose problems were to vex Italian statesmen during the next ten years, or for whom the peace of Lodi was a prelude to disaster. To the landless *condottiere* it was a still greater misfortune, threatening discharge and destitution; and no one felt this more severely than the last of the Piccinini, Giacomo. Deprived of employment, he could only hope to maintain his status by seizing some dominion as the brothers Sforza had done; and for this there was still no more propitious ground than the petty communes and principalities of the Papal States.

At the end of 1454 an attack on the States by Piccinino was already expected, though in what direction, or with what objective, was not yet known. The pope appealed to Sforza, who loathed Piccinino, to prevent him from passing through Lombardy, and when the Bolognese did the same, the duke sent help and tried to combine the lords of Romagna against him. Piccinino himself was equally strenuous in seeking their alliance. But if one or two – Malatesta Novello, Borso d'Este – extended him a welcome, the majority preferred a policy of scrupulous duplicity, and negotiated with all sides indifferently.

The letters seized by the commune of Siena had revealed a tentative correspondence between Sigismondo Malatesta and Piccinino, which included plans for an invasion of Pesaro and for a matrimonial alliance. But it also disclosed that Piccinino was unwilling to offend the count of Montefeltro; and during 1455 there were some signs of a possible (and ominous) alliance between Piccinino and Federigo against Sigismondo. In March therefore Sigismondo offered his services to the pope, and it was rumoured that his were the territories to be attacked. Sforza, Florence and the pope all sent troops for defence, and it was the duke of Milan who persuaded Calixtus III to renew Sigismondo's vicariates in June, although, as his envoy wrote, 'al dispetto del mondo solo per contemplazione de V.S. col mezzo mio et non è stata poca gratia'.[1] By then Piccinino had made up his mind, and, abandoning Cesena where he had spent the spring, he led his forces into Tuscany. For a season Sigismondo was spared.[2]

Events at this time developed erratically, but the warring purposes behind them are clear. To Sigismondo the wayward power of Piccinino

---

bishop's palace (Colucci, vi, p. lxxi; Siena, 136–9), built *rocche* at Verucchio and Sogliano (Bernardy, *ASI* Ser. 5, 29, 1902, 341, 342), and provided for the better defence of Fano and its *contado* (Amiani, i.419).

[1] 15 June 1455: Fumi, 'Sforza', 527; Battaglini, *Vita*, 691 (bull 'super confirmatione Vicariatum et super remissione censuum').

[2] Anon. Veron., 76–8; Pedrino, rub. 1712, 1716, 1719, 1721; Pietro di Giovanni, 113, 115; Simonetta, 407; *Chron. Bon.*, iv.234–5; Clementini, ii.484–5; Battaglini, *Vita*, 463–5; Tonini, v.250–1; Pastor, *Päpste*, i.493; Bernardy, 'Archivio', nn. 303, 304; Fumi, 'Sforza', 527; Massèra, 'Sequestro'; Franceschini, *Urbinum* 1931–2, v.61, vi.1–2.

was both a constant threat and a possible means of defence against his neighbours. Federigo d'Urbino, still in Aragonese service, saw in Piccinino a promising instrument for his own reckoning with Rimini; while Piccinino himself had no decided loyalty or fixed allegiance, simply the aim to acquire himself a state. At the end of two years it was Federigo who triumphed, enlisting Piccinino with Alfonso and himself against an isolated enemy.

During that time he and Sigismondo wavered between peace and war,[1] but this was more an interlude of diplomatic preparation than of open conflict. What resources of intrigue Sigismondo could command were few. From Francesco Sforza, who had just arranged a marriage alliance with Alfonso, he could expect little further help.[2] The pope was sullenly estranged from the king of Naples, but the papal quarrel and his own were not related, and in a desperate search for aid Sigismondo turned to the distant and undependable house of Anjou. An ambassador was sent to Genoa, already threatened with proceedings by Alfonso, and by him Sigismondo was represented in the negotiation leading up to a secret agreement with Jean d'Anjou in May 1456.[3] Federigo's task was simpler: to obstruct any reconciliation between Alfonso and Rimini until his own differences with Sigismondo had been settled, and if no settlement was reached, to obtain freedom of action against him. In a preliminary visit to Naples he secured the support of Alfonso and Piccinino, and word began to circulate that they were forming an alliance. Impatient by now of all treaty with Sigismondo and anxious at all costs for war, he left in April 1457 for Florence and Milan where, according to Filelfo, the duke gave him encouragement and promised help.[4]

From Lombardy Federigo returned by way of Ferrara, and there consented to take part in one last attempt to satisfy his claims by debate and adjudication. Sigismondo was already present – he may have instigated the move; and Borso d'Este, who a month earlier had imposed a truce between them, arranged for them to meet and confer, in the presence of witnesses, at his secluded country seat of Belfiore. At the wish of Sigismondo two representatives of Venice were invited

[1] For details: Clementini, ii. 396, 485–6; Amiani, i. 420–1; Bernardy, n. 319; Aeneas Sylvius Piccolomini, *Epist.* (1475), 29 Dec. 1456; Manaresi, *La Romagna* vi. 164–72.

[2] Although during the autumn of 1456 Sforza and Borso d'Este tried to persuade Alfonso to make peace with Sigismondo: Soranzo, *Pio II*, 42.

[3] Broglio, in Tonini, v. 258–62; Clementini, ii. 399–400; Battaglini, *Vita*, 471–2; Soranzo, *Pio II*, 40–1; Buser, 84–5, 392. Sigismondo also sent envoys inviting René and Jean d'Anjou to attack Naples, assuring them of papal favour.

[4] Guerriero, 65–7; Filelfo, *Commentarii*, 338–9; Sanzio, iv, ch. xvii; Baldi, *Federigo*, i. 175–9. Cf. Franceschini, 'Gentile Brancaleone', 497; 'Alcune notizie', 183.

to attend, whereupon Federigo requested that envoys from Naples and Milan should also be admitted. Never before had the two rivals come face to face, and the record of their meeting has been minutely preserved.

Sigismondo was the first to speak, and soon showed he was not equipped by nature with the qualities effective in discussion. What he delivered was a savage and incoherent indictment of the whole house of Montefeltro, uncovering resentments pent up for years. He first recalled their aggressions in the time of Carlo Malatesta, accused them of complicity in the rising of Giovanni di Ramberto, and denounced them as the influence controlling the policy of Martin V. Federigo himself he charged with negotiating the sale of Pesaro, with the attack on Fano in 1450, and with the trick which decoyed him from Venetian service in the same year. The catalogue of his grievances, he said, could easily be extended, but he would conclude with repudiating the many crimes of which he had been slanderously accused by Federigo, and which, if true, would have made him the greatest rogue alive. Federigo in his reply was cool, containing his anger and dissembling his animosity, and was able judiciously to confute every accusation. Sigismondo then taunted him with cowardice, but again Federigo had his answer ready. It was true, he admitted, that he had refused the first challenge to fight with Sigismondo, but Sigismondo himself had not appeared, and his own challenge later had been frivolously declined. At this Sigismondo started to his feet and seized his sword. Federigo did the same, and their quarrel might have ended there, had the others not intervened and closed the interview.[1]

One accusation repeated by Federigo and repelled by Sigismondo was that he had plotted several weeks earlier to poison Alessandro Sforza. Sveva da Montefeltro, the wife of Alessandro, had been discovered in adultery, and was suspected of a design to make away with him and surrender Pesaro to Sigismondo, 'el quale è solo l'idola di lei'. It is improbable that Sigismondo was personally implicated in what seems to have been an entirely domestic scandal; but he provoked suspicion by protecting the conspirators and convinced Alessandro of

[1] Filelfo, *Commentarii*, 339–50; Pedrino, rub. 1758; Sanzio, IV, chs. XVIII–XIX; Anon. Veron., 91; Baldi, *Federigo*, i. 179–83, ii. 7–29; Soranzo, 'Invettiva' 1911, 270ff. At this time Sigismondo was, or according to Filelfo pretended to be, lame. Immediately after the meeting Borso d'Este sent an account of it to Sforza (12 May, in which it appears that the two lords had been housed in the same building and that precautions had to be taken to prevent them fighting), while Federigo and Sigismondo each circulated the Italian courts with his own version: Soranzo, *Pio II*, 26, 466–7. Sigismondo also made another attempt, as ineffective as those before, to arrange a duel with Federigo, receiving in October the licence of the duke of Savoy to hold it within his territories any time in the ensuing twelve months: G. W. Leibniz, *Codex juris gentium diplomaticus* (Hannover, 1693–1700), 416.

his guilt, although an enquiry only exposed the misconduct of Sveva, which she was compelled to expiate in a monastery.[1]

Malatesta Novello was also present at the conference, and Federigo must have had a private meeting with him, either at Ferrara or at Cesena on his way home. War with Sigismondo was now certain, and Malatesta, who long before had resigned most of his claims in the Montefeltro to his importunate brother,[2] wanted no part in it. On 30 May therefore he came to an agreement with Federigo which respected his neutrality. If Sigismondo attacked either of them, the other was to supply men and provisions, but if Federigo declared war on Sigismondo, Malatesta was free from obligation to either side. He was also free to accept the obedience of any place now held by Sigismondo, unless besieged by the count of Urbino, or numbered among the disputed castles of the Montefeltro. The pretexts for attack on Rimini were of the flimsiest.[3]

After this it remained only for Federigo to return to Naples and perfect the alliance with Piccinino and Alfonso of Aragon for the punishment of Sigismondo. Since the preceding year, Piccinino, whose invasion of Tuscany had been bought off by the neighbouring Italian states, had been the unwelcome stipendary of the king of Naples, idling his time in the kingdom, inactive and unwanted. To send him against Rimini would satisfy a number of aims: land for the *condottiere*, and retribution for Sigismondo. But the two problems were not of interest to Naples alone. They were of general concern to the whole of Italy, and it was to require several years of complex debate and scheming before the long-suffering powers brought both to an impatient and abrupt solution.

For the moment, won over by the tireless argument of Federigo d'Urbino, who arrived in Naples at the end of June, Alfonso was inclined to what seemed an easy settlement. Negotiation with Sigismondo had been tried,[4] and during the summer of 1457 was tried again, but to little effect. Sigismondo was not insensible to the danger threatening him. He appealed for intercession to Rome, Ferrara, Milan, Florence and Venice, and all but the last, cautious and sceptical

[1] B. Feliciangeli, *Sulla monacazione di Sveva Montefeltro-Sforza, signora di Pesaro* (Pistoia, 1903); Madiai, 'Nuovi documenti'; Soranzo, 'Invettiva' 1911, 269–79; *Pio II*, 26–8.

[2] Above p. 204.

[3] Anon. Veron., 90–1; Clementini, ii.284–5; Soranzo, *Pio II*, 28. The disputed castles included Casteldelce, Montecerignone, Monte con la Valle (di S. Anastasio?), Sassocorvaro, S. Ippolito, Montebello. Clementini adds that Malatesta also carried into neutrality with him the Malatesta counts of Sogliano and Ghiaggiolo.

[4] At the end of 1456 Sigismondo's chancellor was in Naples treating with the king: Soranzo, *Pio II*, 42.

of war, readily accepted his appeal. The duke of Milan, averse to any measure which might profit Piccinino, discountenanced the assault on Rimini, urging Alfonso to compound for half the debt; while the pope, anxious to prevent a revival of war, wrote peremptorily to Sigismondo (26 September), commanding him to pay within six days the sum of 1,000 gold florins and appease the king. Sigismondo himself was fertile in proposals, sent envoys to Naples, and used every resource to influence the king, but there was no reference at first to unconditional repayment. He may have wished to insist upon a judicial investigation of the claim; probably he was hoping by diplomacy to hold off hostilities. For that reason he was discovered unprepared and unsuspecting when Piccinino and the count of Urbino, advancing through the March, at last invaded his territory in November.[1] Thereafter war and negotiation proceeded side by side.

The pope still advised Sigismondo to submit and repay,[2] although Alfonso was now demanding the price of his expenses as well.[3] Florence was evasive, Venice indifferent, but both Calixtus and Sforza kept up their pressure on Alfonso, as did Borso d'Este. From Ferrara, the cardinal Colonna and the conte Everso da Anguillara, some help came in secretly to Sigismondo, and before long he included in his service Giulio Cesare da Varano, Antonello da Forlì, Guido de Baglioni, Marco de' Pii, lord of Carpi, and many others. The Venetians refused to release Carlo Fortebraccio, and Astorre Manfredi, likewise threatened by Alfonso and held off by the king with prohibitive demands, returned only a cold reply to an appeal from Sigismondo.[4] A similar appeal to Malatesta Novello was more kindly received. Malatesta was a close friend of Piccinino. He was willing to intercede, and at the end of November visited the two captains in Fossombrone. On

---

[1] Guerriero, 67; Filelfo, *Commentarii*, 351; Malipiero, 199; Baldi, *Federigo*, ii.29; Aeneas Sylvius Piccolomini, *Epist.* (1475), 22 July, 1 Aug., 1 Oct. 1457; *ASI* xv.177; Battaglini, *Vita*, 467–8; Tonini, v.224, 251–5; Nunziante, 'Primi anni' 1892, 331ff.; Fumi, 'Sforza', 585ff.; Soranzo, *Pio II*, 43ff.; Franceschini, 'Gentile Brancaleone', 489. At the end of September Sigismondo did, it is true, announce he was sending the money, and his representatives in Naples offered to repay first 23,000 ducats and then the full 27,000, but by then the attack had begun; and anyway Alfonso was at the end of all patience. He is reported to have said: 'misser Sigismondo mi ha burlato mi tri annj, io voglio mo videre s'el so burlare luij', and promised to hang 'quel tacagno': Nunziante, *loc. cit.* In Sept. also Venice agreed reluctantly to send a letter recommending Sigismondo to Alfonso: Soranzo, *Pio II*, 46.

[2] Letter of 1 Dec. recommending payment, even complete, and pointing out the folly of jeopardising all 'pro modica pecunia': Aeneas Sylvius Piccolomini, *Epist.* (1475), *locc. citt.*

[3] Malipiero, 206.

[4] Soranzo, *Pio II*, 52–3; though both lords had at this time been asking help of Florence, 'et furono confortati di buone parole': Palmieri, 178.

Federigo he could make no impression, but Piccinino was more conciliatory. For him alliance with Urbino was only one of several ways of
satisfying his ambition. Federigo had already had to check his readiness
to welcome offers of mediation, and he did so again now. There were
even rumours of an understanding between him and Sigismondo. And
it was as much to Piccinino's unaspiring and backward conduct of the
campaign, as to any defence put up by himself, that Sigismondo owed
the safety of his state. By the summer of 1458 only Carpegna had been
taken, from the conte Ramberto, and part of the *contado* of Fano.[1]

Until the death of Calixtus III in August, the time was passed in
profitless bargaining and desultory war. Recommended by Sforza to
make any sacrifice for peace, Sigismondo sent his son Roberto to
Naples, and now made offers extravagant and unreserved, though still
unequal to the mounting demands of the king.[2] In the duke of Milan
Sigismondo professed to place every trust,[3] yet he continued to court
Jean of Anjou, whom it was Sforza's resolve to exclude from Italy.[4]
Intrigue with the Angevin made the king of Naples only more intractable, and when Alfonso died on 27 June, no approach to agreement had
been made. The news of his death was received with rejoicing in
Rimini, and Sigismondo's readiness to pay the debt immediately
cooled. But if he hoped to find the new king, Ferrante, better disposed,
he was soon undeceived. Not content with the friendship of Anjou,
Sigismondo had entered into secret dealings with Gianantonio Orsini,
prince of Taranto, who was among the most powerful of the Neapolitan barons, contracting a marriage alliance and urging him to join the
Angevin. Since this was known to Ferrante, Sigismondo had little
ground for complaint, though complain he did, when the envoy he sent
on Sforza's advice to condole with the king on his father's death was
violently handled on arrival in Naples.[5]

[1] As before in 1455 and 1456 there was evidently some fear in the winter of 1457
that Sigismondo would join with Piccinino, even with Federigo, and invade
Tuscany: Anon. Veron., 99–104, 106, 110; Della Tuccia, 254; Pietro di Giovanni,
327, 340; Malipiero, 201–6; Sanzio, v, chs. xx–xxi; Filelfo, *Commentarii*, 353;
Guerriero, 64, 67; Simonetta, 411; *Chron. Bon.*, iv.251; Aeneas Sylvius Piccolomini, *Epist.* (1475), 2, 17, 22 Nov. 1457; *Pii II Commentarii*, 52; Baldi, *Federigo*,
ii.37; Battaglini, *Vita*, 470–1; Tonini, v. 256–8; Amiani, i.423–5; Ugolini, i.381;
Gaye, i.178; Buser, 399; Zampetti, 24; Soranzo, *Pio II*, 49–53, 55–6.

[2] According to Federigo d'Urbino (2 May 1458) Alfonso was intending to exact
not merely the 27,000 ducats, but also a further 70,000 for expenses, to demand
restitution of Federigo's territories in the Montefeltro while withholding those
just taken from Sigismondo: Dennistoun, i. 112–13; Nunziante, 'Primi anni' 1893,
30–1.

[3] Sigismondo to Sforza, 18 June 1458: Soranzo, *Pio II*, 467.

[4] Jean d'Anjou arrived at Genoa on 11 May, and with him was a chancellor of
Sigismondo: *ibid.* 57.

[5] Broglio, in Tonini, v.262–7; Nunziante, 'Primi anni' 1893, 223–5, 449–50;
Cod. Arag., 42–4; Soranzo, *Pio II*, 66, 71, 467–8.

The pope, to satisfy his long-felt hate of the Aragonese, declared the Regno forfeit. But on 6 August he too died, and the papal threat receded. More serious to Ferrante were the first stirrings of rebellion in the kingdom itself.

The death of Calixtus, and the election on 19 August of a new pope, Pius II, friendly to the house of Aragon, might have heightened the danger to Sigismondo Malatesta. Instead it brought him unforeseen relief. The short interregnum of papal vacancy, commonly a time of disorder in the States of the Church, was seized by Piccinino as offering a more certain chance of conquest than the dilatory operations in Romagna. Concluding a hasty truce with Sigismondo, he marched off into Umbria to occupy Assisi, Gualdo and Nocera, and besiege Foligno, and left Sigismondo free to fight Federigo alone.[1]

The relief as it turned out was shortlived. Sigismondo, despairing of success in direct negotiation with Naples, committed his case to the guidance of Sforza. But Ferrante was far from wanting to come to terms, and clung even more obstinately than his father to the design of appeasing Piccinino's craving for land at the expense of the Malatesta. Sforza was equally determined to reach a peace, not only for defence against Anjou, nor merely as a repulse to Piccinino, but also as a check to the evident purpose of the new pope to win control of the dispute himself. He was convinced, he said, that Pius would never withdraw, once he had 'shoved his nose in'.[2] This, however, the pope had already done, and as Sforza predicted he never withdrew.

On 17 October a treaty was reached between Pius II and Ferrante, revoking Calixtus' censures and acknowledging the king legitimate successor to the throne of Naples. In return Ferrante reluctantly promised to obtain from Piccinino surrender of his conquests in Umbria, and resigned to the pope the decision of his quarrel with Sigismondo.[3] The settlement envisaged by the peace of Lodi should now at last have followed. No ruler was better fitted by office than the pope to undertake arbitration. Yet innocent and well-intentioned though it was, this agreement between the papacy and Naples was the mischievous beginning of months of contentious debate which were to

---

[1] Broglio, in Tonini, v. 267; Pietro di Giovanni, 341; Guerriero, 68; Baldi, *Federigo*, ii.49–51; Nunziante, 'Primi anni' 1893, 33; Fumi, 'Sforza', 600–1; Soranzo, *Pio II*, 58–60.

[2] Battaglini, *Vita*, 638–41; Tonini, v/2.214–16; Nunziante, 'Primi anni' 1893, 207–15, 223, 226–8; *Cod. Arag.*, 56; Soranzo, *Pio II*, 70–2. In Oct. Ferrante may have written asking the other states not to interfere in his war with Sigismondo: Pedrino, rub. 1796.

[3] Rayaldus, 1458, n. xx; Dumont, iii/1.251–2; *Pii II Commentarii*, 52; Giampietro, 'Registro aragonese', 79–81; Nunziante, 'Primi anni' 1893, 232; *Cod. Arag.*, 97.

end by wearying every state in Italy, and by turning Pius II into the impassioned enemy of the Malatesta.

The two conditions of the treaty were in practice contradictory. If Sigismondo welcomed gratefully the promise of papal mediation,[1] Piccinino was just as decidedly opposed to it, and made it clear he would never abandon Assisi should peace deny him recompense from the lands of the Malatesta.[2] Compelled to make a choice, the three powers most concerned, Milan, Naples and the papacy, decided to postpone the settlement with Sigismondo, entertaining him with vague and delusive proposals,[3] and tried to soothe the fears of Piccinino, who, as Ferrante later observed, 'essendo capitaneo de ventura et trevandose seneza guerre et seneza ne[x]uno altro evidenti partito cercara omne via che potisse per mantinirese'.[4] No one was more anxious than the pope to see his departure from Umbria, and it was Pius who went to the greatest lengths to secure it. Sometime in January he promised in writing that in the event of peace between Sigismondo and the king, Piccinino should receive compensation. This document he entrusted to Federigo d'Urbino, whose interests he also engaged to protect before publishing any award. And it is probable that Pius was already contemplating a sentence which would compel Sigismondo, if unable to reimburse Ferrante, to give up certain territories in the Montefeltro and the March of Ancona, some of them to Federigo and others to the king of Naples, who, it was known, would immediately transfer them to Piccinino.[5] By this hasty if not disingenuous compact the pope compromised in advance an impartial decision, and introduced into the case committed to him the independent controversy

[1] He sent representatives to Rome and Naples, and asked Sforza to be his surety for accepting the papal decision. He also persuaded the Venetians to write recommending him to Pius and Ferrante: Grigioni, 'Documenti', 373–5; Nunziante, 'Primi anni' 1893, 235, 237, 240; Picotti, 78. He may even have offered to give up Sinigaglia, Mondavio, and other places, to obtain peace: Cod. Arag., 163.

[2] He and Federigo were again fighting Sigismondo and at the end of Dec. refused a truce: Filelfo, Commentarii, 260–1; Cron. Castel delle Ripe, 24; Battaglini, Vita, 481; Tonini, v. 268; Nunziante, 'Primi anni' 1893, 243; Soranzo, Pio II, 72–4.

[3] For details: Giampietro, 'Regestro aragonese', 81–3; Nunziante, 'Primi anni' 1893, 234–44; Cod. Arag., 142–3; Soranzo, Pio II, 83, 86, 90, 468–9; Picotti, 103; Schivenoglia, 132–3.

[4] To Pius II (30 Dec. 1459): Cod. Arag., 367–8.

[5] The territories were to be: vicariate of Mondavio, Sinigaglia, Montemarciano, Morro, la Pergola, Pietrarubbia, Certalto, and a few others: Soranzo, Pio II, 87–8 (who calls it a 'brutto tiro'). There is no evidence that Pius was yet ill-disposed towards Sigismondo (ibid. 61–3), though Sigismondo's ambassador in Rome had given him offence (Cod. Arag., 114; Nunziante, 'Primi anni' 1893, 240). About this time Sigismondo had Filelfo in Rome to engage the pope's sympathy on his behalf: Filelfo, Epist. fam., 104–5; Battaglini, Vita, 482.

between Sigismondo and the count of Urbino. But he gained his objective. Before the end of January Piccinino withdrew from Assisi, and after concluding an armistice with Sigismondo returned to the kingdom of Naples.[1]

To Pius II the way may now have seemed clear to effective mediation. All he needed was assurance that his sentence would be accepted. But when he set out from Rome on 22 January to preside over the European Congress he had convened at Mantua, the desire for a settlement was still not unanimous in Italy. Ferrante and Federigo d'Urbino, with their embarrassing dependent Piccinino, all wished to continue the war. Sigismondo Malatesta saw in the papal arbitration only one possible issue to his difficulties, which might equally be offered by alliance with Anjou or a secret compact with Piccinino, and only the pope and Sforza sincerely wanted peace.[2]

The first attempt at agreement was made by the pope in Florence during April. Here, besides other lords of Romagna, were present Sigismondo[3] and representatives of Piccinino and the count of Monte-feltro; but from the king of Naples, whom Pius had been exhorting for months to send a plenipotentiary, no envoy arrived. In principle perhaps not averse to a compromise with Sigismondo, Ferrante was concerned before everything to provide for Piccinino, to ensure, as he said, that the *condottiere* should have a 'stantia dove potere stare'; and this he still thought best provided at the expense of Sigismondo. A further obstacle to negotiation were the papal terms of peace. In obedience to advice from Sforza, the pope had no intention of lingering over the juridical niceties of the dispute, or of determining whether Sigismondo was truly in debt to the king. He preferred, 'pro bono pacis et concordia', that Sigismondo engage at once either to pay what Ferrante demanded or give up certain lands in pledge to do so. Since it was known to Pius as to everyone else that Sigismondo was in no condition to produce such a sum of money, the sentence implied a partition, possibly permanent, of the Malatesta dominions, and in this

[1] Pietro di Giovanni, 355; Baldi, *Federigo*, ii.52; Nunziante, 'Primi anni' 1893, 245; 1894, 595–6; Soranzo, *Pio II*, 89.
[2] One solution mooted by Sforza was to murder Piccinino: Nunziante, 'Primi anni' 1894, 600–1, 607.
[3] Federigo d'Urbino had already visited Pius in Perugia in Feb. and there, according to Filelfo, embittered his mind against Sigismondo: Filelfo, *Commentarii*, 364; Pietro di Giovanni, 361–2; Soranzo, *Pio II*, 90–1. Sigismondo himself did not join the pope until he came to Florence on 25 April: Anon. Veron., 124; Guerriero, 68; *Pii II Commentarii*, 52; Della Tuccia, 258; Nunziante, 'Primi anni' 1894, 572–3; Soranzo, *Pio II*, 94–100, 470. In Florence the pope was carried ceremonially on the shoulders of Sigismondo and other vicars of the church, and according to one of the passages expurgated from Pius' *Commentaries* Sigismondo then protested: 'En quo deducti sumus! Urbium domini, lecticarii iam tandem evasimus': (*Opera ined.*, 508).

Sigismondo refused to acquiesce.[1] Indignantly he abandoned Florence, and returned to renew his entreaties to Francesco Sforza at Milan; but Sforza only counselled him to accept an agreement, whatever the cost, as the state of opinion in Italy should already have disposed him to do. Where, he asked, could Sigismondo turn for help? What power would compromise itself for his sake?[2]

Another argument for submission came from Rimini itself, where Piccinino, re-established in Neapolitan pay, had resumed his attack in May. Pius had allowed to Sigismondo freedom to follow the alternative course of war, but he seems to have preferred negotiation; and although at the end of the month he paid a hurried visit to Romagna to survey his defences, he left again within a few days for Mantua, to renew discussion with the pope. In his absence Piccinino and the Feltreschi advanced in face of little opposition, and before peace was made in August managed to occupy a wide extent of Sigismondo's territories in the March and the Montefeltro.[3]

Sigismondo reached Mantua on 3 June, and the pope lost no time in stating his preliminary terms. Sigismondo, he decreed, should pay Ferrante within a year the sum of 30,000 ducats together with a jewel of comparably high value which he had formerly promised the king. He was also to restore to Federigo d'Urbino the castles he had taken from him, together with la Pergola, while Malatesta Novello was to exchange whatever he held in the Montefeltro for equivalent properties elsewhere. These conditions Sigismondo accepted; and it was a measure of his wish for peace that he did so. But they were rejected by the Aragonese envoys, who had at last joined the pope, and who insisted, as they had done already in company with Federigo, that Pius should honour the engagement he had made earlier in the year. The pope had no choice but to comply, and therefore proposed in addition that Sigismondo should give him as security for repayment the greater part of his possessions in the March of Ancona, in particular the vicariate of Mondavio, Sinigaglia, and Montemarciano. Now Sigismondo in his turn protested. He feared the lands once pledged would be consigned to Piccinino, though Sforza, who still urged him to give way, undertook to exact from the pope a written promise to restore them, and

[1] Pius in his *Commentaries* later claimed to have expostulated with Sigismondo for his obstinacy, saying that he was acting out of respect for his ancestors and his dynasty, not for him: *Commentarii*, 52; Delfico, i. 210–11; Nunziante, 'Primi anni' 1894, 610–11; Soranzo, *Pio II*, 91, 100–1, 469–70.

[2] Anon. Veron., 124–5; Soranzo, *Pio II*, 103–4; Picotti, 103.

[3] By the first week in August Guerriero says Sigismondo had lost to Piccinino 'tra bone terre et castelli . . . in numero cento quindeci', including Penna Billi, S. Agata, Macerata and Certaldo; *Cronaca*, 68. Cf. *Chron. Bon.*, iv. 268–70; Della Tuccia, 258–9; Filelfo, *Commentarii*, 365; Pedrino, rub. 1807–8, 1814; Amiani, i. 426; Nunziante, 'Primi anni' 1894, 602–7, 636; Soranzo, *Pio II*, 104.

never allow Piccinino or any other *condottiere* within their frontiers. Weeks passed in idle debate, while Sigismondo's subject castles were being overrun. At first Ferrante and Federigo were agreeable to the pope's original terms, but Piccinino, ill-disposed to any peace, especially one neglecting his own interests, stiffened the king's resistance. Ferrante now demanded not merely enforcement of the revised conditions, but that the lands surrendered in the March of Ancona should be entrusted to his keeping. That they would then pass to Piccinino was clear to everyone, and the pope refused. He was no less opposed to the suggestion of Sforza and Sigismondo that they should be held by the duke of Milan; and when at last, at the beginning of August, all parties were brought into momentary agreement, the pope announced he would take custody of them himself.

The final terms accepted at Mantua and drawn up on 6–7 August began with an assurance that the papal sentence would be published within three months. Meanwhile Sigismondo was to accept one of two procedures. By the first he would give guarantees to pay Ferrante 50,000 ducats within a time yet to be determined but not less than one year, or if he failed to offer guarantees, would surrender in pledge to the pope Sinigaglia, Montemarciano, the vicariate of Mondavio, and Morro,[1] which would be transferred on the publication of sentence to a person trusted equally by Pius and Ferrante. By the second Sigismondo gave no guarantees and surrendered the territories immediately. In either case he was to continue drawing the revenue, and all troops, whether of Piccinino or any other, were to be excluded. As soon as the lands were given up hostilities were to cease, and in the interval Piccinino and Federigo would be asked to suspend attacks. What territory had been lost to Sigismondo during the war was also to be committed to the pope, and restored when sentence was issued.

A further group of clauses regulated relations between the Malatesta and Montefeltro. According to these Federigo was to get back all the castles occupied by Sigismondo since 1445–6, with Pergola and Sassocorvaro. Pietrarubbia and Certaldo were to be released by Sigismondo for the pope and Sforza to assign, after investigation, to himself or the count of Urbino, and three other places recently taken from Sigismondo were to be retained by Federigo.[2] The exchange of territories in the Montefeltro which constituted part of Violante's dowry was to take place under the supervision of the pope, and he was to pronounce how much of the dowry was still owed by Federigo, which would then, in accordance with earlier contracts, pass to Sigismondo.

[1] I.e. the territories mentioned in Pius' secret promise of January; above p. 221.
[2] Which with Pietrarubbia and Certaldo had been promised to Federigo by the king of Naples in 1457.

Peace, explained Pius in his *Commentaries*, was his sole object when preparing this award. For that reason it was provided that during a period still to be fixed by the pope, Sigismondo was to undertake no action against the king of Naples. In return he and Sforza promised to try to obtain from Ferrante some mitigation of the terms, a reduction in the money to be paid and a longer time in which to pay it. Even so the sentence was, as Broglio complained, 'molto aspra et indebita'. That the obligations should lie mainly on Sigismondo was perhaps natural, for the initial assumption had been his guilt. But there was little to bind other parties to observance of the terms. They were well received by no one, though all but one accepted them. Only Piccinino, for whom, as Pius admitted,[1] no place had been made, refused to give assent. Yet it was on him that the success or failure of the whole peace was known to depend.[2]

If Sigismondo Malatesta had contravened such principles as governed the relations of fifteenth-century Italian states, by the autumn of 1459 he had made adequate atonement. Not merely had his lands been invaded and laid waste: he himself was bound by solemn sentence to satisfy his enemies. When therefore, as now happened, he saw the sentence imperfectly executed and only partially fulfilled, it was no capricious aggravation of his crimes that he also broke away from his obligations, nor was it, as Pius II was soon to exclaim, the expression of innate perversity. Convinced, as was apparent from the beginning, that the papal peace could never be enforced, he merely turned for defence to other and more hazardous expedients, never lost sight of during the course of negotiation.

It was the intransigence of Piccinino which in the end compelled Sigismondo to give up hope of any equitable settlement by the pope. At first he attempted faithfully to apply the terms of peace, and his readmission into the Italian league was debated among the powers. Federigo was persuaded to abandon his attacks, and by the middle of September most of the lands to be given up in pledge or restitution had been surrendered to papal commissioners. A month later all but a few of the castles claimed by Federigo were made over to him, and only Pietrarubbia, Certaldo and certain others were withheld by Sigis-

---

[1] Picotti, 164.
[2] Pius was certainly disgusted by the obstinacy of Ferrante and Federigo which for so long held up peace: Anon. Veron., 128–9; Pedrino, rub. 1807, 1814; Filelfo, *Commentarii*, 365–6; Pietro di Giovanni, 379; *Diario Ferrar.*, 39; *Chron. Bon.*, iv. 268–79; *Pii II Commentaria*, 74–5; *Cod. Arag.*, nn. 182–3, 197, 201, 206–7, 209; Battaglini, *Vita*, 485, 655; Tonini, v. 269–72; Nunziante, 'Primi anni' 1894, 610–17; Soranzo, *Pio II*, 106–31, 471–4; Picotti, 144, 164. Cf. Pius' account in a later letter listing Sigismondo's crimes and maintaining that but for him this 'fex Italiae' would have perished: *Epist.* (1473), n. VI.

mondo.[1] At this the count of Montefeltro and the papal representatives raised loud protest, but the duke of Milan more judiciously testified to Sigismondo's general goodwill, and was not obviously deceived in doing so. Application of the peace had worked entirely to the disadvantage of Sigismondo, and there was no sign that he would be able to get redress. While, for his part, he had consented to remain impatiently in Mantua and allow the confiscation of his territories, Piccinino had not merely refused to relinquish his conquests, but had carried the invasion further into the Malatesta lands, dismissing all talk of a peace as 'archimie et arte del signor Sigismondo'. In November Sigismondo wrote to his envoy in Milan, expressing fear that Piccinino would winter in his territories. He suspected also that 'quelli preti non ce inganni'.

There was every reason for suspicion. During the summer the prince of Taranto and other magnates of the kingdom of Sicily had at last come out in rebellion, and in October Jean d'Anjou opened his long-delayed offensive on the coast of Naples. An understanding was spoken of between Piccinino and the Angevin leaders, and in his anxiety to keep the *condottiere* away from his frontiers, Ferrante urged him to hold on to the Malatesta dominions (7 November). Pius II, who was growing weary of an endless and fruitless negotiation, may also have agreed secretly to this. If so, he cannot have expected acquiescence when he wrote (27 November) ordering Sigismondo to sanction the sequestration of the remaining castles, and promising to induce Piccinino to withdraw. Sforza, determined as ever to destroy Piccinino, and fearing like Ferrante he would ally himself with Anjou, desired at least that Federigo and Sigismondo should be brought into public alliance and support Pius and himself in preventing Piccinino from attacking the Regno. As a result, on 28 November the lords of Rimini and Urbino came together at Mondaino in a meeting more friendly than the last, and in the presence of the ducal envoy planned the strategy of a campaign. But it is probable that Sigismondo already had his own plans. Forbearance and humility seemed to have yielded few results, and with the advance of winter the idea of direct independent action must have become more appealing. On 2 January he met Piccinino at Cesena, where Malatesta Novello, disobedient from the first to the papal terms of peace, had allowed him winter quarters; and it was concluded that in return for the territories in Piccinino's hands, Sigismondo would leave him free to advance against Naples. Three weeks later Piccinino had come to terms with the Angevin.[2]

[1] S. Costanzo, S. Vito, Montescudo and Morro. Sigismondo feared they would be given to Federigo, although, he said, they were already adjudged to him by Sforza and the pope: Soranzo, *Pio II*, 152; Colucci, xxi/i. 134–5; Baldi, *Federigo*, ii. 66–7.
[2] Anon. Veron., 128–9, 133; Filelfo, *Commentarii*, 365–9; Sanzio, xi, ch. xxii; Pedrino, rub. 1814–16; Guerriero, 69; *Pii II Commentarii*, 74–5; *Epist.* (1473),

These compacts were secret and were followed by no open or immediate declaration of defiance. Sigismondo still welcomed the offer of fresh discussions with Sforza and the pope, and sent his son Roberto to Naples to obtain a relaxation of the terms. An attempt was made as well to reconcile him with Federigo d'Urbino and Alessandro Sforza, but all spirit had long passed from these negotiations and their futility was proved. By the end of February the treaty with Piccinino was suspected if not known, and when Piccinino surrendered his conquests to the Malatesta, and suddenly moved his army south in March, unopposed and possibly helped by Sigismondo and Malatesta Novello, suspicion changed to certainty, although Federigo himself and the papal envoys did little to oppose him, relieved like the Malatesta to see him depart.

Even now the duke of Milan did not despair of peace with Sigismondo. Intent before everything to help Ferrante and defeat Anjou, he endeavoured during the spring and early summer to restrain Sigismondo from joining the enemy or molesting the lands of the count of Montefeltro, absent on behalf of the church in the Neapolitan kingdom, and proposed that he also should enter the service of Naples. His advice received at least a hearing in Rimini, but from Ferrante, whose need of money was greater than his need of troops, he obtained nothing. Nor was the pope any longer conciliatory. His favour was reserved henceforward without disguise for Federigo, and in the face of protest from Sforza, he now introduced the illegitimate condition that the lands made over in pledge by Sigismondo should be restored only when he had paid up as temporal vicar his arrears of papal *census*.[1] It was not therefore without provocation that Sigismondo, who appears at this time in a state of irritated and anxious despondency, at last entered into an agreement with the Angevins (late August or early September), by the terms of which he was probably to receive aid in men and money

nn. VI, XI; Baldi (1473), ii.66; Clementini, ii.412–13; Battaglini, *Vita*, 491, 642–3; Amiani, i.426–7; Tonini, v. 272, v/2.217–19; Ugolini, i.387; Buser, 404; Nunziante, 'Primi anni' 1893, 597; 1894, 328, 431, 440, 442, 619, 647; Bernardy, 'Archivio', nn. 421–2, 427–8; *Cod. Arag.*, nn. 217, 227, 234, 240, 242, 256, 264, 294; Theiner, iii.355; Soranzo, *Pio II*, 133–76, 476–80; Picotti, 191–2, 220, 263, 280, 300, 315, 434, 449, 494; Perret, i.331; Mazzatinti, *MSS di Francia*, ii.339–40.

[1] This had been no condition of the original peace, but the question of *census* owed had already been raised at Mantua in the preceding year: Soranzo, *Pio II*, 120. Calixtus III had remitted the debt as it stood during his pontificate (above p. 214), but by 1460 a new debt of four years' *census* had accumulated. Sigismondo's representatives to the pope requested that the amount be reduced in view of the territories recently given up, while Pius wanted it raised on account of the lands received through Violante, for which *census* had never been paid. The pope was clearly unwilling to contemplate the restitution of the lands at all. He explained to Sforza that they offered a good means of holding the Malatesta in check, and he may already have been meditating giving them to a member of his own family: Soranzo, *Pio II*, 195, 198–9, 201–3.

to recover his alienated territories and conquer Pesaro and Urbino, while engaging on his side to accept service with neither the king, the pope, nor the duke of Milan, to keep up hostilities in the Papal States and to invade the kingdom whenever summoned. Already before this Sigismondo had intervened to prevent the Feltreschi from refortifying the castle of Uffigliano, to which the rival claims of Malatesta and Montefeltro had not yet been decided, and in July he expelled the papal castellan from Montemarciano. By the treaty with Jean d'Anjou he abandoned the last vestiges of restraint, repudiated the treacherous pretence of a negotiated peace and challenged the papacy to war.[1]

In Pius II he had chosen an adversary bitter, obdurate and pertinacious, who for the next three years, unmoved by the remonstrances of the other Italian powers, was to pursue him with blind and absorbing rancour. By joining the Angevin Sigismondo antagonised Sforza as well, who now denounced in his letters the 'tristi modi' of the lord of Rimini; but before the end of the year, resentful though he was of Sigismondo, he was beginning to express uneasiness at the pope's obsessive passion to humiliate the Malatesta.[2] On 15 October 1460 Pius II wrote commanding Sigismondo to remit without delay the 10,000 ducats of *census* owed for the past four years,[3] and the contest was joined. Sigismondo ignored the papal admonitions and, encouraged by the help of the Angevins, the prince of Taranto, Piccinino and Malatesta Novello, opened his attack to recover the vicariate of Mondavio, defeating the papal commissary, Ludovico Mavezzi. Sinigaglia eluded him, but his intervention in a local war between Iesi and Ancona enraged the pope still more: 'et così conseguì e principiò la guerra dal Papa alla Signorìa sua, il quale se infiammò fieramente contra il prefato Signore alia sua disfatione' (Broglio).[4] At the end of December 1460 the two brothers Malatesta were excommunicated, and

---

[1] On all this: Simonetta, 412–13; Guerriero, 70–1; Pedrino, rub. 1838; Della Tuccia, 261; Filelfo, *Commentarii*, 369; Baldi, *Federigo*, ii.69, 83; Lilii, ii.211; Battaglini, *Vita*, 499, 644; Tonini, v/2.220; Dennistoun, i.123; Bernardy, 'Archivio', nn. 432–5, 440, 442, 445, 448, 452, 454; Pastor, *Acta*, n. 97; Nunziante, 'Primi anni' 1894, 647, 655, 657–8; 1895, 224, 230, 453, 457; 1896, 266, 271–2; *Cod. Arag.*, nn. 336, 347, 355; Soranzo, *Pio II*, 177–205; Picotti, 340, 342, 355, 359, 516; Mazzatinti, *Inventari*, xxxix. 79–80. Jean d'Anjou wished the Venetians to guarantee Sigismondo's territories, but the republic clung to its neutrality: Perret, i.340–1.

[2] Simonetta, 449; Soranzo, *Pio II*, 205–7, 217–20.

[3] Although at the instigation of Sforza (who had pressed also many times for a reduction of Sigismondo's *census*), he had just exempted Alessandro Sforza from three-quarters of his *census*, equally owing for 4 years: Soranzo, *Pio II*, 212–13.

[4] Tonini, v.278–80; Guerriero, 71–2; *Chron. Bon.*, iv.276–7; Pedrino, rub. 1844, 1850; Bernabei, 179–81; Raynaldus, 1460, nn. LXX–II; Pastor, *Acta*, n. 104; *Pii II Commentaria*, 108, 112, 124; *Epist.* (1473), nn. VI, XIX; Clementini, ii.417–18, 486; Battaglini, *Vita*, 501–2; Amiani, i.428–9; Nunziante, 'Primi anni' 1896, 271–2; Soranzo, *Pio II*, 211–21.

on 16 January in a public consistory, attended by Federigo d'Urbino and Alessandro Sforza, the Sienese *advocatus fisci*, Andrea di Ugo Benzi, read out a vehement charge against Sigismondo Malatesta, rehearsing his multiple crimes against God and man in a prolix and partisan speech, very much in the taste of the time. The preparation of a more formal indictment was committed to the cardinal of S. Pietro in Vincoli, Nicholas of Cusa, while the pope announced the need for some process, inverting canonisation, which would enrol Sigismondo a citizen of Hell.[1]

Incapable of conducting single-handed an effective attack on Rimini, Pius appealed at the same time to the members of the Italian league, but to little purpose. Florence, Ferrara and Venice all remained stubbornly neutral. Sforza too, who had sent a contingent of troops, continued to urge the pope to circumspection;[2] and it was with his benediction that a profitless attempt to reconcile Sigismondo and Pius was undertaken in the early spring.[3] Preoccupied with the Neapolitan war, the duke refused to countenance extreme proceedings against Rimini, and only went so far to meet the pope's intransigence as to detach from Sigismondo's side two of his leading allies, Antonello of Forlì and Giulio Cesare Varano, and to reopen negotiations with Piccinino.[4] Pius, it was clear, could expect neither aid nor approbation from his Italian confederates in chastising Sigismondo.

This did not make him falter. At the beginning of April he published a further excommunication of the Malatesta, and spent the next few months in conciliating the local enemies of Sigismondo. Montemarciano he promised to Iesi, Pietrarubbia he adjudged to

---

1 'El papa ha formato el processo contro el S. Gismondo che non podeva essere piu terribile' (14 Dec. 1460, letter from Monte Carignone to S. Marino: Bernardy, 'Archivio', n. 467. The excommunication was published on 25 Dec.); Pedrino, rub. 1844; *Pii II Commentarii*, 128–9; *Opera ined.*, 524; *Epist.* (1473), n. VI; Mittarelli, *Cod. S. Michaelis*, 704–14; Raynaldus, *loc. cit.*; Pastor, *Acta*, nn. 105–8, 110: Soranzo, 'Invettiva' 1910, 468–9, 476; *Pio II*, 221, 227–9.

2 For which reason the bishop of Teano and cardinal of S. Cecilia, Niccolo Forteguerra, proposed early in January that the Malatesta state should be partitioned between one of Sforza's sons and a nephew of the pope, the whole proceeding being represented as the action of the league. Pius welcomed the idea: Bernardy, 'Archivio', n. 467; Pastor, *Acta*, n. 109; *Päpste*, ii.93, 95; Soranzo, *Pio II*, 22–6, 231–3, 479–80. Sforza explained that it was out of no love of Sigismondo, who had injured him 'in le carne et sangue', that he still favoured negotiation.

3 Soranzo, *Pio II*, 234–42. Both Pius and Sigismondo were without resources for an effective campaign: cf. Grigioni, 'Costruttori', 198 ff., showing Sigismondo's inability to pay in money the artists at work on the Tempio, although in March he was able to hire Cecco Brandolini on behalf of himself and his brother; *idem*, 'Documenti', 375–6.

4 Who made a prohibitive claim to all of Sigismondo's territories except the vicariate of Mondavio, Sinigaglia, 'e le altre terre adiudicate al sig. conte di Urbino': Soranzo, *Pio II*, 243–5.

Federigo d'Urbino, and in June he renewed to Federigo his vicariates, putting him as well in possession of S. Leo, Pergola, Montecavallo, and certain other places.[1] Nor was he dismayed at the defeat inflicted by Sigismondo early in July on the papal forces at Nidastore.[2] While Pius hastened to repair his losses and reanimate the campaign, Sigismondo, hoping perhaps to have impressed the pope by arms, abstained from exploiting his victory, and turned instead to proposals of peace, only to find the papal terms unacceptably severe.[3] His relations at this time with the Angevins also seemed incalculable,[4] and the autumn and winter of 1461 were spent less in preparations for a second season of war than in tentative negotiations with the contending powers. Envoys were secretly sent from Rimini to Louis XI of France,[5] while locally a marriage alliance was concluded with Taddeo Manfredi of Imola.[6]

Both Pius and Sigismondo were embarrassed by lack of money,[7] and this may have been in part responsible for the slow progress of operations in the early months of 1462.[8] In October Nicholas of Cusa had

[1] *Pii II Commentarii*, 131; Theiner, iii.364; G. Baldassini, 163–4; Colucci, xxi/1. 134–5; Soranzo, *Pio II*, 242, 243 (n. 1), 245–6. In a conversation with the Milanese ambassador in May, Pius alluded to Canossa as showing the force of papal censures: Soranzo, *ibid.* 246.

[2] Branchi, 177; Guerriero, 73; *Chron. Bon.*, iv.283–4; Broglio, in Tonini, v.281–8; Battaglini, *Vita*, 504–8; Filelfo, *Commentarii*, 387; *Pii II Commentarii*, 141–2; Pedrino, rub. 1859; Theiner, iii.363; Pastor, *Acta*, n. 117; *Päpste*, ii.733; Soranzo, *Pio II*, 247–50.

[3] Pius demanded that Sigismondo should sue for pardon, pay arrears of *census* and surrender Mondavio again as a guarantee of the Mantuan terms: Amiani, i.430; Tonini, v.288–9; Pastor, *Acta*, n. 119; *Päpste*, ii.95–6; Soranzo, *Pio II*, 250–3, 255–7, 259–62, 270, 296 (n. 1). Cartoons of Sigismondo now appeared in the Papal States, although Bologna at first, to the pope's indignation, would not allow them.

[4] At the end of July he set out to join Piccinino in an attack in the Abruzzi, but Piccinino did not arrive. However, shortly afterwards Roberto Malatesta's *condotta* was renewed by Piccinino: *Chron. Bon.*, iv.285; Battaglini, *Vita*, 503, 509; Tonini, v.288–9; Grigioni, 'Documenti', 380–1; Soranzo, *Pio II*, 257–9, 262–3.

[5] On Sigismondo's relations with Louis XI (Sept. 1461–Jan. 1462): Perret, 375, 382; Louis XI, *Lettres*, ii, 10–11; *Dépêches des ambassadeurs milanais*, i.124–5, 158, 162, 174; Soranzo, *Pio II*, 268–9, 277.

[6] 10 Nov. 1461: Soranzo, *Pio II*, 273–4. About this time it was rumoured, falsely, that Sigismondo was negotiating with the infidel: Pedrino, rub. 1873–4; Anon. Veron., 148; Yriarte, 286; Baluze, iii.113–14; Soranzo, 'Missione', 43–54, 93–6; 'Matteo de' Pasti', 62–4; Ricci, 41–4; Campana, 'Matteo de' Pasti', 5.

[7] Pius to the legate in the March, Oct. 1461: Pastor, *Acta*, n. 123). On his side Sigismondo was compelled to suspend work on the Tempio, which remained with its roof exposed and snow within its walls. The local friars were persuaded or enjoined to sell some of their properties 'in reparationem dicti tecti ecclesie et capellarum predictarum': Ricci, 225, 592. In Jan. 1462 Sigismondo had to pawn his jewellery: Grigioni, 'Costruttori', 199.

[8] Sforza was still pressing for peace, Sigismondo ostensibly agreeable, and the repudiation by Louis XI of the Pragmatic Sanction may have persuaded Pius to look more kindly on Sigismondo, then negotiating with the French court; but by

presented the results of his enquiry into Sigismondo's transgressions, enabling Pius to discharge against him the greater censures of the church, but at the intercession of others he had withheld them from immediate publication.[1] Impatient at last of Sigismondo's contumacy, he resumed punitive proceedings. In February the subjects of the Malatesta were released by papal bull from their allegiance, and while Sigismondo, supported by French diplomacy and enheartened by receipt of money, negotiated with the prince of Taranto, intrigued to get hold of Pesaro and opened a campaign against the Montefeltro, the pope circulated scurrilous verses against him in Romagna, and prepared his final condemnation.[2] On 27 April 1462, Nicholas of Cusa read out the sentence. In various public places of Rome effigies of Sigismondo were burned, with the words issuing from the mouth: 'Sigismundus hic ego sum Malatesta, filius Pandulphi, rex proditorum, Deo atque hominibus infestus, sacri censura senatus igni damnatus.' Excommunication and interdict were proclaimed, and Sigismondo was deprived of his vicariates in Rimini, Fano, Sinigaglia, and Montefeltro, Cesena and Mondavio. No one was to consort with him, no subject respect his commands, no priest in his territories celebrate the offices of the church. An abstract was made of the censures and distributed throughout Italy.[3]

Far from intimidating Sigismondo, this only angered him.[4] If his own situation was not strong, the papal armies were no better off;[5] and during the spring and early summer of 1462 he proceeded unopposed with his preparations for 'una grande facenda'. With money from the prince of Taranto and the Angevins, he was able to take into his service Niccolo d'Este, Pino Ordelaffi and Gianfrancesco Pico della Mirandola, on the understanding that he took his troops south to help conquer the

February it was clear Sigismondo was only trying to avert the final sentence and hoping events would force Pius to give in: Soranzo, *Pio II*, 274–80, 483–6; Fumi, 'Attegiamento', 158–60.

[1] *Pii II Commentarii*, 184–5; *Epist.* (1473), n. VI; Soranzo, 'Invettiva' 1910, 480, 482; *Pio II*, 270–2. To the earlier accusations, Nicholas added disbelief in immortality, for which Sigismondo was condemned by the college of cardinals as a heretic.

[2] Sigismondo complained of the verses in a letter of 26 March 1462, concluding defiantly: 'uno bello morire tutta una vita honora': Pastor, *Päpste*, ii.736; Pedrino, rub. 1882–3; Giordani, *A. Sforza*, lxiv ff.; Soranzo, *Pio II*, 283–7; Mazzatinti, *Archivi*, Ser. 1, i.335.

[3] *Pii II Commentaria*, 184–5, 202–3; *Epist.* (1473), n. VI; Anon. Veron., 151, 165–9; Amati, 'Notizie', 214; Müntz, i.248; Yriarte, 287; Pastor, *Päpste*, ii.99; *Acta*, n. 133; Soranzo, *Pio II*, 288–92, 486–7; 'Invettiva' 1910, 480, 482.

[4] Even Federigo disapproved of the theatrical violence of these proceedings: Soranzo, *Pio II, locc. citt.*

[5] Early in March Pius reviewed the difficult situation of the papacy and king of Naples: papal revenues, temporal and spiritual, he said amounted only to 150,000 ducats: Pastor, *Acta*, n. 125.

Abruzzi.[1] But whether from reluctance to desert his state, or because he was checked by the papal commissary, or, finally, because he was deceived by the same stratagem practised successfully in 1450, when he was offered Pesaro, he made no serious attempt to cross the March of Ancona and instead attacked Sinigaglia. On 12 August he obtained surrender of the city and its *rocca*, only to be faced a few hours later by the army of Federigo d'Urbino and the pope. Pius had long been negotiating for the count's release from service in the kingdom. Federigo was no less anxious to come to grips with Sigismondo, and in July Sforza and Ferrante at last allowed him to leave. Informed that Federigo's force was strong, Sigismondo tried at first to deflect him by negotiation, arguing that if the Malatesta were dispossessed, the turn of the Montefeltro would soon follow, and pointing out that to 'la ragione del dominare' Pius II had added the power 'da sostenerla'. With a characteristic blend of rectitude and prudence Federigo replied that he came to fight as captain of the church, not as count of Urbino, and a battle was begun close by Sinigaglia in which the Malatesta army was totally defeated.[2]

From this reverse Sigismondo was never permitted to recover.[3] In despair he left by ship from Fano to implore help from the Angevins, and in his absence the papal troops under Federigo and the cardinal of Teano systematically overran his territories. Late in August he was still holding Rimini, Fano, Mondavio, Gradara, Mondaino, Montefiore, S. Leo, Verucchio, Pietrarubbia and Santarcangelo, but by the end of the year the open country around these places had been almost entirely subjected, and Mondavio, Montefiore, Verucchio and Santarcangelo all taken. Montevecchio, where the ruling counts adhered to the Malatesta, had been reduced, and Carlo Malatesta of Sogliano decisively won over to the church.[4] In October Astorre Manfredi entered papal

---

[1] Anon. Veron., 153–4; Cobelli, 241; *Pii II Epist.* (1473), n. xxx; Baldi, ii.195; Amiani, i.430; Battaglini, *Vita*, 647; Tonini, v/2.225–6; Bernardy, 'Archivio', nn. 496, 503, 505; Nunziante, 'Primi anni' 1897, 212; 1898, 145–6; Soranzo, *Pio II*, 292–3.

[2] 13 August 1462: Anon. Veron., 154; Simonetta, 460–1; Guerriero, 75; Branchi, 177; *Chron. Bon.*, iv.295–8; Palmieri, 181; Della Tuccia, 267; Sanzio, CIII–IX; Pedrino, rub. 1891–2, 1904; *Pii II Commentarii*, 258–9; Cagnola, 159; Bernardy, 'Archivio', n. 508; Soranzo, *Pio II*, 296–303; Fumi, 'Attegiamento', 174.

[3] Sforza evidently thought the victory sufficient and wrote (23 Aug.) to Pius stressing the importance of Naples, but also explaining again that he had no personal aversion to punishing Sigismondo, and repeating the story of Polissena's murder: Fumi, 161; *Pii II Commentarii*, 260–1.

[4] Simonetta, 462; Guerriero, 75–6; Anon. Veron., 160–1; Geraldini, 497; Pedrino, rub. 1899–1902; *Pii II Commentarii*, 261–2, 265–6; Baldi, *Federigo*, iii.10–23; *Cron. Castel delle Ripe*, 25–6; Bernardy, nn. 510, 513–14, 516, 518–19, 520–7; Soranzo, *Pio II*, 303–6, 311–12, 318–20, 336–8, 487–8.

service and attacked the lands of Malatesta Novello.[1] S. Marino the pope had already enlisted on his side,[2] and early in December he purchased the support of Antonello da Forlì with the grant in vicariate of S. Marco and other places confiscated from Sigismondo.[3] By a bull of 24 September Pius empowered the cardinal-legate to absolve from interdict any subjects of the Malatesta submitting to the church.[4] But the device was not of great effect. Though the towns which surrendered received generous privileges from the pope,[5] they acted more from fear of pillage than love of the church. During the winter, when effective control was withdrawn, many of them rebelled and returned to the rule of Sigismondo, re-electing him lord.[6]

Meanwhile Sigismondo himself had been unable to do much to encourage such exhibition of loyalty. When he arrived in the Regno early in August he came, in Simonetta's words, as 'victus a victis petiturus' – six days after Sinigaglia Piccinino had been defeated at Troia and the Angevin cause overthrown.[7] At the end of the month a meeting occurred at Trani between Sigismondo, Piccinino and Jean d'Anjou which ended in tears and despair. The prince of Taranto refused any help, and on 21 September made a separate peace with Ferrante.[8] Sigismondo's case was now desperate. To Cosimo de' Medici it appeared at this time 'che sit actum de rebus Andegavensium

---

[1] Pedrino, rub. 1905–6; Geraldini, 495–7; *Chron. Bon.*, iv. 304–5; *Pii II Commentarii*, 265; Mittarelli, *Accessiones*, 343; Rubeus, 642; Soranzo, *Pio II*. 311–12, 326–7. The Ordelaffi stood by the Malatesta but Sforza sent help to Federigo and got Ferrante to pardon the debt of Astorre Manfredi: Pedrino, rub. 1914; *Pii II Epist.* (1473), nn. xxxv, xxxvii; Soranzo, 311–13, 328, 491.

[2] 21 Sept. 1462; with a promise of Malatesta land: Delfico, ii, pp. xciv-viii; Tonini, v/2.227–9; Mazzatinti, *Inventari*, xxxvii.30, 35; Bernardy, 'Archivio', nn. 445, 470, 487, 492, 497; *ASI* 1900, pt. 2, 139; Soranzo, *Pio II*, 296, 315–16. Territorial gains were also promised Federigo.

[3] Fantuzzi, iv.465–8; Mazzatinti, *Archivi*, Ser. 1, i.335.

[4] *Ibid.*; Castellani, *Malatesta*, 41; Soranzo, *Pio II*, 317.

[5] For example, Montefiore: Vitali, 326–7, 351–2, 354–6; Soranzo, *Pio II*, 319–20.

[6] For example, Longiano, and a number of castles in the *contado* of Fano (Dec. 1462); Anon. Veron., 162; Vitali, 356–9; *Pii II Commentarii*, 298; Soranzo, *Pio II*, 338–363. About the same time, however, Malatesta Novello had to dispossess the conte Cocco Malatesta who, like the count of Cusercoli and Valdoppio, had gone over to the church: Pedrino, rub. 1912. Soranzo, *Pio II*, 326–7. And in October, a plot was detected in Rimini by papalist sympathisers: *ibid.* 320.

[7] *RIS*² xxi/i.457.

[8] Sforza was again planning Piccinino's death, as the only cure to an insoluble problem: Simonetta, 462; *Chron. Bon.*, 304–5; Anon. Veron., 156; Broglio, in Tonini, v.291–4; Pedrino, rub. 1893, 1897, 1903; Raynaldus, 1462, n. x; Nunziante, 'Primi anni' 1897, 230–5; Soranzo, *Pio II*, 307–9. Louis XI's envoys pressed for Sigismondo's inclusion, but Pius would hear nothing of it: *Epist.* (1473), nn. xxxv, xxxvii.

in Italia, et che etiam al Magco Sig. Sigismondo dolgha la testa'.[1] An approach to Florence came to nothing,[2] and a second attempt to appease Federigo d'Urbino with an offer of marriage alliance, in any case unlikely to succeed, was checked by the pope.[3] Late in September Sigismondo set out from Trani, and then from Manfredonia by ship for Venice. A storm blew him out of his course and drove him onto the Dalmatian coast, delaying his arrival in Venice until the end of October There he was coldly and cautiously received, and with the impression of having failed again he returned after a few days by way of Ravenna to Rimini.[4]

This time, however, as soon became clear, the failure was only apparent. If help was to come from anywhere, it could only come from the Venetians who, alert to the danger of papal reconquest and the opportunities of Malatesta weakness, decided in the autumn of 1462 to send an embassy to Pius II and try to compel him to peace. Hitherto they had preferred an attitude of vigilant neutrality, in both Romagna and Naples, although a year before, in return for a loan, Sigismondo had pledged them the town of Montemarciano, where a *provveditore* was instantly installed,[5] and earlier still Sforza expressed a fear the Malatesta would assign them at least the protectorate of their territories.[6] Sigismondo had a permanent envoy in Venice, and even before his visit the republic began to show him favour.[7] As a result of the Venetian decision to interfere, the war between Pius II and the Malatesta immediately changed in character. What had been mainly a local conflict, confined to the Papal States, became a concern of the most powerful and dreaded state in Italy.

Two weeks before Sigismondo set foot in Venice the senate had formally voted for intervention.[8] The proposal was to press for peace, in the interest of Italy and of war against the Turk. Fear that the Venetians and not the papacy would replace the Malatesta in Romagna decided Sforza to join his voice with theirs;[9] and on 28 October, when Bernardo Giustinian was receiving his instructions as ambassador to

[1] *Dépêches des ambassadeurs milanais*, i.386.
[2] Possibly owing to papal intervention: Soranzo, *Pio II*, 310–11.
[3] *Pii II Epist.* (1473), n. xxxvii; Dennistoun, i.138–9; Pastor, *Acta*, n. 134; Soranzo, *Pio II*, 316–17.
[4] Anon. Veron., 161; Palmieri, 181; Guerriero, 76; Pedrino, rub. 1909–11; *Pii II Commentarii*, 266; Soranzo, *Pio II*, 334–5.
[5] Raynaldus, 1461, n. x; G. Baldassini, 165, App. LXII; Pastor, *Päpste*, ii.95; Soranzo, *Pio II*, 264; Battaglini, *Vita*, 644–5; Tonini, v/2.220–1.
[6] Early summer 1461: Soranzo, *Pio II*, 246–7.
[7] Pius II, *Epist.* (1473), n. xxxviii; *Commentarii*, 268–9; Soranzo, *Pio II*, 309–10.
[8] 12 Oct. 1462: Soranzo, *Pio II*, 321–2, 489 (which reveals that the saltworks of Cervia were already being mentioned).
[9] Soranzo, *Pio II*, 322–6, 488–91. Florence was less responsive: *ibid.* 327.

Rome,[1] Pius was having already to complain of Venetian interference and reassert his resolve to wipe out the Malatesta.[2] Ten days later Giustinian arrived for audience with the pope, and a debate ensued which is reproduced in Pius' *Commentaries* with a verve and violence quite unsupported by the record of despatches. It was the Venetian envoy's argument that Sigismondo and his brother had already been sufficiently punished, and he invited the Vicar of Christ to show suitable mercy, alluding on the one hand to the loyal tradition of the Malatesta family, of which, he said, Sigismondo was no worthy member, and emphasising on the other the need for immediate action against the infidel. The pope's answer, as related by himself, is a fabrication. He did not, it appears, justify his severity by indelicate reference to Venetian example at home, in Istria, and elsewhere, but rather offered Venice compensation, though remaining firm in his policy.[3] On the way from Venice, Giustinian had secured promises that Milanese and Florentine ambassadors should follow him to Rome. Now, with the representatives of France, they also pleaded for peace, stimulated by Venetian military preparations in Ravenna. Sforza even undertook to protect the Malatesta, if Pius refused them pardon, wrote further letters to the pope, Federigo d'Urbino, Sigismondo and Malatesta Novello, and withdrew what troops he had fighting in the March.[4]

Before the end of November the joint efforts of the Italian ambassadors had succeeded in getting the pope to promise a conditional truce for Malatesta Novello who, Pius allowed, was a less shameful offender than his brother. But to Sigismondo he would concede nothing. The mere mention of his name was still enough to enrage him, and this personal resentment was now wedded also to self-interest, by a plan to install his nephew in Sigismondo's lands.[5] In the event the negotiation miscarried. Though both brothers sent envoys to Rome, neither was

---

[1] Anon. Veron., 162; Soranzo, *Pio II*, 323, 492–5; *Pii II Commentarii*, 268–9. At the same time Venice avoided direct help to the Malatesta: Pastor, *Acta*, n. 136; Soranzo, *Pio II*, 490, 495–6.

[2] *Epist.* (1473), n. xxxviii; Anon. Veron., 157–9; Pastor, *Acta*, n. 138, cf. 137; Soranzo, *Pio II*, 332–4.

[3] *Pii II Commentarii*, 266–9; *Opera ined.*, 540–1; Soranzo, *Pio II*, 345–8; Pastor, *Päpste*, ii. 100.

[4] Anon. Veron., 162, 164–9; *Pii II Commentarii*, 271; Soranzo, *Pio II*, 339–45, 348–52, 362–3.

[5] Anon. Veron., 163; *Pii II Commentarii*, 298–9; Soranzo, 353–63, 364–6. In Jan. his ambassador wrote to Sforza: 'E volgare comune opinione che il papa abbia intrapresa questa guerra per ambitione de novo stato et non per rasone nè per il demeriti del Sig. Sigismondo': *ibid.* 339, 368; Cf. Picotti, 'Sopra alcuni frammenti inediti dei Commentarii di Pio II', *Misc. in onore di G. Sforza* (Lucca, 1920), 103; Filelfo, *Epist. fam.*, lib. xxiii, p. 157t. The Venetians for a time seem to have favoured separating Malatesta Novello and Sigismondo, because, it was said, they had hoped Sigismondo would surrender them his state if reduced to despair.

yet prepared, in the early spring of 1463, to accept terms which within only a few months they were glad to accept without protest. On Good Friday both were again excommunicated.[1]

Venice now began to abandon all reserve in support for the Malatesta,[2] encouraged by their total helplessness. While Sigismondo offered them his state to dispose of in any future peace,[3] Malatesta Novello at the end of April brought to completion a long-suspected secret treaty selling the Venetians Cervia, which they had coveted for more than a century for its profitable saltworks and monopoly.[4] This only maddened the pope still more. He declared the sale null and void, and refused to hear of any agreement with either of the Malatesta.[5]

Since the last days of April the papal campaign against Sigismondo had been resumed in the March, with the support of many local powers. If Siena refused the invitation to avenge its grievances of 1454,[6] Fermo, Iesi, the Manfredi and the Ordelaffi all joined in.[7] Privileges were granted Santarcangelo to ensure its loyalty, and the earlier promises to S. Marino were renewed and reinforced.[8] Avoiding Rimini, which was strongly protected by its defences and an outbreak of plague, Federigo and the legate concentrated their attack on Macerata Feltria, Certaldo and Sasso, and, after taking them, on the castles in the *contado* of Fano which had returned to the Malatesta during the winter.[9] Neither Sigismondo nor Malatesta Novello was in a position to offer serious opposition. Each placed all his hope in intercession by the greater states. Venice in particular grew increasingly urgent for peace as the Turkish threat sharpened in the Balkans. The duke of Milan supported her, and both together pressed the Malatesta to face facts and submit. Their advice finally prevailed. Towards the end of June Sigismondo offered to give up Fano and his other possessions in the March of

[1] Soranzo, *Pio II*, 366–74, 376–9, 383–4.
[2] Refusing to publish the new excommunication, and preparing naval and military forces: *ibid.* 382–5. Sforza, anxious not to offend Venice, seconded her peace offensive but at the same time was reluctant to lose any possible gains in Romagna.
[3] *Ibid.* 380.
[4] Pedrino, rub. 1927; Anon. Veron., 176; Guerriero, 76; *Chron. Bon.*, iv.310–11; *Ann. Forl.*, 98; *Pii II Commentarii*, 299; Battaglini, *Vita*, 648–9; Franchini, 'Annullabilità'; Soranza, 'Cervia', 201–19; *Pio II*, 372, 376–7, 326–8.
[5] *Pii II Commentarii*, 299; Soranzo, 'Cervia'; *Pio II*, 389–91, 497–9.
[6] Soranzo, *Pio II*, 442.
[7] *Pii II Commentarii*, 318–19; Mittarelli, *Accessiones*, 337; Pedrino, rub. 1929; *Cron. Ferm.*, 183, 209; Bernabei, 182; Marchesi, 481. Cf. Battaglini, *Vita*, 647–8; Tonini, v/2.230.
[8] Marini, *Santo Arcangelo*, 62; Castellani, *Malatesta*, 41; Theiner, iii.373; Delfico, ii, pp. xcix–cii; Battaglini, *Vita*, 649–51; Tonini, v/2.230–1, 234–7; Mazzatinti, *Archivi*, Ser. 1., i.335.
[9] Guerriero, 76; Pedrino, rub. 1925; Bernardy, 'Archivio', nn. 572, 580, 582–9; Sanzio, ix, ch. xxxviff; Baldi, *Federigo*, iii.24–5; *Cron. Castel delle Ripe*, 26–7; Vitali, 329–30; Soranzo, *Pio II*, 407.

Ancona, in return for his former holdings in Romagna and a release from all arrears of *census*. Even this, however, Pius II, unmoved by further news of Ottoman advances, was reluctant to accept; and Sigismondo now resigned himself to a fight to the death.[1] It was otherwise with Malatesta Novello. Convinced that continued resistance could only result in total destruction, he surrendered his case without reserve to the Venetians and the pope, and an agreement was quickly reached, even over Cervia. Terms of peace were finally arranged at Tivoli on 26 August.[2] Malatesta then retired from the war, and Sigismondo was left alone.

Without defence or money to purchase defence, Sigismondo could do nothing but watch the steady disintegration of his state. On 25 September, despite the presence of Roberto Malatesta as Sigismondo's lieutenant, the citizens of Fano, who had loyally withstood a siege, capitulated to the papal army under Federigo d'Urbino, and within a few weeks Mondolfo, S. Costanzo, le Caminate, Sinigaglia, Gradara and S. Giovanni in Marignano had all fallen. Only Rimini with a small circle of territory remained to Sigismondo.[3] He continued to issue repeated appeals – to Sforza, to Florence, to Borso d'Este,[4] but the only active help he received came from Jean d'Anjou, Piccinino and Venice. It was the Venetians in the end who saved him from the final ignominy of dispossession and exile.[5] During the summer cardinal Bessarion was in Venice pressing for war on the Turks, but the Venetians made it

[1] *Ibid.* 391, 500.

[2] Ratified by Malatesta Novello on 8 Nov., the main terms were: that Malatesta acknowledge his errors and sue for pardon, accept as friends and enemies the friends and enemies of the church, especially Sigismondo, pay within fourteen months 4,600 gold florins' *census*, and finally allow the vicariate to revert in the event of his death without legitimate male issue (a condition known to be certain): Soranzo, *Pio II*, 403–4; Anon. Veron., 177; Geraldini, 499; Zazzeri, 343.

[3] Anon. Veron., 175, 177, 185, 186, 188–90; Bernabei, 182–3; Pedrino, rub. 1932–3; Simonetta, 466–7; *Ann. Forl.*, 98; *Chron. Bon.*, iv.316–17; Guerriero, 77; *Pii II Commentarii*, 318–19, 337, 342; Baldi, *Federigo*, iii.25–50; Amiani, i.435; Giordani, *A. Sforza*, lxxi; Battaglini, *Vita*, 523–7; Tonini, v/2.236–7; Vitali, 330; Bernardy, 'Archivio', nn. 590, 592–601; Pastor, *Acta*, nn. 145, 149; *Päpste*, ii.101, Anh. 58; P. A. Paltroni, *Assedio de Fano* (ed. Castellani, Fano, 1896); Soranzo, *Pio II*, 408–11, 414–15, 417–33, 500–6, 510. The papal army was now supported by Pesaro, Ancona, Antonello da Forlì, Astorre Manfredi, Cecco Ordelaffi, Carlo Malatesta of Sogliano, Cocco Malatesta and Gianfrancesco di Bagno. On 5 Oct. the Milanese envoys in France wrote applauding the good news from Italy, particularly the defeat of Sigismondo, 'quel perfido tyranno, inimico de Dio et de la pace d'Italia': *Dépêches des ambassadeurs milanais*, i.314, 316.

[4] Soranzo, *Pio II*, 414, 418, 499–500, 501–3; Battaglini, *Vita*, 651–2: Tonini, v/2.238–9. A plan of Sigismondo's in July and Aug. to marry his daughter by Isotta, Alessandra, to a nephew of the pope produced nothing: Battaglini, *Vita*, Tonini, v/2.237; Soranzo, *Pio II*, 502.

[5] He rejected a Venetian offer to purchase his territories: Soranzo, *ibid.* 504 – 'Sigismondo Malatesta in Morea', 244.

clear that first there must be peace in Italy, the pope setting an example
befitting his office.[1] Once again the Italian powers combined in appeal
to Pius. Finally the Venetians obtained a promise that Rimini should
remain unmolested. And it was as the effect of a simple bargain between
Venice and the pope that Sigismondo at last received pardon. Venice
abandoned the siege of Trieste, Pius the war in Romagna, and both
prepared to fight the Turk.[2]

Up to then, both before and after the siege of Fano, Sigismondo
himself, desperate though he was, had been able to make no progress
toward an agreement, neither by embassy to Rome, nor locally with the
legate.[3] Early in October, yielding to the unanimous advice of Venice,
Sforza and Borso d'Este, he again sent to the cardinal of Teano,
entreating pardon and peace. The legate accepted, and in Rome the
pope announced his terms. All but Rimini and a small banlieu was to
be renounced, and these Sigismondo was to keep for his lifetime only
for a *census* of 1,000 florins. In addition he was to sue for pardon,
acknowledge together with his subjects his heretical conduct, and
receive formal absolution. Only then would peace be valid. These
conditions were accepted by Sigismondo's envoy in Rome, and by the
end of November had been fully carried out. The confiscated lands
were in the hands of the pope, and following a three days' fast Sigismondo and the population of Rimini had confessed to their sins and
been absolved. On 2 December the cardinal of Teano was able to lay
down the new boundaries, and release to Sigismondo a Rimini stripped
of territories it had ruled since the age of the commune.[4]

Only one task remained: to distribute the spoils among the victors.
As the progress of the war had worsened for the Malatesta, so the
number and spirit of their enemies had grown. Some had already
received their reward, like Antonello da Forlì, who now got Talamello
and certain other places as well, but most had to wait for peace. The
main beneficiaries were the pope's nephew, Antonio Piccolomini, and

[1] Pastor, *Päpste*, ii.247, 739–41; Soranzo, *Pio II*, 415–16.
[2] October: Malipiero, 208; M. A. Sabellico, *Hist. Ven. Libri XXXIII* (Venice,
1718), 724; Baldi, *Federigo*, iii.51; Soranzo, *Pio II*, 417, 434, 508–9. Second to
Venice Borso d'Este did most to promote peace: Soranzo, *ibid.* 508.
[3] Battaglini, *Vita*, 652; Tonini, v/2.239; Soranzo, *Pio II*, 435–9, 501–6.
[4] Up to the last Pius may have hoped, by protracting negotiations in Rome, to give
papal troops time to get Rimini 'per tractatus': *Opera ined.*, 453–4. Cf. Pastor,
Acta, nn. 160, 171; Soranzo, *Pio II*, 434, 509–10; *Pii II Commentarii*, 344–5;
Chron. Bon., iv.318–19; Palmieri, 182; Anon. Veron., 196–7; Geraldini, 499–500;
Della Tuccia, 268–9; Broglio, in Tonini, v.300; Battaglini, *Corte*, 159; *Vita*,
653–4; Tonini, v/2.239–41; Soranzo, *Pio II*, 403–4, 442–9. According to the Anon.
Veron. (196) Sigismondo was also bound to repeat the *credo* once a day during the
rest of his life, fast every Friday, visit the seven churches in Rome, and then in
time the Holy Sepulchre. The clergy who had continued their ministrations during
the interdict were suspended: *Pii II Commentarii, loc. cit.*

the pope's general, Federigo d'Urbino. The first was given Sinigaglia and the vicariate of Mondavio – Fano the college of cardinals refused to allow him – the second all the castles in the Montefeltro held by Sigismondo, with many more in the former *contado* of Rimini, altogether over fifty *oppida*, among them Penna Billi, the ancestral home of the Malatesta, and S. Leo. To the conti di Bagno, Carlo Malatesta of Sogliano, and the cities of Iesi, S. Marino, Santarcangelo and Montefiore, scraps of territory and privileges were thrown – perhaps also to the Manfredi, the Ordelaffi and the conte Cocco Malatesta. Florence to her disgust received nothing. Nor did Sforza, though his brother Alessandro, disappointed in his hopes of possessing Sinigaglia and Montemarciano, was comforted with Gradara and Castel Nuovo. For the rest, the papacy inherited.[1]

The Malatesta were never to recover from the blows inflicted by Pius II. To many their humiliation was a judgement of God: 'Dio è giusto signore', remarked the Sienese envoy in Rome, 'e tutto fa bene.'[2] Others considered it needlessly severe.[3] Sigismondo himself seems to have enjoyed a new if momentary serenity. He passed his time in hunting. But he was still not without hope of restitution. Papal pontificates were often short, and papal policy mutable. Such at least may have been his thoughts when he wrote to Pier Francesco de' Medici: 'retrovo la conditione mia essere l'opposito de quello che volgarmente se sole dire che chi ha poca roba ha pochi pensieri a mi è remasto poca roba e assai pensieri'.[4]

---

[1] Battaglini, *Vita*, 654–8, 661–3; Tonini, v/2.241–7, vi/2.829ff.; Anon. Veron., 198; Geraldini, 499–500; T. Baldassini, 82; Giordani, *Gradara*, 93; Colucci, xxii.14; Siena, 150; Vitali, 360; Pastor, *Acta*, nn. 170, 176; Bernardy, 'Archivio', nn. 609, 614–19, 622; Soranzo, *Pio II*, 449–56. Ferrante waived Sigismondo's debt so that Antonio Piccolomini could enter the pledged lands without reservation. Another *nipote*, Giacopo Piccolomini, received Montemarciano.

[2] 'questo non avrebbe pensato Sigismundo quando inghanno li Sanesi': Pastor, *Acta*, n. 176. Cf. above p. 237 n. 3.

[3] Even the Urbino chronicler Ser Guerriero describes the terms as 'vituperosi a la sua [Sigismondo's] signoria': *Cronaca*, 77.

[4] 5 Dec. 1463: Rossi, 'Delitto', 382.

8

The papal reconquest

For nearly another forty years the Malatesta kept their remnant lands: a petty principality, isolated among territories which had long forgotten all government but theirs. More than this they never achieved. The limit of their recovery was reached under Sixtus IV, when the agreements of 1463, requiring all territory to revert on the death of Sigismondo and his brother, were so far relaxed as to confirm them in the tenure of Rimini. Complete or ample rehabilitation was never contemplated, or even perhaps expected. However dissimilar the personal affinities or aims of different popes, their office imposed certain principles on all of them which did not allow the work of Pius II to be carelessly undone.

This was the lesson Sigismondo had to learn in the last few years of his life. He did not at first consider his new situation to be final or beyond hope. There were still followers, 'Pandolfeschi', in the cities recently lost, particularly Fano, and with them he was secretly in touch.[1] At the same time he knew that retrieval would be won, if at all, less by violence or intrigue than by conciliation and calculated penitence. For this reason, in spite of the pope, he took service with Venice in the spring of 1464, to fight against the Turks in the Morea, a command refused by every other Italian captain, including Federigo d'Urbino.[2] The campaign which followed, lasting two years, brought neither success nor profit. The period is of interest solely in showing how humble and insecure was the place now left the Malatesta in Italy. Rimini and Cesena had lost all independent standing, and were important only as they engaged the attention or attracted the ambition of the papacy and greater powers. Sigismondo was aware of this. By the terms of his Venetian *condotta* he obtained a promise of protection for his state and family, and a garrison of 150 foot was sent to keep the peace in his absence. But already before his departure, in June 1464, he was called on to provide for the defence of Rimini: against a conspiracy of

---

[1] Geraldini, 501; Amiani, ii. 10–12; Soranzo, 'Morea', 221; Castellani, *Malatesta*, 41; Mazzatinti, *Archivi*, Ser. 1., i. 335.

[2] On the campaign in the Morea, 1464–6; Soranzo, 'Morea'; Massèra in *N. arch. ven.*, 1919.

certain exiles, headed by Giovanni Malatesta, relative of the Ramberto who had fomented revolt in 1431, and against the intrigues of the apostolic legate in Fano and the papal *nipote*, Antonio Piccolomini.[1] And when, early in the following year, it was rumoured that he had died of plague in Dalmatia, he was even granted a foresight of what might happen on his death.

Venice at once sent help to Isotta and her son Sallustio, who had been left in charge of Rimini, hoping perhaps ultimately to displace them. Inside the city itself it became clear that Isotta, who planned to make Sallustio *signore*, could count on little support. Some citizens favoured Roberto, as the eldest surviving son of Sigismondo, a good number were for returning to the church as the treaty of 1463 required, while still others inclined to a strong foreign power such as Milan or Florence. Roberto, who seems already to have been as apt at attracting favour as his father was in losing it, was at this time in the pay of Francesco Sforza. Sigismondo had wanted him to enter Venetian service, but Roberto preferred to remain with a prince who wished to see him established in Rimini; and on the report of Sigismondo's death he prepared to set out from Milan, encouraged by his uncle, Malatesta Novello, by Sforza and by the Medici. The new pope, Paul II, who before his election had been a friend and companion of the Malatesta, was equally alert, held a papal army ready to occupy Rimini, and confirmed by enquiry his right to succeed there. The Venetians finally secured the support, whether feigned or sincere, of Isotta and her followers.

To these strategic preliminaries there was to be no sequel for several years. By the beginning of February 1465 Sigismondo was known to have recovered his health, and the contest was left untried. But the curtain had been momentarily lifted on a question of unsuspected complexity.[2] Isotta degli Atti, who wished to perpetuate her power through her son, had been made to feel her weakness. Vindictively, and in the face of protest from the pope, Malatesta Novello and others, she now imprisoned and after torture put to death one of Sigismondo's most respected counsellors, Giacomo dal Borgo, who had injudiciously opposed the Venetians and planned to give the city to Roberto.[3] But more important was the outburst of general interest in the question of

---

[1] Battaglini, *Vita*, 533–5, 664–6; Soranzo, *Pio II*, 457–60, 510–11; 'Morea', 219, 223–5; Massèra, *loc. cit.* Pius was pondering the final expulsion of Sigismondo from Rimini: Tonini, v.302; Soranzo, 'Morea', 225. It was in this atmosphere of disloyalty that Sigismondo left, taking with him about 40 young men of the leading families of Rimini, ostensibly in his service, in reality as hostages: Soranzo, 'Morea', 227, 277–8.

[2] Malipiero, 209–10; Soranzo, 'Morea', 236–48; *Pio II*, 460.

[3] Zippel in *RIS*[2] iii/16.166; Soranzo, 'Morea', 243–7; Massèra, *N. arch. ven.*, 1919, 232–3.

the Riminese succession. Alarmed by the threat from Venice and Roberto Malatesta, Sigismondo began to agitate for release from service in the Morea. For months the Venetians detained him with reassuring words, as if anxious to prolong his absence; and only when events in Romagna gave them cause to welcome his return was licence granted (25 November 1465). In April 1466 he was back in Rimini.[1]

The events in Romagna again concerned the succession to part of the Malatesta state: to Cesena and Bertinoro. In November 1465, after several months illness, Malatesta Novello died at Bellaria. His vicariate should now have escheated to the papacy. Already in July, when his death was expected, Paul II had alerted Federigo d'Urbino, papal commander, to prepare to occupy Cesena. Sigismondo was anxious to keep the city for the Malatesta who, he said, had held it for over three hundred years. At the same time he had no wish to see it pass to Roberto, whom Malatesta Novello seems secretly to have appointed his successor. As a client of Milan Roberto was equally suspect to the Venetians; and the threat of his accession in Cesena explains their final readiness to grant Sigismondo's discharge. In August Roberto was summoned from Milan by Malatesta Novello, and he was still in Cesena at his uncle's death. At once he had himself proclaimed lord. But most of the Cesenati seem to have favoured returning to the church, though some, including the *podestà*, offered the city to Venice. Roberto, after a fruitless appeal to the pope, Florence, Venice and Milan, allowed them to surrender the government to the papal representative (9 December 1465). Partly in compensation but more in defence against Venice, Paul now took him into papal service, and granted him, in hereditary vicariate, Sarsina, Meldola, Polenta and certain other small lordships of the Malatesta inheritance, while Cesena and Bertinoro were reserved to the church and invested with substantial privileges. More than anything the pope was concerned to check Venetian influence. In February he warned the republic to mind its own affairs and take its eyes off Rimini, which was to fall to the church 'pleno iure'.[2]

By this Paul declared his resolve to implement, when the time came, in Rimini as in Cesena, the full terms of 1463. The most serious resistance, furtive and oblique, he may have expected to come from

[1] Bringing the remains of Gemistos Plethon: Anon. Veron., 228, 230; Clementini, ii.456–8; Battaglini, *Vita*, 540; Soranzo, 'Morea', 250–5, 259–69; Massèra, *N. arch. ven.*, 1919, 233.

[2] Theiner, iii.383, 385, 413; *Stat. Caes.* (1589), 369–71; *Chron. Bon.*, iv.347–8; Guerriero, 81; *Vite Paolo II*, 132; Iac. Piccolomini, in *Pii II Commentarii*, 378; Baldi, iii.76–87; Chiaramonti, 424; Battaglini, *Vita*, 539, 688; Tonini, v.306–8; Zazzeri, 360–71; Ugolini, i.466; Soranzo, 'Morea', 271–7; Mazzatinti, *Inventari*, xxxix.80, 130. Certain possessions and revenues were left to Violante, who in April 1466 finally surrendered her rights in the Montefeltro.

Venice. But he had also first to convince Sigismondo Malatesta that the terms were absolute. While still in the Morea Sigismondo had sent his son Valerio on a fruitless mission to Rome to obtain restitution of his former lands. On his return he seems sincerely to have hoped for some concessions from the papacy, if only in recognition of his service against the Turk.[1] How mistaken he was he soon learned after arrival in Rome in April. Paul II had already expressed irritation at Venetian pressure on behalf of Isotta. Later he showed dismay at the joyful reception given Sigismondo on returning to Rimini, a reception echoed in various places subject now to the church. If he granted Sigismondo a friendly welcome, it was less, therefore, to meet his requests than to detach him from Venice. His private plan was to obtain Rimini with the adjacent territories, against 'un contracambio equivalente e mazore', such as Cesena, together with Cervia, if the Venetians could be induced to surrender it. No gift could be expected from a pope who, according to reports of the time, was bent on depriving all the lords of Romagna.[2] His election *capitula*, he said, forbade him to alienate church property. These had been drawn up by the college of cardinals, and however compliant the pope, the *curia* would have opposed all concession to Sigismondo. A commission of cardinals was appointed to negotiate with him, but they refused to compromise. Many suspected the intention was to beguile Sigismondo in Rome, while papal troops sent to Romagna against Bartolommeo Colleone occupied his and other lands; and Sigismondo circulated a warning to the lords of Imola, Forlì and Faenza. By the end of June he had lost all patience and withdrew, having obtained nothing but fair promises, not even 'una terra o rocha nel destretto de Arimino, da Potere qualche fiata andare a piacere', nor 'in governo a nome de la Chiesa quisti tri lochi solamente, videlicet, Mondavio, Sanlodecio, Montescudelo, per potere avere qualche reductor per sè et per la famiglia sua, accadendo qualche turbatione de peste in Arimino'.[3] On 16 July, Paul appointed a

[1] Soranzo, 'Morea', 256–8, 268–9. Cf. the poem written in 1467 when the sarcophagus of S. Constantius was brought to the Piazza S. Marco in Rome: after a panegyric of Sigismondo, 'Latii decus', 'Aemiliae regionis honor' etc., come the lines:

'Restituet meritis Pauli clementia regnum
Quod furor arripuit non tibi iure Pii.'

E. Müntz, in *Mélanges G. B. de Rossi* (Paris, 1892), 138–43.

[2] 'La Santità de Nostro Signore, havendo facto esaminare le investiture che pretendono havere questi Signori de Romagna, trova che in vero niuno de lor gli ha ragione alcuna e per questo da qui inanti ha deliberato de non acceptare da lor censo, ne videatur approbare e col tempo ha animo de tirarse ugni cosa sotto. Nondimeno queste cose sono fra puoche persone et tengonose molto secrete qui': cardinal Francesco Gonzaga to his father, June 1466: Soranzo, 'Morea', 241.

[3] Anon. Veron., 234; Broglio, in Tonini, v. 308–10; Clementini, ii. 459–60; Battaglini, *Vita*, 541–2; Fossati, *Viglevanum*, v, 1911.

governor to the vicariate of Mondavio, the *contado* of Rimini, and Santarcangelo.[1]

Sigismondo's departure may have alarmed the pope and cardinals, and they determined to send troops into the neighbourhood of Rimini. But Paul also thought it wise to try and soothe his feelings by offering a pension; and on 10 July 1,500 ducats were placed to his credit by the Apostolic Camera.[2] Sigismondo had also promised to return to Rome in the autumn for further talks. He kept his word, and according to Broglio it was during his second visit that he learned, through Giulio Varano, of the projected exchange of territories. His reaction, described at length by the Riminese chronicler, was violent approaching to frenzy. It was now, if the story is true, that he went to the pope in the first fury of outrage, with a weapon concealed to kill him; but Paul, 'comprendendole così furibondo', became suspicious and refused an audience. On the following day he granted an interview in the presence of seven cardinals, and denied any scheme of exchange. He may have learned that Sigismondo, with other lords of Romagna, was in correspondence with the Venetian *condottiere* Colleone; and to isolate him from Venice the pope now took him into his pay.[3]

With this conclusion Sigismondo had to rest satisfied. He made no attempt to reopen negotiation, nor to reverse the defeat by force. But he had at least averted the threat of dispossession. He remained till his death in the papal service; and as late as June 1468, when his *condotta* was further extended, the pope assured him control of Rimini, and assumed a share in the cost of its defences.[4] In other minor ways, too, Paul showed him favour.[5] It was in a house provided by the pope that

[1] *Mem. Santarcangelo*, 19–20.
[2] Fossati, *Viglevanum*, v, 1911; *Vite Paolo II*, 47; Platina, 384.
[3] 'Or considerate voi leggitori che animo fo in quell'ora del Signor mis. Sigismondo! . . . rimase con grave affano e strania disposizione li entrò nella sua mente: et in quel dì non volle più mangiare e manco bere. Pervenuta la tenebrosa nocte, e mai nelli suoi occhi li entrò sonno, volgendo e rivolgendo sopra tale proposta ricevuta dal Papa. Et in tucto fermò la sua opinione di fare vendetta sopra la prava volontà de Papa Paulo. E soprastando nel suo lecto sopra li aspri suoi pensieri vacillando per che modo podesse dare morte al Papa infra se medesimo disanimava, che gionto chel fosse dinanzi alli suoi piedi, avendo da lui audienza, senza alcuna tardazione andarli adosso col suo pugnale bene in ordine a tel mestieri, e metterlo a fine.' This the honour of the house descended from the Scipios demanded, and the perfidious treatment he had suffered from the popes. 'Siate certi, Signori ligitori, che lo sfortunato Signore rugiva e fremiva colla sua mente come el lion selvagio, che ha gran brame di cibare': Broglio, in Tonini, v.310ff. The chronology of Sigismondo's interviews with Paul II is not securely established: *Vite Paolo II*, 47; Platina, 384; Clementini, ii.461, 489; Battaglini, *Vita*, 542–9; Tonini, v.310–18.
[4] Battaglini, *Vita*, 668–70. For cameral payments to Sigismondo, Jan. 1467, Jan. 1468, June 1468: *Vite Paolo II*, 47 and Platina, 384.
[5] He presented him with the golden rose, and when Sigismondo lay ill in Rimini during Sept. 1467 sent him his own doctor, Niccolo da Rimini: *Vite Paolo II*, 47.

Sigismondo passed his frequent visits to Rome. All of which makes
implausible the rumour that he was an accomplice of Pomponius
Laetus.[1] In fact it was while he was engaged in a papal campaign,
against Norcia in the spring of 1468, that he contracted the illness
which caused his death. He died at Rimini on 9 October, at the age of
fifty-one, leaving all his schemes of redemption frustrated and unful-
filled, like the church of S. Francesco, majestically conceived but never
completed, which he continued to plan and hope for to the end.[2]

Just as he provided in his will for work to proceed on the Tempio, so
doubtless Sigismondo expected that efforts to perpetuate the Malatesta
state would also survive his death. According to Clementini, he left
behind him thirteen children, most of them illegitimate.[3] But the contest
for power in Rimini was to lie between only two of them, Roberto
Malatesta and Sallustio, a prince whose character and inclinations the
dominant influence of his mother Isotta never allows to appear distinctly
in the narratives of the time.[4] Roberto, as seen, was already popular in
Italy, though Pius II described him as 'a child worthy of his father'.[5] But
Sigismondo seems never to have considered him as a successor, less from
any personal dislike[6] than from reluctance to offend Isotta. It was Isotta
and her son he appointed his heirs.[7] And it was Isotta, with the support
of a strong Venetian garrison, who tried to secure Rimini on his death.[8]

Roberto at this time was in the neighbourhood of Rome,[9] and while
there, according to Iacopo Piccolomini, received a letter from Isotta
inviting him to come and share the *signoria*.[10] Attracted by the proposal

---

[1] Pastor, *Päpste*, ii.329. Platina was questioned concerning conversations he had
recently had with Sigismondo in Rome, and replied: 'De litteris . . . de armis, de
praestantibus ingeniis tum veterum tum nostrorum hominum' (384).

[2] *Vite Paolo II*, 151; Broglio, in Tonini, v.320; Anon. Veron., 256; Clementini,
ii.468–9, 476; Battaglini, *Vita*, 549, 555–6, 672; Tonini, v.320–1, v/2.248;
Grigioni, 'Costruttori', 197–8.

[3] Clementini, ii.476; A. Battaglini, *Corte*, 12; F. G. Battaglini, *Vita*, 555–6. Two of
his sons, Galeotto and Pandolfo, married daughters of Rodolfo Varano: Lilii,
ii.212; Zampetti, 28.

[4] Lillii (ii.215–16) says Giulio Varano also, as husband of Giovanna Malatesta, had
designs on Rimini; he was certainly attracted into the war against Roberto in the
following year by the hope of securing part of the allodial lands of the Malatesta:
cf. Zampetti, 31–2.

[5] *Commentaries* (tr. Gragg), 364.

[6] Though he had been angered by the surrender of Fano in 1463, and Roberto had
retired not to Rimini but to Ravenna, since when he had gone very much his own way.

[7] Clementini, ii.458, 469; Battaglini, *Vita*, 540–1, 670–3; Tonini, v/2.247–51.

[8] Clementini, ii.489; *Vite Paolo II*, 166. A Venetian garrison seems to have been in
Rimini fairly continuously during the last years of Sigismondo's life.

[9] *Vite Paolo II*, 166.

[10] All other accounts state simply that Paul summoned Roberto to him, when he
learned of Isotta's actions in Rimini.

but unwilling to affront the pope, he went to Paul, showed him the letter, and offered instead to take possession of Rimini for the church. The pope agreed and, in return for a formal renunciation of all claims to Rimini, promised Roberto investiture with Sinigaglia and Mondavio.[1] That Roberto's ambitions did not rest here, however, was quickly proved, for that same night he sent an envoy to Ferrante of Naples, then on no friendly terms with Rome, seeking a *condotta* and revealing an intention to reoccupy the entire heritage of Sigismondo and Domenico Malatesta. Meanwhile, in Rimini itself a number of disaffected notables, among them Matteo Belmonti, Matteo Lazzarini, Pietro Genari and Raimondo Malatesta, all once devoted servants of Sigismondo, had come together in a conspiracy in favour of Roberto, and with their connivance he entered Rimini on 20 October. Isotta, it is said, dissimulated her displeasure, and for a brief period she, Sallustio and Roberto Malatesta governed the city together. But the accord did not last. Isotta soon withdrew from the Castel Sigismondo, the Venetian garrison was dismissed, and undivided power passed to Roberto.[2]

By then the envoy in Naples had arranged a *condotta* with the king and obtained a pledge to defend Rimini during the next two years. Roberto sent frequent despatches to the pope to allay suspicion, promising but always postponing the surrender of Rimini, until Paul discovered his secret compact with Ferrante and publicly denounced his treachery.[3] An open conflict became inevitable. For greater security Roberto appealed to the two allies of Naples, Florence and Milan, and through the intercession of Federigo d'Urbino, who had begun to fear for his own dominions,[4] he was received during April into the league. Besides these formal allies Roberto could look for support to the discontented subjects of Fano and Cesena, where the *contadini* were becoming impatient of the oligarchical restoration which had accompanied the return of papal government; and it was the suppression of a peasant disturbance by the legate in Cesena which marked the beginning of the war. Paul had already taken into his pay Napoleone Orsini and Alessandro Sforza, and at the end of May he concluded an alliance with Venice. A week later Rimini was besieged. The allied powers all pro-

---

[1] Antonio Piccolomini had lost Sinigaglia in 1464.
[2] Anon. Veron., 260; Iac. Piccolomini, *Pii II Commentarii*, 404–5; *Vite Paolo II*, 167; Clementini, ii.491–2; Battaglini, *Zecca*, 271; Tonini, v.325–9, v/2.251–2; Mazzuchelli, 38.
[3] Iac. Piccolomini, *loc. cit.*; Raynaldus, 1468, n. xxxi.
[4] Baldi, *Federigo*, iii.154–5; Franceschini, *Montefeltro*, 505. Another local lord who regarded papal policy with suspicion and favoured Roberto was Giovanni Bentivoglio: Fabronius, *Laurentii Medicis vita*, ii.46–7; Ady, 65; while Iac. Piccolomini states that all the 'minores vicarii' in the papal army saw their own fate involved in Roberto's: *Pii II Commentarii*, 417.

tested, and even Venice was suspicious of the pope's design on Rimini, but Ferrante alone sent effective help. Paul issued copies of Roberto's written renunciation of Rimini, and while the lord of Urbino sent irritated demands for troops to the members of the league, Roberto beguiled the papal captains with insincere negotiations until Federigo was able to come up to relieve him. When on 30 August Federigo and he soundly defeated the papal army near Cerasolo, it was less the result of allied support than of their own military efficiency.[1]

By this victory Roberto was not merely established firmly in Rimini, but encouraged to pass from defence to attack, and during September he was able to occupy the *contado* of Rimini, the district of Fano, and most of the vicariate of Mondavio. Sinigaglia also feared for its independence,[2] and only the intervention of the Venetians, who up to then had been grudging and reluctant allies of the pope, checked his advance.[3] Even so Venice desired Paul to make his peace with Roberto, while the presence of Venetian troops in Romagna caused the other Italian powers, particularly Florence and Milan, to press with greater vehemence for compromise.[4] But the pope was inflexible, and not for another year did he condescend to negotiate. Meanwhile, during the summer of 1470 the rival pretenders to power in Rimini, Sallustio and Valerio Malatesta, were quietly murdered, and Isotta thrust into unprotesting obscurity.[5] Roberto hastened to disclaim all responsibility for their death, giving each a funeral suitable to his dignity, and if he came for a time under suspicion this did nothing to diminish the esteem in which he was held outside Rimini. He was invited by the king to Naples and confirmed as an ally of the league, and in April 1471 he was festively betrothed to Isabetta, the young daughter of Federigo d'Urbino.[6] It was the king of Naples also who a few months earlier

---

[1] Iac. Piccolomini, *ibid.* 405–17; *Pii II Epist.* (1473), 685–6, 690; Branchi, 178; Palmieri, 188; Platina, 393–4; Guerriero, 86; *Chron. Bon.*, iv.385–7; *Vite Paolo II*, 167–8; Anon. Veron., 261–8; Vespasiano da Bisticci, i.278–80; Sanzio, XII, c.XLVI ff.; Baldi, *Federigo*, iii.156; Chiaramonti, 424–5; Clementini, ii.495–508; *Mem. Ripatransone*, 90; Raynaldus, 1469, n. XXVI; Fabronius, *Laurentii Medicis vita*, i.30, ii.44–5; *Cron. Castel delle Ripe*, 27; Amiani, ii.18; Tonini, v.330–41; Zannoni, 'Impresa di Rimini'; Fossati, *AMM* 1905, 423ff. In Meldola, Roberto's mother, Vannetta Toschi, put up an equally strenuous defence: Soranzo, 'Vannetta Toschi', 171–5.

[2] Iac. Piccolomini, *Pii II Commentarii*, 418–20; *Epist.* (1473), 691–9; Sanzio, XII, c. XLVI ff.; Anon. Veron., 267; Baldi, *Federigo*, iii.199; Amiani, ii.20; Zonghi, 179; Mancini, *AMM* 1926, 190–1.

[3] Anon. Veron., 261–8; *Vite Paolo II*, 167; Malipiero, 237–8; Perret, i.521. Paul even got the consistory to agree to the possible cession of Rimini to Venice.

[4] *Vite Paolo II*, 199–201; Fossati, *AMM* 1905; Nebbia, *ASL* 1939, 125–6, 130–1.

[5] Anon. Veron., 274; *Chron. Bon.*, iv.392, 396; Clementini, ii.509–11; Battaglini, *Zecca*, 272–3; Yriarte, 346–8, 450–1; Tonini, v.341–3.

[6] Guerriero, 88; Dumont, iii/1.408, 413, 415, 428–30; Baldi, *Federigo*, iii.208; Clementini, ii.519; Ugolini, i.496; Tonini, v.344–6, v/2.252–3.

obtained for Roberto a truce of forty-eight days.[1] In Rome it was at last agreed that Roberto should surrender the *contado* of Fano, retaining the city and *contado* of Rimini, but when Paul II died on 26 July 1471 these terms had still to be enforced.[2]

During the vacancy Roberto resumed his offensive in the March of Ancona, again causing alarm in Sinigaglia, and he might have imperilled his barely won peace had not Ferrante persuaded him to relinquish his conquests;[3] and in October Paul's successor, Sixtus IV, who felt none of his predecessor's antipathy to Roberto, renewed the previous agreements.[4] They were not applied for another two years, a delay ascribed by some to the urgency of other claims on the pope's attention. In August 1473 instructions were issued for the resumption by the church of the *contado* of Fano, and Roberto was invested with the vicariate of Rimini.[5]

So much, at the end of ten years, were the Malatesta allowed to salvage from the wreck of 1463.

An accomplished soldier ('in al fate del'arma pareva uno conte Rolande'),[6] with a delight in ostentation, Roberto Malatesta remained a prominent and respected figure in Italy until his death in 1482. He was a model of the *condottiere* prince, and the record of his life is consumed in the details of contracts of service, differences over pay, changes of allegiance, and war. He was first in the hire of Naples and Florence,[7] and then in 1476 entered the service of the pope.[8] But his relations were on all sides friendly;[9] and at his marriage to Isabetta da Montefeltro in 1475, which was made the occasion of costly and sumptuous display,

[1] Anon. Veron., 277; Guerriero, 87; Tonini, *loc. cit.* It was the capture of Negroponte by the Turks in July which finally persuaded Paul to peace.

[2] Baldi, *Federigo*, iii.203–7; *Vite Paolo II*, 201; Dennistoun, i.200–2; Amiani, ii.20, 23; Zonghi, 276.

[3] Anon. Veron., 286; Clementini, ii.513–14; Mancini, *AMM* 1926, 191; Mazzatinti, *Archivi*, Ser. 1., ii.219.

[4] Sanzio, XII, c. LIV; Baldi, *Federigo*, iii.207–8; Amiani, ii.23; Tonini, v/2.255; Zonghi, 180–1.

[5] Anon. Veron., 300; Clementini, ii.516; Amiani, ii, LXXXV–VI; Tonini, v.348; Zonghi, 182–3; Mazzatinti, *Archivi*, Ser. 1, i.326. In Feb. 1475 the Fanese had still to prohibit citizens from going to Rimini 'ad loquendum dno Roberto de Malatestis absque licentia dnorum priorum' (Zonghi, 256), and three years later they were fearing the return of the Malatesta (Amiani, ii.44–5; also in 1480, *ibid.* 49).

[6] Bernardi, *Cronache*, i.1.110.

[7] For details: Anon. Veron., 315–16; Clementini, ii.518; Tonini, v. 349–51.

[8] Tonini, v. 373.

[9] For his relations with Milan: Filelfo, *Prose e poesie*, *AMM* 1901, 220; cf. *ibid.* 1908, 400, 420.

ambassadors were present from every power, besides many *signori* of Romagna and the March.[1]

Roberto continued in the pay of the church until 1478, when, being sent by Sixtus against Florence after the Pazzi conspiracy, he retired aggrieved from papal service and transferred his support to the Medici. He wrote to Girolamo Riario to justify his conduct, and again on 28 February (1479) to his representative in Rome, Giovanni Antonio da Fano. His chief complaint was of failure by the papacy to remit his pay regularly, and for several months, he said, he had for that reason made plain his intention to quit: 'Io non naqui de casa che sia usa d'andare mendicando.' He spoke also of broken promises, of unfounded rumours against him at Rome, and concluded by requesting discharge, despite 12,000 ducats owing to him, 'perchè non è al mondo la più dura cosa che servire fidelmente et essere tenuto suspecto'.[2] With Costanzo Sforza he passed from papal into Florentine service, and in June heavily defeated the forces of the church under Matteo da Capua near Perugia. For this he was deprived of his vicariate and his lands were placed under interdict. Similar censures were published against other lords of the Papal States who adhered to Florence, and in November Lorenzo de' Medici and Lodovico il Moro were forming a resolution to ensure that the small *signorie* of Romagna were left undisturbed.[3]

Roberto's separation from the papacy did not last long. At the end of 1479 he entered first secretly and then publicly into the service of Venice, receiving in April the title of supreme commander and an hereditary place in the Maggior Consiglio;[4] and when, in the same month, the pope formed an alliance with the republic, it included Roberto as Venetian general.[5] Girolamo Riario, the most favoured nephew of Sixtus IV, was another signatory of the league, and during the summer of 1480 Roberto Malatesta was sent by Venice to support

---

[1] Clementini, ii.518ff.; Tonini, v. 351, v/2, 269–74. The year before Roberto's sister, Contessina, was betrothed to Cristofero da Forlì, nephew of the cardinal Stefano of Milan, and in 1481 another sister, Antonia, married Rodolfo Gonzaga, only to be put to death two years later for adultery: Schivenoglia, 190, 192; *Diario Ferrar.* 84, 131; *Arch. Gonzaga*, ii.180; Battaglini, *Vita*, 684–6; Tonini, v. 382.

[2] Bernardi, i.1.25; *Cron. Perug.*, 649; Baldi, *Federigo*, iii.249–50; Clementini, ii.541–2; Tonini, v. 376, v/2.275–83.

[3] Anon. Veron., 345, 348; Sigismondo dei Conti, *Storie*, i.63–4, 68ff.; *Diario Ferrar.*, 67; *Cron. Perug.*, 649–50; Sanzio, XII, c. LXXXI–VIII; Baldi, *Federigo*, iii.251ff.; Raynaldus, 1479, 251ff.; Fabronius, *Laurentii Medicis vita*, i.95ff., ii.198; Tonini, v. 376–9, 382; B. Buser, *Lorenzo de' Medici* (Leipzig, 1879), 147; Perret, ii.162; Mazzatinti, *Archivi*, Ser. 1, i.326.

[4] Malipiero, 248–50; Anon. Veron., 354; Sanudo, 68; Clementini, ii.542–4; Fabronius, *Laurentii Medicis vita*, ii.203; Tonini, v/2.283–4; Perret, ii.196.

[5] Sanudo, 1212. It seems Venice may have resisted a plan by the pope and Girolamo Riario to expel the Malatesta from Rimini: E. Piva, *Guerra di Ferrara del 1482* (1893), 29–30.

his attack on Forlì.[1] To the annoyance of Federigo d'Urbino Roberto also welcomed Girolamo's design in the following year to dispossess the Este of Ferrara,[2] and it was perhaps in response to family feeling as much as Venetian pressure that Sixtus absolved Roberto from ecclesiastical censure in March 1481.[3]

The war of Venice and the papacy against Ferrara opened in the spring of 1482, when Roberto Sanseverino and Roberto Malatesta were sent against Bagnacavallo. Roberto Malatesta was irritated by Sanseverino's appointment to a share in the command and does not seem to have taken much part in the campaign in Romagna.[4] But a more exacting enterprise was shortly to claim him. In support of the Este, who were related to the royal house of Naples, Alfonso, duke of Calabria, was sent into the Papal States to threaten Rome. The pope had little defence, and in distress appealed to Venice, asking for the release of Roberto. The republic agreed, and on 23 July Roberto presented himself before Sixtus to await his command. He was entrusted with fifty squadrons of horse and 12,000 foot; and under him he had many distinguished captains, Girolamo Riario and the Venetian *provveditori* among them. Setting out from Rome on 15 August, he occupied Alba on the 18th and Gandolfo and Savello on the 19th, the duke of Calabria retiring to the formidable site of Campomorto (S Pietro in Formis). There, two days later, a furious battle was fought, 'più aspre che mai fossero vedute e fatte in Italia', says Roberto in his report of it, and the Aragonese army was totally routed. News of the victory was sent in all directions, and no contemporary chronicler fails to write it up. But it was Roberto's last engagement. At the end of the month, when the pope summoned him to the defence of Forlì, he was prostrated by exhaustion and dysentery – if not, as was falsely suggested, overcome with poison administered by order of Girolamo Riario. The pope sent his own doctor, invited him to Rome and offered the apartments of the palace. To Rome he was brought, to the house of Stefano Nardini, the cardinal of Milan; and there he died on 10 September, having received the viaticum and extreme unction, it was said, from the pope himself. He was awarded a splendid funeral in St Peter's, where Sixtus caused a monument to be erected in his name, with a magniloquent epitaph to commemorate his victory.[5]

[1] Anon. Veron., 357; Sanzio, xii, c. xcii; Bernardi, i.1.47; Clementini, ii.544; Marchesi, 524; Tonini, v. 381.
[2] Sigismondo dei Conti, i.117–21; Pasolini, iii.91.
[3] Clementini, ii.545; Tonini, v. 382.
[4] Malipiero, 252, 258; Sanudo, 1214–15; Navagero, *Storia Venez.*, RIS xxiii. 1163; Clementini, ii.547; Rubeus, 647D; Messeri and Calzi, 182; Frati, *Gior. stor. lett. it.*, 1888, 333–4.
[5] Sanudo, 1221ff.; Iacopo Volterrano, 176, 178ff.; *Diario Ferrar.* 112–14; *Ann. Plac.*, 967ff.; *Diari sanesi*, 811; Navagero, RIS xxiii. 1176–7; Anon. Veron., 379–

It was remarked by some that Roberto's death came as a relief to the church, since otherwise Rimini, Fano and Sinigaglia would not have sufficed for his greed.[1] But by many in Italy it was felt as an acute loss: 'è stata jattura a tutta Italia'.[2]

Inside Rimini the situation was much as after Sigismondo's death fourteen years earlier. Roberto's children, of whom the eldest, Pandolfo, was only seven years old, were nearly all born of his mistress, Elisabetta Aldovrandini da Ravenna, who, like Isotta but with better success, was to try and make her influence dominant in Rimini;[3] while Isabetta da Montefeltro, afflicted by the death of both her husband and her father, retired to a monastery in Urbino.[4] Roberto had provided for the succession, nominating as regents with Elisabetta Galeotto and Raimondo Malatesta, descendants of Gaspare di Galeotto. And on 1 October Pandolfo 'rode the city' to take ceremonial possession of the government. From the papacy came no threat of interference; and if there had been a plan to reclaim Rimini, it was quietly withdrawn. As early as 11 September, the day after Roberto's death, Sixtus announced to the commune of Rimini and to Venice that he had legitimated Roberto's two sons and invested them with his inheritance; and on the 12th he promised to send a legate, the cardinal of Milan, to deliver the bulls of investiture and ensure peace in Rimini. A fortnight later the troops lately led by Roberto arrived in Rimini, 'pro defensione et securitate status illius Ariminensis'; and on 10 October the legate proceeded to carry out the legitimation and investiture, commanding Pandolfo again to perambulate the city in token of authority. Pandolfo was created sole vicar, paying a *census* of 1,000 *scudi*, while his brother Carlo was assigned instead an annuity. Oaths of fealty were taken from the council of twelve and representatives of the *castelli*; then, the formalities of succession being complete, the cardinal left by ship from Rimini.[5]

84; Infessura, 96–105; Malipiero, 261–3; Cobelli, 271, 280; *Cron. Perug.*, 652–3; Sanzio, XII, c. XCVIII, CII, CV; Sigismondo dei Conti, i.139ff.; Bernardi, i.1.65, 88, 100; G. Marini, *Degli Archiatri Pontifici*, ii (Rome, 1784), 219–21; Tonini, v/2.285–93, 304; *Lettere di Lorenzo*, 261; Pastor, *Päpste*, ii.586–90, 791. On the same day Federigo d'Urbino died near Ferrara, also of fever.

[1] Iacopo Volterrano, 179.   [2] Sanudo, 1224.

[3] The other children were Giovanna and Carlo, the first 5, the second only 2. Roberto also left a son, Troilo, by Elizabetta, the wife of Adimario degli Adimari a Riminese noble, and a daughter, Battista, by Isabetta, his wife: Clementini, ii.539, 543, 563; Battaglini, *Zecca*, 290; Tonini, v/1.477–8.

[4] Dennistoun, i.289.

[5] Until the age of 20 Pandolfo was to have as coadjutor Galeotto Malatesta: Anon. Veron., 384–5; Bernardi, i.1.111; Sanudo, 1224; Clementini, ii.359–61; Battaglini, *Zecca*, 275–7; Tonini, v. 396, v/2.290–8, 301–3; Mazzatinti, *Inventari*, xxxvii.148. Giulio Cesare Varano may again have hoped for the succession of Rimini: Lilii, ii.235–6.

What checked Sixtus from seizing Rimini at so opportune a time is not immediately clear. He may simply have decided to wait, or he may, as Fabronius suggests, have accepted advice from Lorenzo de' Medici.[1] But it is also probable that he acted from suspicion that Venetian influence, arrested for a time under Roberto Malatesta, was reviving in Rimini. In the autumn of 1482 a plot was discovered to surrender the city to Venice.[2] The ringleaders were punished, but relations with Venice continued to be close. There may have been some fear in Rimini of Girolamo Riario, or at least a division of loyalties. In April of the following year the Venetians were reported to have made another attempt on Rimini, and word spread that Pandolfo, a son of Sigismondo, 'con le spalle et genti de' Veneziani hanno corso la terra di Rimini, e che la terra gridava Marco, Marco, la rocca autem Chiesa, Chiesa'.[3] True or false, the rumour was revealing: not the Malatesta, but two outsiders, Venice and the papacy, were now the true contenders for mastery of Rimini. Two years later Innocent VIII asked the Malatesta to admit a papal garrison to Rimini as a defence against the Venetians.[4] Not for another decade, however, did a decisive conflict develop.

During these years the history of the Malatesta, after two centuries of strenuous action in the political life of Italy, dwindles again to details of domestic faction and intrigue. Not that relations with other states were neglected or diminished. Roberto Malatesta had bequeathed to his son the high reputation he enjoyed in Italy, and for this reason, within a few months of accession, Pandolfo was taken into the pay of Florence, Naples and Milan. In 1487 Ferrante, expecting as great things of the son as of the father, offered Pandolfo the protection of the league.[5] It was necessary also to provide for Pandolfo's marriage; and in February 1485 Raimondo Malatesta concluded in Bologna his betrothal to Violante, daughter of Giovanni Bentivoglio, which established friendship between the families for many years to come.[6] With

---

[1] *Laurentii Medicis vita*, i. 124. He also explains in the same way the pope's failure to reoccupy Pesaro on the death of Costanzo Sforza. Cf. Cappelli, *Lettere*, cit., 267–8. A Florentine envoy reported at this time that Rimini was 'ghovernato et recto in modo e da tali homini che ha bisogno della gratia didio et piu che ordinario': ASF, *Mediceo av. principato*, filza 38, n. 504 (12 Oct. 1482).

[2] Clementini, ii. 560; Battaglini, *Zecca*, 277–8; Tonini, v/2, cxxx, pp. 299–301 (proceedings against Alberto de' Pedruzii, one of Pandolfo's counsellors, who tried to raise the city against Pandolfo).

[3] Cappelli, *Lettere*, cit., 266. Cf. Sanudo, 1229.

[4] Tonini, v. 403.

[5] *Diario Ferrar.*, 127; Clementini, ii. 564; Tonini, v. 399. In 1486 Pandolfo and Carlo were knighted by the duke of Calabria on his way back from Lombardy: Clementini, ii. 563–4; Tonini, v. 404.

[6] *Ann. Bon.*, RIS xxii. 905, 908–9; Bernardi, i. 1. 299–300; Ghirardacci, iii. 231–2, 254; Battaglini, *Zecca*, 282; Tonini, v. 407.

the Este, as in previous periods, the Malatesta or the regency remained on the best of terms,[1] as also with the neighbouring lords of Pesaro and Urbino;[2] while the papacy under Innocent VIII, when it noticed the Malatesta at all, seems to have been well inclined.[3] But all these contacts were of small importance beside developments in Rimini itself.

Under Galeotto Malatesta as *gubernator* the regency of 1482 administered affairs for ten years without serious unquiet.[4] And when dissension came it was limited at first to members of the government. While suspicion and jealousy began to separate Galeotto and Raimondo Malatesta, Pandolfo himself, under the direction of his mother Elisabetta, was already developing his later qualities of a petulant, dissolute and hated oppressor. Reports of these conditions began to reach Ferrara, where duke Ercole d'Este decided to do what he could to remedy them. In particular he was anxious to see Pandolfo receive the training proper to a prince, and detach him if possible from the profligate idlers with whom his mother, ambitious for power, had surrounded him. For this purpose he sent to Rimini in 1491 one of his closest counsellors, Bartolomeo Cavalieri, who was able on his arrival to send an account of Pandolfo which showed him to be not yet entirely unregenerate. And in April of the next year the duke himself visited Rimini, taking Carlo Malatesta away with him to be educated in arms with his own sons, but resisting Elisabetta's attempt to remove Cavalieri as well.[5]

A month before this visit the quarrel of Galeotto and Raimondo Malatesta matured in a plot on the part of Galeotto and his sons to assassinate their rival. On the evening of 6 March Raimondo was cut down and murdered as he was leaving Elisabetta's house. The crime was bitterly resented by Elisabetta, whose special favour to Raimondo seems to have caused his death, as well as by Giovanni Bentivoglio, another of his patrons.[6] In self-defence Galeotto conspired the further step of putting Pandolfo to death and seizing power himself. August 1st was the day appointed, but a few hours before the time planned the conspiracy was reported and the leaders were taken and executed. There was no disturbance in Rimini, and help sent by Giovanni Bentivoglio was not required.[7]

---

[1] *Diario Ferrar.*, 180.
[2] Battaglini, *Zecca*, 280–1; Ugolini, ii.59; Cappelli, 'Pandolfo', 422.
[3] Clementini, ii.563–4; Tonini, v. 404, 408; Martorelli, 358.
[4] Only an attempt to raise money in 1487 by granting licence to export corn at a time of dearth threatened a rising among *la plebe* and was abandoned: Cappelli, 'Pandolfo', 423.
[5] *Ibid.* 423ff.; Tonini, v. 410–13.   [6] Gozzadini, *Giovanni II Bentivoglio*, 7 n. 1.
[7] *Diario Ferrar.*, 127; Ghirardacci, iii.265, 267; Clementini, ii.566–7; Battaglini, *Zecca*, 283; Cappelli, 'Pandolfo', 426–9; Tonini, v. 413–19, 491–2. Their confiscated property was restored by Pandolfo to their families, in some cases at least.

Pandolfo Malatesta should now have held sole authority in Rimini. The period of tutelage seemed to be over, and in a letter to the duke of Ferrara he took pleasure in declaring he was at last free, 'dove era servo'.[1] In reality the greater share of power fell to Elisabetta and members of her family, the Aldovrandini, whom she brought into office and influence.[2] The government led by Galeotto Malatesta may have had some merits:[3] it was at least the government of a man and a Malatesta. But no good is spoken of the régime which supplanted it. It was Elisabetta, according to Clementini, who encouraged Pandolfo in the vices and excesses which accustomed him to violence.[4] By the summer of 1493 she had got rid of Cavalieri, who was as glad to leave as she was to see him go.[5] And it was Elisabetta finally who took the serious step of placing Rimini under the protection of Venice, 'essendo questo stato', in Cavalieri's words, 'debole e povero di aderenti'. She went to Venice in March 1493 with Pandolfo and Carlo, and by the spring it had been arranged that Venice should assume guardianship of their state for two years, assigning Pandolfo an annual stipend of 7,000 ducats to maintain a hundred men: not, as Cavalieri remarked, an obvious improvement on the former papal contract providing 6,000 ducats for fifty men. In September Pandolfo presented himself again before the senate.[6]

The Venetian alliance was not exclusive but extended to the papacy, with whose *condottieri* Pandolfo continued to be numbered,[7] and to other local lords and communities of the March and Romagna, with whom Pandolfo had relations.[8] This was his position when the French invasion broke on Italy in 1494. But what part he played in the events that followed does not become clear. The search only shows to what insignificance the small *signori* of the Papal States had now declined; though according to one report, Pandolfo was present at Fornovo and there acquitted himself well.[9] At the end of 1495 he fell into a dispute with Caterina Sforza over the castle of Cusercole. Venice

---

[1] Cappelli, 'Pandolfo', 427.

[2] *Ibid.* 430–1; Tonini, v.457.

[3] Battaglini, *Zecca*, 281; but cf. the petition to Cesare Borgia (1503): Tonini, vi/2. 796–7.

[4] *Raccolto storico*, ii.577.

[5] Cappelli, 'Pandolfo', 431ff.

[6] Clementini, ii.568; Ammirato, iii.191; Tonini, v.420; Cappelli, 'Pandolfo', 433ff. Since 1491 Pandolfo had been agitating for a *condotta* with which to supplement his income and was reported by Cavalieri to be 'dispostissimo all'esercizio militare': a readiness he seems soon to have lost: Cappelli, *ibid.* 423ff., 434.

[7] De Roo, *Alexander VI*, iv.279; Ammirato, iii.191.

[8] Malipiero, 350; Lilii, ii.242; Amiani, ii.72, 75; Gozzadini, *Giovanni II Bentivoglio*, 100–1. They included the Bentivoglio, Montefeltro, and Sforza of Pesaro.

[9] Tonini, v.422–3, v/2.312. Cf. Bernardi, i.1.53; Bembo, ii.37; Battaglini, *Zecca*, 284.

supported him closely, and the cries 'Marco' and 'Pandolfo' were raised indiscriminately by their followers.[1] Venetian 'protection', it was evident, was becoming something more. When, in the following year, Pandolfo refused to go to Naples at the behest of Venice, preferring to remain and foster discontent in Cesena, the republic, on appeal from the Cesenati, sent him a letter of imperious rebuke, as though addressing a peccant officer of its own provincial government.[2] As the months progressed Venetian influence became increasingly pronounced; and early in 1497 Elisabetta and her sons were again in Venice where at her request the grant of protection and *condotta* were renewed, the political advantages of the one outweighing for the Venetians the military uselessness of the other.[3]

The value of the Venetian protectorate was soon put to the test, and not at first by any foreign threat but by events in Rimini itself. At the end of August, during a visit to her daughter in Tuscany, Elisabetta unexpectedly died. Only a year before she had complained to the Venetian government that Pandolfo was plotting to kill his brother and herself; and now the reports inevitably spread that Pandolfo had had her poisoned. In a letter to the duke of Ferrara, however, Pandolfo professed himself inconsolable.[4] And certainly he had reason to grieve. This time he was indeed left in sole command of Rimini; and the freedom was fatal to his rule and the Malatesta principality. 'Homo de mala natura, dissolute in ogni vizio.'[5] Pandolfo was not even accomplished as a tyrant. Within two months of his mother's death he had provoked the only serious conspiracy ever formed against the Malatesta. Not all the blame lies with him. If Sigismondo had kept, to the last, the loyalty of his subjects, Roberto began to forfeit it, and under his successors disaffection grew.[6] But it was the naked misrule of Pandolfo which first turned discontent into revolt. His vindictive

[1] Malipiero, 407–8; Bernardi, i.1.115 ff.; Pasolini, iii.233, 235.
[2] Sanudo, Diarii, i.50, 83, 122–4, 179, 195; *Diario Ferrar.*; Clementini, ii.573–4. The Malatesta still had followers in Cesena, as also Fano (Amiani, ii.65), while in 1491 there had been a dispute between Pandolfo Malatesta and Santarcangelo: Mazzatinti, *Archivi*, Ser. 1, i.321.
[3] Sanudo, *Diarii*, i.588–9, 614, 670–1; *Diario Ferrar.*, 100.
[4] M. Brosch, *Papst Julius II* (Gotha, 1878), 325; Cappelli 'Pandolfo', 436. The Venetian Sanudo naturally gives a good opinion of Elisabetta: 'dona bellissima, giovene et molto saputa, la qual con il suo ingegno governava il stato di Rimano et il fiol signor Pandolfo, reprendendolo che non si portava a modo il padre etc. Et amava più il signor Carlo suo etiam fiol junior, et etiam dicta madonna amava molto la Signoria nostra, vedendo da quella dependeva ogni ben che dicti soi fioli potesseno aspectar': *Diarii*, i.752–3.
[5] Malipiero, 499, who continues: 'l'ha venenà so pare, e ha fatto morire un so fratel menore'.
[6] At least in certain sections of the nobility: Clementini, ii.492, 510; Battaglini, *Zecca*, 285–7, 289–91; Cappelli, 'Pandolfo' 454; cf. also Sigismondo's hostages in the Morea: above p. 241 n. 1.

nature was well known to Rimini, and in 1495 had caused unrest when he and certain ribald companions murdered an envoy of the king of Hungary on his way to Rome and robbed him of his money.[1] According to Caterina Sforza, the citizens rose because offended 'in their property, their honour and their persons'. Marin Sanuto stressed particularly Pandolfo's urge to exercise 'questa tirania di voler haver quelle done li piaceva et con quelle usar'.[2] Pandolfo seems not to have suspected the degree of their hostility, and continued during 1497 to meddle in the faction fights of Cesena;[3] but the Venetians were awake to it and sent a representative to try to keep the peace.[4] The plot was prepared by members of the upper class, families like the Adimari and Belmonti, who had prospered under Malatesta government and served it well, but were most exposed to Pandolfo's licence and slighted by his preference for the court favourites. The plan, formed during October, was to exterminate the whole Malatesta family when gathered in the church of S. Giovanni Evangelista on Sunday, 28 January 1498, and then raise the crowd with cries of 'libertà'. Of a popular insurrection there is no sign. In the event, like the similar Pazzi conspiracy, the attempt miscarried, and like Lorenzo de' Medici, Pandolfo was able to escape after an ignominious climb over the organ and high altar. He took refuge in the *rocca* and owed his safety, says Clementini, to the *plebe* by whom he was 'assai amato'; but Caterina Sforza wrote that after this attack he was 'hated universally'. Some of the conspirators eluded capture, but more were taken and punished with death, expropriation or exile.[5]

For two more uncertain years Pandolfo Malatesta was able to maintain his rule, but it never became secure. Conspiracies, both inside Rimini and among the exiles, were frequent;[6] and it was Venice alone which upheld him. Although inactive as a *condottiere*, he was retained in Venetian service, and on his appeal a Venetian envoy was sent to compose the city, unsettled after the plot, to whom all effective authority was surrendered.[7] The birth of a son, Sigismondo, to Pan-

---

[1] *Diario Ferrar.*, 146; Clementini, ii.572, 583.

[2] *Diarii*, i.861; Pasolini, iii.286.

[3] There were many exiles from Cesena in Rimini: Clementini, ii.576–7; Tonini, v.429; Baldi, *Guidobaldo*, i.85, 123.

[4] Tonini, v.429.

[5] Bernardi, i.1.159–60; Sanudo, *Diarii*, i.861–3; *Diario Ferrar.*, 278; Priuli, i.80; Malipiero, 498–9; Clementini, ii.577–83; Battaglini, *Zecca*, 291; Tonini, v/2.321–30; Pasolini, iii, docs. 781, 788.

[6] Sanudo, *Diarii*, i.957, ii.20, 28, 34, 41, 452; Bernardi, i.1.161. Consequently Pandolfo's government became harsher on the culprits.

[7] 'Di subito al dite Pandolfe se butò neli braze de Sam Marco; bemchè prima lui fuse in lega, tamen di nove se i aricomandò': Bernardi, i.1.160–1; Sanudo, *Diarii*, i.861–3, 872, 877, 884, 1107; ii.84; Priuli, i.80, 228, 231–2; Malipiero, 498–9. As early as May 1498 there were rumours that Pandolfo intended exchanging Rimini

dolfo and Violante in October 1498 was accompanied by no festivity or popular response.[1] That the last Malatesta to govern Rimini would ever have established firm dominion is improbable. The opportunity was never given him. Little more than a year after the insurrection Cesare Borgia appeared in Romagna to evict and destroy all the *signorotti*.

When Pope Alexander VI denounced the temporal vicars of the Papal States for neglect to pay their *census* and sent his son to dispossess them, he was not applying a policy that was new. Other popes before him had complained of non-payment of tribute,[2] or had used this as a pretext for depriving *vicarii*; and many of Alexander's predecessors had been successful, as he was, in reasserting direct dominion of the church. At various times and in various ways since the death of Martin V important cities had been recovered from *signori*: Foligno, Imola, Forlì, Osimo, and the lands of Francesco Sforza and the Malatesta, with many smaller places like Anguillara and Montone; and of these many were made to swear never again to accept the government of despots.[3] Both Paul II and Sixtus IV were held to have planned to eradicate the vicars and feudatories,[4] and although not easy to demonstrate, there is every appearance that during the fifteenth century the authority of the popes in their territories was increasing. Turbulent families there continued to be, particularly in Rome; local warfare could still break out, and the period of vacancy in the see of Rome was regularly disturbed. But the effective power of the pope was felt more immediately and in more places than formerly, whether to impose peace and order, or in works of artistic patronage. The violent extortion of privileges by insubordinate cities had almost ceased, and, together with wider legations in the Papal States, communes could now be offered as bribes in a papal conclave:[5] they must have promised some profit.[6] It was because the popes were now often able to make good their intention of

---

for certain Venetian territories in Friuli: Sanudo, *Diarii*, i. 1041–2; Pasolini, iii. 288, 293. The Este as well offered Pandolfo help after the conspiracy: Cappelli, 'Pandolfo', 436–7.
[1] Sanudo, *Diarii*, ii. 70, 77, 79, 145 (who adds: 'ch'è zà 100 anni la caxa di Malatesti non havea hauto fioli legitimi che havesse dominata Rimano'); Clementini, ii. 583; Tonini, v. 434.
[2] *Magnum Bull. Roman.*, v. 349–50, 369–71; De Roo, iv. 274–5, 295–7.
[3] For example Fano in 1464: Amiani, ii. 10.
[4] Baldi, *Federigo*, iii. 235–6; above p. 243.
[5] As in 1492: Pastor, *Päpste*, iii. 276–7. Under Alexander VI even his daughter Lucrezia received the government of papal cities: *ibid.* 423, 428.
[6] Bauer ('Studi', 336–7) says that by Sixtus IV's pontificate the financial autonomy of many communes had gone completely; almost one-third of papal income now came from the Papal States: Gottlob, 256.

enforcing their authority that neighbouring states – Milan, Venice, Naples and above all Florence – did everything to oppose it, and proceeded in secret to encourage revolt wherever it threatened to appear.

At the same time it was characteristic of the later fifteenth-century popes that they often heedlessly imperilled what they had been at pains to win. Each of them after the death of Nicholas V, with varying diligence, established relatives as territorial dynasts where previously other families had ruled. It was largely a consequence of nepotism that the papal vicariate, instituted more than a century before as a short, terminable office, entered under them into its final phase as a hereditary *feudum perpetuum*; and every pope on election had to face not merely long-established families like the Malatesta and Montefeltro, but others, the Borgia, Piccolomini, Riarii, Della Rovere and Cibò, raised by his predecessors. In seeking to set up relatives as vicars and princes, the popes frequently met resistance from the college of cardinals, who during the fifteenth century seem to have offered with spasmodic zeal to supervise the territorial interests of Rome. Election *capitula* devised by them insisted that land should not be recklessly alienated, which may explain the care with which their assent was mentioned in bulls of investiture to papal *nipoti*; and although at this time the traditional complaint of papal misgovernment continued,[1] if the terms of agreement which were drawn up when cities reverted to the direct government of the church are to be taken literally, it must be concluded that the population at large as well as the *curia* was opposed to grants of fief and vicariate. Nearly all compacts of the kind arranged during the fifteenth century include requests or guarantees that henceforward the city or commune remain *immediate subjecta*.[2] Even where this provision is lacking, the agreements reached, though generally more restrictive than in the past, could also be generous; enough to suggest a new

---

[1] Cobelli, 179ff.; Pedrino, rub. 441, 604, 789ff.; Della Tuccia, 130; Nunziante, 'Primi anni' 1892, 336; Valois, *Pape et concile*, i.332, ii.100–3; Pastor, *Päpste*, i.420ff., 610ff.; Ady, 17–18; Fink, 'Dominicus Capranica', Morpurgo-Castelnuovo, *AR* 1929. Lorenzo de' Medici commented of the Papal States in 1486: 'Questo Stato ecclesiastico è sempre stato la ruina d'Italia perchè sono ignoranti e non sanno modo di governare Stati, però pericolano tutto il mondo': Cappelli, *Lettere*, 291; Machiavelli's opinion is well-known. The popes, particularly Sixtus IV, tried to reassert the Constitutions of Albornoz, but clerical cupidity was difficult to overcome.

[2] For examples of such agreements, largely in the March and Umbria, between *c.* 1430 and 1465: Theiner, iii.51, 60, 250, 256, 260, 307, 325, 329, 374, 380; Dorio, 214–15; Cimarelli, 32, 47; Lilii, ii.180; Benigni, *S. Genesio*, in Colucci, xix, pp. cxx, cxxxi; *Mem. M. Cassiano, ibid.* xxviii.102; *Cod. dip. di S. Vittoria, ibid.* xxix, n. cxxvii; C. Santini, *Mem. di Tolentino* (Macerata, 1789), 368; Pulignani, *Arch. stor. Marche Umb.*, 1886; Sassi, *SR* 1952.

THE PAPAL RECONQUEST 259

reciprocity between *libertas* and authority.[1] Cesare Borgia himself was
to be prompt in granting privileges.[2]

The government of *tiranni* in the Papal States, considered by some at
least less harsh than that of the church,[3] has been condemned outright
by others, among them Machiavelli.[4] But no general estimate is
possible. Conditions varied too much with time and place; while
government which was offensive to *nobili*, by *contadini* might be
regarded as benevolent. Revolts were not infrequent,[5] but it is not
always clear by whom they were led. In 1439 it was the nobility which
welcomed or contrived the expulsion of the Trinci from Foligno where
they soon had the peasants and *popolo minuto* against them,[6] but five
years later it was the same class which called back the Varani to
Camerino.[7] In no city probably could the lord count on equal loyalty
from all classes. In Imola at the end of the century Caterina Sforza's
government seems to have had levelling tendencies, which drove the
leading citizens to desert her for Cesare Borgia.[8] And Priuli's judgement may well have been true that the *tiranni* trembled at the approach
of Borgia, not merely because he had a good army but because he could
expect support from 'le parte contrarie in le citade'.[9] A number were
upheld solely by outside powers like Venice, Florence or Milan;[10] only
Faenza of the cities taken by Borgia stood resolutely by its lord. The
others all accepted or invited his rule, giving a semblance of popular
sanction to his government. First of the papal *nipoti* to be strengthened
by a foreign alliance,[11] Cesare Borgia was irresistible. Nowhere could
the *signorotti* expect to withstand his attack. And least of all in Rimini.

[1] For example, the terms granted Montefiore in 1462: Soranzo, *Pio II*, 319–20; cf.
Sassi, *SR* 1952.
[2] For example, to Imola, Savignano, Castel Durante, Sinigaglia, Bertinoro, Serravalle: Alvisi, docs. 11, 19, 62, 83–5.
[3] Sugenheim, 347–8; M. Brosch, *Geschichte des Kirchenstaates* (Gotha, 1880), i.9.
[4] *Discorsi*, iii.29.
[5] Thus in 1408 Iesi expelled the Simonetti, in 1426 S. Severino the Smeducci, in
1428 Fermo and Montottone the Migliorati, in 1433 Camerino the Varani, in 1435
Fabriano the Chiavelli, in 1444 Urbino assassinated Oddantonio da Montefeltro, in
1460 Sassoferrato killed Luigi degli Atti: Morici, 'Corrado Trinci', 255–6.
[6] Dorio, 234–5, 262ff.
[7] Lilii, ii.197.
[8] Alvisi, 71ff. In Forlì, on the other hand, there is evidence of dissatisfaction among
the *contadini*: *ibid*. 78.
[9] *Diarii*, ii.70.
[10] Thus Sigismondo dei Conti, speaking of the vicars of Rimini, Pesaro and Faenza
(ii.227–8): 'aut ad Venetos, aut Mediolanenses, aut Florentinos respiciebant;
horum nutu gubernabantur et gubernabant, nulla Sedis Aspostolicae ratione
habita, quem et, cum commodum erat, oppugnare non verebantur'. Cf. Alvisi,
65–6.
[11] Cf. Machiavelli, *Decennali, Decennale primo*, 172–4. Cesare also received unpre-
cedentedly large sums from the Camera Apostolica: Pastor, *Päpste*, iii.460, 466.

After the assassination attempt and the ensuing reprisals, it required little to depose Pandolfo Malatesta from power. His enemies or their leaders were gathered in Cesena to organise his expulsion which, according to Priuli, they could have managed with ease.[1] On and off ever since the war with Sigismondo the papacy had aspired to reclaim Rimini, and the conspirators could always sell the city to the church, 'che ha gran desiderio d'averlo'.[2] A convenient excuse lay to hand in the fact that Pandolfo, who in 1495 had complained of his burden of *census*,[3] was behind like other *signori* with his payments to Rome. In constant fear of disloyalty at home, and of attack from outside, he had only one resource: the protection of Venice. And this, he soon learned, was not guaranteed.

At first the Venetians tried actively to preserve Pandolfo from destruction, clearly hoping to become masters in Rimini as elsewhere in Romagna, and in May and June 1498 when the pope threatened with deprivation all feudatories and vicars who had not paid tribute, they asked for Rimini to be left unmolested.[4] In the following spring papal proceedings against the despots were resumed,[5] and Pandolfo, anxious to make his position secure, besought Venice to pay 1,000 ducats of his *census*. The republic agreed, but Alexander only raised his demands, and in August Pandolfo was excommunicated.[6] As autumn advanced and the Borgia programme to evict the *signori* of Romagna and the March became known all over Italy,[7] Pandolfo Malatesta, with the lord of Faenza and other *raccomandati*, was forced into total dependence on Venice. After the fall of Imola and Forlì, a *provveditore* was sent at his request with troops to take command of Rimini. The pope was told that to attack the Malatesta would be to attack the republic. And early in 1500 Venice obtained a respite for Pandolfo and his state by per-suading Louis XII to withdraw his troops from Romagna.[8]

Embarrassments in Lombardy had done as much as Venetian diplomacy to bring Louis XII to this decision. Once they had been overcome he joined with the pope and Cesare Borgia in urging the republic to repudiate its defenceless clients in the Papal States. Through-out the summer of 1500 negotiations went on, Pandolfo Malatesta

[1] *Diarii*, i.228, 231. Pandolfo was also still at loggerheads with Caterina Sforza: Sanudo, *Diarii*, i.861–3, ii.432; Pasolini, iii, docs. 735, 744, 746, 750, 753, 759.
[2] Cavalieri's report to Ferrara: Cappelli, 'Pandolfo', 428.
[3] *Ibid.* 435.
[4] De Roo, iv.296; Bonardi, 'Venezia e Cesare Borgia', 386.
[5] Amiani, ii.78–9; Pasolini, iii, docs. 1012, 1016.
[6] Sanudo, *Diarii*, ii.649, 745, 911, 1370; Tonini, v.435.
[7] Malipiero, 564; De Roo, iv.297; Pastor, *Päpste*, iii.425.
[8] Malipiero, 564, 568; Priuli, i.228, 231–2, 248–9, 257, 271; Sanudo, *Diarii*, iii.57, 67, 90, 122, 131; Alvisi, 87; Bonardi, 'Venezia e Cesare Borgia', 388–9. The pope claimed the Riminese were asking him to recover the city.

helplessly standing by, and only reluctantly did the Venetians at last give way. Unwilling to proceed to extremities with the papacy, they were finally compelled to abandon resistance by the Turkish offensive in the Near East and the capture of Modone. In September Pandolfo failed to obtain a renewal of his *condotta* and was told he must provide for himself. A hurried visit from Carlo Malatesta accomplished nothing, and before the end of October Pandolfo was a fugitive from Rimini.[1]

The end came quickly. Unrest in Rimini had increased as the months went by,[2] leaving Pandolfo no choice but to capitulate. When faced with the threat of siege at the beginning of October, he could only reply by sending his wife and family away to Bologna and retiring passively to the *rocca*. The care of the city and the conduct of affairs he surrendered entirely to the council, which at once sent an ambassador to negotiate with Borgia and the bishop of Isernia, governor of Cesena. An agreement was soon reached, ratified by Pandolfo on 10 October, by which he sold the *rocca* with its munitions and artillery, and renounced Rimini for ever. Meldola, Sarsina, and his other castles were also sold for a further sum, and two days later Pandolfo Malatesta left for Bologna to assume the status of private citizen.[3]

[1] Sanudo, *Diarii*, ii. 271, 282, 343, 403, 409, 426–7, 505–6, 617, 711, 806–7, 828, 861, 868–9; Machiavelli, *Opere* (Milan, 1804–5), v. 162–3; Priuli, i. 189, 200; De Roo, iv. 307–9; Feliciangeli, *Acquisto di Pesaro*, 22, 39–40; Bonardi, 390.

[2] Clementini, ii. 584; Sanudo, *Diarii*, iii. 266, 296, 375, 400, 404, 653, 782.

[3] *Diario Ferrar.*, 301; Priuli, ii. 63; Sanudo, *Diarii*, iii. 911, 938; Bernardi, i. ii. 315; Sigismondo dei Conti, ii. 228; Ghirardacci, iii. 300; Tonini, v/2. 330–5; Alvisi, 129–30, doc. 20; Feliciangeli, *Acquisto di Pesaro*, docs. VIII, X; Ady, 123.

9

The government of the Malatesta

1. The papal vicariate

It was as recreant vicars of the Roman church that the papacy chose to proceed against the Malatesta, and formally it was the forfeiture of this title which precipitated their fall. Among the earliest of *signori* in the Papal States to receive the office of vicar, they were among the last to lose it. To trace the development of the institution under them is, in part at least, to trace a history of the institution itself.

As elaborated during the fourteenth century, the vicariate *in temporalibus* represented in a new form the customary readiness of the popes to make a bad bargain rather than no bargain at all with powerful subjects who might later, under different circumstances, be less disposed or less able to resist their authority. It was granted normally to lords, *tyrampni*, whom it was designed to convert from formal officers of city and commune into formal delegates of the pope. The popular sources of the despot's powers were not always explicitly repudiated, but, in early days at least, the investiture of a vicar was sometimes preceded by token surrender of the city to a papal representative and by an oath of fealty from the citizens; while even later the pope quite commonly addressed letters to the subjects of a *signore*, now vicar, commanding them to obey the new papal officer. By pope and despot alike the vicariate was conceived as a privilege, and this character it long preserved; it was usually awarded or renewed on petition, and in many cases renewal had also to be purchased.

During the course of its development the detailed terms of the papal vicariate underwent considerable variation. New clauses were inserted, older ones omitted. But certain of them, and some of the most important, persisted throughout, even after the vicariate had become 'perpetual'. First among the obligations consistently imposed was a *census* or annual tribute, of several hundred or several thousand gold florins, to be paid usually on the feast of SS. Peter and Paul. This could be and often was remitted or reduced, but *census* remained an inseparable incident of the vicarial office. Equally regular an obligation was the *iuramentum fidelitatis*, the oath of fealty to the pope and his successors, which was usually taken locally in the presence of a legate. Homage is rarely mentioned as accompanying the oath; no bond of reciprocal duties was created between the pope and his vicar, and bulls of investiture were normally careful to insist that the vicar must provide for his own defence out of his own resources. For a long time, and until it had degenerated into a lax and overgenerous concession, the vicariate commonly imposed as well the obligation of military service (*exercitus et cavalcata*), and attendance at *parlamenta*.

For his part the vicar received powers which even from the beginning were in most cases ample. Among these also there were some which recurred in every concession, notably *merum et mistum imperium et omnimoda jurisdictio temporalis*, a comprehensive juridical privilege which was customarily followed by another general formula bestowing wide executive powers: *dispondendi, ordinandi, statuendi, faciendi, corrigendi puniendi, diffiniendi, exequendi*. Very often authority to punish rebels was expressly granted, and the right to appoint or deprive all officials, the *podestà* and so on, specifically mentioned. Except when 'perpetual' vicariates began to be conferred, these rights were usually restricted in several ways. Appellate justice was frequently reserved to the pope and his rectors, as also were cases of heresy, the forgery of papal bulls, and treason against the pope. Similar restrictions were sometimes placed on the fiscal powers of the vicar. Normally he was given the right to impose and collect all *thelonea, pedagia, datia, et gabellas, ac omnes et singulos fructus* pertaining to the church; but often he was cautioned not to impose new or excessive taxes, and in a number of cases the *regalia* of the church such as tallage or *affictus* were excluded, as an obligation to be met in the customary way. Coinage too was a right rarely allowed, and then only by separate concession. One prohibition lay on all vicars alike, whether 'perpetual' or temporary; that forbidding alienation of lands bestowed. To perpetual vicars also could be addressed the vague admonition to govern well, which was more often cast in the form of a command to govern according to the statutes of the city – in theory and perhaps in practice long sanctioned by the pope – and to abolish all enactments contrary to the liberties of the church.

Representing as it did a delegation of authority from above, the papal vicariate should by its nature have always been a temporary concession, and this in the majority of cases it seems to have remained until the second half of the fifteenth century. Vicariates were granted for a term of years, at the end of which, as the bulls of investiture sometimes required the vicar to promise on oath, government was to revert to the papacy. This was a condition not easily relaxed, and although even before that time grants could be made *ad vitam*, or be hereditary within the term of years, it was not until the Schism that vicariates were bestowed, and then not recklessly, for more than one generation. It was during the Schism also that the first hereditary and perpetual vicariates appeared. But even when prolonged in this way the papacy could still lay down, if necessary, how succession to the office should proceed. After the Schism it was still common to set up a vicariate for a term of years and no more, and only when popes began to grant the title to their *nipoti*, or to specially favoured servants like the lords and communities who gathered round Pius II in his attack on the Malatesta, did this rule collapse. In 1463 a vicariate was conceded to Antonio Piccolomini to which female offspring were allowed to succeed. Thereafter, when granted at all, the papal vicariate was usually of that 'perpetual' kind of which Cesare Borgia was the peculiar beneficiary, and the associated obligations were for the most part slight.[1]

The Malatesta of Rimini were one of the families who were able to extend their vicariates beyond a term of years or a single generation.[2]

[1] This general sketch of the papal vicariate is based mainly on the investitures from 1329 to 1501 printed in Theiner, ii, iii and in Lünig, iv.89–98; Fantuzzi, iii, n. CXXIV, iv, n. CLXIV; *Cron. Ferm.*, 113; Pedrino, rub. 1506, 1606; Sigismondo dei Conti, i.382–4, ii.445–7; Ghirardacci, ii.270, 287; L. A. Muratori, *Delle antichità estense* (Modena, 1717–40), ii.80–1, 270–4; Adami, 30–1; G. Baldassini, App. xli; S. Borgia, *Memorie istoriche della pontificia città di Benevento* (Rome, 1763–9), iii.368–82, 391; Battaglini, *Vita*, App. LI; Tonini, v/2, XCV; Morici, *Conti Atti*, doc. iii; Gozzadini, *Nanne Gozzadini*, doc. xii; Guiraud, 132–3; De Roo, iv.306, 547–9; Alvisi, docs. 11, 15, 34; Biscaro, 'Relazioni' 1928, 48–9; Scalvanti, *BU* 1906, 302–7; Pellegrini, Gubbio', 168; Feliciangeli, 'Relazioni', 398; Giordani, *Gradara*, 89–90; *A. Sforza*, xl.

[2] The bulls of investiture to the Malatesta of Rimini are as follows and will subsequently be referred to by their number in Roman numerals here:

    I 1355, grant of Rimini, Pesaro, Fano and Fossombrone (Tonini, iv/2, CXVIII).

    II 1358, grant of certain castles in the dioceses of Rimini, Fano and Fossombrone (*ibid.* CXXXIII).

    III 1363, the preceding grants renewed (*ibid.* CXXXIII).

    IV 2 Jan. 1391, grant of Cesena, Senigallia, Meldola, Castronovo, Dogaria, vicariate of Santarcangelo, Pieve di Sestino, lands, castles and places of the territory of Montefeltro, vicariate of Mondavio, Pergola, Donato, Finigli (Arch. vat., Arm. xxxv, fos. 59v–65r).

    V 3 Jan. 1391, I, II, III, renewed and extended, but without Pesaro (Battaglini, *Vita*, App. I; Tonini, iv/2, CCVII; Theiner, iii.13).

    VI 1399, IV renewed, together with Cervia, Polenta, Culianello, Monte Venere, Bastia dal Fiano, Mondolfo, Corinaldo (Battaglini, *Vita*, App. II; Tonini, iv/2, CCXIX).

    VII 1415, grant of certain castles belonging to the church of Ravenna (Fantuzzi, iv, n. CLXI; Tonini, v/2, XXVII).

    VIII 1448, allusion to recent grant of Senigallia (Battaglini, *Vita*, 574).

    IX 1448, grant of Cervia (*ibid.* App. XIX; Tonini, v/2, LIII).

    X 1450, confirmation of Rimini, Cesena, Fano, Bertinoro, Cervia, S. Leo, vicariate of S. Agata, Pieve di Sestino, vicariate of Penna Billi etc. to Sigismondo and Malatesta Novello, and of Senigallia, Pergola, Gradara, Mondaino, Casteldelce, Talamello etc. to Sigismondo (Battaglini, *Vita*, App. XX; Tonini, v/2, LVIII).

The earliest grants made to them – in 1355, 1358 and 1363 – were for a period of ten years only.[1] The vicariates were bestowed upon Malatesta Guastafamiglia and his brother Galeotto, and were to pass, if they died, to Malatesta's sons, Pandolfo and Malatesta Ungaro. In a sense, therefore, they were from the start hereditary. When Malatesta died in 1364 Galeotto remained sole vicar.[2] As already seen, his rule was prosperous, and before his death (1385) he had extended the family dominion both as vicar and lord over new and important territories; but although he is said to have tried in 1381 to obtain a vicariate of his lands in *terza generatione*, there is no evidence that he was successful.[3] Rather, if the bull of investiture is to be believed which was issued by Boniface IX on 3 January 1391 to Galeotto's sons, the grants of 1355 and 1363 were not renewed till then.[4] It was by this bull that the pope first conceded to the Malatesta their original vicariates for the period of two lives: to Carlo, Pandolfo, Malatesta and Galeotto Belfiore, and their *filios masculos legitimos et naturales immediate descendentes, natos et nascituros*.[5] Eight years later, in 1399, the other territories then governed by the Malatesta – Cesena, Cervia, Sinigaglia, the vicariate of Mondavio and so on – which had been acquired subsequently to the first vicariates, but were themselves held by similar privileges, were in turn converted into a tenure for two generations (VI).

Provided the Malatesta continued loyal to the church, these concessions should have remained in force for sixty years and more, until the death of the heirs, Galeotto Roberto, Sigismondo, and Domenico Malatesta; but, as previously shown, they were challenged by Martin V, despite his bull legitimating the three princes, and by Malatesta of Pesaro who claimed the succession for himself. Most of the lands entrusted to the Malatesta in 1399 were forfeited, together with others held by more precarious titles, and the vicariate of those cities left them in 1430 had to be paid for heavily.[6] For what length of time these were to be retained is not stated. Although it would have been characteristic of Martin V to have restored the more severe restrictions of the earlier grants, it is certain that before the pontificate of Nicholas V, if not

---

[1] Before their defeat and submission in 1355 the Malatesta had hoped to obtain an hereditary grant of all the extensive lands they were holding, or expected still to conquer: above p. 73.

[2] Above p. 86.

[3] *Lucca, Regesti*, ii/2, n. 801.

[4] There are however two notices that the vicariates were confirmed by Gregory XI when the 10 years' term ran out (Battaglini, *Vita*, 691; Mazzatinti, *Inventari*, xxxvii.92, n. 53), and there is some evidence that *census* continued intermittently to be paid between 1373 and 1391: Bib. Gamb., *Cod. Pand.*, fos. 113–15, 120, 126, 138.

[5] No. v. Pesaro was now separate and so omitted: above p. 102.

[6] Above p. 170.

already in the time of Martin, Sigismondo and his brother had succeeded in reviving the conditions of tenure allowed their father and
their uncle. From the bull of confirmation by Nicholas (29 August
1450) it can be seen that popes Martin, Eugenius, and Nicholas himself,
had already all or some of them conceded to Sigismondo, Malatesta
Novello, and their heirs and successors the vicariates of Rimini,
Cesena, Fano and other towns, while to Sigismondo in particular, his
heirs and successors, had been granted Sinigaglia and other places
within or neighbouring on the March (x). 'Heirs and successors' is an
imprecise formula, but one other document at least may be cited to
illustrate it: that of 13 June 1448, by which the two Malatesta received
the investiture of Cervia for three generations: *vobisque, aut altero
vestrum cedentibus vel decedentibus, filios et nepotes legitimos et naturales* (ix).
Shortly after making these grants Nicholas proceeded to legitimate
certain of Sigismondo's sons, which rendered them eligible to succeed
to all *dominia, honores, dignitates ac officia secularia.*[1]

It was not therefore until the peace concluded with Pius II in 1463
that the right of succession to the vicariate was withheld from the
Malatesta. By the grudging concessions of that year Malatesta Novello
and then Sigismondo were allowed to remain vicars in their shrunken
domains only until their death. This condition Sigismondo's son,
Roberto, was able in part to circumvent when in 1465, after failing to
win the succession to Cesena, he obtained the heritable vicariate of
Sarsina, Meldola and other small towns in Romagna. Later he was
created vicar of Rimini, and it may be presumed that it was from a
vicariate granted for more generations than one that Pandolfo Malatesta was expelled in 1500. This may be inferred both from the provision made by Roberto for the inheritance of his son, and from the
promptitude with which Sixtus IV made Pandolfo the legitimate
successor. Many years afterwards, during the pontificate of Paul IV,
Roberto and Ercole Malatesta, grandsons of Pandolfo, made a claim in
Rome to the 'fief' of Rimini, and invoked in support the bull of
investiture which had granted hereditary tenure – though their pleas
were unsuccessful.[2]

Full or 'perpetual' inheritance the Malatesta never secured, and
the grant of Cervia in 1448 appears by its terms of succession the most
generous ever made them. Neither did they obtain any title more
honourable than vicar, in contrast with the Montefeltro, created dukes
in 1443 and 1474, or the Este, who received the ducal dignity first under
Paul II and then from Alexander VI.[3] Unlike their rivals of Urbino they

[1] Tonini, v/2, LIX.
[2] Above p. 251; Cappelli, 'Pandolfo', 448. On his brief return to Rimini in 1527,
Sigismondo II Malatesta described himself as vicar: Battaglini, *Zecca*, 299.
[3] Theiner, iii. 298, 427; Pastor, *Päpste*, ii. 476.

had never been counts,[1] and Sigismondo's attempt in 1452 to raise his dominion in Rimini to the level of a marquisate seems to have led to nothing.[2] Only the office and emoluments of rector of Romagna distinguished them for a time in the persons of Galeotto and Carlo Malatesta. Knighthood they shared with all signori.[3]

The vicariate was normally granted to more than one member of the family at a time,[4] and those receiving it seem to have had almost unrestricted freedom to dispose of internal administration as they wished.[5] The periodic partition of their territories has already been noticed. The first was made by Malatesta Guastafamiglia and Galeotto, and shortly before his death Malatesta arranged for the division by lot of the government of his cities between Pandolfo and Malatesta Ungaro, under the supremacy of Galeotto. A similar partition took place among Galeotto's sons in about 1390, followed by further divisions when the two youngest of them died in 1400 and 1416; and their example was adopted by Galeotto Roberto, Sigismondo and Malatesta Novello upon the death of their uncle, Carlo.[6] Even after partition each, certainly, continued to call himself papal vicar of all the cities, since the grants had been received in common,[7] and a close community of government was maintained.[8] But there is little evidence that this tended to any unification of their dominions. Rather did partition acknowledge the traditional autonomies and distinctness of the individual communes. The administrative and financial organisation of each city or group of

[1] Although Sigismondo was pleased for a time to call himself 'count of Montefeltro': above p. 204. Certain subsidiary branches of the family were, of course, counts: below p. 296.

[2] Above p. 209.

[3] There were also of course external honours such as the membership of the Venetian nobility bestowed on a number of the Malatesta.

[4] Although the Ravenna lands, for example, received by Malatesta de' Malatesta in 1415 were granted to him alone (xii), as were Sinigaglia, and then Montemarciano and Monte Cassiano to Sigismondo (x); and in 1482 Pandolfo was created sole vicar of Rimini: above p. 251.

[5] However, in 1422 Malatesta of Pesaro evidently thought it wise or necessary to obtain papal authority to divide his lands among his sons: Mazzatinti, *Inventari*, xxxvii. 124. Again in 1450 Nicholas V ratified the partition of territory by Sigismondo and Malatesta Novello: Soranzo, 'Cervia', 201. And similar authority may have been needed for disposal of lands by will: Battaglini, *Vita*, 691, 692, 693; Zazzeri, 351–3, 364.

[6] Above pp. 86, 102, 169.

[7] Thus in Dec. 1406 Malatesta of Cesena describes himself as vicar of Rimini: ACF, *Cod. mal.* 3, fos. 16r–v. Again Pandolfo, who governed Fano and was lord of Brescia and Bergamo, continued so to be described: ACF, *Canc.*, *Cons.* i, fos. 5r, 7r; *Cod. mal.* 3, fo. 12r; Theiner, iii. 212. Later Malatesta Novello also continued to be addressed as vicar of Rimini: see above p. 179.

[8] Above p. 103.

cities remained separate,[1] each paid a quota to the collective *census*,[2] and
the special conditions of each were allowed in large measure to persist.
Carlo and Pandolfo Malatesta even issued separate coinages.[3]

In many ways investiture with a vicariate only corroborated authority
already inherited, or received or extorted by the Malatesta from the
communes. It was not, nor did it become, the sole source of signorial
power. It was a concomitant one, a confusion which makes it sometimes difficult to determine how the *signori* are acting, as representatives
of the city or as representatives of the pope[4] – an ambiguity which may
have had advantages. Thus in Rimini, and possibly in Fano, Fossombrone and Cervia as well, the Malatesta had obtained control over
finance, legislation and the appointment of the *podestà* and other
officials, before the vicariate was granted.[5] Such control the papacy
refused to recognise as legitimate, and in 1355, before the Malatesta
were formally created vicars, the representative of Rimini had to
acknowledge the illegality of having made them *protectores, defensores, et
rectores* without papal licence.[6] By this the papacy reminded the commune of the limits of its privileges. For the communes also were widely
privileged, and their franchises in turn, conceding or ratifying as they
did powers to which those of the Malatesta owed their origin, went a
long way to anticipate the authority now bestowed on individuals by
the vicariate. Both Fano and Pesaro had since 1200 enjoyed full
criminal and civil jurisdiction with the right to appoint the chief magistrates, being bound in return only to *expeditionem et parlamentum,
pacem et guerram* (at the discretion of the papacy), rectorial procurations,
a periodic oath of allegiance, the appellate juridiction of the church, and
the payment of a small *census*;[7] while Rimini itself had obtained concessions still more generous, though continuing well into the four-

---

[1] Cf. below p. 320.
[2] That of Fano (e.g. 1367) was 750 gold ducats (Amiani, i.290), the quota of
Fossombrone and Castelgagliardo 800 fl. (Vernarecci, *Fossombrone*, i.310). Later
Pandolfo's contribution for the cities was 1,500 fl.: Amiani, i.327. Under Sigismondo and Malatesta Novello, Malatesta (1451) paid 1,600 out of the 4,000
ducats: Rossi, 'Nuove notizie', 169–72.
[3] Battaglini, *Zecca*, 219–20.
[4] A difficulty increased when Galeotto and Carlo Malatesta become also papal
rectors of Romagna.
[5] In Pesaro circumstances regarding the *podestà* may have been distinct: Vaccai,
51–2. In Cesena, where the church had recently enjoyed direct control, and
Galeotto Malatesta was established with papal support, the position was at first
singular; in 1380 the *podestà* is described as acting *pro S.R.E. et Magnif. et excel. d.d.
Galaotto de Malatestis*: Lucca, *Regesti*, ii/2, n. 769.
[6] Above p. 77.
[7] Theiner, i.43, 238, 472, 490; *Liber Censuum*, i.89; Amiani, ii, XXIII, XLVIII;
Zonghi, 167–9.

teenth century to quarrel with the papacy over their limits and implications.[1] At the same time all three cities together with Fossombrone had extended an authority over the neighbouring *castra* which the church had been constrained to recognise.[2]

It is not evident that when bestowing the vicariate the papacy sought to invalidate such established privileges;[3] but it did by the very terms and act of investiture make the authority exercised clearly emanate, at least in part,[4] from Rome. By conceding ample legislative, judicial, executive and fiscal powers, the pope created a new sanction, superseding the old, for rights long enjoyed by the communes and surrendered by them to the Malatesta. The bulls of investiture provided unfailingly that all statutes offensive to ecclesiastical liberty should be suppressed (I–VII, IX), while that of 1355 even stipulated that whenever the pope or his successors should reside in the subject cities of the Malatesta, they should have power, *praeter et ultra jurisdictionem solitam*, to exercise *merum et mistum imperium* through *podestà* and other officials of their choice.[5] The papacy was here claiming the right, if only temporary, to use a greater authority than it had done since the expulsion of the Hohenstaufen from Romagna and the March.

The bull if investiture itself was usually addressed to the newly created vicars, rehearsing their titles and proclaiming their special fitness to undertake the government of papal subjects, whose wellbeing came first among the *varias multiplicesque curas* that beset the church.[6] Sometimes the grant was said to be made in answer to petition,[7] at other times on the initiative of the pope.[8]

So much was by way of preamble. The body of the document was occupied with laying down the terms and conditions of the privileges bestowed, and began by making over to the Malatesta, either by papal authority alone or with the counsel of cardinals as well (III, V, VII), the *vicariatum, gubernationem, administrationem, et regimen in temporalibus* of the

---

[1] Above pp. 23, 53.

[2] Above p. 24. For the *castra* beyond the Metauro which in 1283 'non respondent ecclesie Romane set Comuni Fani': Theiner, i.269.

[3] Thus each bull of investiture safeguarded whatever privileges with regard to judicial appeals the communes might already hold (below p. 272); and if in 1355 the papacy condemned the election of the Malatesta as *defensores*, it allowed municipal officials to be appointed by the commune as usual: above p. 77.

[4] The papacy was always careful only to concede powers 'pertaining' to the church, but it is open to question whether these were always as extensive as the bulls of investiture imply: below p. 273.

[5] Tonini, iv/2.216.

[6] II–VII, IX. A similar formula was already in use during the thirteenth century for grants of privileges to communes, e.g. to Rimini in 1284: Theiner, i.438.

[7] E.g. II: *vestris in hac parte supplicationibus inclinati.*

[8] E.g. IX: *motu proprio, non ad ipsius Sigismundi Pandulfi vel alterius pro eo nobis super hoc oblate petitionis instantiam.*

territories defined.[1] The authority conveyed was not limited to the Malatesta, but could be delegated by them to others: *per vos vel alium seu alios quem seu quos ad hoc deputandum vel deputandos duxeritis*,[2] and of this right of devolution the Malatesta made liberal use. Not merely did they establish, as was natural, a superior bureaucracy with extensive powers, 'vicars', 'governors' and officials to represent them in their absence or superintend local government in the different cities;[3] they were generous also in granting lands great and small, often with rights of jurisdiction, to leading citizens, servants military and civil, and members of their own widely ramified family. Many of the properties they drew on were doubtless patrimonial – castles, estates, mills, vineyards, which in some cases they had held from the earliest days, or houses they had purchased, built or received by gift or forfeiture.[4] But others were certainly parts of the vicariate, and the records are many, particularly during the fifteenth century, of followers of the Malatesta being invested, often by feudal contract, with a castle or group of castles, *cum eius curia et cum omni suo iure et jurisdictione et mero et misto imperio et gladii potestate et cum omnibus suis pertinentibus*.[5] Frequent though these grants seem to have been, the Malatesta were careful always to reserve the rights of the church when making them. In 1433 Sigismondo, in the name of himself and his brother, conceded the 'Castrum Monleonis, cum sua curia' to the conte Ramberto Malatesta and his heirs, 'ad habendum, regendum quam etiam gubernandum salvo semper iure Sanctae Romanae Ecclesiae ac Vicariatus ipsorum magnificorum dominorum quod ius vicariatus non intendit ipse magnificus dominus [Sigismondo] a se abdicare nisi quatenus processerit ex dispositione S.D.N. Pape'.[6] On occasion the beneficiary of such grants

---

[1] I–III, VII–VIII; VI granted only *curam, regimen, et gubernationem ac administrationem*, and IX, *regimen et gubernationem*.

[2] I–III, V–VII, IX; VIII says that Sinigaglia was granted *cum potestate et facultate concedendi dictam civitatem eiusque comitatum in regimen et gubernationem spectabili ac generoso militi Dno Petro Johanni Burniolo de Cesena pro se ac etiam filiis* (Giovanni dei Bugnoli was one of Sigismondo's principal secretaries). V and VI envisage the delegation of government to *salariati, consanguinei* and others.

[3] Below pp. 302, 316.

[4] Below p. 295.

[5] Grant by Sigismondo in 1441 of Castel di Barte and other places to his governor and lieutenant in Fano and elsewhere, Bartolomeo da Palazzo: Battaglini, *Corte*, 145; cf. below p. 300.

[6] Franchini, 'Annullabilità', 218 (with other examples). In 1441 Sigismondo gave Rodolengo da Iseo the villa of S. Mauro with *ius regendi et gubernandi d. villam et homines cum mero et misto imperio et gladii potestate salvo iure Romanae Ecclesiae et D. Papape et vicariatus ipsius magnif. dom.*: Battaglini, *Saggio*, 41; Fantuzzi, VI.243. Franchini (*loc. cit.*), who insists the vicariate was a feudal institution, describes these concessions as subinfeudations. He adds that rights of the church were consistently reserved and that this was legitimate practice according to the doctrine of Baldus.

seems to have turned directly to the pope for investiture or confirmation.[1]

Such direct recourse to the papacy combines with other factors to
show that, however general a delegation of authority the pope may have
made by granting the vicariate to the Malatesta, he did not intend to
abandon all communication with their subjects. The formalities
accompanying the original investiture of 1355 gave some premonition
of this, when oaths of obedience to the papacy were taken not only
from the Malatesta but also from the communes,[2] and the grant of that
year provided that each *podestà* on appointment should take a similar
oath in the presence of the local bishop. The later bulls of Boniface IX
and Gregory XII in turn required the inhabitants of the subordinate
cities to take the same oath of obedience to the papacy and its vicars,
the Malatesta, before the Malatesta themselves or their representatives
(IV–VII), while those of Boniface IX laid down further that all men to
whom office was given by the Malatesta should take an oath to the
legate or rector promising to keep their cities obedient to the vicar and
the church, and ensure that they reverted to the papacy when the period
of the grant had been reached (IV–VI). Accordingly in 1416, and later in
1418 and 1419, the general council of Fano sent representatives to
swear obedience to the Council of Constance, then to Martin V, and
finally, at the provincial parliament of 1419, to the church and to the
Malatesta as its vicars.[3] It was customary also for the pope when
granting or renewing the vicariate to write to the subject communes,
commanding them to obey the papal *vicarii* (II, IV–VII, IX), and it was
in this spirit that Eugenius IV in 1432 wrote to the Riminese, congratulating them on their loyalty to the Malatesta.[4] After the appointment of the Malatesta as vicars, papal letters addressed directly to the
councils and communes of their cities were certainly infrequent, but
they did not cease altogether,[5] and even become common again during
the minority of Pandolfaccio.[6] In the eyes of the church the Malatesta
were only papal officers in a specially privileged position, and from the

---

[1] Thus in 1422 Martin V confirmed the gift by Pandolfo Malatesta of certain lands to
Ugolino de' Pili: Castelucci, 'Regesto', 187; and when Sigismondo ceded S.
Costanzo to Bartolomeo da Palazzo, Bartolomeo in 1437 got investiture from the
pope: Amiani, i.381.

[2] Above p. 77.   [3] Above p. 154.   [4] Above p. 179.

[5] For example letters to the commune of Fano in 1377, 1388 and 1445: Amiani,
i.299–300, 312, 401; ii, lxxi. In March 1448 the newly nominated governor and
treasurer of the March and Massa Trabaria wrote to Fano, Sinigaglia and Mondavio
announcing his appointment and commanding their obedience: ACF, *Canc.*, *Reg.*
ii, fo. 30v; cf. for similar letters *ibid.* fos. 27r, 39r, 1447, 1449. Sometimes the pope
wrote at the vicar's request, as when Eugenius IV, in June 1432, on petition from
Galeotto, ordered the bishop of Rimini to see that Jews wore distinctive dress:
Battaglini, *Vita*, 609–10.

[6] Tonini, v/2, CXXIV, CXXXI, CXXXIV.

pope as sovereign the cities and communes – which he continued to describe as 'his' – were never wholly separated.[1]

Having conveyed in general terms the privilege of 'vicariate, government' etc., the bull of investiture went on to elaborate, in what quickly became a formal and regular sequence, the various powers involved. The first of these were judicial. The Malatesta were entrusted with *omnimoda potestate auctoritate et Jurisdictione ac mero et misto imperio*',[2] as well as particular authority to punish rebels. These grants bestowed nothing new. In Rimini the Malatesta were already empowered by the commune to punish traitors against themselves,[3] while the general right to administer justice implied in *merum et mistum imperium* had long been enjoyed by the Malatesta as *signori*. And so later grants by Boniface IX and his successors claimed only to confer the jurisdiction 'que inibi per dictam Ecclesiam seu alios pro ea diutius exercita fuerunt' – in which 'alios' must be construed to mean the magistrates of the communes themselves. Certainly the terms of the vicariate can have implied little change in the existing organisation of justice, and can have been important only in giving a new title to control it.

It was not the custom of the Roman church to concede unlimited jurisdiction in its privileges. Certain cases were regularly reserved,[4] notably heresy and treason, and the same restriction was extended to vicars like the Malatesta.[5] It was in obedience to tradition also that the church retained a superior appellate jurdisdiction within the territory of the vicariate,[6] though excepting any particular rights of the commune (I, III–VII, IX). This did not prevent the Malatesta from issuing statutes about appeals, nor from establishing their own appeal justices;[7] but this may have been a local expedient of government which did not affect the prerogative, though it may have curtailed the power,[8] of the church.

Implied in jurisdiction was the right to appoint the *podestà* whose work was mainly judicial, together with all other officials, and the next

---

[1] As appears from cardinal Anglico's *Descriptio Romandiolae* (1371) which gives a detailed account of the Malatesta territories, though it concludes: 'Non potuit haberi plenior informatio de predicta civitate Arimini, concessa est dictis dominis de Malatestis': Theiner, ii. 515.

[2] I–VI, VIII–X. VII grants only *omnia iura et iurisdictiones*.

[3] Above p. 63; cf. also Cervia: *Stat. Cerviae*, 23.

[4] Above p. 5.

[5] V, VI–IX. VI includes also forgery of bulls. Treason of course meant treason to the church.

[6] Above pp. 5, 9. The privileges granted Fano and Pesaro in the thirteenth century reserved appeals.

[7] Bib. sen., *Stat. Rim.*, fo. 3; *Stat. Fani*, II, ch. lxxxiiii; *Stat. Caes.* (1589), 89ff.; Bartoccetti, 'Liber', 18, 45–6; ACF, *Cod. mal.* 4, fo. 206r.

[8] Partner, 128, 191.

privilege granted was that of setting up *potestates et iudices ac ceteros officiales*, to deal with local justice: *cases cujuscunque generis motas et movendas inter cives incolas habitatores* (I–VII, IX). This again only ratified a power already held by the communes, and alienated by them, or the most important of them, to the Malatesta, except perhaps at Pesaro where during the pontificate of Eugenius IV the Malatesta were appointing the *podestà* by their authority as vicars.[1] Rather than convey rights that were new, the bull of vicariate, by the various oaths to the church and the *vicarii* it imposed on all officials of the Malatesta, made clear that from being servants and magistrates of the commune or the *signori* they were held to have become the subordinates of papal officers. How rigorously these conditions were applied it is impossible to judge.[2] Here again no doubt the practical effect of the vicariate was not great. The *podestà* continued as before to hold his office on behalf of (*pro*) the reigning lord (*dominus*), although in solemn documents at least the lord seems now to have been qualified as vicar-general of the Holy Roman Church.[3] In the same way, when proceeding with other electors to renew the *consiglio generale* of Rimini in 1398, Carlo Malatesta described himself as doing so *tamquam Vicarius Civitatis Arimini pro Domino nostro Papa et Sancta Romana Ecclesia Generalis*.[4] Yet this need imply no more than formal scruple; and it is probable that the authority over officials they held of the commune was more important to the Malatesta than that held of the church, in the early days of the vicariate at least.

To judicial and administrative prerogatives was added the right to collect all revenues: *potestas colligendi omnes et singulos redditus ad eamdem Ecclesiam pertinentes*.[5] This formula raises the same problem as the preceding clauses, in that the bulk of revenues, the indirect taxes (*datia, gabellae* etc.) had long passed into the hands of the communes, and so could not have been construed, unless recovered by forfeiture, as 'pertaining' to the church. The taxes owed the papacy by Rimini and the other towns were few, and from all but one of these the Malatesta were granted no immunity. Only from payment of tallage were they exempted, and even this exemption did not always pass unmolested by the

---

[1] Vaccai, 52.

[2] Vaccai, speaking of Pesaro, says the *podestà* took an oath, first to the pope in the presence of an episcopal vicar, and then to the Malatesta in the presence of the chancellor: 54–5. The practice in Fano may have been similar: Amiani, i. 177.

[3] Thus at Fano in 1353 the *podestà* is described as officiating *pro Magnifico illustri et excelso Dno. Dno. Gallaotto de Malatestis de Arimino*, but in 1359, after concession of the vicariate, Galeotto is called vicar of the Roman Church as well: Zonghi, 475. After that the formula was probably usual.

[4] Tonini, iv/2.422.

[5] In various forms: I–VII, IX. v and vi state also that the Malatesta were not obliged to render account of their fiscal administration.

pope and his provincial officials.[1] On the other hand the Malatesta were obliged to pay *census* each year, and were expected to meet all expenses incurred by them as vicars unaided by the papacy (IV–VII, IX). From this it may be seen that if the vicariate added a new authority to their fiscal powers, it did not promise to increase in any way the profit to be drawn from them.

The last vicarial privilege explicitly granted was legislation: the right *faciendi, statuendi, ordinandi, mandandi, corrigendi, diffiniendi, sententiandi, et exequendi* (V–VII, IX). The papacy had never ceased to take interest in the statutes published by the communes, claiming both to approve them and to supervise their correction.[2] In the bulls investing the Malatesta this claim assumed the modified form of a command to repeal all statutes hostile to the church.[3] There is no sign that the Malatesta ever complied with the command, but in other directions they found it useful to record the new source of their legislative authority beside the old, as when in 1365, before introducing certain amendments into the statutes of Rimini, Galeotto Malatesta referred to the *potestatem et arbitrium sibi concessum a sancta matre Ecclesia iuxta formam vicariatus eiusdem Nec non a comune conscilio et hominibus Civitatis Arimini*.[4] In 1365 the vicariate was still only a recent honour, and therefore one to which Galeotto may have thought it proper to allude. Later on, when revising statutes or issuing decrees, the Malatesta were usually satisfied to use the simple title *dominus* and ignore the style of 'vicar'.[5] Once again it would appear that they were more alive to their prerogatives as *signori* than their privileges as vicars.

One reason for this may have been that the terms of the papal vicariate did not, expressly at least, authorise every right exercised by the Malatesta.[6] Such was the privilege of castle-building, sometimes mentioned in bulls of vicariates to other families, and by tradition requiring papal licence.[7] There are cases, it is true, of licences granted

[1] Below p. 283.

[2] Calisse, 'Costituzioni', 60–1.

[3] *Et quod omnia Statuta si qua in dictis Civitatibus Comitatibus et districtibus fuerint vel sunt edita contra eamdem Romanam Ecclesiam et Collegium et Ecclesiasticam libertatem Ecclesias Ecclesiasticasque personas seu earum bona cassabunt et facient totaliter amoveri*: 1; cf. IV-VII, IX.

[4] Bib. sen., *Stat. Rim.*, fo. 365v. Cf. decrees (1367): ACF, *Cod. mal.* 1.

[5] *Stat. Caes* (1494): *Haec sunt quaedam additiones aeditae et factae per homines et consilium communis Cesenae signatae et confirmatae per magn. dominum nostrum Malatestam novellum de malatestis*. Cf. below p. 289. There may however have been a tendency to use the vicarial title when promulgating laws of a solemn or permanent character.

[6] It must be remembered that almost until the end of their rule, but particularly in the time of Galeotto and Carlo, the Malatesta governed other lands beside those they held in vicariate, only some of which had been received from the papacy.

[7] For example: Theiner, i. 116, 254.

the vicars of Rimini.[1] But the Malatesta were tireless military builders,[2] and there is no evidence that they normally sought papal authorisation.

Another unauthorised privilege of the Malatesta was coining money.[3] This was already a right of the communes in Rimini, Pesaro and Fano, and the Malatesta inherited it.[4] For a long time the papacy did not challenge the practice, although Sigismondo was accused by Andrea di Ugo Benzi in his speech before the papal consistory in 1461 of having debased the currency;[5] but in the second half of the fifteenth century the popes started to attack the unlicensed issue of coin by *vicarii* and others.[6] The Malatesta territories were then reduced to insignificance and the local coinage began to lose such importance – of prestige more than utility – as it had ever had.[7]

On analysis the privileges of papal vicariate indicate little increase of actual power to the Malatesta. Not only were they in most cases already invested with a similar authority by the communes; that authority was more useful in the daily conduct of business, was not restricted in time, and implied rights of which the vicariate made no mention. In addition, the vicariate, while offering authority, also imposed duties. At first these were no mere formality, and reminded the Malatesta in a number of ways that their position, if privileged, was not to be extraordinary. They were told, for example, to govern justly and well (IV–VII, IX), to abide by municipal statute (III–VII, IX), to avoid exacting *talias illicitas*, and even to introduce no taxes *ultra consuetum modum*, without the consent of their subjects.[8] They were also expected to observe papal and

---

[1] By a bull of 28 Nov. 1431 Eugenius IV authorised Galeotto Roberto to fortify his palace of Gattolo in Rimini, the precursor of the *rocca* built by Sigismondo: Tonini, v/2, xxxix.

[2] On the building activities of Sigismondo cf. above p. 213. According to Clementini (ii. 373) and Ricci (142) he constructed castles and fortification at Rimini, Fano, Gradara, S. Leo, Monte Fiore, Santarcangelo, Sinigaglia, Montescudolo, Pennabilli, Sassocorvaro, Sogliano, S. Cristoforo, Carignano and Verucchio, but in most cases he was only perfecting work begun by his predecessors, particularly Galeotto. In 1453 (?) Sigismondo ordered a general investigation of the conditions of all fortifications: ACF, *Canc., Reg.* ii, fo. 75.

[3] Although Battaglini (*Zecca*, 218) was of the opinion that the vicariate implicitly sanctioned the right of coinage. In Pesaro Costanzo Sforza first received licence to coin money in 1475 (Giordani, *Zecca*, 184).

[4] The right is clearly proved only for Rimini and Pesaro: Battaglini, *Zecca*, 163–4, 187; Castellani, 'Zecca', 29–30.

[5] Mittarelli, *Bibliotheca*, 705, 710; Battaglini, *Zecca*, 269.

[6] Theiner, iii. 382; Battaglini, *Zecca*, 77, 187; Pastor, *Päpste*, ii. 301–2, 603.

[7] Battaglini, *Zecca*, 77, 187. On the small economic importance of the Riminese and similar local currencies: Vasina, *Romagna*, 274; Larner, 229.

[8] I, III–VI, IX: an injunction which the fiscal records of the Malatesta do not suggest they respected: below pp. 306, 313.

rectorial constitutions[1] and this on occasion they clearly did.[2] But the restriction most important to Rome was certainly the traditional one, now extended to *vicarii*, forbidding alienation of church land and property (I–VII, IX); and with this during the critical period of their history the Malatesta of both Rimini and Pesaro came into serious conflict. It applied, first, to ecclesiastical estates, in particular the *enfiteusi* of local churches, which, despite papal prohibition, did not always escape interference by the Malatesta;[3] but it referred equally to the whole territory in vicariate, and it was against the clause in this sense that the Malatesta offended most. Among themselves perhaps they were free to exchange their lands. Fossombrone seems to have passed without papal censure from the Malatesta of Rimini to those of Pesaro,[4] although it was with papal sanction that the vicariate of Mondavio was reunited with Fano in 1446,[5] and Cervia annexed to Cesena in 1450.[6] What the papacy was most concerned to prevent was the transfer of territory to a neighbouring power. When Galeazzo Malatesta in 1445, abdicated the vicariate of Pesaro and Fossombrone to Alessandro Sforza and Federigo d'Urbino, all parties to the contract were at once excommunicated.[7] Similarly when Malatesta Novello ceded Cervia to Venice in 1463, the pope exclaimed in protest to the Venetian envoy: 'obstat natura feudi, obstant Apostolicae litterae investiturae quae omnem alienationem prohibent', and the Auditores Rotae supported him with arguments drawn from feudal law.[8] In both transactions the papacy was later brought to acquiesce, but only from political weakness.

[1] IV–VII; cf. the vicariate of S. Agata granted in 1430: Marini, *Saggio*, 19.
[2] For example the *Cost. Egid.* laid down that the papal arms should be erected in every city; when Galeotto Malatesta in 1379 placed the Malatesta arms above his palace in Cesena (built by Albornoz) he first obtained papal licence to do so: Zazzeri, 239. Again the *Cost.* (110–12) repeated the severe prohibition against export of victuals from the Papal States; in 1421 Pandolfo Malatesta got papal permission to export 2,000 *some* of corn: Feliciangeli, 'Relazioni', 403.
[3] Especially if it lay across the site of fortifications projected by the Malatesta: Siena, 137–9; Castellani, *Malatesta* 33–4; Coleschi, 60. In this connection too must be noticed the clause in the peace concluded between Pius II and Malatesta Novello in 1463, by which Malatesta engaged to restore all lands taken from the churches of Ravenna and Sarsina since the first day of Eugenius IV's pontificate: Soranzo, *Pio II*, 404. In 1413, however, the Malatesta of Pesaro obtained from John XXIII a bull secularising emphyteutic properties of their churches to reduce the amount of land exempt from taxation: Giordani, *S. Tommaso*, 130–1, App. XXXVIII, XXXIX, XLIV–V.
[4] Above p. 166.
[5] Above p. 195.
[6] Soranzo, 'Cervia', 201.
[7] Above p. 195.
[8] *Pii II Commentarii*, 299; Franchini, 'Annullabilità', 232–40; Soranzo, 'Cervia'. The year before there was a rumour that Sigismondo was negotiating to surrender Citerna and other places to Florence; Pius II warned the Florentines any such sale would be invalid: Soranzo, *Pio II*, 310–11.

The vicariate, as already shown, was intended to transform *signori* into official delegates of Rome. In granting it, therefore, the popes were just as anxious to clarify its obligations and sanctions as to elaborate its powers; and from the first the Malatesta were bound to certain duties which they were solemnly engaged to perform. It was laid down that they should receive into their territories no 'prince' or 'potentate' 'de quo seu da qua possit verisimiliter dubitari seu presumi mutatio status vel occupatio Civitatum', a restriction common to all papal subjects (I); they were to proceed against heretics (I, IV) and give no protection to rebels or *banniti* of the church, but place them in custody if ordered by the provincial officers (IV, V, VI, IX); they were to provide billets and supplies, though not without payment, to papal and rectorial troops (IV, VII). The grant of 1355 enjoined also that all exiles from the Malatesta cities should be readmitted and receive back their properties; but this was a temporary condition, not subsequently repeated. More important than these occasional services, and more clearly defined were the positive obligations: an elaborate oath of fealty, attendance in provincial armies and parliaments, the payment of an annual *census*.

The oath of fealty differed little from the general oath of obedience owed by all papal subjects: the *iuramentum fidelitatis consuetum et de conservando et defendendo et recuperando terras castraque.*[1] In 1355 the whole investiture was cast in the form of sworn promises by the Malatesta: to respect ecclesiastical liberty, govern according to the statutes, and fulfil all the other duties placed upon them, as well as to surrender the vicariate at the end of ten years; but it mentioned also the various articles of the oath of fealty itself, which bound the Malatesta to exercise the vicariate 'fideliter', and to repeat the oath to each new pope within a year of election. After this it became established practice to place at the end of the bull of vicariate the *forma iuramenti* the Malatesta were to take. By that of 1358, in addition to the oath *alias fidelitatis debite*, they were to swear to observe all the conditions of the grant and promise to relinquish it *finito vicariatus tempore*. Should they fail first to take the oath, the bull was inoperative. In 1391 when the Malatesta received their vicariates for two generations, new details had to be introduced *per expressum*: thenceforward it was to be taken every ten years by Carlo Malatesta and his brothers, and after them by their heirs, who were also bound to take it within six months of succeeding. The oath itself now took the extended form which became current during the Schism, and included a promise to resist the heretic Robert of Geneva, never rebel against the church, or allow any emperor, king or duke etc. to assume office in papal cities, and to receive the pope or his

---

[1] Battaglini, *Vita*, App. xxxix; Franchini, 'Annullabilità', 232ff.; cf. Tonini, iv/2.222.

legates *reverenter et humiliter, quotiens ad partes illas accesserint.* If the
Malatesta failed to abide by the spirit of the oath, even after admonition,
they were to be excommunicated, suspended, and then deprived (v).
In the grant of Cervia in 1448 this threat of excommunication had dis-
appeared, but otherwise the form of oath established in 1391 remained
unaltered thereafter.[1]

The conditions for taking the oath were not in general stringent. At
first perhaps the Malatesta were expected to come and swear personally: *ad apicem summi Apostolatus personaliter*;[2] although they took the
oath locally in 1355 to the legate (i), Galeotto had to obtain exemption
in 1362 from visiting Avignon to swear obedience to the new pope,
receiving permission to do so to the papal representative instead.[3] This
subsequently was the usual practice. The grant of 1358 laid down that
the oath should be taken to the legate in Italy; so did that of1363,which
demanded also that a record of the oath be sealed and sent to the
Camera Apostolica. When Galeotto in 1383 was awarded in expectation
the vicariate of lands taken from Guido da Polenta, it was to the bishop
of Rimini, as papal commissioner, that he was to swear.[4] By then there
were popes in Italy again, and Carlo Malatesta was able and ready to
take the oath personally to Boniface IX, for himself and his brothers.[5]
But the bulls of vicariate continued to allow the Malatesta to perform
the ceremony locally (v–vii, ix) and even by proxy (vi, vii, ix). In
practice they seem to have followed convenience. In February 1431, on
the election of Eugenius IV, Galeotto Roberto sent the leading officials
of his territories to swear obedience to the pope on behalf of the
dynasty;[6] but in 1434 and 1435 Malatesta Novello and then Sigismondo, who were entering papal service as *condottieri*, swore to
Eugenius in person, as did Sigismondo again in 1459 when he was with
Pius II in Ferrara.[7] There is no record of whether the Malatesta complied fully with the rules governing the frequency of the oath, particularly that requiring it every ten years, but it is clear that political
expediency would counsel them to do so whenever a new pope was
elected. It was certainly not a formality to neglect. By the papacy the
oath was held to be the sanction on which the vicariate rested, estab-

[1] vi, vii, ix. The clause against the anti-pope appears first in the oath of Galeotto
in 1383 for lands to be conquered from Guido da Polenta: Bib. Gamb., *Cod.
Pand.*, fo. 137. Later of course Roberto of Geneva is replaced by other schismatic
popes – in 1448 Felix V.

[2] Tonini, iv/2.255.

[3] *Ibid.* cxxxiv. Malatesta Guastafamiglia made the journey: above p. 83. A letter
was also sent congratulating the pope on his election: *ibid.* cxxxii.

[4] Bib. Gamb., *Cod. Pand.*, fo. 137; Tonini, iv/2.365.

[5] *Ibid.* 391, 393. Malatesta of Pesaro also took the oath *in manibus nostris*: Theiner,
iii.47, 84.

[6] Clementini, ii.243; Amiani, i.366.

[7] Tonini, v/1.269; above p. 182.

lishing a relationship akin to vassalage,[1] and breach of the oath invited immediate censure. One reason advanced by Pius II in condemning the sale of Cervia was the oath sworn by the Malatesta,[2] and the last Malatesta was judged to have forfeited his 'fief' by betraying the duty of vassal to lord.[3]

Like the oath of fealty, military service, even if commuted, was a general duty in the Papal States,[4] and in 1355 it was imposed automatically on the Malatesta as vicars of the church. By the provisional agreement of 2 June it was proposed that 150 knights be produced each year to serve for three months in Romagna and the March,[5] but Malatesta Guastafamiglia rejected this as too heavy, and in the final bull the number was reduced to 100. It was made clear that in return for this and other services the papacy was itself obliged in no way to protect the Malatesta (I–VII, IX), but it was understood that the contingent would not be needed every year, and allowed, though only when the pope decided, that service could be commuted (I). These conditions remained, substantially unaltered, throughout the fourteenth century, and they seem to have been the only military duties expected of the Malatesta and their subjects.[6] But during the fifteenth century there are signs of a change. After the grant of 1399 all explicit mention of military service by the Malatesta themselves ceases, while in the bull of 1448, relating to Cervia, it is stated instead that such duties shall be performed by the 'inhabitants' of the city in the customary way.[7] The reason may be that in the fifteenth century the Malatesta became professional *condottieri* who might be in the service of the church or equally that of some other Italian government. This was particularly true of Sigismondo. During the earlier period the Malatesta had met papal demands adequately, above all under Albornoz, and in the Eight Saints war;[8] but even then it was the subject communes that inevitably

---

[1] In 1418 (?) Pandolfo Malatesta described himself as '*homo* et vicarius Ecclesie'.

[2] *Propter iuramentum Investiturae que iurarunt se restiturum*: Franchini, 'Annullabilità', App. II.

[3] Cappelli, 'Pandolfo', 448. On the wider question whether the vicariate was 'feudal' it may be noted that in 1463 the Auditores Rotae concluded, though hesitantly enough, that it should be classified a fief: Franchini, 'Annullabilità'.

[4] *Cost. Egid.*, ii.40; 'Description of the March', Theiner, ii.325; above p. 5. By the middle of the fourteenth century it was normally fixed in amount and in length and locality of service.

[5] Theiner, ii.303; above p. 76.

[6] I, II and by implication III exempted the Malatesta and their subjects from all other military service (*exercitus*).

[7] Tonini, v/2.167: *Volumus insuper, et hujusmodi Vicariatus constitutioni adjicimus per presentes, quod incole et habitatores predicti ad parlamenta generalia accedere, ac exercitus et cavalcatas more solito sicut alii de dicta provincia facere consueverunt, facere teneantur.*

[8] Above chap. 4. In 1373, however, the pope had to urge Galeotto to produce his military contingent (Tonini, iv/1.192), and in 1401 Boniface IX ordered the

bore the burden.[1] Their obligation was not new, and it was only a reversion to older practice if in the fifteenth century papal officers occasionally sent them requests for troops directly.[2] Not that the Malatesta ceased altogether to receive demands for men,[3] but after 1432, when they appear at all in the service of the church it is as mercenary captains of the pope. Sigismondo died a papal *condottiere*, as did Roberto his son, and Pandolfaccio was for long an idle military pensioner of the popes.[4]

A parallel development is traceable in the equally traditional obligation to attend provincial *parlamenta*, which the terms of vicariate at first imposed on both the Malatesta and their subjects (I, II, III); but in the grants of 1391 and later it was their subjects whom the popes seemed most concerned to oblige to visit *parlamente*.[5] By the end of the fourteenth century provincial parliaments had become infrequent, and it is not easy to say how readily the duty was performed, or even when it was exacted, but on occasion certainly the obligation was met;[6] while at an earlier period it was in a general parliament convened in a palace of the Malatesta that the fundamental laws of the Papal States had been published.[7]

As already seen, military service and parliament were two closely associated obligations – for one main purpose of parliament had always been to supply troops or money for troops.[8] In practice therefore it involved a duty that was financial, and when imposed on the Malatesta took its place beside other, more formidable claims on their revenues. Principal of these was the *census* to be paid annually to the Camera Apostolica. But more than *census* was demanded. In 1355, and again in 1358 and 1363, certain provincial taxes were reserved to the church,

---

    treasurer of Romagna to compel the Malatesta, on pain of excommunication and
    loss of all vicariates, and fiefs held of the papacy, empire or any other, to supply
    the 1,000 lances they owed. He was given power to exempt them: Theiner,
    iii.65. In 1392 Carlo Malatesta was able to commute his services: Amiani, i.316.
[1] For example: Amiani, i.286–7, 303–4; Vernarecci, *Fossombrone*, i.337.
[2] For example: Amiani, i.381; *Mem. Santarcangelo.* n. XVII. When submitting to the
    Malatesta in 1450 Monte Alboddo asked to be allowed to do military service at the
    request of the church: Rossi, *Monte Alboddo*, 112–13, 147–52.
[3] Battaglini, *Vita*, App. IX; Tonini, v/2, XXXVIII (1431).
[4] Above pp. 245, 250, 254. Even when serving other powers the Malatesta would
    not fight against the church (e.g. the contract with Piccinino, 1440: *Atti canc. visc.*,
    ii.103). Of course in the fourteenth century too the Malatesta had received pay if
    serving the papacy for a long time.
[5] V–VI, IX; cf. above p. 279 n. 7.
[6] Notably, but not only, in the March of Ancona: ACF, *Cod. mal.* 21, fo. 178r
    (1407); Amiani, i.348 (1419); Favier, 190ff.
[7] Above p. 80.
[8] Above pp. 6, 9.

fumantiae in Romagna, *census* and *affictus* in the March of Ancona. From the later grants such detail disappears: all distinction between Romagna and the March is ignored, and the bulls of 1391 and 1399, though concerned with both these provinces, specify only *affictus*. The same is true of the bull granting the Ravenna lands in 1415, while that of 1448, for Cervia, makes no allusion to these traditional taxes at all.

Of the four cities originally granted the Malatesta, Rimini alone belonged to Romagna, and alone therefore owed what the bull of 1355 called *fumantiae*. *Fumantiae*, *focaticum*, the hearth-tax, was one of the two charges to which the Riminese had been brought to submit after the popes recovered Romagna.[1] It was therefore no innovation to expect them to pay it, and as far as may be judged the tax continued to be collected unopposed after the vicariate had been set up.[2] From Fano, Pesaro and Fossombrone, on the other hand, the bull of 1355 required *census et affictus*. In the thirteenth century Pesaro and Fano had purchased privileges of government from the papacy in return for an annual *census* of £50.[3] In these privileges no mention is made of *affictus*, but in the accounts of the March of Ancona for 1344 both cities are charged with this rent,[4] and it is this second tax which the places held in vicariate by the Malatesta in the March are recorded as paying later. In 1356,[5] and again between 1409 and 1421, in 1422 and 1426, *affictus* or *fito* is rendered by all or some of them;[6] but of *census* there is hardly word, nor in the privileges of 1391 and later is there reference to it as due from these communities in the March.[7] Yet it was a distinct tax, it

---

[1] Tonini, *Imposte*, 6–8. In 1330 it amounted to £650 *Rav.* (Theiner, i.588), in 1336 to £600 (Tonini, iv.100).

[2] Theiner, ii.515. In 1404 Boniface IX granted Giovanni di Ramberto Malatesta for 5 years the collection of *fumentaria* in Rimini and Santarcangelo, in return for an annual payment of 200 gold fl., a grant confirmed in 1405, 1407, 1409, 1413 and 1417: Castellani, *Malatesta*, 40–1.

[3] 'vel si mallemus novem denarios pro unoquoque fumante, ut more vestro loquamur': Theiner, i.43, 238, 472, 490; *Liber Censuum*, i.89. The same was true of other communities destined to come under the Malatesta – Staffolo, Offagna, Castelfidardo etc: Theiner, i.p.269 and nn. 482, 484, 489; Pastori; Aloisi, *AMM* 1905, 414–21, 1906, 326.

[4] Fano with 15 fl. 13 *sol.* 4 *den. Rav.*, Pesaro with 22 fl. £1 12 *sol.*: Theiner, ii.144–5 (44 *sol. Rav.* equalled 1 fl.).

[5] In *c.* 1356, Fano (£33 13 *sol.*), Fossombrone (£10) and Pesaro (£50) all paid *affictus* (Theiner, ii.347–8). The figure £50 for Pesaro would suggest the *affictus* represented under a new name the *census* imposed in the thirteenth century. Like Pesaro Iesi had been paying £50 *census* (Theiner, i.43), which now became £50 *affictus*. That Fano paid only £33 results from the fact that part of its *contado* had been detached: above p. 55.

[6] Arch. vat., *Arm.* xxxiii, n. 11; ACF, *Cod. mal.* 21, fo. 186; Fumi, 'Inventario', 6–7. The subjects of the Malatesta of Pesaro also paid *affictus*: Theiner, iii.275 (1435).

[7] In 1402 however the Malatesta apparently claimed that Fano, Pesaro, Fossombrone, Mondavio, Orciano and Corinaldo, which were held in vicariate, were

was paid by other towns which the Malatesta governed, though not as vicars of the church,[1] and, more important, even after 1391 cities like Fano, over which the vicariate did extend, were frequently vexed by demands for *census* traditionally owed in the March of Ancona, in addition to *affictus*, and on one occasion for *fumantiae* as well.[2]

Officials of the Malatesta did their best to repel injunctions of this kind, but it was not the only threat against which they had to defend their lords' immunity. The papacy also demanded, and at times may have succeeded in collecting, tallages. To *taleae*, as one of the principal papal taxes,[3] all the Malatesta cities had originally been subject.[4] But the first bulls of vicariate granted them a general (and in practice unusual) exemption from it,[5] while those of the later fourteenth century and after made no reference to tallage at all. With the concession of Cervia in 1448 went no other financial obligation than the payment of *census* by the Malatesta. For a time the immunity was respected by the papacy and its officers,[6] but before the end of the

liable only to attend parliaments and pay *census*: Theiner, iii.63. This is contrary to the bull of 1399 which mentions only *affictus* (VI). The inference that they were the same thing is ruled out by the fact that in 1385 Mondavio, and in 1422 and 1426 Corinaldo, paid both: Arch. vat., *loc. cit.*; Fumi, *loc. cit.*; ACF, *Canc., Castelli* i, fo. 6v.

[1] Thus Staffolo, Castelfidardo, Cittanova etc.: Arch. vat., *loc. cit.*; Fumi, *loc. cit.*; Gianandrea, 'Staffolo', doc. liii.

[2] Provoking protests (as in 1447 and 1448) from Malatesta officials: ACF, *Canc., Castelli* i, Ser. 1386ff., fos. 70v–71r, *Reg.* ii, fos. 22r–26v, 31r–32r; Zonghi, 176 n. xvi. In 1406 Innocent VII renewed a bull of Boniface IX invalidating all grants of vicariate, *gubernatio*, fief or emphyteusis, to the extent that they reduced the *census antiqui, affictus, fumantiae, salinae, tracta quorumcymque victualium, aut alia regalia Beati Petri*, but nothing seems to have resulted. By this time revenue from hearth-tax, *affictus* and *census* had shrunk to negligible proportions: Partner, 117.

[3] Above p. 5.

[4] Thus Fano in 1344 (ACF, *Depos., Entrata/uscita* 1), other places in the March in 1342 (Theiner, ii.190), and, grudgingly, Rimini: Tonini, iv/1.100ff.; *Imposte*, 6–8; above p. 53.

[5] Above p. 273; cf. Partner, 188.

[6] The survey of the March (*c.* 1356) states: 'Forosinfronium et Fanum non fuerunt taxate quia sunt dnorum de Malatestis [qui] debent solvere pro Vicariatu' (i.e. *census*): Theiner, ii.348 (similarly Pesaro). Rectorial tallages disappear from the accounts of Fano after 1355, and neither Fano, Pesaro nor Fossombrone appear among Albornoz' provisions for *tallia militum*: *SS* xii.309–10, xiii.22–4. Of Rimini cardinal Anglico wrote in 1371: 'Consuevit solvere in anno pro tallia libr. 14,500 set hodie non solvit quia dni de Malatestis solvunt censum supradictum': Theiner, ii.515. He gives the same reason for non-payment of *tallia* by Imola (vicariate of the Alidosi), and Ravenna and Cervia (vicariate of the Polenta: *ibid.* pp. 492, 513); and when the Malatesta received early in the fifteenth century the 'government' but not the vicariate of Osimo and other places they were obliged to pay all taxes, including *tallia*, but had no *census* to pay. Yet a document of 1389–90 gives a different reason for the Malatesta's immunity: 'Fanum, Pensaurum, Forosinpronium non fuerunt taxate quia domini de Malatestis tenebant serviebant cum personis et equitibus': Amati, 'Notizie', 191–2.

fourteenth century it began to be challenged, as it continued to be during the century that followed.[1] From certain lands of the Malatesta, those not held in vicariate, tallage was incontestably due,[2] and when necessary paid.[3] The liability of their other lands was much less certainly established, and when asserted by the provincial representatives of the pope, drove the Malatesta or those under them to protest against violation of their liberties. In 1402 they had to remind the papacy that the places they governed in the March as vicars were exempt from *tallie vel collecte*, and have their immunity affirmed.[4] Even so their privileges do not always seem to have resisted invasion, and it is perhaps safest to assume that however reticent the phrasing of bulls of vicariate, tallages of some kind were from the late fourteenth century exacted on occasion from all the Malatesta lands, in the March of Ancona at least, which could, if the pope desired, be made over to the Malatesta themselves.[5] Beyond the obvious possibility that papal

[1] Already in 1367 the Malatesta were obtaining exemption from 'war taxes': Amiani, i.290; while in 1390 Fano, Pesaro and Fossombrone were among the cities of the March to whom the local officials wrote demanding tallage: ACF, *Canc.*, *Castelli* i, Ser. 1386ff., fo. 70r; similar letters seem to have been received in 1439, 1447 and 1448: above p. 282 n. 2.

[2] Notably the cities and towns (Osimo, Castelfidardo, Montefilottrano, Staffolo, Offagna etc.) of which in 1400 and 1407 Pandolfo Malatesta received the temporary *regimen, gubernationem et administrationem*. These grants were very similar to the vicariate, but in addition to parliaments and military service reserved 'census seu affictus et regalia nec non omnes et singulas talias tam impositas quam imponendas pro conductis gentium armorum': Battaglini, *Vita*, App. iv, v; Cecconi, 'Sommario', n. xxiv; Gianandrea, 'Staffolo', 325.

[3] Thus at various times between 1405 and 1426: Cecconi, 'Sommario', nn. xii, xxv; Gianandrea, 'Staffolo', 326; Amiani, i.331; Nicoletti, 163 n. 3; Maraschini, nn. 76, 92; Arch. vat., *Arm.* xxxiii, n. 11; ACF, *Cod. mal.* 5, fos. 29, 30, 37 .

[4] Theiner, ii.63; Favier, 192; for other cases: above n. 1.

[5] The list of places paying tallage in the March in 1426 includes several towns held by the Malatesta in vicariate (Arch. vat., *loc. cit.*), and in 1435 tallage was among the dues remitted in the peace of the Malatesta of Pesaro with the church (Theiner, iii.275). Some years earlier (1421) Pandolfo Malatesta is recorded as having received tallage from Fano, Mondavio, Pergola and Scorticata (Amiani, i.350), and in 1414 Malatesta of Cesena ordered *taglie* to be paid by Pandolfo's territories for hire of troops (ACF, *Cod. mal.* 5, fos. 29–30; Zonghi, 18). Here the question arises whether Malatesta and Pandolfo were acting for themselves or for the church: whether immunity from rectorial tallage had transferred the tax to the vicar? From lands not held in vicariate tallage could be transferred by the pope to a lord, as by Gregory XII to Carlo Malatesta (Eubel, *RQ* 1896, 100; Valois, *Schisme*, iv.144; Cutolo, ii.198). Pandolfo Malatesta also between 1410 and 1423 was receiving tallages from Osimo and other places, probably by papal grant (Martorelli, 241; Cecconi, 'Sommario', n. xlviii; cf. ACF, *Cod mal.* 21, fos. 125r, 126v, 150r–152r; 24). But the fiscal records of Fano register also payments of *taglie* from lands held in vicariate (ACF, *Canc.*, *Castelli* xv; *Cod. mal.* 87 (fo. 60r), 104–6). It is not certain these taxes remained in the vicar's hands: in 1438, when the community of Monterolo petitioned Sigismondo to be free of 'taglie, salva in

officials were simply trying to override franchise, or the conservative belief, sometimes stated,[1] that tallage was still in commutation of military service, to which the Malatesta lands were liable, the most likely explanation lies in some change in the nature of papal taxation itself: that the old *tallia militum*, from which exemption was granted, had become fixed and regular and was being superseded, especially after the Schism, by other extraordinary taxes, *subsidies* or *tallie*, similar in purpose, and sought perhaps in parliaments of the kind to which the Malatesta and their subjects were still bound to send representatives.[2]

By contrast with these lesser impositions, there was no question about the obligation to pay an annual *census* in return for the vicariate. Together with the oath of fealty, it was fundamental to the whole institution, however small in amount. That of the Malatesta (and the Este) was for long by far the highest. By the first grant of 1355 they were engaged to pay each year 6,000 gold florins, to be delivered at their own cost and risk to the Camera Apostolica *ubicumque fuerit*,[3] half at Christmas and half in June on the feast of SS. Peter and Paul. For their original lands this figure continued with slight variations for nearly a century, though later, in the mid-fifteenth century, the more normal rule was imposed of paying it in one sum, in June.[4] When, near the end of the fourteenth century, the Malatesta of Pesaro received a separate investiture, they were bound to a *census* of 1,800 florins.[5] But that did not serve to lessen the amount due from the Malatesta of Rimini, who meanwhile had extended their territories raising the total sum due to 10,000 florins, reduced in 1421 to 8,000 and at some subsequent date to 6,000. Only after their defeat by Pius II did their *census* shrink to a mere 1,000 ducats, which it remained until their fall.[6]

Failure to pay *census* carried threat of excommunication, interdict and ultimately deprivation (I–VI); and of all vicarial obligations it was

quella forma fanno quelli del vicariato [Mondavio] cio e letaglie de la Marca', he could only promise his help (ACF, *Canc.*, Reg. ii, fo. 45v; cf. 34v for a similar request from Rupola five years later). The records are the more difficult to interpret in that the Malatesta themselves imposed war taxes, sometimes called *taglie*. The papal levy would seem also limited to the March: Larner, 291.
[1] Above p. 282 n. 6.
[2] Anzilotti, *AR* 1919; Bauer, 'Studi', 334; Nina, *Finanze*, iii.203; Favier, 191ff. *Subsidies* were paid for example on request by Galeotto in 1374, demanded in 1439: Tonini, iv/2, CLXXXII; Zonghi, 176. Another tax of the kind was a levy on the Jews: it was against this that the Malatesta and their officials protested in 1402, 1447 and 1448: ACF, *Canc.*, Reg. ii, fos. 22v, 24r, 32r.
[3] As an exception to this particular rule the Malatesta were allowed in 1364 to pay their *census* locally in Bologna: Tonini, iv/2, CXL.
[4] The grant of 1358 added another 300 fl., that of 1415 a further 150. The Cervia investiture of 1448 carried its own *census* of 200 ducats.
[5] Mazzatinti, *Inventari*, xxxvii.92; Theiner, iii.87; Ugolini, ii.192.
[6] Above pp. 157, 203, 238; Partner, 69–70, 189; Favier, 184.

perhaps the one the papacy interpreted most strictly. It was therefore in the interests of the Malatesta to meet it as regularly as they could, if their revenues only permitted. To the Florentine Villani, as already seen, the *census* laid on the Malatesta in 1355 seemed trifling, but not so to the Malatesta themselves. The sum of 8,000 florins first proposed by the papacy was rejected by Guastafamiglia as beyond his resources, and it was reduced at his request by one-quarter.[1] With the subsequent basic *census* the Malatesta seem to have remained satisfied, until a century later in 1450 Sigismondo obtained from Nicholas V a further reduction in recognition of his services.[2] Previously, down to his accession at least, the tribute cannot have been embarrassingly onerous. Rimini alone, according to cardinal Anglico, had been accustomed before the vicariate to pay each year £14,500 in tallage,[3] and the income of the city, as far as was in his power, he estimated in 1371 to be £73,700 *Rav.*[4] The late fourteenth and the early fifteenth centuries seem to have been a period of prosperity for Rimini. The city was populous and yielded an ample revenue,[5] but so also did the other towns of the Malatesta: Cesena,[6] Pesaro,[7] Cervia,[8] and Fano,[9] to name only the most important and disregard the lords' patrimonial receipts. Small wonder that Braccio in 1416 considered the Malatesta rich enough to pay a

---

[1] Above p. 76. Even then taxes imposed to pay the legate and other expenses caused a peasant disturbance: *Cron. mal.* 20.

[2] From 6,000 to 4,000 fl. (above p. 203) of which Malatesta Novello was to pay 1,600, Sigismondo the rest (Rossi, 'Nuove notizie', 169–72). In 1460 he tried for a further reduction: above p. 227. For the Malatesta of Pesaro, overtaken by poverty more quickly than the Malatesta of Rimini, the papacy had already reduced the *census* twice, in 1407/8 and 1426: Ugolini, ii.192; Theiner, iii.163; Mazzatinti, *Inventari*, xxxvii.86–7; Partner, 189; above pp. 166, 167.

[3] Theiner, ii.525, but cf. Tonini, iv.100ff. In 1337 Rimini was prepared to pay as much as 2,400 fl. each year to keep out one of its *signori*: Larner (223) believes *census* was a lighter burden than tallage.

[4] Theiner, ii.525. The expenses of collection must have raised the total to £80,000: Tonini, *Imposte*, 19.

[5] Despite the heavy mortality caused by the Black Death (*Cron. mal.* 17; Tonini, iv/1.130–1), in 1371 Rimini had 2,240 *foc.*, which the *contado* made up to 5,505: Theiner, ii.525. Though demographically imprecise (Larner, 209ff.), these figures agree fairly well with the sixteenth-century estimate of the population in the time of Carlo Malatesta as between 20,000 and 30,000 souls, rendering an annual revenue of about 40,000 ducats: Tonini, vi/1.191–2; Clementini, ii.224.

[6] With an estimated revenue in 1371 of £24,120, plus £3,000 from the sale of salt: Theiner, ii.525.

[7] For the year 1373 the revenues of Pesaro amounted to £36,072: Tonini, iv/1.193; *Imposte*, 38–9.

[8] With a revenue in 1371 of £3,200, excluding the immense profits of its saltworks: Theiner, ii.525.
Where, in 1404, public (as distinct from patrimonial) income amounted to £78,024 *sol.* 17 *den.* 4 (with payments from Mondavio, S. Sepolcro, Pergola, and other places, but the bulk from Fano): ACF, *Cod. mal.* 16.

heavy ransom;[1] and at this time the papal *census* can have claimed only a small proportion of their income: in 1404, if the accounts are complete, it took no more than a tenth part of the revenues of Fano.[2]

Census, however, was only one of many claims on the resources of the Malatesta, too numerous and diverse to enumerate.[3] In a single year, 1404, the money paid out in Fano alone amounted almost to £75,000.[4] During the early fifteenth century, at a time of continual war in the Papal States, as well as of Pandolfo Malatesta's costly adventures in Lombardy, the expenditure of the Malatesta was particularly great, and between 1411 and 1414 to only one of his captains, Martino de Faenza, Pandolfo made over nearly £50,000.[5] In consequence the Malatesta, like other vicars, sometimes allowed their payments to the Camera to fall into arrears, though less frequently in the fourteenth century than the fifteenth, when the status of vicar had become habitual. Down to the confused period which opened with the pontificate of Gregory XII the records of *census* paid, both in Rimini[6] and in Fano,[7] are fairly complete; but subsequently, although the surviving accounts are imperfect, all such local record ceases.[8] This does not mean that the Malatesta consistently evaded the duty,[9] but it does suggest their payments became fitful and uncertain. On a number of occasions, it is true, the papacy was willing to remit arrears of *census*:[10] Sigismondo

[1] Above p. 147.

[2] For income: above p. 285. The *census* amounted to £7,434 *sol.* 19 *den.* 14 (ACF, *Cod. mal.* 17), but this may have included arrears: below n. 6.

[3] Cf. below pp. 314, 324.

[4] ACF, *Cod. mal.* 17.

[5] *Ibid.* 21, fo. 241.

[6] Bib. Gamb., *Cod. Pand.*, fos. 106-15, 117, 119-21, 123-6, 138, 145-8; Clementini, ii.131, 230, 234; Tonini, iv.140, iv/2, CLXXXII; Schäfer, *Ausgaben, Urban V und Gregor XI*, 502, 568-9, 575-6. Even in this period the Malatesta were sometimes in arrears and under papal censure for non-payment: *Cod. Pand.*, fos. 108, 114; Tonini, iv.192, 416; Theiner, ii.652. In 1362 the Malatesta met their obligation by replenishing Bologna with corn: Tonini, *Imposte*, 34.

[7] ACF, *Depos.*, *Entrata/uscita* 17, 56, 57, 59; *Cod. mal.* 13 fo. 31r, 14 fo. 48r, 17 fo. 48r, 21 fo. 186r; Castellucci, 'Regesto', 185-7. In 1404 the Malatesta had to impose new taxes to pay off *census*: Vernarecci, *Fossombrone*, 346.

[8] At Fano the volumes of the *Depositaria* for 1398-1432, 1436-9, 1441 and 1446-9 are all missing, but in the other accounts of the Malatesta following 1407 there is no allusion to *census*.

[9] Battaglini, *Vita*, App. XXIX, LXIX; *Zecca*, 236; Partner, 69-70, 189. During much of the Schism the Malatesta were prompt, even previous, with their payments: Favier, 186, 434.

[10] Thus in 1367 (Amiani, i.290; cf. Mazzatinti, *Inventari*, xxxvii.92), 1390 (for service in recovering Bertinoro: *Cod. Pand.*, fo. 139), and 1419 (above p. 156; Battaglini, *Vita*, 692); while Martin V's remission of the debts owed by Pandolfo Malatesta may have included *census* (Battaglini, *Vita*, 693). The Malatesta of Pesaro were just as anxious for relief (Mazzatinti, *Inventari*, xxxvii.92, *a.* 1390); in 1435, acknow-

in particular availed himself of this privilege at least twice, in 1450 and again in 1455;[1] yet haphazard and intermittent payment of this kind exposed the Malatesta to a threat of papal reprisals, and whenever during the fifteenth century the popes attempted to recover Rimini, they found a legitimate reason ready every time in the failure of the Malatesta to pay their tribute punctually.[2] It was used by Martin V against the heirs of Carlo Malatesta, and again by Pius II against Sigismondo and Malatesta Novello, who, although released from debt in 1455, were still unable or unwilling to meet papal claims.[3] After Sigismondo's defeat the Malatesta's capacity to pay was seriously reduced. It seems still to have taken no more than one-tenth of revenue, but revenue was now sadly diminished.[4] By the end of the fifteenth century Rimini had ceased to be populous and wealthy,[5] and both Roberto and Pandolfo Malatesta complained that their *census* was more than they could afford.[6] Payment doubtless remained irregular,[7] and among the vicars of the church denounced by Innocent VIII and Alexander VI for not paying tribute, the Malatesta must have been included. This at least was the excuse invoked when in 1500 the papacy proceeded for the third time to attack them. Pandolfo's agitated efforts to raise the *census* in Venice availed nothing, and he went down helplessly before the onslaught of Cesare Borgia.

As will be seen, the events of 1500 virtually ended the government of the Malatesta. Yet the blow need not have been fatal, if only the Malatesta had preserved the affection of their subjects. Condemned as vicars of the church, they might have survived as *signori* and later recovered papal favour. This they had succeeded in doing before, and other

---

ledging them to be 'non solum pauperes, sed mendici', Eugenius IV pardoned all arrears. (Theiner, iii.275; Mazzatinti, *Inventari*, xxxvii.93), but in 1444, the year of the sale to Sforza and Federigo d'Urbino, *census* was still unpaid: Giordani, *A. Sforza*, xxii–iii, xxv–xxix.

[1] x: above p. 203.

[2] Franchini ('Annullabilità', 221) says only refusal to pay *census* could justify deprivation, but this is not confirmed by bulls to the Malatesta.

[3] Above pp. 170, 228. In 1464, after peace with the pope, Malatesta Novello was owing 2,000 fl., at his death 6,000: Mazzatinti, *Archivi*, Ser. 1, i.335; Robertson, 'Cesena', 137.

[4] See the Venetian survey (1504) of Pandolfo's income and expenses: Sanudo, v.497.

[5] Below p. 327.

[6] In 1479 Roberto complained that the *census* of 1000 ducats 'fo molto più et magior taglia che non pagò mai homo de casa mia per quello che tengo', and in 1495 Pandolfo made a similar protest: Tonini, v/2, cx; Cappelli, 'Pandolfo', doc. i and 235.

[7] Thus in the brief balance of revenues of Sixtus IV's reign the *census* of Rimini does not appear beside those of Ferrara, Bagnacavallo, Urbino, Faenza, Pesaro, Forlì and Imola: Gottlob, 254.

despots dispossessed by the Borgia were to do it again. The fact that the expulsion of the Malatesta was permanent and all their endeavours to return unsuccessful, was due not only to their relations with the papacy. Much more was it a consequence of their conduct as princes, of the older relations between lord and commune, upon which the vicariate had been imposed.

10

The government of the Malatesta

2. The *signoria*

It was inevitable that the papacy when seeking to evict the Malatesta should describe them as subjects, disobedient subjects, of the church, for such in law they were. But in the political life of Italy they were much more than this, as Pius II quickly found. They were members of a princely dynasty who could raise armies, despatch embassies and conclude alliances independently of their papal sovereign.[1] They could regard themselves as lords in their own right, and were not therefore content, when issuing decrees or publishing laws, merely to adopt the title of vicar. 'Vicars' indeed they did on occasion call themselves,[2] but it was not the style that they or their officials made use of most. 'Rector' or 'gubernator' were equally favoured, and still more 'dominus' or 'signore',[3] which, in all its vagueness, remained supreme among the titles of the Malatesta, until at the end of the fifteenth century 'princeps' began to appear in public documents and inscriptions.[4]

---

[1] Sometimes, it is true, the Malatesta alleged the need of papal consent before entering an alliance, as did Carlo Malatesta in 1423 (*Commiss. Albizzi*, i.471, 494), and other powers could desire papal approval before employing them: *Lucca, Regesti*, ii/2.1769, 1771–3 (1397); Battaglini, *Vita*, 455 (Siena 1454).

[2] This was particularly the case during the early years of the vicariate under Guastafamiglia and Galeotto (Bib. sen., *Stat. Rim.*, fos. 193v–194v; ACF, *Cod. mal.* 3, fos. 17r–19v; Mariotti, *Bandi mal.*, 11; Grimaldi, 'Bandi') and Galeotto's four sons (*Stat. Caes.* (1589), 81, 86, 252; *Stat. Rim.*, fos. 190–1, 340r, 349r; Battaglini, *Vita*, App. vi; Tonini, v/2, xxxiii), and in 1432 the *officialis custodie dampnorum datorum* in Fano is said to hold his office *pro magnificis et potentibus dominis generalibus Vicariis*: ACF, *Depos., Zocco del Danno Dato*, 4). But there seems to be no rule in the usage, and under Sigismondo it declines.

[3] As late as April 1378 Galeotto Malatesta was still calling himself *dominus et defensor* of Rimini (Bib. sen., *Stat. Rim.*, fo. 187); but this soon gave way to other titles, already in use, such as *dominus generalis* (*Stat. Cerviae*, 112; Vitali, 235), *Magnifico et Possente Signore* (*Stat. Rim.*, fos. 349r ff.) etc. On their coins the Malatesta simply called themselves *domini*: Battaglini, *Zecca*, 220, Tav., 'Monete di Rimini', nn. 11–16.

[4] E.g. 1484 and 1490: Battaglini, *Zecca*, 280–1; Corte, 170. 'Princeps' characteristically became common under Sigismondo, though it had been used earlier by the jurist Baldus when addressing Carlo Malatesta (Battaglini, *Corte*, 54, 126 n. 45). It found particular favour with the humanists in Sigismondo's patronage (Affò,

The Malatesta had been *domini*, both formally and in fact, before ever they gained the papal vicariate, and earlier still they had been landed magnates of prominence. It is as landowners that the Malatesta first appear, and landowners they all remained. Their private estates lay thickly everywhere and lasted as a source of income and influence as long as the *signoria*. Possessed of property from the earliest times in Rimini and Verucchio, the Malatesta are seen from the middle of the thirteenth century to be acquiring lands indefatigably both there and further afield, in Bellaria, Santarcangelo, Gradara, Savignano, Roncofreddo, Montescudolo, Montefiore, and many other castles and villages.[1] Similar accretions of property preceded or accompanied their establishment in Pesaro, Fano, Fossombrone, S. Sepolcro, Cesena, Sinigaglia, Montalboddo and elsewhere, in all of which they gained lands.[2] Round Fano alone the Malatesta held properties in Saltara, Serrungarina, Cartoceto, Fogliano, Mondolfo, Ripalta, Montegiano, Pezzolo, Issola, S. Costanzo and Roncitello.[3] La Caminata and Stacciola near Fano, and Fiumesino, Bellaria, Bordonchio, Castel Liale and Gerlendeta near Rimini, the Malatesta seem to have possessed entire,[4] while outside their own dominions they had property in Bologna,[5] Florence, Ferrara, Lombardy and for a time Venice.[6] The separation of the Malatesta of Pesaro did not affect their possessions outside that city;[7] and even when they were humiliated, stripped of their terri-

---

16, 28–9; Battaglini, *Corte*, 62, 134–5, 194; Yriarte, 318, 386–7), who also called him *divus* or *rex* (Affò, 16–17; Battaglini, *Zecca*, 258; Guarino da Verona, *Epistolario* (ed. R. Sabbadini, Venice, 1915–19), ii.634; Ricci, 435–6 etc.). Sigismondo and Malatesta were the first to use the elephant as a symbol, presumably of regal splendour (Battaglini, *Zecca, loc. cit.*; Ricci, 320–2). Yet sometimes, as in 1453, Sigismondo gave only his military title in a decree: ACF, *Cod. mal.* 93, fo. 25r (*ducalis capitaneus generalis*).

[1] The titles to these lands covering the years 1259 to 1374 were collected together early in the fifteenth century by Pandolfo III Malatesta, and are now preserved in the *Codice Pandolfesco* at Rimini.

[2] For Pesaro see for example Amiani, i.295; Fano: *ibid.* 289; Zonghi, 248–50; Fossombrone: Vernarecci, *Fossombrone*, i.316; S. Sepolcro: Mazzatinti, *Archivi*, Ser. 2, iv.128, 148; Sinigaglia: ACF, *Cod. mal.* 72 and below p. 291 n. 3; Montalboddo: *Cod. mal.* 4, fo. 5r.

[3] ACF, *Cod. mal.* 27.

[4] For Caminata: ACF, *Cod. mal.* 9, 10 (fo. 175r), 80; *Canc., Reg.* ii, fo. 67r; for Stacciola: *Cod. mal.* 10 (fo. 226r), 37–8; for the other places: Sanuto, v.494–5. The income from Meldola and Polenta seems to be purely patrimonial: *Cod. mal.* 39; though the distinction between private and public land is not easily drawn.

[5] Where Galeotto Malatesta had a house: Bosdari, 'Giovanni da Legnano', 62–3, 117–20.

[6] Giordani, *Notizie*, xxx–i; Tonini, iv/2.318, v/2.197; Lucca, *Regesti*, ii/2.1848; above p. 134.

[7] The Malatesta of Pesaro continued to hold properties in Fano and elsewhere: Amiani, i.386; Giordani, *Gradara*, 82; Fantuzzi, v.197; Mazzatinti, *Inventari*, xxxviii.7.

tories and expelled from power, the papacy still guaranteed to the Malatesta their private estates.[1]

The properties were of every kind, comprising agricultural land, houses, shops and palaces, woods, water-courses and mills. Mills were especially profitable and seem almost to have become a monopoly of the Malatesta. In Pesaro and Fano at least, and probably elsewhere, even the mills of the commune passed into their hands.[2] Some land the Malatesta held emphyteutically or otherwise of the church,[3] but most they acquired by purchase or by exchange,[4] wills[5] or outright gift, though not all gifts seem to have been voluntary.[6] Finally there were properties which came to the Malatesta not as private owners but by virtue of their powers as *signori* and papal vicars, from rebels, traitors and offenders against their laws.[7]

This private demesne was usually administered apart by specially appointed factors,[8] and yielded a valuable return for consumption and sale. In 1409 the income of Pandolfo Malatesta's factor in Fano amounted to nearly £11,000, apart from large quantities of wine, oil and other produce,[9] and at the end of the fifteenth century Pandolfaccio

---

1 As for example in 1430: above p. 170. In 1465 Paul II ratified the gifts by Malatesta Novello before his death: Theiner, iii.385; Zazzeri, 364–5, 370–1. Similarly in 1500 Cesare Borgia permitted Pandolfo to retain his properties, and dispossessed those who had rushed to grab them on his expulsion: Bernardi, i/2.315; Sanudo, *Diarii*, v.560. In Fano by contrast Paul II gave the city the Malatesta palaces: Amiani, ii.24; Zonghi, 177, 181.

2 For Fano: Amiani, i.381 (and 190, which suggests the commune retained the monopoly after the Malatesta). For Pesaro and Fossombrone: Vaccai, 200–2; Giordani, *A. Sforza*, xxvi. Cf. further: ACF, *Cod. mal.* 21, fo. 300v; 38. At Urbino also mills, fulling mills and mines were all in the lords' hands: Franceschini, *Montefeltro*, 304.

3 Theiner, ii.144, iii.61; Giordani, *S. Tommaso*, 154–5; Mazzatinti, *Inventari*, xxxix.175; Vernarecci, *Fossombrone*, ii.61, 79–80; Fantuzzi, vi.170.

4 Above p. 290 n. 1. Guastafamiglia may have been rather summary in his methods of buying property: Tonini, iv/2.263.

5 Above p. 290 n. 1. The goods of the intestate also may on occasion have fallen to the *signore*: Zonghi, 141. Not only land was bequeathed: in 1375 Galeotto Malatesta received nearly 3,500 gold ducats from a citizen of Ravenna dying in Rimini: Rubeus, 592, and Bib. Gamb., *Cod. Pand.*

6 Vernarecci, *Fossombrone*, i.317–18.

7 Chiaramonti, 396; Clementini, ii.217, 219, 583–4; Battaglini, *Corte*, 173ff., 181; Tonini, v/1. 491–2, v/2, CXLII, vi/2.849. For lands forfeit for disobedience cf. an act of Sigismondo's (10 April 1443) disposing of 'certe terre de uno da pesaro Rechadute ala mia camera per contrabando de grano': Bib. Gamb., *Arch. notarile, Atti Fr. Paponi*.

8 Or *gastaldi* or *massari*. There are references also to *soprastanti* of the lords' mills (*Cod. mal.* 87, fo. 79r) and to an *exactor generalis* (Fantuzzi, vi.243). But the commonest term is factor: *Cod. mal.* 4, 9–10, 19 etc. In Sinigaglia the *depositario* or public treasurer controlled also the Malatesta estates: *Cod. mal.* 72, 107–8. Some property of course was farmed, for example (1398) Pandolfo's income from mills *ultra et citra metaurum*: ACF, *Canc., Cons.* i, fo. 3r.

9 *Cod. mal.* 19.

was still drawing one-ninth of his revenue *di le sue possessione.*[1] Most of this money was spent locally in paying manorial officials and wage labourers, buying beasts and crops, repairing or hiring buildings, or providing hospitality.[2] The main sources of income were rents (*fiti*) and the proceeds from the sale of livestock and produce: timber, flax, wine and, especially, corn (wheat, barley, spelt, beans).[3] The mills controlled by the Malatesta probably increased their grain receipts[4] and in 1409 money from corn sales formed the largest single item in the factor's income.[5] As seen, Romagna and the March were grain-exporting regions, though subject to recurrent restrictions on *tratte.*[6] So the Malatesta disposed of their corn not only locally[7] but also abroad. On one occasion Pandolfo III Malatesta received nearly £22,000 from corn sales to Venice.[8]

As a source of income trade in corn was of less account than the Malatesta's lucrative control over the distribution and sale of salt, which brought in more than any other category of revenue public or private. There had been a salt-tax already under the commune,[9] and even before they acquired Cervia, the Malatesta may have had their salt

[1] Of a total 9,224 ducats £3 14 *sol.* they supplied 1,190 ducats: Sanuto, v. 489.

[2] ACF, *Cod. mal.* 10, 19, 39, 72, 80-3, 88-91, 111-12. In 1409 over £1,500 were spent on meat alone: *Cod. mal.* 19. The factor's accounts of 1436-8 show the Malatesta could employ thousands of labourers in the course of a year or more: *Cod. mal.* 80.

[3] *Cod. mal.* 4 (fos. 5r, 203v-204v), 19, 27, 38-9, 80-3, 89-91, 111-12.

[4] In the thirteenth century payment for grinding corn seems to have been made in kind (Amiani, i.190), and this practice continued under the Malatesta. The manorial income of Stacciola 1398-1406 (*Cod. mal.* 38) records grain contributions from individuals and communities round Mondolfo, from Fano, Sinigaglia and the vicariate of Mondavio, said to be 'di ragione del signore', but these may have been food rents.

[5] £3,209 7 *sol.* 7 *den.*: *Cod. mal.* 19. In 1372 Malatesta Ungaro bequeathed his wife and daughter 10,000 *star. Arim.* of corn in his granaries: Tonini, iv/2, CLXVI, 316, 318.

[6] Above pp. 7, 13. In 1524 it was calculated that the territory of Rimini normally produced 24,000 *stara.* of wheat of which the city took at least 12,000 'per il manzare', leaving 4,000 for seed and a surplus of 8,000: ASF, *Carte Strozziane*, Ser. 1, 238, fo. 141.

[7] As was usually the case; thus *Cod. mal.* 78 deals with the grain received and distributed between 1430 and 1433 by Bartolomeo da Sassoferrato, the official *sopra li biavi del Segniore*. Some is given out, some sold, some sent to Rimini, some to the miller, etc., as the lord directs.

[8] *Cod. mal.* 21, fo. 238r. In 1406, on the other hand, Pandolfo Malatesta formed a *compagnia* with a certain Bernardo di Giovanni Bottini, to buy corn and import it tax-free, taking half the profits: *ibid.* 4, fos. 4v-5r. Corn-rings by others the Malatesta could act to suppress: Tonini, *Imposte*, 33.

[9] Tonini, iv/1.100-8; *Imposte*, 14, 38-9. In Rimini in the first half of the fourteenth century it was imposed at the rate of £15 *Rav.* for every 1,000 lbs. and in 1371 yielded £5,000: Theiner, ii.515.

depots (*canipae salis*),[1] just as later, when Cervia was in their hands, they continued to procure salt from other places.[2] Nevertheless with Cervia, which they governed for nearly a century, their opportunities for gain must have increased enormously.[3] It was now that they established a salt monopoly,[4] which those who became their subjects were expected to recognise.[5] Special officials were set up to administer it,[6] and the profits were substantial. In 1404 it was the richest of the ordinary revenues recorded, amounting to almost £11,000,[7] and so it probably remained: in 1480 the salt of Fano, Cesena and Sinigaglia still yielded a quarter of the income from the lands surrendered by the Malatesta twenty years before.[8] Proceeds from local sales were increased still more by contracts with neighbouring lords and communities;[9] and its value to the Malatesta is stressed by the care with which they shared the Cervia salt supplies when dividing up their dominions.[10] Even when

[1] Tonini, iv/2.317. Already in 1354–6 there was a company in Fano for purchase and sale of salt, with which the *signori* doubtless had something to do: *ACF, Depos., Ufficio del Sale*, 1.

[2] Thus in 1396 salt was purchased in Dalmatia for Pandolfo Malatesta's *chaneva: Cod. mal.* 21, fos. 221r ff., 270r. Salt was also brought from Venice to Fano, then sent out to the subject villages, the lord sharing the proceeds: Zonghi, 45. Cf. further: *Cod. mal.* 4, fo. 3, 205.

[3] In 1330 Cervia salt was the richest source of revenue in Romagna: Theiner, i.757–8. In 1371 Anglico wrote: 'fieret de sale in tanta quantitate quod fulciret Lombardiam, Tusciam, et Romandiolam': *ibid.* ii.513. Cf. N. Spinelli (1393): 'fit ibi sal de quo vivit Bononia et tota Romandiola': Durrieu, *Royaume d'Adria*, Pièces Justif. II, 54. According to Giovanni Pedrino, the church 'ne chavava più frua che de nessuna altra çittade che fosso 'l suo regimento' (rub. 784), which was probably true before the discovery of the Tolfa alum mines.

[4] Pandolfo III Malatesta issued a decree, confirmed by Sigismondo in 1437, asserting the complete monopoly in Fano, the vicariate of Mondavio, etc., of his *canipa salis*: ACF, *Cod. mal.* 3, fo. 12r. In the fifteenth century financial records mention only salt belonging to the lord or received from companies with which he was connected: *Cod. mal.* 16, fo. 107r; 20, fos. 127r ff.; 24, etc. The same is true of Rimini: Sanuto, v. 448, 489, 495. All traffic in salt was dependent on the lord's licence: *Stat. Cerviae*, 112–15.

[5] Thus Montalboddo: Menchetti, i. 252. In an act of commendation to the Malatesta in 1439, Luigi degli Atti promised to receive salt from the *canipa* of Sigismondo 'pro pretio quo venditur aliis': Battaglini, *Vita*, 567; Morici, *Conti Atti*, 39–40.

[6] In Rimini from *c.* 1390: Battaglini, *Zecca*, 223, 232–6; *Vita*, 612; Tonini, v/i.525, v/2, XLIV, 143–6. For Fano cf. ACF, *Cod. mal.* 16, fo. 107r; *Canc., Reg.* ii, fos. 23v, 25v; Bartoccetti, 'Liber', 20–1. For S. Sepolcro: *Cod. mal.* 16, fo. 109r; Bartoccetti, 'Liber', 40.

[7] ACF, *Cod. mal.* 16, fos. 107r, 109r; cf. *ibid.* 24.

[8] Bauer, 'Studi', 387–8.

[9] For example with Bologna (Carlo and Sigismondo): Bosdari, 'Comune', 142; Battaglini, *Zecca*, 232–6, *Vita*, 612; Tonini, v/2, XLIV. For evidence that the Malatesta supplied the rest of Romagna: *Pii II Commentarii*, 299; Battaglini, *Zecca*, 236; Rossi, 'Prodromi' 1906, 213. Malatesta Novello seems to have supplied Cosimo de' Medici: Yriarte, 427. Cf. Partner, 145.

[10] Battaglini, *Zecca*, 222–3, 232–6; Rossi, 'Nuove notizie', 169–72.

the Malatesta sold Cervia they retained their salt monopoly. It yielded Pandolfaccio about one-fifth of his income; and one concession by Cesare Borgia in 1500 was to reduce the price enforced by the Malatesta in salt sales to Rimini and *contado*.[1]

Rights over property were frequently combined with rights over men, and it is not always easy to distinguish the private lands of the Malatesta from the larger territories, villages and castles of which they were hereditary lords or were created *signori* and then vicars.[2] From their earliest days the Malatesta had united lordship with land ownership; and by the year 1311, when Malatesta da Verucchio drew up his will, they were firmly established in the neighbourhood of Pesaro and Rimini, at Verucchio, Roncofreddo, Ceola, Trebbio, Gradara, Giovedia and Monte Cagnano.[3] To these original *castra* they made continual additions, permanent or temporary, during the next century and a half. They gained much by direct conquest in the frontier warfare of the March, Romagna and the Montefeltro, but certain towns accepted them by formal acts of commendation,[4] while still others they received by investiture from the emperor,[5] papacy[6] and archbishops of Ravenna. From the church of Ravenna in 1356 Guastafamiglia received a number of places in the *comitatus* of Rimini and Pesaro, which in violation of the archbishop's rights had long been subject to the communes.[7] In effect they were now detached by the Malatesta from the *contado* and made tributary to themselves, but after the rise of the

---

[1] Sanudo, *Diarii*, v. 494–5. Later, during the brief restoration of the Malatesta to Rimini in 1503, the salt monopoly was revived, and Pandolfo, when selling the city to Venice, was guaranteed the existing stocks of salt: *ibid.* 333, 375, 632. Similar monopolies were exercised by the Montefeltro, Alidosi and Ordelaffi: Franceschini, *Montefeltro*, 304; Partner, 145.

[2] Thus in the Torre di Gualdo, assigned in 1419 to Parisina Malatesta as dowerland and then 8 years later to Margherita d'Este, they and their factors were to have jurisdiction, civil and partly criminal, while their *coloni* and *homines* were to be exempt 'ab omni gravamine reali et personali seu misto': Fantuzzi, v. 423–6. Cf. la Stacciola: Zonghi, 64–5.

[3] And possibly other places: Tonini, iv/2, x; above pp. 28, 35.

[4] As Pergola or Monte Cassiano.

[5] S. Sepolcro and Citerna by Charles IV as *feuda nobilia in perpetuum*: Tonini, iv/2. 307.

[6] As Montemarciano and Montecassiano in 1453.

[7] Giordani, *Gradara*, 114–15; *Novilara*, 35–6; Fantuzzi, iv.447–8; Mazzatinti, *Inventari*, xxxv. 154. In 1367 investiture was renewed to Pandolfo Malatesta: Clementini, ii.93; Rubeus, 590; while the castles granted in vicariate to Malatesta of Cesena in 1415 are described as having long been held by the Malatesta in conjunction with the *vicecomes* of the church of Ravenna (v). The archbishops continued to have or share territorial interests in the lands of the Malatesta right down to 1500: Tarlazzi, ii.422–6; Tonini, iv/2.333; Pasolini, iii, doc. 604; Sanudo, v. 605, 606. Cf. above p. 25.

signoria it was not unnatural that the new authority should supersede the old. Long before this the commune had itself surrendered a part of the *contado* to them. Two of the earliest castles held by the Malatesta, Verucchio and Gradara, may have been granted to them, the first by Rimini, the second by Pesaro;[1] and in 1332 they received from Rimini four other dependencies: Montefiore, Castelnuovo, Scorticata and Sogliano.[2] Accompanied by full powers of *merum et mixtum imperium*, these places passed from the general jurisdiction of the commune to the particular *seigneurie* of the Malatesta.[3] In that relation they remained until the war with Pius II. Gradara, Verucchio and Montefiore were *signorie* in miniature, enclosed within the larger lordship of Rimini and Pesaro.[4] But as the power of the Malatesta grew these small hereditary lordships must have lost much of their original distinctness, tending again to merge with the *contado*; and, although belonging in a special sense to the Malatesta, they did not, like the private estates, escape general forfeiture to the papacy.

At no time did the Malatesta keep their demesne properties and castles to themselves. They renewed the habits of feudal lordship and monarchy. So land and jurisdiction (and not only demesne) was given to maintain a wife or mistress,[5] to make up a marriage portion,[6] or most often to reward clients and officials, and hold together in loose dependence on the lord the many branches, inconspicuous but impor-

---

[1] Above pp. 26, 48

[2] Battaglini, *Vita*, 692; Tonini, iv/2, LXXIX.

[3] As appears from the 1380 list of Galeotto Malatesta's *colligati* etc.: Ansidei, 'Tregua', 36. There is evidence in the fifteenth century that the Malatesta got possession of places formerly belonging to the commune of Cesena: Zazzeri, 341.

[4] Verucchio and Monte Fiore were both *castra* possessed, like the cities, of communes and councils (at Verucchio a general and 2 smaller councils, of 12 and 36, at Monte Fiore (in the late fifteenth century) a council of 60 and another (*credenza*) of 30). In the first Ferrantino Malatesta appears, in 1341, as *dominus et defensor*, governing, as was later practice, through a *capitano*. In Monte Fiore also, where Malatesta Ungaro is described as *dominus naturalis et perpetuus*, the chief magistrate was a *capitano*, paid but not elected (as they claimed in 1462) by the local population: Antonini, *Supplemento*; Vitali, 81, 305, 326–7, 370–5; Battaglini, *Corte*, 251; Tonini, iv/1.96, iv/2.267–8, 315; Pecci, 'Verucchio'; Bernardy, 'Archivio', nn. 28, 62, 167, 211, 330; Soranzo, *Pio II*, 319–20. For Gradara: *Stat. Grad.*

[5] Thus in 1454, and the period following, the revenues of Montemarciano were being administered on behalf of 'Dompna Ysopta de limalatesti': ACF, *Cod. mal.* 111. Malatesta Novello too assigned lands for the upkeep of his wife, Violante, and her court: Theiner, iii.385; Mazzatinti, *Archivi*, Ser. 1, i.326; Zazzeri, 365, 370–1; and in 1481 Roberto Malatesta gave Isabetta da Montefeltro the revenues of Saludeccio in the Riminese *contado*: Clementini, ii.545.

[6] As Gualdo: above p. 294 n. 2. Le Fratte, in the vicariate of Mondavio, was also used by Sigismondo as part of the dower of his daughter Giovanna: Zampetti, 104–5.

tant, of the Malatesta *consorteria*. During most of their history the
Malatesta were a prolific family, and for *signori* of their kind numbers
meant strength. Though the record of their many offspring, legitimate
and illegitimate, is reticent or still obscure, it is enough to indicate
the existence beside or behind the reigning members of the house of the
indistinct figures of others *de ipsa progenie*,[1] who, barely noticed by the
chroniclers, often gave active service and cooperation.[2] Such was
Giuliozzo Malatesta who in 1339 and 1343 was Malatesta vicar in
Fossombrone, and whose sons had lands and castles both there and in
Rimini.[3] Another was Giovanni di Tino di Gianciotto, who served the
Malatesta loyally from 1334 to his death in 1375.[4] Eight of his nine sons
were adherents of Carlo Malatesta in 1389,[5] and five members of the
Riminese *consiglio generale* in 1398.[6] All held property in Rimini and
elsewhere, and possessed the privileges – tax immunity, the right to
carry arms, and so on – accorded to the Malatesta by the commune,
until in 1431 Giovanni di Ramberto tried to seize power himself and
was exiled.[7] Not dissimilar was the history of another cadet branch: the
descendants of Gaspare, an illegitimate son of Galeotto. They too were
generously endowed with land in Rimini and Cesena,[8] until after a
century of unpretentious service they were tempted during Pandolfaccio's minority to make their authority as regents permanent.[9] Even
the Malatesta counts of Ghiaggiolo and Sogliano, whose independent
lordship went back to the thirteenth century, sometimes took office
and held land of their greater cousins in Rimini. Malatesta of Ghiaggiolo was *podestà* of Rimini in 1405, vicar of S. Sepolcro in 1410 and

---

[1] Tonini, iv/2.422.
[2] For details see the works of Clementini, the Battaglini, and above all Tonini.
Many of their tombs in S. Francesco were destroyed by Sigismondo, who indiscriminately collected their remains into a common 'arca degli Antenati': Ricci,
217, 498, 568, 569, 570, 574.
[3] Theiner, ii, p. 343; Tonini, iv/1.362, iv/2, ccxxxi; Vernarecci, *Fossombrone*,
i.297–8, 316–18, 321–2, 331; Mariotti, *Serrungarina*, 28.
[4] *Cron. mal.*, 35; Clementini, i.588–90; Tonini, iv/2.163. He was a member of the
consiglio generale: A. Battaglini, *Saggio*, 54; F. G. Battaglini, *Zecca*, 312; Tonini,
iv/2.201.
[5] Osio, i.285.
[6] Tonini, iv/2.423, cf. iv/1.293–4; Clementini, i.590–1.
[7] Above p. 172; *Cron. mal.*, 35, 62, 124; A. Battaglini, *Saggio*, 38ff.; *Corte*, 118;
F. G. Battaglini, *Zecca*, 307; *Vita* 286, 559–60; Tonini, iv/1.280–95. From 1430,
through Lodovica, great granddaughter of Giovanni di Tino, this line was inter-
married with a dissident branch of the Montefeltro, settled in Rimini under Carlo
Malatesta.
[8] Tonini, iv/1.339, iv/2.408–9; Massèra, *RIS*[2] xv/2.62 n. 1. Other illegitimate offspring of Galeotto Malatesta and their descendants held properties too: Battaglini,
Corte, 125.
[9] Above p. 253. Cf. Tonini, iv/1.338ff., v/1.486ff.; Gamurrini, ii.345; Zonghi, 68,
75, 79.

podestà of Osimo in 1414;[1] while his brother Galeotto served as one of Carlo Malatesta's captains.[2] His son Niccolo was sent as commissary to Fano by Sigismondo Malatesta in 1445,[3] and another of his sons, Ramberto, was given lands for his services by Sigismondo in 1433 and 1434.[4] Of the Malatesta of Sogliano Giovanni was granted several castles by Sigismondo and his brother *cum mero et misto imperio et gladii potestate*,[5] and collaborated ably in the government of Cesena under Malatesta Novello, as his son Carlo continued to do after him.[6] But these two families, like the counts of Cusercole[7] and Carpegna,[8] who were related to the Malatesta stock, never belonged to the class of paid dependants of the Malatesta. They were rather political clients, who might now follow the interest of Rimini and now desert it,[9] with a place, if only modest, beside the Malatesta themselves in the territorial baronage of Romagna, Montefeltro and the March. The Malatesta

---

[1] Clementini, i.627; ii.261; Tonini, v/1.440; Bartoccetti, 'Liber', 37, 45. Another member of the family, Cecco, was *podestà* in Faenza, 1414–15, where the Malatesta were influential: Mittarelli, *Accessiones*, 336; Tonduzzi, 469.

[2] Maraschini, *Lettere*, nn. 50, 58, 60, 74. Galeotto had been guardian of the two brothers: Tonini, iv/2.331.

[3] Amiani, i.400. In 1447 he received from Sigismondo the castle of Talacchio 'ob ejus grata servitia': Tonini, iv/1.305.

[4] Clementini, i.627–8, ii.304, 306; Franchini, 'Annullabilità', 218; cf. further on him: Pedrino, rub. 166, 267; *Commiss. Albizzi*, i.538, 540–65 *passim*. In 1460 Galeotto, Ramberto's brother, was given Giovedia by Sigismondo 'pro expensis', 'cum omnibus immunitatibus a quibuscumque factionibus oneribus', but he lost it through supporting Sigismondo against Pius II: Battaglini, *Vita*, 533. Another of the family, Antonio, was bishop of Cesena and used by Malatesta Novello in negotiations with Pius II: Zazzeri, 334, 476; Soranzo, *Pio II*, 397. For their original lands, Ghiaggiolo etc., the counts remained tenants of the church of Ravenna, until their line died out late in the fifteenth century: Fantuzzi, vi.258; Tonini, iv/1.295–307.

[5] Clementini, ii.312; Battaglini, *Zecca*, 315, 316; Mazzatinti, *Archivi*, Ser. 1, i.335.

[6] Sansovino, 238v; Tonini, iv/1.356–9; Clementini, ii.284–5; Battaglini, *Zecca*, 314.

[7] A branch of the Malatesta of Ghiaggiolo. Dispossessed of their castle of Valdoppio by the Malatesta of Rimini in 1437 (Pedrino, rub. 994), they later became friendly with Rimini: Soranzo, *Pio II*, 499; and just before his expulsion Pandolfaccio exchanged Castel Liale with them for Cusercole: Sanudo, *Diarii*, v. 494.

[8] Traditionally allies of the Malatesta of Rimini, they married early in the fifteenth century into the lines of Gianciotto and Sogliano, and took the family name: M. Salvadori, *Compendio della famiglia dei Conti di C.* (Urbino, 1880), 43, 61; Massèra, *RIS²* vi/2.62 n. 5. Their loyalty to Sigismondo Malatesta cost them dear: Nunziante, 'Primi anni', xix, 650; Soranzo, *Pio II*, 130–1, 403–4, 453, 498.

[9] For their changing relations see on Ghiaggiolo: Tonini, iv/1.295–307; Ansidei, 'Tregua', 38; Osio, i.285; Cutolo, ii.226; on Sogliano: Battaglini, *Zecca*, 308–14; *Vita*, App. XLIX, LII; Tonini, iv/1.351–62; Zazzeri, 341; Ansidei and Osio, *locc. citt.*; *Commiss. Albizzi*, i.14; Soranzo, *Pio II*, 403–4, 499; Sanudo, *Diarii*, ii.172, 209; v. 605–6.

attracted many clients from this class[1] and they illustrate the means of influence by which the *signoria* was developed and maintained.

How this influence was exercised is still better shown by the record of the citizen families, noble or bureaucratic, who helped the Malatesta govern their state. Every subject commune had its nobles, *cittadini* in the fullest sense. By tradition leaders of municipal life, they not only commanded a natural place in the councils of the communes, but also expected and obtained employment with the Malatesta. Some were long-established families, at least by the fifteenth century, like the Benci or Belmonti, Castracani, Adimari, Perleoni, Atti and Roelli;[2] others, like the Andarelli, Maschi or Valturi, came from small places in the Malatesta state: Gradara, S. Agata, Macerata Feltria;[3] while a few had migrated from the Malatesta castles of Montefiore and Verucchio.[4] Besides these native families, however, there were migrants from further afield. Throughout most of their history the Malatesta attracted able and ambitious men from all over Italy to enter their service and settle with their relatives in Romagna. At Cesena the families most employed by the Malatesta were all first established there by Galeotto Malatesta and his successors.[5] Others came from Lombardy with Pandolfo III Malatesta, like the Brescian family of Iseo, of whom Goffredo Rodolenghi da Iseo gave consistent service to the Malatesta before the papal victory of 1463, receiving in reward a succession of investitures from Sigismondo and his brother.[6] Bartolemeo da Palazzo, who earned the

---

[1] For example: the conti Bandi of Monte in the Montefeltro, for a time vassals of the Malatesta, then of the Montefeltro, finally of Rimini, (Clementini, ii.565; Battaglini, *Zecca*, 282; Tonini, v/1.407; P. Franciosi, *Vicende di S. Leo* (S. Marino, 1928), 60–5), or the Gambacorti of Bagno, *raccomandati* of the Malatesta (Battaglini, *Corte*, 89), or Luigi degli Atti (above p. 293 n. 5).

[2] Mazzuchelli; Gamurrini, ii.343–4; Battaglini, *Corte*, 81, 154, 198ff., 245; *Vita*, 401, 566ff.; *Zecca* 231; Tonini, iv/1.118, 135, 331, 368, 374, 379, 532, 537–8; v/1.186, 249, 255, 363, 415, 430–1, 515ff., 600; Massèra, *RIS²* xv/2.61, 124; Ricci, 592. For others, the Sagramori, Galiani, Ramussii, Ricciardeli etc.; Clementini, ii.451–2, 517–18; Battaglini, *Corte*, 181ff.; Tonini, iv/1.366–8, v/1.515ff.

[3] A. Battaglini, *Corte*, 163–5, 171, 179–81, 225–6; F. G. Battaglini, *Zecca*, 286; Tonini, v/1.98, 108–10, 176, 184, 192, 347, 358, 409–10, 530, 532, 545–7, 589–96, 695; Massèra, *RIS²* xv/2.107. Similar, even if of higher social condition, were the Paganelli, former lords of Montalboddo: Rossi, *Monte Alboddo*, 94–7. For Cesenati in the service of Sigismondo: Vasina, *Romagna*, 262, 286.

[4] Battaglini, *Corte*, 186, 212; Vitali, ch. VI; Tonini, v/1.527–8. On similar use of the nobility in Pesaro: Feliciangeli, 'Acquisto di Pesaro', 64.

[5] Chiaramonti, 417; Zazzeri, 236–9, 268, 278–9, 355–6.

[6] At various times Goffredo was given S. Ippolito, the Tomba and Villa of S. Mauro, Giovedia, Fratta, Castelnuovo, Bosco and Gambettola. The two last here continued to hold after 1463, and his family retained them until 1680: A. Battaglini, *Saggio*, 41–2; F. G. Battaglini, *Vita*, 533, 576; Fantuzzi, vi.243–4; Tonini, v/1.281, v/2.32–3, 197; Vernarecci, *Fossombrone*, i.367; Zonghi, 71, 141; Zazzeri, 279, 364; Soranzo, *Pio II*, 454, 498, 499.

special favour of the Malatesta by acting promptly in the riots at Fano in 1431, was also Brescian. He was employed by Sigismondo as councillor and lieutenant in Fano, and was in return endowed by him with a number of lands in the vicariate of Mondavio.[1]

Whether of foreign or local origin, many who served the Malatesta could expect, like Bartolomeo and Goffredo, to receive some recompense in property or land. Sometimes the motive of reward was explicit, as when Giuliano Arnolfi was given land in 1486 by Galeotto Malatesta 'ob sinceram et integram fidem qua usus est ad prefati Illmi. Dni. Nri. Dni. Pandulfi personae statusque salutem'.[2] At other times the grant was in place of money.[3] Most obvious were gifts of land and franchise to men in daily intercourse with the *signori*: their secretaries, chancellors, *aulici* and *commensales*,[4] together with military officers or mercenary captains.[5] But they were not alone. Patrician families also benefited, such as the Paganelli, Atti and Valturi.[6] And when land was not directly given, it might come by way of marriage. The Malatesta, and more especially the cadet branches and illegitimate offspring, never wholly disdained alliances with the local nobility, and so in time became connected with many leading families of their subject towns: in Rimini,[7]

---

[1] A. Battaglini, *Corte*, 82; Amiani, i.381, 387; above p. 270. To the same immigrant class belonged Giovanni Antonio da Monticolo of Faenza who between 1457 and 1459 was *podestà* of Rimini, settled in the city, and founded the noble family of the Monticoli (Battaglini, *Corte*, 118) or political exiles like Benedetto Gambacorti of Pisa, who became one of Sigismondo's counsellors and *raccomandati* (*ibid.* 89), the Migliorati of Fermo, who during the fifteenth century held office under the Malatesta (*ibid.* 144; Tonini, v/1.601; Yriarte, 340), or the Brancaleoni (Clementini, ii.313; F. G. Battaglini, *Zecca*, 315; Massèra, RIS² xv/2.83 n. 9, 84 n. 10, 103 n. 1; above p. 160.

[2] Tonini, v/1.575; above p. 297 n. 3.

[3] As the grants of land to the artists at work on the Tempio: above p. 229. A gift of land could also clear a debt: Clementini, ii.384.

[4] For example the grant by Sigismondo of castles, and then (1448) of Sinigaglia, to his 'summus segretarius', P. G. Brugnoli (F. G. Battaglini, *Vita*, 348; A. Battaglini, *Corte*, 71–3, 138; Zazzeri, 364; Massèra, RIS² xv/2.86 n. 7), or to 'Ser Cichino mio cancellere' of the lands forfeit for contraband in 1443 (above p. 291 n. 7). Cf. further: Clementini, ii.311–12; Grigioni, 'Costruttori', 124; Massèra, RIS² xv/2.131 n. 6, 135 n. 1.

[5] For example, letter of Malatesta of Pesaro to the officials of Fano, 13 April 1415: 'Egregii Amici carissimi. Io voglio che voi me advisate per vostra litera se el mio magnifico fradello S. messer Pandolfo ha conceduto la staciola Anicolo datolintino liberamente cum tucte le soe ragione overamente che ello se abbia reservato ase le condamnagione': ACF, *Cod. mal.* 5, fo. 41r. Cf. Tonini, v/1.523, 553 (1496).

[6] Paganelli: Pedrino, rub. 29, 89; Rossi, *Monte Alboddo*, 94, 97; Valturi: Clementini, ii.327; Battaglini, *Corte*, 226; Tonini, v/1.590 ('Castrum Torite cum omni suo jure ac mero et misto imperio'); Atti: *Cron. mal.*, 124–5.

[7] Where, from the late fourteenth century, connections are attested with the Agolanti, Bandi, Belmonti, Brancaleoni, Faitani, Gualdi, Migliorati, Ricciardelli, Roelli, Ronconi and others: Tonini, iv/1.338, 341, 364–5, v/1.407, 478, 487–8, 490, 494, 503, 509, 518, 524, 526–7; Gamurrini, ii.344; Sercambi, iii.253.

Fano[1], Cesena,[2] Pesaro,[3] Santarcangelo,[4] S. Sepolcro[5] and Fossombrone.[6] In the days of their supremacy therefore the Malatesta might be represented as occupying the centre of a wide class of vassals, feudatories and urban *otttimati*, a Malatesta 'interest' related to their family and to the property on which their family had thriven.[7]

Up to the last the Malatesta continued to give away lands,[8] but at no time were the lands all patrimonial. Some, like Castelnuovo, Giovedia or Gambettola, doubtless were. So too were the countless smaller properties acquired by purchase or inheritance. But many, and perhaps the most important, were theirs to grant only as *signori* and vicars of the church.[9] As vicars, as has been shown, they possessed complete authority to delegate.[10] But as *signori* equally they had been empowered to dispose freely of communal revenue and property.[11] Their influence as patrons and landed magnates is therefore inseparable from their formal prerogatives as despots.[12]

[1] Thus Malatesta of the Tramontani married Bernardina di Giovan Duranti da Fano: Tonini, v/1.501.

[2] Polissena, illegitimate daughter of Andrea Malatesta of Cesena, married a leading noble of Cesena, Anastasio Tiberto: Braschi, 284.

[3] Raimondo de Gaspare di Galeotto married Antonia di Almerico degli Almerici of Pesaro, whose Malatesta descendants took the name of Almerici: Tonini, v/1.487.

[4] One of Galeotto Malatesta's illegitimate daughters married the son of Muzolo Balacchi of the leading family of Santarcangelo: *RIS*[2] xv/2.40–1, and notes; Marini, *Santo Arcangelo*, 88.

[5] Andronico di Gaspare di Galeotto married Bianca de' Bifolchi of Borgo S. Sepolcro (Tonini, iv/1.340), Ricca di Raimondo di Gaspare di Galeotto an Ettore de' Roberti of the same city (*ibid*. v/1.487).

[6] Giacomo, illegitimate son of Galeotto Malatesta, married Margarita de Paolo Monalducci of Fossombrone: Tonini, iv/1.341. A place should also be found for such figures as Isotta degli Atti and Vanetta Toschi of Fano.

[7] The words 'vassals' and 'feudatories' were used by Pius II when releasing Sigismondo's subjects from obedience to him (*Epist.*, n. VI).

[8] Two days before surrendering Rimini in 1500 Pandolfo assigned Castel Leale 'cum mero et misto imperio' to Ceseare Borgia's representative, Roberto Bencini of Cesena: Tonini, v/1.434. The Venetian survey of 1504 records certain citizens of Rimini 'quali dicono el signor Pandolpho averli alienato alcune tornature de dicte possessione': Sanudo, *Diarii*, v. 495.

[9] Which may explain the distinction drawn by Paul II when resuming possession of Cesena: 'Volumus ut omnes donationes, venditiones et concessiones facte per Malatestam Novellum in suo robore firme persistent, exceptis terris et fortilitiis': Theiner, iii.385.

[10] Above p. 270.

[11] For Rimini: above p. 63, Similar rights were conferred on Galeotto Malatesta by Cervia (below App. VI), and on Pandolfo III Malatesta by Corinaldo: Battaglini, *Corte*, 80–1.

[12] In one sphere, the ecclesiastical, Malatesta influence seems to have been slight. Although, like all magnates, they possessed rights of patronage and family connections with particular churches and monasteries (Mittarelli, *Ann. Camald.*, v. 457–9; Zazzeri, 276–7; Vasina, *Romagna*, 274, 290) and had occasional disputes with the church over candidates to benefices (N. Traversarii, ii.242–3; *Commiss.*

By 1355, when they first received the papal vicariate, the Malatesta seem to have been created *signori* or *defensores* in only two of their cities: Rimini and Fano.[1] Rimini had made Malatesta Guastafamiglia *defensor ad vitam*, and Fano conferred the same office on his brother, Galeotto.[2] Galeotto evidently succeeded as *defensor* in Rimini,[3] but neither in his lifetime nor later is there sign of any new or recurrent mandate from the communes, as in other Italian despotisms. And once the vicariate was firmly established it became unnecessary.[4] It was common, if not customary, for the Malatesta to perform a succession ceremony in their subject cities, which then took an oath of allegiance;[5] but this also was prescribed by the terms of vicariate.[6] The title *defensor* was soon abandoned by the Malatesta as a relic of their rise to power.

Outside Rimini and Fano they had at first to be content with the office of *podestà*. Such at least was the case of Pesaro where, except for one short interlude in 1356, Pandolfo II Malatesta was *podestà* until the accession of his uncle Galeotto in 1373. Only then did the *podestà* appear as acting 'pro magnifico et excelso domino nostro domino Galaocto da Malatestis': a formula thereafter constant.[7] In Fossom-

Albizzi, i.300), they never secured anything like regular control of higher church appointments in their dominions, where Rimini, Pesaro and neighbouring dioceses had always depended directly on Rome (*Liber Censuum*, ii.105) and, with the rest of the Papal States, all prelacies, by the early fourteenth century, were reserved to papal provision (J. Haller, *Papsttum und Kirchenreform* (Berlin, 1903), 109, 111; Tonini, iv/1.408–9; above p. 9). Nearly all bishops of the Malatesta state were therefore outsiders; only 3 were ever Malatesta themselves: Leale in Pesaro (1370–4) and Rimini (1374–1400), Bartolomeo in Rimini (1445–8), and Antonio in Cesena (1435–75): Eubel, i.108, 414; ii.107, 127; Tonini, iv/1.418–19, v/1.617–18. In its judicial and fiscal immunities also (except for extraordinary taxes sanctioned by bishop or pope) the church preserved relative independence, though Sigismondo was accused of interfering with both (Mittarelli, *Biblioteca*, 712; Battaglini, *Vita*, 671; Tonini, v/2.248); in all of which the *signoria* of the Malatesta (and seemingly of other lords of Romagna and the Papal State) contrasted sharply with the duchy of Milan (Cognasso, 'Note', 116ff.) and possibly all the greater Italian states, republican or despotic.
[1] They had of course held the title in other places during their brief period of expansion in the March before 1355 (above p. 65); also in Verucchio (above p. 294 n. 4). Similarly, in Cervia Bernardino Polenta had been created *defensor*, and his powers were transmitted to Galeotto Malatesta, but not apparently the title (below App. VI).
[2] Above pp. 64–5; ACF, *Depos., Catasti* 1 (1348); Zonghi, 483 (1354).
[3] Above p. 289 n. 3.
[4] In exceptional circumstances the grant might be renewed as when the Malatesta reconquered Cervia in 1433: below App. VI.
[5] Above pp. 173, 251. Cf. Chiaramonti, 393; Amiani, i.311–12, 371; Battaglini, *Corte*, 73; ACF, *Canc., Cons.* v, fos. 98r ff., 131r ff., 147r. In Milan also, after the duchy was created (1395), there were no further formalities of election, merely an oath: Giulini, *Contin.*, iii.91–2.
[6] Above p. 271.
[7] Giordani, *Orazioni*, XIII ff.; Tonini, iv/1.328; cf. Vaccai, 51–2.

brone also, before 1355, Galeotto Malatesta was no more than *podestà*, ruling through a vicar.[1]

By tradition the *podesteria* was the chief magistracy of the commune. To dominate this was to dominate the state, and in every city the Malatesta governed it was subordinate to their will. In Rimini and Cervia, and probably Fano also, they had been granted control by the commune; elsewhere the right of appointment was conveyed by the papal vicariate.[2] And so from the second half of the fourteenth century all *podestà* in the greater communes were formally and almost regularly recorded as installed 'on behalf of' the lords Malatesta,[3] as were the miscellaneous vicars, *podestà* and *capitani* who administered lesser places like Amandola, Mondolfo, Santarcangelo, Corinaldo, or the villages and *castra* of the *contado*.[4] This does not seem always to have implied that the *podestà* was nominated by the Malatesta. Often, perhaps normally, he was;[5] but on occasion they conceded a right to elect subject to confirmation,[6] or accepted the recommendation of local communities. Thus in April 1415 Malatesta of Pesaro, as representative of Pandolfo, granted a request from the commune and people of Monte

[1] Vernarecci, *Fossombrone*, i.306. As late as 1431 one of the Malatesta of Pesaro was occupying the *podesteria* of Fossombrone: Fantuzzi, v.197.

[2] Except in places, like Iesi in 1408, which fell to them by conquest. At Rimini, after 1342, and Fano, after 1336, no Malatesta was ever *podestà*: Tonini, iv/1.254ff., v/1.450ff.; Amiani ii.348ff. (who also speaks of Galeotto allowing Fano to elect the *podestà*: i.264). For Cervia: below App. VI.

[3] In Rimini, Fano, Cesena, Sinigaglia, Iesi, Osimo: Bib. sen., *Stat. Rim*, fos. 355–6; ACF, *Canc., Cons.* i, fo. 7v, *Bandi* i.; *Stat. Caes.* (1589), 252; Tonini, *locc. citt.* (which shows during the fifteenth century there were often *vicepodestà*, 'pro domino Carolo', 'Sigismundo' etc.); Bagli, 79–82; Mariotti, *Bandi mal.*, 35–6; Bartoccetti, 'Liber', 29–30, 41, 44–5; Gianandrea, 'Potestà', 153; Loevinson, 'Sunti', 275; etc. For Pesaro: above p. 301.

[4] ACF, *Canc., Castelli, passim, Reg.* ii, fos. 34v, 71, *Cons.* i, fo. 7v; *Cod. mal.* 21, fos. 64r, 70r ff.; Bartoccetti, 'Liber', *passim*; Vitali, 235, 284; Castellani, *Malatesta*, 33–4; etc. The Malatesta also provided 'lochapitano gienerale delcontado de fano', a new centralised authority of their creation: ACF *Cod. mal.* 16, fo. 99r, 21, fo. 36r, *Canc., Cons.* i, fos. 7v, 35r; *Depos., Entrata/uscita* 76; Amiani, i.217, 272, 317. In the Riminese *contado* similarly they reduced the number of *capitani*: *Stat. Rim.*, fo. 388v (1349).

[5] For example letter of Pandolfo III Malatesta nominating the *podestà* of Fano (1407): below App. VII. Other examples are a letter (1415) by Carlo Malatesta to 'officiales nostri' in Fano recommending candidates as *podestà* in Staffolo and Castelfidardo (ACF, *Cod. mal.* 5, fo. 36v), and short notes to his officials in Fano from Sigismondo (1446, 1448) instituting *podestà*: *ibid. Canc., Reg.* ii, fos. 6v, 29v. In the *Liber Offitiorum* (Bartoccetti), which gives a detailed survey of officials in the territories of Pandolfo Malatesta (1410), many are said to be 'provided' (by the *signore*). For similar *mostre* (1406–9, 1434, 1463): ACF, *Cod. mal.* 8, 94–6.

[6] Cases occur at Cesena, S. Sepolcro, Osimo, Montalboddo and various minor places: Chiaramonti, 386; Coleschi, 62; Rossi, *Monte Alboddo*, 112–13, 147–52; Bartoccetti, 'Liber', 23–4, 37–8, 45, 50–2; ACF, *Cod. mal.* 94–6.

Filottrano to retain the existing *podestà* for another term.[1] Such a violation of the statutory limit of six or twelve months' tenure was common under the Malatesta, who frequently renewed or extended the appointment of their nominees.[2] The *podestà* themselves came from all parts of North and Central Italy, and though sometimes chosen from among the local nobility – a Ronconi of Rimini to serve as *podestà* in Fano, an Aguselli of Cesena to serve in Rimini – the practice never became common.[3] For this reason the petitions of the fifteenth century to grant offices only to natives may have been meant to include the *podesteria*:[4] in Rimini certainly, after the papal reconquest, the *podestà* was always a citizen.[5] At the same time, beside the *podestà*, or above him, the Malatesta frequently appointed a vicar or lieutenant to govern the larger communes. Even when they divided their territories they were persistent absentees; and, since the *podestà* had lost all political importance and become mainly a justiciar,[6] a grander, plenipotentiary official was created to represent them. Such were the 'vicars' whom Guastafamiglia and Galeotto, when still only *defensores*, set up in Rimini and Fano: the first of a long if intermittent series in Fano, Rimini, Pesaro, Cesena and Osimo.[7] Like the *podestà*, the vicar-general enjoyed judicial powers, but he had authority also to issue laws and statutes and was in every way vice-regent of the Lord.

However represented, by a vicar or *podestà*, the Malatesta always reserved some jurisdiction to themselves.[8] Routine justice was certainly never their concern, but they could intervene to pardon offences or remit fines, and frequently did so.[9] They decided what crimes could be

---

[1] *Ibid.* 5, fo. 41v. Cf. Bartoccetti, 'Liber', 51–2. Similarly in 1386 Santarcangelo, desiring to have 'uno valente homo giurista', requested extension of the vicar in office 'per longo tempo': Castellani, *Malatesta*, 33–4.

[2] ACF, *Cod. mal.* 5, fo. 40v; Bartoccetti, 'Liber', *passim*; Menchetti, i.156–7. Between 1416 and 1429 the same man was *podestà* or *vicepodestà* of Rimini: Tonini, v/1.443.

[3] Amiani, ii.348ff.; Tonini, iv/1.254ff., v/1.439–59.

[4] Below p. 331.

[5] Tonini, vi/2.102ff.

[6] Cf. below App. VII; also ACF, *Canc., Cons.* v, fo. 98r; Vaccai, 51.

[7] *Stat. Rim.*, fos. 187, 193–4, 203r, 263v, 278v, 285, 333, 341, 361v; *Stat. Caes.* (1494), lib. 1; ACF, *Depos., Enirata/uscita* 17, 56–9, 72, 74; *Canc., Cons.* i, fo. 54v, *Reg.* ii. fo. 70r; *Cod. mal.* 4, fo. 206r; Amiani, i.270, 286–8, 304, 317, 330, 335, 347 etc.; Vernarecci, *Fossombrone*, i.331; Grimaldi, 'Bandi'; Maraschini, *passim;* Giordani, *S. Tommaso*, 59; Gianandrea, 'Potestà', 153–4. Sometimes vicars replaced the *podestà*, sometimes were not appointed at all: in Rimini and Fano Sigismondo used his sons to represent him.

[8] For example App. VII below: 'exceptis gratiis et remissionibus quas nobi omnimodo reservamus'. Again in 1453 (?), writing to his officials in Fano, Sigismondo reserved control of the death penalty: ACF, *Reg.* ii, fo. 74v.

[9] A. Battaglini, *Corte*, 144; below p. 321. In 1446 on the completion of the Castel Sigismondo, Sigismondo proclaimed it a sanctuary for criminals (except offenders

compounded for and by what authority,[1] and suspended statutory penalties or granted immunity from particular laws.[2] Interference with the statute was no abuse of powers, since both as lords and then as vicars the Malatesta were fully invested with control of legislation,[3] and from the earliest period they are recorded as issuing decrees and amending statutes, either directly or through their vicars and *referendarii*. The decrees (*bandi*) of the Malatesta, both in Latin and the vernacular, were incessant and innumerable, covering all possible business, mercantile, judicial, military and civil: the sale and movement of goods and value of currency, the violation of curfew, payment of taxes, observance of holy days, the conduct of prostitutes.[4] A large number simply reaffirmed statute, or were merely temporary, and the formulas used – *volumus et mandamus, sancimus, decernimus, et mandamus, fanno bandire et comandare* – lacked the solemnity of permanent law. But the distinction between decree and statute was not sharp. Decrees are interspersed among the statutes, and many modified statute, even permanently,[5] or were given statutory force.[6] In this way a corpus of *reformationes*, supplementary to the statute, developed during Malatesta rule, which may have been collected into separate books,[7] and which

against the state): F. G. Battaglini, *Zecca*, 246. Carlo Malatesta seems to have interested himself in law and corresponded with Baldus on the subject: A. Battaglini, *Corte*, 54, 126.

[1] ACF, *Depos., Entrata/uscita* 2 (1344) records compositions by order of Galeotto. In 1453 Sigismondo's vicar-general in Rimini wrote to Fano forbidding composition for severe crimes without the lord's licence: ACF, *Canc., Reg.* ii, fo. 70v; but a few years later (1461) Sigismondo allowed his *depositario, referendario* and *cancelliere* in Fano authority to compound: *ibid.* fo. 127v.

[2] Mariotti, *Bandi mal.*, 35; Maraschini, n. 16; Bib. sen., *Stat. Rim.*, fos. 264r ff. For certain offences (e.g. usury) penalties were wholly at discretion of the lord: *Stat. Rim.*, fo. 351v; Bagli, 84–5 (1398).

[3] Above p. 274 and below App. iii, vi. The edition of the statutes of Pesaro issued by Malatesta de' Malatesta in 1412 freed the Malatesta from all obedience to them: Vaccai, 13.

[4] Many are in Bib. sen., *Stat. Rim.*, fos. 190–3, 348r–368v; ACF, *Cod. mal.* 1, 3, 5, 92, 93; *Canc., Reg.* ii, fo. 55r ff.; *Stat. Cerviae*, 111–15; Giordani, *Zecca*, 203, 205; Tonini, *Porto*, 145; Zazzeri 291; Grimaldi, 'Bandi'; Mariotti, *Bandi mal.*; Zonghi, 10–12; Bagli. Decrees were usually announced by the town crier (*publicus tubator*): ACF, *Canc., Carteggio, Bandi* i, *passim*; Bagli, *passim*.

[5] Thus, one of the Malatesta decrees on the *gabelle* of Fano passed into statute even after their fall: Zonghi, 10–12. Again, a decree of Carlo Malatesta (21 May 1387) doubled the statutory penalties in Rimini against *rissantes*: Bib. sen., *Stat. Rim.*, fo. 349v.

[6] As when Carlo Malatesta issued an edict on notarial abuses which he intended 'havere et fare observare como lege et statuti' (1398): Bib. sen., *Stat. Rim.*, fos. 359v–360r; Bagli, 82–3. Similarly, in 1417, the decree reducing by half the statutory duties on merchandise into Fano: *Stat. Fani, Tractatus Gabellarum*. In 1478 Fano decided to remove from statute all decrees of the Malatesta: Amiani, ii.45.

[7] At Rimini (Bib. sen., *Stat. Rim.*, fo. 366v) and Fano (ACF, *Canc., Reg.* ii, fo. 29r).

included, in addition, more solemn amendments to statute by the *signori*. Such amendments, particularly common in the fourteenth century, were as miscellaneous as decrees, but were more obviously concerned with institutional and judicial regulation: the functions of the lord's general vicar, the method of appointing the municipal *massarius*, the duties of the subject, details of the *extimum*.[1] The growing number of *reformationes* may have led in places to confusion.[2] This helps to explain why, under the Malatesta, new editions of the statutes were compiled in many communes they governed. A few of these clearly related to phases in the rise and consolidation of the Malatesta *signoria*: as at Rimini (1334) and Pesaro (1343, 1412 and 1423), where each records the special powers conferred on the *signori*.[3] But most have no political reference at all. By the middle of the fifteenth century the statutes had been renewed, once or more times, with the sanction or desire of the Malatesta, in Fano, Bertinoro, Savignano, Scorticata, Longiano, Serravalle and Verucchio.[4]

Among the matters most often dealt with by both decrees and statutes were military and related obligations. The movement of private individuals was controlled,[5] the curfew regulated and enforced,[6] and the carrying of arms forbidden.[7] The ban on arms, common though it was, implied no immunity from military service. Apart from certain police duties – the ancient service of watch, presentment and hue and cry[8] – the subjects of the Malatesta, like those of other *signori*, were

---

[1] Bib. sen., *Stat. Rim.*, fos. 1ff., 187, 262v ff., 278v ff., 285, 286r ff., 317r ff., 325r-339r, 341, 363, 375v ff.; ACF, *Cod. mal.* 3, fos. 17r-19v; *Stat. Caes.* (1494), lib. 1; *Stat. Fani*, lib. 11, ch. LXXXIII; Clementini, ii.130-1; Battaglini, *Zecca*, 60; Giordani, *Zecca*, 191-4; Vernarecci, *Fossombrone*, ii.178; Tonini, iv/1.378; *Imposte*, 15; Mariotti, *Bandimal.*, 49-50. The formulas used were various; until about 1365 the phrase *provisum et ordinatum est* was common, and the amendments called *ordinamenta provisiones et addictiones*; but from the closing years of Galeotto the form was: *statuimus et firmamus, statuimus et ordinamus, ordeniamo et perpetualmente statuimo*, etc.
[2] One of Carlo Malatesta's decrees (1413) refers to a 'derogatio provisionis derogantis statutum': Bib. sen., *Stat. Rim.*, fos. 340r, 349v; Bagli, n. 7, p. 86.
[3] Above p. 63; Vaccai, 13-14; Feliciangeli, 'Relazioni', 395.
[4] *Stat. Fani, proemium*; Amiani, i.374, 409; Zonghi, 254-5; Borgogelli, 'Statuti'; Battaglini, *Zecca*, 226; Gasperoni, 'Savignano', 252, 260; Fontana, *Statuti*, iii.101; Bernardy, 'Frammenti sanmarinesi', 343. Cf. for further cases: Tonini, vi/2.877, cl. 1; ACF, *Canc., Reg.* ii,fo.45v; Nicoletti,665-6; Clementini,ii.564; Marcucci,17.
[5] ACF, *Cod. mal.* 5; Zonghi, 15ff.
[6] Bib. sen., *Stat. Rim.*, fos. 264r ff. (1351); Chiaramonti, 399 (1393); Zazzeri, 291 (1436, 1437); Grimaldi, 'Bandi' (1367).
[7] Bib. sen., *Stat. Rim.*, fos. 262v-263r (1351); Zazzeri, 291 (1436); ACF, *Cod. mal.* 5; Grimaldi, 'Bandi'; Vaccai, 154-5.
[8] At Rimini reorganised by Guastafamiglia, against some local protest, by a system of elected *gualdarii* to make regular presentments of *danni dati*: Bib. sen., *Stat. Rim.*, fos. 278v ff., 287v, cf. 285v-286r. For arrangements generally, in town and

liable in emergency to conscription for general defence. This service was owed to the Malatesta both as successors of the commune and as vicars of the pope. It fell mainly, though not exclusively, on the country districts, and more than once the Malatesta had to call out *uno homo per casa* and make what use they could of *fanterie paesane*.[1] They were not therefore solely dependent on mercenary soldiers or afraid to see their subjects armed. But the levy of peasants and townsmen was never more than an extraordinary measure, and the permanent forces of the Malatesta were always paid. In Rimini the Malatesta had been granted power to hire mercenaries,[2] and from the time of Malatesta Guastafamiglia always kept a body of *stipendarii* who alone had freedom to carry arms.[3] They also appointed the castellans of the numerous castles and *rocche* reconstructed or built by them in every corner of their territories.[4] In time of war these forces were expanded, and the main duty of the subject was then to pay the service of others rather than to serve himself. Taxes for troops (*gradi, taglie*) were frequent and sometimes onerous.[5] When not raised for troops, they were used to

country, of watch, presentment, pursuit and collective responsibility for crime: Vasina, *Romagna*, 285; Mariotti, *Bandi mal.*, 11ff.; Zonghi, 485; Vaccai, 111ff., 149–50; Sorbelli, *Comune*. In 1429 Fano asked for citizens to be relieved of watch and ward and replaced by hired guards paid by the Malatesta: ACF, *Canc., Cons.* v, fo. 10r.

[1] For details on urban and rural militias: *Cron. mal.*, 39; *Commiss. Albizzi*, i.565; Clementini, ii.255, 389–99, 484–5; Amiani, i.299, 308–10, 352, 421; Zonghi, 20, 435; Martorelli, 229; Vernarecci, *Fossombrone*, i.363; Soranzo, *Pio II*, 283. Some importance the Malatesta must have attached to these untrained forces, since *cavalcate* were the one duty from which Galeotto Belfiore in 1386 withheld immunity from immigrants to Cervia: *Stat. Cerviae*, 111 (though Monterolo the Malatesta seem to have exempted from *hoste*: ACF, *Canc., Reg.* ii, fo. 45v; Nicoletti, 665–6). The militia, however, was not very reliable (e.g. Cecconi, *Castelfidardo*, 102–3); and one grievance under Pandolfaccio was a survey (1497) of men fit to bear arms: Clementini, ii.576.

[2] *Stipendarios conducendj*: Bib. sen., *Stat. Rim.*, fo. 339r.

[3] In Rimini it was ordained in 1351 that no one should carry arms except the *stipendarii* of the Malatesta and the commune, or those specially licensed by the *defensor*: *ibid.* fos. 262v–263r. In 1371 Anglico reports in Rimini *quatuor banderie peditum ad custodiam dominorum*: Theiner, ii.515. Constables and *squadrerii* of the Malatesta often appear in the records, suggesting there were permanent subordinate commands: A. Battaglini, *Corte*, 87; F. G. Battaglini, *Vita*, 557; *Zecca*, 275–7; Tonini, iv/1.366–8, v/1.515, 523, 553.

[4] For example ACF, *Cod. mal.* 9; Bartoccetti, 'Liber', *passim*; Zonghi, 32–3, 148–50; below App. vi. Already in 1356 (?) the 'Description of the March' shows the Malatesta to be holding the *rocche* in the *contado* of Fano, those in Fossombrone territory being held by the sons of Giuliozzo Malatesta: Theiner, ii.343. In 1415, however, Malatesta told the Fanese to send two castellans to Amandola, presumably chosen by them: Zonghi, 19.

[5] The fiscal records of the Malatesta are filled with accounts of such taxes 'per lo subsidio de legiente darme' (*Cod. mal.* 100, Dec. 1450) or 'per li fanti' (*ibid.* 97, fo. 3r, July 1439). At Fano, from the first appearance of treasury books (1344:

meet the expenses of purveyance. Purveyance was a universal practice, a source of grievance in Romagna under the Malatesta as elsewhere in Italy and Europe, and the subject population, particularly the country people, were more often expected to furnish arms and supplies, or billets, than take part in war themselves.[1] It was the *contadini* also who bore the burden of *corvées* (*factiones*): digging ditches, repairing roads, building and maintaining fortifications[2] – in their turn a frequent cause of complaint.[3]

Corvées, purveyances, taxes for payment of mercenaries were only part of the claims made by the Malatesta on the resources of their subjects. Allied, if independent, were the endless items of regular public revenue. But fully to evaluate these it is necessary first to emphasize a feature of Malatesta government, common to all Italian despotisms: the survival beside the *signoria*, in dependent partnership, of the commune with its councils and particular officials.

It was not merely that the term 'commune' itself continued in use: that officials were still denominated officials of the 'commune',[4] rights

---

Depos., Entrata/uscita 1), they are almost annual to the end of Malatesta rule: *Cod. mal.* 5, 13–14, 17, 21, 97–100; *Canc., Cons.* ii, fos. 100r ff.: Amiani, i.270, 297, 305, 309, 316, 320, 327–8, 336, 348, 350, 386; Zonghi, 18–19, 151–2. For similar payments by Cesena: Chiaramonti, 398. They were levied also by Pandolfo Malatesta in Brescia and Bergamo (Zonghi, 120ff.), and by the Visconti in their dominions (Tagliabue, 'Politica', 185ff.). Local communities also bore garrison costs (Maraschini, n. 64), which probably explains the regular *taxe per cavali* charged on the places of the Riminese *contado* at the monthly rate of 20 *sol.* per horse *ad taxas stipendiariorum*: Sanudo, *Diarii*, v. 55off.

[1] Maraschini, nn. 52–4, 63, 67; Zonghi, 20; Martorelli, 229; Anselmi, 5–8. For example of a tax to pay supplies (Jan. 1442): 'Libro de uno grado e doy terzi posta Aragione de Cinque denari e doy terzi per libro per donare Al Nostro M.S. per prestanze che avia fatte y Ciptadine di questa terra Alla sua S. per renderle ayditti Ciptadine. Et per pagare quilli che Anno dato le vettovarie alle giente darme': *Cod. mal.* 99. For petitions to restrict purveyance, billeting etc. from Rimini and other towns: Bib. sen., *Stat. Rim.*, fos. 375v, 376v (1461); Sanudo, *Diarii*, v. 645, cl. 11 (1503); Tonini, vi/2.844, 852 (1509); Martorelli, 231–6 (1416); Rossi, *Monte Alboddo*, 147ff. (1450).

[2] Clementini, ii.252; Tonini, iv/1.108; iv/2, CXCII, CCIII; v/1.20; *Imposte*, 22; Alvisi, 489–90; Amiani, i.381; Chiaramonti, 398, 401; Menchetti, i, *passim*; Siena, 136. The records suggest that whereas *contadini* had to serve in person on public works citizens met their obligations in money: *Cod. mal.* 3, fo. 16r–v; Amiani, i.301, 303, 307, 354, 419; Soranzo, *Pio II*, 410; Clementini, ii.562; Tonini, v/1.403.

[3] The Riminese petition of Dec. 1461 says the *contadini* had been so oppressed by works and requisitions that a number had been compelled to migrate: Bib. sen., *Stat. Rim.*, fo. 374v; Ricci, 224. Cf. further ACF, *Canc. reg.* ii, fos. 45v, 110; Tonini, vi/2.879, cl.9; Sanudo, *Diarii*, v. 491.

[4] *Cancellero del Comuno de arimino, Cancelleria Audientie Comunis, offitialis viarum et pontium ac stratarum Comunis Arim., Officialis major Custodie Comunis Arim., vicarius et judex gabellarum et appelationum Comunis Arim.* etc.: ACF, *Canc., Reg.* ii, fos. 69v, 122r; Tonini, iv/2.372, v/1.539, 559–60, 590, v/2.231, 261. For Fano: ACF. *Canc. Reg.* ii, fos. 68r, *Cons.* v, fo. 98r; *Cod mal.* 3, fos. 20v–21v, 4, fos. 6r–7r; etc.

ascribed to 'lord and commune',[1] or exiles declared enemies of both lord and commune.[2] The structure of communal government also persisted without radical change. At Montalboddo, a typical township of the March, the *priori*, Otto di Credenza and *consiglio generale* all retained a working place in the administration under the tutelage of the lord and his vicar.[3] Exactly similar conditions recur at Santarcangelo, Pergola, Savignano, Mondavio, Monte Cassiano, S. Sepolcro and Osimo.[4] At Pesaro the two municipal councils, the greater and the smaller *di credenza*, and for a time also the four *capitani del popolo*, were kept by the Malatesta as component parts of the administrative system,[5] as were the Anziani and *consiglio* of Cesena.[6] At Fano finally and at Rimini itself government with the aid of greater and lesser councils was also regular practice.[7]

The meetings of the greater council (*consiglio generale*), if irregular, were never merely formal, nor were its powers, though variable from commune to commune, of no account. It still chose some officials, in most cases lesser officials, of the kind with whom citizens had day-to-day dealings. At Pesaro, however, this privilege was unusually wide, including the right to nominate the *ufficiali di danno dato* and captains of the *contado*.[8]

[1] As when, in May, July and Sept. 1442, Sigismondo granted lands with all rights and jurisdiction pertaining to himself or the commune of Rimini: Bib. Gamb., *Arch. notarile, Atti Fr. Paponi*. The fifteenth-century notarial acts of Rimini continue to treat the commune and its laws as the governing authority; while financial provisions of the Malatesta refer to *estimi* as *del Comuno de arimino* (Bib. sen., *Stat. Rim.*, fo. 363r), and to *gabelle* as *del Comuno di Fano* (*Cod. mal.* 3, fo. 2r).

[2] As by Guastafamiglia, Galeotto and Sigismondo: Bib. sen., *Stat. Rim.*, fos. 200v, 201r; ACF, *Canc., Carteggio, Bandi*, fo. 13; Mariotti, *Bandi mal.*, 48–9.

[3] Menchetti, *passim*.

[4] In all of which are found functioning general and smaller councils (of 10, 24 etc.), sometimes *parlamenta* or *arenghi* of all heads of families, and commonly under *priori, anziani* and similar elected colleges, to whom the Malatesta addressed correspondence: Castellani, *Malatesta*, 33–4; Nicoletti, 190–1; Gasperoni, 'Savignano', 261–3; Battaglini, *Saggio*, 40; ACF, *Canc., Castelli* i, *passim*; *Mem. M. Cassiano*, 57, 61–3; Coleschi, 62–3; Mazzatinti, *Archivi*, Ser. 2, iv.124; Maraschini, nn. 22, 28.

[5] Vaccai, 24–8. Cf. also Fossombrone: Vernarecci, *Fossombrone*, i.468. The authority of the *capitani del popolo* at Pesaro was eventually limited by Pandolfo II and then *omnino sublata* by his son, Malatesta: Vaccai, *loc. cit.*; Giordani, *Orazioni*, ix.

[6] *Stat. Caes.* (1589), 81ff.; Chiaramonti, 387, 400–2, 419; Zazzeri, 239. The Anziani were expected to collaborate with the *podestà* in the administration of justice and decisions regarding public works.

[7] At Rimini the four Ufficiali also survived to the end of Malatesta rule as a commission of the general council: Amiani, i.362–3; Battaglini, *Vita*, 606–7; Tonini, iv/2.161, 200–3, 432; v/2.129–31, 233, 321; Predelli, xii, n. 100; Vitali, 291; below App. v.

[8] As well as the overseers of roads and bridges, 3 notaries to make an annual census of the city, the schoolmaster and certain doctors: Vaccai, 25, 84, 123, 168, 174, 227. For the purpose of election the *consiglio* could assemble without licence: *ibid.* 30–1.

In Rimini such offices were perhaps fewer.[1] In 1461 Sigismondo was petitioned and agreed to 'remit' offices which previously *se solevano cavare pro brevi*.[2] In 1405 the *consiglio generale* of Fano submitted a similar request for officials formerly elective to be chosen by the general council, or in a smaller council which the same petition asked to be set up;[3] although in the event the appointments passed to the smaller council, the *consiglio generale* continued regularly to fill a number of places.[4] The same right is in evidence at Cervia, Santarcangelo, Montalboddo and Savignano.[5] And from time to time, as we have seen, communes were permitted even to elect to the greater magistrates as well.[6] In finance, too, and law-making the citizen council preserved a modest part. Statutes, if often initiated by the lord, were normally drafted or collected by commissions of the council;[7] decrees or provisions were not only addressed to the council, or read, published and approved in the council, but also proposed and prepared by the council;[8] and the

---

[1] Bib. sen., *Stat. Rim.*, fos. 214r, 278v, 360v; Tonini, v/1.544–5; *Porto*, 117–18. Carlo Malatesta allowed the *consiglio* to present 5 candidates for choice as *massarius*: *Stat. Rim.*, fo. 256v.

[2] *Ibid.* fos. 374v, 377r–v. The Venetians regranted and extended the right (1504): Sanudo, *Diarii*, v. 644, 650.

[3] 'Ancora adimandano jdicti suoy Citadinj ala Exa. sua S. che sedegne volere che gli offitij delcomuno jqualj solevano essere di Citadinj delconseglio delodananza siano remissi nelo consiglio di citadinj che ordinara S. Segnore siche havendo di disdagij e delefatighe havesseno ancora delautilitate e Incaso non fosse depiacere de remectere idicti offitij inlo consiglio didictj Citadinj che novamente se ordinara. Supplicano che se digne fargli remectere almeno in lo consiglio generale dela citade como gia furono anticamente. Sperando che didictj offitij gli toccara inloconsiglio general predicto alcuna volta qualche utilitade dessi offitij': ACF, *Canc., Cons.* i, fo. 35v. There follows a list of a dozen or so minor officials, with their fees and perquisites, including the *notario dela gabella, notario dicatasti, offitiale dela bolla dela bechari* and the *mazzarolo depigni.*

[4] ACF, *Canc., Cons.* v, fos. 9r, 20v. Cf. vol. 8, 10 (*notarii judicis maioris, notarii judicis minoris, iudices minores, Extimatores comunis, procuratores comunis*, etc.); *Cod. mal.* 21, fo. 194.

[5] See App. VI below; Castellani, *Malatesta*, 31–2; Menchetti, i, *passim*; Gasperoni, 'Savignano', 261–3.

[6] Above p. 302. In 1416, following rebellion, Osimo was empowered to elect the *offitialis damnorum datorum* and the *cancellarius*, Castelfidardo the *cancellarius*, and Montefilottrano three candidates for the *podesteria*: Bartoccetti, 'Liber', 45–7, 49, 51–2.

[7] As at Rimini (1349, 1360, 1378), Fano (1434, 1436–7, 1448), and Pesaro (*temp.* Malatesta di Pandolfo): Bib. sen., *Stat. Rim.*, fos. 278v, 285v, 325r; Amiani, i.374; Zonghi, 261; Borgogelli, 'Statuti'; Giordani, *S. Tommaso*, 59–60; Feliciangeli, 'Relazioni', 395.

[8] Mariotti, *Bandi mal.*, 39–40; Bib. sen., *Stat. Rim.*, fos. 280v, 341; Amiani, i.387, 419. There is also evidence that in Rimini, Pesaro and Fano the communal seals and stamps continued in regular use under the Malatesta: ACF, *Cod. mal.* 105; Battaglini, *Zecca*, 190; Vaccai, 43; although the Malatesta also issued decrees etc. under their own seals, 'sub nostro consueto sigillo': *Stat. Rim.*, fos. 190–3. Cf. below p. 316.

council could be implicated in the issue of *acta decreta et Reformationes*.[1] It might also, with the lord's assent, impose, vote and apportion taxes.[2] In short the general council was intermittently involved in most government business: despatching envoys, granting troops and organising defence, presenting and hearing petitions, raising loans, farming taxes, and even, in Fano, electing new councillors.[3] And, something of the same residual self-rule was preserved in the *contado*, where certain officials were elected, certain matters left to local decision.[4]

The sum of these activities may not have been great, but this was partly because the routine work of the general councils had passed in almost all communes to a smaller derivative body (*di credenza* etc.), sometimes specially authorised by the greater assembly, but conceived all the same as fully representative of the city.[5] In Rimini the smaller council comprised twelve members, in Fano thirty-three or twenty-four, though fewer than this normally attended.[6] It is not always clear when such commissions were created, but in Fano at least the smaller council seems first to have been regularised in response to a petition presented in 1405.[7] However established, the smaller council was the point of articulation between commune and *signoria*: it stood for the

---

[1] For example: ACF, *Canc., Cons.* i (1398–1411): 'In hoc libro scribuntur acta decreta et Reformationes fienda et fiendas in Civitate fani tam per Magnificum et potentem dominum Pandulfum quam per Consilium Adunantie et generale Comunis Civitatis Fanj.' Cf. *Cons.* vi (1434–6): 'Reformationes provisiones decreta et ordinamenta fienda per Cives Consiliarios'.

[2] For example in Fano, Cesena, S. Sepolcro, Montalboddo and Pesaro: ACF, *Canc., Cons.* v, fos. 61v–62r etc.; *Cod. mal.* 98–100; Amiani, i. 329, 351, 359; Coleschi, 62; Menchetti, i. 281, ii/2.93; Giordani, *Porto*, 16; Vaccai, 27–8; Robertson, 'Cesena', 129. In the vicariate of Mondavio the council's main work seems to have been the vote and disposal of taxes (*collecte*): ACF, *Canc., Castelli* i (1385–95).

[3] Chiaramonti, 401–2, 419; Amiani, i.413–16; Menchetti, i.32; ACF, *Canc., Cons.* ii, 168r ff., 170r ff., 186r–187r; v, 9r–11v, 87, 90r ff. In S. Sepolcro (1390) the commune was allowed to determine the membership of the *consiglio* – 15 lists of 20 each: Coleschi, 62; Battaglini, *Saggio*, 54; Grigioni, 'Documenti', 379–80. It also seems to have fallen to the general council of Rimini to give particular powers to public notaries: Tonini, iv/1.260, iv/2.431–2.

[4] For example Verucchio and Montefiore, above p. 295.

[5] In Rimini the members of the small council were described in the fifteenth century as *totum comune et totam universitatem representantes*: Battaglini, *Corte*, 228 n. 18; Tonini, v/2, LXXXV, CXXIX. Cf. for Fano: ACF, *Canc., Cons.* i, fos. 48r, 52r. For the *consiglio generale* giving authority to the smaller in Fano: *Cons.* v, fo. 71v; in Montalboddo: Menchetti, i.281.

[6] For further examples: above p. 308; below p. 319.

[7] Asking Pandolfo Malatesta to 'determinare certo numero de Consiglerj Citadinj I quali sopra ifacti del comuno e bisognj che tucto eldi occurreno haybano a provedere con liOffitialj Vostrj. e che loro aybano elpensiero de dicti facti Insieme con li Offitialj.V. per che savendolo staranno piu attenti e solicciti alaobedientia deli Offitiali e piu presti alefacende e bisognj dela comunita predicta': ACF, *Canc., Cons.* i, fo. 34r.

commune beside the officials representing the lord,[1] and took a regular part in government, at Fano meeting almost monthly.[2] Like the *consiglio generale*, but with greater freedom, it chose officials,[3] issued decrees and *reformationes*,[4] levied taxes and appointed treasurers (*depositarii*) to collect them.[5] At times it had every appearance of real independence: writing to other cities, petitioning the pope, and governing in the lord's absence.[6]

[1] As shown by the fact that the lords' officials were always distinct from the members of the smaller council, and by the practice of addressing letters to the officials and council jointly, for example: Sigismondo (2 March 1448) to 'Spectabilibus et Egregiis tamquam patribus et Amicis carissimis Consilio XXIIII nostre Civitatis Fani et officialibus nostris': Amiani, i.409; Borgogelli, 'Statuti'; cf. Mariotti, *Bandi mal.*, 28–9.

[2] ACF, *Canc., Cons., passim*.

[3] At Fano, in addition to the offices petitioned for in 1405 (above p. 000; cf. ACF, *Canc., Cons.* i, fo. 43, v, fos. 11, 23–4), the council came, by further concessions (1415, 1437), to fill offices including the *offitium Amici Comunis* (or *massaro*), *offitium extimacionis carnium* and *offitium pontium et viarum* (*Cons.* ii, fo. 82v; Amiani, i.169–70, 381). It also nominated masters of grammar and inspected the 'carte del dottorato' of the *podestà* and his vicar (*Cod. mal.* 4, fos. 4r, 7v; *Canc., Cons.* i, *Carteggio, Minutario* i; Amiani, i.364). In Pesaro and Rimini there is less evidence of conciliar appointment (Vaccai, 167; Tonini, v/1.558, v/2, CI), but at Urbino most offices were still elective: Luzzatto, 'Comune e principato', 191–3.

[4] For example: ACF, *Canc., Cons.* ii (1413–20): 'Hic est liber sive quaternus in quo scribentur Acta et Refformationes que fient per Consilium tragintatrium consiliariorum Civitatis Fani'; cf. above p. 310 n. 1. Also: below App. VII. Borgogelli, 'Statuti'.

[5] At Fano it raised taxes (*gradi, mezzi gradi*) to pay the doctors and masters it appointed (ACF, *Depos., Collette*, vols. 68, 70, 112 etc.) and for a variety of other purposes, making up the *intrada del Comuno*, which by a grant of Sigismondo (1442) included the duty on exported oil (*Cod. mal.* 3, fos. 20–1, 23; *Depos., Collette*, 75, 121; *Canc. Cons.* ii, fos. 148ff.). As well it handled details of the *estimo*, tax immunities etc. (*Canc., Cons.* i, fos. 46v, 57r, *Reg.* ii, fo. 75r; Amiani, i.386; Soranzo, *Pio II*, 410; Borgogelli, 'Statuti'). Rimini also had its limited *intrada* and *spexa*, which it tried to increase after the fall of the Malatesta: Sanudo, *Diarii*, v. 496, 559, 644; Tonini, vi/2.805–6, 842. In smaller places, like Santarcangelo, there was still revenue 'che expecta al comuno': Castellani, *Malatesta*, 33–4 (1386).

[6] Thus 1429–31 and later Fano was in negotiation with Venice concerning the annual oil tribute owed since the twelfth century (Amiani, i.366–7, 338, 413); 21 July 1430 the *podestà, domini quattuor, consilium* and commune of Rimini addressed a letter to the officials, council and commune of Fano (Amiani, i.362–3); 1431 Fano petitioned the pope (*ibid.* 365); 1438 Sigismondo committed Fano to the care of the 33 (*ibid.* 382); 1446–7 Fano and Rimini took the initiative in transactions with Sforza (Zonghi, 271; Mariotti, *Bandi di tregua*, 11–17); 1452 the Venetians incensed at the passage of Sigismondo to the Florentines, wrote to the Riminese (who in turn wrote to the Fanese), and then began commercial reprisals; the Fanese protested they were not responsible for Sigismondo's change of sympathy, and were ready to abide by all agreements; Venice revoked its ban (Amiani, i.416–17; Zonghi, 272); June 1461 the council of 24 corresponded with Federigo d'Urbino, the council of 12 in Rimini, Sigismondo, etc. (ACF, *Canc., Carteggio, Minutario* i); 1463 the council of 33 (Roberto Malatesta present) decided on capitulation to Federigo d'Urbino (Amiani, i.435).

The survival of the councils shows that the Malatesta, like most Italian despots, long remained satisfied with the exercise of power, disinclined to institutional change. The creative era of government lay behind in the period of communal independence, and what the communes had created was now used, as local opportunity suggested, but not replaced by the despot.

This indifference to forms marked especially the financial relations of lord and commune. In Rimini Guastafamiglia and Galeotto were granted complete control of revenue,[1] though in the early days of their rule, it is suggested, special payments may have been made for the upkeep of their courts.[2] At Pesaro certainly, despite the wide authority conferred by the vicariate, the Malatesta remained to the end salaried lords of the city, with a monthly *provisio*.[3] Similar *provedigioni* were also paid in the early fifteenth century by Mondolfo, Pergola, Mondavio, S. Sepolcro, Monterolo and Montebello;[4] and down to 1389 by Fano as well.[5] Many communes continued to pay the *podestà* and other chief officials; at Pesaro all salaries were paid by the commune and only at Rimini, Fano and possibly Cesena were most eventually paid by the lord.[6] The main items of public revenue also remained unchanged,

[1] Above p. 63. This was probably true of Cervia also: below App. VI.

[2] Tonini, referring to the years 1336–7, conjectures about £12,000 annually: iv/1.100ff.

[3] A system preserved by the Sforza and only suppressed by Cesare Borgia who took over all revenue (and the obligation of papal *census* and most other expenditure): Giordani, *Porto*, 17–19; *Zecca*, 217–18; Tonini, *Imposte*, 37–9; Vaccai, 119, 176; Feliciangeli, 'Relazioni', 405; Alvisi, 248.

[4] ACF, *Cod. mal.* 15, 16 (fos. 100r, 102r, 108r, 118r, 119r), 20, 24, 74, 75, 76, 77, 79, 84, 87; Zonghi, 154–5; Coleschi, 59. After 1429 only Mondolfo, Pergola and Mondavio are mentioned as paying 'provisions', and after 1430, when Martin V recovered so much of the Malatesta territory in the March, only Mondolfo.

[5] In 1344 Galeotto was receiving £310 a month, in 1358 200 ducats: ACF, *Depos.*, *Entrata/uscita* 1 and 17. Payment is last recorded in 1389 (*ibid.* 69), about which time the Malatesta may have assumed the formal control of revenue they already had in Rimini, just as the Visconti were doing at the same period in Lombardy: Tagliabue, 'Politica', 43ff. Even after 1389 special provisions were occasionally paid the Malatesta: to Galeotto Roberto in 1429, Sigismondo 1430–1, Roberto 1461–3 (ACF, *Cod. mal.* 76, 79, fos. 51r ff., 95), as well as to the Malatesta court (*ibid.* 74, 76, 87, fo. 91r). Cf. a letter of Pandolfo Malatesta, April 1415: 'Io ho sentido che de presente se domanda oltra la rata usata per quelli magnifici mei fradelli a fano ducati mille e perche io ho magior bisogno che io havesse mai Vecomando che guardiate che delemei intrate voi non tochate niente', etc.: *ibid.* 5, fo. 40v.

[6] For Pesaro: above p. 308. In Rimini the Malatesta seem to have paid all officials except the *oficiale de la guarda, notari de la guarda, canzellier* and *soprastante del comun*; the *vicario de gabella* received only one-third of his stipend from the lord: Bib. sen., *Stat. Rim.*, fos. 221v–223r, 265v ff.; Sanudo, *Diarii*, v. 445–7, 489, 496, 559, 645, 649. In Cesena, in 1368, the church was paying the chief officials and the Malatesta probably did the same: Theiner, ii.461. In Fano also the fifteenth-century Malatesta accounts regularly include salaries of the *podestà, refferendario, vicario generale delle gabelle*, chancellor of the commune and many more: *Cod. mal.* 13–14, 17, 24,

chief among them being *dazii* or indirect levies on bread, wine and numerous other commodities, the proceeds of justice (*danni, dati, malefici, capisoldi* and so on) and various direct taxes (*colte* etc.), supported by the *estimo* or property tax.[1] And finally, as seen, the communes retained some share in the raising and spending of taxes, or received assignments on revenue.[2] But whatever the forms or conventions in use, ultimate control of all revenue belonged to the Malatesta. Even if they had a 'provision', no rule forbade their use of other income.[3] If communal councils took decisions touching finance, it was by leave of the Malatesta.[4] Where formerly the general council had imposed all taxes, most were now imposed by the lord.[5] While special *colte* or *gradi* were voted to satisfy an active and importunate government,[6] the older revenues, *dazii* and *estimi*, were closely regulated from above.[7]

73–4, 76, 79, 84–5, 87; *Canc., Reg.* ii, fos. 68r ff. By contrast all officials were paid by the communes (at rates controlled by the lord) in Osimo, Corinaldo, Pergola, Staffolo, Montefiore, the *contados* of Rimini and Fano and many other places: ACF, *Canc., Cons.* i, fo. 35r, *Reg.* ii, fos. 34v, 45v, 113r, 116v, *Castelli* i; Bartoccetti, 'Liber', 23–4, 57–8; Sanudo, *Diarii*, v. 491–3; Mariotti, *Bandi mal.*, 32–3; etc.

[1] For details: ACF, *Cod. mal.* 16, 18, 20–4, 73–7, 79, 84–5, 97–100; *Depos., Entrata/ uscita, passim, Collette, passim*; Sanudo, *Diarii*, v. 448, 489ff., 496, 558ff.; Tonini, iv/1.100–8, vi/2.842; *Porto*, 125; *Imposte*, 6–19, 38–9. *Dazii* were normally farmed (ACF, *Canc., Protocolli de' canc.*, i–ii; Battaglini, *Zecca*, 226; Gasperoni, 'Savignano', 265) but the country districts of Rimini, Fano and possibly Pesaro seem to have compounded for at least some of them (*Cod. mal.* 16, 20; Theiner, ii.515; Sanudo, *Diarii*, v. 55off.; Tonini, *Imposte*, 28–9). On the various debated meanings of *capisoldi* cf. Zonghi, 5; Robertson, 'Cesena', 147; Waley, 257; Partner, 118; in the Malatesta accounts they seem partly charges on litigation, partly sums deducted from salaries. At Sinigaglia and Montemarciano an additional source of income were transhumant grazing rents: *Cod. mal.* 70–2, 107–9, 111; *Canc., Reg.* ii, fo. 112v.

[2] As for example Ripa, in 1460, which received on petition the income from *malleficia* (as well as exemption from pasture rents at Sinigaglia, 'de eo quod al Cameram ipsorum Dominorum pertinet'): ACF, *Canc., Reg.* ii, fo. 112v.

[3] Not even at Pesaro: Giordani, *Zecca*, 217–18. Though S. Sepolcro, Mondavio and Pergola paid a fixed *provigione*, other parts of their revenue were at the disposal of the Malatesta as well: ACF, *Cod. mal.* 15, 16 (fos. 100–3, 109–10), 21 (fos. 75, 130, 144–6, 154–5), 24.

[4] For example *Cod. mal.* 3, fo. 20v; Amiani, i.329.

[5] Cf. Zonghi, 316. Montalboddo, however, in 1449 obtained a condition that the Malatesta were to impose no taxes there: Rossi, *Monte Alboddo*, 112–13, 147–52.

[6] ACF, *Depos., Collette, passim*. As an example, vol. 103, Sept. 1439: 'Libro de uno grado del nostro Magnifico e possente S. Segnore Messer Sigismondo pandolfo di Malatesti posto del mexe deseptembre . . . el quale se scotera per mano de Jacomo di Britij da fano depoxitario delprelibato nostro Magco. Segnore.' Particularly common seem to have been the *gradi* imposed on strangers (*foresteri*); cf. *Cod. mal.* 16, fos. 113r–114v, 123r; 21, fos. 78, 128; 24.

[7] *Dazii*, though described indifferently as 'del Comune' and of the lord, were minutely controlled from the first (Bib. sen., *Stat. Rim.*, fo. 367r; ACF, *Cod. mal.* 3, fos. 2r, 5r, 12r, 25r etc., 92–3; *Stat. Cerviae*, 132; Mariotti, *Bandi mal.*, 41, 44–5; A. Battaglini, *Saggio*, 3; F. G. Battaglini, *Zecca*, 267; Vaccai, 14) and so a subject of

Tax immunities, already common before the *signoria*, were now the lord's concern; in course of time they spread far beyond the Malatesta family and became a theme of common petition and complaint.[1] The lord decided how income should be spent, and the communal accounts, though basically unaltered, now listed endless payments *dichomandamento delsignore*, to the lord's *depositario* or to the factors who managed his estates.[2] It was finally the lord's prerogative to appoint the officials in charge of revenue; and even when they were described as being 'of the commune', they always exercised their office 'on behalf of' the Malatesta. In Rimini during the fifteenth century they were the *magister introitum*, the *referendarius*, the *depositarius* and the *vicarius gabellarum* who was usually also *judex appelationum*.[3] At Fano the hierarchy was the same, except for the *maestro de l'intrate*.[4] Elsewhere there were only

constant petition, especially in the fifteenth century (*Stat. Rim.*, fos. 375, 377–9; ACF, *Canc.*, *Cons.* ii, fos. 180–1, *Reg.* ii, fo. 71; Rossi, *Monte Alboddo*, 112–13, 147–52). Revisions of the *estimo* and the regulations governing it were taken in hand by the Malatesta from the 1340s on, though more frequently in Rimini than in Fano, where there seems to have been no serious reassessment between the mid-fourteenth and mid-fifteenth century (*Stat. Rim.*, fos. 325r, 326r ff., 354v–5r, 363v–65v; ACF, *Depos.*, *Catasti*; Tonini, iv/1.122–6). It too was a subject of petition (*Stat. Rim.*, fo. 376, *a.* 1461), though the communes shared in its administration.

[1] To the traditional and unchallenged immunities of justices, doctors, students etc. the Malatesta soon added others granted to their *familiares*, *domestici*, *aulici* etc. (ACF, *Canc.*, *Reg.* ii, fo. 29v; Battaglini, *Corte*, 262–3), as well as to immigrants (*Stat. Cerviae*, 111; Menchetti, i.18–19), clients like the Malatesta of Sogliano (ACF, *Depos.*, *Collette*, 77; *Canc.*, *Reg.* ii, fo. 133r; Tonini, iv/1.359, 379; v/1.407), and even, for certain taxes, whole communities (for example Santarcangelo: Castellani, *Malatesta*, 19–20, 31–3, *a.* 1373). At Rimini already by 1349 there were exempt *ex gratia domini* as well as *ex beneficio statuti comunis* (Bib. sen., *Stat. Rim.*, fo. 333). Their numbers so grew that the Malatesta themselves had to restrict exemption to certain classes and check their acquisition of property (*Stat. Rim.*, fos. 349r, 363–4; Bagli, 86–7; Clementini, ii.244–5; Tonduzzi, 450: *a.* 1394, 1413, 1431). Even so Fano in 1413, Rimini in 1461, Ripa and other places in 1460, all desired a reduction of immunities: ACF, *Canc.*, *Cons.* ii, fos. 17r, 109v, 112v; *Stat. Rim.*, fo. 376r.

[2] For these infinitely various payments which were always the most extensive if not the most expensive entry: ACF, *Cod. mal.* 11, 13, 14 (fos. 51r ff., 62r–v, 64r–68r), 17, 21 (fos. 176–85, 205r, 219r–220v, 330ff.), 24, 74, 76, 79, 84–5, 87; *Depos.*, *Entrata/uscita*, *passim*. For payments to the lord's *depositario* or factor, which in 1409 for example, were the factor's largest source of income: *Cod. mal.* 13, 14 (fos. 56r–57r, 69r), 19, 21 (fos. 187r, 211r), 74, 85; *Depos.*, *Entrata/uscita* 73, 80, vol. 73, 80.

[3] Bib. sen., *Stat. Rim.*, fos. 361v, 367r; Bagli, 90; ACF, *Canc.*, *Reg.* ii, fos. 118r–122v; Sanudo, *Diarii*, v. 445–6; Battaglini, *Corte*, 73, 81, 138–9, 144, 149, 154, 171ff., 184, 212, 240; *Zecca*, 275–7, 286; *Vita*, 567, 671; Tonini, v/1.511, 535, 539, 541, 545–6, 552, 566, 584, 601; v/2.249, 336; Massèra, *RIS*[2] xv/2.107 n. 4, 124 n. 2; Ricci, 592.

[4] ACF, *Canc.*, *Reg.* ii, fos. 55r ff., 68r–69v, 70v, 127v, *Cons.* i, fo. 61r–v; *Cod. mal.* 3 (fos. 2r, 25r), 76, 93, 94 (fo. 18r), 95, (fo. 4r), 102; Amiani, i.270, 329; ii, lxxv; Battaglini, *Corte*, 73, 139; Zonghi, 153–4, 261, 405; Grigioni, 'Documenti', 371, 392; Gianandrea, 'Staffolo', 326; Bartoccetti, 'Liber', 19–20, 21–2; Borgogelli,

depositarii.[1] There seems in fact to have been some attempt to centralise the revenue. Pandolfo III Malatesta made all his income tributary to Fano;[2] and under Sigismondo, who held both Fano and Rimini, the revenues from his lands in the March were in turn made subordinate to Rimini. In supreme control was the *magister introitum* who collected all receipts, transferring them to the general *depositario*. Under him were the *refferendario generale d'arimino*, who accounted to the lord for all income and expenditure, and the *depositario generale de Arimino*, who received all revenues appropriated to the Camera, but could make no payment without written authority from the *maestro* or the *refferendario*. Beside these was the *cancellero del commune*, whose duty it was to affix *bollecte* to all warrants for payment.[3] The same system prevailed at Fano, but with the added provision that the *refferendario* there was to send a monthly statement of accounts to the *generale maestro de Lintrada* at Rimini.[4]

Like the *podestà* these fiscal magistrates were without exception Malatesta nominees; and so, as far as can be judged, were all other leading officials of communal administration. In Rimini and Cervia at least this was in obedience to powers surrendered before the papal vicariate.[5] At Rimini the list of officials appointed by the Malatesta was very long and included, among the more notable, the *oficiale de la guarda* (*major officialis custodie*), in control of the night watch, the *massaro*, the *oficiale di danni dadi*, the constables of the gates and the chancellor of the commune.[6] Malatesta Guastafamiglia and Galeotto

'Statuti', 243; App. VII below. At Fano there was also a 'Revisor seu Ratiocinator rationum camere Domini et communis Fani': *Cod. mal.* 4, fo. 7r; Bartoccetti, 'Liber', 20. To illustrate appointment cf. letter of Pandolfo Malatesta (26 June 1406) nominating Moldutio de Bocatii of Meldola 'nostrum Referendarium et generalem regulatorem omnium et singularum Civitatum terrarum et locorum nostrorum Romandiole Marchie Ducatus et Tuscie' etc.: *Cod. mal.* 4, fos. 6r–7r.

[1] As at Mondavio (ACF, *Canc.*, *Reg.* ii, fos. 66r–67v; Zonghi, 125; Bartoccetti, 'Liber', 27), Sinigaglia (ACF, *Canc.*, *Reg.* ii, fos. 72r–73r; Zonghi, 127; Bartoccetti, 'Liber', 29), and S. Sepolcro (Mazzatinti, *Archivi*, Ser. 2, iv.106; Bartoccetti, 40).

[2] As appears from the office of *referendarius* and general *regulator* (Gianandrea, 'Staffolo', 325–6; above p. 314 n. 4), and the Fano accounts of this period which contain receipts from Mondavio, Pergola, Corinaldo, Montalboddo, S. Sepolcro, Sinigaglia, Osimo etc.: ACF, *Cod. mal.* 16, 18, 20, 21, 24; *Depos.*, *Entrata/uscita* 76.

[3] ACF, *Canc.*, *Reg.* ii, fos. 118r–122v (1453?).

[4] *Ibid.* 69r-v, 1453. Cf. *Depos.*, *Entrata/uscita* 79 (1435). The *depositario* at Fano was also to send to Rimini all income from the *tracte de le biave* in the March. Cf. *Canc.*, *Cons.* i, fo. 61 (1406); *Cod. mal.* 4, fos. 6r–7r (1406); Zonghi, 405–7.

[5] Above p. 63; below App. VI.

[6] The Venetian survey of 1504 enumerates the officials paid and presumably appointed by the Malatesta: Sanuto, v.445–8. Anglico's description of 1371 is shorter and mentions beside the *podestà* and vicar only the *officialis custodie* and *officiales dampnorum*: Theiner, ii.515. Cf. *Stat. Rim.*, fos. 278v, 349r-v; A. Battaglini, *Corte*, 228, 237; F. G. Battaglini, *Zecca*, 278; Tonini, v/1.358, 488, 590; v/2, LXXXV, CIII; above p. 309.

had been specially empowered to choose the chancellor in the time of the *defensoria*. As then defined his duty was to keep the minutes of meetings of councils and other bodies, and write letters on behalf of the *signori* or the commune; he held the communal seal, but could use it only with authority from the Malatesta or their officials; and he was to be paid by the commune. Once established these rules seem to have remained permanently in force.[1] The records at Fano agree in general with those of Rimini. There also the chief officials appointed by the Malatesta, apart from the *podestà* and cameral officers, were the *officialis dempnorum datorum, officialis custodie*, captains of the gates, castellan and chancellor of the commune.[2] And it was much the same in the other subject towns.[3] Even when the communes were allowed to fill certain offices, it was only with the lord's sanction.[4]

It was on these officials, with the *podestà, vicarii* and castellans, and their capacity for local initiative that the *signoria* depended for effective government. It was to them that the mass of Malatesta letters were directed, and with them also that the provincial *curia* of the papacy had often to negotiate;[5] and their delegated powers were of the amplest.[6] Their personal dependence was correspondingly strict. All were answerable, by an oath of office, exclusively to the Malatesta,[7] and many were drawn from their intimate entourage. Like all *signori*, the Malatesta were surrounded by a permanent group of familiars: counsellors, secretaries, chancellors, *aulici, commensales, camerarii* and others, who were employed in the most important and delicate business.[8] They were also by origin the most cosmopolitan. If some were of local birth,[9] a large proportion were recruited from outside,

---

[1] *Stat. Rim.*, fos. 221v–223r.

[2] ACF, *Depos., Zocco del Danno Dato*, 4; Amiani, i.316; ii, LXXV; Zonghi, 339, 403, 483, 485; Bartoccetti, 'Liber', 19–23; Borgogelli, 'Statuti', 243.

[3] For example Osimo, Iesi, Mondavio, Montolmo, Pergola, Castelfidardo, Monte-lupone: ACF, *Canc., Cons.* i, fo. 7v; Bartoccetti, 'Liber', 25–6, 32, 42, 46–50; Maraschini, n. 78; Martorelli, 231–6.

[4] As shown by the Fano petition: above p. 309 n. 3. Even the hire of a new doctor or town-crier had first to be sanctioned: ACF, *Canc., Cons.* i, fos. 88r ff., v, fo. 1v. Cf. Vaccai, 167. And the *signore* could influence appointment of elected officials as well: ACF, *Canc., Reg.* ii, fo. 104v.

[5] Above p. 282.

[6] Cf. Sigismondo's instructions regarding officials in Fano (1453?): ACF, *Canc., Reg.* ii, fos. 74r–75v.

[7] Chiaramonti, 393, 400; Vaccai, 54–5, 227; Gasperoni, 'Savignano'; ACF, *Cod. mal.* 94, fos. 2r, 6r; below App. VI.

[8] For examples of such men and their careers: Clementini, ii.451–2, 517–18; A. Battaglini, *Corte*, 71, 89, 93, 116, 138–42, 171ff., 181–3; F. G. Battaglini, *Zecca*, 286; *Vita*, 348, 350, 671; Tonini, v/2.448, 450–1, 545–6, 562, 581, 589–95, 695, 706–8; Massèra, *RIS*² xv/2.86 n. 7, 107 n. 4, 119 n. 3, 131 nn. 6, 7, 134 n. 5, 135 n. 1; *Roberto Valturio 'omnium scientiarum doctor et monarcha'* (Pesaro, 1927).

[9] Above p. 298.

which explains the wide regional diversity among officials of the Malatesta state. Those serving Pandolfo III Malatesta in the March of
Ancona derived variously from Brescia, Pavia, Cremona, Bologna,
Florence, Vigevano, Trento and a number of other cities;[1] and something of the same is to be suspected also of the government in Rimini.[2]

That behind the dual structure all effective power was despotic is
confirmed by every other aspect of Malatesta government. Thus
although in Rimini and Fano the Malatesta did not place their names on
the coinage until the time of Carlo and his brothers, minting, currency
and exchange matters had long been subject to their control; previously
they had been satisfied to issue money in the name of the city.[3] Again,
where formerly it had been the prerogative of the commune or general
council to admit foreigners to citizenship and the right to acquire
property, it was now enough to obtain the lord's personal sanction.[4]
The *signoria*, in summary, was the commune operated by the will of one
family: the inherited privileges, institutions, traditional procedures that
remained were all governed in the last resort by the Malatesta. Nothing
shows this better than the councils, which, whatever their initiative in
administration, were basically compliant and subordinate assemblies.
The general councils especially, at one time the focus of municipal
government, had little real power left. Their meetings were infrequent,
and their membership fixed in various ways by the lord. At Fano,
Cesena, Pesaro and Fossombrone the Malatesta were responsible for
reducing the number of councillors,[5] though it was later raised again
in Fano by Pandolfo III.[6] In Rimini attendance at the council may
already have been limited to 300 before the Malatesta became formally

[1] Bartoccetti, 'Liber', 14.

[2] Bib. sen., *Stat. Rim.*, fo. 374v; cf. below p. 331.

[3] ACF, *Cod. mal.* 5, fos. 2ff.; Battaglini, *Zecca*, 60, 220; Castellani, 'Zecca'; Amiani,
i. 379–80. At Pesaro it was the same: Giordani, *Zecca*, 190–4. Anonymous also was
control of the communal seals (cf. above p. 309), though in Fano during the
fourteenth century Galeotto's initial found its way onto public seals: Borgogelli,
'Stemmi', 71ff.

[4] For servants and followers of the Malatesta receiving the citizenship of Rimini:
Affò, 23; Battaglini, *Corte*, 172, 190; Vitali, ch. VI *passim*. For Sinigaglia: ACF,
Canc., *Reg.* ii, fos. 72r–73v. At Fossombrone Vernarecci claims that pre-signorial
forms at least of admission to citizenship continued: *Fossombrone*, i. 363. Cf. also:
Grimaldi, 'Bandi'; below p. 336.

[5] At Pesaro (1343) from 400 to 200, at Fossombrone from 100 to 33, at Cesena from
96 to 72, reverting, after the papal reconquest, to 96: Vaccai, 13, 27; Vernarecci,
Fossombrone, i. 364; Zazzeri, 239; Robertson, 'Cesena', 131–2. Cf. Zonghi,
317.

[6] 11 Aug. 1417: 'Reformatio Consilij Generalis Civitatis Fanj facta de mandato
dominj pandulfi de malatestis quj Jussit quod Consilium generale Ampliaretur in
maiorj numero' etc. There follow 158 names of which 53 are crossed through:
ACF, *Canc.*, *Cons.* ii, fos. 172r–3r. These figures suggest membership was to be
c. 100: cf. *Cons.* v, fos. 87, 90, vi.

supreme;[1] but they were nonetheless free to control its membership. In February 1398, with the help of seventeen electors, Carlo Malatesta chose and published the list of councillors: 197 in all, of whom eleven were members of the Malatesta family, while others were dependants or adherents.[2] The same control of recruitment was exercised at Fano, Pesaro and Cervia.[3] And with recruitment went a like control of conciliar proceedings. All sessions, in every town, were convened and led by the lord's *podestà* or vicar.[4] At Pesaro the Malatesta *locumtenens* proposed the matters for debate; he, or the lord if present, possessed a casting vote; while the *podestà*, when occasion arose, selected the committees to decide disputed questions.[5] At Fano similarly the general council proceeded *cum consensu atque deliberatione Officialium Magnif. dnorum*, or *cum consensu et voluntate. dominj Potestatis*.[6] And such action as the council took, in Fano and elsewhere, seems in time to have consisted largely of drafting and presenting petitions. To the communes this may have appeared its most important function.[7]

The smaller council was more active and more regular, but it was also more intimately associated with the rise and maintenance of the Malatesta *signoria*. At Rimini it was the publication in 1295 of statutes enlarging the powers of the *consiglio di credenza* at the expense of the Quattro Officiali which gave the first indication in law of growing Malatesta influence. In the years following much important business is found transacted in the smaller council and in the presence of the Malatesta; and in the critical legislation of 1334–5 it was a session of the

---

[1] Tonini, iii.196, vi/1.10; though figures of the later fourteenth century suggest rather 200: *ibid*. iv/2, CXVI. The Venetians later reduced it to 100.

[2] Such as Antonio da Mondaino, Carlo's doctor, Francesco Certaldo, the Perleoni (5 members), Faitani (5), Brancaleoni, Agolanti, Gualdi, Roelli: Tonini, iv/2, CCVII.

[3] The statutes of Pesaro (1423) provide that the *consiglio generale* shall be 100, the *credenza* 30, or more or less, as the Malatesta please, since they approve the choice: Vaccai, 14. For Cervia: below App. VII. For Fano: above p. 317 n. 6.

[4] Bib. sen., *Stat. Rim.*, fo. 280v (1360); ACF, *Cod. mal.* I, fo.13 (1367); *Canc., Cons.* i, fo. 14 (1401), v (1429ff.); Tonini, iv/2, CXVI (1355), v/2, XXXIII (1425). At Savignano there were fines for absence or withdrawal without the vicar's permission: Gasperoni, 'Savignano'.

[5] Giordani, *Zecca*, 202–5; Vaccai, 31.

[6] ACF. *Cons.* vi (1434–6); *Canc., Cons.* i, fo. 13: 'Idem dominus potestas una cum consensu et voluntate hominum dictj Conscilij et dictum Conscilium totum cum consensu et voluntate dicti dominj Potestatis unanimiter et concorditer fecerunt' etc. (20 April 1401). For Rimini: Tonini, v/2.129–31 (1425).

[7] ACF, *Canc., Cons.* v, fo. 9r, *Castelli* i, fos. 35r ff.; above p. 309. The *consiglio generale* was also summoned of course on ceremonial occasions, as when Carlo Malatesta left for Constance in 1415, or on specially solemn occasions, as when peace was made with the church in 1355 and Carlo Malatesta was captured by the Visconti in 1425: Battaglini, *Vita*, App. VI; Tonini, iv/2, CXVI, v/2, XXXIII. Cf. Zonghi, 243, n. ix.

smaller council which empowered the Malatesta to elect a *consiglio* of *sapientes* with full freedom to manage all communal affairs.[1] The Riminese statutes show them to be doing this before the number of councillors came to be fixed at twelve.[2] At Fano also, before the council of thirty-three was finally set up, the Malatesta were making use of a small *consilium Adunantie*.[3] The smaller council was a more wieldy instrument of government than the *consiglio generale*, and found more favour with the *signori*. It was consistent with their policy that the statutes of Pesaro drawn up in 1343, at the desire of Pandolfo II Malatesta, *podestà*, established a *consiglio di credenza* of sixty citizens.[4] At Cesena, along with the general council, the Malatesta sought to reduce the Anziani from twelve to eight members;[5] and at Sinigaglia in the middle of the fifteenth century Sigismondo provided twenty-four councillors to govern the city.[6] As a general rule the small council was nominated by the lord;[7] where, as at Savignano, it was chosen by lot from the greater assembly, its members were bound immediately to take an oath to the Malatesta vicar.[8] It was normal also for the smaller council to be summoned by the *podestà* or other signorial official.[9] At Rimini during the fifteenth century this was commonly the *officialis custodie*;[10] but sometimes it was a member of the *consiglio segreto*, a restricted body of courtiers in close attendance on the lord, who debated with him all matters of general policy.[11] Whoever presided, much of the business, in the smaller as in the greater council, came to

[1] Above p. 63; below App. III.

[2] *Stat. Rim.*, fos. 193v–194v. When the council of 12 was introduced is not clear. By the time of Sigismondo it was already well established, while the regency council set up on the death of Carlo, in 1429, comprised 12 members. The Visconti had councils of 12 in Milan and other towns and it is possible that Carlo copied their example. Once instituted the council survived the fall of the Malatesta.

[3] Above p. 310 ACF, *Canc., Cons.* i, fos. 8r (1399), 17 (1404). Meetings sometimes had as few as 12 members.

[4] Vaccai, 13.

[5] In 1398 a proposal by Malatesta di Galeotto to limit the council to 48 and the Anziani to 8 was defeated by 38 votes to 11: Chiaramonti, 404.

[6] Mancini, *AMM* 1926, 210.

[7] 'Consciliarij nominati ellecti per magnificum et potentem dominum nostrum': ACF, *Canc., Cons.* v, fo. 64r (1432); cf. i, fo. 30r (1406), viii (1445–9), fo. 60r; Tonini, v/2.154 (1442); Soranzo, 'Invettiva' 1911, 160–1. On the special as on the general council there were members of the Malatesta family in both Rimini and Fano: ACF, *Cons.* vi ff., *passim*; Battaglini, *Corte*, 229; Tonini, v/1.510.

[8] Gasperoni, 'Savignano'. on Pandolfo Malatesta's accession in 1482 the council of 12 in Rimini also took an oath: above p. 251.

[9] ACF, *Cod. mal.* 92, fo. 11r (1420); *Canc., Cons.* i, fo. 8r (1399), 17 (1404) etc.

[10] Battaglini, *Corte*, 228 (1463); Tonini, v/1.488, v/2, CI (1471), CIII (1472).

[11] Battaglini, *loc. cit.* Reference to the lords' personal *consiliarii* or *consiglio segreto* are elusively scattered; in July 1449 it seems to have comprised only 5 members: A. Battaglini, *Corte*, 138. Cf. F. G. Battaglini, *Vita*, 664; *Zecca*, 275–7; A. Battaglini, *Corte*, 141; Tonini, v/1.583; above pp. 198–9.

consist of framing petitions, and its activity, though extensive, was commonly safeguarded first by a request for licence to proceed.[1] Altogether, it may be supposed, the same easy conventions prevailed as in neighbouring Urbino, where the duke intervened directly in local government only when his interest was involved.[2]

Combined in common dependence on one ruling family, it might at least be thought that the various communes of the Malatesta state, however much unaltered in their local institutions, would have slowly undergone some rudimentary unification. In fact very little was done. At times, certainly, laws were issued for general application.[3] or the statutes of one commune made the model for those elsewhere.[4] A higher appellate jurisdiction was introduced,[5] and during the fifteenth century, as already seen, the control of revenues was centralised. This was all. And such unity as developed did not extend beyond the territory assigned by partition to each member of the family.[6] Communal loyalties remained lively; old jealousies between cities survived, and squabbles over boundaries could still exasperate the feelings of neighbouring towns.[7] It is said the *signorie* began to evolve something new when groups of communes become tributary to a single, central

[1] For petitions on all conceivable subjects (including, from Fano, request for help in promoting a candidate to an episcopal see: ACF, *Canc., Cons.* ii, fo. 92v, 1415) cf. Bib. sen., *Stat. Rim.*, fo. 374v; ACF, *Cons., passim*; Mariotti, *Bandi mal.*, 51–2. Care to seek permission for even the smallest actions is paralleled from other *signorie*: cf., on Vigevano, Fossati, *ASL* 1914.

[2] Luzzatto, 'Comune', 195.

[3] Thus Galeotto published certain statutes for all his subject cities: ACF, *Cod. mal.* 3, fos. 17r–19v; Bib. sen., *Stat. Rim.*, fos. 1ff.; *Stat. Fani*, lib. ii, ch. LXXXIII; *Stat. Caes.* (1589), 86ff. Cf. below p. 000; ACF, *Canc., Reg.* ii, fos. 55r–58r. On the other hand laws could just as often be confined to one city and *contado*: *Stat. Rim.*, fos. 349r–350v, 355r–356v, 359v–360r, 361v (1395–1421).

[4] As in 1434 when Sigismondo ordered the statutes of Fano to be revised according to those of Cesena: Amiani i.374; Borgogelli, 'Statuti'.

[5] Probably by Galeotto: ACF, *Cod. mal.* 4, fo. 206r; *Canc., Cons.* i, fos. 97r ff.; *Stat. Caes.* (1589), 86ff.; Maraschini, nn. 2, 4, 7, 9, 10, etc.; Bartoccetti, 'Liber', 18–19; above, p. 272. There are also records (1406, 1408) of parliaments of the Malatesta cities in Fano and Rimini: Amiani, i.328, 330.

[6] When Malatesta of Cesena was governing Fano for his brother, petitions continued to be addressed to Pandolfo at Brescia: ACF, *Cod. mal.* 4, fo. 31 n. 3.

[7] Between 1362 and 1369 there were boundary disputes between Fossombrone and Cagli (Vernarecci, *Fossombrone*, i.324–5), in 1410, 1412 and 1426 between Osimo and Castelfidardo (Cecconi, *Castelfidardo*, docs. XII–III; Maraschini, nn. 1–2), and in 1439 between Fano and the vicariate of Mondavio (Zonghi, 177, n. XVII). There were also differences between Rimini and Cesena (Tonini, v/2.198); but most persistent perhaps was the refusal of Santarcangelo to be subordinate to Rimini: Clementini, ii.633; *Mem. Santarcangelo*, nn. XIX, LII, 17–18, 31; Marini, *Santo Arcangelo*, 62; Sanudo, *Diarii*, v.509–10; Alvisi, 250, docs. 26,44; Tonini vi/2.783, 844–5. Similarly (1460) Ripa was allowed independence of Sinigaglia: ACF, *Canc., Reg.* ii, fo. 112v.

city.[1] But there are few traces of such amalgamation under the Malatesta. Rimini was never a capital or even head of a feudal honour. Union was purely personal and, as at Urbino once again, there was more centralisation of authority than unity of administration.[2] The Malatesta state was conservative (not to say 'reactionary'), and the Malatesta had neither the power nor the desire to impose uniformity from town to town. In some places they administered the revenues themselves, in others they used direct control. In some the officials were paid by them, in others by the commune. But everywhere a communal constitution survived to resume independent life should despotism fail in power or popularity. In the end the Malatesta stood or fell by the quality of their government.

Among the despotisms of Romagna the Malatesta *signoria* was for long the most settled and peaceful.[3] For generations they seem to have avoided tactless, partisan or provocative proceedings. Carlo Malatesta in particular was a conscientious ruler, and well into the reign of Sigismondo the family continued to be known as popular with all subjects. As *signori* they were constantly called on to exercise their prerogative of pardon, by remitting or reducing judicial penalties.[4] More than once they courted favour by granting corporate privileges to towns.[5] To their interest in public works the Tempio at Rimini and the library at Cesena were not the only testimony.[6] And where, as at Cervia or Sinigaglia, a community had fallen into poverty and decay, they did everything to restore and promote a robust economic life.[7] With time

---

[1] P. S. Leicht, *Storia del diritto italiano* (Milan, 1944), 255, 285; Cognasso, 'Note', 23–8, 64.

[2] Luzzatto, 'Comune e principato', 195–6.

[3] Tonini, iv/1.385. Cf. Sacchetti, writing of the Malatesta late in the fourteenth century (*Rime*, 332):

> 'Giusto governo in questi sempre giace
> e di lor terre poca guardia fanno
> perché a' terrieri tal signoria piace.'

[4] The Malatesta records at Fano are full of petitions arising from judicial fines, which it seems to have been customary to reduce: Zonghi, 12–22; cf. Sanudo, *Diarii*, v. 496. Sometimes they granted also a general amnesty: Amiani, i.360–1, 415–16; above p. 85.

[5] As to Santarcangelo (Mazzatinti, *Archivi*, Ser. 1, i.334), Fano (Amiani, i.371), S. Vito and Monterolo (ACF, *Canc.*, Reg. ii, fo. 116v).

[6] Zazzeri, 268–9, 292, 338–9; Coleschi, 60; Amiani, i.355; Zonghi, 140; Battaglini, *Zecca*, 281. For their upkeep of the port at Rimini: Clementini, ii.252; Battaglini, *Zecca*, 226, 281.

[7] Sinigaglia was described in 1371 as being decayed and abandoned owing to the *infectionem aeris* (Theiner, ii, 535); but in the middle of the fifteenth century Sigismondo took steps to rehabilitate the town, with such success that the present Sinigaglia has been described as his foundation: ACF, *Canc.*, Reg. ii, fos. 72r–3r;

a 'native and genuine reverence' began to gather round them,[1] such that in 1446 the Venetians thought it wise to warn Francesco Sforza that their lands would be difficult of attack: 'sonno terre forti et molto affectionati ad li Signori loro'.[2] The truth of this opinion was later confirmed during Sigismondo's war with the papacy, when Rimini, Fano and the smaller centres round all stood firm as long as possible despite inadequate defences; and during the winter of 1460, when things were getting desperate, Sigismondo even received petitions from certain subject communities to remain forever under Malatesta rule.[3] This was not their only demand, however, nor theirs' the only petition. In the emergency of a last stand to save the *signoria*, complaints flowed in from many places which, loyally but emphatically, declared how much was felt to be wrong, and not only of recent date, in the governemnt of the Malatesta.[4]

Such criticism was not new. Grievances had always abounded, many of a kind common to all medieval régimes. They derived in part from the low level of public morality, which more than once united the Malatesta with their subjects against misgovernment by officials. Although, in agreement with general practice, all leading officials were scrutinised (syndicated) before retiring, by representatives of either the Malatesta or the commune,[5] such inquests were neither reliable[6] nor a certain restraint on misconduct. Quite early, in 1365, Galeotto Malatesta had to take measures against official abuses in Rimini,[7] and in 1415 Pandolfo III Malatesta had to issue a series of decrees for Fano prohibiting delays in criminal justice, and rebuking financial officials, quicker in paying themselves once or twice over than in collecting the

Battaglini, *Vita*, 574; Nicoletti, 35; Mancini, *AMM* 1926, 210. Similar measures were taken at Cervia by Galeotto Belfiore and Carlo Malatesta, but in Malatesta Novello's day the town was still largely depopulated and under water: *Stat. Cerviae*, 111, 114; Battaglini, *Zecca*, 222; Soranzo, 'Cervia', 201.

[1] See the interesting letter of the bishop of Rimini, June 1522: Clementini, ii.682–6.
[2] Osio, iii.428ff. The name 'Malatesta' and, in the fifteenth century specifically 'Sigismondo', was commonly adopted by the Riminese: Vasina, *Romagna*, 275.
[3] ACF, *Canc.*, *Reg.* ii, fos. 112v, 116v.
[4] Petitions were submitted to Sigismondo by Ripa (7 Nov. 1460), Monterado, Roncitello and Scapezzano (3 Dec. 1460), the 'vicariate' (of Mondavio? 5 Jan. 1461), S. Vito and Monterolo (Jan. 1461?), and Rimini (8 Dec. 1461): ACF, *Canc.*, *Reg.* ii, fos. 109r–10v, 112v–13v, 114v, 116; Bib. sen., *Stat. Rim.*, fos. 374v–9v.
[5] In Pesaro and Savignano by delegates of the Malatesta (Vaccai, 56; Gasperoni, 'Savignano'), but in Fano, on occasion at least, by elected scrutineers: ACF, *Canc.*, *Cons.* ii, fo. 130r; Mariotti, *Bandi mal.*, 32; Amiani, i.304. The Malatesta maintained a close watch over officials and, like other *signori*, compiled periodic 'musters' (*mostre*), recording even details of personal appearance: *Cod. mal.* 9; Zonghi, 32–3; Bartoccetti, 'Liber.'
[6] Maraschini, 13.
[7] *Stat. Rim.*, fos. 366r ff. About the same time Pandolfo II took similar action in Fossombrone: Vernarecci, *Fossombrone*, i.338.

public revenue.[1] His censures can have had little effect, for the same grievances recur in a petition from Fano only two years later.[2] During this period Pandolfo was still preoccupied with affairs in Lombardy, and on his return the administration may have improved. But Sigismondo, who replaced him and was like him a frequent absentee, was similarly obliged to publish *bandi*, for all parts of his state, against judicial abuses by *podestà* and associated officials: in particular bribery and the irresponsible use of torture, which he reserved to his discretion.[3]

A still more irritating cause of discontent, for which the Malatesta themselves were answerable, was the minute control by government over trade, the details of indirect taxation, and the movement of all commodities.[4] Not that the Malatesta neglected the interests of trade and industry[5] and whenever possible they did reduce customs duties and make trade more free. At Rimini under Carlo Malatesta it is recorded that there were no restrictions on the sale of bread and wine.[6] At Fano in 1417, owing to the distressed state of the city, Pandolfo III halved the duties on incoming merchandise,[7] and in 1439 Sigismondo, on petition, limited the *passagium* in Fano to what it had been in his

[1] Mariotti, *Bandi mal.*, 33–4. For other decrees and complaints (1399, 1407): ACF, *Canc., Cons.* i, fos. 5, 88r ff. Cf. further: Maraschini, n. 78.

[2] ACF, *Canc., Cons.* ii, fos. 179ff.

[3] *Ibid. Reg.* ii, fos. 55r–8r.

[4] All import and export required signorial licence: Giordani, *Zecca*, 202–10; Vaccai, 193ff., 215ff.; *Stat. Cerviae*, 132–3; ACF, *Canc. Reg.* ii, fos. 72v, 75r; *Cod. mal.* 5, fo. 2, 92 (fo. 25v, licence by Sigismondo to Cosimo de' Medici to export corn: Feb. 1437), 93; Maraschini, *passim*. For the vexation arising: Cecconi, *Castelfidardo*, 98–9. Transit trade was equally regulated and the customs' charges could be relatively high: *Commiss. Albizzi*, i. 10–9 (1402: request by Florence to Carlo Malatesta for 'il passa del suo Porto').

[5] This is a subject in itself, but among relevant details it may be noted that Pandolfo III and Carlo Malatesta established annual fairs at Fano and Cesena (ACF, *Canc., Cons.* ii, fo. 180v; Amiani, i. 381; Zazzeri, 272–3); that Carlo, followed by Sigismondo, was successful (where the commune had failed) in promoting woollen cloth and possibly other trades in Rimini which, in Carlo's day, exported manufactures to Dalmatia and had 30 or 40 merchants ships, and, under Sigismondo, maintained some 25 trade guilds (Bib. sen., *Stat. Rim.*, fo. 368v; Clementini, ii. 224, 245–6; F. G. Battaglini, *Zecca*, 154, 226–7; A. Battaglini, *Corte*, 159, 243; Tonini, iii. 110–11; *Porto*, 104; Vasina, *Romagna*, 259, 285); and that wool and silk production also prospered under the Malatesta at Fossombrone, where Pandolfo II may have encouraged the start of paper manufacture (Vernarecci, *Fossombrone*, i. 459). At the same time nothing was attempted to relieve dependence on Venice and Florence which, if anything, increased during the fifteenth century: Vasina, *Romagna*, 277–8, 292; above p. 21.

[6] Battaglini, *Zecca*, 226–7. Carlo also lifted *dazi*, wholly or in part, in times of crisis or dearth: Clementini, ii. 231–2. Far less considerate, by contrast, was the food policy of the last Malatesta in the 1480s and 1490s: *ibid.* 568; Cappelli, 'Pandolfo', 423.

[7] *Stat. Fani*, 'Tractatus Gabellarum'.

father's time, because it was keeping away merchants trading between Tuscany and the Marches.[1] Two years earlier Sigismondo had also suppressed at one stroke fourteen *dazi* imposed in Rimini,[2] and later in 1454 local freedom of traffic between the two dominions was an article in the peace between Sigismondo and his brother.[3] In 1468, finally, perhaps to curry favour, Isotta, Roberto and Malatesta de' Malatesta granted a general liberty to anyone, native or 'foreign', wishing to import *panni pignolati*, skins, spices, hosiery and other merchandise, 'et questo perchè per molte rasone et experientie se intende esser grande bonificatione de questa terra'.[4] These concessions if maintained were doubtless well received, at least by consumers, but indirect taxes were too rich a source of income to be lightly surrendered,[5] and the Malatesta could never long relax and were reluctant even to delegate their control of trade. The only resource of the discontented was to petition at least for freedom of traffic within the Malatesta state or with friendly powers outside.[6]

It was not in practice possible for the Malatesta to grant any extensive commercial freedom or relief from taxation. Economic sanctions were a normal consequence of war, and the Malatesta were constantly at war. For this and their schemes of territorial expansion, they needed every *soldo* and ducat that could be raised, and there is no doubt that the numerous demands of the Malatesta often became oppressive. As seen already, war taxes by the Malatesta, particularly under Pandolfo III, were frequent[7] and more than once provoked appeals for alleviation.[8] In the spring of 1415 the commune of Monte Cassiano was so drained of money that it was reduced to raising loans.[9] But war and the

[1] ACF, *Cod. mal.* 3, fo. 21v.

[2] Bib. sen., *Stat. Rim.*, fos. 367r ff.; Battaglini, *Zecca*, 267; Bagli, 90ff. In addition he granted liberty to import all 'mercantia o Robbe excepti pannj de lana el cui valore sia de soldi 24 in giuso'; but this must have been infringed if it needed to be repeated in 1468. He also, alone of the Malatesta, allowed sumptuary laws to lapse: Vasina, *Romagna*, 275.

[3] Tonini, v/2, LXVI.

[4] *Ibid.* XCIX; *Porto*, 145. Under Pandolfo 'ultimo' there was still a tax on *robe conducte in Arimano*: Sanudo, v. 448.

[5] The check to protectionism may reflect also growing dependence on outsiders: Vasina, *Romagna*, 276, 292.

[6] Thus in 1416 one desire of the rebel Osimani was freedom of trade with lands friendly with the Malatesta (Martorelli, 231–6); in 1417 Fano petitioned without success that the August fair be free *fino in XXV lib. de bol.*, as had been the case at Rimini under Galeotto (ACF, *Canc., Cons.* ii, fo. 180v); and in 1460–1 all the petitions included a request for free or freer trade inside the Malatesta dominion. The Riminese seem to have secured this later from Venice. Cf. further: ACF, *Cons.* ii, fo. 45r; Rossi, *Monte Alboddo*, App. viii.

[7] Cf. above p. 306.

[8] For such petitions by Fano during the early fifteenth century: ACF, *Cod. mal.* 3, 4; *Canc., Cons.* ii, fos. 7v–8r, 17r ff., 179r ff.; Amiani, i.335; Zonghi, 12.

[9] *Mem. M. Cassiano*, 60.

pay of troops were not the only occasion for extraordinary levies. When the Malatesta bought S. Sepolcro in 1370 for 10,000 florins it was the subject cities that had to pay,[1] as it was when Bertinoro was pledged to the Malatesta in 1394.[2] The taxes requested in 1417 to ransom Carlo Malatesta from Braccio were so untimely as to cause open unrest in S. Sepolcro and the *contado* of Fano.[3] The communes also paid the papal *census* and other subsidies to Rome,[4] shared the cost of embassies, and were expected to provide gifts (*exenia*) when Malatesta (and neighbouring *signori*) were born, married or died.[5] When taxes did not yield enough or were slow of collection, the Malatesta had recourse to loans, either locally or from abroad,[6] and if the loans were large the subject communes were obliged to guarantee repayment.[7] Loans were taken also from the Jews who, though generally detested by their subjects as 'blood-sucking' usurers,[8] never lost the interested favour of the Malatesta.[9] Finally, and wholly distinct, there were the receipts the Malatesta drew from mercenary arms. When good and remitted regularly, they clearly helped finance such works as the

---

[1] Fano made a *prestanza* of 1,000 gold ducats, the Jews of Fano another 1,000; in 1373 more money for the same purpose had to be raised: Amiani, i. 295.

[2] *Ibid.* i. 319.

[3] ACF, *Canc.*, *Cons.* ii, fos. 148r ff.; Amiani, i. 341–2; Coleschi, 64. In S. Sepolcro the *gabelle* were doubled, trebled and quadrupled to pay the ransom.

[4] Amiani, i. 290; Tonini, iv/2. 385–6; Vernarecci, *Fossombrone*, i. 346.

[5] In Dec. 1459, when Federigo d'Urbino married Battista Sforza, the *consiglio di credenza* of Pesaro declared it was usual on such occasions to present an *ensenium* to the lords (Giordani, *A. Sforza*, xlviii, lviii), and this was certainly the custom under the Malatesta: *Cod. mal.*, 39, 101; Zonghi, 152–3; Amiani, i. 312, 319–20, 326, 332, 381, 406–7; Vernarecci, *Fossombrone*, i. 339; above p. 81. Pertile (ii/1. 450) suggests the *signori* were aping feudal monarchy.

[6] For loans in Fano and other communes: ACF, *Cod. mal.* 21, fos. 133–8, 142v (for expenses in taking Bergamo and Iesi), 147r–149v, 153r–154v etc.; *Cod.* 99: Vasina, *Romagna*, 291; above p. 307 n. 1. Among loans outside may be noted the money borrowed from the wealthy Gozzadini of Bologna (Gozzadini, *Nanne Gozzadini*, 24–5), and the Scaligeri: above p. 111.

[7] Predelli, x, n. 212 (1415), xi, n. 83 (1421), xii, n. 100 (1429); Amiani, i. 350; Soranzo, *Pio II*, 403–4 (1463). Sigismondo got involved in debt to Venice for jewelry for Isotta; Fano was made surety and in 1476, 13 years after passing to the church, was let off part of a papal tallage to make repayment: Amiani, i. 388, ii. 8, 16, 22–3; Grigioni, 'Documenti', 367ff. The communes were also pledges, in their persons and property, for treaties made by the Malatesta: Battaglini, *Vita*, 606–7, 618–19 (1425, 1435).

[8] So in the Riminese petition, Dec. 1461, to which the laconic reply was 'providebitur': Bib. sen., *Stat. Rim.*, fo. 375r.

[9] ACF, *Cod. mal.* 16 (*sub Intrada Straordinaria*), 21 (fo. 270r), 74; Chiaramonti, 419; Battaglini, *Vita*, 289, 609–10; *Zecca*, 71; Mariotti, *Bandi mal.*, 40; Grigioni, 'Costruttori', 199; Borgogelli, 'Istanza'. Favour to the Jews may explain why Monti di Pietà were introduced in Rimini and Fano only after their expulsion, though at Gubbio, 1463, and Pesaro they were established under despots: Pellegrini, 197; Vaccai, 139.

Tempio Malatestiano and Sigismondo's reconstruction of Sinigaglia. But pay was insecure, and by the early fifteenth century said to be declining. Yet precisely from this time the evidence is that the Malatesta, with other lords of Romagna, became dependent more than anything on just this source of income.[1]

There is every sign in fact that during the fifteenth century, whatever expedients were tried – extraordinary taxes, loans or *condotte* – the financial state of the Malatesta steadily deteriorated. This financial weakness first overtook the Malatesta of Pesaro. In 1373 Pandolfo II Malatesta, lord of Pesaro and Fossombrone, is said to have died a rich man: 'signore de molta moneta e altri grandi texori';[2] but his son Malatesta died heavily in debt. In 1413 he was reduced to having church properties secularised to limit tax exemptions,[3] and he seems never to have been able to pay the dowry of his daughter, Paola Agnesi, wife of Gianfrancesco Gonzaga.[4] Galeazzo, who succeeded him and finally sold the city, lacked the competence or the power to repair his finances. He was perpetually harassed by creditors, and for a time had to commit certain of his territories to foreign hands.[5]

The Malatesta of Rimini suffered a similar if slower impoverishment. Early in the fifteenth century Fano still yielded Pandolfo III a considerable revenue exceeding his expenditure,[6] but this favourable balance was soon unsettled by his costly conquests in Lombardy.[7] Rimini also provided an ample income at this time, estimated in 1371 at about £80,000 *Rav.* or over 47,000 ducats, roughly the sum that Carlo Malatesta was held a century after his death to have received each year from Rimini.[8] By the end of the fifteenth century this income had contracted to less than 10,000 ducats.[9] Petty economies were tried at various times

[1] So for example Battaglini, *Zecca*, 71. The same was true of Urbino: Dennistoun, i.175–6. For rates and difficulties of pay: Partner, 155–6; above pp. 198ff. Under Galeotto and Carlo income was also increased by their salaries as rectors of Romagna, whose monthly pay in 1368 and 1371 was 120 fl.: Theiner, ii.460, 495.

[2] *Cron. mal.*, 35. [3] Above p. 276.

[4] Tarducci, 'Gianfr. Gonzaga', pt. i. 327–8. Cf. his remissions of *census*: above p. 286.

[5] Mazzatinti, *Inventari*, xxxviii.100, xxxix.222; Vernarecci, *Fossombrone*, i.348–9; F. Tarducci, *Cecilia Gonzaga ed Oddantonio da Montelfeltro* (Mantua, 1897); above p. 187.

[6] Above p. 285; but it included arrears of taxes, some dating from 1377 and 1378: ACF, *Cod. mal.* 16, fos. 113r–14r (*entrate de cholte e grade vecchi* – a common item in the Malatesta accounts).

[7] ACF, *Cod. mal.* 24. The patrimonial income for 1409–10 (£10,550 *sol.* 5 *den.* 6) was also exceeded by the factor's expenses £12,797 *sol.* 5 *den.* 2), though he had received nearly £6,000 from the public *depositaria*: *Cod. mal.* 19.

[8] See above p. 285.

[9] Sanudo, *Diarii*, v.489. During the pontificate of Clement VII the Riminese Balacchi complained that the income of Rimini had fallen to as little as 4,000 ducats: Tonini, vi/1.192.

by the Malatesta. They checked the practice of pardoning fines,[1] reduced official salaries[2] and restricted tax immunities.[3] At the same time they ceased to remit the papal *census* regularly.[4] But nothing availed to remedy a weakness from which the whole Malatesta state seems to have suffered, lord and subject alike. In 1524 Balacco Balacchi of Rimini complained with some extravagance that whereas in the time of Carlo Malatesta one suburb alone had numbered 10,000 people, the entire city of Rimini could not now muster so many, and that while in Carlo's day the city had boasted sixty ships it now had none.[5] This decay he ascribed to the effects of misgovernment and harsh taxation; but although there is some evidence that oppressive government had caused men to migrate,[6] those contemporaries were doubtless nearer the truth who blamed pestilence and war.[7] In 1417 the Malatesta were

[1] In 1406 Malatesta de' Malatesta ordained that pardon of fines in his territories (Cesena, Bertinoro etc.) was to cease owing to loss of revenue: ACF, *Cod. mal.* 21. In Dec. Pandolfo Malatesta extended the same order to his lands: *Cod. mal.* 3, fo. 16; *Stat. Fani, Tractatus Gabellarum.*

[2] At Fano the salaries of the *podestà, revisor rationum* and officials *super sale domini* all fell between *c.* 1400 and 1424 (App. VII below; Bartoccetti, 'Liber', 17, 20–1, 58–9); under Sigismondo the *podestà*'s establishment was also reduced (ACF, *Cod. mal.* 94, fos. 2r, 6r etc.). At Rimini a large reduction is evident in the *podestà*'s salary between the late fourteenth and late fifteenth century: Theiner, ii.515; Sanudo, *Diarii*, v.445.

[3] Above p. 314. Enfeoffments must also have abridged Malatesta revenue: above pp. 295ff.

[4] Above p. 286.

[5] Tonini, vi/1.192. From being possibly the largest and wealthiest Romagnol city in the later fourteenth century (above p. 285; cf. Larner, 6,220ff.) Rimini was certainly much contracted by 1500. In 1511 the number of 'mouths' in Rimini was put at 4,933 and *c.* 1524 the population over 5 years of age was estimated at 5,500 in the city, 6,500 in the *contado*: ASF, *Carte Strozziane*, Ser. I, 238, fo. 140; Tonini, vi/1. 85, 191. There was a similar decline at Fano: F. Bonasera, *Fano (SP* xx, 1951), 86. And in both cities, as well as Cervia, the Malatesta, from the late fourteenth century, placed total or partial restrictions on foreign marriages by women, *ut civitas liberis repleatur*: Amiani, i.381, 410; Mariotti, *Bandi mal.*, 39–40; Vasina, *Romagna*, 276, 288.

[6] Above p. 307.

[7] 'Quoniam civitas haec Ariminea bellorum turbinibus et epidemiarum infortuniis, quibus saepe perturbata retroactis temporibus ac vexata fuit, non solum divitiis verum etiam civibus et personis eam incolentibus exhausta et fere denudata reperitur': Tonini, vi/2.835 (*a.* 1508). Sigismondo introduced his tax reliefs in 1437 (above p. 324) to meet what he called the 'danni, detrimenti, et diminutioni' suffered by Rimini 'già longo tempo fo per morie, per guerre, et per altre male condictione de tempi' – fair definition of late medieval 'crisis'. At Rimini and Fano a local expression of decline was the progressive silting up of their seaports, which neither the Malatesta nor later rulers could arrest: Guicciardini, *Opere inedite* (Florence, 1866), viii.406; Tonini, *Porto*, 106; Bonasera, *Fano*, 73. A description of Romagna, 1578, blames this lowland sedimentation on highland deforestation, though in a later account (1621–34) Rimini is still reported the most commercial city in Romagna: Dal Pane, 49; Zoli and Bernicoli, 28.

already granting financial concessions to Fano, exhausted by their continuous war in the March of Ancona.[1] Later on the wars waged locally under Sigismondo from the time of Sforza's invasion all brought hardship, if only because of the expenses of hire and billeting. The local skirmishes with the Montefeltro all took their toll. In 1443 the men of Rupola begged exemption for twenty years from the *taglie* and *salarii* owed to the vicar and chancellor of Mondavio, because shortly before they had been sacked and dispersed by the count of Urbino, and a year later Sigismondo had to offer indemnity to all citizens of Fano who had suffered losses during the recent war.[2] The final struggle with Piccinino and Pius II made irreparable the damage of earlier years, undoing any good to be expected from the liberal fiscal policy announced in 1437.[3] By the end of 1461 Rimini was crippled. Complaints came in as well from the March of Ancona,[4] and Sigismondo had to renounce all hope of keeping the *literati* he had attracted to his court, or of paying his artists with money.[5] After 1463, with most of his territory gone, he was more than ever bound to his pay as *condottiere*,[6] and the purchase-money of Cervia which was still outstanding can, if paid at all, have brought him small relief.[7] When he came to make his will Sigismondo had little to bestow,[8] and the inventory of his goods in 1468 does not indicate a man of wealth or ostentation.[9] His son Roberto attempted greater display and is said by Broglio to have spent 35,000 ducats on his wedding with Isabetta da Montefeltro;[10] but he too had to live as a mercenary captain and found a *census* of 1,000 ducats burdensome.[11] Even his heir Pandolfo, although no active soldier, frequently contracted *condotte in aspetto*.[12] His revenues were slight, and from either poverty or meanness he failed to pay the handsome dowry due by her father's will to his sister Giovanna.[13] Against the richly subsidised Borgia he was powerless.

[1] Above p. 323. The Malatesta were also directly responsible for war damage: in 1399 much of Montalboddo was destroyed during conquest by Galeotto Belfiore: Menchetti, i.7, 14.
[2] ACF, *Canc.*, *Reg.* ii, fo. 34v; Mariotti, *Bandi di tregua*, 10.
[3] See above p. 324 n. 2. Cf. Battaglini, *Zecca*, 267; *Vita*, 553.
[4] Bib. sen., *Stat. Rim.*, fo. 376r; ACF, *Canc.*, *Reg.* ii, fo. 116v.
[5] Battaglini, *Corte*, 200, 206; Grigioni, 'Costruttori', 197–200.
[6] Above p. 240.
[7] Battaglini, *Vita*, 666–7. Malatesta Novello died in financial difficulty: Robertson, 'Cesena', 137.
[8] Tonini, v/2, xcvii. It is much shorter than those of earlier Malatesta.
[9] Battaglini, *Vita*, lxii; Ricci, doc. xvii.
[10] Tonini, v/1.364: this was more than 3 times the annual revenue drawn from Rimini by his son Pandolfo.
[11] Above p. 287.
[12] Above p. 254.
[13] Sanudo, *Diarii*, v.1012.

All classes suffered by the wars and exactions of the Malatesta; but whether all suffered equally, and how in general they were affected by Malatesta government, are difficult questions. During most of their history the Malatesta escaped the charge of harsh and violent rule. The heavy punishment of Ugolino de' Pilii and his sons, which was cast in the teeth of Sigismondo, seems to have been deserved;[1] and although in 1509 the Riminese secured annulment of the confiscations made by Pandolfo Malatesta after the rising of 1493, they asked that all other *alienationes ac bonorum confiscationes* enforced by the Malatesta and their officials for fifty years before he upheld, *et perpetuum silentium imponatur*.[2] Insurrections were few. The rising of 1431 was not, as already shown, a popular movement, though it led to acts of irresponsible destruction;[3] and the rebel Osimani in 1416 were soon induced to accept terms.[4] Once in power the Malatesta sought, like other *signori*, to rise above the loyalties and feuds of faction. The Parcitadi, or some of them, may have been readmitted to Rimini, though under a different name. With the exiled Carignani of Fano the Malatesta ultimately made peace; and in Fossombrone they mediated between members of hostile families.[5] At Cesena, however, and S. Sepolcro the Ghibelline factions conspired against them and had to be suppressed.[6]

It is sometimes alleged that the Italian despots were kinder in government to the peasantry than were the communes before them,[7] and at least it may be admitted that the *contadini* had less incentive to rebel than the urban families who might expect by successful revolution to assume control themselves. Such a view may best reflect the state of popular feeling under the Malatesta. On occasion certainly they acted in favour of the peasantry, as when Malatesta *defensor* in 1349 reduced

[1] Battaglini, *Corte*, 79–81; Sigismondo was not always severe to traitors: *ibid.* 81, 144.

[2] Tonini, vi/2.849, cl. 40, 850, cl. 43.

[3] Above p. 171. At Rimini the foreigners were chased out, and the records of the *podestà* burned: Clementini, ii.246; Battaglini, *Vita*, 288–9; at Cesena the *libri Emphiteuticorum* were destroyed: Chiaramonti, 419; at Fano the records of the *gabelle*: Zonghi, 399.

[4] Martorelli, 231–6; Vernarecci, *Fossombrone*, i.346–7.

[5] Battaglini, *Saggio*, 54 etc.; Amiani, i.324–5 (*a.* 1399); Vernarecci, *Fossombrone*, i.319. Pandolfo Malatesta also tried to reconcile the factions of Bergamo: Belotti, i.599.

[6] Under Galeotto and Carlo Malatesta: Theiner, iii.61; Chiaramonti, 382, 395–6, 404, 406–7; Zazzeri, 248, 252; Coleschi, 65, 201. Cf. letter of Martin V to Galeotto Roberto and his brothers, complaining of the detention in prison for 18 years of certain nobles of Montevecchio: Tonini, v/2, xxxvi.

[7] For example Feliciangeli, 'Relazioni', 401–2, 415–18, 426ff., with reference to the Varani (cf. Lilii, ii.219). At Faenza under Galeotto Manfredi the discontented were a noble faction (Messeri and Calzi, 191); at Forlì the *contadini* seem to have been the class best affected toward the *signoria*: Cobelli, 191–2, but cf. 303; Pasolini, i.330–1.

the number of *capitanei* in the *contado* of Rimini, 'pro exhoneratione rusticorum'.[1] At Corinaldo Pandolfo III Malatesta instructed every landowner to provide suitable housing for farm workers, who were crowded into hovels round the city walls and gates; and at Fano refused a petition that the rule applied by his brothers in the country districts subject to them, by which the places of the *contado* could agree upon no expenses without the assent of the city government, should also apply to Fano, as had formerly been the practice. To him it did not appear 'lecito'.[2] Finally, Sigismondo made some provision to relieve the Riminese *contadini*,[3] and was ready in 1460 to meet the requests of Ripa in the March of Ancona.[4]

None of these measures argues a coherent policy, nor is one to be expected. If the Malatesta were content to leave unaltered much in the communal constitution, they were no more concerned to change the inherited relations of city and *contado*. It was innovation enough that they now normally appointed the local officials. They directed the administration, but the administration proceeded much as before. The captains of the *castelli* preserved their limited civil jurisdiction,[5] and the rural commune kept up its subordinate activity;[6] but the *contadini* continued to suffer the burden of *corvées* and purveyance,[7] and the periodic rural outbreaks caused by taxation suggest that according to custom the urban population was making the *contado* pay a disproportionate part.[8] At Sinigaglia, under the Malatesta, the established

---

[1] Bib. sen., *Stat. Rim.*, fo. 338v. For other enactments for relief of *laboratores*: fo. 337v.

[2] Cimarelli, 28–9; ACF, *Canc., Cons.* ii, fos. 17r ff.

[3] His decrees of 1437 include the statement: 'Ultimo accioche i dicti Contadini de la dicta Cita non siano ultra El debito gravati vole et comanda che niuno Contadino possa senza suo comandamento essere sostenudo in Arimino per debita de la sua comunità, o per alcuno resto, havendo lui pagado el debito suo, E che per la dicta caxione non possano essere sequestrade ne retenude alcune sue cose'; Bib. sen., *Stat. Rim.*, fo. 368v; Bagli, 94.

[4] Above pp. 313, 320. There are also cases under the Malatesta of rural representatives attending city councils on tax and harvest matters: Amiani, i.270; ACF, *Canc., Cons.* ii, fos. 102, 103, 104v, 186–7.

[5] Sanuto, v.55off., 644–5; Gasperoni, 'Savignano'; Vaccai, 228; Bartoccetti, 'Liber', 12–14; ACF, *Canc., Cons.* v., fos. 98ff., 131ff. (showing how syndics of the *contado* take an oath, not as formerly to the commune, represented by the *podestà* (Amiani, i. 177), but to the *vice-podestà* as representative of the lord and commune or the lord alone); Tonini, v/2.297–8.

[6] Above p. 310.

[7] Above p. 307.

[8] Cf. particularly the disputes over tax apportionment between town and *contado* at Fano, 1385 and 1433; Clementini, ii.272–3; Amiani, i.308. For tax revolts in the *contado* of Rimini (1355) and of Fano (1410, 1416, 1425): *Cron. mal.*, 20; Amiani, i.334, 341–2, 354. Vernarecci (*Fossombrone*, i.349) says the poverty of the Malatesta of Pesaro was particularly felt by the *contado* to which the citizens merely transferred the burden.

practice remained that the *contadini* and *forenses* alone should pay pasture dues, citizens being exempt.[1] At best the Malatesta may have moderated urban domination; which will explain why, when they fell from power, it was particularly the *contadini*, as at Cesena in 1469 or Rimini after 1500, who desired their return.[2]

There is no sign that the urban aristocracy resented the way in which the *contado* was managed by the Malatesta. Yet it was the aristocracy which finally drove the Malatesta out. And, given the close connections formed between many nobles and the *signoria*, it is urgent to ask why. At first it might seem sufficient to argue, with Aristotle in his account of Greek tyranny, that they acted from hatred and contempt, contempt for the last Malatesta, a weak capricious tyrant, addicted to every outrage against the honour of his subjects. This was the explanation of some contemporaries, like Sanudo. Hints of a deeper reason, however, were added by another contemporary, Priuli, when he said that Cesare Borgia in his attack on the *tiranni* was encouraged by disaffected parties in the towns.[3] The self-evident fact is that, however popular the Malatesta, however strong their aspiration to repudiate faction, they could never hope fully to satisfy the ambition, the expectation of patronage, of the native nobility. They did employ them, certainly, both at home and abroad,[4] and also followed the general practice of seeking offices for their subjects in other states.[5] But it was still a subject of complaint that local office was not reserved to local men,[6] and in 1431 what encouraged Giovanni di Ramberto Malatesta to attempt his *coup d'état* was discontent among the councillors of Rimini, replaced by 'foreigners' from Ferrara.[7] In every town a class

---

[1] ACF, *Cod. mal.* 70 (1402).

[2] Chiaramonti, 424–5. Cf. above p. 246, below pp. 333, 336. Luzzato has shown that at Urbino also in the fifteenth and sixteenth centuries the city retained its administrative and economic hegemony over the *contado* ('Per la storia delle relazioni fra città e contado nel medioevo', *Le Marche* ii. 52–5). The Visconti and Sforza were unable to check the exploitation of the *contado* which continued to bear most taxes (Tagliabue, 'Politica', 228ff.; Cusin, 'Aspirazioni', 284–90), and the same seems to have been true under the Medici in Tuscany (Anzilotti, *ASI* 1915).

[3] Above p. 259.

[4] Above p. 298. Pandolfo Malatesta employed many Fanese nobles in his Lombard dominions: Borgogelli, *SP* 1927, 2.

[5] As of Paolo Guinigi, the Polenta, Lorenzo de' Medici: *Carteggio Guinigi*, i n. 55; Rubeus, 617; ASF, *Mediceo av. principato*, filza 26, n. 299, filza C ins., n. 167, filza Guid., nn. 157, 159. In 1414 the Perugians applied to Carlo Malatesta for *unum probum et expertum militem pro potestate*: Cutolo, i. 424.

[6] Bib. sen., *Stat. Rim.*, fo. 374v (1461).

[7] Above p. 172. It has recently been argued by Vasina (*Romagna*, 257–8, 267ff., 288) that at Rimini, down at least to Sigismondo's time, a schism existed between the Malatesta, their court circle and government, and the old native patriciate, which was bridged neither by patronage nor occasional intermarriage; but the conclusion

existed proud and jealous of its status which, if lifted into power, would form a natural oligarchy. There is nothing to suggest that this class was deeply discontented throughout the two hundred years of Malatesta rule, and only held in check by repressive measures. But when, as happened under Sigismondo, the Malatesta were discredited and humbled, when the government passed into the hands of doting women like Isotta and Elisabetta Aldovrandini, and when the Malatesta fell out among themselves or adopted tyrannical ways, then the dominant families were instinctively provoked to look for other and more capable rulers, who might bring them greater liberty or more assured prosperity. There were already signs of disaffection under Sigismondo, both at Fano and at Rimini, and after his death there began to develop, beside the adherents of the Malatesta, groups who saw in Venice or the papacy the promise of a milder and more stable government.[1] Their attitude, no doubt, was that of the Milanese *ottimati* who, impatient equally of popular excess and ducal *signoria*, attained under Charles V the easy and remote surveillance they desired.[2] So in Cesena after 1465 and in Rimini after 1500, an oligarchy was established under the tutelage of the church.[3] At Rimini it was the *ottimati*, or some of them, who planned the rising of 1498.[4] It was the *ottimati* who most resented the loss of territories by the Malatesta which had once been governed by the commune,[5] and it was probably the *ottimati* to whom the papacy addressed its promises that they should ever afterwards be governed by the church.[6] It was this class which negotiated the surrender of Rimini in 1500.[7] And finally, it was this class which prevented the Malatesta from ever regaining power.

is rather forced. At Cesena much the same group (some 30 families) were associated with government before and after the expulsion of the Malatesta: Robertson, 'Cesena', 140 (their defection was possibly caused by war expenses which reduced the Malatesta capacity for patronage: *ibid*. 137).

[1] Above pp. 241, 252.
[2] Cusin, 'Aspirazioni', 280, 283, 314.
[3] Chiaramonti, 424–5; Zazzeri, 360, 364, 368–9; Robertson, 'Cesena'; below p. 335.
[4] Above p. 253.
[5] Petition to Cesare Borgia, 1502 (Clementini, ii.592), and to the pope, 1509 (Tonini, vi/2, xxxviii, 840): 'quod omnes Terrae Comitatus, Ariminensis de praesenti sub dominio S. Rom. Ecclesiae restituantur'.
[6] Thus in 1431 the commune of Civita Nova petitioned the pope to annul all privileges granted the Varani and then the Malatesta, and to remain *immediate subjecta*: Theiner, iii.250. The request was granted, and the same promise was made to all cities of the Malatesta recovered by the church: Santarcangelo (Marini, *Santo Arcangelo*, 63), Bertinoro (Garampi, *Illustrazione*, 41; Theiner, iii.383), Fano (Amiani, ii.60), Cesena (Robertson, 'Cesena', 126) and Rimini (below p. 336). Cf. statutes of Montefiore: 'cum enim sub annis domini 1462 de mense Octobris Terra nostra non sine magno labore tyrannicum iugum D.D. de Malatestis excussisset': Vitali, 351–2.
[7] Above p. 261.

Despite the contrary testimony of Priuli,[1] Rimini does not seem, like neighbouring Urbino, to have been restive under the shortlived government of Cesare Borgia. It rather appears that the new duke of Romagna set out to court the nobility which had prepared the way for his invasion. He reinstated the exiles of 1498 and gave them back their properties. He took a number of Riminese notables into his service, and when a dispute broke out between the commune and the *contado* over the partition of taxes, he pronounced in favour of the commune.[2] The peasantry resisted his levies, and in October 1502 certain castles rose in revolt with the cry 'Pandolfo Malatesta'.[3]

Pandolfo, who a year before had been driven from Bologna to Venice,[4] may have had some part in these disturbances. He was certainly intriguing in Romagna, but may have been persuaded that no return was possible while Alexander was alive.[5] He therefore kept aloof from the conspiracy of La Magione, and only when the news of the pope's death arrived in August 1503 did he and the other disinherited despots, supported by Venice, make a resolute attempt at recovery. On 26 August he left Venice for Romagna. At once the *contadini* rose again, and sought Pandolfo for lord.[6] In the *contado*, clearly, the Malatesta were still assured of popular support, and Carlo Malatesta, who was of a different stamp from his feeble brother, could claim a large following there.[7] But in the city there were few who wanted the Malatesta back. While Urbino welcomed its duke, 'Rimino par non vio el signor Pandolfo Malatesta', and according to Sanudo there were only two effective parties in the city, one for the church and one for Venice – but 'pochi il suo signor'.[8] The balance of forces remained what it had been since Sigismondo's collapse, Venetian facing papal partisans, and each with one objective: a distant and benevolent government. In the contest the first round went to Venice.

During September and October Pandolfo made a series of attempts on the city, and not until 22 October could he finally report success to

---

[1] Who says that already in Nov. 1500 the people of Rimini and Pesaro were anxious to return to their former lords: *Diarii*, ii.69.

[2] Clementini, ii.583–90; Tonini, v/1.434ff., vi/1.2, vi/2.767–72; Alvisi, 142, 515.

[3] Tonini, vi/2.786–7; Sanudo, *Diarii*, iv.378 (who adds that Rimini too became restless and 'zercha il so signore': 384).

[4] Alvisi, 220; Ady, 123.

[5] Sanudo, *Diarii*, iv.409, 439, 455; *Mem. Santarcangelo*, 32; Alvisi, 238–9; B. Feliciangeli, *Lettere di Galeazzo Sforza* (Sanseverino, 1915), 15, 16, 25, 32.

[6] Sanudo, *Diarii*, v. 70, 72: 'In questi zorni, li villani si sublevono e par brusaseno li libri e altro, e voleno il signor Pandolfo per signor.' Cf. Ghirardacci, RIS² xxx/1.324.

[7] Report of the Venetian *provveditore* in Rimini, 21 Jan. 1504: 'li villani dil territorio amano forte il signor Carlo Malatesta': Sanudo, *Diarii*, v. 751.

[8] *Ibid*. 70, 79; Battaglini, *Zecca*, 288.

Venice.[1] In this letter he said he had been well received in Rimini, and that all his enemies had fled. But he ignored the advice of his wife Violante and confidential followers to adopt conciliatory measures and make peace with the exiles, and according to Baldi acted harshly against them.[2] It is probable that the exiled leaders would have refused negotiation: the very day that Pandolfo wrote glowingly to Venice, three of them put proposals before the *podestà* of Cervia for turning over Rimini to the Venetians.[3] The idea was not only theirs, but had been abroad in Romagna for several weeks; and although the Venetians were confident of Pandolfo's total dependence,[4] it met with their active encouragement. On 12 October Guidobaldo, duke of Urbino, was commissioned by the senate to persuade Pandolfo to surrender Rimini in return for land elsewhere. Pandolfo hesitated and sent for the opinion of his wife and Giovanni Bentivoglio. Even when he had entered Rimini, the Venetians did not yield but resolved at least to seize the *rocca* which, Guidobaldo claimed, would soon force Pandolfo to negotiate. As it happened Pandolfo got the *rocca* for himself, in spite of Venetian intrigue, but he decided nonetheless to leave for Venice at the end of October and submit to her protection.[5]

On 2 November he appeared before the senate and commended his family and state to Venetian guardianship. He was followed by representatives of the council of twelve who asked the republic to protect the Malatesta *signoria*, pointing out that Pandolfo 'era mutato di quello era'; but they received only an evasive reply. Venetian influence was advancing in Romagna. Montefiore had already submitted to S. Marco; Santarcangelo and Verucchio were on the point of surrender; and on 6 November it was learned that Savignano and Gatteo had also welcomed the Venetians. Pandolfo Malatesta had no course but capitulation. 'Vedendo il Stato suo tuto comquasato et lui ettiam malissimo voluto dali sui populli' (Priuli), Pandolfo accepted the exchange proposal, and on 16 November an official answer was published to his demands. Not everything he asked for was granted.

---

[1] The *rocca* did not surrender for another week. For details: Giustinian, 173–4, 334, 477; Sanudo, *Diarii*, v. 86, 91, 111, 118–19, 122, 124, 128, 139, 146, 154, 162, 173, 189, 193, 201, 203, 235–6; Priuli, 290, 300, 303, 311; Bembo, 135; *Diario di Urbino*, 445–9; Bernardi, ii.49, 51, 56–7; Castellani, *Dominazione veneta*, 13; Alvisi, 411–12, 415, 419, 427; Bonardi, 'Venezia e Cesare Borgia', 402, 406. Priuli adds that Pandolfo was not wanted back by Rimini 'per averli facto dele insolentie et violentie non conveniente; et cum veritate hera legiere di zervello' (290).

[2] Clementini, ii.597–8; Baldi, *Guidobaldo*, ii.125ff., 138.

[3] Sanudo, *Diarii*, v. 203.

[4] Giustinian, ii.224: 'lo potemo reputar nostro senza nostra spexa'.

[5] For details: Giustinian, ii.224; Sanudo, *Diarii*, v. 163, 165, 199, 200, 205, 206–8, 212–15, 226, 228; Bembo, 134; Baldi, *Guidobaldo*, ii.140–2. Giustinian, Bembo and Bonardi all speak of the proposal of exchange as coming originally from Pandolfo. Cf. Clementini, ii.597–8.

As lord of Rimini, commanding a revenue of 10,000 ducats, he sought equivalent compensation. However, the senate only allowed him an endowment one-third of the size and finally assigned him Cittadella, which he feared would provide an income of only 2,000 ducats. He was also given a small *condotta* and a sum of money in cash. His wife was assigned an annuity, his brother Carlo an annuity and *condotta*, and he and his descendants were created Venetian nobles. Carlo Malatesta, who had stayed in Rimini, was now instructed to surrender the city. With reluctance he complied, and on 24 November the *provveditore* Malipiero was received tumultuously in Rimini.[1]

Between 1503 and 1509 Rimini was governed by Venice and became one of the component oligarchies of the Venetian territorial state. In general the Venetian rector, like the papal governor later, took over the powers of the Malatesta, but wider privileges were allowed to the commune. The citizens could now elect to more offices. They were free to appoint the council of twelve and to 'reform' the general council, which was reduced to a select body of a hundred, but their power to issue statutes was subject to Venetian ratification. A greater freedom of trade was also granted, and some provision made for the repair and rehabilitation of the city. This régime was well suited to the nobility and gave them little cause for grievance. The lands possessed near Rimini by Pandolfo Malatesta were restored on petition to the jurisdiction of the commune, and the sentences against the Adimari and Belmonti were suspended.[2] Yet when Venice was compelled to surrender Rimini to the church in May 1509, the news was received by the population with great rejoicing: bonfires were lit, muskets and artillery fired off, and bells, tambourines and trumpets sounded. A triumphal arch was erected to Julius II, all monuments of the Venetian government were slighted, and the day of the papal reconquest was proclaimed an annual festival.[3]

The papal government confirmed and extended the liberties accorded by Venice. Under the jurisdiction of a resident governor, the citizens were now permitted to elect, subject to papal confirmation, all municipal officials, including the *podestà* and two consuls or *priores*. Henceforward they would be men of local birth, and even clerical benefices, it was promised, should be bestowed on natives or *idonei*. The commune was

---

[1] Giustinian, ii.310, 335; Sanudo, *Diarii*, v. 234, 236, 244–5, 272, 276, 279, 295, 308, 311–12, 319–20, 332–3, 357, 367, 375, 380–1, 383–4, 389, 402–4; cf. 469–70, 519, 540, 687, 708, 793–4; *Diario Ferrar.*, 353; Sanudo, 73; Priuli, ii.314, 322–3; Bembo, 135–6; *Diario di Urbino*, 450; Bernardi, ii.116; Sigismondo dei Conti, ii.335–6; Cappelli, 'Pandolfo', 454–6; Tonini, vi/2.801–4; Romanin, 11–12; below App. v, vi, vii.

[2] Sanudo, *Diarii*, v. 643–51; Tonini, vi/2.804–13; Clementini, ii.606.

[3] *Ibid.* 622; Tonini, vi/1.55, 58; vi/2.855–6.

given a preponderant share in revenue, and granted a salt monopoly throughout its territories. The power to issue statutes, if confirmed by the church, was also upheld, and it was provided that the council general only, apart from the governor, should license foreigners to acquire property in the city. All effective power of the commune was vested on petition in a small council conscripted *de genere Nobilium, Doctorum, Mercatorum, nec non Artificum ad regimen idoneorum*: a hundred chosen from the nobility, thirty from the commoners. This body was to elect the consuls and the council of twelve. Vacancies were to be filled by cooptation *de melioribus vel magis idoneis vel artificibus*, and no more than three at any time were to be of the same family (*parentela sive casata*). All these changes were introduced in answer to petitions from Rimini itself. Twelve months later (December 1510) the *contadini* submitted a similar petition; but wherever it conflicted with the privileges granted to Rimini it was overridden or modified.[1] The oligarchical nature of the new régime is too obvious for emphasis. It represented a consummation checked by the *signoria*; and the regulation restricting multiple membership in the council was designed to prevent any relapse into despotism. Other measures were directed to the same end. Pandolfo Malatesta's properties round Rimini were transferred to the commune,[2] and a promise exacted from the pope never to grant Rimini again, in fee or vicariate, to the Malatesta or anyone else.[3]

Every defence had seemingly been erected against further Malatesta restorations. One common result, however, of renewed civic freedom was a revival also of faction, if only through the persistence of a despotic *clientela*. In Rimini there were still Pandolfeschi, as previously in Fano and Cesena.[4] Partly to hide their sympathies they took the nostalgic name of 'Guelfs', obliging their opponents, the Ecclesiastici, by a final twist of terminology, to call themselves 'Ghibelline'. Periodically there was open conflict between the parties and by 1520 it was plain the city would never know peace or security until, either by force or disillusion, the Pandolfeschi had been eclipsed. The infatuated conduct of the Malatesta was to make it quite unnecessary to rely on force alone.

Carlo Malatesta, the only able and respected member of the family, had been killed fighting for the Venetians in 1508. Pandolfo, who lacked all steady purpose and had also quickly forfeited the friendship

---

[1] Clementini, ii.623; Tonini, vi/2.836–57, 877–82.
[2] Clementini, ii.636; Tonini, vi/1.82–3, vi/2.849.
[3] The promise was first made in reply to the petition of 1509 and then repeated in 1511 to Galeotto de' Gualdi, one of the notables alienated by Pandolfo: Battaglini, *Zecca*, 284–5; Tonini, vi/2.840.
[4] Above p. 240.

of Venice, was kept alert by his wife Violante and his son Sigismondo, a man as brutal as himself, and with their encouragement he maintained close contact with the Malatesta faction in Rimini. An approach to the pope in 1513 was predictably without result. They had better success, by direct action, nine years later, following the death of Leo X (December 1521) and the absence from Italy of Adrian VI. In May 1522, after two failed attempts, Sigismondo was admitted in disguise into Rimini by a wealthy client of the Malatesta, the Bolognese Bonazzolo Bonazzuoli, who took him to his house. From there the Pandolfeschi easily seized control of the city, and word was sent into the *contado* that it had been done with papal sanction. At this, says Clementini, the 'vulgar people, ever desirous of change', and dissatisfied with papal administration, proclaimed support for the revolution, and the rival faction escaped only with difficulty. When Pandolfo Malatesta joined his son, he received a cordial welcome from the city.

The second brief restoration of the Malatesta opened with festivities; but the initial peace was soon disturbed when a number of *contadini* invaded Rimini and burned the municipal records. At the same time levies were exacted from clergy and laity, the former Malatesta estates reclaimed, enemies expropriated, friends enriched, and everything sacrificed to a policy of petty partisan violence. An appeal to Rome by Pandolfo for reinvestiture with his *tenue stato* was brushed aside by the cardinals. Rimini was threatened with interdict, a papal army was assembled, with reinforcements from the Riminese exiles, and by January 1523 Pandolfo had been forced to surrender to the arbitration and sentence of the pope. The sentence was adverse. He was told his family had lost all claim to Rimini when they sold the city to Venice. He was convicted of treason, and only escaped with his life through the intercession of certain cardinals and the duke of Urbino. While heavy penalties were imposed on the Malatesta faction, Pandolfo was reduced to selling his meagre properties round Rimini, merely in order to live.

On one further and final occasion the Malatesta reimposed their rule. They still had followers in Rimini, enough at least to enable Sigismondo, now charged with the family affairs, to harass the papal authorities, pending a chance to return. It came in the turbulent summer of 1527 when, fighting with the Banda Nera, he and a group of mercenaries contrived to force an entry into the city and raise the cry 'Malatesta'. Once again Pandolfo was sent for, but this time every class was turned against him, 'si cittadinj, artifficj, plebei e contadinj, commo altrj'; in a last feeble spasm of tyranny he spent his time in the Rocca Malatestiana, ingeniously torturing his enemies. Many fled the city. Many were imprisoned or put to death. And there were few Malatesta supporters left when Clement VII despatched Lautrec to reconquer Rimini in January 1528. The papal terms were generous, granting even the possibility of a renewed vicariate; but the citizens in desperation besought the pope to set them free, and in June 1528 a papal army once more expelled the Malatesta from Rimini, this time for ever.[1]

Blame for the final calamity can only rest with the Malatesta themselves. Had Carlo Malatesta ruled or even survived with his brother, they might have re-established power and re-formed a working alliance with the urban *ottimati*. The attitude of the *ottimati* can perhaps be inferred from the history of Rimini and the Malatesta written, nearly a century later, by a member of the class, Cesare Clementini. Clementini spares no praise of the Malatesta who were capable and worthy: their names were part of his civic heritage. But for the last of the family he has few good words. He presents no general indictment of the Malatesta as despots or dynasty; and that he was not alone in this is shown by the long survival in Rimini of Malatesta stock and kin.[2] Primarily it was the misrule of Pandolfo and his sons which cost the Malatesta their principality, by antagonising every class and group of society. When in 1532 Roberto di Pandolfo invaded again it was now the *contadini* who took him prisoner. For another ten years and longer the Malatesta continued to plan and intrigue, causing disquiet in the city, but those few of their supporters who remained there offered no hope of return.[3]

[1] Clementini, ii.619, 627, 654, 658–62, 672–8, 682–96, 701–13, 744; Battaglini, *Zecca*, 292–301; Tonini, vi/1.45, 50–2, 112–13, 132, 134, 138–40, 159–78, 197, 201–17; vi/2, LV–VIII, LXXI, LXXV, LXXIX; Ugolini, ii.224; Cappelli, 'Pandolfo', 438ff.; *Arch. Gonzaga*, ii.181.

[2] Clementini, ii.635, 641, 665; Battaglini, *Zecca*, 306ff.; Tonini, iv/1.338–43, v/1.486–508. Others (Sogliano etc.) survived, together with Alidosi and Manfredi, in the irreducibly feudal Apennines; the *signori* returned to the hinterland from which they had sprung: Dal Pane, 32ff.; Zoli and Bernicoli, 13ff., 22ff.

[3] Clementini, ii.714ff.; Battaglini, *Zecca*, 301ff.; Tonini, vi/1.233, 242–5, 253–4, 259.

Appendix

I

(*Statuto di Rimini*, Biblioteca del Senato, fo. 215v. Cf. Battaglini, *Zecca*, 185–6)

Statutum et ordinatum est quod magnifici millites domini Malatesta et Gallaotus nati quondam generosi millitis domini Pandulfi de mallatestis et eorum descendentes non sint ligati nec ligari possint ad observationem aliquorum statutorum ordinamentorum provissionum et refformationum dicti comunis nec ad ipsa observanda teneantur aliquo modo. Et ei possint uti contra quemlibet ad sui comodum pro libito voluntatis. Set non alii contra ipsos. Et hoc auctoritate et vigore praessentis statuti non obstantibus alliquibus statutis provissionibus et ordinamentis dicti comunis factis et factiendis in contrarium. Quibus quantum ad predictos dominos et suos descendentes sit omnimodo derogatum. Et hoc statutum habeat locum in pressentibus preteritis et futuris.

II

(*Statuto di Rimini*, fos. 198r-v)

Statutum et ordinatum est de cetero et perpetuo ad offitium generalis potestarie et rectorie dicti civitatis comitati et districtus Arimini eligatur et eligi debeat in potestatem et rectorem praedictum per consilium et comune Civitatis praedicti solummodo alter ex magnificis et generosis militibus et dominis dominis Mallateste et Galaotti nati olim bone memorie magnifici et gienerosi militis domini Pandolfi de Malatestis de Arimino et non alius civis vel comitatinus districcualis vel forensis dicte Civitatis Cuius ellecti offitium duret et durare debent [*sic*] de anno in annum per unum annum ex vice ellectionis semel facte de ipso. Et ellectio ad offitium supradictum de altero ex predictis dominis celebretur et celebrari debeat singulis annis ante finitum tempus ellectionis proxime precedentis per duos menses vel circha in dicto concilio supradicto que ellectio possit efficaciter celebrari de pressedente in offitio supradicto. . . Ita quod pressedens et exercens offitium supradictum iure vel statuto aliquo non obstante possit dictum offitium acceptare continuare et exercere de anno in annum subcessive iuxta ellectionem de ipso factam in dicto conscilio et secundum beneplacitum ipsius ellecti dicto tempore in dicto offitio pressendentis non obstante quod tunc temporis vel quandocunque tali similli maiori vel minori offitio fungeretur vel functus sit per se et suos submissos ac vicarios exercere potestariam et regimen supra-dictam dum modo saltim semel in edomeda in palatio comunis Arimini ad banchas ubi iura reduntur debeat . . . personaliter assedere ad audiendum querelas viduarum pauperum et etiam opresorum per potentiam vel calumpnias quorum qunque ut sit dictas calumpnias et cavilaciones possit tollere et dictos opresos viduas et pauperes possit in suis iuribus et iusticia confovere Teneatur etiam et debeat suis sumptibus et expensis dictus electus pro exercitio dicti offitii habere continue tres iudices in utroque iure.

III

(Statuto di Rimini, fos. 215v–218r. Cf., with variations, Battalgini, *Zecca*, 183–5)

De potestate et arbitrio concessis dominis Mallateste et Gallaoto de mallatestis in ipsorum consilio sapientum.

Statutum et ordinatum est pro conservatione pressentis status civitatis plani comictatus et districtus arimini nec non etiam amicorum omnium status predicti quod magniffici milites domini Mallatesta et Gallaotus et unus ex ipsis altero se abssentante possint sibi assumere aliquos de dicta civitate in quocunque numero in sapientes et consiliarios pro libito voluntatis et conscilium credentie parvum vel magnum ex dictis amicis facere ad eorum et cuiuslibet ipsorum domos coaddunare et facere coaddunari ad omnem eorum voluntatem. Et quicquid deliberatum firmatum vel dispositum in aliquo de consciliis supradictis fuerit in pressentia et consensu dictorum dominorum vel alterius eorum etiam si illud deliberatum firmatum vel dispositum sit contra formam vel preter formam alicuius iuris comunis vel statutorum refformationum et ordinamentorum comunis predicti sit firmum et perpetuo robur obtineat et efficatiam habere debeat sive delliberatum fuerit vel firmatum vel dispositum de gravaminibus et sumptibus novis vel usitatis imponendis sive de expedendo de avere dicti comunis in quacunque quantitate parva vel magna sive de quacunque causa vel re que respiciat comodum vel incomodum comunis et singularum personarum ipsius. Et in tantum valeat et debeat omnino valere et provari tale deliberatum vel firmatum vel factum in alio de consciliis supradictis quod non egeat nec ei necesse sit ad efficatiam ipsius poni firmari vel deliberari in aliquo alio conscilio parvo vel magno sapientium dicte civitatis vel in conscilio generali dicte civitatis. Nec etiam sit necessaria pressentia vel consensus dominorum quattuorum offitialium comunis arimini vel alterius cuiuscunque offitialis dicti comunis vel alterius cuiuscunque persone. Quorum dominorum quattuor et cuiuslibet alterius offitialis dicti comunis offitium quantum ad id quod delliberatum firmatum et dispositum fuerit in alio ex consciliis supradictis suspensum sit et esse intelligatur perinde ac si predictorum offitium non fuisset inductum per formam alicuius statuti dicte civitatis nec reperiretur in rerum natura. Ut sic predicti domini vel alter eorum altero abssente cum dictis sapientibus ex amicis predictis quos secum in quocunque numero votare voluerint omnia possint delliberare firmare et refformare statuta et provisiones facere et omnia alia que posset

Comune Ariminj cum omnibus et singulis hominibus dicte Civitatis comitatus et districtus arimini. Et que posset facere generale conscilium Civitatis predicte. Ut sic etiam predicti domini et alter eorum ex plenitudine potestatis et arbitrii sibi concessi et adtributi vigore presentis statuti possint statuta dicti Comunis cassare mutare et suspendere pro libito voluntatis eorum et cuiuslibet eorum cuiuscunque condictionis existant statuta predicta. Possint etiam in hiis que deliberata firmata vel disposita fuerint per eos cum aliquibus sapientibus dicte Civitatis vel sine defectu admisse solempnitatis que requireretur ex forma alicuius juris comunis vel municipalis comunis predicti supplere et adimplere ex plenitudine potestatis et arbitrii predicte [*sic*]. Ut perinde predicta omnia valeant et teneant ac si in eis essent servate omnes solepnitates iuris Comunis vel municipalis comunis predicti. Et hoc si de contingentibus nichil fuisset obmissum in eis. Hoc addito quod quedam per dictos dominos vel alterum eorum cum dictis sapientibus contingi posset deliberari tractari firmari vel disponj resspitientia vel non respitientia conservationem paciffici status pressentis. Que secreta perpetuo vel ad tempus teneri expediens forte esset. Et propterea non bene factum esse testium vel alicuius notarij pressentiam adhibere per quos possint perpetua probari vel sciri preditta sic facta fuisse ut supra et infra in pressenti statuto comprehenditur. Statutum et ordinatum est quod de predictis non requiratur alliqua scriptura vel probatio plena vel semiplena. Set ad plenissimam probationem eorum [que] dicerentur sic deliberata vel disposita vel firmata in alio de consciliis supradictis in pressentia dictorum dominorum vel alterius eorum suffitiat solum quod ad dictorum dominorum vel alterius eorum mandatum vel consensum executionj mandata fuerint. Et quod omne id quod mandatum fuerit per dictos dominos vel alterum eorum super quibuscunque rebus vel factis dicti comunis eius comodum vel incomodum respitientibus pressumatur firmatum deliberatum et dispositum in omnibus consciliis supradictis et cum omni solepnitate que eidem esset necessaria vel oportuna ad efficatiam. Et ad esse suum perfectum. Contra quam pressuntionem non possit neque debeat admicti aliqua probatio in contrarium. Ut sic in predictis et in quolibet predictorum vel habentibus similitudinem vel conexitatem cum predictis ad prestandum perpetuam efficatiam eisdem suffitiat solum probare vel per assertionem simplicem dictorum dominorum vel alterius eorum vel per testes vel per acta vel per instrumenta predicta vel aliqua predictorum facta fuisse de mandato vel consensu dominorum predictorum vel alicuius eorum sine alia delliberatione vel refformatione vel alia quacunque solepnitate. Et predicta omnia et singula perpetuo valeant et serventur auctoritate pressentis statuti. Quod tam per presens statutum et per aliquam eius partem non intelligatur derogatum vel abstractum aliquod de dominio libero et perpetuo dicto magniffici milliti domino Mallateste predicto et de potestate et offitio sibi concesso in dictione dominij supraditti per refformationem conscilij generalis dicte Civitatis. Quod presens statutum in qualibet suj parte reguletur et coartetur secundum refformationem predictam in quantum ei in alliquo derogaret et contradiceret et habeat et vendicet sibi locum presens statutum in pressentibus pendentibus et futuris et in omnibus preteritis negotiis et factis et dispositis de consensu vel mandato dittorum dominorum ab eo tempore citra quo regimen Civitatis predicte fuit sub sola cura et regimine ipsorum non obstantibus aliquibus statutis refformationibus ordinamentis et provissionibus dicti comunis alliqualiter adversantibus pressenti statuto in aliqua sui parte vel quomodo libet directe vel indirecte impedientibus effectum pressentis statuti in aliqua sui parte. Quibus iuribus statutis ordinamentis refformationibus et provissionibus omni modo sit et esse intelligatur derogatum auctoritate et vigore pressentis statuti.

IV

(Statuto di Rimini, fos. 224v-225r. Cf., with variations, Battaglini, *Zecca*, 186; Tonini, iv/2.134-5)

De confirmatione concessionis bailie et arbitrii atributi domino Mallateste et de aprobatione gratiarum factarum per ipsum vel dominum G[allaotum] eius fratrem.

Statutum et ordinatum est quod reformatio conscilii generalis Civitatis predicte per quam concessum et datum fuit per homines dicte Civitatis dominium et deffensorium Civitatis et districtus ariminj ad vitam magniffico militi domino Mallateste nato quondam magniffici millitis dominj pandulfi de mallatestis. et scripta manu talis notarij in quacunque forma sit. et quicquid potestatis tribuat domino supradicto et secundum quod scripta est perpetuo firma permaneat absque spe revocationis adnullationis [vel] reffutationis alicuius ex quacunque causa vera vel falsa. Et quicquid factum gestum vel dispositum est usque nunc vel in futurum fiet per supradictum dominum pretestu sui offitij et dominij, sive contineat comodum vel incomodum dicti Comunis sive de avere rebus vel pecuniis dicti Comunis sive de processibus vel condenationibus cancellatis vel suspensis de mandato ipsius sive de banitis dicti Comunis quacunque de causa exemptis vel extractis de banno et condempnationibus de mandato dicti domini sive de aliis quibuscunque rebus vel negotiis dicti Comunis sit ratum et firmum irrevocabiliter et perpetuo debeat ratum et gratum haberi per Comune predictum. Et quod quicquid super predictis factum gestum vel dispositum fuerit per dominum supradictum intelligatur semper factum pretestu sui offitij et dominij. Etiam si hoc non exprimatur et de hoc non admictatur probatio in contrarium. Hoc addito quod gratie facte per magnifficum millitem dominum Gallaotum fratrem supradicii dominj super quibuscunque processibus pendentibus vel finitis super malleffitiis cancellandis vel abollendis et super condempnationibus corumcunque expectantibus ad exationem dicti Comunis. Et super eximendis nannitis de banno et condempnationibus dicti Comunis et de aliis quibuscunque rebus vel predittis similibus perpetuo sint firme et rate et per Comune ariminj vel alium non possint infringi adnullarj vel etiam casarj quocunque colore quesito. Et predicta perpetuo valeant et serventur in preteritis pendentibus pressentibus et fucturis. non obstantibus quibuscunque statutis refformationibus ordinamentis et provissionibus dicti Comunis factiendis in contrarium. Quibus quantum ad predicta contenta in hoc statuto sit omni modo derogatum detruncatum dum tamen refformationi predicte in qua et per quam traslatum at concessum fuit dominium et offitium supradictum dicto domino Mallateste per presens statutum nichil derogetur vel detrunchetur set semper in suo esse perfecto et sua stabillitate duret et permaneat.

V

(Tonini, iv/2.137–8)

In Χρι nomine, amen. Hec sunt reformationes facte in Consiliis generalibus Civitatis tempore pot' nobilis militis Dni egani de Lambertinis de Bononia, et pro parte tempore Pot.' nobilis viri Galaotti de Lambertinis de Bononia Pot.' Civitatis et Districtus Arim. et scripte per me Blasium notarium filium quondam Muzoli ser Blaxii de Arimino, et pro parte per Johannem q. Lendani notarium et nunc Notarium dictorum Dnorum Pot. sub annis Dni Millo. CCC. XXXV. Ind. tertia, Arim. tempore Dni Benedicti PP. XII, diebus et mensibus infrascriptis.

Die . . . Aprilis

Coadunato Consilio generali Civitatis Arimini . . . banitoris in Palatio d. Comunis more solito congregato de mandato . . . egani de Lambertinis de Bononia Honorabilis Potestatis Civitatis et Districtus Arim . . . pres. consensu et voluntate Dnorum . . . Leonis Hominis S. Andree et Rainerii . . . Johis Guilli Jud. eorum nomine . . . Dni Bartoli de Lazaris et Bartoli de Faitano eorum sociorum quatuor officialium d. Civitatis proposuit Sapiens vir Dnus Johes de Li . . . vicarius d. dni Potestatis, quid placet dicto Consilio providere, deliberare . . . infrascripta posta [sic], tenor cujus talis est.

Cum hoc sit, quod pred. Dnus Eganus Potestas Civitatis praefate finiat regimen . . . pot. in Kall' Madii proxime venturis, et expedit de futuro Potestate providendo pro utilitate d. Comunis quid placet d. Consilio generali providere et reformare super electione novi Pot. fienda, proponit d. dnus. Vicarius et pred. Dnus eganus Pot. cum . . . sotii et familia possit offitium Potestarie exercere usque ad eventum [sic] novi Potestatis tam in Civilibus quam in Criminalibus super qua petitione petit sibi salubre consilium exiberi.

In quo quidem consilio surrexit Tuttolus Marabottini unus ex consiliariis dicti consilii et arengando dixit et consiluit, quod electio dicti . . . Pot. debeat . . . in Magnificum et Potentem Militem Dnum Mallatestam defensorem dicte Civitatis cum illis Sapientibus, quos secum habere voluerit et quicquid per ipsos factum fuerit in pred. valeat et plenum robur obtineat ut . . . pred. pres . . . factum fo . . . et quod d. dnus eganus Potestas cum ejus Iudicibus, sotiis, et familia possit officium Pot. exercere usque ad eventum novi Potestatis tam in Civilibus quam in criminalibus, et in omnibus quae spectant ad officium Dni Potestatis et ejus Curie, non obstantibus aliquibus Statutis, reformationibus, vel provisionibus in contrarium loquentibus.

In reformatione cujus consilii facto partito per d. Dnum Vicarium de sedendo placuit omnibus de d. Consilio dictum consilium d. Tuttoli consul . . . nemine in contrarium surgente et sic extitit reformatum.

Presentibus testibus Dno Rainerio et Gianghino fratribus Iud. filiis q. Ugolini Guillelmi, Johe L . . . Notario, Accorsino Bla . . . Notario, et G. . . a . . dino Girardini publico Banitore d. Comunis et aliis.

VI

Statutory powers of the Polenta and then Malatesta in Cervia (*Statuta Civitatis Cerviae*, ed. Ravenna, 1588)

According to the statutes of Cervia drawn up in 1328 the assent of Ostasio di Bernardino da Polenta, 'defensor' of Cervia, was necessary in the election of the *podestà* (p. 2). Most other officials (i.e. the lesser ones) seem to have been freely elected; but the *massarius* was allowed to make no payments without the licence of Ostasio (p. 8), while the chancellor was appointed by Ostasio, his duties being to keep all documents, fiscal, judicial etc., to inspect the accounts of the *massarius* on behalf of the 'defensor', register the names of all officials, and 'cancellare condemnationes' (pp. 9–10). The 'defensor' could also have a 'vicar' if he so desired (*ibid.*).

As to the *consiglio generale* of 200 it is stated: 'correctio dicti consilii spectet ad dominum defensorem, cum consilio quatuor bonorum virorum elegendorum per dictum dominum defensorem' (p. 15). Nothing was to be proposed in the council except in the presence of the *podestà* or his vicar, and of the 'defensor' or his vicar (p. 16).

The making of statutes was surrendered wholly into the hands of the 'defensor': 'Statuimus et ordinamus quod dominus defensor communis Cervie vel eius vicarius, singulis annis, de mense Ianuarii, proponere teneatur in consilio generali utrum expediat communi Cerviae statuta facere et deliberatum fuerit quod fiant statuta, tunc ipse dominus defensor eligere debeat quatuor bonos viros et illi potestatem habeant statuta condendi, et omnia statuta confecta per eos et approbata per dictum dominum defensorem et debeant in generali consilio publicari et facta publicatione pro statutis perpetuo habeantur' (pp. 16–17).

Ostasio was also placed in complete control of all gates and fortifications, with full power to proceed against traitors (p. 23).

Chapter 40 of the statutes seems to define these privileges still further. It provides that Ostasio shall have full charge of the collection of revenues. He alone of the communal officers may interfere with communal property. Any expenses incurred by him shall be as valid as if they had been confirmed by the council according to the statutes. The *podestà* and other officials are to be held by oath to defend Ostasio and his descendants. No assemblies of the council are to meet without the assent of Ostasio. Only he, his family and his adherents may carry arms. Only he may build where he pleases. As 'defensor' finally he is to receive from the commune a fixed stipend (pp. 23–5).

This chapter (no. 40) is *headed*: 'De immunitate et arbitrio concessis D. Malatesta Novello, suis filiis et descendentibus . . .' It probably indicates the powers renewed to the Malatesta when they recovered Cervia in the time of Sigismondo, and may therefore be taken as a summary of their privileges there when first they took the city from the Polenta.

However, later in the published Statuto (p. 118) there is a chapter entitled: 'De auctoritate et potestate tradita domino Galeotto de Malatestis', which runs:

'Statuimus et ordinamus quod magnificus . . . dominus Galeottus natus domini . . . habeat plenam et liberam potestatem faciendi, precipiendi concedendi, ordinandi, et totum quod sibi placuerit, et voluerit in his quae tangunt seu tangent commune Cervie . . . et omnes officiales communis Cervie eligendi et mutandi, in eis salaria constituendi ad suam liberam voluntatem, et omnia et singula statuta corrigendi, interpretandi, emendendi, et de novo faciendi, et quicquid fecerit concesserit, atque eligerit, correxerit, preceperit, interpretatus fuerit, emendaverit et de novo fecerit, habeatur pro lege, et executioni mandetur in omnibus et per omnia ac si per consilium generale communis Cervie factum esset, non obstantibus statutis, vel reformationibus seu ordinamentis in contrarium loquentibus, tam factis quam faciendis, de quibus oporteat, vel non oporteat expressam fieri mentionem, quae quantum ad hoc pro expressis et specificatus plene habeantur et hoc intelligatur in praeteritis postquam et futuris.'

VII

11 August 1407: Pandolfo III Malatesta nominates the *podestà* in Fano
(ACF, *Codici malatestiani* 4, fo. 5v)

'. . . tenore presentium te elegimus ac deputamus nostrum potestatem Civitatis fanensis commictens tibi totales vires nostras in omnibus et singulis causis tam civilibus quam criminalibus occurentibus in dicta civitate comitatu atque districtu pro tempore et termino sex mensium . . . mandamus quod omnibus et singulis hominibus incolis et habitatoribus dicte Civitatis et comitatus quatenus tibi tuisque offitialibus pareant pariter et intendant in omnibus et singulis ad tuum offitium spectantibus et pertinentibus et in omnibus volumus et mandamus te posse agere, facere et expedire nomine nostro ac si personaliter essemus exceptis gratiis et remissionibus quas nobis omnimoda resservamus. Item quod possis sententias et condempnationes atque bampna in civilibus et criminalibus dare atque perferre cum consilio tui vicarij ac assensoris tam in civilibus quam in criminalibus quibuscunque:

Condennationes autem sententias banna et penas quascunque vite tuleris tu et offitiales tui contra inhobedientes et delinquentes ratas et rata atque firmas habebimus et faciemus auctore deo inviolabiliter obsservari et similiter quecunque tua gesta ad tuum offitium spectantia durante tempore supradicto: debes autem in tuo offitio tenere continuo unum Iudicem seu collateralem licentiatum et doctoratum in Jure vel saltem licentiatum valentem . . .'; also a 'sotius miles', two notaries, two 'domicelli', eight 'famuli' or 'bernarii acti ad arma', one 'paggius', and three horses. He is to receive £189 each month from 'depositario nostro civitatis fani' for himself and his subordinates, with certain fruits of office. All fines and revenues of justice he is to assign to the depositario.

'Item teneris obsservare et obsservari facere decreta nostra et Reformationes factas et fiendas per Consilium nostrum Civitatis fanj et nostro mandato et maxime decreta et ordines officij nostri refferendarij fani.'

Finally he and his officials are to be syndicated.

Bibliography

I. SOURCES

A. DOCUMENTARY

Acta Aragonensia, ed. H. Finke, Berlin, 1908–23.

Acta Concilii Constanciensis, ed. H. Finke, Münster, 1896–1928.

Amati, G., 'Notizie di MSS dell'archivo secreto vaticano', *ASI* 1866.

Anselmi, A., *Documenti sulla guerra dei Malatesta contro Roccacontrada, 1413–5*, 1896.

L'Archivio Gonzaga di Mantova, ed. P. Torelli, A. Luzio, Mantua, 1920–2.

Atti cancellereschi viscontei, ed. C. Vittani, Milan, 1929.

Bagli, G., *Bandi malatestiani*, Modena, 1885 (also *AMR* 1885).

Baluze, E., *Miscellanea novo ordine digesta* (G. D. Mansi), Lucca, 1761.

Bartoccetti, V., 'Liber offitiorum civitatum terrarum atque locorum Magnifici et Excelsi domini nostri Pandulfi de Malatestis in Marchia (Codici Malatestiani 7). Scriptus in millioccccdecimo de mense Novembris Tertie Indictionis', *SP* 1925.

'Traduzione integrale del Codice 12 dell'Archivio Malatestiano di Fano', *SP* 1926.

Bernardy, Amy A., 'Dall'archivio governativo della repubblica di S. Marino', *AMM* 1912.

Bonaini, F., *Acta Henrici VII*, Florence, 1877.

Bullarium Franciscanum, ed. K. Eubel, Rome, 1898 etc.

Canestrini, G., 'Di alcuni documenti risguardanti le relazioni politiche dei Papi d'Avignone coi Comuni d'Italia', *ASI* App. vii, 1849.

Capitoli del comune di Firenze, ed. C. Guasti, A. Gherardi, Florence, 1866, 1893.

Carteggio di Paolo Guinigi, ed. L. Fumi, E. Lazzareschi, Lucca, 1925.

Castellucci, A., 'Regesto di documenti vaticani della storia medievale e moderna delle Marche', *SP* 1931.

Cecconi, G., 'Sommario cronologico delle pergamene osimane', in Ciavarini, *Collezione, cit.*, iv, 1879.

Ciavarini, C., *Collezione di documenti delle città e terre marchigiane*, Ancona, 1870–84.

Cipolla, C., *Documenti per la storia delle relazioni diplomatiche fra Verona e Mantova nel secolo xiv.*, Venice, 1907.

Cocquelines, C., *Bullarum romanorum pontificum amplissima collectio*, Rome, 1741.

Codice Aragonese, Le, ed. A. A. Messer, Paris, 1912.

Codice diplomatico della terra di S. Vittoria, in Colucci, *Antichità, cit.*, xxix.

'Codici malatestiani', *Le Marche* 1901–2.

Cola di Rienzo, *Briefwechsel*, ed. K. Burdach, P. Piur, Berlin, 1912–28.

Commissioni di Rinaldo degli Albizzi per il comune di Firenze, ed. C. Guasti, Florence, 1867–73.

Concilium Basiliense, ed. J. Haller, Basel, 1896 etc.

Costituzioni Egidiane dell'anno MCCCLVII, ed. P. Sella, Rome, 1912.

Dal Pane, L., *La Romagna dei secc. xvi e xvii in alcune descrizioni del tempo*, Bagnacavallo, 1932.

Degli Azzi Vitelleschi, G., *Le relazioni tra la repubblica di Firenze e l'Umbria nel secolo xiv*, *BU* App. vol. x, Perugia, 1904.

Dépêches des ambassadeurs milanais en France sous Louis XI et François Sforza, ed. B. de Mandrot, Paris, 1916–23.

Déprez, M. E., *Recueil de documents pontificaux conservés dans les diverses archives d'Italie, QF* 1900.

Deutsche Reichstagsakten, ed. L. Weizsäcker, Munich, 1867 etc.

Documenti dell'archivio Caetani, ed. G. Caetani, Perugia, 1922–30.

'Documenti sulle relazioni tra Galeazzo Maria Sforza e Federigo d'Urbino per l'assedio di Rimini', *AMM* 1905.

Doenniges, G., *Acta Henrici VII*, Berlin, 1839.

Dumont, J., *Corps universel diplomatique du droit des gens*, Amsterdam, 1726–31.

Epistolae saeculi xiii e regestis pontificum romanorum selectae, ed. G. H. Pertz, *MGH* 1883–94.

Fantuzzi, M., *Monumenti ravennati*, Venice, 1801–4.

Ficker, J., *Urkunden zur Geschichte des Römerzugs Kaiser Ludwig des Baiern*, Innsbruck, 1865.

Finke, H. *Forschungen und Quellen zur Geschichte des Konstanzer Konzils*, Paderborn, 1889.

Frati, L., 'Raccolta di lettere politiche del secolo xiv', *ASI* 1893.

Fumi, L., 'Inventario e spoglio dei registri della tesoreria apostolica della Marca', *Le Marche*, 1904.

Gaye, J., *Carteggio inedito d'artisti dei secoli xiv, xv, xvi*, Florence, 1839–40.

Giampietro, D., 'Un registro aragonese nella Biblioteca Nazionale di Parigi', *ASN* 1884.

Giustinian, A., *Dispacci*, 1502–5, ed. P. Villari, Florence, 1876.

Göller, E., *Die Einnahmen der apostolischen Kammer unter Johann XXII*, Bonn, 1910. *Die Einnahmen der apostolischen Kammer unter Benedikt XII*, Paderborn, 1920.

Gorrini, G., 'Lettere inedite degli ambassadori fiorentini in Avignone', *ASI* 1884–5.

Grigioni, C., 'Documenti inediti intorno a Sigismondo Malatesta', *La Romagna*, 1910.

Grimaldi, G., 'Due bandi di messer Cortesia de' Lambertini vicario di Fano nel 1367', *Le Marche*, 1900.

Hardt, H. von der, *Magnum oecumenicum Constanciense concilium*, Frankfurt etc., 1696–1742.

Kern, F., *Acta imperii, Angliae et Franciae, 1267–1313*, Tübingen, 1911.

Lattes, E., *Repertorio diplomatico visconteo*, Milan, 1911–18.

Lettere di Lorenzo il Magnifico, ed. A. Cappelli, *Atti e Mem. Dep. Stor. Pat. prov. Parm. Mod.*, 1863.

Lettres communes, Jean XXII, ed. G. Mollat, Paris, 1904 etc.

Lettres closes etc., Benoît XII, ed. G. Daumet, Paris, 1899–1920 (cited as *Lettres Ben. XII*).

Lettres communes, Benoît XII, ed. J. M. Vidal, Paris, 1902–11.

Lettres secrètes etc., Urbain V, ed. P. Lecacheux, Paris, 1902 etc.

Lettres secrètes etc., Gregoire XI, ed. L. Mirot, H. Jassemin, Paris, 1935 etc.

Liber Censuum de l'Eglise Romaine, Le, ed. P. Fabre, L. Duchesne, Paris, 1889 etc.

Loevinson, E., 'Sunti delle pergamene marchigiane conservate nell'archivio di stato di Roma', *AMM* 1915.

Louis XI, *Lettres*, ed. J. Vaesen, Paris, 1883 etc.

Lucca, R. *Archivio di Stato, Regesti*, ed. L. Fumi, G. degli Azzi Vittelleschi, Lucca, 1903–13.

Lünig. J. C., *Codex Italiae diplomaticus*, Frankfurt, Leipzig, 1725–35.

Magnum Bullarium Romanum, Turin, 1857–72.

Mansi, G. D., *Sacrorum conciliorum collectio*, Florence etc., 1759 etc.

Maraschini, L., *Lettere malatestiane dirette ai rappresentanti dei Malatesta nella Marca*, Osimo, 1902.

Mariotti, R., *Bandi malatestiani nel comune di Fano, 1367–1463*, Fano, 1892.
Bandi di tregua fra i Malatesta, gli Sforza, e Federigo da Montefeltro.
Martène, E., Durand, U., *Thesaurus novus anecdotorum*, Paris, 1717.
Veterum scriptorum amplissima collectio, Paris, 1724.
Mazzatinti, G., *Inventari dei MSS italiani delle bibliotecha di Francia*, Florence, 1886–8.
Inventari dei MSS delle biblioteche d'Italia, Turin etc., 1887 etc. (cited as Inventari).
Gli archivi della storia d'Italia, Rocca S. Casciano, Ser. 1, 1897–1907, Ser. 2, 1910–15.
Mittarelli, G. B., *Biblioteca codicum S. Michaelis prope Murianum*, Murano, 1779.
Mohler, L., *Die Einnahmen der apostolischen Kammer unter Klemens VI*, Paderborn, 1931.
Morbio, C., *Codice visconteo-sforzesco*, Milan, 1846.
Mucciolo, G. M., *Catalogus codicum malatestianae caesenatis bibliothecae*, Casena, 1780.
Osio, L., *Documenti diplomatici tratti dagli archivi milanesi*, Milan, 1864–72.
Pastor, L., *Acta inedita hist. pontif. roman. sec. xv, xvi, xvii illustrantia*, i, Freiburg i.B.), 1904.
Pastorello, E., *Il copialettere marciano della cancelleria carrarese, 1402–3*, Venice, 1915.
Piccolomini, Aeneas Sylvius, *Epistolae*, Milan, 1473.
Epistole in cardinalatu edite, Rome, 1475.
Piccolomini, Iacopo, *Epistolae*, in *Pii II Commentaria*, Frankfurt, 1614.
Pius II: see Piccolomini, Aeneas Sylvius, above.
Predelli, R., *I libri commemoriali della repubblica de Venezia*, Venice, 1876 etc.
Preger, W., *Die Politik des Papstes Johann XXII, Abhand. Hist. Kl., Bayer. Akad.*, Munich, 1886.
Raynaldus, O., *Annales ecclesiastici*, Lucca, 1747–56.
Regesta Honorii Papae III, ed. P. Pressutti, Rome, 1888, 1895.
Regesta pontificum romanorum, ed. A. Potthast, Berlin 1873–5.
'Regesto di documenti relativi a Città di Castello', *BU* 1900.
Regesto di S. Appollinaire Nuovo, ed. V. Federici, Rome, 1907.
'Regesto e documenti di storia perugina', *ASI* xvi 2, 1851.
Regestum Clementis papae V, Rome, 1885–92.
Registres d'Innocent IV, ed. E. Berger, Paris, 1884 etc.
Registres de Nicolas III, ed. M. J. Gay, S. Vitte, Paris, 1898–1938.
Registres de Martin IV, various editors, Paris, 1901 etc.
Registres d'Honorius IV, ed. M. Prou, Paris, 1888.
Registres de Nicolas IV, ed. M. E. Langlois, Paris, 1886–1905.
Registres de Boniface VIII, ed. C. Digard etc., Paris, 1884 etc.
Registri dell'ufficio degli statuti in Milano, ed. N. Ferorelli, Milan, 1920.
Registri viscontei, ed. C. Manaresi, Milan, 1915.
Riezler, S., *Vatikanische Akten zur deutsche Geschichte in der Zeit Kaiser Ludwigs des Baiers*, Munich, 1891.
Romano, G., 'Registri degli atti notarili di C. Cristiani', *ASL* 1894.
Santoro, C., *Registri dell'ufficio di provvisione e dell'ufficio dei sindaci sotto la dominazione viscontea*, Milan, 1929, 1932.
Il registro di G. Besozzi, cancelliere di G. M. Visconti, Milan, 1937.
Schäfer, K. H., *Deutsche Ritter und Edelknechte in Italien während des 14 Jahrhunderts*, Paderborn, 1911–41.
Die Ausgaben der apostolischen Kammer unter Johann XXII, Paderborn, 1911.
Die Ausgaben der apostolischen Kammer, 1335–62, Paderborn, 1914.
Die Ausgaben der apostolischen Kammer unter Urban V und Gregor XI, Paderborn, 1937.
Statuta Civitatis Caesenae, Venice 1494, Cesena, 1589.
Statuta Civitatis Cerviae, Ravenna, 1588.

Statuta Civitatis Fani, Fano, 1568.
Statuta terrae Graderiae, ed. G. Vanzolini, in Ciavarini, *Collezione*, cit., iii, 1874.
Tarlazzi, A., *Appendice ai Monumenti Ravennati*, Ravenna, 1869, 1876.
Theiner, A., *Codex diplomaticus temporalis S. Sedis*, Rome, 1861–2.
Werunsky, E., *Excerpta e registris Clementis VI et Innocentii VI historiam S.R. Imperii sub regimine Karoli IV illustrantia*, Innsbruck, 1885.
Winkelmann, E., *Acta imperii inedita*, Innsbruck, 1880–5.
Wolkan, R., *Briefwechsel des Eneas Sylvius Piccolomini*, Vienna, 1909 etc.
Zimmermann, F., *Acta Karoli IV imperatoris inedita*, Innsbruck, 1891.
Zoli, A., Bernicoli, S., *La Romagna nel principio del sec. xvii*, Ravenna, 1899.
Zonghi, A., *Repertorio dell'antico archivio comunale di Fano*, Fano, 1888.

B. NARRATIVE AND LITERARY

Acciaiuoli, P., *L'Impresa di Rimini* (1469), ed. G. Zannoni, *Acc. Lincei, Rendiconti, Cl. Sc. Morali*, Ser. v, vol. v, 1896.
Annales Aretini, RIS xxiv.
Annales Caesenates, RIS xiv.
Annales Estenses, RIS xviii.
Annales Forolivienses, ed. G. Mazzatinti, RIS² xxii/2.
Annales Mediolanenses, RIS xvi.
Annales Parmenses Maiores, MGH SS xviii.
Annales Placentini, RIS xx.
Annales Placentini Gibellini, MGH SS xviii.
Anonimo Veronese, *Cronaca (1446–88)*, ed. G. Soranzo, Venice, 1915.
Azarius, P., *Liber gestorum in Lombardia*, ed. F. Cognasso, RIS² xvi/4.
Basinii Parmensis Poetae opera praestantiora, Rimini, 1794.
    Le Poesie liriche, ed. F. Ferri, Turin, 1925.
Battagli, Marco, *Marcha 1212–1354*, ed. A. F. Massèra, RIS² xvi/3.
Benvenuti de Rambaldis de Imola, *Comentum super Dantis Aldigherii Comoediam*, ed. G. F. Lacaita, Florence, 1887.
Bernabei, L., *Croniche Anconitane*, in Ciavarini, *Collezione*, cit.
Bernadi, A., *Cronache Forlivesi dal 1476 al 1517*, ed. G. Mazzatinti, Bologna, 1895–7.
Billii, A., *Historia*, RIS xix.
Biondo, Flavio, *Hist. ab inclinatione Romanorum*, Basle, 1559.
    Triumphantis Romae, Basle, 1559.
    Scritti inediti e rari, ed. B. Nogara, Rome, 1927.
Bonincontri, L., *Annales*, RIS xxi.
Borghi, T., *Continuatio cronice dominorum de Malatestis*, ed. A. F. Massèra, RIS² xvi/3.
Branchi, Baldo, *Cronaca malatestiana*, ed. A. F. Massera, RIS² xv/2.
Broglia, G., *Estratti dalla cronaca universale di Broglia di Tartaglia da Lavello*, ed. A. F. Massèra, RIS² xv/2.
Bruni, L., *Historia*, ed. E. Santini, RIS² xix/3.
Buoninsegni, P., *Historia fiorentina*, Florence, 1580.
Cambi, C., *Istorie*, in *Delizie degli eruditi toscani*, ed. Ildefonso di S. Luigi, xx, Florence, 1785.
Campanus, J., *Vita Braccii Perusini*, RIS² xix/4.
Cantinelli, P., *Chronicon*, ed. F. Torraca, RIS² xxviii/2.
Capponi, Neri di Gino, *Commentari*, RIS xviii.
Cavalcanti, G., *Istorie fiorentine*, Florence, 1838–9.
Chronicon Bergomense, RIS xvi.

Chron. Bon.: see *Corpus Chronicorum Bononiensium*, below.
Chronicon Cortusiorum, *RIS* xii.
Chronicon Estense, *RIS* xv, *RIS*² xv/3, ed. G. Bertoni, A. P. Vicini.
Chronicon Forlivense, *RIS* xix.
Chronicon Placentium, *RIS*, xvi.
Chronicon Regiense, *RIS* xviii.
Chronicon Siculum, ed. G. de Blasiis, Naples, 1887.
Cobelli, L., *Cronache forlivesi*, ed. G. Carducci, E. Frati, Bologna, 1874.
Compagni, D., *Cronica*, ed. I. del Lungo, *RIS*² ix/3.
Corpus Chronicorum Bononiensium, ed. A. Sorbelli, *RIS*² xviii/1.
Cribelli, L., *Vita Sfortiae*, *RIS* xix.
Cronaca di Mantova (Aliprandi etc.), ed. O. Begani, *RIS*² xxiv/13.
Cronaca di Perugia ('Graziani'), *ASI* xvi/1, 1851.
Cronaca malatestiana, ed. A. F. Massèra, *RIS*² xv/2.
Cronache Fermane, ed. G. de Minicis, Florence, 1870.
Croniche senesi, ed. A. Lisini, F. Iacometti, *RIS*² xv/6.
Dati, Gregorio, *Istoria di Firenze*, ed. L. Pratesi, Norcia, 1902.
Decembrio, P. C., *Opuscula historica*, ed. F. Fossati etc., *RIS*² xx/1.
Della Tuccia, Niccolo, *Cronache di Viterbo*, Florence, 1872.
Diari sanesi (Allegretti), *RIS* xxiii.
Diario d'anonimo fiorentino, ed. A. Gherardi, Florence, 1876.
Diario delle cose di Urbino, ed. F. Madiai, *Arch. stor. Marche Umb.*, 1886.
Diario Ferrarese (B. Zambotti), ed. G. Pardi, *RIS*² xxiv/7.
Diatriba preliminaris ad Fr. Barbari epistolas, Brescia, 1741.
Dubois, P., *De recuperatione Terrae Sanctae*, ed. C. V. Langlois, Paris, 1891.
Fazio, B., *Rerum gestarum Alphonsi regis*, ed. J. G. Graevius, *Thesaurus Antiquitatum Italiae*, ix/3, 1723.
Filelfo, F., *Epistolae familiares*, Venice, 1502.
    Commentarii de vita Frederici comitis Urbanitis, *AMM* 1901.
    Prose e poesie volgari, *AMM* 1901.
Finke, H., 'Eine Papstchronik des XV Jahrhunderts', *RQ* 1890.
Gatari, G. and B., *Cronaca Carrarese*, ed. A. Medin, G. Tolomei, *RIS*² xvii/1.
Geraldini, A., *De vita P. Angeli Geraldini*, ed. B. Geraldini, *BU* 1896.
Griffoni, M., *Memoriale historicum*, ed. L. Frati, A. Sorbelli, *RIS*² xviii/2.
Ser Guerriero da Gubbio, *Cronaca*, ed. G. Mazzatinti, *RIS*² xxi/4.
Guicciardini, F., *Le cose fiorentine*, ed. R. Ridolfi, Florence, 1945.
Iacopo Volterrano, *Diarium romanum*, *RIS* xxiii.
Infessura, *Diaria rerum romanorum*, ed. O. Tommasini, Rome, 1890.
Istoria dell'assedio di Piombino, *RIS* xxv.
Johannis Ferrariensis, *Excerpta*, ed. L. Simeoni, *RIS* xx/2.
John of Segovia, *Hist. Gen. Synodi Basil.*, ed. E. Birk. *Mon. Conc. Gen. sec. decimi quinti*, Vienna, 1857 etc.
Liber Pontificalis, ed. L. Duchesne, Paris, 1886–92.
Malipiero, D., *Annali veneti*, ed. F. Longo, *ASI* vii/2, 1843.
Manni, D. M., ed., *Cronichette antiche*, Florence, 1733.
Mattiolo, P. di, *Cronaca Bolognese*, ed. C. Ricci, Bologna, 1885.
Mazzei, Ser Lapo, *Lettere di un notaio*, ed. C. Guasti, Florence, 1880.
Minerbetti, *Cronica Volgare già attribuita a P. Minerbetti*, ed. E. Bellondi, *RIS*² xxvii/2.
Minuti, A., *Vita di Muzio Attendolo Sforza*, ed. G. B. Labertenghi, *Misc. stor. ital.*, vii, 1869.
Mittarelli, G. B., *Ad script*, RR. II. SS. Cl. Muratorii Accessiones Historicae Faventinae, Venice, 1775.

Morelli, G., *Cronica*, Florence, 1718.

    Ricordi, in *Delizie degli eruditi toscani*, ed. Ildefonso di S. Luigi, xix, Florence, 1785.

Morelli, L., *Cronica*, in *Delizie, cit.* above, xix, Florence, 1785.

Naldi, N., *Iannotii Manetti Vita*, *RIS* xx.

Nerli, A., *Breve Chronicon*, xxx, ed. O. Begani, *RIS*² xxiv/13.

Niem, Dietrich V., *Vita Johannis XXII*, in Hardt, *Magnum Concilium, cit.*, ii, 1697.

Palmieri, M. *Liber de temporibus*, ed. G. Scaramella, *RIS*² xxvi/1.

Pedrino, G. R., *Cronica del suo tempo*, ed. A. Pasini, Rome, 1929, 1934.

Piccolomini, Aeneas Sylvius (Pii II), *Commentarii*, Frankfurt, 1614.

    Commentaries, tr. F. A. Gragg, Smith College Studies in History, xxii, xxv, xxx, Northampton, Mass., 1937 etc.

    Opera inedita, ed. J. Cugnone, Rome, 1883.

Pietro di Giovanni, *Cronaca perugina inedita*, *BU* 1898.

Pius II: see Piccolomini, above.

Platina, *Liber pontificum*, ed. G. Gaida, *RIS*² iii/1.

Poggio Bracciolini, *Historia*, *RIS* xx.

Priuli, G. *Diarii*, ed. R. Cessi, *RIS*² xxiv/3.

Ristretto di fatti d'Italia e specialmente d'Urbino dal 1404 al 1444, ed. G. Baccini, in *Zibaldone* (Florence), i, 1880.

S. Caterina da Siena, *Lettere*, ed. N. Tommaseo, Florence, 1860.

Sacchetti, F., *Libro delle rime*, ed. A. Chiari, Bari, 1936.

    Lettere, ed. A. Chiari, Bari, 1938.

Salutati, C., *Epistolario*, ed. F. Novati, Rome, 1891–1911.

Sanudo, M., *Vite de' Duchi*, *RIS* xxii (cited as Sanudo).

    Diarii, ed. F. Stefani, Venice, 1879 etc.

Sanzio, G., *Cronaca*, ed. H. Holtzinger, Stuttgart, 1893.

Scalvanti, O., 'Frammenti di cronaca perugina inedita', *BU*, 1905.

Schivenoglia, A., *Cronaca di Mantova*, ed. C. d'Arco, Milan, 1856.

Sercambi, G., *Cronache*, ed. S. Bongi, Rome, 1892.

Ser Naddo, *Memorie storiche*, in *Delizie, cit.* above, xviii, Florence.

Sigismondo dei Conti, *Storie dei suoi tempi, 1475–1510*, Rome, 1883.

Simonetta, G., *Rerum gestarum Fr. Sfortiae commentarii*, ed. G. Sorenzo, *RIS*² xxi/3.

Sozomenus, *Specimen historiae*, *RIS* xvi.

Stefani, Marchionne, *Cronaca fiorentina*, ed. N. Rodolico, *RIS*² xxx/1.

Traversarii, A., *Epistolae*, ed. L. Mehus, Florence, 1759.

Velluti, D., *Cronica domestica*, ed. I. del Lungo, G. Volpi, Florence, 1914.

Vergerio, P. P., *Epistolario*, ed. L. Smith, Rome, 1934.

Vespasiano da Bisticci, *Vite di uomini illustri*, ed. L. Frati, Bologna, 1892 etc.

Villani, Giovanni, Matteo e Filippo, *Croniche*, ed. A. Racheli, Milan, 1857–8.

Vitae paparum avenionensium, ed. F. Baluze, G. Mollat, Paris, 1914–27.

Vite di Paolo II, ed. G. Zippel, *RIS*² iii/16.

Zambeccari, P., *Epistolario*, ed. L. Frati, Rome, 1929.

II. SECONDARY WORKS

Adami, F., *De rebus in civitate Firmana gestis*, in J. G. Graevius, *Thesaurus*, vii/2, 1722.

Ady, C. M., *The Bentivoglio of Bologna*, Oxford, 1937.

Affò, P. R., *Notizie intorno la vita di Basinio Basini*, in *Basini opera, cit.*

Alvisi, E., *Cesare Borgia*, Imola, 1878.

Amettler y Vinyas, D. J., *Alfonso V. de Aragon en Italia*, Gerona, 1903–28.

Amiani, P. M., *Memorie istoriche della città di Fano*, Fano, 1751.

Ammirato, S., *Istorie fiorentine*, Florence, 1647.

Angelita, G. F., *Origine della città di Ricanati*, Venice, 1601.

Annibaldi, C., 'Podestà di Iesi, 1197–1447', *AMM* 1916.

Ansidei, V., 'La tregua del 21 marzo 1380 fra Galeotto Malatesta e Antonio di Montefeltro', *BU* 1916.

Antonelli, M., 'Una relazione del vicario del Patrimonio a Giovanni XXII', *AR* 1895.

'Vicende della dominazione pontificia nel Patrimonio dalla traslazione della Sede alla restorazione dell'Albornoz', *AR* 1903–4.

'I registri del tesoriere del Patrimonio (1326–31)', *AR* 1922.

Antonini, F., *Supplemento della chronica di Verucchio*, Bologna, 1621.

'La pace di Lodi', *ASL* 1930.

Antonini, F., Avicenna, O., *Memorie della città di Cingoli*, Iesi, 1644.

Baldasseroni, F., 'La guerra tra Firenze e G. Visconti, *SS* 1902–3.

La pace tra Pisa, Firenze e Lucca nel 1343, Florence, 1904.

'Le relazioni tra Firenze, la Chiesa, e Carlo IV', *ASI* 1906.

Baldassini, G., *Memorie istoriche dell'antichissima città di Iesi*, Iesi, 1765.

Baldassini, T., *Notizie historiche della reggia città di Iesi*, Iesi, 1703.

Baldi, B., *Della vita e de' fatti di Guidobaldo da Montefeltro*, Milan, 1821.

Vita e fatti di Federigo di Montefeltro, Rome, 1824.

Bartoccetti, V., 'Il comune di Fano cattivo pagatore nel "400"', *SP* 1927

'L'elezione di un medico a Fano nel 1421', *SP* 1927.

Bartolucci, P. G., 'Legenda B. Galeoti Roberti de Malatestis', *Arch. francisc. hist.*, 1915.

Battaglini, A., *Saggio di rime volgari di G. Bruni de Parcitadi*, Rimini, 1783.

Della corte letteraria di Sigismondo Pandolfo Malatesta, Rimini, 1794.

Battaglini, F. G., *Memorie istoriche di Rimino e de' suoi signori artatamente scritte ad illustrare la zecca e la moneta riminese*, Bologna, 1789.

Della vita e de' fatti di Sigismondo Pandolfo Malatesta, Rimini, 1794.

Bauer, C., 'Studi per la storia delle finanze papali durante il pontificato di Sisto IV', *AR* 1927.

'Die Epochen der Papstfinanz', *Hist. Zeitschrift*, 1928.

Belotti, B., *Storia di Bergamo*, i, Milan, 1940.

Bembo, P., *Historiae Venetae Lib. II*, in J. G. Graevius, *Thesaurus*, v/1, 1722.

Benadducci, G., *Della signoria di F. Sforza nella Marca*, Tolentino, 1892.

Barnady, Amy A., 'Frammenti sanmarinesi e feltreschi', *ASI* 1902.

Biscaro, G., 'Le relazioni dei Visconti con la Chiesa', *ASL* 1919–20, 1927–8, 1937.

Blumenthal, H., 'Johannes XXIII, seine Wahl und seine Persönlichkeit', *Zeitsch. f. Kirchengeschichte*, 1900.

Bock, F., 'Der Este-Prozess von 1321', *Archivum fratrum praedicatorum*, 1937.

'I processi di Giovanni XXII contro i Ghibellini delle Marche', *Boll. ist. stor. it.*, 1941.

Bonardi, A., 'Venezia e Cesare Borgia', *N. arch. ven.*, 1910.

Bonoli, P., *Istorie della città di Forlì*, Forlì, 1661.

Borgogelli, P. C., 'Degli statuti di Fano', *SP* 1933.

'Degli stemmi e del siglo della citta città di Fano', *SP* 1936.

'Istanza di un'ebrea Fanese per l'esercizio della medicina', *SP* 1938.

Bosdari, F., 'Giovanni da Legnano', *AMR* 1901.

'Il comune di Bologna alla fine del secolo xiv', *AMR* 1914.

'Giovanni I. Bentivoglio', *AMR* 1915.

Bouard, M. de, *La France et l'Italie au temps du Grand Schisme d'Occident*, Paris, 1936.

Braschi, G. B., *Memoriae Caesenates*, Rome, 1738.

Buser, B., *Die Beziehungen der Mediceer zu Frankreich, 1434–94*, Leipzig, 1879.

Caggese, R., *Roberto d'Angiò*, Florence, 1922, 1930.

Cagnola, *Storia di Milano*, *ASI* 1842.

Calisse, C., 'La costituzione del Patrimonio di S. Pietro in Tuscia nel secolo xiv', *AR* 1892.

Campana, A., 'Una ignota opera di Matteo de' Pasti e la sua missione in Turchia', *Ariminum*, i, 1928.

'Atti, Isotta degli', in *Dizionario biografico degli Italiani*, iv, 1962, pp. 547–56.

Canetta, C., 'Il congresso di Roma nel 1454', *ASL* 1882.

'La pace di Lodi', *Riv. stor. it.*, 1885.

Cappelli, A., 'Di Pandolfo Malatesta ultimo signore di Rimini', *Atti e Mem. Dep. Stor. Pat. prov. Mod. Parm.*, 1863.

Castellani, G., *La dominazione veneta a Santarcangelo*, Santarcangelo, 1894.

'La zecca di Fano', *Riv. it. di numismatica*, 1899, 1901.

I Malatesta a Santarcangelo, Venice, 1906.

Cecconi, G., *Storia di Castelfidardo*, Osimo, 1882.

Ceci, G., *Malatesta di Pandolfo Malatesta e il comune di Todi*, Todi, 1890.

Chiaramonti, S., *Historiae Caesenae Libri XVI*, in J. G. Graevius, *Thesaurus*, vii/2, 1722.

Chroust, A., *Beiträge zur Geschichte Ludwig des Baiers, i. Die Romfahrt, 1327–9*, Gotha, 1887.

Ciaccio, L., 'Il cardinal legato Bertrando del Poggetto in Bologna', *AMR* 1905.

Ciapessoni, P., 'Per la storia dell'economia e della finanza pubblica pavesi sotto F. M. Visconti', *Boll. stor. pavese*, 1906.

Cimarelli, V. M., *Istorie dello stato d'Urbino, Corinalto* etc., Brescia, 1642.

Clementini, C., *Raccolto storico della fondatione di Rimino e dell'origine e vite de' Malatesti*, Rimini, 1617.

Cognasso, F., 'Note e documenti sulla formazione dello stato visconteo', *Boll. stor. pavese*, 1923–4.

Coleschi, L., *Storia della città di Sansepolcro*, Città di Castello, 1886.

Colini, F., *Memorie storiche della città di Iesi*, Iesi, 1890.

Colini-Baldeschi, E., 'Comuni, signorie e vicariati nella Marca d'Ancona', *AMM* 1924–5.

Colini-Baldeschi, L., 'Le "Constitutiones Romandiolae" de Giovanni d'Appia', *N. studi medievali*, ii, 1925.

Collino, G., 'La politica fiorentino-bolognese dall'avvento al principato del conte di Virtù alle sue prime guerre', *Mem. Acc. Torino*, 1904.

'La guerra viscontea contro gli Scaligeri', *ASL* 1907.

'La preparazione della guerra veneto-viscontea contro i Carraresi', *ASL* 1907.

Colucci, G., *Delle antichità picene*, 31 vols., Fermo, 1786–94.

Compagnoni, P., *La reggia Picena*, Macerata, 1661.

Compagnoni, P., *Memorie della chiesa di Osimo*, Rome, 1782.

Contelorio, F., *Martini quinti vita*, Rome, 1641.

Corio, B., *Storia di Milano*, Milan, 1855–7.

Cronaca di Castel delle Ripe e della terra di Durante, in Colucci, *Antichità, cit.*, xxvii.

Cusin, F., 'Le aspirazioni straniere sul ducato di Milano e l'investitura imperiale', *ASL* 1936.

'L'impero e la successione degli Sforza di Visconti, *ASL*, 1936.

Cutolo, A., *Re Ladislao d'Angiò-Durazzo*, Milan, 1936.

Dainelli, A., 'Niccolo d'Uzzano nella vita politica, *ASI* 1932.

Daverio, M., *Memorie sullo stato dell'ex-ducato di Milano*, Milan, 1804.

Davidson, R., *Forschungen zur Geschichte von Florenz*, Berlin, 1896 etc.

Geschichte von Florenz, Berlin, 1896 etc.

Delfico, M., *Memorie storiche della repubblica di S. Marino*, Florence, 1843.

Dennistoun, J., *Memoirs of the dukes of Urbino*, London, 1909.
De Roo, P., *Material for a history of pope Alexander VI*, Bruges, 1924.
Dorio, D., *Istoria della famiglia Trinci*, Foligno, 1638.
Dupré-Theseider, E., *I papi d'Avignone e la questione romana*, Florence, 1939.
Durrieu, P., *Le royaume d'Adria*, Paris, 1880.
   Les Gascons en Italie, Auch, 1885.
Eitel, A., *Der Kirchenstaat unter Klemens V.*, Berlin, 1907.
Ercole, F., *Dal comune al principato*, Florence, 1929.
   Da Bartolo ad Althusio, Florence, 1932.
Ermini, F., 'Gli ordinamenti politici e amministrativi nelle Costituzioni
   Egidiane', *Riv. it. scienza giur.*, 1894.
Ermini, G., 'Le relazioni fra la Chiesa e i comuni della Campagna e Marittima
   in un documento del sec. xiv', *AR* 1925.
   'La libertà comunale nello Stato della Chiesa, 1198–1367', *AR* 1926.
   I parlamenti dello Stato Chiesa delle origini al periodo Albornoziano, 1930.
   'I rettori provinciali dello Stato della Chiesa', *Riv. stor. dir. it.*, 1931.
   'Stato e chiesa nella monarchia pontificia dei secc. xiii e xiv', *ibid.* 1932.
   'Aspetti giuridici della sovranità pontificia nell'Umbria nel sec. xiii', *BU* 1937.
   'Caratteri della sovranità temporale dei papi nei secc. xiii e xiv', *ZRG Kan.*
   Abt., 1938.
Eubel, K., *Hierarchia catholica medii aevi*, Münster, 1913.
Fabre, P., 'Un registre caméral du cardinal Albornoz en 1364'. *Mélanges
   d'archéologie et d'histoire*, 1887.
Fabretti, A., *Biografie dei capitan venturieri dell'Umbria*, Montepulciano, 1842–6.
Fabronius, A., *Laurentii Medicis magnifici vita*, Pisa, 1784.
   Magni Cosmi Medici Vita, Pisa, 1789.
Falco, G., 'L'amministrazione papale nella Campagna e nella Marittima dalla
   caduta della dominazione bisantina al sorgere dei comuni', *AR* 1915.
   'I comuni della Campagna a della Marittima', *AR* 1919, 1924–6.
Faloci-Pulignani, M., 'Il vicariato dei Trinci', *BU* 1912.
Fattori, M., *Ricordi storici della repubblica di S. Marino*, Foligno, 1911.
Favier, J., *Les finances pontificales à l'époque du grand schisme d'occident*, Paris, 1966.
Feliciangeli, B., 'Notizie di Costanza Varano-Sforza', *Gior. stor. lett. it.*, 1894.
   Sull'acquisto di Pesaro da Cesare Borgia, Camerino, 1900.
   'Delle relazioni di Fr. Sforza coi Camerti', *AMM* 1908.
Ferranti, P., *Memorie storiche della città di Amandola*, Ascoli Piceno, 1891.
Ficker, J., *Forschungen zur Reichs- und Rechtsgeschichte Italiens*, Innsbruck, 1868 etc.
Filippini, F., 'La riconquista dello stato della Chiesa per opera di Egidio Albornoz',
   SS v–viii, 1896–1900.
   Il cardinale Egidio Albornoz, Bologna, 1933.
Fink, R. A., 'Dominicus Capranica als Legat in Perugia, 1430–1', *RQ* 1931.
Finke, H., 'Zur Vorgeschichte des Konstanzer Konzils', in *Forschungen und
   Quellen, cit.*
Fontana, L., *Bibliografia degli statuti dei comuni dell'Italia superiore*, Turin, 1907.
Franceschini, G., 'Il poeta Urbinate Angelo Galli e i duchi di Milano', *ASL*
   1936.
   'Ancora alcune notizie su Angelo Galli, *ASL* 1938.
   'Gian Galeazzo Visconti arbitro di pace fra Montefeltro e Malatesti', *ASL* 1938.
   'Lo stato d'Urbino dal tramonto della dominazione feudale all'inizio della
   signoria', *AMM* 1941.
   'La signoria di Antonio da Montefeltro sesto conte d'Urbino dagl'inizi
   all'annessione di Gubbio', *AMM* 1943.
   'Alcuni documenti su la signoria di Galeotto Malatesta a Borgo San Sepolcro',
   SR 1951.

'Alcune lettere inedite del cardinale Galeotto da Pietramala', *Italia medioevale e umanistica*, 1964.

I Montefeltro, Varese, 1970.

Franchini, V., 'L'annullabilità della cessione di Cervia', *La Romagna*, 1911.

Franciosi, P., *Vicende storiche di S. Leo, antico Monteferetro*, S. Marino, 1928.

Frati, L., 'La lega dei Bolognesi e dei Fiorentini contro Gian Galeazzo Visconti', *ASL*, 1889.

Fumi, L., 'Eretici e ribelli nell'Umbria', *BU* 1897-9.

'Francesco Sforza contro Iacopo Piccinino', *BU* 1910.

'L'atteggiamento di Francesco Sforza verso Sigismondo Malatesta in una sua istruzione del 1462', *ASL* 1913, pt. i.

Gamurrini, E., *Istoria genealogica delle famiglie nobili toscane e umbre*, Florence, 1668-85.

Garampi, G., *Memorie ecclesiastiche appartenenti all'istoria e al culto della Beata Chiara di Rimini*, Rome, 1755.

Illustrazione di un antico sigillo della Garfagnana, Rome, 1759.

Gaspari, D., *Memorie storiche di Serrasanquirico*, Rome, 1883.

Gasperoni, G., 'Il comune di Savignano', *AMR* 1907-8.

Gherardi, A., 'La guerra dei Fiorentini con papa Gegorio XI', *ASI* 1867-8.

Ghirardacci, C., *Historia di Bologna*, i, ii, Bologna, 1597, 1657; iii, *RIS*[2] xxxiii/1.

Gianandrea, A., 'Della signoria di Francesco Sforza nella Marca', *ASL* 1881.

'Le pergamene di Staffolo', *Arch. stor. Marche Umb.*, 1886.

'Della signoria di Francesco Sforza nella March secondo le memorie dell'archivio fabrianese', *ASI* 1888.

'Potestà e capitani lombardi nella Marca', *ASL* 1896.

Giordani, A. degli Abati Olivieri, *Memorie della badia di S. Tommaso in Foglia*, Venice, 1755.

Illustrazione della rubrica 152 libro III dello statuto di Pesaro, Pesaro, 1768.

Memorie del porto di Pesaro, Pesaro, 1774.

'Della zecca di Pesaro', in G. A. Zanetti, *Nuova raccolta delle monete e zecche d'Italia*, i, Bologna, 1775.

Memorie di Gradara, Pesaro, 1775.

Memorie di Novilara, Pesaro, 1777.

Notizie di Battista da Montefeltro, Pesaro, 1782.

Orazioni in morte di alcuni signori di Pesaro della casa Malatesta, Pesaro, 1784.

Memorie di Alessandro Sforza, Pesaro, 1785.

Giorgio, D., *Vita Nicolai V pontificis maximi*, Rome, 1742.

Giovanardi, P. G., 'Un frate minore martire del sigillo sacramentale', *Studi francescani*, 1912.

'Ancora sul martire del sigillo sacramentale a Rimini', *ibid.* 1916-20.

'Vitae duae B. Galeoti Roberti de Malatestis', *Arch. francisc. hist.*, 1928.

Giulini, G., *Continuazione delle memorie spettanti alla storia di Milano*, Milan, 1771 etc

Göller, E., *König Sigismunds Kirchenpolitik, 1404-10*, Freiburg i.B. 1902.,

'Untersuchungen über das Inventar des Finanzarchivs der Renaissancepäpste', *Miscellanea Ehrle*, v, Rome, 1924.

Gottlob, A., *Aus der Camera Apostolica des 15 Jahrhunderts*, Innsbruck, 1889.

Gozzadini, G., *Memorie per la vita di Giovanni II Bentivoglio*, Bologna, 1839.

Nanne Gazzadini e Baldassare Cossa, Bologna, 1880.

Grigioni, C., 'I costruttori del Templo Malatestiano in Rimini', *Rassegna bib. dell'arte*, 1908.

Gritio, P., *Dell'historia di Iesi*, Macerata, 1578.

Guiraud, J., *L'état pontifical après le Grand Schisme*, Paris, 1896.

Hefele-Leclercq, *Histoire des conciles*, vi-vii, Paris, 1907 etc.

Hofmann, W. von, *Forschungen zur Geschichte der kurialen Behörden vom Schisma bis zur Reformation*, Rome, 1914.

Hollerbach, J., 'Die gregorianische Partei, Sigismund und das Konstanzer Konzil', *RQ* 1909.

Jarry, E., *La vie politique de Louis de France*, Paris, 1889.

Jordan, K., 'Das Eindringen des Lehnwesens in das Rechtsleben der römischen Kurie', *Archiv f. Urkundenforschung*, 1932.

Kirsch, J. P., 'Die Rückkehr der Päpste Urban V. und Gregor XI. von Avignon nach Rom', *Quellen u. Forsch. aus dem Gebiete der Geschichte*, 1898.

Koelmel, W., *Rom und der Kirchenstaat im 10 und 11 Jahrhundert*, Berlin, 1935.

Lanciani, R., 'Il patrimonio della famiglia Colonna al tempo di Martino V.', *AR* 1897.

Larner, J., *The Lords of Romagna*, London, 1965.

Lazzari, A., *De' conti feltrechi d'Urbino*, in Colucci, *Antichità, cit.*, xxi.

Leicht, P. S., 'Staatsformen in der italienischen Renaissance', *QF* 1940, reprinted *Scritti vari*, i, 1943.

Lilii, C., *Dell'historia di Camerino*, Macerata, 1652.

Loye, J. de, *Les archives de la chambre apostolique au XIVe siècle*, Paris, 1899.

Luzi, E., *Compendio di storia ascolana*, Ascoli Piceno, 1889.

Luzzatto, G., 'Comune e principato in Urbino nei secc. xv a xvi', *Le Marche* 1905.
    'Le sottomissioni dei feudatari e le classi sociali in alcuni comuni marchigiani (sec. xii e xiii)', *Le Marche* 1906; cf. 1907.

Madiai, F., 'Nuovi documenti su Sveva di Montefetro-Sforza', *Le Marche* 1909.

Malavolti, O., *Historia de' fatti e guerre de' Sanesi*, Venice, 1599.

Marchesi, S., *Supplemento istorico dell'antica città di Forlì*, Forlì, 1678.

Marcucci, R., *L'antico archivio comunale di Senigallia*, Senigallia, 1902.

Marini, A., *Storia della terra di Montottone*, Fermo, 1863.

Marini, G., *Saggio di ragioni della città di S. Leo*, Pesaro, 1758.

Marini, M., *Memorie istorico-critiche della città di Santo Arcangelo*, Rome, 1844.

Mariotti, R., *Serrungarina nel sec. xiv*, Fano, 1890.

Marongiù, A., *Il parlamento in Italia nel Medio Evo e nell'età moderna*, Milan, 1962.

Martorelli, L., *Memorie historiche dell'antichissima e nobile città d'Osimo*, Venice, 1705.

Massèra, A. F., 'Note malatestiane', *ASI* 1911.
    'I poeti Isottei', *Gior. stor. lett. it.*, 1911, 1928.
    'Il serventese romagnolo del 1277', *ASI* 1914.
    'Amori e gelosie in una corte romagnola del Rinascimento', *La Romagna* 1916.
    'Il sequestro di un corriere diplomatico malatestiano nel 1454', *La Romagna* 1928.
    rev. of Soranzo, 'S.P.M. in Morea', *N. arch. ven.*, 1919.

Mazzuchelli, G., *Notizie intorno ad Isotta da Rimino*, Brescia, 1759.

Memorie di Monte Cassiano, in Colucci, *Antichità, cit.*, xxviii.

Memorie istoriche di Ripatransone, *ibid.* xviii.

Memorie risguardanti la terra di Santarcangelo (N.N.), 1817.

Menchetti, A., *Storia di un comune rurale della Marca Anconitana, Montalboddo oggi Ostra*, Iesi etc., 1913 etc.

Mesquita, D. M. B. de, *Giangaleazzo Visconti*, Cambridge, 1941.

Messeri, A., Calzi, A., *Faenza nella storia e nell'arte*, Faenza, 1909.

Mirot, L., *La politique pontificale et le retour du Saint Siège à Rome en 1376*, Paris, 1899.

Mittarelli, G. B., *Annales Camaldulenses*, Venice, 1755–73.

Moeller, R., *Ludwig der Bayer und die Kurie im Kampf um das Reich*, Berlin, 1914.

Morici, M., *Dei conti Atti, signori di Sassoferrato*, Castelplanio, 1899.
    'Di Corrado Trinci, tiranno e mecenate umbro del Quattrocento', *BU* 1905.
    'Il vicariato dei Trinci', *BU* 1912.

Muller, C. F. F., *Der Kampf Ludwig des Baiers mit der römischen Kurie*, Tübingen, 1879–80.

Müntz, E., *Les arts à la cour des papes*, Paris, 1878 etc.

Muzi, G., *Memorie di Città di Castello*, Città di Castello, 1842–4.

Nicoletti, L., *Di Pergola e dei suoi dintorni*, Pergola, 1899, 1903.

Nina, L., *Le finanze pontificie nel medio evo*, Milan, 1929–32.

Nucci, R., 'L'arte dei notari a Cingoli nel secolo xiv, *AMM* 1913.

Nunziante, R., 'I primi anni di Ferdinando d'Aragona e l'invasione di Giovanni d'Angiò', *ASN* 1892–7.

Odorici, F., *Storie bresciane*, Brescia, 1853–62.

Partner, P., *The papal state under Martin V*, British School at Rome, 1958.

Pasolini, P., *Caterina Sforza*, Rome, 1893.

Pastor, L., *Geschichte der Päpste seit dem Ausgang des Mittelalters*, Freiburg i.B., 1886 etc.

Pastori, L., *Memorie storiche di Montelparo*, in Colucci, *Antichità, cit.*, xvii.

Pecci, A., *Cenni storici di Verucchio*, Rimini, 1920.

Pecci, G., 'Il governo di Verucchio e gli statuti della meta del secolo xv', *AMR* 1938.

Pellegrini, A., 'Gubbio sotto i conti e duchi d'Urbino', *BU* 1905.

Pellini, P., *Dell'historia di Perugia*, Venice, 1664.

Perret, P. M., *Histoire des relations de la France avec Venise*, Paris, 1896.

Pertile, A., *Storia del diritto italiano*, ed. P. del Guidice, Turin, 1896 etc.

Picotti, G. B., *La dieta di Mantova e la politica dei Veneziani*, Venice, 1912.

Pirchan, G., *Italien und Kaiser Karl IV in der Zeit seiner zweiten Romfahrt*, Prague, 1930.

Pochettino, G., 'La repubblica di S. Marino avanti il sec. xv', *AMR* Ser. 3, xxviii, 1910.

Re, *Vita di Cola di Rienzo*, Forlì, 1828.

Ricci, C., *Il tempio malatestiano*, Milan, Rome, 1924.

Ricotti, E., *Storia delle compagnie di ventura in Italia*, Turin, 1844–5.

Robertson, I., 'The return of Cesena to the direct dominion of the church after the death of Malatesta Novello', *SR* 1965.

Rodolico, N., *Dal comune alla signoria: saggio sul governo di Taddeo Pepoli in Bologna*, Bologna, 1898.

Romanin, S., *Storia documentata di Venezia*, Venice, 1855–61.

Romano, G., 'Niccolo Spinelli', *ASN* 1899 etc.

Rondini, S., 'Memorie istoriche di Monte Filottrano', in Colucci, *Antichità, cit.*, xxii.

Rossi, A., *Notizie istoriche di Monte Alboddo*, in Colucci, *Antichità, cit.*, xxviii.

Rossi, L., *La guerra in Toscana del 1447–8*, Florence, 1903.

'Sull'abbandono di Piombino da parte del Re d'Aragona nel 1448', *ASI* 1903.

'Federigo da Montefeltro condotto da Fr. Sforza', *Le Marche* 1905.

'Venezia e il Re di Napoli, Firenze, e Fr. Sforza dal novembre del 1450 al giugno del 1451', *N. arch. ven.*, 1905.

'I prodromi della guerra in Italia del 1452–3, i tiranni di Romagna e Federigo da Montefeltro', *AMM* 1905–6.

'Niccolo V. e le potenze d'Italia', *Riv. scienze stor.*, 1906.

'Nuove notizie su Federigo da Montefeltro, Sigismondo Malatesta e i Manfredi d'Imola e di Faenza (1451)', *AMM*, 1906–7.

'Di un delitto di Sigismondo Malatesta', *ibid.* 1910.

'Un nuovo documento su "Di un delitto di S.M."', *ibid.* 1910.

Rubeus, Hieronymus, *Historiarum Ravennatum Libri XI*, ed. J. G. Graevius, *Thesaurus*, vii/1, 1722.

Salvelli, C., *Pandolfo Malatesta, signore di Bergamo*, 1932.

Salvioli, G., *Gli statuti inediti di Rimini, anno 1334*, Ancona, 1880.
Salzer, E., *Über die Anfänge der Signorie in Oberitalien*, Berlin, 1900.
Sansovino, F., *Origine e fatti delle famiglie illustri d'Italia*, Venice, 1582.
Sautier, A., *Papst Urban V. und die Soldnerkompagnien in Italien in den Jahren 1362–7*, Zürich, 1912.
Savioli, L. V., *Annali Bolognesi*, Bassano, 1784–95.
Scalvanti, O., 'Il vicariato di N. Fortebraccio a Borgo S. Sepolcro', *BU* 1906.
Schneider, F., *Kaiser Heinrich VII.*, Greiz, Leipzig, 1924, 1928.
Siena, L., *Storia di Sinigaglia*, Sinigaglia, 1746.
Sighinolfi, L., *La signoria di Giovanni da Oleggio in Bologna*, Bologna, 1898.
Soranzo, G., 'La cessione di Cervia e delle sue saline a Venezia nel 1463', *La Romagna* 1909.
  'Una missione di Sigismondo Pandolfo Malatesta a Maometto II nel 1461', *La Romagna* 1909.
  'Ancora sulla missione di Sigismondo Pandolfo Malatesta a Maometto II e Matteo de' Pasti', *La Romagna* 1910.
  'Un invettiva della curia romana contro Sigismondo Malatesta', *La Romagna* 1910–11.
  Pio II e la politica italiana nella lotta contro i Malatesti, Padua, 1911.
  'Due delitti attribuiti a Sigismondo Malatesta', *Atti ist. Ven. di Sc., Lett., Arti*, 1914–15.
  'Sigismondo Pandolfo Malatesta in Morea e le vicende del suo dominio', *AMR* 1917–18.
  'Ultima mia parola sul martire del sigillo sacramentale a Rimini', *Studi francescani*, 1921.
  'Un atto pio della Diva Isotta', *AMR* 1925.
  'Una piccola ignorata signora di Romagna, Vannetta Toschi', *AMR* 1933–4.
Sorbelli, A., *La signoria di Giovanni Visconti a Bologna*, Bologna, 1902.
  Il comune rurale dell'Appennino Emiliano nei secc. xiv e xv, Bologna, 1910.
Sugenheim, S., *Geschichte der Entstehung und Ausbildung des Kirchenstaates*, Leipzig, 1854.
Tagliabue, M., 'La politica finanziaria nel governo di Giangaleazzo Visconti', *Boll. stor. pavese*, 1915.
Talleoni, M., *Istoria dell'antichissima città di Osimo*, Osimo, 1808.
Tanursi, F. M., *Memorie istoriche della città di Ripatransone*, in Colucci, *Antichità, cit.*, xviii, 1792.
Tarducci, F., 'Gianfrancesco Gonzaga, signore di Mantova', *ASL* 1902.
Temple-Leader, G., Marcotti, G., *Giovanni Acuto*, Florence, 1889.
Tonduzzi, G. C., *Historie di Faenza*, Faenza, 1675.
Tonini, C., *La coltura letteraria e scientifica in Rimini dal sec. xiv ai primordi del xix*, Rimini, 1884.
Tonini, L., *Il porto di Rimini*, Bologna, 1864 (from *AMR* 1864).
  Le imposte pagate in Rimini nel sec. xiv, Bologna, 1872 (from *AMR* 1872).
Tonini, L., Tonini, C., *Storia civile e sacra riminese*, Rimini, 1848–82.
Torelli, P. P., *Sulle antiche memorie di Castel Durante*, in Colucci, *Antichità, cit.*, xiii.
Torre, A., 'Le controversie fra l'arcivescovo di Ravenna e Rimini nel sec. xiii', *SR* 1951.
  I Polentani fino al tempo di Dante, Florence, 1966.
Ugolino, F., *Storia dei conti e duchi d'Urbino*, Florence, 1859.
Vaccai, G., *La vita municipale sotto i Malatesta, gli Sforza, e i Della Roverere, signori di Pesaro*, Pesaro, 1928.
Valeri, G., 'Della signoria di Fr. Sforza nella Marca', *ASL* 1884.

Valeri, N., 'L'insegnamento di Giangaleazzo Visconti e i consigli al Principe di Carlo Malatesta', *Boll. stor. bib. subalpino*, 1934.

L'eredità di Giangaleazzo Visconti, Turin, 1938.

Valois, N., *La France et le Grand Schisme d'Occident*, Paris, 1896–1908.

Le pape et le concile, 1418–50, Paris, 1909.

Vancini, O., *La rivolta dei Bolognesi al governo dei vicari della Chiesa*, Bologna, 1906.

'Bologna della Chiesa', *AMR* 1906–7.

Vasina, A., *I Romagnoli fra autonomie cittadine e accentramento papale nell'età di Dante*, Florence, 1965.

Romagna medievale, Ravenna, 1970.

Vecchiazzani, M., *Historia di Forlimpopoli*, Rimini, 1647.

Vergottini, G. de, 'Richerche sulle origini del vicariato apostolico', *Studi in onore di E. Besta*, ii, Milan, 1937–9.

'Note per la storia del vicariato apostolico durante il sec. xiv', *Studi in onore di C. Calisse*, iii, Milan, 1939–40.

Vernarecci, A., *Del comune di S. Ippolito*, Fossombrone, 1900.

Fossombrone dai tempi antichissimi, Fossombrone, 1903, 1914.

Vicinelli, A., 'L'inizio del dominio pontificio in Bologna', *AMR* 1920–2.

'La famiglia dei conti di Bologna', *AMR* 1924–5.

Vitali, V., *Il dominio della parte guelfa in Bologna*, Bologna, 1901.

Vitali, G., *Memorie storiche risguardanti la terra di Monte Fiora*, Rimini, 1828.

Volpi, G., 'La vita e le rime di Simone Serdini', *Gior. stor. lett. it.*, 1890.

Waley, D., *The Papal State in the thirteenth century*, London, 1961.

Werunsky, E., *Geschichte Kaiser Karls IV. und seiner Zeit*, Innsbruck, 1880–92.

Yriarte, C., *Un condottière du XVe siècle, Rimini. Etudes sur les lettres et les arts à la cour des Malatesta*, Paris, 1882

Zampetti, T., *Giulio Cesare Varano*, Rome, 1900.

Zannoni, G., 'L'impresa di Rimini', *Rendiconti, Acc. Lincei, Cl. Sc. Morali*, 1896.

Zazzeri, R., *Storia di Cesena*, Cesena, 1889.

Index

Acciaiuoli, Niccolo, 70, 76
Adimari, family of, 256, 298, 335
   Adimario, 251n
afflictus, 5, 77, 263, 281–2
Aimery de Châtelus, 53, 71
Albizzi, Rinaldo degli, 121, 139, 161, 163
Albornoz, Egidio, cardinal, 44, 46–7, 66, 70, 73–83, 87, 91–3, 96, 106n, 148, 276n
   Gomez, 81, 88
Aldovrandini, Elisabetta, 251, 253–5, 332
Alexander V, pope, 132, 135, 138, 139n
Alexander VI, pope, 257, 260, 266, 287, 333
Alfonso V, king of Aragon, Naples and Sicily, 188, 193–5, 198–9, 204–12, 215–19
Alfonso, duke of Calabria, 250, 252n
Alidosi, lords of Imola, 17, 19, 47, 93, 112, 113, 121, 135n, 149n, 150n, 153n, 212, 282n, 294n, 338n
   Bertrando, 106
   Lucrezia, 157–8
   Ludovico, 158
   Rengarda, 106
   Roberto, 79
Amadeo VII, count of Savoy, 100
Amadeo VIII, count of Savoy, 141
Amandola, 16n, 145n, 302, 306n
Amelius de Lautrec, 52
Ancona, 13, 14, 65, 75, 76, 145, 147, 209, 212, 228, 237
Ancona, March of (*see also* Pentapolis), 1–2, 7n, 8n, 12 ff., 19, 45, 46, 47, 60, 64–6, 72, 79, 97, 116, 123, 126, 135, 137–8, 143–8, 152, 153n, 154, 170, 180–1, 188, 193–4, 197, 221, 223, 280–1
Anglico, *see* Grimoard
Anjou, counts and dukes of
   Charles, king of Sicily, 30, 33

Jean, duke of Calabria, 215, 219–20, 222, 226–8, 230–3, 237
Louis I, 100, 101n
Louis II, 133–4
René, 215n
Arezzo, 58, 59, 74
Argenta, 60
Artechini, family of, 56
Ascoli Piceno, 13n, 14, 65, 66, 74n, 75, 76, 126, 149, 153, 188
Assisi, 120, 160
Atti, family of, 298–9
   Isotta degli, 204, 213, 241, 243, 245–7, 295n, 300n, 324–5, 332
   Luigi degli, 293n, 298n
Atti, of Sassoferrato, 109–10, 162n
   Giovanni di Ungaro, 109
   Luigi, 259n
   Ungaro, 74, 173
Attoni, family of, 19

Baglioni, Braccio, 213n
   Guido, 218
Bagnacavallo, 14, 183n, 287n
   counts of, 16, 17n, 18
Bagno, counts of, 121, 237n, 239, 298n
Balacchi, Mucciolo de', 97n
Baligano, Tano, lord of Iesi, 49, 53
Barbiano, Alberigo da, 101n, 107, 117, 119n, 120, 121–2
   Giovanni da, 133, 114, 121
Basinio Basini, of Parma, 194
Basle, council of, 142n, 151, 152n, 174, 180, 183
Bastia dal Fiano, 264n
Belfiore, 123
Bellaria, 242, 290
Belmonti, family of, 256, 298, 299n, 335
   Belmonte, 123n
   Matteo, 246
Benci, family of, 298

Benedict XII, pope, 43, 45, 46n, 60, 70
Benedict XIII, pope of Avignon, 126–7, 139–40
Bentivoglio, lords of Bologna, 254n
  Giovanni I, 118–19
  Giovanni II, 246n, 252, 253, 334
  Violante, 252, 257, 261, 334, 337
Bergamo, 125, 155, 307n, 325n, 329n
Bertinoro, 18, 48, 50n, 54, 98, 104–5, 144, 170, 179, 203, 242, 259n, 264n, 286n, 305, 325, 327n, 332n
Boccaccio, Giovanni, 67, 73
Bologna, 1, 3, 12, 13, 14, 37n, 42, 49, 50n, 52, 57, 60, 66, 67, 68–9, 80–1, 84, 87–8, 89, 91, 92, 111–14, 117–20, 132, 135–7, 149, 153, 168, 183, 214, 230n, 286n, 290, 293n, 317
Boniface VIII, pope, 34, 40, 54n
Boniface IX, pope, 104, 109, 113, 115–17, 119–20, 149, 151–2, 265, 279n, 281n, 282n
Bordonchio, 290
Borghi, Tobia, 200n
Borgia, family of, 258, 288
  Cesare, 254n, 257, 259–61, 264, 287, 291n, 294, 300n, 312n, 328, 331–3
  Lucrezia, 257n
Bosco, 298n
Brancaleoni, family of, 17, 93, 107, 110n, 150n, 160–2, 299n, 318n
  Alberigo, 160–1, 171, 187, 191n
  Bartolomeo, 160
  Branca, 107
  Galeotto, 160
  Gentile, 160, 164, 185
  Venanza, 101
Brescia, 103, 124, 142, 155–6, 307n, 317
Bulgaria, 112
Buscareto, 109
  Niccolo da, 53n, 66, 74, 75

Cagli, 18, 92n, 94, 97, 106, 109, 320n
Calcinara, 183
Calixtus III, pope, 212, 214–15, 217–20, 227n
Calliscesi, family of, 56
  Rodolfino, 33
Calpolo, Francesco da, 121
Camerino (see also Varano, Da), 19, 78, 127, 146n, 150n, 154, 192
Caminate, le, 123, 237, 290
Campagna, province of, 1, 8n, 47, 99n, 126
Campiano, 123
Campomorto, 250

Candelara, 194
Cane, Facino, 124–5, 155
Canetoli, family of, 168
Cantiano, 108–10
Carignano, 275n
  family of, 64, 329
  Giacomo, 55, 64
  Guido, 55
  Teresino, 71n
Carmagnola, Francesco da, 155–6, 179
Carpegna, 98n, 219
  counts of, 17, 25n, 27n, 162n, 212, 297
  Francesco, 180
  Giovanni, 173
  Ramberto, 219
Carrara, Da, lords of Padua, 60, 69n, 81, 87, 113, 114
  Ubertino, 60n
Cartoceto, 290
Casalbone, 112
Casalecchio, 119
Cascina, 85
Castel Bolognese, 183
Casteldelce, 185, 203, 217n, 264n
Castel di Barte, 270n
Castel Durante, 107n, 160, 162–4, 171, 259n
Castel Fidardo, 66n, 116, 145n, 168, 171, 281n, 282n, 283n, 302n, 309n, 316n, 320n
Castelfranco, 59
Castelgagliardo, 268n
Castellacia, 98n
Castel Liale, 290, 297n, 299n
Castelnovo, 185n, 239, 264n, 295, 298–9
Castracani, family of, 298
Castrocaro, 13, 98n, 116
  counts of, 16
Cattolica, 62
census, of towns, 5, 10, 54, 74, 77, 144, 268, 281–2
  of vicars, 73n, 76–7, 82, 86n, 91n, 102n, 103, 104n, 156, 157n, 160, 166n, 167n, 170, 203n, 209, 227–8, 230n, 237–8, 251, 257, 260, 262, 265n, 268, 274, 284–7, 312n, 325
Ceola, 294
Certaldo, 221n, 223n, 224–5, 236
Cervia, 5n, 17, 19, 48, 51, 55n, 101, 102, 110n, 116, 168, 170–1, 181–2, 201, 203, 209n, 212–13, 234n, 236–7, 243, 264n, 266, 268, 272n, 276, 278–9, 282n, 285, 292–4, 300–2, 306, 312n, 315, 318, 321–2, 327–8, 334

Cesena, 17, 18, 23, 24, 25n, 28n, 33, 37n, 48, 49, 50n, 51, 55–6, 64, 79, 95, 97, 100, 102, 104, 112, 113, 117n, 118n, 122, 144, 145, 154, 155, 156, 169–72, 179, 183, 203, 209n, 212, 214, 231, 242–3, 246, 255–6, 260, 264n, 266, 276n, 285, 290, 293, 295–8, 300–3, 307–8, 310, 312, 317, 319, 320–1, 323, 327n, 329, 331–2

Cesenatico, 97, 100, 119n, 134, 142

Charles IV, emperor, 43, 69, 73–5, 87, 88–90, 93

Charles III of Durazzo, king of Naples and Hungary, 99–100, 107

Chiavelli, lords of Fabriano, 66, 127, 259n
  Alberghetto, 74
  Chiavello, 127

Cima, lords of Cingoli, 138n
  Bartolomeo, 66
  Giovanni, 127

Cingoli (see also Cima), 49, 65, 127, 145n

Citerna, 90, 98n, 212, 276n, 294n

Città di Castello, 89, 90, 92n, 149, 151n, 153n, 174

Cittadella, 335

Cividale, 132

Civita Nova, 145n, 147, 282n, 332n

Civitella, 74n

Clement V, pope, 42, 43n, 49, 54n

Clement VI, pope, 43, 44, 47

Clement VII, pope of Avignon, 99, 100, 104, 277–8

Clement VII, pope, 337–8

cloth industry, 13n, 323n

coinage, 268, 275, 289n, 317

Colleone, Bartolomeo, 243–4

Colonna, family of, 173–4, 218
  Caterina, 160
  Giovanni Andrea, 153
  Vittoria, 166

Comacchio, 18, 20n

companies, mercenary, 65–8, 72–3, 75, 80, 84–6, 94–5, 100, 111, 112, 181

Constance, council of, 135, 137, 139, 140–3, 145, 146, 148, 150n, 151–3, 154
  Peace of, 4, 53n

Constantine, Donation of, 1, 2, 46n, 151

Corinaldo, 98n, 109, 116, 168, 170, 264n, 281n, 300n, 302, 313n, 315n, 330

corn trade, 7, 13, 292

Correr, Angelo, cardinal (see also Gregory XII, pope), 129n, 141, 143–5, 148
  Antonio, cardinal, 182n

Cossa, Baldassare (see also John XXIII, pope), 120, 121–3, 127, 130, 132, 135–6

councils, communal, 22–3, 38, 62–4, 77, 103n, 142, 251, 271, 273, 307–13, 316–20, 325n, 330n, 331, 334–6

Cuglianello, 101, 112, 116, 264n

Cunio, counts of, 16, 36

Cusa, Nicholas of, cardinal, 229, 230–1

Cusercole, 37n, 254
  counts of, 233n, 297

despotism (see also Papal State and Malatesta of Rimini, signoria), 10–12, 16 ff.

Dogaria, 264n

D'Oleggio, Giovanni, 69, 99

Donato, 98n, 264n

Dubois, Pierre, 1–2, 46n

Duraforte, Astorgio da, 45, 47, 68, 70

Eight Saints, War of, 93–6, 106

emperors, see under proper names

Empire, Holy Roman, 2–4, 42–4

Este, lords of Ferrara, 47, 52, 59, 60n, 64, 68–9, 74, 79, 81, 87, 96, 111, 113, 149n, 150n, 180, 213, 229, 250, 253, 284
  Alberto d', 213
  Borso d', 212–18, 237–8
  Costanza d', 81
  Ercole d', 253–5
  Ginevra d', 176, 186
  Lionello d', 190–1, 194
  Margherita d', 168, 172, 175, 213n, 294n
  Niccolò II, d' 81, 87, 88, 89
  Niccolò III d', 117–19, 124–5, 135n, 137, 155n, 168–70, 172–4, 179, 182, 186n
  Niccolò di Lionello d', 231
  Ugo di Niccolò III d', 155n
  Ugo d'Obizzo d', 81, 90n

Eugenius IV, pope, 152n, 172, 173, 179, 182–4, 188–9, 190, 194–6, 266, 271n, 275n, 287n

Fabriano (see also Chiavelli), 39, 58, 74, 127, 259n

Faenza (see also Manfredi), 13, 17, 18, 19, 31, 47, 48, 57, 59, 95, 104, 117, 121–2, 135–6, 243, 259–60, 287n, 329n
  Martino da, 127, 147–8, 286

Faggiola, 185
　family of, 40
　Neri della, 74
　Uguccione della, 18, 48, 52
Fano, 13, 24, 43n, 49, 51, 55–6, 59, 64–5,
　66, 68, 71, 76, 80, 81n, 82, 86, 98n,
　102–3, 129, 133n, 145, 147, 154n,
　165, 166n, 169–74, 179, 182n, 188–
　9, 194, 195, 203, 208, 210n, 214n, 216,
　219, 231–3, 236–7, 239, 240–1, 246–
　8, 251, 255n, 264n, 266–9, 271,
　272n, 275n, 281–3, 285–6, 289–93,
　297, 299–332
Felix V, anti-pope, 194
Fermo, 39, 51, 58, 66, 69, 73n, 74, 126,
　138, 144–5, 149, 153, 186, 187, 194,
　236, 259n
Ferrante I, king of Sicily, 211, 219–28,
　231n, 232–3, 239n, 246–8, 252
Ferrara (see also Este), 1, 50, 59, 87, 89,
　114, 215–17, 287n, 290
　Antonio da, 80n
Filelfo, Francesco, 221n
Finigli, 98n, 264n
Fiumesino, 290
Florence (see also Medici), 13, 33, 37, 49,
　50–1, 52, 66–9, 71, 73, 74, 76, 84–5,
　89, 93–6, 99n, 107–8, 110–21, 130,
　131, 133, 135, 136, 137, 147, 150n,
　151n, 156n, 158–64, 172, 184–5,
　188–9, 193–5, 199–201, 204–12,
　214, 217–18, 222–3, 229, 234–5,
　237, 239, 242, 246–9, 276n, 290,
　311n, 317, 323n
focaticum, 5, 77, 281–2
Fogliano, 290
　Tommaso da, 23
Foligno, 74, 153, 257
Fondulo, Gabrino, 124–5, 155
Forlì (see also Ordelaffi), 11n, 17, 18, 19,
　31, 34, 48, 49, 51, 54, 57, 61, 73, 80,
　98, 104, 112, 121–3, 135–6, 145,
　153, 154, 158, 164, 173n, 180, 182,
　183–4, 197n, 243, 250, 257, 260,
　287n, 329n
　Antonello da, 218, 229, 233, 237–8
Forlimpopoli, 136, 180, 183–4
Fortebraccio, Carlo, 194, 213, 218
　Niccolò, 152, 169-70, 174, 181
Fossombrone, 49, 59, 60, 64, 65n, 71,
　76, 77n, 82, 86, 98n, 102, 103, 104,
　106n, 154n, 166, 174, 187n, 191–3,
　195, 197–8, 218, 264n, 317, 320n,
　322–3, 329

Francavilla, 138
Fratte, Le, 295n, 298n
Frederick I, emperor, 17, 23, 24
Frederick II, emperor, 3, 21, 24, 28, 29,
　30
Frederick III, emperor, 177n, 203, 207
Frontone, 191

Gabrielli, family of, 66, 107–10
　Francesco, 191
　Gabriele, 107
　Giovanni, 191
Gaetani, Onorato, 99
Gambacorti, Benedetto, 299n
Gambancerri, family of, 29, 30
Gambettola, 298n, 299
Gatteo, 334
Geneva, Robert of, cardinal, 95, 100
Gerlendeta, 290
Ghiaggiolo (see also Malatesta, counts of),
　35, 37, 38
　Orabile di, 37
　Uberto, count of, 37
Ghibellinism, see under Guelf
Giovanna I, queen of Naples, 69, 87,
　100
Giovanna II, queen of Naples, 154
Giovedia, 28, 294, 297n, 298n, 299
Gonzaga, lords of Mantua, 81, 87, 113,
　118, 124, 158, 184, 212
　Alda, 113n
　Feltrino, 81
　Francesco, 111, 113–15, 117, 118, 120,
　124, 128
　Gianfrancesco, 124–5, 147n, 187n, 326
　Isabetta, 103n, 111, 117, 128–9, 146,
　168–9, 173, 175n
　Ludovico, 212
　Rodolfo, 249n
Governolo, 114
Gozzadini, family of, 120, 325n
　Gabione, 119n, 149n
　Nanni, 149n
Gradara, 35, 48n, 59, 60, 86, 169, 174–5,
　180, 187n, 192, 195–6, 203, 207n,
　212, 213, 232, 237, 239, 264n, 275n,
　290, 294–5, 298
Granarola, 195n
Gregory IX, pope, 2n
Gregory XI, pope, 89–90, 94, 95, 97, 99,
　153, 265n
Gregory XII, pope (see also Correr,
　Angelo), 123, 126 ff., 166n, 173,
　283n

Grimoard, Anglico, cardinal, 87, 90, 92, 97
Gualdo, Torre di, 294n, 295n
Gubbio, 66, 75, 76, 77, 107–9, 145, 325n
Guelf and Ghibellinism, 8, 9, 14–15, 19, 28–30, 31, 33–4, 45–6, 47, 48 ff., 66, 67, 84, 117n, 122, 124–5, 197n, 329, 336
Guidi, counts, 16
Guinigi, Paolo, 331n

Hawkwood, Sir John, 86n, 87, 89, 91, 93, 101
hearth-tax, *see focaticum*
Henry VI, emperor, 24, 26, 50–1
Henry VII, emperor, 42, 43
heresy, 9, 24n, 45–6

Iesi (*see also* Simonetti), 65, 74, 75, 127, 137, 145n, 147, 154, 166, 212, 228, 229, 236, 239, 259n, 302n, 316n, 325n
Imola (*see also* Alidosi), 13, 15, 17, 18, 31, 57, 61, 104, 153, 158–9, 164, 173n, 183, 243, 257, 259n, 260, 282n, 287n
imperium, merum et mixtum, 5, 10, 54, 146n, 263, 269, 270, 272, 295, 297, 299n
Innocent IV, pope, 23
Innocent VI, pope, 45, 70, 72, 74, 93
Innocent VII, pope, 126, 151–2, 282n
Innocent VIII, pope, 252–3, 287
Iseo, family of, 298
    Goffredo Rodolenghi da, 202, 298
    Rodolengo da, 270n
Issola, 290

John XXII, pope, 44n, 46n, 54, 55, 65n, 72, 150, 195
John XXIII, pope, 132–40, 142, 144, 145, 151, 161, 276n
Julius II, pope, 335

Ladislas, king of Naples, 126–7, 131–9, 144
Laetus, Pomponius, 245
Lando, conte Lucio, 84, 100–1
Lavello, Tartaglia da, 146
Legnano, Giovanni da, 92n
Lodi, Peace of, 157, 210–11, 214, 220
Longiano, 168, 233n, 305
Louis, king of Hungary, 69–70, 72, 84
Louis XI, king of France, 230, 233n
Louis, duke of Savoy, 216

Louis of Taranto, 69–70, 74
Louis of Touraine, 104
Lucca, 66, 68, 103
Ludwig of Bavaria, emperor, 42, 43, 52, 67, 71n
Ludwig, duke of Bavaria, 140–1
Lugo, 158, 182
Lunano, 171

Macerata, 14, 75, 138, 145
Macerata Feltria, 162, 223n, 236, 298
Malatesta, count of Dovadola, 121
Malatesta, counts of Ghiaggiolo, 37n, 212, 217n, 296
    Antonio, 297n
    Cecco, 297n
    Cocco, *see* Niccolo
    Galeotto, 297
    Galeotto di Malatesta, 297n
    Giovanni, 110n
    Malatesta, 296
    Niccolo, 180, 233n, 237n, 239, 297
    Ramberto di Malatesta, 270, 297
    Ramberto di Uberto, 56, 64n, 75
    Uberto, 48, 56
Malatesta, lords of Pesaro, 102, 145n, 154n, 166–7, 169, 171, 173–5, 180, 186–93, 276, 281n, 283n, 284, 285n, 286n, 290, 302, 326, 330n
    Carlo di Malatesta, 146, 166–7, 169, 172, 174, 186
    Galeazzo di Malatesta, 141n, 146, 166n, 169, 174, 186–7, 189–93, 195, 199–200, 207n, 326
    Malatesta di Pandolfo, 90, 102, 105, 109, 116, 130, 139, 146, 166–7, 169, 265, 267n, 278n, 302, 304n, 308–9, 326
    Pandolfo di Malatesta, 169, 174, 186–7
    Paola, 212n, 326
    Taddea, 148n
Malatesta of Rimini (*see also* Rocca Malatestiana, Tempio Malatestiano)
    origins, 26 ff., 35, rise to power, 29 ff., expansion of, in March of Ancona, 48–9, 55, 64–6, 123, 137–8, 144–5, 161, in Romagna, 47–8, 50–1, 97–101
    signoria, 38–40, 61–4, 71–2, 103, 289–332; jurisdiction, 272, 303–4, 320–1, 327; legislation, 272, 274, 304–5, 309–11, 320; police and military organisation, 305–7, 315, 330; taxation and revenue, 71–2, 273–4, 275, 291–4, 306–7, 310–15, 323–8, 330–1

Malatesta of Rimini (*cont.*)
  papal vicariate, 43, 71n, 73, 76–8,
    82–3, 91n, 98n, 100, 102–4, 116,
    144, 156–7, 159, 190n, 195, 201,
    203, 214, 227–8, 230n, 231, 237,
    238, 242, 248, 249, 251, 262–88,
    336–8
  Alessandra, 237n
  Andrea, 91, 102, 106, 113, 114, 115n,
    116, 118, 120, 122, 125, 133, 135,
    136, 137, 138, 144–6, 154–5, 165,
    265, 267n, 283n, 294n, 300n, 319–
    20, 327n
  Andronico di Gaspare, 200n
  Anna, 60n
  Antonia di Andrea, 125, 155
  Antonia di Sigismondo, 249n
  Antonio, 301n
  Bartolomeo, 194n, 301n
  Battista, 251n
  Carlo di Galeotto, 91, 99, 102–68, 170,
    173, 177n, 216, 265, 267–8, 278,
    280n, 283n, 289n, 293n, 296n, 297,
    302n, 304–5, 309n, 317–19, 321–3,
    325–7, 329n, 331n
  Carlo di Roberto, 251–5, 261, 333,
    335–6
  Caterina, 68
  Contessina, 249n
  Costanza, 90
  Domenico (Novello), 165, 168–9, 172,
    178–80, 182–8, 190, 193–4, 196,
    203–5, 208–10, 212–14, 217–18,
    223, 226–9, 233, 235–7, 241–2,
    264n, 265–8, 276, 278, 285n, 287,
    290–1, 293n, 295n, 297–8, 300n,
    322n, 324, 328n
  Ercole, 266
  Ferrantino di Malatestino, 49, 50, 51,
    52, 53n, 55, 56, 57–8, 60–1, 62, 67,
    68, 71, 106, 295n
  Ferrantino Novello, 57, 60–1
  Galeotto Belfiore, 91, 102–3, 105, 110,
    114, 116, 154, 161n, 265, 306, 322n,
    328n
  Galeotto di Almerico, 251, 253, 296,
    299
  Galeotto di Andrea, 138n, 141n, 146
  Galeotto di Pandolfo, 51n, 59–101,
    104n, 106–8, 112, 128n, 265, 267–8,
    273n, 274–6, 278, 279n, 284n, 289–
    91, 295n, 296, 298, 300n, 301–5,
    308, 312, 315, 317n, 320, 322, 324,
    329n

  Galeotto di Sigismondo, 245n
  Galeotto Roberto, 129, 165, 168–70,
    172–5, 265, 267, 271n, 275n, 278,
    312n, 329n
  Gaspare di Galeotto, 296
  Gentile, 106, 156, 161
  Giovanna di Sigismondo, 213, 245n,
    295n
  Giovanna di Roberto, 251n, 328
  Giovanni di Lancilotto, 240
  Giovanni di Malatesta, 26, 27
  Giovanni 'Sciancato', Gianciotto, 31,
    33n, 35, 36, 37, 48, 57, 168
  Giovanni di Pandolfo I, 58n, 89
  Giovanni di Ramberto (descendant of
    Gianciotto), 168, 171–3, 216, 281n,
    296, 331
  Giovanni di Ramberto, count of Sogli-
    ano (*see also* Malatesta, counts of
    Sogliano), 27, 31, 36
  Giovanni di Tino di Gianciotto, 57,
    75, 77, 296
  Giuliozzo, 296, 306n
  Guido, 60
  Leale, 301n
  Lodovica, 296n
  Lucrezia, 197n, 209, 213
  Maddalena, 36
  Margarita di Galeotto, 113
  Margherita di Sigismondo, 209, 213
  Malatesta da Verucchio, 28–41, 56,
    72
  Malatesta 'della Penna', 26n, 27–8, 35
  Malatesta di Giovanni, 26
  Malatesta di Pandolfo ('Guastafamig-
    lia'), 51n, 55, 57–86, 99n, 106, 265,
    267–9, 289n, 291n, 294, 301, 303,
    305–6, 308, 312
  Malatesta di Sigismondo, 204, 212, 324
  Malatesta 'Ungaro', 66, 70, 72n, 79–
    86, 88–90, 128n, 265, 267, 292,
    295n
  Malatestino 'dall' Occhio', 31, 36,
    37, 40, 41, 49, 50, 51, 56n, 61n
  Malatestino di Ferrantino, 52, 57–8,
    60
  Masia, 68
  Pandolfo I, 36, 41, 48, 51, 53n, 54, 55,
    56n, 57, 61n
  Pandolfo II, di Malatesta Guasta-
    famiglia, 58n, 64, 65n, 69n, 71n,
    72n, 80n, 84, 86, 87, 89, 90, 168,
    265, 267, 294, 301, 308n, 319,
    322n, 326

Malatesta of Rimini (*cont.*)
Pandolfo III, di Galeotto, 91, 102–3, 105, 190n, 111n, 112, 113, 114, 115n, 116, 117n, 118, 119, 123–5, 128n, 129, 134, 137n, 142, 146–7, 154–8, 163–7, 265, 267n, 268, 271n, 276n, 283n, 286, 290–3, 298, 300n, 302, 310n, 312n, 315, 317, 320n, 322–4, 326–7, 329n, 330–1
Pandolfo IV, di Roberto, 251–7, 260–1, 266, 267n, 271, 280, 287, 291, 294, 297n, 299n, 306n, 324n, 328–9, 333–8
Pandolfo di Sigismondo, 245n, 252
Paola Bianca, 99
Paolo 'il Bello', 33n, 36, 37, 57
Parisina, 122, 155n, 168, 179, 213n
Polissena, 300n
Raimondo di Almerico, 246, 252–3, 296
Raimondo di Gaspare, 300n
Ramberto di Gianciotto, 57–8
Ramberto di Giovanni, 27
Rengarda (I) di Galeotto, 90
Rengarda (II) di Galeotto, 110, 160, 161
Rengarda di Malatesta da Verucchio, 36
Ricca, 300n
Roberto di Pandolfo IV, 338
Roberto di Sigismondo, 'il Magnifico', 177, 186n, 204, 210, 212, 219, 227, 230n, 237, 241–2, 245–51, 255, 266, 280, 287, 295n, 311n, 312n, 324, 328
Roberto di Sigismondo II, 266
Sallustio, 241, 245–7
Sigismondo Pandolfo, 165, 168–9, 171–2, 174–245, 264n, 265–8, 270–1, 275, 276n, 278–80, 285, 287, 289–91, 293, 295–9, 301–4, 308–9, 311–12, 315–16, 319–25, 327–32
Sigismondo II, 256, 266n, 337
Simona, 36
Taddea, 68, 99n
Troilo, 251n
Valerio, 209, 243, 247
Malatesta, counts of Sogliano, 40, 41, 56n, 71n, 162n, 171n, 217n, 296, 314n, 338n
Carlo, 232, 237n, 239, 297
Giovanni, 180, 297
Manfred, 3, 33
Manfredi, lords of Faenza, 17, 19, 36, 47, 69n, 73n, 79–80, 93, 101, 106, 112, 113, 117–18, 121–2, 149n, 156, 158, 164n, 169, 183–5, 212, 236, 239, 338n

Alberghettino, 40
Astorgio I, 97, 106, 113, 117, 119n, 121–2
Astorgio II, 180, 195n, 196n, 211n, 212, 218, 232, 233n, 237
Galeotto, 329n
Gian Galeazzo, 106, 117, 135–6
Giovanni, 46n
Guglielmo, 46n
Guidaccio, 195
Guidantonio, 184, 186n
Taddeo, 230
Mantua (*see also* Gonzaga), 222–4, 226, 227n
Congress of, 222
Marittima, province of, 1, 99n, 126
Marsano, Bernardo count of, 58n
Martin IV, pope, 8, 18, 36
Martin V, pope, 152–71, 173, 174, 216, 265–6, 271n, 286n, 287, 329n
Mary of Savoy, duchess of Milan, 201n
Maschi, family of, 298
Massa di Romagna, 183n
Massa Trabaria, 96n, 106, 144, 160, 171, 185n
Matelica, 19, 145n
Mecla, 74n
Medici, family of, 241, 249
Cosimo de', 177–8, 201, 206–7, 233, 293n, 323n
Lorenzo de', 249, 252, 258n, 331n
Pier Francesco de', 239
Meldola, 98, 102, 104, 154, 179, 242, 247n, 261, 264n, 266, 290n
Mengardoni, Pandolfo de', 168
Mercatello, 160, 164, 185n
Michelotti, Biordo, 116, 152
Migliorati, lords of Fermo, 150n, 259n, 299n
Ludovico, 126, 138, 144–8, 152, 156
Mogliano, Gentile da, 66, 69–70, 73n, 74, 76
Mondaino, 58, 60–1, 203, 232, 264n
Mondavio, 102, 104, 116, 168, 170, 174, 181n, 182n, 190n, 195, 210n, 213, 221n, 223–4, 228, 229n, 230n, 231–2, 239, 243–4, 246, 247, 264n, 271n, 276, 281n, 283n, 285n, 292n, 293n, 295n, 299, 308, 310n, 312–13, 315–16, 320n, 322n, 328
Mondolfo, 66n, 98n, 102, 109, 116, 237, 264n, 290, 292n, 302, 312
Monlione, 58, 270

Montalboddo, 116, 123, 147, 154, 203n, 213n, 280n, 290, 293n, 298n, 302n, 308–10, 313n, 315n, 328n
  Carlo, da, 123n
Montebello, 98n, 108n, 109n, 110n, 217n, 312
Monteboaggine, 193, 195n, 204
Monte Cagnano, 48n, 294
Monte Cassiano, 137, 147, 154, 209, 267n, 294n, 308, 324
Montecavallo, 230
Montecerignone, 195n, 197n, 204, 217n
Montedoglio, counts of, 17
Montefano, 116, 170
Montefeltro, 12, 26, 30, 51n, 98, 104n, 106, 108n, 116, 157n, 161–2, 170n, 185, 187, 191, 193–5, 197, 200, 202–4, 213, 219n, 221, 223–4, 231, 239, 242n, 264n
  counts of, 17 ff., 20n, 25n, 27n, 37–8, 45, 48, 55, 60, 64, 66, 89n, 92–4, 97, 101n, 106–10, 111, 149n, 150n, 153, 154, 174, 180, 186–7, 190, 253, 254n, 294, 296n, 326
  Anna, 110
  Antonio, 94, 107–10, 112, 115n, 118, 150n, 161n
  Battista, 166n
  Federigo, 48, 50, 51, 54, 55
  Federigo di Guidantonio, duke of Urbino, 164–5, 171, 177, 185, 187–8, 190–7, 199–200, 202–8, 210–12, 214–37, 239, 240, 242, 246–7, 250, 266, 276, 311n, 325n, 328
  Giovanni, 144n
  Guidantonio, 110, 134n, 136, 147, 151, 159–68, 171, 174, 181, 184–5, 190, 193
  Guido, 17–18, 19, 30, 31, 33–4, 37–40
  Guidobaldo, duke of Urbino, 334, 337
  Isabetta, 247–8, 251, 295n, 328
  Oddantonio, duke of Urbino, 190–1, 193, 266
  Speranza, 51
  Sveva, 216–17
  Violante, 181, 187, 193, 197, 204, 227n, 242n, 295n
Monte Filottrano, 116, 145n, 283n, 302–3, 309n
Montefiore, 86, 232, 233n, 239, 259n, 275n, 290, 295, 298, 310n, 313n, 332n, 334
Montefotogno, 185n

Montegello, 110, 185n, 193, 195n
Montegiano, 290
Montegiorgio, 138n
Montegrimano, 195n, 197n, 204
Montelocco, 171
Montelupone, 147, 171, 316n
Monteluro, 188, 195, 200, 206n, 207n
Monte Marciano, 209, 221n, 223–4, 228, 229, 234, 239, 267n, 294n, 295n, 313n
Montenovo, 98n
Monterado, 322n
Monterolo, 213, 283n, 306n, 312, 321n, 322n
Monte Rubbiano, 138
Montescudolo, 226n, 243, 275n, 290
Monte Tassi, 195
Montevecchio, 187n, 232, 329n
Montevenere, 116, 264n
Monti di Pietà, 325n
Monticoli, family of, 299n
Montolmo, 138, 145n, 189, 316n
Montone, Braccio da, 127, 137, 145–8, 152–4, 160, 161
Montottone, 259n
Moriale, Fra, 66, 70, 73
Morro, 221n, 224, 226n

Naples, kingdom of (*see also under* Anjou *and* individual rulers), 75, 76, 85, 87, 100
Narni, 116, 160n
Nicholas III, pope, 34
Nicholas IV, pope, 10, 32
Nicholas V, pope, 170n, 196–8, 200–4, 209–12, 266, 267n, 285
Nidastore, 230

Offagna, 116n, 145n, 171, 281n, 283n
Omodei, family of, 29, 30
Orciano, 281n
Ordelaffi, lords of Forlì, 17, 19, 20n, 48, 51, 53n, 55, 56, 68, 73, 76, 80, 93 ff., 98–9, 101, 104n, 105–6, 111, 114n, 115, 117, 121, 136, 149n, 153n, 182–5, 212, 233n, 236, 239, 294n
  Antonio, 122, 136, 180, 182–3, 197n
  Cecco di Antonio, 197n, 237
  Cecco di Giovanni, 99n, 105, 122
  Francesco, 46n, 64, 66, 67, 70n, 74, 76n, 79–80
  Giorgio, 122, 136, 157
  Giovanni di Francesco, 68, 98
  Giovanni di Ludovico, 99n, 112
  Lucrezia, 122

Ordelaffi, lords of Forlì (*cont.*)
Ludovico, 68, 76n, 98
Pino I, di Giovanni, 99n, 101, 105, 118n
Pino II, di Antonio, 231
Scarpetta, 50n
Sinibaldo, 97, 98–9, 105
Tebaldo di Giorgio, 157–8
Tebaldo di Ludovico, 99n
Orsini, family of, 90n, 138, 153
Aldobrandino, count of Pitigliano, 210–11
Bertoldo, 36
Gianantonio, prince of Taranto, 219, 226, 228, 231, 233
Napoleone, cardinal, 49–50
Napoleone, 246
Paolo, 120, 135n, 138, 144n
Rinaldo, 99n
Orvieto, 74, 147, 152
Osimo, 51, 53n, 65, 72, 116, 123, 145n, 157, 168, 170–1, 257, 282n, 297, 302n, 303, 308–9, 313n, 315–16, 320n, 324n, 329
Ottrano, 116n

Paderno, 60, 75
Paganelli, 298n, 299
Pagani, Maghinardo, da Susinana, 18, 19, 178
Palazzo, Bartolomeo da, 270–1, 298–9
Palterieri, Margherita, 35
Papacy (*see also* Papal State)
and communes, 3–4, 7 ff., 46n, 92, 149–50, 153, 257–9
and despots, 1, 10–11, 45–6, 92 ff., 149–50, 152–3, 257
and empire, 2–4, 42–4
and feudatories, 3, 11, 47
at Avignon, 42–5
Papal state
origins and boundaries, 1–2, in the thirteenth century, 1–11, during the Avignonese papacy, 42–7, 91–6, during the Schism, 96–7, 99, 104–5, 119, 148–52, in the fifteenth century, 152–4, 257–9
cardinals and, 6, 151, 153, 239, 243, 258
government of, 4–5, 8–9, 44–7, 91–3, 148, 257; jurisdiction, 5, 9, 77, 263, 272; legislation, 5, 6, 44, 46, 91, 258n; military service, 5, 53, 73n, 76–7, 82, 263, 279–80; parliaments, 5, 6, 31, 34, 36, 54, 59, 70–1, 77, 80, 104, 156, 263, 280; rectors, 4, 6, 7n,

31–3, 34–7, 44, 46n, 51, 71, 99, 103, 149; revenue and taxation, 5, 44n, 46n, 53–4, 92, 105, 149, 151–2, 257n; vicariate (*see also* Malatesta of Rimini, vicariate), 43, 97, 98–9, 100, 104–5, 109, 127, 135–6, 138, 149–50, 152–3, 160, 164, 165, 166n, 182, 183, 197, 231, 233, 257–8, 262–88, 336
'Parcitade' (*Pater civitatis*), 21, 30, 329
Parcitadi, family of, 28, 29, 30, 37–40, 62, 71n
Concordia, 28, 30, 35
Galassino, 40
Giovanni, 40
Montagna, 32, 40
Parcitade, 30, 33
Parcitadino, 40
Ugolino, 29, 30
Ugolino 'Cignatta', 40, 62n
Pasti, Matteo de', 194
Patrimony, Tuscan, province, 1, 2, 8n, 47, 108, 116, 180
Paul II, pope, 241–8, 257, 266, 291n, 300n
Paul IV, pope, 266
Penna Billi, 26, 163, 170n, 203, 223n, 239, 264n, 275n
Pennarossa, 185n
Pentapolis, 2, 21
Pepoli, lords of Bologna, 47, 60, 68
Obizzo, 68
Taddeo, 68, 104
Perfetti, Niccolo de', 191, 195n
Pergola, 65n, 66n, 104, 108, 168, 170–1, 181n, 190n, 194, 195n, 203, 205, 213, 221n, 223–4, 230, 264n, 283n, 285n, 294n, 308, 312–13, 315–16
Angelo della, 159, 162
Perleoni, family of, 298, 318n
Perugia, 8n, 47, 49n, 52, 58, 60, 61, 68–9, 74, 75, 87, 92, 101n, 107–8, 112, 116n, 119, 120, 127, 133n, 134, 138n, 145–7, 150n, 153, 331n
Pesaro (*see also* Malatesta of), 25, 34, 37n, 43n, 48, 55, 58, 59, 64, 65n, 67, 71, 72n, 76, 86, 90n, 98n, 102, 104, 129, 145, 174, 180, 187, 189–93, 195, 196–7, 199–202, 206–8, 213–14, 216, 228, 231, 237n, 252–3, 259n, 264n, 265, 268–9, 272n, 273, 275n, 281–3, 285, 287n, 290–1, 294–5, 298n, 300–5, 308–13, 317–19, 322n, 325n, 330n, 333n
la Tojmba di, 195

Petrarch, 84n, 90
Pezzolo, 290
Philargos, Peter, of Candia (*see also* Alexander V, pope), 123n, 127, 131
Piccinino, family of, 152
  Francesco, 183, 186n, 189, 190n
  Giacomo, 214–15, 217–30, 233, 237
  Niccolo, 181–6, 188
Piccolomini, family of, 176, 258
  Aeneas Sylvius (*see* Pius II, pope)
  Antonio, 238–9, 241, 246n, 264
  Giacopo, 239, 245
Pico della Mirandola, Gianfrancesco 231
Pietramala, family of, 162n
  Galeotto de' Tarlati da, 98
  Masio da, 90
Pietramaura, 185n
Pietrarubbia, 108n, 163, 221n, 224–5, 229, 232
Pieve di Sestino, 98n, 203, 264n
Pii, lords of Carpi, 212
  Marco, 218
Pili, Ugolino de', 189n, 271n, 329
Piombino, 153, 200
Pisa, 67, 68, 76, 84, 120
  Council of, 130–3, 138–9, 151
Pisanello, 194
Pius II, pope, 26n, 172n, 175, 176–7, 180n, 186n, 189n, 199n, 202, 203, 204n, 211, 220–39, 241n, 245, 264, 266, 276n, 278, 279, 287
Plethon, Gemistos, 242n
podestà, podesteria, 9–10, 14, 16, 18, 36, 48, 62–3, 71, 77, 121, 159, 272–3, 301–3, 315–16, 319, 327n, 335
Polenta, castle of, 18, 101, 112, 116, 184, 242, 264n, 290n
Polenta, Da, lords of Ravenna, 17, 18–19, 20n, 31, 36, 48, 53n, 55n, 66, 67, 68n, 97, 112, 120, 150n, 154, 169, 183–5, 282n, 331n
  Bernardino, 35, 36, 48, 301n
  Francesca, 36–7
  Guido di Lamberto, 34, 36, 51
  Guido di Ostasio, 96, 97, 100–1, 104
  Obizzo, 146
  Ostasio, 56n, 60, 66, 71, 344
popes, *see under* individual pontiffs
Pouget, Bertrand du, cardinal, 45, 57, 59–60, 67, 70
Pozzo Alto, 195

Ranchio, 123

Ravenna (*see also* Da Polenta, Traversari), 13, 15–16, 18–19, 31, 36, 49, 57, 61, 112, 142, 183, 234, 235
  church of, 3, 9n, 14n, 15, 18, 23, 24–5, 27n, 30, 37n, 48n, 82n, 100–1, 104, 112, 144, 179n, 264n, 267n, 276n, 294, 297n
  Exarchate of, 2
Recanati, 75, 138, 144n, 145n, 147
Riarii, family of, 258
  Girolamo, 249–50, 252
Rienzo, Cola di, 72
Rimini, 11n, 14, 17, 21 ff., 43n, 49, 50n, 51n, 53–5, 57–64, 71, 76, 82, 85–6, 87n, 102, 104, 128, 129–30, 134, 145, 147–8, 159, 169–73, 203, 231–3, 236–48, 251, 256, 260–1, 264n, 266, 268–9, 275n, 281–2, 285–7, 289–90, 293–6, 298–9, 301–38
  church of, 24
  commune of, 21 ff., 53–4, 61–4, 71–2, 83, 163, 179, 251, 307 ff.
  contado of, 23 ff., 59, 60–2, 75, 144, 248
  economy of, 21, 323–4, 327
  guilds in, 22, 323n
  population of, 13, 21, 285, 327
  port of, 117n, 119n, 321
  privileges of, 7n, 23, 24, 53–4
  statutes of, 22, 62, 63, 71–2
Ripa, 313–14, 320n, 322n, 330
Ripalta, 108n, 109, 204, 290
Ripatransone, 65n
Robert, king of Naples, 42, 50–3, 56n, 60
Rocca Malatestiana, 30, 183n, 194, 213n, 275n, 303n
Roccacontrada, 65n, 74, 105, 138, 145n, 181n, 188, 190n, 194
Roccasecca, 133
Roche, Androin de la, 80–81
Roelli, family of, 298, 299n, 318n
  Leonardo, 168, 172, 179
Romagna, 1–3, 5–8, 10–21, 32–4, 42, 46, 50, 54, 58–60, 67, 72, 79–80, 97, 103, 110, 112, 116–17, 121–3, 135–7, 145, 148, 152, 157–9, 197, 281–4
Rome, 1, 46, 87–8, 94, 95, 96, 116, 117n, 126–7, 133, 153
Romsey, Richard, 101
Roncitello, 290, 322n
Roncofeddo, 56, 58, 60, 102, 290, 294
Rontagnano, 185n, 193
Rovere, della, family, 258

Roversano, 105
Rupert III of Bavaria, Count Palatine, 118, 130, 140
Rupola, 284n, 328

Sacchetti, Franco, 92
Salimbeni, of Siena, 88–9
salt, saltworks, 234n, 236
    tax, 5n, 292–4, 336
    trade, 13, 285n, 293
Saltara, 290
Saludeccio, 243, 295n
Salutario, 121
Sanatello, 185
San Costanzo, 174, 226n, 237, 271n, 290
San Cristoforo, 275n
San Giovanni in Galileo, 58
San Giovanni in Marignano, 237
San Giovanni in Persiceto, 118, 119n, 120n, 136–7, 154
San Leo, 37n, 55n, 97, 98, 108n, 109n, 162, 170n, 187, 203, 230, 232, 239, 264n, 275n
San Lorenzo in Campo, 190n
San Marino, 26, 39, 55, 97, 162, 185, 187, 206, 212, 229n, 233, 236, 239
San Mauro, 28, 270n, 298n
San Procolo, 17, 34
San Ruffilo, 81, 82n
San Sepolcro, 90, 98, 102, 103n, 117n, 128, 157n, 170, 183, 285n, 290, 293n, 294n, 296, 300, 302n, 308, 310, 312–13, 315n, 325, 329
San Severino, 66, 74, 127, 145n, 153, 259n
    Polissena da, 103n
Sanseverino, Roberto, 250
Sant'Agata, 156n, 162, 170n, 179, 203, 223n, 264n, 276n, 298
Sant'Anastasio, 195n, 197n, 204, 217n
Sant'Angelo in Vado, 160, 164, 185n
Santa Caterina of Siena, 92
Santarcangelo, 24, 35, 55, 82, 97–8, 104, 175, 179, 232, 236, 239, 244, 255n, 264n, 275n, 281n, 290, 300, 302, 303n, 308–9, 311, 314n, 320–1, 322n, 334
Sant'Ippolito, 180, 217n, 298n
San Vito, 226n , 321n, 322n
Sarsina, 144, 242, 266, 276n
Sassocorvaro, 170, 171, 195n, 205, 217n, 224, 236, 275n
Sassoferrato (see also Atti), 74, 109, 259n
Savignano, 30, 82, 290, 305, 308–9, 318–19, 322n, 334

Savignano di Rigo, 185n, 193
Scala, Della, lords of Verona, 43n, 68, 81, 111, 112
    Antonio, 111n
    Bartolomeo, 111n
    Cansignore, 88, 111
    Mastino, 47
Scapezzano, 322n
Scorticata, 26, 102, 179, 283n, 295, 305
Serra dei Conti, 123, 170
Serrasanquirico, 49
Serravalle 259n, 305
Serrungarina, 174, 290
Sforza, 138
    of Buscareto, 109
    Caterina, of Forlì, 254, 256, 259, 260n
    Michele Attendolo, 146n
    lords of Milan, 246–7, 312n; Francesco, 124, 152, 165n, 177n, 181–97, 199–203, 205–12, 214–29, 232n, 233n, 234–9, 241–2, 311n, 322; Ippolita, 212n; Ludovico, il Moro, 249; Polissena, 176, 186, 187, 201, 206n, 213n, 232n
    lords of Pesaro: Alessandro, 187, 191–2, 195, 197, 200–1, 206–7, 209, 212, 216–17, 227, 228n, 229, 239, 246, 276; Battista, 325n; Costanzo, 249, 252n , 275n
Siena, 68, 69, 74, 75, 87, 88–9, 124n, 150n, 151n, 210–11, 214, 236
    Council of, 166
Sigismund of Hungary, emperor, 130, 134–5, 139–43, 155, 180
Simonetti, lords of Iesi, 53n, 94n, 109, 127, 150n, 259n
    Lomo, 65n, 66, 74
Sinigaglia, 25, 49, 53n, 65n, 98, 104, 147, 168, 170–1, 180, 181n, 190, 192, 195–6, 203, 210n, 213, 221n, 223–4, 228, 229n, 231–2, 237, 239, 246–8, 251, 259n, 264n, 266, 267n, 270n, 271n, 275n, 290–3, 299n, 302n, 313n, 315n, 319–21, 326, 330
Sixtus IV, pope, 240, 248–52, 257, 266, 287n
Smeducci, lords of San Severino, 93n, 138n, 259n
    Ismeduccio, 66, 74
    Onofrio, 127
Soanna, 195n
Sogliano (see also Malatesta, counts of), 26, 40, 48, 51, 214n, 275n, 295
Solara, 81, 83n

Spoleto, 47
   duchy of 1, 2, 9n, 105, 116n, 160
Stacciola, 290, 292n, 299n
Staffolo, 116n, 281n, 283n, 302n, 313n
sumptuary laws, 324n

Talacchio, 297n
Talamello, 203, 238, 264n
tallage, *tallia militum*, 5, 53–4, 61, 77,
   153n, 263, 273, 282–4, 325n
Tartalti, Pietro, lord of Arezzo, 59
Tausano, 185n
Tempio Malatestiano, 177, 201n, 202n,
   204, 209n, 229n, 230n, 245, 296n,
   299n, 321, 326
Terzo, Ottobuon, 124–5
Todi, 105, 116, 152, 153
Torelli, Guido, 162
Toschi, Vannetta, 186n, 204, 247n,
   300n
Traversari, of Ravenna, 15, 18
   Paolo, 15
   Pietro, 26
Trebbio, il, 26, 294
Trinci, lords of Foligno, 150n, 259
   Corrado, 153, 160

Ubaldini, Giovanni D'Azzo degli, 100–
   1, 112
   Ottaviano degli, 29
   Ubaldino degli, 105
Ubertini, Andreino degli, 121
Uffigliano, 228
Umana, 66n
Urban V, pope, 83, 86, 87, 89, 92n
Urban VI, pope, 96, 98, 99, 103,
   108
Urbino (*see also* Montefeltro, counts of),
   12, 14, 17–18, 20n, 25n, 30, 37, 38,
   52, 53n, 55, 58, 64, 71, 89, 92n, 94,
   106–9, 138, 139, 190, 194–5, 228,
   287n, 291n, 311n, 320–1, 331n,
   333

Valdeponde, 37n
Valdoppio, 233n , 297n
Valturio, family, 298, 299
   Roberto, 199

Varano, Da, lords of Camerino, 19, 45,
   46n, 66, 68, 91n, 93n, 94, 127, 138n,
   145, 147, 150n, 151n, 192, 259,
   329n, 332n
   Costanza, 191–2
   Gentile, 90, 101
   Giulio Cesare, 213, 218, 229, 244,
      245n, 251n
   Niccola, 138n
   Rodolfo di Berardo, 75, 87, 90–1, 94,
      99, 101
   Rodolfo di Gentile, 138, 145
   Rodolfo di Piergentile, 245n
Venice, 13, 14n, 50, 55, 69, 74, 84n, 109,
   114, 115n, 117, 124, 130, 133n, 137,
   140, 142, 146, 147, 150n, 155–6,
   164, 169, 172–4, 179–80, 183–4,
   186, 188–9, 194, 196, 198–204,
   206–10, 212, 215, 217–18, 221,
   228n, 229, 234–8, 240–7, 249–52,
   254–6, 260–1, 276, 287, 290, 292,
   293n, 309n, 311n, 318n, 322–5,
   332–5
Verme, Jacopo del, 114
Verucchio, 26–7, 214n, 232, 275n, 290,
   294–5, 298, 301n, 305, 310n, 334
Viano, 185n
Visconti, lords of Milan, 43n, 47, 68–9,
   74, 80–1, 84, 87–9, 91, 93, 102,
   111 ff., 124, 150n
   Agnese, 113n
   Ambrogio, 87
   Bernabò, 80, 84, 86, 95, 113n
   Bianca, 190
   Filippo Maria, 142, 146, 152, 154–9,
      162–4, 167, 174, 177, 180–6, 188,
      194–8, 201n
   Galeazzo, 84
   Gian Galeazzo, 87, 101, 102n, 108, 109,
      111–19, 121, 123, 161n
   Giovanni, archbishop, 47, 68–9
   Giovanni Maria, 124–5, 154–5

Werner, duke of Urslingen, 65, 68
William of Holland, emperor, 23

Zagonara, 159
Zappolino, 52